# A Comprehensive Spanis

**Reference Grammars**
**General Editor: Glanville Price**

*Published:*

A Comprehensive French Grammar
Fourth Edition
L. S. R. Byrne and E. L. Churchill
Completely revised and updated by Glanville Price

A Comprehensive Russian Grammar
Terence Wade
Edited by Michael J. de K. Holman

A Comprehensive Spanish Grammar
Jacques De Bruyne
Adapted with additional material by Christopher J. Pountain

A Comprehensive Welsh Grammar
David A. Thorne

*In preparation:*

A Comprehensive German Grammar

A Comprehensive Italian Grammar

A Comprehensive Portuguese Grammar

A French Grammar Workbook

A Russian Grammar Workbook

# A Comprehensive Spanish Grammar

*Jacques De Bruyne*

*Adapted with additional material
by Christopher J. Pountain*

BLACKWELL
*Publishers*

English version copyright © Jacques De Bruyne and Christopher Pountain, 1995

First published in Dutch as *Spaanse Spraakkunst*
by Uitgeverij De Sikkel, N.V. 1979
Second edition 1985

First published in English 1995
Reprinted 1996, 1997, 1998, 1999, 2000

Blackwell Publishers Ltd-
108 Cowley Road
Oxford OX4 1JF, UK

Blackwell Publishers Inc
350 Main Street
Malden, Massachusetts 02148, USA

*British Library Cataloguing in Publication Data*
A CIP catalogue record for this book is available from the British Library

*Library of Congress Cataloging in Publication Data*
Bruyne, Jacques De.
[Spaanse spraakkunst. English]
A comprehensive Spanish grammar./Jacques De Bruyne: adapted,
with additional material, by Christopher J. Pountain.
p.   cm. – (Reference grammars)
Includes bibliographical references and index.
ISBN 0–631–16803–6 — ISBN 0–631–19087–2 (pbk)
1. Spanish language – Grammar. I. Pountain, Christopher J.
II. Title. III. Series: Blackwell reference grammars.
PC4112.B7913   1995                         94–46863
468.2'421–dc20                              CIP

Typeset in 10 on 12pt Times New Roman
by Typesetting Solutions, Slough, Berks
Printed and bound in Great Britain by T. J. Press Ltd, Padstow, Cornwall

This book is printed on acid-free paper

# Contents

## Indefinite Pronouns and Adjectives

# Foreword

The second edition of Jacques De Bruyne's *Spaanse Spraakkunst* was published in Belgium in 1985. It received wide acclaim and interest, and so it was logical that a wider readership should be sought: a German version appeared in 1993, and a French version is also planned. De Bruyne's grammar springs from a tradition which considers at every point the notion of the linguistic norm, a norm established partly by prescriptive grammar and partly by the usage of 'good' literary authors. At the same time, it captures a remarkably wide range of usage which gives the flavour of the immense variety which is to be found in the Spanish-speaking world. This English version incorporates many additions and amendments made by Professor De Bruyne himself to the second edition, together with substantial reorganization and supplementation by myself; in the latter, however, I have been at pains to preserve the style and spirit of the original work, and I must thank Professor De Bruyne for very generously giving me a free hand in this.

In the Preface to the second Dutch edition, De Bruyne explains that he has given more attention than is usual to what he perceives as the important trends in present-day Spanish, especially usage of the non-finite forms of the verb. He illustrates established rules as far as possible from works dating from after 1960 and from the modern press. The chief sources of the 'normativist' position are the Real Academia's *Esbozo de una nueva gramática de la lengua española* of 1973 and the work of Alcina Franch and Blecua, Fernández Ramírez, Seco and Marsá. Authors from many areas of the Spanish-speaking world are represented, principally: Cela (Galicia), Zunzunegui (Basque Country), Riera and Vázquez

Montalbán (Catalonia), Sender (Aragon), Delibes and Chacel (Old Castile), García Pavón (La Mancha), Quiñones and Pemán (Andalusia), Cabrera Infante and Carpentier (Cuba), Fuentes and Rulfo (Mexico), García Márquez (Colombia), Cortázar and Puig (Argentina), Onetti (Uruguay), Allende (Chile), Icaza (Ecuador), Vargas Llosa and Bryce Echenique (Peru), Roa Bastos (Paraguay). Care was also taken to ensure a range of register and style, the chief concern always being to give the broadest possible survey of usage.

Examples quoted have sometimes been abbreviated or slightly modified without, however, changing the essential point illustrated.

CJP

# Abbreviations

Non-standard abbreviations have been kept to a minimum in this book. Abbreviated references to books are listed in the Bibliography.
The asterisk (*) indicates an unacceptable Spanish example.

*Informants*

| | |
|---|---|
| ALV | Manuel Alvar, Universidad Complutense, Madrid |
| BUS | Eugenio de Bustos Tovar, Universidad de Salamanca |
| CAR | Fernando Lázaro Carreter, Universidad Complutense, Madrid |
| HER | César Hernández, Universidad de Valladolid |
| LAP | Rafael Lapesa, Universidad Complutense, Madrid |
| LLO | Antonio Llorente Maldonado de Guevara, Universidad de Salamanca |
| LOP | Juan M. Lope Blanch, Universidad Nacional Autónoma de México (a native of Spain) |
| MON | Félix Monge, Universidad de Zaragoza |
| MOR | Humberto López Morales, Universidad de Puerto Rico (a native of Cuba) |
| RAB | Ambrosio Rabanales, Universidad de Chile |
| SEN | Ricardo Senabre, Universidad de Salamanca |
| VAQ | María Vaquero, Universidad de Puerto Rico (of Spanish origin) |
| VAR | Beatriz Varela, University of New Orleans (a native of Cuba) |
| ZOR | María Antonia Martín Zorraquino, Universidad de Zaragoza |
| | |
| JdeB | Jacques De Bruyne |

# Pronunciation

## The Alphabet

**1** In the traditional Spanish alphabet, *ch, ll,* and *ñ* (and sometimes *rr* – see under **RR** in 2) are considered to be separate letters. In many Spanish-language publications, alphabetical order takes this into account, *ch, ll* and *ñ,* whether at the beginning of a word or within a word, following *c, l* and *n* respectively in many dictionaries (thus *charla* comes after *criar, rellenar* after *reloj*).[1] In April, 1994, the Asociación de Academias de la Lengua Española agreed no longer to consider *ch* and *ll* as separate letters. However, since the traditional alphabetical order is observed in the majority of current publications, we describe the traditional system here. The future of *ñ* was also under threat for a time because of pressure within the European Union to standardize typewriter keyboards; but it was vigorously defended as an emblem of Spanish individuality.[2]

| Capital letters | Small letters | Name[3] |
|---|---|---|
| A | a | *a* |
| B | b | *be* |
| C | c | *ce* |
| CH | ch | *che* |
| D | d | *de* |
| E | e | *e* |
| F | f | *efe* |
| G | g | *ge* |
| H | h | *hache* |
| I | i | *i* |

| Capital letters | Small letters | Name |
|---|---|---|
| J | j | *jota* |
| K | k | *ka* |
| L | l | *ele* |
| LL | ll | *elle* |
| M | m | *eme* |
| N | n | *ene* |
| Ñ | ñ | *eñe* |
| O | o | *o* |
| P | p | *pe* |
| Q | q | *cu* |
| R | r | *ere* |
| RR | rr | *erre*[4] |
| S | s | *ese* |
| T | t | *te* |
| U | u | *u* |
| V | v | *uve* or *ve* |
| W | w | *uve doble* or *ve doble* |
| X | x | *equis* |
| Y | y | *i griega* |
| Z | z | *zeta* or *zeda* |

## Pronunciation

**2** Pronunciation will be represented in the following sections by the International Phonetic Alphabet.

Indications of the pronunciation of the letters are of necessity concise, and do not take account of all possibilities and variants. As in other languages, the pronunciation of a letter in Spanish is sometimes also partially determined by the letters or sounds which precede or follow it.

Differences within Peninsular Spanish and between Latin-American and Peninsular pronunciation are sometimes considerable, and only the most general and striking differences are mentioned here.[5] Since this book is being published in Europe, the Peninsular variant (which is also widely regarded as the 'standard') is given first. But the 'standard' pronunciation is constantly changing: recently, there have been cries of alarm concerning the growing 'relaxation' of Spanish pronunciation.[6]

**A** Single vowels in Spanish are pronounced monophthongally (in English, on the other hand, a single letter often corresponds to a diphthong, e.g. *a* in *plate* [ej], *u* in *mute* [ju]). Spanish *a* [a] falls between the *a* of *hat* and the *a* of *father*, but is more open than either:

| | |
|---|---|
| *Salamanca* [salamanka] | Salamanca |
| *pagar* [paɣar] | to pay |

**B** There is no distinction in the pronunciation of the letters *b* and *v*, except in some bilingual areas, notably Paraguay.[7]

At the beginning of a word (unless preceded by a vowel without a break) and after *n* or *m*, both letters are pronounced like English *b* [b]; in other positions, they have a fricative pronunciation [β]:

| | |
|---|---|
| *basta* [basta] | it is enough |
| *envidiar* [embiðiar] | to envy |
| *Amberes* [amberes] | Antwerp |
| *la vida* [laβiða] | life |
| *beber* [beβer] | to drink |
| *vivir* [biβir] | to live |

There is thus no difference in pronunciation between pairs like *revelarse* 'to reveal oneself' and *rebelarse* 'to rebel'. Spanish speakers are also likely to mis-spell *b* for *v* and vice versa: on the 1987 New Year's Eve menu at the Hotel Montico (Tordesillas), for example, there appeared *sorvete* (for *sorbete*) *vodka-limón*.

**C** has two quite different pronunciations according to the letter following:

(1) When followed by an *e* or an *i*, *c* is pronounced approximately like voiceless English *th* in *thing* [θ]:

| | |
|---|---|
| *la celda* [la θelda] | cell |
| *la cima* [la θima] | top |

(See also **6** on *seseo*).

(2) Elsewhere, *c* is pronounced like English *k* [k] in kite, except that the 'aspiration' (puff of air) which accompanies the English voiceless plosives (*p*, *t* and *k*) before vowels is absent in Spanish.

| | |
|---|---|
| *la cama* [la kama] | bed |
| *clemente* [klemente] | clement, merciful |

| | |
|---|---|
| *comer* [komer] | to eat |
| *cruel* [kruel] | cruel |
| *curar* [kurar] | to cure |

Where (exceptionally) *c* appears in final position, e.g. *coñac*, it is either pronounced as *k* or is silent.[8]

Note the different pronunciations of *c* in the following words:

| | |
|---|---|
| *la acción* [la akθjón] | action |
| *Cáceres* [káθeres] | Cáceres |

**Ch** (see **1**) is pronounced like English *ch* [tʃ] in *church*, *child*.

| | |
|---|---|
| *charlar* [tʃarlar] | to chat |
| *muchacho* [mutʃatʃo] | boy |

As a capital letter, only the *C* is written as a capital when the rest of the word is in lower case: *China* (not: *CHina*).

**D** At the beginning of a word (unless preceded by a vowel without a break), and after *n* or *l*, *d* is pronounced like English *d* except that the tongue is just in contact with the top of the back of the teeth.

| | |
|---|---|
| *¡dime!* [dime] | tell me! |
| *la falda* [la falda] | skirt |
| *la tienda* [la tjenda] | shop |

In other positions, it has a fricative value similar to that of voiced English *th* [ð] in *the*, *there*, *they*, etc., though Spanish [ð] is shorter and weaker.

| | |
|---|---|
| *cada* [kaða] | each |
| *la defensa* [laðefensa] | defence |

At the end of a word, *d* is hardly pronounced (in Madrid and some parts of Castile it is regularly heard as [θ]) or is even completely unpronounced, although it does tend to be retained in the second person plural of the imperative.

| | |
|---|---|
| *la bondad* [laβonda(ð)] | goodness |
| *la pared* [la pare(ð)] | wall |
| *Madrid* [maðri(ð)] | Madrid |
| BUT *¡Trabajad!* [traβaxað] | Work! |

There is an increasing tendency in speech for intervocalic *d* not to be pronounced at all in the sequence *-ado*(s) (though it is retained in very careful speech).

| | |
|---|---|
| *el soldado* [el soldao] | soldier |
| *morado* [morao] | purple |
| *demasiado* [demasiao] | too much |
| *trabajado* [trabaxao] | worked |
| *silbado* [silbao] | whistled |
| *lado* [lao] | side |

The loss of intervocalic *d* is even more widespread in some regions: in *La chanca*, in which the speech of a poor district of Almería is represented, J. Goytisolo uses forms like *Estaos Uníos* (for *Estados Unidos* 'United States') (1981: 34) and *toavía* (for *todavía* 'still') (p. 59). A revealing comment concerning this feature is found in *A la sombra de las muchachas rojas* by F. Umbral:

> *Suárez* (Prime Minister-President of Spain after the Franco period) *hablaba con la correcta pronunciación castellana, pero cayendo en los populares y democráticos 'aos'* (1981: 154).
> Suárez spoke with correct Castilian pronunciation, but lapsed into the popular and democratic *aos*.

In many Latin-American countries this pronunciation is felt to belong to an inferior social level. In Mexico and Argentina. for example, intervocalic *d* is even pronounced with special emphasis by some speakers, as is final *d*.[9] There is also a marked tendency to reinforce the pronunciation of final *d* in Catalan-speaking areas (Baleares, Cataluña, Valencia).

**E**  See **A**. The pronunciation of *e* [e] is similar to that of the first element of the *ay* of English *play* [ej]; it is not as open as the *e* [ɛ] of English *yet*.

| | |
|---|---|
| *eliminar* [eliminar] | to eliminate |
| *fenomenal* [fenomenal] | phenomenal |

The *e* is slightly more open in closed syllables:

| | |
|---|---|
| *comer* [komer] | to eat |
| *la embajada* [la embaxaða] | embassy |

*Note:* There is no 'silent' *e* in Spanish (as, for example, in English *hose*).

Spanish historically has resisted an initial group of *s* + another consonant (*esporádico* 'sporadic', *escandinavo* 'Scandinavian'), and speakers tend to introduce an *e* in foreign words beginning with *s* + another consonant, even when it is not written. In *estrés* 'stress'[10] and *eslogan* 'slogan', which have been fully absorbed into the language, the spelling has been modified to reflect this. Even proper names may be hispanized in this way: the name of the singer Bruce Springsteen appeared as *Brus Esprinstin* in *Cambio 16*, 5 February 1990, 130 and in the 1992–3 season Real Madrid had an Argentine player whose surname was spelt *Esnaider* (clearly a Hispanic version of *Schneider*).

**F** As in English.

| | |
|---|---|
| *faltar* [faltar] | to be lacking |
| *fofo* [fofo] | flabby |

**G** As for **C**, there are two quite different pronunciations according to the following letter.

(1)    The *g* is pronounced like the *ch* in Scots *loch* or German *doch* [x] when it is followed by an *e* or an *i*.

| | |
|---|---|
| *gemir* [xemir] | to moan, to wail |
| *ginebra* [xineβra] | gin |

In Andalusia and Latin America, [x] is often weakened to [h].

(2)    Otherwise:

(a)    At the beginning of a word (unless preceded by a vowel without a break – see **B** and **D**), or when preceded by a nasal, *g* has the same pronunciation as English *g* in *game* [g]:

| | |
|---|---|
| *la gloria* [la gloria] | glory |
| *la manga* [la maŋga] | sleeve |

(b)    In other positions it has a voiced fricative pronunciation [ɣ]:

| | |
|---|---|
| *el agua* [el aɣwa] | water |
| *el lago* [el laɣo] | lake |
| *la goma* [laɣoma] | rubber |
| *digno* [diɣno] | worthy |

**Gu** followed by *i* or *e* is similarly pronounced [g] or [γ]:

| | |
|---|---|
| *la guerra* [laγerra] | war |
| *guiar* [giar] | to guide |
| *ceguera* [θeγera] | blindness |
| *seguir* [seγir] | to follow |

**Gu** before *a* is pronounced [gw]: *Guadalajara* [gwaðalaxara]. See also under **U**.

**Gü** is always pronounced [gw]: *argüir* [argwir] 'to argue'.

**H** *H* is not pronounced in standard Spanish.

| | |
|---|---|
| *hacer* [aθer] | to do, to make |
| *el honor* [el onor] | honour |
| *prohibir* [proiβir] | to forbid |

Only exceptionally is *h* pronounced in standard speech (as, for example, in *holgorio*. 'binge'). Attention is drawn to such exceptions in *DRAE*[11] by the mention 'la *h* se aspira' ('the *h* is aspirated'). However, the *h* which is derived from Latin *f* and which continued to be pronounced as an aspiration in the standard language into the Golden Age is preserved in certain parts of the Spanish-speaking world, e.g. in parts of Andalusia (F. Quiñones regularly writes *h* as *j* in *Las mil noches de Hortensia Romero* (1979: 53 and passim). in the Canary Isles and in some Latin-American countries, principally in popular speech.[12]

The following pairs thus have the same pronunciation: *hola*, 'hello'/*ola*, 'wave'; *hierro*, 'iron'/*yerro*, 'error'.

**I** Spanish *i* resembles the *ee* of English *feet* [i]; it is never as open as the *i* of English *fit* [ɪ].

| | |
|---|---|
| *el vino* [el bino] | wine |
| *dimitir* [dimitir] | to resign |

As part of a diphthong (see **9**). *i* is pronounced like the English *y* in *yet* or the second element in the *ay* of *play* [j].

**J** Like *ch* in Scots *loch*, German *doch* [x].

| | |
|---|---|
| *empujar* [empuxar] | to push |
| *el jefe* [el xefe] | head. boss |
| *el ojo* [el oxo] | eye |
| *jugar* [xuγar] | to play |

See also **G** above. It will be noted that the letter which follows *j* does not influence its pronunciation (by contrast with *g*, which before *e* and *i* is pronounced the same way as *j* [x]).

At the end of a word, *j* tends not to be pronounced.

>   *el reloj* [el rreló][13]          clock, watch

>   *A mí, en Canarias, una me regaló este reló.* (J. Goytisolo, 1981a: 17).
>   One girl in the Canaries gave me this watch.

**K** As in English (but see **C**).

This letter is not very common, however, in Spanish.[14] It is found today chiefly in foreign words.

>   *el kilo* [el kilo]          kilogram
>   *kaki* [kaki]              khaki

Words like *kilo(gramo)*, *kilómetro*, etc., where *k* precedes *i*, are sometimes also spelt with *qu*: *quilogramo*, *quilómetro*.[15]  *Kaki* 'khaki' is alternatively spelt *caqui*.

**L** Always like the English 'clear' *l* of *fly* [l]; only regionally (notably Catalonia) like the English velar or 'dark' *l* of *full* [ɫ].

>   *Lima* ]lima]          Lima
>   *loco* [loko]          mad

**Ll** (see **1**) In standard pronunciation, this is a 'clear' *l* which is palatalized (i.e. the tongue is pressed up to the palate as the sound is pronounced): [ʎ]. Unlike the *lli* of English *million*, [ʎ] in Spanish is thought of as a single unit, and never divided between syllables or words (in either speech or writing):

>   *llamar* [ʎamar]                      to call
>   *Sevilla* [seβiʎa] (syllabified *Se-vi-lla*)   Seville
>   *lleno* [ʎeno]                        full
>   *bullir* [buʎir] (syllabified *bu-llir*)      to boil

Where capitalization is necessary, only the first *L* is written with a capital when the rest of the word is lower case:

>   *Lloró toda la noche*
>   He cried all night
>   (not *LLoró*)

*Antonio Llorente no ha venido*
Antonio Llorente has not come

In much of southern Spain and in Latin-America[16] *ll* is pronounced [j], a phenomenon known as *yeísmo*. In *yeísta* pronunciation,
there is no distinction between pairs such as *callado* 'silent'/*cayado*
'crook' [kajaðo], *halla* 'finds'/*haya* (subjunctive of *haber*) [aja] and
*pollo* 'chicken'/*poyo* 'stone bench' [pojo].

In much of Argentina and Uruguay, *ll* is pronounced like the *s* of
English *measure* or the *j* or French *jamais* [ʒ]:[17]

 *calle* [kaʒe]      street

**M** As in English:

 *la mancha* [la mantʃa]   stain
 *el camello* [el kameʎo]   camel

**N** As in English:

 *nacer* [naθer]     to be born
 *el enano* [el enano]    dwarf

As in English, the pronunciation of *n* is affected by a following
consonant: thus *en vez de* [embeθde], *angosto* [aŋgosto]. In some
areas, notably Galicia, final *n* is regularly pronounced [ŋ]: *comen*
'they eat' [komeŋ].

**Ñ** (see **1**) A palatalized *n* (see **L1**): [ɲ]. Unlike English *ny* in *canyon*,
Spanish [ɲ] is always thought of as a single unit.

 *la montaña* [la montaɲa] (syllabified *mon-ta-ña*) mountain
 *España* [espaɲa] (syllabified *Es-pa-ña*)  Spain
 *ñoño* [ɲoɲo] (syllabified *ño-ño)*   silly

The mark ñ is known as *la tilde.*[18]

**O** See **A**. Pronounced like the first element in the diphthong *ow* of
English *show* [ʃow]:

 *Barcelona* [barθelona]  Barcelona
 *vanidoso* [baniðoso]   vain, conceited

Although *o* tends to be more open in a closed syllable or before *r* or
*rr*, it is never as open as the *o* of English *hot* [ɔ].

| | |
|---|---|
| *donde* [donde] | where |
| *correr* [korrer] | to run |

**P** As in English (but see **C**).

| | |
|---|---|
| *el apartamento* [el apartamento] apartment | |
| *la pipa* [la pipa] | pipe |

In the group *ps-, p* is silent (e.g. *psicología* [sikoloxía] 'psychology'), and a variant spelling with *s- (sicología)* is sometimes used.

**Q** This letter is always followed by *u*, and the group *qu* is pronounced like *k*:[19]

| | |
|---|---|
| *Don Quijote* [doŋ kixote] | Don Quixote |
| *quedar* [keðar] | to stay |
| *equipar* [ekipar] | to equip |

**R** Spanish *r* is a 'flap' produced by the tip of the tongue at the front of the mouth, like the *r* of Scots *free*:

| | |
|---|---|
| *pero* [pero] | but |
| *Marta* [marta] | Martha |

Spanish also has a double *r (rr)*, and this is sometimes considered to be a separate letter. Note that *rr* is never split between syllables and is only found between vowels. It is a 'trill' or 'roll', a longer version of *r*, like the *r* of Scots *red*.

| | |
|---|---|
| *el perro* [el perro] (syllabified *pe-rro*) | dog |
| *serrar* [serrar] (syllabified *se-rrar*) | to saw |

At the beginning of a word, *r* is pronounced like *rr*.

| | |
|---|---|
| *la rata* [la rrata] | rat |

and in compound words, this pronunciation is represented by *rr*:

| | |
|---|---|
| *el vicerrector* (*vice + rector*) | vice-rector (deputy |
| [el biθerrektor] | vice-chancellor) |
| *infrarrojo* (*infra + rojo*) | infrared |
| [infrarroxo] | |
| *autorretrato* (*auto + retrato*) | self-portrait |
| [autorretrato] | |

Note also the spelling *pavorreal* (normally *pavo real*) 'peacock' used by G. García Márquez in *El amor en los tiempos del cólera* (1985: 40).

There is thus a clear distinction in pronunciation between words like *pero* [pero] 'but' and *perro* [perro] 'dog', *caro* [karo] 'dear' and *carro* [karro] 'cart'.

In many areas of Latin America, notably Chile, *rr* (and initial *r-*) are 'assibilated', i.e., pronounced somewhere between standard English *r* and *z*.

**S** In Spain, the standard pronunciation of *s* is 'apical' (i.e., with the tip of the tongue, or with the tongue very slightly curled back); in Andalusia and Latin America, it is more like English *s* in *sit*. It is never pronounced [z] between vowels as in the *s* in English *reason*.

| | |
|---|---|
| *la casa* [la kasa] | house |
| *sesenta* [sesenta] | sixty |

Before *r* [rr], *s* is not usually pronounced, except in very deliberate speech:

| | |
|---|---|
| *las rosas* [larrosas] | roses |
| *las ratas* [larratas] | rats |
| *Israel* [irrael] | Israel |

See also *ceceo* (**6**).

In Andalusia and Latin America, *s* at the end of a syllable is often 'aspirated', i.e. pronounced like an English *h*, or dropped altogether: [tjɛnɛ(h)] *tienes*, [otrɔ(h)] *otros*.

**T** As English *t* in *tea* (but see **C**).

| | |
|---|---|
| *el tomate* [el tomate] | tomato |
| *setenta* [setenta] | seventy |

*T* at the end of a word (there are few such words in Spanish) may or may not be pronounced, and the same applies to foreign words: Carmen de Mora, in her edition of J. J. Arreola's *Confabulario definitivo* (1986, 117, note), writes *Utrech* for *Utrecht*.

**U** Like English *oo* [u] in *fool*; never like English *u* [ju] in *fume*.

| | |
|---|---|
| *el usurero* [el usurero] | usurer, profiteer |
| *Cuba* [kuβa] | Cuba |

As part of a diphthong (see **9**), *u* is pronounced as English *w* in *well* or the second element in *ow* of *cow* [w].

The 'silent' nature of *u* in the groups *gue*, *gui* and *que*, *qui* has already been noted under **G** and **Q** respectively. When the *u* is to be pronounced after *g*, it carries a diaeresis (*una diéresis*) (¨):

| | |
|---|---|
| *la vergüenza* [la βergwenθa] | shame |
| *la cigüeña* [la θigweɲa] | stork |
| *el pingüino* [el piŋgwino] | penguin |

**V** See **B**.

**W** Some grammars do not include this letter in the Spanish alphabet. It does, however, appear in *Esbozo* 122–3.

*W* is found exclusively in loanwords (often proper nouns). It is generally pronounced like English *w* in *win*, though it is sometimes pronounced (and also written) like *v*.

| | |
|---|---|
| *el wáter*[20] [el báter] | loo, WC |
| *el whisky* (also *uiski*, *güiski* [el (ɣ)wiski] | whisky |
| *el windsurf* [el wínsurf] | windsurfing |

Loanwords such as *vagón* [baɣón] 'carriage' and *valón* [balón] 'Walloon' are now regularly spelt with *v*. DRAE, 468, and DUE, I, 861, give both *darvinismo* and *darwinismo* 'Darwinism' as possibilities.

**X** The following distinction is sometimes made:

(1)    *X* is pronounced [ks] intervocalically and sometimes at the end of a word:

| | |
|---|---|
| *el examen* [el eksamen] | exam |
| *exacto* [eksakto] | exact |
| *el taxi* [el taksi] | taxi |

(2)    *X* is often pronounced *s* when it precedes a consonant and sometimes when it is the last letter in a word:

| | |
|---|---|
| *el texto* [el teksto or el testo] | text |
| *extraño* [estraɲo] | strange |
| *Félix* [félis] | Felix |

In practice, at least in careful speech, there is a tendency for *x* to be pronounced in all cases as [ks], and there is a systematic preference for this pronunciation in Latin America.[21]

In some Mexican words, *x* is pronounced like *j* [x]. The best-known case is *México* itself (and its derivatives *mexicano*, *mexi-*

*canismo*, etc.).[22] Indeed, although *México* is sometimes spelt *Méjico* in Spain, Mexicans always spell it with an *x*, being the *x* is viewed almost as a symbol of national identity:

> – *México es una equis* – *le dijo Félix cuando eran muy jóvenes* –, *España es una eñe, no se entiende a esos dos países sin esas letras que les pertenecen a ellos* (C. Fuentes, 1979: 46)
> 'Mexico is an x', Félix said to him when they were very young, 'Spain is an ñ; you can't understand those two countries without those letters that belong to them'

**Y** As English *y* in *yet* [j]. At the end of a word, the *y* forms a diphthong with the preceding vowel and is pronounced like the second element in the *ay* of English *play* [ej]. At the beginning of a word, [j] is strengthened to [dʒ] by some speakers.

| | |
|---|---|
| *yo* [jo] or [dʒo] | I |
| *el rayo* [el rrajo] | ray |
| *la ley* [la lej] | law |

In some Latin-American countries (principally Chile and Argentina), initial or intervocalic *y* is pronounced like English *s* in *measure* [ʒ]:

| | |
|---|---|
| *yo* [ʒo] | I |
| *ayer* [aʒer] | yesterday[23] |

**Z** Like English *th* in *thing* [θ]:

| | |
|---|---|
| *Zaragoza* [θaraɣoθa] | Zaragoza |
| *la cruz* [la kruθ] | cross |

See also *ceceo*, **6**.

## 3 Remarks

Spanish spelling is particularly straightforward by contrast with English or French, which have etymological spelling systems which are not based on present-day phonetic reality. This does not mean that it could not be simplified further, for example, by using *j* for *g* and *z* for *c* before *e* or *i* (see the private spelling systems invented by the nineteenth-century grammarian Andrés Bello and the twentieth-century poet Juan Ramón Jiménez). Some words admit variant spellings, e.g. *acimut/azimut* 'azimuth', *cinc/zinc* 'zinc'.[24] In Spanish, as a general principle, only letters which are pronounced are written (but see **H, U** and **P** in **2** above) and only letters which are written are pronounced.

**4** Note particularly that the English spellings *ch*, *ph* and *th* in words borrowed from Greek are represented as *c*, *f* and *t* in Spanish:

| | |
|---|---|
| *coro* | chorus |
| *filosofía* | philosophy |
| *teatro* | theatre |

*B*, *n* and *p* are sometimes suppressed in pronunciation when they come at the end of a syllable and are followed by another consonant, and as a result variant spellings have been admitted: *oscuro* or *obscuro*, *setiembre* or *septiembre*, *trasportar* or *transportar*.[25]

**5** In general there are phonetically no double consonants in Spanish, and the spelling reflects this, by contrast with English:

| | |
|---|---|
| *efecto* | effect |
| *imposible* | impossible |
| *ilegal* | illegal |
| *amoniaco* | ammoniac |

The only exception to this is *nn*:

| | |
|---|---|
| *ennoblecer* [ennobleθer] | to ennoble |
| (syllabified *en-no-ble-cer*) | |

In spelling, however, *cc* and *rr* are found; but *cc* always represents two different sounds and *rr* (see **R** in **2** above) is considered to be a single element.

| | |
|---|---|
| *la acción* [la akθjón] | action |
| (syllabified *la ac-ción*) | |
| *el perro* [el perro] | dog |
| (syllabified *el pe-rro*) | |

Only very exceptionally are double vowels found (for example, the names *Saavedra*, *Feijóo*).

## 6 *Ceceo* and *Seseo*

By *ceceo* and *seseo* is meant, respectively, the tendency to pronounce [s] as [θ] and [θ] as [s]:

*Ceceo*:
 *la iglesia* [la iɣleθja]   church
*Seseo*:
 *decir* [desir]     to say
 *la caza* [la kasa]    hunting

*Ceceo* is found in much of Andalusia and is often reflected in speakers' spelling: JdeB reports the spelling *Campoviejo cocecha* (for *cosecha*) *1964* on a menu in the well-known Granada restaurant La Ruta del Veleta. *Seseo* occurs in other parts of Andalusia (notably in the city of Seville) and is more or less generalized in Latin America, where pronunciations like [θjelo] and [θurdo] would be considered an affectation.[26]

## 7 *Sinalefa*

When a vowel at the end of one word is followed by a vowel at the beginning of another, the two vowels are pronounced together (there is no intervening glottal stop or *r* as sometimes appears in English *there is* [ðɛːɹɪz], [ðɛːʔɪz] *law and order* [lɔːɹəndɔːdə], [lɔːʔəndɔːdə])and are thought of in poetry as belonging to the same syllable. This phenomenon is called *sinalefa*.

 *veinte años* [bejnt(e)aɲos]  twenty years
 (syllabified *vein-tea-ños*)
 *la edición* [laeðiθjón]   edition[27]
 (syllabified *lae-di-ción*)

In some cases this fusion of vowels can lead to ambiguity, as in

 *Santa Ana* (Saint Anne) – *Santana* (Spanish surname)
 *está hablando* (he/she is speaking) – *está blando* (it is soft)

## 8 'Strong' and 'Weak' Vowels

Spanish vowels may be classified as 'strong' (*a, e, o*) or 'weak' (*i(y), u*).
 This distinction is important for the correct application of the following accentuation rules.

## 9 Diphthongs

The following groups of vowels give rise to diphthongs in Spanish:

Strong + weak

| | | |
|---|---|---|
| el *aire* [el ajre] (syllabified *ai-re*) | air |
| la *deuda* [la ðewða] (syllabified *deu-da*) | debt |
| *oigo* [ojɣo] (syllabified *oi-go*) | I hear |

Weak + strong

| | |
|---|---|
| el *labio* [el laβjo] (syllabified *la-bio*) | lip |
| *pues* [pwes] (one syllable) | so, then |
| la *gloria* [la glorja] (syllabified *glo-ria*) | glory |

Weak + weak

| | |
|---|---|
| el *viudo* [el bjuðo] (syllabified *viu-do*) | widower |
| el *ruido* [el rrwiðo] (syllabified *rui-do*) | noise |

There is thus no diphthong in words like *oasis* (*o-a-sis*) 'oasis', *chimenea* (*chi-me-ne-a*) 'chimney, fireplace', *traer* (*tra-er*) 'bring', *roer* (*ro-er*) 'gnaw', etc.: two strong vowels together always constitute separate syllables.

A diphthong is considered to belong to one syllable. This is important for the application of the rules of stress.

## 10 Stress

Spanish words are classified according to the position of the stress into *agudas* (stress on the final syllable), *llanas* or *graves* (stress on the penultimate syllable), *esdrújulas* (stress on the antepenultimate syllable) and – limited to verb forms with enclitic pronouns (see **265**) – *sobresdrújulas* (stress on the third syllable from the end).

The following rules govern the placing of stress in Spanish:

(1)    In words which end in a vowel, a diphthong, *-n* or *-s*, the stress falls on the penultimate syllable. The majority of Spanish words fall into this category:[28]

| | |
|---|---|
| el *muchacho* | boy |
| la *industria* | industry |
| *joven* | young |
| la *crisis* | crisis |

(2)   In words which end in a consonant (apart from -*n* or -*s*), the stress falls on the last syllable.

| | |
|---|---|
| la mu<u>jer</u> | woman |
| el alba<u>ñil</u> | mason |
| la volun<u>tad</u> | will |

If by virtue of the above stress rules the stress falls on a syllable which consists of a diphthong, the strong vowel in this diphthong is stressed. If the diphthong consists of two weak vowels, the stress falls on the last vowel of the diphthong. The same principle holds for monosyllabic words.

| | |
|---|---|
| el m<u>ie</u>do | fear |
| el <u>a</u>ire | air |
| lu<u>e</u>go | then, next |
| el pi<u>e</u> | foot |
| di<u>o</u> | he/she gave |
| f<u>ui</u> | I was; I went |
| tr<u>iu</u>nfo | triumph |

**11** If there is deviation from the stress rules given in **10**, an accent mark (*el acento ortográfico*) (´) must indicate the syllable on which the stress falls.

| | |
|---|---|
| el kil<u>ó</u>metro | kilometre (US kilometer) |
| los <u>jó</u>venes | young people |
| el <u>ré</u>gimen | regime, diet |
| dif<u>í</u>cil | difficult |

The accent mark also indicates when a combination of weak and strong vowels do not form a diphthong, even when the word is from other points of view regularly stressed:

| | |
|---|---|
| el ba<u>ú</u>l<br>(syllabified *ba-úl*; without the accent it would be mono-syllabic \**baul*.) | trunk |
| contin<u>ú</u>o<br>(syllabified *con-ti-nú-o*; without the accent it would be *con-ti-nuo* 'continuous'.) | I continue |

## 12 Remarks

Some words have an accent mark which strictly speaking is superfluous as far as pronunciation is concerned. The purpose is to signal a difference in meaning.

| | |
|---|---|
| *tú* (you) | *tu* (your) |
| *él* (he, him) | *el* (the) |
| *sí* (yes; himself, herself, itself, themselves) | *si* (if) |
| *más* (more) | *mas* (but) |
| *sé* (I know) | *se* (himself, herself, itself, themselves) |
| *cómo* (how) | *como* (as, since) |

However, the accent has a secondary function in suggesting the difference between the stressed and unstressed nature of these words: contrast *tú/tu*, *él/el* in <u>*tú*</u> *sueñas* 'you dream', <u>*él*</u> *trabaja* 'he works' (stress on the pronouns), but *tu* <u>*sueño*</u> 'your dream', *el* <u>*trabajo*</u> 'the work' (stress on the noun).

The written accent is used with interrogative and exclamatory words used in direct or indirect questions and exclamations (see **Interrogative and Exclamatory Pronouns and Adjectives**):

*¡Cuánto lo siento!*
How sorry I am!

*¿Cuánto cuesta?*
How much is it?

*No sabes cuánto lo siento*
You don't know how sorry I am

*Me preguntó cuánto costaba*
She asked me how much it was

**13** In the formation of plurals an accent may need to be added or omitted if the number of syllables in the word is changed. This follows from the fact that the stress must in principle remain on the same syllable.

*el* <u>*examen*</u> (exam)          *los exámenes*

(If no accent were used in the plural, the stress would be assumed to fall on the penultimate syllable (i.e. the second *e*, since the word ends in an *s*)

*la razón* (reason)                *las razones*
(In the plural the accent becomes superfluous: the stress falls regularly on the *o* in the penultimate syllable, since the word ends in *s*)

*el chico holgazán* (the lazy boy)   *los chicos holgazanes*

See also **266** on the place of the written accent in verb forms with a clitic pronoun.

Note also the use (or non-use) of the stress accent in compound words: the accent is not used in the first word of unhyphenated compounds (*tiovivo* 'roundabout') but is used in both words of hyphenated compounds (*guía-catálogo* 'catalogue-guide').[29]

**14** The importance of the written accent[30] is evident from examples like the following, where the meaning of the forms distinguished is fundamentally different:

*arteria* (artery)            *artería* (cunning)
*la calle* (street)           *callé* (I kept quiet)
*el revólver* (revolver)      *revolver* (to revolve)
*el cálculo* (calculation)    *calculo* (I calculate)
                              *calculó* (he/she calculated)[31]

– *En esta película está guapa* (F. Umbral, 1980: 57)
'She looks pretty in this film'

**15** Variation in the use of the accent occurs in only a restricted number of words.

| | |
|---|---|
| *la anémona* or *la anemona* | anemone |
| *austriaco* or *austríaco* | Austrian |
| *cardiaco* or *cardíaco* | cardiac |
| *el cártel* or *el cartel* | cartel[32] |
| *el conclave* or *el cónclave* | conclave |
| *el chófer* or *el chofer* | driver |
| *el/la dinamo* or *el/la dínamo* | dynamo |
| *etíope* or *etiope* | Ethiopian |
| *la exégesis* or *la exegesis*[33] | exegesis |
| *el fútbol* or *el futbol* | football |

| | |
|---|---|
| *el gladíolo* or *el gladiolo* | gladiolus |
| *la medula* or *la médula* | medulla, marrow |
| *la olimpiada* or *la olimpíada* | Olympiad, Olympic Games |
| *el omóplato* or *el omoplato* | shoulder blade |
| *la ósmosis* or *la osmosis* | osmosis |
| *el pabilo* or *el pábilo* | wick |
| *el pentagrama* or *el pentágrama* | stave (in music) |
| *el período* or *el periodo* | period |
| *una novela policiaca* or *una novela policíaca* | detective novel |
| *el reuma* or *el reúma*[34] | rheumatism[35] |
| *Rumania* or *Rumanía*[36] | Romania |

The forms *austríaco, chofer* and *policíaco* are customary chiefly in Latin America.

**16** *Élite* is now very commonly pronounced [élite] in the Peninsula, and is generally so pronounced in Latin America, although *DRAE*, 564, gives the form *elite* implying the preservation of the French stress pattern as [elíte].[37]

**17** The accent (´) is usual, though optional, with capital letters. The tilde (˜), however, is never omitted.

## Punctuation

**18** The principal punctuation marks are:

| | |
|---|---|
| . | *el punto* |
| , | *la coma* |
| : | *los dos puntos* |
| ; | *el punto y coma (el semicolón)* |
| ... | *los puntos suspensivos* |
| « » | *las comillas* |
| ¡ ! | *los signos de exclamación* or *admiración* |
| ¿ ? | *los signos de interrogación* |
| - | *el guión* |
| — | *la raya* |
| ( ) | *los paréntesis* |

Punctuation in English and Spanish is broadly similar, but there are some important differences.

**19** The inverted question mark and exclamation mark are placed where the question or exclamation properly begins, or before the phrase or word which is to be stressed.

| | |
|---|---|
| *¿Quién es este hombre?* | Who is this man? |
| *¡Cuánto me alegro!* | How delighted I am! |

*Argentina ¡campeón!*     Argentina Champions!
(Text which appeared on the electronic scoreboard in the Buenos Aires stadium when Argentina won the World Cup in 1978)

| | |
|---|---|
| *Sin haber leído el periódico, ¿cómo podría saberlo?* | Without having read the paper, how could I know? |
| *Tengo que decirle ¡muchas gracias! otra vez* | I must thank you again very much |

*Idos, y dejadme en paz, ¡so cretinos!* (A. Roa Bastos,1977: 213)
Go away and leave me in peace, you cretins!

*En una corrida de la feria de Valencia, cortó dos orejas, rabo y ¡dos! patas* (F. Vizcaíno Casas, 1976: 145)
In a bullfight during the Valencia festival, he was awarded two ears, a tail and two(!) feet

A sentence can be interrogative as well as exclamatory; this will be evident from the different punctuation marks used:

*¡Qué persecución es esta, Dios mío!* (*Esbozo*, 149)
Good gracious, what sort of persecution is this?!

A greater number of question and exclamation marks may be used, and may be placed 'asymmetrically' as in (iii) below:

(i)   *¡¡¡Basta!!!* (J. A. de Zunzunegui, 1971: 674).
      Enough!!!

(ii)  *¡¡¿Qué os habéis creído los psiquiatras que es el ministro de la Gobernación?!!!* (J. A. Vallejo-Nagera, 1980: 81).
      What do you psychiatrists think a Home Secretary is?!!!

(iii) *¡Usted, ¿quién es?!* (A. Berlanga, 1984: 170).
      Who are you?!

**20** After the opening words of a letter or similar document (third example below), the Spanish convention is to use a colon.

| | |
|---|---|
| *Muy Señor mío:* | Dear Sir, |
| *Querido amigo:* | My dear friend, |
| *Madrileños:* | People of Madrid! |

(The well-known Mayor of Madrid, Enrique Tierno Galván, began his famous *Bandos* in this way)

**21** Direct speech is introduced by a dash; the end of direct speech is marked by a change of paragraph. Any interpolated material is separated from the direct speech by dashes, which may be used in conjunction with other punctuation marks:

> – *¿Enfadado conmigo? – exclamó el Gorila –. Si es un pedazo de pan* ... (J. Goytisolo, 1988: 55)
>
> 'Cross with me?' exclaimed Gorilla. 'It's only a hunk of bread ...'

New paragraphs in direct speech are opened by "or '; direct speech or quotation within direct speech is usually enclosed in *comillas* (« »):

> *"Al llegar a bordo el pobrecillo quería abrazarme... Se volvía hacia mí y me decía: «Gorila, ya voy para viejo ... Si algo me quieres, prométeme una cosa: que cuando yo muera continuarás en ella pase lo que pase»* (ibid., 56).
>
> 'When he arrived on board the poor fellow wanted to embrace me... He turned towards me and said, "Gorilla, I'm getting an old man... If you have any feeling for me at all, promise me one thing: that when I die you will carry on with it [the boat] come what may" '

Otherwise, English inverted commas (' ', " ") are both traditionally rendered in Spanish by « », although double inverted commas (" ") are increasingly finding favour:

> *Según Arias, Cristiani no descartó que el asesinato de Ellacuría lo cometiera un "elemento militar incontrolado" y reconoció haber oído "versiones" de que los asesinos eran unos 30 uniformados* (*El País*, international edition, 20 November 1989: 1)
>
> According to Arias, Cristiani did not deny that the murder of Ellacuría was committed by an 'uncontrolled military element' and he admitted having heard 'accounts' that the murderers were a group of about thirty soldiers in uniform

**22** The comma is used in much the same way in English and Spanish, although in Spanish, it is sometimes used to mark the end of a long subject noun phrase in a way that is not usual in English: see, for example, the second example in **41** below.

A comma may be used before the conjunction *y* if the phrases involved are fairly long and involve different subjects:

> *La Guardia Civil patrulla por los pueblos, y la Policía Nacional, por las ciudades* (*MEU*, 29)
> The Guardia Civil patrols villages and the Policía Nacional the towns

## Capital Letters

**23** The following have capital letters (*letras mayúsculas*) in English but lower case letters (*letras minúsculas*) in Spanish:[38]

(1)  *Gentilicios* (i.e. nouns or adjectives indicating inhabitants of continents, countries, regions and towns, etc.) and their derivatives:

|   |   |
|---|---|
| *los americanos* | Americans |
| *la industria belga* | Belgian industry |
| *una andaluza* | an Andalusian woman |
| *un londinense* | a Londoner |
| *un anglicismo* | an Anglicism |

(2)  Nouns or adjectives denoting members of political parties or religious groups:

|   |   |
|---|---|
| *los conservadores* | the Conservatives |
| *los cristianos católicos* | Catholic Christians |

(3)  Days of the week and months of the year:

|   |   |
|---|---|
| *lunes el 3 de enero* | Monday 3 January |

(4)  Points of the compass unless abbreviated (*N,S,E,O*) or part of a place-name (*Estación del Norte, América del Sur, Berlín del Oeste*).

(5)  English tends to use capitals for all nouns and verbs in titles, whereas in Spanish capitals are not used after the first word:

> *El coronel no tiene quien le escriba* (title of a novel by G. García Márquez)
> No One Writes to the Colonel.

(See also the remarks on sigla like EEUU, CCOO, FFCC, etc. in **149.**)

## 24 Remark

In the Spanish press, there is a fashion for referring to well-known dates of political significance in the following way:

> *el 23-F*
> 23 February, 1981, the date of the attempted coup d'état by Lt.-Col. Tejero.

> *El BBV y el Banco de Comercio inauguran una nueva devaluación después del 6-J* (*Ya*, 19 May 1993: 1)
> The BBV (Banco de Bilbao y Vizcaya) and the Banco de Comercio begin a new devaluation after the 6 June (the date of the Spanish General Election)

# The Article

**25** Spanish, like English, distinguishes definite and indefinite articles.

## 26 Forms

### The Definite Article

| | |
|---|---|
| *el* (masculine singular) | *los* (masculine plural) |
| *la* (feminine singular) | *las* (feminine plural) |

To this list is traditionally added the so-called 'neuter' form *lo*, although this is never used with nouns (except in the expression *a lo* + proper noun, see **66**), all nouns in Spanish being either masculine or feminine. (For the use of *lo*, see **63–70**; for gender, see **86**ff.)

## 27 Contraction with prepositions

*a* + *el* contracts to *al*
*de* + *el* contracts to *del*

*Mañana iremos al museo*
Tomorrow we shall go to the museum

*Hemos hablado del caso*
We have spoken about the case

*El año pasado fuimos al Brasil.*
Last year we went to Brazil.
(On the use of the definite article with geographical names, see **38**)

In the written language there is a tendency to avoid the use of two contracted forms together:

> *Los sublevados se apoderaron de el (palacio) del duque de Ascoli* (*Esbozo*, 216)
> The rebels took possession of the Duke of Ascoli's (palace)

Before proper nouns (certain place-names, names of people, surnames, titles of books, etc.) the contracted forms are generally not used.

> *Voy a El Ferrol*
> I am going to El Ferrol
> (F. Franco Salgado-Araujo, 1977: 14, 15 and passim, uses contracted forms: *la llegada al Ferrol* 'arrival at El Ferrol', *los alrededores del Ferrol* 'the outskirts of El Ferrol')

> *Te enseño los mejores cuadros de El Greco*
> I'll show you El Greco's best pictures

> *Al padre de El Cordobés le llamaban «El Renco»* (F. Díaz-Plaja, 1966: 172)
> El Cordobés's (a well-known bullfighter of the 1960s and 1970s) father was called 'El Renco'

> *Los caminos de El Señor*
> The ways of the Lord (title of a novel by J. A. de Zunzunegui)

> *José-Luis Cebrián, director de El País* (F. Umbral, 1985: 8).
> José-Luis Cebrián, the editor of *El País*.

## 28 Use of *el* for *la*

The form *el* is used instead of *la* if the following three conditions are simultaneously fulfilled:

1 the article stands immediately before the noun
2 the noun is feminine singular
3 the noun begins with a stressed *a-* or *ha-*

| | |
|---|---|
| *el agua* | water |
| *el arma* | weapon |
| *el habla* | speech, language |
| *el hacha* | axe, hatchet |
| *el hambre* | hunger |

Nouns such as those above remain feminine, however, as is shown by their agreeing adjectives (see, however, **160**):

> *el agua fría*                       cold water

But:

> *la pequeña hacha*            the little axe
> (the article is not immediately before the noun)
>
> *las armas*                      the weapons
> (the feminine noun is used in the plural)
>
> *la abeja*                       the bee
> (the first syllable of the noun is unstressed)
>
> *la alta traición*             high treason
> (*alta* is an adjective)

This rule does not apply to girls' names (Christian names or surnames), the letters of the alphabet (*la a, la hache*) and to nouns denoting female people or animals. Another exception is the place name *La Haya* 'The Hague'.

> *¿Ha venido la Ángela?*       Has Angela come?
> (See **41-2** on the use of the article with proper nouns.)
>
> *el árabe*    Arab (man)      *la árabe*    Arab (woman)
>
> *el ánade*    male duck       *la ánade*    female duck

*Note:* The use of *agua* as the first element in a number of compound nouns gives rise to *el* sometimes being used with these nouns; the gender of such words is also liable to variation.

> *el* or *la aguanieve* (f)         sleet[1]
>
> *el aguafuerte* (usually m)     etching
> *el aguafuerte* (f)              nitric acid
>
> *el aguardiente* (m)            liquor
>
> *la aguamarina* (f)             aquamarine

Another such word is *el avemaría* ('Ave Maria') which is feminine (plural *las avemarías*).

> *Saber uno como el avemaría alguna cosa* (*DRAE*, 167)
> To know something like the back of one's hand

*Haz*, which is feminine in its meaning of 'face, surface' is found with both *el* and *la*: *el/la haz de la tierra*[2] 'the face of the earth'. (*Haz* is masculine in its meaning of 'bundle, sheaf', in which case the article is of course always *el*.)

(See also **160** and **299** on the use of *este* and *otro* with such nouns.)

### Usage

### 29  Definite Article in Spanish: Indefinite Article or No Article in English: Nouns with a General Meaning

'Mass' nouns (nouns denoting a substance):

> *La nicotina perjudica a la salud*
> Nicotine is damaging to health

Plural nouns used generically:

> *A veces los animales son más fieles que los hombres*
> Animals are often more faithful than people.

> *Los niños tienen que acostarse pronto*
> Children have to go to bed early

Abstract nouns:

> *La sinceridad es importante en la vida*
> Sincerity is important in life

### 30  Nouns denoting parts of the body

A definite article is used with 'essential' parts of the body after the verb *tener* and the preposition *con*. The English translation may involve a possessive adjective in such cases:

> *Tenía la cara ancha; la cabeza, pesada; los ojos, bovinos* (A. M. de Lera, 1970: 33).
> He had a broad face, a heavy head and bovine eyes (or: His face was broad, his head heavy and his eyes bovine)

> *Tenía las manos pálidas* (G. García Márquez, 1977: 335).
> He had pale hands

> *Lola, bella a la manera asturiana, con los ojos, la boca y la nariz grandes, vigilaba el nivel etílico de su marido* (F. Umbral, 1981: 25)

Lola, a typical Asturian beauty with her big eyes, mouth and nose, was watching over her husband's alcohol level

*Asunción tenía el pelo oscurísimo* (J. Fernández Santos, 1977: 109).
Asunción had very dark hair (or: Asunción's hair was very dark)

In the following sentence, however, no article is used with *trenzas* 'plaits', since plaits are not an 'essential' part of the body:

*Tenía trenzas grises, los ojos brillantes y burlones, la piel sucia. . .* (J. C. Onetti, 1979: 151).
She had grey plaits, bright, mocking eyes and dirty skin.
(One could, however. say *unas trenzas grises*: see **84**.) Note also that this sentence is not so appropriately translated by 'Her plaits were grey', since not everyone has plaits.

## 31 Titles and similar expressions

The definite article is used with titles and words which are used in courtesy expressions (like *capitán, doctor, general, padre* (religious), *presidente, profesor, reina, rey, señor, señora, señorita*. . .), when they are followed by names.
   The definite article is not used when such expressions are used as forms of address.

*El general Sharon presentó ayer su dimisión* (*El País*, 12 February 1983: 1).
General Sharon tendered his resignation yesterday

*Por la mañana llegó el doctor Pozuelo* (R. Garriga, 1979: 350).
Doctor Pozuelo arrived in the morning

*Estaba presente la reina Fabiola*
Queen Fabiola was present

*El profesor De Bruyne no pretende molestar a nadie* (*Aragón Expres*, 21 May 1981: 14)
Professor De Bruyne does not intend to upset anyone

*Mañana jugaré al tenis con el señor Muñoz*
Tomorrow I shall play tennis with Mr Muñoz

*Me envía el Padre Rivero* (M. Delibes, 1987: 219)
Father Rivero has sent me

But:

*¡Oh, disculpe usted, Padre!* (M. Delibes, 1987: 218)
Oh, excuse me, Father!

*¿Le gusta este libro? – Sí, señor García*
'Do you like this book?' 'Yes, Mr García'

*Señor Martínez, el señor Climent le llama* (E. Parra, 1981: 60)
Mr Martínez, Mr Clement for you

The definite article is not usually used before such titles when they appear in apposition.[3]

*Ha venido el mejor médico de la ciudad, doctor García*
The best doctor in the town, Doctor García, has come

*El coronel de mi regimiento, señor Castro, reunió a toda la oficialidad* (F. Franco Salgado-Araujo, 1977: 32)
The colonel of my regiment, Castro, called a meeting of all the officers

However, it is not impossible in such cases to find a definite article; in the same work, the author refers to

*Mi compañero de ayudantía, el comandante Bastard*
My fellow adjutant, Major Bastard

## 32  Don, Doña, San(to), Santa, Fray, Sor

Before *don* and *doña* (see **250**), no definite article is normally used (though see **41**).

*El Rey recibió ayer a don Felipe González* (*El Alcázar*, 16 February 1983: 17)
The King received Mr Felipe González yesterday

Similarly, no definite article is used with *san(to), santa* 'saint', *fray* 'brother (religious)' and *sor* 'sister (religious)' (but *hermano* 'brother' and *hermana* 'sister' do take the article in the same way as the titles in **31**).

*He leído la obra completa de San Pablo*
I have read the entire work of Saint Paul

*Santa Teresa nació en Ávila*
Saint Theresa was born in Avila

*La hermana San Sulpicio* (title of a novel by A. Palacio Valdés)
Sister San Sulpicio

## 33 *Tío, Tía*

A definite article may be used before *tío* 'uncle', and *tía* 'aunt'. In present-day Spanish, however, especially in the spoken language, there is a tendency for it to be omitted.

*La tía María me lo ha dicho* (or: *Tía María me lo ha dicho*)
Aunt Mary told me

*En aquella sala, tía Matilde recibió a sus amigas* (J. García Hortelano, 1967: 39)
Aunt Matilde received her friends in that room

*Ni tía Elisa, ni los muchachos, ni mucho menos tío Pedro, dejaban de presentarse en la mesa* (D. Medio, 1958: 26)
Neither Aunt Elisa, nor the boys, and still less Uncle Pedro, failed to appear at the table

As with titles (**31**), the article is not used in forms of address:

*Sí, tía María*
Yes, Aunt María

In referring to members of a family, the definite article is used in Spanish where English uses the title on its own:

*La abuela y Juan estaban sentados en el borde de la gran cama de matrimonio* (C. Laforet, 1966: 168)
Granny and Juan were sitting on the edge of the big double bed

## 34 Chapters, Parts of Books, Etc.

Reference to chapters, parts of books, etc., usually requires the definite article in Spanish by contrast with English:

| | |
|---|---|
| *en el capítulo once* | in chapter 11 |
| *véase la página 213* | see page 213 |

although the article is not used in a title:

| | |
|---|---|
| *CAPÍTULO XX* | CHAPTER XX |

(See also **227**.)

## 35 *(Nosotros/Vosotros)* + Definite Article + Noun

A definite article is used before a plural noun in apposition with
the personal pronouns *nosotros, vosotros, ustedes*:

> *Nosotros los aragoneses somos muy testarudos*
> We Aragonese are very stubborn

> *Vosotros/ustedes los estudiantes queréis/quieren un mundo mejor*
> You students want a better world

The personal pronoun can also be omitted. The sense is not
obscured, since the meaning is carried unambiguously by the
verb-form.

> *Los hombres dominamos mejor nuestras alegrías* (J. A. de Zun-
> zunegui, 1959a: 209)
> We men control our happiness better

> *Los españoles en América cometemos a veces pifias sociales* (D.
> Alonso, 1981: 424)
> We Spaniards in Latin America often make social blunders

(For further examples, see **245** and **1287**.)

## 36 Use of the Article in the Expression of Age and Time

A definite article is used in Spanish in many expressions of age
and time, and in expressions of time with days of the week or
words like *semana* 'week', *mes* 'month', *año* 'year'.

> Age

> *Él me enseñó a leer a los veintisiete años* (A. M. Matute,
> 1977: 165)
> He taught me to read when I was twenty-seven

> *Encuentra la postal de Eugenia cuando a los quince se fue a
> veranear a Cartagena* (R. H. Moreno-Durán, 1981: 48)
> He finds Eugenia's postcard when she went to spend the
> summer in Cartagena at the age of fifteen

*Note:* In the expression *tener + X años* 'to be X years old', no article
is used after the verb *tener*:

> *Mi hermano tiene veinte años*
> My brother is twenty

Time

*Es la una*
It's one o'clock

*¡Ya son cerca de las seis!* (M. Mihura, 1981: 132)
It's nearly six!
(Note the plural verb)

*Te lo diré a las once y veinte*
I'll tell you at twenty past eleven

(In cases like the three above, the word *hora(s)* is understood. Constructions like *El tren sale a las once horas*, although not unusual in administrative language, are considered Gallicisms.)

The definite article is often omitted in expressions where two different times are mentioned in the same phrase. The connection is indicated by prepositions (*de . . . a*; *entre . . .* ).

*De siete de la mañana a tres de la tarde* (J. Izcaray, 1961: 139)
From seven in the morning to three in the afternoon

– *¿A qué hora son las clases?*
– *De seis a ocho.* (M. Puig, 1980: 216)
'What time are the lessons?'
'From six to eight'

*Entre las dos y media de la tarde y tres y media, el marqués de Villaverde estuvo en Presidencia* (*Heraldo de Aragón*, 24 October 1975: 1)
Between half past two and half past three in the afternoon, the Marquis of Villaverde was with the Prime Minister

Otherwise the article may sometimes be omitted for stylistic reasons:

*Y ya suena el timbre. Seis y cuarto. No puede ser* (A. Carpentier, 1976: 11)
And now the bell is ringing. Quarter past six. Impossible

Note also the expression

*¿Tiene hora?*
Do you have the time?

which is very common in colloquial Spanish.

## Days of the Week

The definite article with days of the week, etc.:

> *El martes subirá la gasolina* (*El País*, 5 January 1980: 9)
> Petrol is going up on Tuesday

> *El miércoles voy al mercado*
> On Wednesday I'm going to the market

> *El año próximo mi hermano tiene que hacer el servicio militar*
> Next year my brother has to do his military service

> *Los martes me levanto a las seis*
> On Tuesday(s) I get up at six

(See also **668–669**.)

The article is omitted in appositional usage, however:

> *El Rey recibirá mañana, lunes, la Orden de la Jarretera* (*El País*, 18 June 1989: 15)
> The King will receive tomorrow, Monday, the Order of the Garter

In many Latin-American countries the variant *(el) día lunes, (el) día martes...* (with or without an article) is found for *el lunes, el martes...*:

> *Mal hecho que trabajes día domingo* (mentioned by Kany, 1951: 24)
> A shame you have to work on Sunday
> (One could also say ... *el día domingo*)

## The Year

When the noun *año* is omitted in referring to a year, the definite article is used in Spanish standing immediately before the numeral:

> *La guerra del catorce* (S. Lorén, 1971: 70)
> The war of 1914

> *La generación del 98*
> The generation of 1898 (an important group of Spanish writers)

**Seasons**

The definite article is used with the names of the seasons:

> *El otoño es la mejor estación del año*
> Autumn is the best season of the year

The use of the article is optional after prepositions:

> *Aquí nieva con frecuencia en (el) invierno*
> It frequently snows here in (the) winter

except when the season is further qualified, when the article is required:

> *En la primavera de su amor* (*DUE*, II, 841)
> In the springtime of their love

## 37  The Definite Article with the Object of *jugar* and *tocar*

The verb 'to play' is translated in Spanish by *jugar a* (if a game) or *tocar* (if an instrument). A definite article is normally used with the following noun in both cases.

> *Mi amigo Juan juega bien al fútbol*
> My friend Juan plays football well

> *Jugaban a las cartas* (G. García Márquez, 1985: 497)
> They were playing cards

> *La dueña de la casa tocaba el piano* (I. Allende, 1984: 17)
> The lady of the house was playing the piano

> *Mi primo aprende a tocar la trompeta*
> My cousin is learning to play the trumpet

In American Spanish the object of *jugar* often has no article (and no preposition *a*):

> *Comían manzanas, jugaban ajedrez, tocaban acordeón* (P. Neruda, 1976: 360)
> They were eating apples, playing chess and playing the accordion

> *Jueguen fútbol, que es buen ejercicio para las piernas* (M. Vargas Llosa, 1973: 216)
> Let them play football: it's good exercise for their legs

## 38 The Definite Article with Proper Nouns (Names of Countries and People)

No article is normally used with names of continents, countries or regions:

(i)   *Vamos a hablar de África*
      We are going to talk about Africa

(ii)  *España es un país rico en tesoros artísticos*
      Spain is a country rich in artistic treasures

(iii) *Bélgica es una monarquía constitucional*
      Belgium is a constitutional monarchy

(iv)  *¿Usted peleó en Vietnam?* (M. Puig, 1980: 26)
      Did you fight in Vietnam?

(v)   *La asistencia médica en Cataluña* (*El País*, 16 February 1983: 12)
      Medical assistance in Catalonia

Both *Estados Unidos* and *los Estados Unidos* 'the United States' are used (perhaps with a preference nowadays for the former (which is treated as singular), but the article is always used in the full name (*los Estados Unidos de América*) and the article was always used in *la Unión Soviética* 'the Soviet Union'. These remarks hold also for the abbreviations *(los) EEUU* (see also **149**) and *la URSS*. *USA* is normally used without an article.

(vi)  *Pérez de Cuéllar confía en USA y la URSS* (*El Alcázar*, 16 November 1983: 15)
      Pérez de Cuéllar has confidence in the USA and the USSR

*El Reino Unido* 'the United Kingdom', *los Emiratos Árabes Unidos* 'United Arab Emirates' and similar names of countries generally retain the article.

The article is still also used in *El Salvador* (where it is really part of the name of the country) and *la India* 'India' (but see the example after the next). It is also retained for the Spanish regions *la Mancha* and *la Rioja* (although one always speaks of *los vinos de Rioja* 'Riojan wines').

The following names of countries may still take the definite article: *la Argentina* 'Argentina, the Argentine',[4] *el Brasil* 'Brazil', *la*

*China* 'China', *el Canadá* 'Canada', *el Ecuador* 'Ecuador', *el Japón* 'Japan', *El Paraguay* 'Paraguay', *el Perú* 'Peru', *el Uruguay* 'Uruguay'.[5]

(vii) *La Argentina está compuesta principalmente por inmigrantes* (M. Puig, 1980: 31)
Argentina consists mainly of immigrants

The absence of the article is especially characteristic of journalistic usage, which here appears to be moving towards grammatical simplification.[6]

(viii) *El Rey visitará India y Japón* (*Informaciones*, 6 February 1978: 10)
The King will visit India and Japan

(ix) *Se estrella un avión en Canadá y otro en Uruguay* (*La Vanguardia*, 14 February 1978: 31)
One plane crashed in Canada, and another in Uruguay

(x) *Esas chinchas han reaparecido en Zaire* (*El Norte de Castilla*, 3 August 1988: 3)
Those bugs have reappeared in Zaire

But there is still variation, as can be seen clearly from examples like the following:

(xi) *Quieres conquistar para Cristo un imperio. – ¿El Japón, China, la India, Rusia . . . ?* (J. M. Escrivá de Balaguer, 1965: no. 315)
You will conquer an empire for Christ. Japan, China, India, Russia . . . ?

(xii) *Queremos que vengas a Brasil (. . .) Se fue al Brasil* (M. Alvar, 1982: 137)
We want you to come to Brazil (. . .) He went to Brazil

Conversely, the article is sometimes used in archaistic language and in high style, especially with names of exotic countries:

(xiii) *Sabemos que nunca llegó a la Polinesia* (M. Vázquez Montalbán, 1979b: 22)
We know that he never reached Polynesia

Similar variation in the use of the definite article occurs with acronyms denoting organizations, as, for example, *ETA*, the Basque separatist movement.

**39** The definite article is used if the name of the country or region is qualified by an adjectival phrase, unless the whole expression is thought of as the name of a country or region.

> *La Francia del Sur*
> Southern France

> *El Flandes de Erasmo* (G. Díaz-Plaja, 1981:136)
> The Flanders of Erasmus

> *Le voy a contar una biografía: la de un hombre que sólo ha conocido la España gobernada por Vd.* (F. Arrabal, 1972a: 111)
> I'm going to tell you someone's life story: a man who has only known Spain governed by you

> *Un pueblo de Castilla del Norte* (I. Aldecoa, 1970: 310)
> A village in North Castile

> *Te conocí cogiendo margaritas en las praderas de Carolina del Sur* (C. J. Cela, 1963b: 355)
> I met you picking daisies in the prairies of South Carolina

> *China Popular abrirá sus puertas* (*Informaciones*, 6 February 1978: 15)
> The People's Republic of China will open its doors

**40** The definite article is used with the names of mountains and volcanoes:

> *el Everest*            Everest
> *el Etna*              Etna

(See also **89**.)

*Sierra Bermeja*, *Sierra Morena* and *Sierra Nevada* (names of mountain ranges) are generally used without the article:

> *Lanjarón. Agua Mineral de Sierra Nevada* (on bottles of mineral water)
> Lanjarón. Mineral Water from the Sierra Nevada

although the article is used when *Sierra* is followed by *de*:

> *Al fondo, la nieve de la Sierra de Béjar sonríe como una cara doncella* (C. J. Cela, quoted in Coste and Redondo, 1965: 153)
> In the distance, the snow of the Sierra de Béjar smiles like a young girl's face

**41** In the spoken language a definite article is used before personal names, especially when people of a lower social status are referred to or where someone is mentioned contemptuously.

> *El Pepe*                    Pepe

> *La Consuelito y su sargento, tuvieron siete nenes – el Eduardo, el Pepito, la Consuelín, la Piedrita, la Conchita, el Paquito y la Merceditas . . .* (C. J. Cela. 1973: 97)
> Consuelito and her sergeant had seven children – Eduardo, Pepito, etc.

Such usage is frequent in rural areas:[7]

> In M. Delibes's *Las ratas,* where the author describes the life of individual peasants and renders their speech, almost all the characters are named in this way: *El José Luis, la Simeona, el Justito, el Antoliano, el Pruden, el Rosalino, la Sabina,* etc.

and here a definite article may even be used before the combination of Christian name and surname:

> *El Anselmo Llorente* (M. Delibes, 1987: 44 and passim).

A definite article may sometimes also be found before *don, doña,* as in older usage.[8] These constructions have a pejorative (or at least an ironical) meaning, as in the following example, where the writer may also be intending to surprise:

> *El tras de la doña Nati era otra cosa* (F. Umbral, 1980: 64)
> Doña Nati's posterior was something else

**42** At the same time, a definite article can be found before surnames (also, exceptionally, Christian names, and sometimes both together) of women (especially foreigners) who have achieved celebrity in the world of art or literature.[9]

> *Se dice que la Gardner solía acabar enamorándose locamente de un guitarrista* (F. Umbral, 1972: 184)
> It is said that (Ava) Gardner used to end up falling madly in love with a guitarist

> *Guiles llega a afirmar que la Monroe, después de Chaplin y la Garbo, ha sido la figura más famosa del séptimo arte* (M. Delibes, 1972: 122)
> Guiles even says that (Marilyn) Monroe, after Chaplin and

(Greta) Garbo, has the most famous figure in the cinema
(Note the distinction in usage between males and females)

> *La Greta Garbo, la Marlene Dietrich, la Greer Garson* (S. Fernández, 1951: 299)

> The Spanish writer Emilia Pardo Bazán was often referred to as *la Pardo Bazán*

Today, the definite article is used fairly frequently with the names of (male) politicians: this may be to give an ironical or colloquial tone (putting the least possible distance between the reader and those in power), or perhaps the surname is considered a kind of nickname, as may be the case with *el Guerra* (i.e. Alfonso Guerra, the Spanish Vice-President in the 1980s and early 1990s).

The masculine definite article is also used with an author's name to signify a book:

> *Lo consulté en el Casares y en el Moliner* (F. Marsá, 1986: 128)
> I looked it up in Casares (*Diccionario ideológico de la lengua española*) and Moliner (*DUE*)

**43** The definite article is used when an adjective precedes a name:

> *el pequeño Mateo*　　　　　　little Mateo

**44** A definite article is also sometimes used with names of animals.

> *Actualmente tengo dos perros (la «Dina», ya hecha, y el «Choc II», todavía cachorro . . .)* (M. Delibes, 1972: 169)[10]
> I have at the moment two dogs ('Dina', now fully grown, and 'Choc II', still a puppy)

## 45　Names of Languages

Names of languages are preceded by the (masculine) article:

> *El chino es difícil*　　　　　Chinese is difficult

> *Traducir al español*　　　　　Translate into Spanish

However, after *en* and certain common verbs associated with language (*aprender, enseñar, entender, estudiar, escribir, hablar, saber,* etc.), the article is normally omitted, except when the language is further specified:

> *Este libro está escrito en francés*
> This book is written in French

> *Hablo francés y español*
> I can speak French and Spanish

> *Habla el español de Chile*
> She speaks the Spanish of Chile

## 46 Names of Colours

Names of colours are preceded by the (masculine) article (see also **93**):

> *El rojo es mi color preferido*
> Red is my favourite colour

But there is no article after a preposition:

> *Pintó la pared de rojo*
> He painted the wall red

## 47 Heaven and Hell

| | |
|---|---|
| *el cielo* | heaven |
| *el infierno* | hell |

## 48 *En (la) cama*

There is a difference in meaning between *estar en cama* and *estar en la cama*, *estar en cama* implying 'to keep to one's bed' and *estar en la cama* simply 'to be in bed':

> *Mujer, me quieres ver en cama para toda la vida* (J. Fernández Santos, 1977: 65)
> You want to see me stuck in bed all my life, woman

> *Estaban en la cama él y la cuñada* (J. Goytisolo, 1981: 64)
> He and his sister-in-law were in bed

## 49 Idiomatic Expressions

A definite article is used in numerous idiomatic expressions in Spanish, e.g.:

| | |
|---|---|
| *dar la bienvenida a alguien* | to welcome someone |
| *por las buenas o por las malas* | by fair means or foul |
| *dar los buenos días a alguien* | to say good morning to someone |
| *ir a la cama* | to go to bed |
| *a/en la cárcel* | to/in prison |
| *a/en la ciudad* | to/in town |
| *dar la enhorabuena a alguien* | to congratulate someone |
| *ir a la escuela* | to go to school |
| *al/en el espacio* | into/in space |
| *dar las gracias a alguien* | to thank someone |
| *al/en el hospital* | to/in hospital |
| *a/en la iglesia* | to/in church |
| *al mercado* | to market |
| *dar el pésame a alguien* | to express one's condolences to someone |
| *dar la razón a alguien* | to admit someone is right |

## 50 More than One Noun

When two or more nouns are linked by a conjunction (such as *y* or *o*), or appear in a list, Spanish often uses a definite article in each case, whereas the article before the second and subsequent nouns is omitted in English. Purists insist on this when the first noun is feminine and subsequent nouns are masculine:

*Las mujeres, los viejos y los niños fueron acomodados en carros* (DUE, I, 265)
The women, old people and children were put in carts

However, there is considerable flexibility when the sequence of nouns includes a mixture of genders:

*Una guía de las calles, plazas, parques y paseos de la ciudad* (ibid.)
A guide to the streets, squares, parks and avenues of the town

In a group of two nouns, the absence of an article with the second noun may imply that both refer to the same thing:

> *La villa y corte* (soubriquet for Madrid)
> The town and the capital (both designate Madrid)

An article is therefore used with the second noun to make clear that the two nouns do *not* refer to the same thing; contrast:

> *Ésta es la iglesia o capilla de San Lorenzo*
> This is the church or (rather) chapel of San Lorenzo
>
> *¿Quiere ver la iglesia o la capilla?*
> Do you want to see the church or (instead) the chapel?

## 51 With the Infinitive

The infinitive often functions just like a noun in Spanish (see **1178**) and in such cases it may be preceded by *el*:

> *El fumar es peligroso*  Smoking is dangerous

## 52 As a Possessive

On the use of a definite article with the value of a possessive, see **323**.

## 53 Definite Article in English, No Definite Article in Spanish

The definite article is often not used in Spanish with a noun which is in apposition (see also **73**):

> *Lolo Sainz, nuevo entrenador de la selección nacional de balon-cesto* (*Gente*, supplement to *Diario16*. 6 June 1993: 3)
> Lolo Sainz, the new national basketball team coach
>
> *Seis cortesanos, únicos testigos de la boda Imperial* (*ABC*, 10 June 1993: 31–2).
> Six courtiers, the only witnesses of the Imperial wedding

**54** With some words denoting 'residence' or 'seat (of government, etc.)', no article is used after the prepositions *a*, *de* and *en*, unless such words are qualified by an adjectival phrase or clause.

> *Estas gentes van a asaltar Palacio – temió Ramón* (J. A. de Zun zunegui, 1952a: 238)

'These people are going to attack the Palace,' said Ramón fearfully

*Hace un par de meses asistí a una reunión en Palacio* (C. Fuentes, 1979: 12)
A couple of months ago I attended a meeting at the Palace

*Vete a Estado Mayor y te enterarás* (J. L. Castillo Puche, 1956: 302)
Go to Staff HQ and you'll find out

*Camino de Capitanía* (F. Umbral, 1987: 105)
On the way to the Captaincy General (the building where the offices of a *capitán general*, the highest rank in the Spanish Army, are situated)

Occasionally, *el* is found with *Palacio*, but in such cases it seems that it is the building that is being alluded to (rather than the institution or its functional aspects):

*Fuimos los primeros en dejar el Palacio* (F. Franco Salgado-Araujo, 1977: 127)
We were the first to leave the Palace

Omission of the definite article with names of Ministries and other administrative bodies is a characteristic of journalistic language:

*Interior informará a los partidos de nuevo sobre los contactos con ETA* (*Diario 16*, 10 February 1989: 5)
The Ministry of the Interior will brief the parties again on their contact with ETA

*Tráfico grabará en vídeo las infracciones de los conductores* (*ABC*, 10 February 1989: 13)
The Traffic Police will record driving offences on video

*Con esta evolución – explica Trabajo – el descenso del paro es del 10,84 por ciento* (*El Norte de Castilla*, 13 August 1989)
With this development, the Ministry of Labour explains, unemployment has gone down by 10.84 per cent

## 55 *Casa, escuela*, etc.

The use of the article with *casa* is similar to that described in **54**.

*Al salir de casa, tropezó con don Rufino* (J. A. de Zunzunegui, 1958: 177)

As he left home, he bumped into Don Rufino

However, in Latin America and Andalusia a definite article is often used with *casa*:

*Volvimos a la casa* (J. C. Onetti, 1979: 62)
We went home
(See also Kany, 1951: 20).

No article is used in the expressions *a casa de, en casa de, de casa de*, in spite of the fact that *casa* is followed by an adjectival phrase in such cases.

*Aureliano había dejado a su novia en casa de sus padres* (G. García Márquez, 1977: 221)
Aureliano had left his girlfriend at her parents' house

There is a clear difference between *ir a escuela* and *ir a la escuela*, the first denoting a habitual activity and the second referring to a specific occasion.

## 56 *A principios*, etc.

There is no definite article in the expressions *a principios de* 'at the beginning of', *a mediados de* 'in the middle of', *a fines de* 'at the end of'.

*A principios de noviembre* (*DUE*, II, 844)
At the beginning of November

But *al principio de, al comienzo de*:

*Al principio de la guerra* (*DUE*, II, 844)
At the start of the war

## 57 *Más, meños, mejor* and *peor* used Adverbially as Superlatives

No definite article is used in Spanish when *más, menos, mejor* and *peor* are used as adverbs in a superlative sense.

*Nos abandonó cuando más lo necesitábamos*
He left us in the lurch when we needed him (the) most

> *Esto es lo que menos nos ha divertido en la película*
> This is what amused us (the) least in the film

> *Éste es el producto que mejor se ha vendido*
> This is the product which has sold (the) best

But:

> *Este producto me parece el peor*
> This product seems to me the worst
> (Here *peor* is being used adjectivally)

## 58 In Titles of Kings and Queens

For the absence of the Spanish article before a numeral in the titles of kings and queens, etc., see **229**.

## 59 Optional Use of the Article

The definite article is optional in a number of idiomatic expressions, e.g. *con (el) pretexto de* 'on the pretext of', *con (la) intención de* 'with the intention of', *con (el) deseo de* 'with the desire to'.[11]

For the use of the article with the term *por cien* 'per cent' (%), see **1285**.

## 60 Definite Article as a Pronoun

In some usages, the Spanish definite article forms are translated by a pronoun in English.

## 61 Definite Article before *de*

The definite article forms are used before *de* noun:

> *Este libro y el de la cubierta verde*
> This book and the one with the green cover

## 62 Special Meanings of *la de*

*La de* has one or two established elliptical meanings:

> *La de Bringas* (title of novel by B. Pérez Galdós)
> Bringas's wife

*Fuimos a la de Martín*
We went to Martín's place

*Paco tiene el cuerpo como una criba, la de metrallazos, no puedes hacerte idea* (M. Delibes, 1969a: 276)
Paco's body is riddled like a sieve, you just can't imagine the number of shrapnel wounds

*Siempre había creído que su hijo era un botarate. ¡Con la de mujeres que hay en Madrid, ir a escoger a esa espingarda!* (M. Aub, 1971: 134)
He had always believed his son was an idiot. Fancy, with all the women there are in Madrid, going and choosing that beanpole!

(Compare a similar meaning of *la que*, **345**.)

## 63 The Use of the 'Neuter' Article *lo*: Nominalized Adjectives and Past Participles

Definite article + adjective in Spanish corresponds to definite article + adjective + 'one' in English:

*Este libro y el verde*
This book and the green one

*No en la casa antigua sino en la nueva*
Not in the old house but in the new one

The usage extends to past participles, which, especially when qualified, may be expanded to relative clauses in translation into English:

*Este problema y los ya referidos*
This problem and the ones (which have) already (been) referred to

## 64 Nominalization with *lo*

Adjectives, some ordinal numerals, past participles (see **1222**) and even adverbs can be nominalized with *lo*, when they are used in a general or abstract sense.

*Lo seguro es lo primero* (F. Umbral, 1969: 79)
Certainty is the first thing

*¿Qué es lo argentino?* (E. Sábato, 1981: 65)
What is typically Argentine?

*Felisberto Hernández y la escritura de «lo otro»:* title of a book
by F. Lasarte (mentioned in *Insula*, 425: 19)
Felisberto Hernández and the writing of 'the other thing'.
(*Lo otro* here has the meaning of *el misterio*)

*Es gente muy ocupada, déjelos venir según lo convenido*
(M. Puig, 1980: 65)
They're very busy people; let them come as agreed

*Lo perfecto es inalcanzable* (Alcina Franch and Blecua,
1975: 570)
Perfection is unattainable
(The authors point out that in a case like this *lo perfecto* could
be replaced by *la perfección. Esbozo,* 408–9, observes that *lo
bueno, lo útil, lo rápido, lo oscuro*, etc., are synonymous with *la
bondad* 'goodness', *la belleza* 'beauty', *la utilidad* 'usefulness',
*la rapidez* 'speed', *la oscuridad* 'darkness', etc., if these nouns
are used in 'their most abstract and general sense'; and for S.
Fernández[12] there is practically no difference in modern
Spanish between *el contrario* and *lo contrario* 'contrary'.

*Ese poeta ya nos conocía en lo lejos del tiempo* (J. Cortázar, 1973:
140)
That poet knew us already far back in time

*Lo más que haremos es darnos unos besos* (G. Cabrera Infante,
1979: 453)
The most we will do is kiss a bit

*Alonso Fariños pertenecía a lo mejor de Vigo* (R. Garriga,
1980: 314)
A. F. belonged to the cream of Vigo society

It will be noted that English rarely has a simple equivalent for such
expressions, and translation usually involves nouns like *thing* or
*matter*, or the use of a clause.

The noun-like nature of *lo* + adjective, etc. is clearly shown in
the following examples, where the construction is used in conjunction with 'true' (masculine or feminine) nouns:

*En ambas poetisas cuenta la ternura, lo apasionado, lo religioso*
(C. Conde, 1979: 21)

In both poetesses, the tender, the passionate and the religious are important

*Las palabras y lo indecible*: title of an essay by R. Gómez de la Serna.
Words and the unsayable

*La Nada y lo Absoluto* (E. Sábato, 1981: 135)
Nothingness and the Absolute

*Lo* + adjective may be qualified by a further adjective:

*Resulta evidente la dependencia cervantina de lo italiano renacentista* (C. Blanco Aguinaga *et al.,* 1979-81: I, 330)
Cervantes's dependence on the (ideas of) the Italian Renaissance is evident

## 65 *Lo* + Adjective with Adverbial Value

*Lo* + adjective has an adverbial value in constructions like the following:

*Carmen Elgazu se emocionó lo indecible* (J. M. Gironella, 1966a: 163)
Carmen Elgazu was unutterably moved.
(One could also say: ... *se emocionó indeciblemente*)

Note also

*Abandone lo antes posible esta posición* (F. Franco Salgado-Araujo, 1977: 52)
Abandon this position as quickly as possible

## 66 *A* + *lo* + Adjective

*A* + *lo* followed by an adjective or by a masculine or feminine noun used adjectivally has the same meaning as *a la manera (de)*. In these frequent combinations a feminine noun or a proper noun (perhaps preceded by words like *don, Infanta,* etc.) can also be found.

*Saludar a lo militar*
To salute in the military fashion

*– Tú, con tu novio, ¿qué harías con él?*
*– Quererle mucho.*
*– Pero ¿a lo alegre o a lo funeral?*
*–A lo serio* (J. García Hortelano, 1979: 177)
'What will you do with your boyfriend?'
'Love him a lot.'
'But cheerfully or miserably?'
'Seriously'

*La mujer llegó a lo hombre y con traje de amazona* (A. Roa Bastos, 1977: 230)
The woman arrived riding like a man and dressed like an Amazon

*Esperará en un coche muy a lo señorona* (J. A. de Zunzunegui, 1954: 67)
She will wait in a car very like a great lady

*Este hombre llevaba grandes bigotes a lo Napoleón III* (P. Baroja, 1951: 42)
This man had a large moustache à la Napoleon III

*La batalla del Ebro se prolongó durante varios meses en una tremenda carnicería a lo Verdun* (J. L. Comellas, 1967: 634)
The Battle of the Ebro went on for several months in a tremendous butchery that was reminiscent of Verdun

*A lo don José Gutiérrez* (F. Umbral, 1985: 15)
Like Don José Gutiérrez

*Sus hijas Elisa y Blanca traían el pelo cortado «a lo Infanta Cristina»* (D. Medio, 1958: 80)
Her daughters Elisa and Blanca had their hair cut short à la Infanta Cristina

The construction is similar in meaning to *a* + *la* + feminine adjective (see **671**). Sometimes the two expressions are found in the same sentence:

*Guillermina era una escritora a la francesa, a lo parisino, una escritora de verdad* (F. Umbral, 1981: 52)
Guillermina was a writer in the French tradition and in the Parisian tradition – a real writer

## 67 Set Phrases with *lo* + Adjective

*Lo* appears in a number of adverbial phrases beginning with the prepositions *a*, *de* and *por*, such as:

| | |
|---|---|
| *a lo largo* | lengthways |
| *a lo mejor* | perhaps |
| *a lo primero* | at first, initially |
| *a lo sumo* | at (the) most |
| *a lo vivo* | vividly |
| *de lo lindo* | wonderfully |
| *por lo contrario* | on the contrary |
| *por lo general* | in general |
| *por lo regular* | usually |

## 68 *Lo* + *de* + Noun

In combinations which consist of *lo* + an adjectival phrase introduced by *de*, the article/pronoun refers to facts, events, states of affairs, etc., of which the hearer or the reader is assumed to have prior knowledge. In translation into English, expansion is always necessary. In these constructions a neuter demonstrative pronoun could also be used instead of *lo* (see **309**).

> *Recordé lo de Encarna* (J. García Hortelano, 1967: 32)
> I remembered the Encarna business
> (This is an allusion to an abortion)

> *Venía por lo de la ginebra* (F. Umbral, 1966: 80)
> He came about the gin
> (The speaker had been promised a bottle of gin)

> *Lo del cerdo fue un martes* (I. Allende, 1984: 29)
> The business with the pig took place on a Tuesday
> (An election candidate had been sent a roast pig by his supporters)

(See also **620**).

## 69 Intensifying Use of *lo* . . . *que* Corresponding to English 'How'

*Lo* has an adverbial value when it is used before an adjective or past participle that qualifies a noun or a pronoun. In such cases the adjective or past participle agrees in number and gender with the word to which it refers.[13] The adjective or past participle is always followed by the relative *que*.

> *Sabido es lo sobrios que son los españoles* (P. Baroja, 1951: 159)
> It is well known how sober the Spanish are

> *¿No ves lo solas que estamos?* (J. M. Gironella, 1966b: 641)
> Can't you see how alone we are?
> (In this example, the adjective *solas* qualifies the understood subject of *estamos*, which is *nosotras*)

> *Da pena ver lo abandonado que está eso* (J. Icaza, 1980: 7)
> It grieves one to see how neglected it is

> *Su hermano se escandalizaba recordando lo desdeñoso y cruel que Carlos Marx había sido con su hijo ilegítimo* (R. J. Sender, 1979: 54)
> His brother got agitated as he remembered how (very) scornful and cruel Karl Marx had been towards his illegitimate son

Related to this usage is the following, where *lo* + adjective has an emphatic meaning:

> *Es gente de lo más sencilla y comprensiva* (J. Edwards, 1971: 49)
> They are the simplest and most understanding of people

*Lo ... que* may also be used with adverbs:

> *La gente sonríe, sin meditar en lo deprisa que envejecemos* (F. Umbral, 1972: 92)
> People smile, without thinking how fast we age

> *Ella se confundió en elogios sobre lo «en condiciones» que había llegado el señor de París* (A. Carpentier, 1976: 49)
> She stumbled in her praise of how the gentleman had returned from Paris in such 'good form'

or with no intervening element at all, in which case a general adverb like *mucho* or *bien* is implied: *Ya sé lo que trabaja = ya sé lo mucho/bien que trabaja* 'I know how much/well he works'.

> *Apreté el paso lo que pude* (E. Parra, 1981: 72)
> I quickened my step as much as I could

*Llora lo que quieras* (C. Martín Gaite, 1980: 126)
Cry as much as you like

One may even find *lo . . . que* used with a noun, though such nouns
are clearly being used in an adjectival way:

> *Hoy – pensaba –, hoy seré todo lo mujer que puede llegar a ser
> una mujer* (I. Agustí, 1944: 136)
> 'Today', she thought, 'today I shall be as much a woman as a
> woman can become'

### 70 *Lo que, lo cual*

The definite article forms are also used to form the relative pronouns *el que*, etc. and *el cual*, etc. See **Relatives**.

## The Indefinite Article

Forms

**71**

| | |
|---|---|
| *un* (masculine singular) | *unos* (masculine plural) |
| *una* (feminine singular) | *unas* (feminine plural) |

### 72 Use of *Un* for *Una*

The masculine form *un* is generally used before a feminine noun
which is in the singular and begins with a stressed *a* or *ha* (compare the use of *el* in **28**).

> *un hacha*                    an axe

> *A menudo un teléfono resulta un arma asesina* (E. Parra,
> 1981: 102)
> A telephone often turns into a murder weapon

But:

> *una abeja*          a bee
> (The stress falls on the second syllable)
>
> *una sola arma*       a single weapon
> (There is an adjective between the article and *arma*)

## Usage

### 73 Indefinite Article in English, No Indefinite Article in Spanish

In both English and Spanish, nouns in apposition may be introduced by the definite or the indefinite article, or no article at all. In Spanish, the following rules apply:

(1) Using the definite article with the noun in the appositional phrase is possible when the preceding noun is already identified or known about:

> *Ocaña, el chófer, se limpiaba el sudor con el pañuelo*[14]
> Ocaña, the chauffeur, was mopping his perspiration with a handkerchief
> (Ocaña is known to the speaker, perhaps as 'the chauffeur' who works for him/her)

(2) Using the indefinite article with the noun in the appositional phrase indicates that the preceding noun is considered as representing a class:

> *Ocaña, un chófer, se limpiaba el sudor con el pañuelo*
> Ocaña, a chauffeur, was mopping his perspiration with a handkerchief
> (Ocaña is thought of as one of a group of chauffeurs, perhaps the chauffeurs who work in the same town)

(3) Absence of an article with the noun in the appositional phrase means that the appositional phrase makes a simple additional comment on the preceding noun:

> *Ocaña, chófer, se limpiaba el sudor con el pañuelo*
> Ocaña, a chauffeur, was mopping his perspiration with a handkerchief
> (This simply tells us that Ocaña was a chauffeur by profession)

The use or non-use of the article in such cases depends to a certain extent in both languages on style and register, and it is therefore difficult to give hard and fast rules for usage. On the whole, it seems that Spanish is more likely to omit the article than English, and that cases which an English speaker might feel fall under rules 1 and 2 above are regularly felt by Spanish speakers to fall under rule 3:

*Susanita Rey Expósito, jefa de la comunidad* (J. Marsé, quoted in Nieves, 1984: 85)
Susanita Rey Expósito, the head of the community

*El 12 de diciembre, día de la Virgen de Guadalupe* (C.-J. Cela, quoted in Nieves, 1984: 86)
12 December, the day of the Virgin of Guadalupe

*Aquel militar – presunto amante de María Timoner – que todas las noches se jugaba las fincas de sus tías* (J. Benet quoted in Nieves, 1984: 133)
That soldier – the presumed lover of María Timoner – who every night gambled with his aunts' estates

*El hombre fue juez de una lejana provincia, oficio que ejerció con dignidad hasta el nacimiento de su segundo hijo* (I. Allende, 1990: 35)
The man was a judge in a distant province, a post he discharged with dignity until the birth of his second child

Use of an indefinite article in Spanish for cases which fall under rule 3 above is considered an anglicism.[15] S. Gili Gaya observes that in the following announcements the indefinite article is 'superfluous':

*«Fortia», Un específico contra la anemia*
'Fortia', a specific (medicine) for anaemia

*«Vidas errantes», Una película de emoción, una intriga interesante, una realización espléndida*
'Roaming lives', a moving film, a compelling plot, a magnificent production
(Both examples are taken from Gili Gaya, 1964: 243)

## 74 No Indefinite Article before certain Adjectives

The indefinite article is not used before *otro* '(an)other', nor, in the majority of cases, before *igual* 'such (a)', *medio* 'half (a)', *semejante* and *tal* 'such (a)' (but see **516**), *tamaño* 'so great a, such (a) great', when these adjectives precede a noun.

### Medio

> *He comprado medio kilo de patatas*
> I've bought half a kilo of potatoes

Attention should be paid to expressions of measurement like *centímetro y medio* 'one and a half centimetres', *kilo y medio* 'one and a half kilos', *minuto y medio* 'a minute and a half', etc., where there is no indefinite article before the noun.

> *He comprado kilo y medio de patatas*
> I've bought one and a half kilos of potatoes

But:

> *Joaquín era algo menos que ella: un año y medio menos* (J. Edwards, 1985: 143)
> Joaquín was a bit younger than her: a year and a half younger

With some nouns the meaning of *medio* is changed if it is preceded by an indefinite article. There is a difference between

> *Beber media botella de vino*
> To drink half a bottle (i.e. half the contents of a whole bottle) of wine

and

> *Pedir una media botella de vino*
> To ask for a half bottle (i.e. a bottle half the size of a whole one) of wine

### Otro

> *Me serví otro té* (E. Parra, 1981: 109)
> I poured myself another cup of tea

### Semejante

> *Semejante explicación no me satisface*
> Such an explanation does not satisfy me

### Igual

> *Durante varios años siguió haciendo igual vida* (R. Altamira, cited in J. Coste and A. Redondo, 1965: 166)
> He continued the same way of life for several years

Note also:

> *¿Has visto cosa igual?*
> *¡No había oído en mi vida cosa igual!* (*DUE*, I, 788)
> 'Have you ever seen the like?'
> 'I've never heard the like in my life!'

### Tamaño

> *Esta historia no caerá en tamaña omisión* (R. de la Cierva, 1975: 19)
> This history will not make such a great omission

### Tal (see **515–516**)

But:

> *No me satisface una explicación semejante*
> Such an explanation does not satisfy me
> (The adjective *semejante* comes AFTER the noun)

## 75 Cierto

When *cierto* '(a) certain (= a particular), a little' precedes the noun. the indefinite article is considered by some authorities to be incorrect, though it is frequently found nowadays.[16] The construction with the article is more emphatic, as shown in the third example below:

> Françoise Sagan's novel *Un certain sourire* was translated into Spanish as *Una cierta sonrisa.* 'A Certain Smile'

> *No abandona uno sin cierta melancolía a estos buenos gallegos* (F. Umbral, 1966: 183)
> One doesn't leave these nice Galicians without a certain melancholy

> – *Le tenía usted cierto cariño*
> – *Ríase si quiere. Un cierto cariño* (M. Vázquez Montalbán, 1979b: 2)
> 'You felt a certain affection for him'
> 'Laugh if you want. A *certain* affection'

Contrast the use of *cierto* 'certain, true' *after* the noun: *una señal cierta* 'a definite sign'.

## 76 *Tan* + Adjective

There is no indefinite article in the construction *tan* + adjective + noun. but the construction is restricted to the written language, and is archaic in tone.

> *En tan difícil situación se acuerda de su compañero* (F. Franco Salgado-Araujo. 1977: 119)
> In such a difficult situation he remembers his companion

## 77 *¡Qué . . . !*

Spanish *¡qué!* + noun corresponds to English 'what a' + noun (see below **367–370**).

## 78 No Indefinite Article with certain Nouns

There is often no indefinite article before nouns which denote a quantity, such as *cantidad* 'quantity. amount', *número* 'number', *parte* 'part', *porción* 'portion', etc., whether or not they are preceded by an adjective.

> *Parte del público se levantaba* (P. Baroja, 1952: 14)
> A section of the audience stood up
> (One could also say: *Buena parte del público se levantaba*)
>
> *Había caído gran cantidad de nieve*
> A great quantity of snow had fallen

But also:

> *Aún le quedaba por velar una buena parte de la noche* (J. Fernández Santos, 1977: 28)
> There was still a good part of the night left for him to keep watch

## 79 No Indefinite Article after certain Verbs

The indefinite article is omitted with *unqualified* nouns after the verbs given below.

*Ser*

> *La oración del cristiano nunca es monólogo* (J. M. Escrivá de Balaguer, 1965: no. 114)
> The Christian's prayer is never a monologue

With professions:

> *Mi padre es ingeniero*
> My father is an engineer

Where membership of a category is indicated, even a qualified noun is used without an article:

> *Yo soy hermano de Isabel* (C. Martín Gaite, 1980: 124)
> I'm a brother of Isabel's

*Haber*

> *Para ti hay cama – me advirtieron* (M. Delibes, 1976: 102)
> 'There's a bed for you,' they informed me

*Tener*

> *¿Tienes revólver?* (R. J. Sender, 1965–6:II, 404)
> Have you got a revolver?

> *¿Tiene hora?*
> Have you got the time?

> *Tener coche sería el sueño del pueblo español durante las décadas siguientes* (R. de la Cierva, 1975: 84)
> Owning a car became the Spanish people's dream during the following decades

> *Tenía casa grande, esposa y cuatro hijos* (J. Ibargüengoitia, 1981: 71)
> He had a big house, a wife and four children

But:

> *Mi amigo Juan tiene un coche muy potente*
> My friend Juan has a very powerful car

The difference between the presence and absence of the indefinite article with the object of *tener* is difficult to state accurately. The absence of an article often indicates the idea of a category rather than an individual item: in the third example under *tener* above, *tener coche* has the fuller meaning of 'to achieve the status of car-ownership' rather than simple 'to have a car'.[17] The indefinite article also sometimes has the idea of number associated with it: the difference between *¿Tienes suegra?* 'Have you a mother-in-law?' and *¿Tienes una cuñada?* 'Have you a sister-in-law?' appears to depend on the fact that one normally has only one mother-in-law but may have several sisters-in-law.

### Llevar

> *Mi tío lleva gafas*
> My uncle wears glasses

But:

> *Tienes unas gafas elegantes*
> You've got (some) elegant glasses

### Usar

> *Yo no uso abrigo para salir a la calle*
> I don't wear an overcoat to go out

## 80 After certain Prepositions and Prepositional Phrases

The objects of the following prepositions often have no article when they refer to general categories:

### Como

> *Sentirse como pez en el agua*
> To be like a fish in water

### Con

> *Un hombrecillo con cara de gitana* (M. Vázquez Montalbán, 1990b: 15)
> A little man with a face like a gipsy's

> *Esta noche va a ser la primera que Antonio pasará con mujer nueva* (F. García Pavón, 1980: 156)
> Tonight will be the first Antonio spends with a new wife
> (An ironical example, conveying the idea that *mujer nueva* is regarded by Antonio as a 'category')

### Por

> *Querer por esposa* (*DD*, 294)
> To want as a wife

*Sin*

> *No salgas sin abrigo*
> Don't go out without a coat

But:

> *Nos hemos quedado sin un céntimo*
> We haven't got a (single) cent
> (Here the idea of number is important)

## *A modo/manera de*

> *Llevaba la toalla a modo de bufanda* (*DUE*, II, 432)
> She was wearing the towel like a scarf
>
> *Llevaba un capazo a manera de sombrero* (*DUE*, II, 335)
> She was wearing a basket like a hat

### 81 Other Uses of the Indefinite Article in Spanish

The use of an indefinite article can render the idea of 'approximately'.

> – *¿Cuánto tarda el tranvía?*
> – *No sé; supongo que una media hora* (R. Chacel, 1981: 76)
> 'How long is it before the tram comes?'
> 'I don't know; about half an hour, I suppose'

This is one of the principal uses of the plural form *unos, unas* (see **379**).

**82** Sometimes the noun is omitted and only the indefinite article is found. Such cases are similar to the examples given in **62**, where clearly a word like *cantidad* 'quantity' is omitted.

> *Arlequín contaba una de mentiras tremendas de lo que había visto en el mar* (P. Baroja, 1956: 238)
> Arlequín was telling a whole string of lies about what he had seen at sea.

**83** The article is sometimes suppressed in certain registers of Spanish, as in English, for reasons of economy (notices, newspaper headlines, etc.):[18]

A frequent Spanish notice forbidding parking in front of a garage or exit runs:
*LLAMAMOS GRÚA*
We call the breakdown truck (US tow car) (i.e. vehicles parked here will be towed away)

*Según se ha visto en capítulo anterior* (J. Caro Baroja, 1969: 148)
As seen in a previous chapter

*Recuerde color. Entrada tienda* (notices in underground car park for a department store)
Remember your colour. Entrance to the shop

*Madre víctima* (subtitle on television news)
The mother of the victim

## 84 Use of the Plural

*Unos (unas)* is also encountered before nouns used in the plural which suggest the idea of 'a pair'.

*Gloria tenía los labios gruesos y unos ojos grandes y claros* (C. Martín Gaite, 1980: 70)
Gloria had thick lips and (a pair of) large, clear eyes

*Un cuello que se deslizaba hacia unos senos oprimidos por esa camiseta blanca* (A. Skármeta, 1986: 46)
A neck sliding down towards (a pair of) breasts which were tightly held by that white T-shirt

In 1981 a poster issued by the Banco Español de Ojos (Spanish Eye Bank), which was widely distributed in Spain, read as follows:
*¿CUÁNTO PUEDEN VALER UNOS OJOS?*
What can the value of a pair of eyes be?

*Los generales no veían la necesidad de acumular las funciones militares y civiles en unas solas manos* (R. Garriga, 1980: 89)
The generals could not see the need to accumulate military and civil functions in a single pair of hands

## 85 Emphatic Use of the Indefinite Article

In constructions where an adjective is nominalized by means of *un* (*una, unos, unas*), the indefinite article appears to have an emphatic value. In sentences like *eres un tonto* 'you're an idiot'. *sois unos tontos* 'you're idiots', *un tonto*, etc.. carries the idea of a type rather than simply an attribute:

> – *Eres un tonto* – *gritó don Cosme.* – *Tendrás que hacer dos viajes.*
> – *No soy ningún tonto, jefe. Veré al poeta dos veces* (A. Skármeta, 1986: 36)
> 'You're a real fool,' yelled Don Cosme. 'You'll have to make two journeys.'
> 'I'm no fool, boss. I'll see the poet twice.'
> (Note that *unos* becomes the singular *ninguno* in a negative sentence: see **406**)

# The Noun

## Gender

**86** All Spanish nouns are either masculine or feminine (for 'neuter' nominalizations with *lo* see **64**).

### 87 Rules for Determining Gender

The gender of Spanish nouns is essentially arbitrary, although a number of helpful 'rules' can be given.

Gender Associated with Meaning

### 88 Masculine: Nouns Denoting Male Persons or Animals, Professions or Titles Traditionally Associated with Men

| | |
|---|---|
| *el hombre* | man |
| *el elefante* | (bull) elephant |
| *el sastre* | tailor |
| *el rey* | king |
| *el general* | general |

(See also **105** on *granuja*, *mierda*, etc.)

The first four have the feminine counterparts *la mujer*, *la elefanta*, *la sastr(es)a*, *la reina* (see also **120–122**).

## 89 The Names of most Rivers, Mountains, Volcanoes and Mountain Ranges

It may be that such words as *(el) río, (el) monte, (el) volcán* are felt to be understood here.[1]

| | |
|---|---|
| *el Ebro* | the Ebro |
| *el Támesis* | the Thames |
| *el Amazonas* | the Amazon |
| *el Sena* | the Seine |
| *el Pirineo, los Pirineos* | the Pyrenees |
| *el Etna* | Mount Etna |

But a name which includes a feminine noun, e.g. *sierra* 'mountain range' as its nucleus is feminine in its entirety:

| | |
|---|---|
| *la Sierra Nevada* | the Sierra Nevada |

## 90 Days of the Week

| | |
|---|---|
| *un martes del mes pasado* | one Tuesday last month |

## 91 Months

| | |
|---|---|
| *un septiembre muy lluvioso* | a very rainy September |

## 92 Points of the Compass

| | |
|---|---|
| *el norte de España* | the north of Spain |

## 93 Colours

| | |
|---|---|
| *el rojo* | red |

## 94 Musical Notes

| | |
|---|---|
| *el do* | doh, C |

## 95 Other Parts of Speech which are Nominalized

| | | | |
|---|---|---|---|
| *ahora* | now | *el ahora* | the present |
| *cinco* | five | *el cinco* | five (the figure) |
| *sí* | yes | *el sí* | consent, approval |

| | | | |
|---|---|---|---|
| *pero* | but | *el pero* | objection |
| *deber* | to have to | *el deber* | duty |

The title of a work by C. Sánchez-Albornoz reads: *Del ayer y del hoy de España* 'Spain past and present' (see also **150**)

An important exception is *la nada* 'nothing(ness)':

*Pues, partiendo de la nada, había hecho millones* (D. Fernández Flórez, 1973: 86)
Since starting out from nothing, he had made millions

## 96 Feminine: Nouns which Indicate Female Persons or Animals, Professions or Titles Traditionally Associated with Women

| | |
|---|---|
| *la mujer* | woman, wife |
| *la vaca* | cow |
| *la costurera* | seamstress |
| *la reina* | queen |
| *la modelo* | (female) model |

*Va usted a ser mi modelo preferida* (F. Umbral, 1980: 174)
You will be my favourite model.

*Note:* the noun *marimacho* 'mannish woman, lesbian' is generally masculine (*un marimacho*), although there is some variation.

*Nunca he conocido a ningún marimacho de verdad. A pesar de que dicen que hay tantas, nunca he visto a ninguna* (M. Vargas Llosa, 1986: 40)
I've never known any really butch woman. Despite the fact that people say there are so many of them, I've never seen one.

## 97 Letters of the Alphabet

| | |
|---|---|
| *la a* (see also **28**), *la b* | a, b |

However, in aeroplanes, seats are referred to as *el a, el b*, etc. (presumably because *asiento* 'seat' is understood).

## 98 Special Cases: Names of Towns

Names of towns are generally masculine unless they end in *-a*. But a 'masculine' town may be treated as feminine when the idea of *ciudad* is in the speaker's mind:[2]

*Nos veremos pues en la bella Amberes* (M. Vargas Llosa to JdeB,
25 October 1984)
See you in beautiful Antwerp, then
(But in one of R. Navas Ruiz's poems (*Insula*, 469, December
1985, p. 2) we find twice the sequence *viejo Amberes* 'old
Antwerp')

*¡Es la Nueva Bizancio!* (S. Lorén, 1971: 110)
That's New Byzantium!

'Feminine' towns are treated as masculine when preceded by *todo,
medio, un, propio* or *mismo,*[3] which explains the changing gender of
Pisa in the following examples:

> *Todo Pisa estaba en las calles. Y no quedó un tejado en todo Pisa
> en donde no se viera un grupo de ciudadanos* (E. Jardiel Pon-
> cela, 1959: IV, 535)
> *Pisa entera se puso de rodillas* (ibid., 539)
> *Y Pisa quedó desierta . . .* (ibid., 541)
> All Pisa was in the streets. There was not a single rooftop in
> Pisa where a group of townspeople could not be seen.
> The whole of Pisa knelt down.
> And Pisa lay deserted.

## 99  Names of Ships

Names of ships are treated as masculine, even when they are
feminine nouns or carry a woman's name, which sometimes leads
to apparently odd combinations, as in examples (i)–(iii) below.
But if the boat in question is being thought of as a feminine noun
(e.g. *barca, fragata*, etc.), the name may also be treated as feminine
(even when the noun is masculine, as in (v) below).

(i)   *El «Nueva Fidelidad»* (G. García Márquez, 1985: 471)
      The 'New Fidelity'

(ii)  *El Virgen de África* (A. Grosso, 1978: 133)
      The African Maid

(iii) *Nos encontrábamos felices en la cubierta del Paulina* (F.
      Franco Salgado-Araujo, 1977: 26)
      We were happy on the *Paulina's* deck

But:

> (iv)   *La Cornucopia* (P. Baroja, 1960: 35, 45, etc.)
>
> (v)   *La Zafiro* (P. Baroja, 1955: 108 – here an abbreviation of *la fragata Zafiro* 'the frigate Zafiro')
>
> (vi)   *La Plencitarra* (ibid., 181)
>
> (vii)   *La Hope* (P. Baroja, 1959: 65)

## 100  Compound Nouns

Compound nouns denoting males are usually treated as masculine even when the constituent nouns are feminine:

> *Fulano es un mala leche*
> So-and-so is a nasty piece of work

However, there is hesitation in this area:

> *Juan es un(a) cabeza de turco* (E. de Bustos Gisbert, 1986: 81)
> Juan is a scapegoat

The reverse situation is more strongly resisted:

> *Juana es un/\*una culo de mal asiento*
> Juana is a real fidget

### Gender Associated with Ending

### 101  Masculine: Nouns Ending in -*o*

| | |
|---|---|
| *el libro* | book |
| *el armario* | cupboard |
| *el matrimonio* | marriage; married couple. |

Common exceptions are:

| | |
|---|---|
| *la mano* | hand |
| *la modelo* | (female) model |

and abbreviations of words the full forms of which are (or were) feminine, such as

| | |
|---|---|
| *la foto (<la fotografía)* | photograph, |

| | |
|---|---|
| *la moto (<la motocicleta)* | motorbike, |
| *la polio (<la poliomielitis)* | polio, |
| *la radio (<la radiotelefonía)* | radio (see also **109**). |

Some Spanish girls' names likewise end in *-o*. These names are often ellipses for *Nuestra Señora de . . .* 'Our Lady of . . .' or have some other clear religious allusion, such as *Consuelo* 'consolation', *Rosario* 'rosary', *Patrocinio* 'patronage', etc.

## 102 Feminine: Nouns Ending in *-a*

The majority of nouns ending in *-a* are feminine:

| | |
|---|---|
| *la cabeza* | head |
| *la casa* | house |
| *la maleta* | suitcase |

However, there are a large number of exceptions, including very commonly used words like

| | |
|---|---|
| *los antípodas* | the Antipodes |
| *el clima* | climate |
| *el día/el mediodía* | day/midday |
| *el mapa* | map |
| *el pijama* | pyjamas |
| (but also *la piyama* in Latin America) | |
| *el planeta rojo* | the red planet (Mars) |
| *el problema* | problem |
| *el sistema* | system |
| *el tema* | theme, topic |
| *el tranvía* | tram |

## 103 'Learnèd' Words Ending in *-ma*

Most 'learnèd' words ending in *-ma* are masculine:

| | |
|---|---|
| *el diagrama* | diagram |
| *el enigma* | enigma |
| *el síntoma* | symptom, etc. |

But there are several exceptions:

| | |
|---|---|
| *el asma* (f) | asthma |
| *la diadema* | diadem |
| *la enzima* | enzyme |

> *la estratagema*                   stratagem
> *la flema*                         phlegm

*El eccema* 'eccema', *el enema*[4] 'enema', *el fantasma* 'ghost' and *el reuma/reúma* (see **15**) 'rheumatism' are often treated as feminine in popular speech.[5]

Note also that *el alma* (f) and *la rima* are feminine.

## 104 Nouns Ending in *-a* which Denote Males

Nouns which end in *-a* but which denote males are normally masculine:

> *el cura*                              priest
> *el dentista* (and other *-ista* nouns) dentist
> *el impresionista*                     impressionist
> *el poeta*                             poet
> *el recluta*                           recruit (male), etc.

> *¿Iba yo a dejarte hacer de él un marica?* (R. Chacel, 1981: 98)
> Was I going to let you make a pansy of him?

> *El fiscal pide una pena de 45 años para el brigada acusado de violación* (*El Mundo*, 8 March 1990: 1)
> The prosecutor demands a forty-five year sentence for the warrant officer accused of rape

However, the following are feminine:

> *la criatura*                          child, creature
> *la estrella*                          (film) star
> *la persona*                           person
> *la víctima*                           victim

**105** Into this category also fall a number of feminine nouns used figuratively of people, such as:

> *el cabecilla*                         hothead
> *el cámara*                            cameraman
> *el piel roja*                         redskin, Red Indian
> *el camisa vieja* (a term used to refer to old members of the Spanish Falangist party)

and several pejorative feminine words which similarly are masculine when used of male persons:

| *el bestia* | beast (feminine when used non-figuratively) |
| *el carroza* | in colloquial usage amongst young people, an old man who looks, or tries to look, spruce (feminine when used non-figuratively in the meaning of 'carriage') |
| *el granuja* | rascal, urchin |
| *el mierda* | shit (feminine when used non-figuratively) |
| *el sinvergüenza* | scoundrel, cheeky person |

*Además, ella y su hijo son unos mierdas* (R. H. Moreno-Durán, 1981: 109)
Besides, she and her son are a pair of shits

But the following remain feminine:

| *la fiera* | wild animal |
| *la calamidad* | disaster[6] |

## 106 Colours and Wines

Feminine nouns in -*a* are masculine when they refer to a colour or a wine:

*(la) rosa* 'rose', but

*El rosa es su color preferido*
Pink is his/her favourite colour

*El rosa no me gusta en este cuadro*
I don't like the pink in this picture

also

| *el lila* | lilac (colour) |
| but | |
| *la lila* | 'lilac (flower)' |
| *el naranja* | orange (colour) |
| but | |
| *la naranja* | 'orange (fruit)' |

*(la) Rioja* 'Rioja (region)'
but
*Hemos comprado un rioja muy bueno*
We've bought a good Rioja wine

*(la) Borgoña* 'Burgundy (region)'
but
*El borgoña de 1978 es excelente*
1978 Burgundy is excellent

*(la) Champaña* 'Champagne (region)'
but
*Y el champaña es hermoso* (M. Mihura, 1981: 128)
And champagne is nice
(*El champán* is more commonly used)

## 107 Nouns Ending in *-triz, -ie, -umbre, -(i)dad, -tad, -tud, -sión, -ción, -gión*

These are always feminine:

| | |
|---|---|
| *la cicatriz* | scar |
| *la serie* | series |
| *la muchedumbre* | crowd, multitude |
| *la bondad* | goodness |
| *la caridad* | charity |
| *la lealtad* | loyalty |
| *la virtud* | virtue |
| *la profesión* | profession |
| *la nación* | nation |
| *la región* | region |

## 108 Nouns Ending in *-ión, -zón, -z, -d*

Words with the above endings which have an abstract meaning are usually feminine:

| | |
|---|---|
| *la opinión* | opinion |
| *la razón* | reason |
| *la paz* | peace |
| *la pared* | wall |

But many common nouns with these endings are masculine, e.g.:

| | |
|---|---|
| *el gorrión* | sparrow |
| *el corazón* | heart |
| *el pez* | fish |
| *el césped* | lawn |

## 109 Words which may be either Masculine or Feminine: Different Genders with the Same Meaning

Such words are often described as belonging to a *género ambiguo* 'ambiguous gender'. However, in modern Spanish, a clear preference for one gender or the other can be perceived,[7] and in the list below, the more unusual form is given in brackets.

Sometimes the use of a masculine or feminine form is linked to register, as in the case of *calor* and *color* below.

| | |
|---|---|
| *el/(la) análisis*[8] | analysis |
| *el/(la) azúcar* | sugar |

(but often found with a feminine adjective, e.g. *azúcar fina* 'castor sugar', *azúcar morena* 'brown sugar').[9]

| | |
|---|---|
| *el/(la) calor* | heat |
| *el(la) color* | colour |

(*La calor* and *la color* are typical of the spoken language of some areas of Spain. In C. J. Cela's *Mazurca para dos muertos* (1983), in which the popular speech of Galicia is represented, *calor* and *color* are regularly feminine.)[10]

| | |
|---|---|
| *el/(la) centinela* | sentinel |
| *(el)/la dote* | dowry[11] |
| *el/(la) énfasis* | emphasis |
| *(el)/la linde* | boundary |
| *(el)/la pringue* | grease |
| *el/(la) puente* | bridge |
| *(el)/la tilde* | tilde (˜)[12] |

Some nouns which are feminine in Peninsular Spanish have masculine equivalents in Latin-American Spanish:

| | |
|---|---|
| *un llamado* for *una llamada* | call |
| *el radio* for *la radio* | radio |
| (*el radio* is also 'radius') | |

*el sartén* for *la sartén*          frying pan[13]
*el vuelto* for *la vuelta*          change[14]
etc.

*Le avisaron que tenía un llamado telegráfico urgente* (G. García Márquez, 1985: 135)
They told him he had an urgent telephone call

*Pijama* and *bikini*,[15] which are masculine in the Peninsula, may be feminine in Latin America (the former sometimes with the spelling *piyama*):

> *La piyama debajo de la almohada* (ibid., 83)
> Pyjamas underneath the pillow

## 110 Arte

*Arte* can be either masculine or feminine in the singular, but in the plural it is almost always feminine.

> *el arte romántico*          Romantic art

but, most commonly,

> *el arte* (f) *poética*          poetic art
> (See **28** for the use of *el* here)
>
> *las bellas artes*          the fine arts
>
> *Las artes de los llamados primitivos no son las más antiguas* (O. Paz, 1971: 25)
> The artistic manifestations of the so-called primitives are not the oldest

Note, however, *(los) artes de pesca* 'fishing tackle'.[16]

## 111 Mar

The case of *mar* is far from clear-cut. It is usually masculine: *el mar mediterráneo* 'the Mediterranean', *se cayó al mar* 'he/she fell in the sea'.[17] In the plural *mar* is nearly always masculine: *los mares*.[18]

However, sailors and people who live by the sea tend to use the feminine form. In I. Aldecoa's *Gran sol*, for example, which describes the life of fishermen, *mar* is almost exclusively feminine.[19] *La mar es mala mujer* is the title of a book by Raúl Guerra Garrido (announced in *Ínsula*, 538, October 1991, p. 32). It has been suggested that the masculine form tends to have a more 'concrete' meaning; but many modern writers use both *el* and *la mar* in this sense.[20] The hesitation between the two is evident from the fact that both sometimes appear in the same context:

> *¿Por qué no te vas a la mar?*
> *El mar únicamente hace a los hombres* (J. A. de Zunzunegui, 1958: 148)
> Why don't you go to sea?
> Only the sea makes a man of you

> *Admiré en el señor Guillén su fidelidad al mar – o a la mar como él prefería y solemos decir quienes en ella hemos vivido* (M. Delibes, 1976: 14)
> What I admired in Sr Guillén was his faithfulness to the sea: *la mar* as he and those of us who have lived on it usually say
> (Guillén was an admiral in the Spanish navy)

> *El mar. La mar.*
> *El mar – ¡Sólo la mar!* (R. Alberti, 1981: 84)
> (Usage in this example may be due to Alberti's alternating vision of the sea from a distance (*el mar*) and from El Puerto de Santa María, where he was born (*la mar*).)

In the following expressions, *mar* is always feminine:[21]

| | |
|---|---|
| *la bajamar* | low tide |
| *la ple(n)amar* | high tide |
| *en alta mar* | on the high seas |
| *las mares gruesas* | heavy seas |
| *hacerse a la mar* | to put to sea |
| *mar llana* | smooth sea |
| *mar picada* | choppy sea |

It is also used in the feminine in weather forecasts:

> *En la mar soplarán vientos flojos . . .*
> Winds will be light over the sea . . .

It is feminine in the expression *la mar (de)* 'a lot (of)':

| | |
|---|---|
| *los pies me duelen la mar* | my feet hurt me a lot |
| *divertirse la mar* | to have a great time |
| *nuestro vecino sabe la mar de cosas* | Our neighbour knows a great deal |

## 112 Different Genders with Different Meanings

Many words have a different meaning according to whether they are masculine or feminine. Some common examples are:

| | |
|---|---|
| *el capital* | capital (money) |
| *la capital* | capital (city) |
| *el cólera* | cholera |
| *la cólera* | anger |
| *el coma* | coma |
| *la coma* | comma |
| *el cometa* | comet |
| *la cometa* | kite |
| *el corte* | cut |
| *la corte* | capital (city), court |
| *el cura* | priest |
| *la cura* | cure |
| *el editorial* | leading article |
| *la editorial* | publishing house |
| *el frente* | front (part), political or military front |
| *la frente* | forehead |
| *el moral* | mulberry tree |
| *la moral* | morals, morale |
| *el orden* | order (in sense of series, or good behaviour), and note *orden del día* 'dispatches' |
| *la orden* | order (in sense of command); also (religious) order: *la orden de los jesuitas* 'the Jesuit order' |
| *el parte* | report |
| *la parte* | part |
| *el pendiente* | earring, pendant |
| *la pendiente* | slope |
| *el pez* | fish |
| *la pez* | pitch, tar |
| *el policía* | policeman |
| *la policía* | police force |

(and many other similar pairs, e.g. *el guardia* 'guard (individual)', *la guardia* 'guard (collective)')

(See also **106**.)

**113** Masculine and feminine sometimes indicate respectively a tree and its fruit:

| | |
|---|---|
| *el cerezo* | cherry tree |
| *la cereza* | cherry |
| *el ciruelo* | plum tree |
| *la ciruela* | plum |
| *el manzano* | apple tree |
| *la manzana* | apple |
| *el naranjo* | orange tree |
| *la naranja* | orange. |

In popular speech, a more marked distinction is sometimes made in this area: for example, *manzanero* and *naranjero* may be used for *manzano* and *naranjo*.

**114** In other cases, the feminine denotes a larger or broader object or concept than the masculine. (Spanish grammarians sometimes refer to this phenomenon as *género dimensional*.)

| | |
|---|---|
| *la banca* | banking (system) |
| *el banco* | (individual) bank |
| *la bolsa* | bag (e.g. a shopping bag) |
| *el bolso* | handbag |
| *el cubo* | bucket |
| *la cuba* | tub, barrel |
| *la huerta* | large kitchen garden |
| *el huerto* | smaller kitchen garden; orchard[22] |

In some cases, the situation is reversed, with the feminine noun denoting a smaller object than the corresponding masculine:

| | |
|---|---|
| *el cesto* | basket (large or small) |
| *la cesta* | basket (generally smaller)[23] |
| *la barca* | (fishing) boat |
| *el barco* | boat, ship |

With names of machines, the feminine often indicates the larger or more complex type: *el aspirador/la aspiradora* 'vacuum cleaner', *el computador/la computadora* 'computer', *el secador* 'hairdryer'/*la secadora* 'tumble dryer'.[24]

## 115 Formation of the Feminine

In a relatively small number of cases, the feminine form is quite different from the corresponding masculine:

| | |
|---|---|
| *el hombre/la mujer* | man/woman |
| *el yerno/la nuera* | son-/daughter-in-law |
| *el toro/la vaca* | bull/cow |

**116** However, the majority of feminines are formed by changing the ending of the noun to the characteristic *-a*.

**117** The *-o* and *-e* of a masculine form change to *-a* as follows:

| | |
|---|---|
| *el muchacho/la muchacha* | boy/girl |
| *el viudo/la viuda* | widower/widow |
| *el presidente/la presidenta* | president (male/female), chair(man/woman) |

*Yo soy la jefa – respondió la peluquera* (I. Aldecoa, 1970: 203)
'I'm the boss,' replied the hairdresser
(The masculine form is *jefe*)

*He traído a una clienta* (F. Umbral, 1966: 216)
I've brought a customer
(The masculine form is *cliente*)

**118** An *-a* is added to nouns which end in a consonant:

| | |
|---|---|
| *el español/la española* | Spaniard |
| *el alemán/la alemana* | German |
| *el doctor/la doctora* | doctor |
| *el burgués/la burguesa* | middle-class man/woman |
| *el profesor/la profesora* | teacher |

Note that in the second and fourth of these the written accent is not needed in the feminine forms (see **13**).

**119** In a limited number of words, the feminine is marked by other endings.

| | |
|---|---|
| *el actor/la actriz* | actor/actress |

(*la actora* exists, but in the legal sense of 'plaintiff')

| | |
|---|---|
| *el alcalde/la alcaldesa* | mayor/mayoress or mayor's wife (see **123**) |
| *el conde/la condesa* | count/countess |
| *el gallo/la gallina* | cockerel/hen |
| *el héroe/la heroína* | hero/heroine |
| *el rey/la reina* | king/queen |
| *el poeta/la poetisa* | poet/poetess |

(but *la poeta* tends to be preferred nowadays)[25]

**120** Sometimes the feminine noun has no distinctive ending:

| | |
|---|---|
| *el/la artista* | artist (male/female) |
| *el/la guía* | guide (male/female) |
| *el/la joven* | young man/woman |
| *el/la pianista* | pianist (male/female) |
| *el/la testigo* | witness (male/female) |
| *el/la imbécil* | imbecile (male/female) |
| *el/la reo* | convict (male/female) |

Terms like *abogado* 'lawyer', *catedrático* 'professor', *ingeniero* 'engineer', *médico* 'doctor', *ministro* 'minister', referring to professions to which for a long time women had no access, belonged until recently to this category. However, new forms like *la abogada*, *la médica*, etc. are gradually finding acceptance as more and more women join these professions.[26]

> *La primera ministra, Margaret Thatcher* (*El País*, 5 August 1982: 40)
> The Prime Minister, Margaret Thatcher

> *La médica Carmen Guiraldo.../Carmen Conde... académica* (*El País*, 9 February 1978: 48)
> Doctor Carmen Guiraldo.../Carmen Conde, the academician

> *La señora Cardosa, catedrática de latín* (R. Montero, 1979: 155)
> Señora Cardosa, the professor of Latin

Note also *diputada* 'deputy' (*El País*, 12 August 1981: 36) and *secretaria de Estado* 'secretary of state' (ibid., 7 December 1982: 1); *DRAE*, 1415, also mentions the form *torera* 'lady bullfighter'.[27]

But the preservation of the masculine form is also possible:

> *Tú serás mi mejor crítico* (C. Riera, 1987: 68)
> You will be my best critic (the person referred to is a woman)

> *Mi hija es médico*
> My daughter is a doctor

and still there is a good deal of variation in usage: note, for example, the mixing of feminine and masculine forms in the following examples:

> *A Unga la ensimismaba su decisión de llegar a ser simultáneamente una pintora famosa, una novelista famosa, una actriz famosa y un arquitecto famoso* (J. García Hortelano, 1979: 434)
> Unga was absorbed by her decision to become a famous painter, novelist, actress and architect all at the same time

> *Unas nacen para ser médicos y ejercen, otras para abogadas, muchas para modelos* (C. Tellado, 1984: 80)
> Some are born to be doctors and practise, others to be lawyers, many to be models

> On 5 August 1986 JdeB read a notice from *la Jefe de sección* (signed E. Asensio) in the Facultad de Filosofía y Letras in the University of Valladolid

The pattern of adjective agreement is also open to variation:

> *Entrevista con la ministro francesa, que llega hoy a Madrid* (*Diario 16*, 11 February 1978: 1)
> Interview with the (lady) French minister, who is arriving in Madrid today

> *Hoy llega a Madrid la ministro francés de Sanidad* (*Diario 16*, 11 February 1978: 15)
> The (lady) French health minister is arriving in Madrid today[28]

However, such forms as those in the above two examples are not to be imitated, and the 'normal' agreement is generally considered the correct one. Indeed, *la ministra francesa* would now be more normal.

Naturally, there is difficulty with words such as *travestí* 'transvestite': this is in fact generally treated as feminine:[29]

> *Travestí viciosa – única en Barcelona* (*La Vanguardia*, 15 February 1989: 26)
> Wicked transvestite – unique in Barcelona

**121** In Latin-American Spanish the *-a* ending is used much more readily than in the Peninsula, especially in popular speech, and we find words like *una criminala* for *un criminal* 'criminal', *una intelectuala* for *un intelectual* 'an intellectual', and *una individua* and *una tipa* as feminine variants of *un individuo* 'an individual' and *un tipo* 'a character'.[30]

> *Telefoneaba a una serie interminable de tipos y tipas* (J. Cortázar, 1973: 37)
> He was telephoning an endless string of guys and girls

At the same time, the reverse process is found: in some words *-o* is used for *-a* to refer unambiguously to a male, e.g. *el cuentisto* for *el cuentista* 'storyteller', *el maquinisto* for *el maquinista* 'mechanic', *el pianisto* for *el pianista* 'pianist'.[31]

In *El supremísimo* by the Spanish-Cuban author L. Ricardo Alonso, the form *un prostituto* '(male) prostitute', as a counterpart to the feminine *prostituta*, is found (1981: 138), and from F. Umbral's comments (1983: 66) it is clear that the form *puto*, with the same meaning, can be found, corresponding to the feminine *puta* (see also **255**, fourth example).

**122** *GRAE*, 14, also mentions a 'common' gender (*género epiceno*), to which belong names of animals which are used only in the masculine or the feminine.

| | |
|---|---|
| *el águila* (f) | eagle |
| *la llama* | llama |
| *la rata* | rat |

The only way of stressing the sex of such animals is to use *macho* 'male' or *hembra* 'female' after the noun: the gender of the noun remains unchanged and *macho* and *hembra* are invariable.

**123** In some cases, although masculine/feminine pairs exist, the words do not refer to male/female counterparts:

| *el asistente* | assistant |
| *la asistenta* | charwoman |
| *el químico* | chemist |
| *la química* | chemistry[32] |

In other cases, the feminine form has, or had. the meaning 'wife of', as in

| *el embajador* | ambassador |
| *la embajadora* | ambassador's wife |
| *el general* | general |
| *la generala* | general's wife |

However, *embajadora* and *gobernadora* (and no doubt in time *generala*) may now refer to women who carry out these functions. *Alcaldesa* and *jueza*[33] are regularly used in the sense of 'lady mayor' and 'lady judge' respectively.

# Number: Plural Formation

## 124 General Rules

Plurals of nouns in Spanish are formed in the following way:

(1)   When the noun ends in an unstressed vowel, *-s* is added:

| *la casa/las casas* | house/houses |
| *el hombre/los hombres* | man/men |
| *el libro/los libros* | book/books |

(2)   When the noun ends in a consonant, a stressed vowel or *-y, -es* is added:

| *el árbol/los árboles* | tree/trees |
| *el israelí/los israelíes* | Israeli/Israelis |
| | (*Note:* to be distinguished from *israelita* 'Israelite') |
| *la ley/las leyes* | law/laws |
| *el mal/los males* | evil/evils |

(*Note: malos* is the masculine plural of the adjective *malo*)

| *el maniquí/los maniquíes* | mannequin/mannequins |
| *el pan/los panes* | loaf/loaves |

## 125 Remarks

The *-z* of a singular form becomes *-c-* before *-es* in the plural:

| | |
|---|---|
| *la nuez/las nueces* | (wal)nut/(wal)nuts |
| *el lápiz/los lápices* | pencil/pencils |

**126** Plural formation usually causes no variation in stress. Consequently, a written accent must sometimes be added or dropped in the plural, according to the rules given in **13**.

| | |
|---|---|
| *el joven/los jóvenes* | young man/young men |
| *el interés/los intereses* | interest/interests |

Exceptions are:

| | |
|---|---|
| *el carácter/los caracteres* | character/characters |
| *el régimen/los regímenes* | regime, diet/regimes, diets |
| *el espécimen/los especímenes*[34] | specimen/specimens |

## 127 Exceptions

All nouns which end in a stressed *-e* and some which end in other stressed vowels do not follow the rule given in **124** but simply add *-s* in the plural (instead of *-es*):

| | |
|---|---|
| *el café/los cafés* | coffee/coffees |
| (In popular speech, *los cafeses* is also found)[35] | |
| *el esquí/los esquís* | ski/skis |
| *el menú/los menús* | menus/menus |
| *el papá/los papás* | daddy/daddies |
| *el pie/los pies* | foot/feet |

There is, however, a good deal of variation in this area, e.g. for *esquí*:

> *Con grandes facilidades puedes obtener unos esquíes* (F. Umbral, 1973a: 94)
> You can get skis easily on credit

*Esbozo*, 184–5, gives double forms for other nouns: *bigudís* or *bigudíes* 'curlers', *bantús* or *bantúes* 'Bantus', *tabús* or *tabúes* 'taboos', etc., although nowadays nouns in *-ú* almost always form their plural in *-s*: *ambigú* → *ambigús*, *tisú* → *tisús*, etc.

**128** Nouns ending in *-s* remain unchanged in the plural unless the stress falls on the last syllable, when the general rule applies and *-es* is added:

| | |
|---|---|
| *la crisis/las crisis* | crisis/crises |
| *el lunes/los lunes* | Monday/Mondays |
| *el análisis/los análisis* | analysis/analyses |

But:

| | |
|---|---|
| *el autobús/los autobuses* | bus/buses |
| *el mes/los meses* | month/months |
| *el país/los países* | country/countries |

## 129 Remark

The rules given in **124–128** also hold when other parts of speech are nominalized.

*Un 10 por ciento de «noes»* (F. Vizcaíno Casas, 1979b: 244 – describing the outcome of a referendum)
A 10 per cent 'no' vote

*Hablaban de tiempos diferentes, de ayeres y de anteayeres* (J. Asenjo Sedano, 1978: 145)
They spoke of different times, of all our yesterdays

*¿Estamos de acuerdo? Los síes no se hicieron de rogar* (M. Aub, 1971: 209)
Are we agreed? Assent came spontaneously

*Por aquellos entonces* ... (M. Delibes, 1969a: 176–7)
In days of yore ...

## 130 Special Cases: The Plural of Compound Nouns

Usually, only the last part of a compound noun carries the plural ending.

| | |
|---|---|
| *el ferrocarril/los ferrocarriles* | railway/railways |
| *la bocacalle/las bocacalles* | turning/turnings |
| *el librepensador/* | freethinker/freethinkers |
| *los librepensadores* | |
| *el sordomudo/los sordomudos* | Deaf-and-dumb person/people |

*Reza seis padrenuestros y seis avemarías* (J. Edwards, 1971: 189)
Say six Our Fathers and six Ave Marias[36]

**131** The word remains unchanged when the second element is already plural:

| | |
|---|---|
| *el mondadientes/los mondadientes* | toothpick/toothpicks |
| *el paraguas/los paraguas* | umbrella/umbrellas |
| *el sacacorchos/los sacacorchos* | corkscrew/corkscrews |

**132** There are only very few, relatively scarcely used, combinations in which both components take the plural ending.

*el gentilhombre/los gentileshombres*  gentleman/gentlemen

**133** Neologisms consisting of two component nouns which, in contrast to the foregoing examples, are not written as a single word, behave differently. Only the first noun is pluralized in such cases,[37] the second (which may be viewed as an invariable adjective) remaining in the singular (see also **122**).

| | |
|---|---|
| *el hombre masa/los hombres masa* | the average man/men |
| *el hombre rana/los hombres rana* | frogman/frogmen |
| *un caso límite/unos casos límite* | borderline case/cases |
| *la hora punta/las horas punta*[38] | rush hour/rush hours |

In practice, however, there is a good deal of variation in this area. In Blanco Aguinaga, Rodríguez Puértolas and Zavala (1979–81) we read both *puntos clave* (III, 11) and *puntos claves* (II, 222) 'key points', *los años clave* (III, 234) 'key years' and *novelas claves* (II, 236) 'key novels' (admittedly, three different authors are involved). G. Torrente Ballester of the Real Academia Española speaks of *palabras-clave* (1975: 33), but the linguist F. Marcos Marín (1978: 191) writes *palabras-claves* (both these with a hyphen). C.-J. Cela uses both *figuras-clave* (1983) and *figuras-claves* (1988) 'key figures'.

**134** Some compound nouns are invariable in the plural. They are always forms involving verbs or invariable words. *Esbozo* refers to them as 'syntactic' compounds.

| | |
|---|---|
| *el correveidile (< corre +* | gossip/gossips |
| *ve + y + dile)/los* | |
| *correveidile* | |

| | |
|---|---|
| *el sin trabajo/los sin trabajo* | unemployed person/ people |
| *el sabelotodo/los sabelotodo* | know-all/know-alls |

**135**  However, a few compound forms of this type have become so common that they are apparently considered as simple nouns, and their plural forms follow the general rules.

| | |
|---|---|
| *el pésame/los pésames* | expression/s of condolence |
| *el vaivén/los vaivenes* | seesaw/seesaws |
| *el cargareme/los cargaremes* | receipt, voucher |

## 136  The Plural of Proper Nouns, Surnames and Christian Names)

Use of the plural for surnames tends nowadays to be more typical of the spoken language, the literary language preferring to leave the name invariable (cf. the title of D. Medio's *Nosotros, los Rivero*). Baroja uses both *los Aguirres* and *los Aguirre* in *Las inquietudes de Shanti Andía* (1958), pp. 20 and 21 respectively, both *los Beamontes* and *los Beamonte* in *El mayorazgo de Labraz* (1964a), pp. 92 and 109 respectively.[39]

> *los Mendozas*
> *los Osorios*
> *Aquellos Lénines o Marxes* (J. Asenjo Sedano, 1978: 44)
> Those Lenins or Marxes

However, the following names are always invariable in the plural:

(1)  Names ending in *-z*
(2)  Names ending in *-s* in which the stress falls on the last syllable
(3)  Foreign names

> *los Sánchez*
> *los Muñoz*
> *los Valdés*
> *los Solís*
> *los Thompson*
> *los Schmidt*

**137** Christian names nearly always take the appropriate plural ending, even when they are further qualified.

> *Los que creen ser Don Juanes* (J. Ortega y Gasset, 1959: 34)
> Those who think themselves a Don Juan

> *Dejaba a los Sanchos Panzas de la ciencia el mandil y el laboratorio* (M. de Unamuno, 1967a: 58)
> He left the apron and laboratory to the Sancho Panzas of science

> *Las Erikas, Hildas, Bertas y Elfriedas reían en bandadas* (T. Salvador, 1968b: 69)
> Whole groups of Erikas, Hildas, Bertas and Elfriedas were laughing

> *Ya no había Mecenas, ni Luises catorce* (A. Carpentier, 1976: 29)
> There were no more Maecenases or Louis XIVs

**138** The plurals of English loanwords are subject to a great deal of variation.[40]

The key to the use of apparently inconsistent plural forms is the way in which individual Spanish speakers handle foreign words. Someone who knows English can without further ado borrow both *ticket* and the plural *tickets*. But otherwise, the loanword is 'hispanized' in pronunciation and spelling, and it is therefore not to be wondered at that a plural form like *tiquetes* is found (as, for example, in M. Aub, 1970: 25).[41]

L. Carandell (1970: 127) and A. Skármeta (1986: 98), write *films*, but a Belgian Foreign Ministry brochure intended for Spanish-speaking countries is entitled *filmes belgas*[42] (see also **538**, fourth example).

F. Umbral talks of *pósters* (1973a: 27), but M. Aub has *girles* as the plural of *girl* (1970: 24).

F. Marcos Marín observes that *club* has the plural *clubs* in Spain, but *clubes* in Latin America.[43] According to this linguist, at least four ways of making the plural of *recordman* 'record holder' are encountered in the Spanish press: *recordmen*, *recordman*, *record-mans*, *recordmanes*.[44]

Another oddity is the form *whiskyes*, seen in the window of the Bar Woody in Madrid.[45] One would also expect to find *whiskys* and *whiskies*.[46]

**139** Latin and Greek words also present problems in the formation of the plural.[47] Most are invariable:

| | |
|---|---|
| *el déficit/los déficit* | deficit/deficits |
| *el desiderátum/ los desiderátum* | desideratum/desiderata |
| *el médium/los médium* | (spiritualist) medium/ mediums |
| *el memorándum/ los memorándum* | memorandum/memoranda |
| *el réquiem/los réquiem* | requiem/requiems |
| *el superávit/los superávit* | surplus/surpluses |

although forms with *-s* (e.g. *los memorándums*) and hispanized plurals in *-os* (e.g. *los memorandos*) can be found in the written language.[48] *El álbum* 'album' has the plural los *álbumes*[49] and the recommended plural for *el hipérbaton* 'hyperbaton' is *los hipérbatos*.

**140**   Some masculine plural nouns which denote family relationships or an office[50] carry the idea of male(s) and female(s) as well as being the straightforward plural of the masculine singular:

| | |
|---|---|
| *el hijo* 'son' | *los hijos* 'sons' but also 'children' |
| *el duque* 'duke' | *los duques* 'dukes' but also 'duke and duchess' |
| *el padre* 'father' | *los padres* 'fathers' but also 'mother and father; parents' |
| *el rey* 'king' | *los reyes* 'kings' but also 'king and queen; monarchs' |
| *el suegro* 'father-in-law' | *los suegros* 'fathers-in-law' but also 'mother- and father-in-law' |

*Nuestros hijos puede que sean distintos* (C. Martín Gaite, 1981: 136–7)
Our children may be different

*Los Reyes de España serán invitados a visitar oficialmente la Unión Soviética* (*La Vanguardia*, 14 February 1978: 11)
The King and Queen of Spain will be invited to make an official visit to the Soviet Union

**141** A number of nouns in Spanish are found only in the plural: this phenomenon is called the *pluralia tantum*.

Some of the words given below do appear in the singular, but with a quite different meaning (*el celo* 'zeal', *la esposa* 'wife, spouse', *el polvo* 'dust', *la vacación* 'vacancy'. *la víspera* 'eve, the day before').

| | |
|---|---|
| *las afueras* | outskirts |
| *los celos* | jealousy |
| *los calzoncillos* | pants (US shorts) |
| *las esposas* | handcuffs |
| *las gafas* | spectacles |
| *los prismáticos* | binoculars |
| *las tenazas* | pliers |
| *las tijeras* | scissors |
| *las tinieblas* | darkness |
| *las vacaciones* | holidays |
| *las vísperas* | vespers |
| (but *en vísperas de* 'the day before') | |
| *los víveres* | supplies, provisions |

**142** Plurals are also found in a number of prepositional expressions, e.g.

| | |
|---|---|
| *a espaldas (de alguien)* | behind (someone's) back |
| *a horcajadas* | astride |
| *(estar) a sus anchas* | (to be) at one's ease |
| *a tientas* | gropingly |
| *de bruces* | face downwards |
| (e.g. *caer de bruces* 'to fall headlong') | |
| *de espaldas (a alguien)* | with one's back towards (someone) |
| *a duras penas* | with great difficulty |

In Latin America, plurals are often used with nouns (particularly with an abstract meaning) which in the Peninsula would tend to be singular:

| | |
|---|---|
| *mis entusiasmos* | my enthusiasm |
| *no me eches las culpas* | don't blame me |
| *sin miedos* | unafraid |
| *los altos* | the first floor |
| *los bajos* | the ground floor |

The word *hora* is regularly encountered in the plural in expressions like *¿Qué horas son?* 'What time is it?', *¿A qué horas llegó?* 'What time did he/she arrive?', whereas in Spain one would say *¿Qué hora es?*, *¿A qué hora llegó? Las casas* is also sometimes found for *la casa* 'house'.[51]

**143** The words *día, tarde, noche* are almost always in the plural when part of greetings: *¡Buenos días!* 'Good morning!', *¡Buenas tardes!* 'Good afternoon/evening', *¡Buenas noches!* 'Good evening/ night'.

In Latin America, the forms *buen día* and (exceptionally) *buena noche* are heard.[52]

**144** In some instances singular and plural can be used more or less interchangeably:[53]

| | |
|---|---|
| *barba* → *barbas* | beard |
| *pantalón* → *pantalones* | trousers |
| *nariz* → *narices* | nose |
| *bigote* → *bigotes* | moustache |
| *escalera* → *escaleras* | stairs |

## 145 Singular for Plural

An interesting feature of Spanish, principally the spoken language, is that a singular noun is often used in a collective sense where it is clear from the context that the meaning is properly plural.[54]

It will be noticed that in most of the examples given below the noun is preceded by a word consistent with the collective idea (*mucho, tanto, cuanto,* etc.).

*¿Hay mucha trucha en este río?* (J. Fernández Santos, 1977: 44)
Are there many trout in this river?

*Había leído mucha novela en inglés* (F. Umbral, 1977: 211)
He had read many novels in English

*¡Qué hermoso! ¡Cuánto coche!* (P. Baroja. 1951: 168)
How wonderful! What a lot of cars!

*El profesor de Química lo sigue; parece asustado entre tanto uniforme* (M. Vargas Llosa, 1973: 47)
The chemistry teacher followed him; he seemed frightened amongst so many uniforms

*Le parecía un milagro ante el desfile de tanta mujer hermosa, que aquel hombre fuese sólo de ella* (J. A. de Zunzunegui, 1956a: 156)
It seemed miraculous to her, as she watched so many beautiful women passing by, that that man was hers alone

*Hubo aspirante que abandonó la sala con lágrimas en los ojos* (F. Franco Salgado-Araujo, 1977: 81)
There were candidates who left the room with tears in their eyes

**146** In the following examples, a plural form used alongside the singular noun reflects its plural meaning.

*¡Cuánta estrella! – dijo Manuel.*
*¿Qué serán?*
*Son mundos y mundos sin fin* (P. Baroja, 1946–51: I, 507)
'What a lot of stars!' said Manuel.
'What can they be?'
'They are worlds, endless worlds'
(The verb form *serán* (plural) clearly shows that in the mind of the hearer the preceding *(cuánta) estrella* is logically if not grammatically plural.)

*Hay mucha mujer guapa, y una de ellas, rubia, baila con un negro* (P. Baroja, 1946–51: VIII, 314)
There are a lot of pretty women, and one of them, a blonde, is dancing with a negro
(Here also the form *ellas* indicates that *mujer (guapa)* implies a plural)

## 147 *Gente*

The feminine noun *gente* is used chiefly with a plural meaning corresponding to English 'people':

*Había mucha gente en la plaza*
There were a lot of people in the square

Nevertheless, the word is found in the plural as well, with approximately the same value.[55]

*Tengo la conciencia tranquila.*
*No basta con la conciencia para vivir entre las gentes* (J. A. de Zunzunegui, 1956a: 114)

My conscience is clear.
Conscience isn't enough for living amongst people.
(See also the first example in **54**)

*Gente* may also be equivalent to *persona* 'person', in which case it can be used in the plural and the singular. This meaning is particularly common in Latin America.[56]

> *Algunas gentes – pocas – prefieren el inglés* (M. Alvar, 1982: 23)
> Some people – not very many – prefer English

> *Soy la única gente que tiene para hacerle sus necesidades* (J. Rulfo, 1981: 67)
> I'm the only person he's got to do the necessary for him

> *Cien gentes* (*Esbozo*, 187)
> A hundred people

> *Yo, en cambio, que soy buena gente, un romántico* (M. Vargas Llosa, 1986: 74)
> I, on the other hand, am a good person, a romantic
> (Note the singular complement *un romántico*)

## Special Cases

### 148 Surnames

The use of a double surname, consisting of paternal surname + maternal surname, is frequent in Spanish-speaking countries, as consulting any telephone directory will show.

> *Federico García Lorca* (Spanish author, 1898–1936)
> *José Gutiérrez Solana* (Spanish painter and writer, 1886–1945)
> *Gabriel García Márquez* (Colombian author. Born 1928, Nobel prizewinner for literature, 1982)

The mother's surname is optional; but people may sometimes be referred to only by their maternal surname, especially when their paternal surname is considered too common (thus people refer to 'Lorca' and 'Solana' in speech and writing). In other cases, the use of the maternal surname avoids confusion. The Spanish linguist Manuel Alvar has a son who is in exactly the same profession; the son uses the name Manuel Alvar Ezquerra in publications.

## 149 Acronyms (*siglas*)

The use of acronyms is more extensive in Spanish than in English,[57] and one peculiarity of Spanish is that the plural is often expressed by doubling of letters.

> In Spain, signs like the following can often be seen:
> *FC Burgos – Madrid*
> *FC* is an abbreviation for *Ferrocarril* 'railway'. To refer to the railway network, *FF.CC.* = *ferrocarriles* can be used.

> *EEUU* is the abbreviation for *Estados Unidos* 'United States'

> *FF.JJ.FF.* signified *Falanges juveniles de Franco* (cf. J. L. Alcocer, 1978: 60 – a pro-Franco youth organization)

> *CCOO* is the abbreviation for *Comisiones Obreras* (a communist trades union in Spain)

> *Toda la población no pudo ser más cariñosa con SS.MM. y AA.RR.* (F. Franco Salgado-Araujo, 1977: 14 – *SS.MM.* and *AA.RR.* is the plural of *Su Majestad y Alteza Real*)
> None of the people could have been more affectionate towards Their Majesties and Royal Highnesses.

Sometimes a new noun or adjective is derived from acronyms, giving rise to terms like *cegetista* from *CGT* (*Confederación General del Trabajo*, a Spanish trade union), *jonsista* from *JONS* (*Juntas de ofensiva nacional sindicalista*, the most extreme right-wing group in Franco's time), *pecero*, a member of the *PCE* (*Partido Comunista Español*), *penene*, from *PNN* (*Personal no numerario*, i.e., non-tenured civil servants, especially in education), *ucedero* from *UCD* (*Unión de Centro Democrático*, a Spanish political party), etc.[58]

## 150 Other Parts of Speech Used as Nouns

Many other parts of speech and phrases can be used as nouns in Spanish.

> *Yo* 'I' is found as a noun (and in the plural) in M. de Unamuno (as *yos*, cf. Fernández, 1951: 170) and F. Umbral (as *yoes*, 1979: 116)

M. Delibes talks of *aquellos entonces* 'those times (in the past)' (1981: 40) (see **305**), and J. R. Jiménez nominalizes the pre position *después* in *Luis Cernuda, después de sus despueses* 'Luis Cernuda, after all his afters'

*Los adioses* . . . 'Farewells' is the title of a poetry anthology by G. Díaz Plaja (Barcelona, 1962)

*Qué cuerpo y qué abajo más bravío tenía el Antonio* (F. Quiñones, 1979: 135)
What a body Antonio had, and what a wild underpart

The nominalization of interjections is also frequent, as in *¡Ahs! y ¡ohs!* (C. J. Cela, 1967b: 85), *ayes* (R. del Valle-Inclán, 1963: 87), *los vivas, mueras, etc.* (F. Franco Salgado-Araujo, 1977: 145 and 172)

In C. Fuentes we read: *es mi peoresnada* 'my better than nothing' (1979: 115)

*Agustín es un vivalavirgen* (C. J. Cela, 1969: 78)
Agustín is a wastrel

# The Adjective

## Agreement

**151** In Spanish, the adjective agrees in number and gender with the noun to which it relates (though some adjectives have identical masculine and feminine forms: see **158**). This constitutes an important difference from English, where adjectives are invariable.

| | |
|---|---|
| *un hombre sano* | a healthy man |
| *una mujer sana* | a healthy woman |
| *dos hombres sanos* | two healthy men |
| *dos mujeres sanas* | two healthy women |
| *un cura simpático* | a sympathetic priest |

(*Cura* is masculine, although it ends in *-a*)

Note, however, that with titles agreement follows the sense:

*Su Santidad está enfermo*
His Holiness is ill.

### 152 Formation of the Feminine

Feminine adjectives are formed from the masculine by adding or substituting *-a* as the last letter. Some adjectives, however, have only one form for both genders. This also applies to adjectives which act as nouns.

## 153 First Possibility: -a.

Adjectives in -o

The feminine of adjectives ending in -o is formed by changing -o to
-a.

| | |
|---|---|
| un plato apetitoso | a tasty dish |
| una paella apetitosa | a tasty paella |
| un vestido blanco | a white dress |
| una blusa blanca | a white blouse |

## 154 Adjectives Ending in a Consonant, -ete or -ote

An -a is added to adjectives which end in -án, -ín, -ón. -or and substituted for the final -e of the affective suffixes (see **1321**) -ete or
-ote.

The written accent of -án, -ín and -ón is not needed in the
feminine.

| | |
|---|---|
| mi hermano es muy charlatán | my brother is very talkative |
| su amiga es muy charlatana | his (girl-)friend is very talkative |

(and as a noun: un charlatán/una charlatana 'a chatterbox')

| | |
|---|---|
| un gato chiquitín | a tiny little cat |
| una casa chiquitina | a tiny little house |
| este perro es muy comilón | this dog is very greedy |
| esta muchacha es muy comilona | this girl is very greedy |
| un hombre trabajador | a hard-working man |
| una mujer trabajadora | a hard-working woman |
| el profesor era regordete | the teacher was plump |
| una persona regordeta | a plump person |
| un joven grandote | a gawky young man |
| una joven grandota | a gawky young woman |

**155** Important exceptions to the rule in **154** are comparative
adjectives in -or (*mayor* 'bigger' or 'older', *menor* 'smaller' or
'younger', *mejor* 'better' and *peor* 'worse'), which are invariable in
the feminine. The same applies to some adjectives ending in -or
which derive from Latin comparatives (although they usually

have a non-comparative sense in present-day Spanish): *superior* 'higher' or 'very good', *exterior* 'exterior', *inferior* 'inferior' or 'lower', *anterior* 'anterior' or 'former', *interior* 'interior', *posterior* 'posterior' or 'later', etc.

> *Férula, cinco años mayor, lavaba y almidonaba...* (I. Allende, 1984: 47)
> Férula, who was five years older, was washing and starching ...

> *La rueda anterior era mucho más grande que la posterior* (G. García Márquez, 1977: 350)
> The front wheel was much bigger than the back one

Note, however, the form *superiora* in *madre superiora* 'mother superior (of a convent)'.

## 156 Adjectives of Nationality (*Gentilicios*)

Most of these have -*a* in the feminine.

| | |
|---|---|
| *un coche español* | a Spanish car |
| *una máquina española* | a Spanish machine |
| *un libro inglés* | an English book |
| *una firma inglesa* | an English firm |
| *un pueblo andaluz* | an Andalusian village |
| *una ciudad andaluza* | an Andalusian town |

(Note the use of lower-case letters in Spanish – see **23**.)

Similarly with adjectival nouns:

> *En el centro de Palma, discurren suecas, alemanas, inglesas, noruegas, danesas y francesas* (M. Tudela, 1970: 94)
> Girls from Sweden, Germany, England, Norway, Denmark and France wander around the centre of Palma

**157** However, the following nationality adjectives have the same form for both genders: *belga* 'Belgian', *iraní* 'Iranian', *iraquí* 'Iraqi', *israelí* 'Israeli', *marroquí* 'Moroccan', etc.

> *Banisadr asegura que Irán ha frustrado la invasión iraquí* (*El País*, 4 December 1980: 4)
> Banisadr assures us that Iran has frustrated the Iraqi invasion

**158** Second Possibility: Adjective Remains Unchanged

Adjectives not falling into the above categories have only one ending for both genders:

| | |
|---|---|
| *un espectáculo brillante* | a glittering show |
| *una función brillante* | a glittering function |
| *un artículo optimista* | an optimistic article |
| *una nota optimista* | an optimistic note |
| *un ejemplo fácil* | an easy example |
| *una tarea fácil* | an easy task |
| *un camarero cortés* | a polite waiter |
| *una azafata cortés* | a polite air-hostess |
| *un niño feliz* | a happy child |
| *una mujer feliz* | a happy woman |

**159** *Gandul*

The adjective *gandul* 'lazy, good-for-nothing' has a feminine in *-a*, heard chiefly in the popular speech of Madrid,[1] although the following recent example suggests a broader usage:

> *Estamos hablando de una burguesía incluso más gandula que la actual* (M. Vázquez Montalbán, 1979a:38)
> We are speaking of a middle class who were even more indolent than the present day

**160** Remark

The masculine adjective form is sometimes used before or even after feminine nouns beginning in a stressed *a-* or *ha-* by analogy with the article *el* (see **299**).[2]

| | |
|---|---|
| *otro aula* | another lecture hall |
| *un aula pequeño* | a small lecture hall |
| *mucho hambre* | great hunger |
| *un hambre tremendo* | tremendous hunger |
| *tanto agua* | so much water |

The above forms are considered incorrect.

Formation of the Plural

**161** The plural is formed from the singular in the same way as for nouns (see **124–126**).

| | |
|---|---|
| *la casa blanca* | the white house |
| *las casas blancas* | the white houses |
| *el pan duro* | the hard bread |
| *los panes duros* | the hard loaves |
| *una región agradable* | a pleasant region |
| *unas regiones agradables* | pleasant regions |
| *la falda azul* | the blue skirt |
| *las faldas azules* | the blue skirts |
| *el camarero cortés* | the polite waiter |
| *los camareros corteses* | the polite waiters |

(Note the absence of the written accent in the plural)

| | |
|---|---|
| *el niño feliz* | the happy child |
| *los niños felices* | the happy children |

(Note the change of -*z* to -*c*- in the plural)

**162** The relatively small number of adjectives which end in stressed -*í* add -*es* in the plural just like nouns in -*í*.

| | |
|---|---|
| *un detalle baladí* | a trifling detail |
| *unos detalles baladíes* | trifling details |
| *la fruta marroquí* | Moroccan fruit |
| *las frutas marroquíes* | Moroccan fruits |

*las selvas bengalíes* (J. Cortázar, 1984: 74)
the Bengali jungle

## 163 Special Cases: Colours

Nouns signifying a colour (sometimes figuratively, as in the second example below) which are used as adjectives are invariable. Such words are *la rosa* 'rose' → *rosa* 'pink', *la violeta* → *violeta* 'violet', *la naranja* → *naranja* 'orange', etc., and may be thought of as ellipses for *color de rosa*, *color de violeta*, etc.[3]

*La niña se desmayó en el sofá malva de la sala rosa* (M. Mihura, 1981: 136)
The girl fainted on the mauve sofa in the pink room

Such words are usually treated as invariable in the plural too:

*Cuánto me gustaban las novelas rosa* (C. Martín Gaite, 1981: 39)
How I loved sentimental novels

although analogical agreements are sometimes made:

*Las ropas grises, marrones, negras* (F. Umbral, 1980: 131)
Grey, brown, black clothes

*Paisajes malvas* (S. Fernández, 1951: 120)
Mauve landscapes

*Esos ojos cafés* (A. Skármeta, 1986: 46)
Coffee-coloured eyes

**164** In compound adjectives denoting shades of colour, both components are usually invariable:

| | |
|---|---|
| *ojos azul claro* | light blue eyes. |
| *labios rosa pálido* | pale pink lips |

Alternatively, the second adjective may agree with the noun:

| | |
|---|---|
| *en sus ojos, azul verdosos* | in her green-blue eyes[4] |

## 165 One Adjective Qualifying Two or More Nouns

When the nouns are of the same gender, the adjective is in the plural and agrees in gender with both nouns.

*Gastón era un hombre de una constancia, una habilidad y una paciencia infinitas* (G. García Márquez, 1977: 361)
Gaston was a man of infinite constancy, ability and patience

When the nouns differ in gender, the adjective is usually in the masculine plural (but see the second and third examples below); but for the sake of euphony, speakers avoid putting a feminine noun next to the masculine adjective.

*He comprado una camisa y un sombrero blancos*
I've bought a white shirt and hat
(*He comprado un sombrero y una camisa blancos* is to be avoided)

It is precisely because of considerations of euphony that there is deviation from the general rule in the following examples, where the masculine noun appears only as the third in a series:

*Frente a otras cosas, personas, grupos* . . . (*Esbozo*, 226).
Faced with other things, people and groups . . .[5]

There is a certain tendency to make the adjective agree (in gender and in number) with the noun standing immediately next to it, especially when the adjective precedes the noun:

*Llegó con el rostro y las manos tiznadas*
He arrived with his face and hands blackened with soot

*Con su distinguida actitud y porte* (but *con su actitud y porte distinguidos*)
With his distinguished attitude and bearing
(Both the above examples are from F. Marsá, 1986: 125, who calls attention to the danger of ambiguity to which the lack of agreement can give rise, as, for example, in the sentence *vestía sucia camisa y pantalón* 'he was wearing a dirty shirt and (dirty?) trousers': such sentences should therefore be avoided.)

## The Place of the Adjective and its Effect

**166** The adjective may precede or follow the noun in Spanish; choice of position often creates an effect which is difficult to render adequately in English translation. Appropriate placing of the Spanish adjective is difficult for English speakers, and it is often helpful to try and decide if any different effect would be achieved by placing the adjective differently.

### 167 The 'Regular' Situation

The Adjective Following the Noun

The adjective follows the noun for 'neutral' descriptions in which none of the effects to be described in **171–172** is sought:

| | |
|---|---|
| *una reunión breve* | a short meeting |
| *una chica guapa* | a pretty girl |
| *unos libros interesantes* | interesting books |
| *dos edificios blancos* | two white buildings |

Adjectives of nationality and colour are usually treated in this way, as are 'technical' adjectives:

| | |
|---|---|
| *un periódico belga* | a Belgian newspaper |
| *un jersey rojo* | a red sweater |
| *un problema geométrico* | a geometric problem |

## 168 Distinctive or Contrastive Adjectives

The adjective is also placed after the noun when it has a distinctive or contrastive value. In this use it often corresponds to a restrictive relative clause.

> *La idea de retirarse a una vida más convencional no se le había ocurrido todavía* (I. Allende, 1990: 49)
> The idea of retiring to a more conventional way of life had not yet occurred to her.
> ('More conventional' as distinct from the unconventional life she is leading at the moment; '... a way of life that was more conventional ...')

The contrastive value of an adjective following the noun is often rendered by contrastive stress in English:

> *Ésa es la parte difícil*
> That's the DIFFICULT part (as opposed to other parts)

## 169 The Adjective Before the Noun:[6] Inherent Attributes

An adjective denoting a property that is considered inherent precedes the noun.

| | |
|---|---|
| *la dulce miel* | sweet honey |
| *la blanca nieve* | white snow |
| *las mansas ovejas* | gentle sheep |

*Esbozo*, 410, points out that in such examples placing the adjective after the noun would give a strange impression: only with difficulty could one imagine honey that was not sweet or snow that was not white, etc. *La miel dulce*, for example, would have the contrastive meaning (see **168**) of 'SWEET (not SOUR) honey'. which would be most unusual.

*Las mansas ovejas* implies 'all sheep. which are gentle', while *las ovejas mansas* implies 'those sheep (a sub-group) which are gentle'. Thus *las ovejas mansas* is. in normal circumstances, inappropriate, while *los animales mansos* 'tame animals' (as opposed to *los animales fieros* 'wild animals') is perfectly normal.

## 170 Adjectives which Generally Precede the Noun

The following adjectives generally precede the noun:

Quantifying adjectives:

| | |
|---|---|
| *ambos* | both, |
| *mucho* | much. many, a lot of, |
| *poco* | little, few, |
| *tamaño* | such a great. |
| *tanto* | so much, so many |
| *tengo muchos libros* | I've got a lot of books |
| *había poca gente* | there were few people |

Adjectives with the meaning of 'so-called, supposed'

*llamado*
*denominado*
*supuesto*
*pretendido*

| | |
|---|---|
| *un supuesto experto* | a supposed expert |

(but note *un nombre supuesto* 'an assumed name')

Other adjectives:

| | |
|---|---|
| *mero* | mere |
| *otro(s)* | another, other |
| *sendos* (see **534–535**) | each |
| *dicho* | the aforementioned |
| *una mera casualidad* | a mere chance |

## 171 The Manipulation of Adjective Position for Stylistic Effect:

Subjective Value of the Adjective Preceding the Noun

Placing an adjective before the noun often makes the value of the adjective more subjective. intense or ironical.[7]

Since in English the adjective always precedes the noun, literal translation sometimes cannot communicate the full force of the Spanish. The translations given below are expanded in an attempt to suggest the full meaning of the Spanish examples.

> *las breves horas que hemos pasado juntos*
> the all too short hours we have spent together (even many hours would seem a short time)

(Contrast

> *es un cuento breve pero interesante*
> it is a short but interesting story (a neutral description))

> *Se queja de su negra suerte* (*DUE*, I. 502)
> He complains of his usual rotten luck (a figurative use of *negro*)

(Contrast

> *La raza negra*
> The negro race (*negro* is here used with literal meaning))

The examples given above are also related to the idea of 'inherentness' described in **169**. In the first example of this paragraph it is implied that any time spent in each other's company will be too short; in the third there is an implication that the person in question generally has bad luck. If it is wished to use these adjectives in a distinctive or contrastive way (**168**), then they will follow the noun even though retaining their 'subjective' meaning: *las horas breves como un suspiro que pasamos juntos* 'the hours we spent together, which were as short as a sigh', *hoy está de humor negro* 'he's in a bad mood today (as distinct from his normal behaviour).'

Further examples:

'Subjective' value of adjectives before the noun:

> *Manolo el Pollero se fue a morir a su asturiana tierra* (*Estafeta literaria*, 613, 1 June 1977: 14)
> Manolo el Pollero went to his beloved native Asturias to die
> (*Asturiana* would normally follow the noun, as an adjective of 'nationality'. The meaning here is more intense or subjective)

*Me senté en una terraza a tomar una carísima cerveza fresca* (F. Umbral, 1977: 98)
I sat down on a terrace to have one of their extremely expensive cold beers
(The writer is struck more by the price of the beer than by its coldness)

*Sólo el loro 'Mambrú' se desazonó, revolviendo sus crueles ojos* (A. M. Matute, 1977: 48)
Only 'Mambrú' the parrot showed any sign of disturbance, rolling those cruel eyes of his. (The parrot's eyes are not 'objectively' cruel; they strike those present as such)

*Rechaza el gris departamento de un gris profesor que vive en la calle Charcas* (E. Sábato, 1981: 63)
He rejects the colourless apartment of a colourless teacher who lives in the Calle Charcas. (Not literally 'grey', but figuratively 'colourless')

*Es una sabrosa bella durmiente blanca ciudad* (G. Cabrera Infante, 1968: 354)
It is one of those delightful white sleeping-beauty towns
(The striving after stylistic is also apparent here from the absence of commas in the series of adjectives. The suggestion is that these qualities are inherent in the town; hence it is not simply an objective description but gives the idea of 'pretty-pretty')

*La cincuentona Rosa adopta un misterioso tono para decir la cosa más sencilla* (S. Lorén, 1955: 385)
Rosa, even though in her fifties, adopts a mysterious tone of voice to say even the simplest thing

'Intensifying' use of adjectives before the noun:

*El infante don Juan Manuel era un cristianísimo caballero* (J. A. Gómez Marín, 1972: 46)
Prince Juan Manuel was a most Christian knight

Ironical value of adjectives preceding the noun:

*Recordarán toda su vida el originalísimo viaje* (L. Carandell, 1970: 53)
They'll remember that really original journey all their lives

*Una bonita escena*
A pretty (= disgusting) scene
(But *una escena bonita* 'a pretty scene (literal)')

*¡Valiente amigo eres!*
You're a fine friend (i.e. behaving badly)!

The adjective before the noun may represent an attribute which is strange or exceptional in a particular circumstance, and as such merits special attention:

*Heidi enredaba sus morenos dedos entre sus cabellos foscos* (D. Medio, 1958: 64)
Heidi twisted her dark hair around her brown fingers
(Heidi is a half-caste girl living in Oviedo)

The 'heavier' the adjective is (because of its length or particular meaning), the more unusual or marked in effect its coming before the noun will appear:

*Los rubenianos cisnes* (F. Umbral, 1972: 65)
The swans Rubén Darío talked about

## 172 Literary and Journalistic Style

Placing the adjective before the noun is more frequent in literary style: sometimes the 'inherentness' implicit in an adjective which precedes the noun is exploited to indicate a feature that is well-known, although preceding adjectives seem to be increasingly common in journalistic style:

*La inteligente y fuerte mujer así gana su propia batalla* (C. Blanco Aguinaga et al., 1978–81: I, 308)
This intelligent, strong woman thus wins her own battle
(Of Saint Teresa of Ávila – the adjective sequence is strengthened by being placed before the noun)

*Su poetísimo padrino* (A. Skármeta, 1986: 129)
His godfather the great poet (of the Chilean poet Pablo Neruda)

*En la yanqui Florida* (C. J. Cela, 1963b: 17 and 19)
In the Florida of the Yankees

Journalistic style, too, exploits this device:

> *Ellas y sus dos acompañantes eran de la madrileña barriada de Palomeras* (F. Umbral, 1972: 65)
> She and her two companions came from the Palomeras quarter of Madrid
> (Here, *madrileña barriada* is probably an (ironical) allusion to a standard cliché of the Spanish press, where, in emulation of a falsely elevated or elegant style, the place-name adjective is usually put before the noun, e.g. *la zaragozana prisión de Torrero* 'Torrero prison in Zaragoza' (*El Norte de Castilla*, 27 July 1987: 19), *la madrileña calle de Serrano* 'the Calle Serrano in Madrid' (F. Umbral, 1985: 97))

> *El comunicado de la exiliada familia imperial iraní* (*El País*, 18 October 1980: 3, cited by R. Eberenz in a lecture given on 12 March 1994 in the Instituto de Estudios Hispánicos, Antwerp)
> The communiqué from the exiled Iranian imperial family

## 173 Adjective Position Leading to Differences in Meaning

Some adjectives have a very different meaning according to whether they precede or follow the noun, and often need to be translated by different English adjectives. Here also it can be seen that in general adjectives preceding the noun tend to be more 'subjective' in meaning:[8]

*Alto*

| | |
|---|---|
| *alta sociedad* | high (= high in status) society |
| *un edificio alto* | a high (= tall) building |

*Antiguo*

> *Ha venido un antiguo alumno mío*
> An old (= former) pupil of mine has come

> *Hemos comprado una casa antigua en Andalucía*
> We have bought an old house in Andalusia

*Bueno*

| | |
|---|---|
| *un buen obrero* | a good worker (= good at the job) |
| *un obrero bueno* | a good worker (= a good person) |

*Cierto*
    *un cierto hecho* — a certain (= particular) fact
    *un hecho cierto* — a certain (= sure) fact

*Diferentes*
    *en diferentes libros* — in several books
    *en libros diferentes* — in different books

*Distintos*
    *por distintas razones* — for various reasons
    *por razones distintas* — for different reasons

*Grande*
    *Es una gran orquesta* — It is a great (= very good) orchestra
    *Dirige una orquesta muy grande* — He conducts a very large orchestra.

*Medio*
    *media botella* — half a bottle
    *la clase media* — the middle class

*Negro* (see above **171**)

*Nuevo*
    *un nuevo libro* — a new (= different) book
    *un libro nuevo* — a (brand) new book

*Pequeño*
    *un pequeño zapatero* — a small (= modest) shoemaker
    *un zapatero pequeño* — a small (= short) shoemaker

*Pobre*
    *¡La pobre mujer!* — The poor (= unfortunate) woman!
    *Es una mujer pobre* — She is a poor (= poverty-stricken) woman

*Puro*
    *por pura casualidad* — by pure (=sheer) chance
    (cf. *mero*, **170**.)
    *oro puro* — pure (100 per cent) gold

*Simple*

| | |
|---|---|
| *un simple camarada* | a simple colleague |
| | (= simply a colleague) |
| *un camarada simple* | a simple colleague |
| | (= a simpleton) |

*Único*

| | |
|---|---|
| *la única oportunidad* | the only opportunity |
| *una oportunidad única* | a unique opportunity |

*Varios*

| | |
|---|---|
| *varios colores* | several colours |
| *colores varios* | varied, varying colours |

**174** Spanish authors sometimes play on these differences:

*Es que me gusta ver a los viejos amigos, pero no a los amigos viejos* (S. Lorén, 1971: 226)
I like to see old friends, but not friends who are old

*Yo soy católico, como Dollfuss, sólo que él es un gran hombre pequeño y yo un pequeño hombre grande* (R. J. Sender, 1969b: 162–3)
I am a Catholic, like Dollfuss, with the only difference that he is great in reputation though small in stature and I am small in reputation though great in stature

*De Girald era un alto funcionario de la Magistratura. Era también un funcionario alto* (D. Medio, 1958: 38)
De Girald was a high-ranking civil servant in the magistrature. His height was in keeping with his rank

In 1981 a play with the following title was announced:
   *Hombre rico . . .*
   *¡pobre hombre!*
Rich man . . . poor (= unfortunate) man!

## 175 *Mayor, menor, mejor, peor*

The forms *mayor, menor, mejor, peor* precede the noun when they are used with the definite article as superlatives.

| | |
|---|---|
| *la mayor parte de mis libros* | the majority of my books |
| *es el peor libro de los cuatro* | it is the worst book of the four |

However, when they are used with a comparative meaning, they generally follow the noun, especially when they are further qualified by *alguno*, *ninguno*, *otro* or *uno*.

| | |
|---|---|
| *¡Hay cosas peores!* | There are worse things! |
| *No conozco ningún libro mejor* | I know no better book |
| *No existe otra empresa mayor* | There is no larger firm |

*Mayor* and *menor* also follow the noun when used as comparatives in the sense of 'older' and 'younger':

| | |
|---|---|
| *mi hermano menor* | my younger brother |

and note

| | |
|---|---|
| *un hombre mayor* | an old (elderly) man |

*Mayor* and *menor* also follow the noun in a number of set phrases, such as:

| | |
|---|---|
| *la calle mayor* | the high street |
| *un colegio mayor* | a college, hall of residence |
| *jefe de estado mayor* | chief of staff |
| *en re menor* | in D minor (music) |

## 176 'Optional' Position of the Adjective

Despite the principles given above, in some cases the adjective can precede or follow the noun without any significant change of meaning.

*las buenas obras* or *las obras buenas*
good works

*el común denominador* or *el denominador común*
the common denominator

Sometimes adjective position is associated with register. *La primera vez* 'the first time' is more typical of the spoken language whereas *la vez primera* is more likely to be found as a written form. On the other hand, such a distinction does not hold for *primer piso* and *piso primero* 'first floor' (i.e. 'one floor up from ground' in Peninsular and British usage and 'ground-level floor' in Latin-American and US usage).[9]

## 177 Adjective Position in Exclamatory Sentences

Adjective position in exclamatory sentences, e.g. *¡Qué animal más feo!* 'What an ugly animal!', is discussed in **369**.

## 178 Apocope

The last letter of the following adjectives falls immediately before a masculine singular noun:

| | |
|---|---|
| *uno* | a(n), one |
| *alguno* | some |
| *bueno* | good |
| *malo* | bad |
| *ninguno* | no |
| *primero* | first |
| *postrero* | last |
| *postrimero* | last |
| *tercero* | third |

Note that apocope takes place even when another adjective intervenes before the noun, e.g. *un buen amigo*.

*Es el primer ejemplar de mi libro*
It is the first edition of my book

*Ya me lo explicará algún amigo*
Some friend will explain it to me

But:

*El primero y el último capítulo*
The first and the last chapter
(*primero* does not stand immediately before the noun)

*Te lo digo por tercera vez*
I'm telling you for the third time
(*vez* is feminine)

In Latin America, *primera*, *tercera* and *postrera* are sometimes apocopated before a feminine noun,[10] reflecting an older Peninsular usage.

– *¿Qué viento te trae? – fue su primer pregunta* (R. Güiraldes, *Don Segundo Sombra*, quoted in Kany, 1951: 30)
'What's blown you in?' was his first question

All the above words are sometimes apocopated before a feminine noun beginning with stressed *a-* or *ha-*, e.g.:

| | |
|---|---|
| *ningún aula* | no lecture hall (*DD*, 269) |
| *ningún arma* | no (fire)arm (ibid.) |

## 179 *Grande*

*Grande* is generally apocopated to *gran* before both masculine and feminine nouns.

| | |
|---|---|
| *el gran pintor* | the great painter |
| *la gran reina* | the great queen |

But *grande* is often left unapocopated, especially in the written language, when it is intended to create an emphatic effect:[11]

*El Quijote es un grande libro*
*Don Quixote* is a great book

*Un director de orquesta alemán, grande amigo suyo en sus tiempos de Austria* (G. García Márquez, 1985: 56)
A German orchestral conductor, a great friend of his from his Austrian days

It is even possible to find both apocopated and unapocopated forms with the same meaning:

*Estaba sola en aquel grande piso, en aquella gran ciudad* (I. Agustí, 1957: 290)
She was alone in that big apartment, in that big city[12]

There is no apocope in a case like the following, because *grande* does not immediately precede the noun:

*Una grande y concurridísima Feria* (E. Tierno Galván, 1984: 38)
A large and very crowded fair

*Más grande* does not apocopate:

*El más grande saqueo* (*Esbozo*, 194)
The greatest looting

## 180 *Santo*

Before the name of a male Saint *Santo* is apocopated to *San*:[13]

| | |
|---|---|
| *San Francisco* | Saint Francis |
| *San Juan* | Saint John |

There is no apocope before names beginning with *To-* or *Do-*:

| | |
|---|---|
| *Santo Domingo* | Saint Dominic |
| *Santo Tomás* (or *Tomé*) | Saint Thomas |
| *Santo Toribio* | Saint Toribius |

*Las pruebas están a disposición de cualquier santotomás que quiera verlas* (J. Cortázar, 1973: 48)
The proofs are available for any Doubting Thomas who wants to see them

*Santa* does not apocopate. and neither does *santo* when used in the full sense of 'holy':

| | |
|---|---|
| *Santa Teresa* | Saint Theresa |
| (because a female Saint) | |
| *el Santo Padre* | the Holy Father |
| *el Santo Espíritu* | the Holy Spirit |

# Degrees of Comparison

## The Comparative

**181**  The comparative of the vast majority of Spanish adjectives is formed by placing *más* (or *menos*) before the adjective.

*Este muchacho es más fuerte que su hermano*
This boy is stronger than his brother

*La última edición de este libro es menos cara que la anterior*
The last edition of this book is dearer than the previous one

*Las lágrimas de una mujer son más poderosas que los ríos* (F. Marcos Marín, 1978: 214)
A woman's tears are more powerful than rivers

For the 'pleonastic' use of *no* in comparisons, see **639**.

## 182 Irregular Comparatives

A very few Spanish adjectives have irregular comparative forms:

*bueno*   →   *mejor*
(*Más bueno* may be used of people in a moral sense, and is also used in the set comparison *más bueno que el pan* 'as good as gold')[14]

*grande*   →   *mayor* (also *más grande*, see **183**)

*malo*          →    *peor*
(*Más malo* may occasionally be found)[15]
*mucho*        →    *más*
*pequeño*     →    *menor* (also *más pequeño*, see **183**)
*poco*          →    *menos*

*Más* is not used with these comparative forms:

> *La segunda explicación es mejor que la primera*
> The second explanation is better than the first one

> *Este verano es aún peor que el del año pasado*
> This summer is even worse than last

> *Un caballo es mayor que un perro* (R. Chacel, 1981: 88)
> A horse is bigger than a dog

### 183 Mayor/más grande, menor/más pequeño

*Mayor/menor* are always used for age ('older/younger'):

> *Ella pareció más joven que él, a pesar de que era tres años mayor*
> (A. M. Matute. 1977: 88)
> She looked much younger than him, in spite of her being
> three years older

*Mayor* also appears in a number of set phrases: *calle mayor*, 'high
street'; *colegio mayor*, 'college, hall of residence'; *estado mayor*,
'military staff'.

*Mayor* and *menor* also have the absolute meanings 'of age' and
'under age' (sometimes in combination with *de edad*):

> *Antonio es mayor de edad* (*Esbozo*, 418)
> Antonio is of age

> *Entrada prohibida a los menores*
> No admittance for minors

Otherwise, *más grande/mayor*, *más pequeño/menor* are more or less
interchangeable, although the forms *más grande*, *más pequeño* are
more common in speech.[16]

### 184 Inferior, superior, anterior, posterior[17]

These forms. which derive from Latin comparatives, have ceased
to be true comparatives in modern Spanish, where they have no

positive counterparts. Purists insist, however, that they should be used without *más*, and regard forms like *más superior* (which are fairly common) as solecisms.[18] These words cannot be used in comparative constructions with *que*: they are instead followed by the preposition *a*.[19] *Anterior* 'before' and *posterior* 'after' (both used of time or space) belong to formal register.

> *Esta obra es superior a la otra* (*DD*, 32)
> This work is superior to the other one
> *El bar anterior al restaurante* (F. Umbral, 1985: 136)
> The bar before the restaurant

## The Superlative

**185** Spanish does not distinguish comparative and superlative degree as English does: thus *Juan es el más/menos inteligente* may mean either 'Juan is the more/less intelligent (one)' or 'Juan is the most/least intelligent (one)'. The exact English equivalent is usually clear from the context.

> *Juan es el alumno más inteligente de su clase*
> Juan is the most intelligent pupil in his class

> *El profesor dice: «Juan es mi alumno menos aplicado»*
> The teacher says, 'Juan is my least diligent pupil'

> *Nos enfrentamos ahora con la más grave pregunta* (J. L. Alcocer, 1978: 115)
> We are now faced with the most serious question

## 186 *-ísimo*

The *-ísimo* form, which derives from the Latin superlative, is sometimes described as a superlative in Spanish grammar. It intensifies the meaning of the adjective or other part of speech to which it is attached, and is more or less equivalent to *muy* 'very' (for other ways of expressing this idea, see **190–198**).

> *Juan es muy inteligente/inteligentísimo*
> Juan is very intelligent

In fact, the *-ísimo* form is generally felt to be slightly stronger in force than *muy*, although it appears that the *-ísimo* forms are finding increasing favour both in the modern spoken and written language.[20] In some Latin American countries the suffix -*azo* has the same value as -*ísimo*, e.g. *cansado* 'tired' → *cansadazo* 'very tired', *feo* 'ugly' → *feazo* 'very ugly'.[21]

In the Peninsula, -*azo* does not have this meaning (see **1321, 1327**).

**187** The -*ísimo* suffix replaces the final vowel of the adjective stem, e.g. *dulce* → *dulcísimo*. *tenue* → *tenuísimo*, *frío* → *friísimo*; when the stem ends in the unstressed diphthong -*io*, the whole diphthong is replaced: *amplio* → *amplísimo*. Any written accent on the original adjective falls: *fácil* → *facilísimo*, *rápido* → *rapidísimo*, etc.

Changes in the spelling of the adjective stem are also sometimes needed, e.g. *blanco* → *blanquísimo*, *feliz* → *felicísimo* (cf. **125**), etc.

In some cases, the form of the adjective stem itself changes:

| | | |
|---|---|---|
| *agradable* | → | *agradabilísimo* |
| *áspero* | → | *aspérrimo* and *asperísimo* |
| *amable* | → | *amabilísimo* |

(and similarly the majority of adjectives in -*ble*. with the exception of *feble* → *feblísimo* and *endeble* → *endeblísimo*)

| | | |
|---|---|---|
| *antiguo* | → | *antiquísimo* |
| *bueno* | → | *óptimo, bonísimo* or *buenísimo* |
| *cierto* | → | *certísimo* or *ciertísimo* |
| *cursi* | → | *cursilísimo* |
| *diestro* | → | *destrísimo* or *diestrísimo* |
| *fiel* | → | *fidelísimo* |
| *fuerte* | → | *fortísimo* or *fuertísimo* |
| *grande* | → | *máximo* or *grandísimo* |
| *grueso* | → | *grosísimo* or *gruesísimo* |
| *inicuo* | → | *iniquísimo* |
| *joven* | → | *jovencísimo* |
| *malo* | → | *pésimo* or *malísimo* |
| *nuevo* | → | *novísimo* or *nuevísimo* |
| *pequeño* | → | *mínimo* or *pequeñísimo* |
| *pobre* | → | *paupérrimo* and *pobrísimo* |
| *tierno* | → | *ternísimo* or *tiernísimo*[22] |

Where there are irregular and regular alternatives. the regular form is usually preferred in the spoken language.[23] *Muy* + adjective can of course always be used instead.

Some examples of the use of the 'irregular' forms:

*El juicio general del libro es óptimo* (A. García Berrio, 1976: 22)
The general opinion of the book is excellent

*Pedro despertó sintiéndose pésimo por la borrachera de anoche* (A. Bryce Echenique, 1981: 15)
Pedro awoke feeling dreadful from last night's drinking

Such forms are often used for stylistic effect:

*El mínimo y máximo Dámaso Alonso* (F. Umbral, in *Interviú*, 227, 18–24 September 1980: 13)
The inconspicuous but unsurpassed Dámaso Alonso
(The contrasting superlatives refer respectively to the physical appearance and the intellect of the great Spanish writer and linguist)

*Mínimo* is commonly used in the spoken language in the following expression:

*No tengo la más mínima idea*
I haven't the faintest idea[24]

and may even take the *-ísimo* ending:

*Tengo una minísima radio japonesa debajo de la almohada* (A. Skármeta, 1986: 159)
I have a tiny Japanese radio under my pillow

Such examples show that highly irregular forms like *máximo*, *mínimo*, *óptimo* and *pésimo* are not really thought of as *-ísimo* forms at all nowadays. *Más* is not normally possible with an *-ísimo* form, and the common use of *más* with *óptimo* has been censured by purists.[25]

**188** The suffix *-ísimo* is also widely used in religious terminology and in courtesy formulae, of both individuals and institutions:

| | |
|---|---|
| *la Santísima Trinidad* | the Holy Trinity |
| *el Santísimo Sacramento* | the Holy Sacrament |
| *el Altísimo* | the Almighty |
| *la Purísima* | the Virgin (lit. the Most Pure) |

*el corazón sacratísimo de Jesús*   the Most Sacred Heart of Jesus

*Excelentísimo Señor:*   Dear Sir (to a minister, etc.)

*el Excelentísimo Ayuntamiento de Madrid*
the Madrid City Council

*la Excelentísima Diputación Provincial de Alicante*
the Alicante County Council

*Ilustrísimo* or *Reverendísimo* is used for a bishop; General Franco (head of state in Spain 1939–75) adopted the title *Generalísimo*

**189** The use of *-ísimo* has become so widespread that the suffix is not only used with adjectives, but also with past participles, nouns and even proper nouns, adverbs and adverbial phrases, demonstrative, interrogative and indefinite pronouns:[26]

> *Gracias, Josechu, no sabes cuantísimo te lo agradezco* (M. Delibes, 1969a: 293, quoted in De Bruyne, 1974: 11)
> Thanks, Josechu, you don't know just how grateful I am for that

## Other Intensifying Elements

**190** Spanish has a number of other ways of expressing intensity with adjectives. They should be handled with care by foreigners, and are perhaps best avoided, especially in writing.

## 191 *Re-, rete-, requete-*

*Re* + adjective is frequently encountered in speech.

> *Robertito está relimpio, repeinado, casi elegante* (C. J. Cela, 1967b: 149)
> Robertito is sparkling clean, with his hair carefully combed – he looks almost elegant

Forms like *relimpio*, *repeinado* and similar examples in the sections below have affective overtones of approval or admiration.

**192** *Re-* can in its turn be strengthened by *-te-* or (more often) *-quete-*: thus *bueno* → *rebueno* → *retebueno* → *requetebueno*. Forms in *rete-* are very common in Mexican Spanish.[27]

> *Fueron retemuchas* (J. Rulfo, 1981: 109)
> There were ever such a lot of girls
>
> *¡Qué requetefinas son las brasileñas!* (J. A. de Zunzunegui, 1958: 217)
> How fantastic Brazilian girls are!

**193** Even such combinations are not expressive enough for some speakers, and one sometimes finds in the same word:

> prefix + adjective + *-ísimo*
> 2 or 3 prefixes + adjective + *-ísimo*
> 2 or 3 prefixes + adjective + double suffix *-ísimo*.

Thus *retemonísima*, *requetemonísima* and *requetemonisísima* may be derived from *mona*.[28]
Muy + *requete* + adjective may also be found.

> – *Ellas siempre lo llamaban así.*
> – *¿Pero en broma?*
> – *No, señor; muy requeteserias* (F. García Pavón, 1971: 38)
> 'That's what they always called it.'
> 'But surely as a joke?'
> 'Not at all; they were deadly serious'

## 194 *Super-*

The prefix *super-* is also found in combinations ending in *-ísimo*:

> ... *época de realidades gigantescas, superavanzadísimas en tantos aspectos* (L. Carandell, 1970: 189)
> A period of gigantic realities, in many respects very advanced

## 195 Intensifying Meaning through Repetition

Adjective + *que* + adjective (e.g. *muerto que muerto* 'stone dead', *vivo que vivo* 'alive and kicking', *tonto que tonto* 'really stupid') provides another means of intensifying an adjective in the colloquial language.

*Más* is sometimes added before *que*, especially in exclamatory sentences where the adjective has a pejorative meaning, e.g. *¡tonto, más que tonto!* 'what a bloody idiot!'.

**196** In other cases, *que* is not used, and the adjective is simply repeated (with no comma).

> *Eran unos versos rarísimos, unos cortos cortos y otros largos largos* (M. Delibes, 1969a: 272)
> They were very odd poems, some really short and others really long

### 197 Es más malo ...

Constructions of this type look like comparatives but in fact have an intensifying value. They are generally elliptical exclamatory sentences with the second part of the comparison missing, such as *¡Es más malo!* 'He's a good-for-nothing!', *Era más bonita* 'She was unbelievably pretty', *¡Es usted más antipático!* 'You're really horrid!'. They are typical of the spoken language.[29]

### 198 Other Intensifiers

See also *la mar (de)* in **111** and the apparently paradoxical use of diminutive suffixes with intensifying force in **1323**.

## Adverbial Use of the Adjective

**199** Spanish sometimes uses an adjective where English would use an adverb or adverbial expression.[30] Such adjectives usually agree in number and gender with the subject of the verb, which may lead to an apparent lack of agreement, as in the fifth example below.

A suffix can be added to an adjective used in this way, as in the fourth example.

> *El Cádiz jugó durante todo el encuentro muy nervioso* (*La Vanguardia*, 14 February 1978: 43)
> Cadiz played very nervously for the whole of the match

> *Virginia siempre caminó rápida* (G. Cabrera Infante, 1979: 287)
> Virginia always walked fast

*En general las avefrías volaban altas* (M. Delibes, 1972: 108)
Lapwings generally flew high

*Su vida transcurrió suavona* (F. García Pavón, 1980a: 29)
His life went on without incident

*He pasado una semana intranquilo* (T. Salvador, 1968a: 177)
I have spent an uneasy week (lit. I have spent a week
uneasily).

**200** There is, however, a tendency nowadays for the adjective to
be left invariable in its adverbial use.

Even in the work of important modern writers, strictly incorrect
constructions like the following are found:

*Hablaron muy largo y lamentoso* (F. García Pavón, 1971: 233)
They spoke at length, dolefully

*(En un tapiz) Aparecen unos señores vestidos muy raro*
(C. Martín Gaite, 1968: 86–7)
(On a tapestry) Some very strangely dressed people can
be seen

*Podemos pasárnoslo soberbio* (R. Sánchez Ferlosio, 1971: 134)
We can have a whale of a time
(Here the author is deliberately rendering everyday speech)

*Varios hombres lo miran indiferente, apoyados en la pared
externa de los urinarios* (F. Aínsa, 1984:61)
Several men looked at him indifferently, as they leaned on
the outside wall of the lavatories

**201** An adverb in *-mente* and an adjective used adverbially may
even stand together, and this is similarly considered incorrect:

*Vestía pobremente y desarrapado* (M. Delibes, 1948: 156)
He was poorly and shabbily dressed

**202** Some adjectives and adverbs have the same form.

| | |
|---|---|
| *un producto barato* | a cheap product |
| *comprar barato* | to buy cheaply |
| *un libro caro* | an expensive book |
| *vender caro* | to sell at a high price |
| *derecho como un pino* | as straight as a die |
| *caminar derecho* | to walk straight |

| | |
|---|---|
| *pan duro* | hard bread |
| *trabajar duro* | to work hard |

Words like *bestial, distinto, fatal, fenomenal, genial, igual* and *rápido* are regularly used adverbially in the spoken language, and as such are invariable:

> In the Residencia of the Consejo Superior de Investigaciones Científicas in Madrid, the porter had put up a notice in February 1983 which read:
> *LA CENTRALITA FUNCIONA FATAL*
> The exchange doesn't work properly

> *En Puebla las mujeres hablan distinto* (M. Alvar, 1982: 69)
> In Puebla, women speak differently

> *Lo hizo bestial* (quoted by C. Hernández in a lecture to the Instituto de Estudios Hispánicos of Antwerp, 11 March 1989)
> He did it in an extaordinary fashion

This tendency is stronger in spoken American Spanish where indeed a word like *diario* 'daily' is generally used instead of *diariamente*.[31]

**203** In other cases the adverbial adjective and adjective have the same form but a different meaning, while an adverb in *-mente* (which may or may not have the same meaning as the adjectival adverb) also exists:

| Adjective | Adverbial adjective | Adverb |
|---|---|---|
| *alto* | *alto* | *altamente* |
| high | (a) loud (e.g. *hablar alto* 'to speak aloud') | to a high degree |
| *bajo* | *bajo* | *bajamente* |
| low | quietly | low, meanly |
| *claro* | *claro* | *claramente* |
| clear | clearly | clearly |
| *hondo* | *hondo* | *hondamente* |
| deep | deep(ly) | deeply |
| *limpio* | *limpio* | *limpiamente* |
| clean | clean, fairly | cleanly, fairly |

(e.g. *jugar limpio* or *limpiamente* 'to play clean(ly)')

Such adjectives are restricted to certain verbs with which they are closely associated: thus *alto* is used with *hablar, gritar, pensar,* etc., *bajo* with *hablar, cantar,* etc., *claro* with *hablar, hondo* with *respirar, limpio* with *jugar.*

# Numerals

## Cardinal Numerals

**204**

| | |
|---|---|
| 0 | *cero* |
| 1 | *uno, una* |
| 2 | *dos* |
| 3 | *tres* |
| 4 | *cuatro* |
| 5 | *cinco* |
| 6 | *seis* |
| 7 | *siete* |
| 8 | *ocho* |
| 9 | *nueve* |
| 10 | *diez* |
| 11 | *once* |
| 12 | *doce* |
| 13 | *trece* |
| 14 | *catorce* |
| 15 | *quince* |
| 16 | *dieciséis/diez y seis* |
| 17 | *diecisiete/diez y siete* |
| 18 | *dieciocho/diez y ocho* |
| 19 | *diecinueve/diez y nueve* |
| 20 | *veinte* |
| 21 | *veintiuno/veinte y uno* |
| 22 | *veintidós/veinte y dos* |
| 23 | *veintitrés/veinte y tres* |
| 24 | *veinticuatro/veinte y cuatro* |

| 25 | *veinticinco/veinte y cinco* |
| 26 | *veintiséis/veinte y seis* |
| 27 | *veintisiete/veinte y siete* |
| 28 | *veintiocho/veinte y ocho* |
| 29 | *veintinueve/veinte y nueve* |
| 30 | *treinta* |
| 31 | *treinta y uno* |
| 40 | *cuarenta* |
| 42 | *cuarenta y dos* |
| 50 | *cincuenta* |
| 60 | *sesenta* |
| 70 | *setenta* |
| 80 | *ochenta* |
| 90 | *noventa* |
| 100 | *ciento, cien* (see **212**) |
| 101 | *ciento uno, una* |
| 102 | *ciento dos* |
| 200 | *doscientos(-as)* (see **215**) |
| 300 | *trescientos(-as)* |
| 400 | *cuatrocientos(-as)* |
| 500 | *quinientos(-as)* |
| 600 | *seiscientos(-as)* |
| 700 | *setecientos(-as)* |
| 800 | *ochocientos(-as)* |
| 900 | *novecientos(-as)* (*nuevecientos* is also commonly used, but is not accepted by purists[1]) |
| 1000 | *mil* |
| 10,000 | *diez mil* |
| 25,000 | *veinticinco mil* |
| 100,000 | *cien mil* |
| 200,000 | *doscientos mil* |
| 1,000,000 | *un millón* |

*Un billón* 'a billion' is a million million ($10^{12}$), not a thousand million ($10^9$) as in the US (and increasingly in Great Britain).

For the alternatives *dieciséis/diez y seis*, etc., the single word spelling is preferred.[2]

In writing Spanish, the numbers one to thirty are written out in full unless they are dates; numbers above thirty are written as figures.[3]

Note that *y* is used only between tens and units: *cuarenta y tres* 43 but *ciento uno* 101, *quinientos setenta* 570. This rule also applies in larger numbers, e.g. *ciento cincuenta y cuatro mil quinientos treinta y ocho* 154,538. However, deviations from this rule sometimes occur in set phrases:

> *las mil y una noches*        the thousand and one nights

> *No es un Mingote sino mil y un Mingotes* (*ABC*, international edition, 3 February 1987: 19)
> He is not one Mingote, but a thousand and one Mingotes (Mingote is a well-known cartoonist – now a member of the Real Academia Española)[4]

## 205 The Numbers 1,100 to 1,999

In contrast with English, which optionally uses the hundreds system for the numbers 1100 to 1999, and obligatorily uses it for dates, Spanish always uses a numeral involving *mil*.

> *Este libro tiene más de 1.200* (read *mil doscientas*) *páginas*
> This book has more than one thousand two hundred / twelve hundred pages

> *El Emperador Carlos murió en 1558* (read *mil quinientos cincuenta y ocho*)
> The Emperor Charles died in 1558 (fifteen (hundred and) fifty-eight)

## 206 Decimals

Note that in Spain and Latin America the functions of the comma and full stop in figures are the reverse of those used in the English-speaking world: thus Spanish *1.745 mil setecientos cuarenta y cinco* = English 1,745 'one thousand seven hundred and forty-five' and Spanish *1,745 uno coma siete cuatro cinco* = English 1.745 'one point seven four five'.

## 207 Teens

It is impossible to render the notion of English 'teens' in Spanish except by paraphrase. The term *quinceañero* is sometimes used for 'teenager'.

## 208 *Y pico*

*Y pico* may be added to the numeral to express an approximate amount (see also **490**). When followed by a noun, the expression is sometimes (though more correctly is not) followed by *de*.

*Ciento y pico pesetas* (R. Montero, 1979: 20)
A hundred odd pesetas

*Un país de treinta y pico millones de policías* (J. Goytisolo, 1988: 229)
A country of upwards of thirty million policemen

*Ahora tiene noventa y pico de años* (J. L. Vilallonga, 1980: 39)
He's now over ninety

*La segunda mitad del XIX significa un enorme crecimiento de la población: de casi 300.000 habitantes en 1860 a 470 y pico mil en 1887* (C. del Moral, 1974: 7)
The second half of the nineteenth century saw an enormous increase in the population from almost 300,000 inhabitants in 1860 to over 470,000 in 1887

## 209 *Escaso, largo*

The adjectives *escaso* 'scarce' and *largo* 'long' are used to indicate respectively a bare or a generous measure:

*Tres metros escasos de tela* (*DUE*, I, 1177).
A bare three metres of cloth

*(El escritor) tiene más de sesenta, sesenta «largos», pero conserva algo inefablemente juvenil* (A. Posse, 1990: 82)
(The writer) is sixty, a good sixty, years old, but he retains something ineffably juvenile

## 210 Apocopation of *uno*

*Uno* becomes *un* before a masculine singular noun (whether or not preceded by an adjective). The same applies when *uno* is the last element in a compound numeral preceding a plural noun.

| | |
|---|---|
| *un país* | a, one country |
| *un solo país* | a single country |
| *setenta y un verbos* | seventy-one verbs |
| *Dos mil cincuenta y un pesos* (J. C. Onetti, 1979: 157) | |
| Two thousand and fifty-one pesos | |

## 211 Order of Numerals Involving *uno* or *una*

If the first of two numerals pertaining to a noun is *uno* or *una*, and if both numerals are connected by *y* or *o*, then the second numeral comes after the noun.

> *Esto durará un año o dos*
> This will last one or two years

## 212 *Ciento, cien*

*Ciento* is apocopated to *cien* before a noun (whether or not preceded by an adjective) and before any numeral which it multiplies.

| | |
|---|---|
| *cien dólares* | a hundred dollars |
| *cien casas* | a hundred houses |
| *las cien mejores poesías* | the hundred best poems (*Esbozo*, 239) |
| *cien mil pesetas* | a hundred thousand pesetas |

But:

| | |
|---|---|
| *ciento cincuenta libros* | a hundred and fifty books |

(Here another numeral, not multiplied by *ciento*, comes between *ciento* and the noun.)

In reality these rules are not always adhered to. Forms like *cien quince* for *ciento quince* 'a hundred and fifteen' are regularly found,[5] and conversely the apocopated form is used increasingly today in expressions like *cien por cien* 'a hundred per cent' (also *ciento por ciento* and even *cien por ciento* (A. Bryce Echenique, 1981: 202)) and *cien y cien veces* 'countless times'.[6] In F. Umbral, 1980: 237, we read *cien o doscientos años* 'one or two hundred years'.

American Spanish frequently uses *cien* where Peninsular Spanish uses *ciento*.[7]

*Cien* or *el número cien* is sometimes used in the sense of 'loo, lavatory', deriving from the fact that toilets in hotels were often given this number.[8]

## 213 Agreement of Cardinal Numerals

The cardinal numerals are invariable. except for *uno* and multiples of a hundred, which agree in gender with the noun to which they pertain. For *mil* and *millón*, see **216–217**.

## 214 *Veintiuno*, etc.

Forms like *veintiuno*, *treinta y uno*, etc., in which *uno/a* is the last element, agree in gender with a following noun: *veintiún kilos* '21 kilos', *treinta y una toneladas* '31 tons'. In other positions within a compound numeral, the agreement of *uno* appears to be optional: both *treinta y un mil toneladas* and *treinta y una mil toneladas* are used.[9]

Note that in such cases the noun itself is always in the plural: *veintiún días* '21 days', NOT *\*veintiún día*.

## 215 *Doscientos*, etc.

The hundreds from 200 to 900 agree in gender with the noun to which they pertain, even if, as in the second example below, they are multiplied by another numeral.

| | |
|---|---|
| *doscientas páginas* | two hundred pages |
| *cuatrocientas mil pesetas* | four hundred thousand pesetas |
| *mil doscientos árboles* | one thousand two hundred trees |

## 216 *Millón*

*Millón*, which as in English is a noun, has a plural *millones*. *De* must be used between *millón* and the noun.

| | |
|---|---|
| *dos millones de soldados* | two million soldiers |

## 217 *Ciento* and *mil* as Nouns

*Ciento* (*cien* in some areas[10]) and *mil* can also be used as nouns, especially in the plural. In this usage, *de* must precede the noun. *Cientos* when used as a noun is invariable when followed by a feminine noun (see second example below).

*Cientos y cientos de bachilleres* (C. J. Cela, 1963a: 218)
Hundreds and hundreds of arts students
(*Centenares* (see **236**) can also be used instead of *cientos*)

*Cientos de aventuras* (A. Grosso, 1978: 102)
Hundreds of adventures
(NOT *\*Cientas de aventuras*)

> *Miles de alumnos canadienses usan a diario el periódico en la escuela* (*Ya*, 9 February 1978, supplement entitled *Prensa didáctica*, 1)
> Thousands of Canadian students use the paper every day in school
> (*Millares* could be used instead of *miles*)

In the following example, the two constructions *mil lecciones* and *miles de lecciones* appear to have been confused:

> *Y aquel libro contenía las miles lecciones amorosas de las cuales se podía sacar todo el provecho del mundo* (C. Tellado, 1984: 65)
> And that book contained the thousands of lessons in love from which all the benefit in the world could be derived.[11]

### 218 The Plural of Cardinal Numerals

Other cardinal numerals form their plural, when needed, in exactly the same way as nouns.

> *Añada todos los ceros que usted quiera*
> Add all the noughts you like

> *Cuatro cuatros seguidos*
> Four fours one after the other

The plural of *dos* is *doses*:[12]

> *Tengo tres doses* (*DRAE*, 549)
> I've got three twos (cards)

*Note: Dos* is the plural of *do* 'doh (musical note)'.

### 219 Miscellaneous Expressions with Numbers

| | |
|---|---|
| Six plus four is ten | *Seis y/más cuatro son diez* |
| Ten minus seven is three | *Diez menos siete son tres* |
| Seven times three is twenty-one | *Siete veces tres/Siete por tres son veintiuno* |
| Fourteen divided by two is seven | *Catorce dividido por dos son siete* |
| Ten minus twenty is minus ten | *Diez menos veinte es menos diez* |
| Thirty-seven over twenty | *Treinta y siete sobre veinte* |

| | |
|---|---|
| Six out of ten | *Seis sobre diez* |
| Twelve squared | *Doce al cuadrado* |
| Ten cubed | *Diez al cubo* |
| Ten to the power of five | *Diez a la quinta potencia* |
| Ten to the minus fifteenth | *Diez elevado a menos quince* |
| The square root of sixteen is | *La raíz cuadrada de* |
| four | *dieciséis es/son cuatro* |
| The cube root of twenty- | *La raíz cúbica de veintisiete* |
| seven is three | *es/son tres* |
| Eleven square metres | *Once metros cuadrados* |
| Twelve metres square | *Doce metros al cuadrado* |
| Twenty cubic centimetres | *Veinte centímetros cúbicos* |

## 220 Percentages

Percentages usually have a definite or indefinite article in Spanish (but see the first example under **1285**):

> *El diez por ciento de los encuestados no lo sabían*
> Ten per cent of those interviewed did not know

> *El coste de la vida ha subido en un ocho por ciento*
> The cost of living has gone up by eight per cent

> *El último sondeo de opinión mostró que los partidarios del no alcanzan el 50%, mientras que a favor del sí se pronuncia un 33%, y los indecisos suman el 17% (El País Internacional,* 8 February 1993: 4)
> The last opinion poll showed that the no vote reached 50 per cent while the yes vote was 33 per cent and the don't knows 17 per cent

For number agreement between verb and subject, see **1285**.

## 221 Expressions of Time

| | |
|---|---|
| What time is it? | *¿Qué hora es?* |
| It is one o'clock | *Es la una* |
| It is two o'clock | *Son las dos* |

In Latin America, plural forms such as *¿Qué horas son?* 'What time is it?', *a las doces* 'at twelve o'clock', etc., are some-times used.[13]

| | |
|---|---|
| It is midday | *Es mediodía* |

| | |
|---|---|
| It is midnight | *Es medianoche* |
| It is five past five, ten past five, quarter past five, twenty past five, twenty-five past five, half past five, twenty-five to six, twenty to six, quarter to six, ten to six, five to six | *Son las cinco y cinco, las cinco y diez, las cinco y cuarto, las cinco y veinte, las cinco y venticinco, las cinco y media, las seis menos veinticinco, las seis menos veinte, las seis menos cuarto, las seis menos diez, las seis menos cinco* |
| It is 8.23 a.m./p.m. | *Son las ocho y veintitrés minutos de la mañana/de la tarde* |
| The bus leaves at 0600 hours and arrives at 2345 | *El autobús sale a las 6 y llega a las 23.45* |
| At about six o'clock | *Sobre las seis/A eso de las seis* |
| At about ten past six | *Sobre las seis y diez* |

See also **36**.

*Note:* In Latin America, *am* and *pm* are often used as in English.

## 222 Expressions of Date

The cardinal numeral is used for the expression of dates, with the exception of the first of the month, for which an ordinal numeral may be used.

*Nos veremos en Madrid el 8 (ocho) de marzo*
We'll meet in Madrid on the 8th of March

*Nueva York, 21 (veintiuno) de noviembre de 1969*
(read: *Nueva York, veintiuno de . . .*)

*Me marcharé a España el 1 de mayo*
(read: *el uno de mayo* or *el primero de mayo*)[14]

See **36** for the use of the numeral in the expression of time. For dates in letters, see also **706**.

**223** 'Fortnight' is *quince días* or, as a noun, *una quincena.*

## 224 Decades

Decades are often referred to nowadays in the following way: *los treinta* (or *los años treinta, los treintas*) 'the thirties', *los sesenta* (or *los años sesenta, los sesentas* 'the sixties', etc. The use of such plurals is also common in American Spanish.[15] Purists[16] consider such forms to be Anglicisms and recommend the use of the terms *decenio* or *década*, which gives rise to such constructions as *en el segundo decenio, en la tercera década*, etc.[17]

> *No consta quién fue el crítico que llamó «tremendismo» lo que hacía Cela en los primeros cuarenta* (F. Umbral, 1987: 151)
> It is not known who the critic was who called what Cela was doing in the early forties 'tremendismo'

> *Los terroristas judíos de los cuarenta* (C. Fuentes, 1979: 127)
> The Jewish terrorists of the forties

## Ordinal Numerals

## 225 Forms

| | |
|---|---|
| 1st | *primero*[18] |
| 2nd | *segundo* |
| 3rd | *tercero* |
| 4th | *cuarto* |
| 5th | *quinto* |
| 6th | *sexto* |
| 7th | *sé(p)timo* |
| 8th | *octavo* |
| 9th | *noveno* (*nono*, an archaism, is used in *Pío Nono* 'Pius IX')[19] |
| 10th | *décimo* |
| 11th | *undécimo* (*decimoprimero* is also used, but is considered incorrect)[20] |
| 12th | *duodécimo* (*decimosegundo* is also used, but is considered incorrect) |
| 13th | *decimotercero* (less commonly *decimotercio*) |
| 14th | *decimocuarto* |
| 15th | *decimoquinto* |
| 16th | *decimosexto* |

| 17th | *decimosé(p)timo* |
|---|---|
| 18th | *decimoctavo* |
| 19th | *decimonoveno* (less commonly *decimonono*) |
| 20th | *vigésimo* |
| 21st | *vigesimoprimero* |
| 22nd | *vigesimosegundo* |
| 23rd | *vigesimotercero* |
| 30th | *trigésimo* |
| 31st | *trigesimoprimero* |
| 40th | *cuadragésimo* |
| 50th | *quincuagésimo* |
| 60th | *sexagésimo* |
| 70th | *septuagésimo* |
| 80th | *octogésimo* |
| 90th | *nonagésimo* |
| 100th | *centésimo* |
| 101st | *centesimoprimero* |
| 102nd | *centesimosegundo* |
| 200th | *ducentésimo* |
| 300th | *tricentésimo* |
| 400th | *cuadringentésimo* |
| 500th | *quingentésimo* |
| 600th | *sexcentésimo* |
| 700th | *septingentésimo* |
| 800th | *octingentésimo* |
| 900th | *noningentésimo* (or *nongentésimo*) |
| 1000th | *milésimo* |
| 2000th | *dosmilésimo* |
| | etc. |

The forms from *decimotercero* to *decimonono* may be written as two words, e.g. *décimo tercero*, in which case the accent is used with *décimo*.

Many of the above forms are not actually used, however. Only *primero* to *décimo* inclusive, *centésimo* and *milésimo* are generally known and used to any extent. The others are only used in a technical context,[21] and many Spanish speakers do not know them or make mistakes with them.

There is hesitation over 'the Tenth': both *el siglo décimo* and *el siglo diez*, *Alfonso Décimo* and *Alfonso Diez* are read and heard.[22]

In titles and notices, etc., Roman figures are sometimes used to express the ordinal.

*¡Prepárese para la III guerra mundial!* (read *la tercera guerra mundial*) (on the title-page of the satirical magazine *Muy señor mío*, 24 January 1980)
Prepare for the third World War!

*I Jornadas de Solidaridad con Centro América* (read *Primeras Jornadas . . .*) (notice seen in Granada, 1 March 1984)
First Congress for Solidarity with Central America

## 226 *Sesqui-*

The prefix *sesqui-* (of learned Latin origin) means 'one and a half'. Thus *sesquicentenario* means '150th anniversary' or relates to something 150 years old.

## 227 Alternative Ways of Expressing Ordinal Numerals: Cardinal Used for Ordinal

Spanish speakers generally simply replace unfamiliar ordinal numerals with a cardinal numeral placed before the noun, both in spoken and written language. The numeral is sometimes simply written as a figure, as in the fourth example.

*La cien representación* (M. Delibes, 1948: 21)
The hundredth performance

*Su cuarenta y cinco cumpleaños* (M. Delibes, 1969b: 237)
Her forty-fifth birthday

*La diecisiete prueba de la existencia de Dios* (P. Baroja, 1946–51: I, 1132)
The seventeenth proof of God's existence

*El Rey don Juan Carlos celebró su 39 cumpleaños* (*Heraldo de Aragón*, 6 January 1977: 1)
King Juan Carlos celebrated his 39th birthday

*No era la primera vez, sino la dos millones ciento cuarenta y seis mil veintiocho* (E. Parra, 1981: 101–2)
It wasn't the first time but the 2,146,028th time

The cardinal numeral follows the nouns such as *página* 'page', *capítulo* 'chapter' and *siglo* 'century'.

*Esto se puede leer en el capítulo quince*
One can read this in Chapter 15

*Vivimos en el siglo XX* (read *el siglo veinte*)
We live in the twentieth century

## 228 *-avo*

A common way increasingly favoured by modern speakers[23] of rendering ordinal numbers is to use the forms in *-avo*, which properly denote fractions (**234**):

> *Soy el catorceavo ministro* . . . (Javier Solana, Minister of Culture, on television)[24]
> I'm the fourteenth minister . . .
> (The 'correct' form is *Soy el decimocuarto ministro*, more usually *Soy el ministro número catorce*)

> . . . *al último piso, al treintavo* . . . (C. Fuentes, 1979: 152)
> . . . to the top floor, the thirtieth . . .

## 229 Titles of Kings and Queens, etc.

With names of kings and queens, etc., and Popes, the ordinal numeral is used as far as the tenth (but see **227**), and then the cardinal numeral. In contrast with English, the definite article before the numeral is not used.

> *Isabel II* (read *Isabel Segunda*)
> Elizabeth the Second

> *Carlos V* (read *Carlos Quinto*)
> Charles the Fifth

But:

> *Juan XXIII* (read *Juan Veintitrés*)
> John the Twenty-Third

## 230 Apocope

*Primero* and *tercero* lose the final *-o* before a masculine singular noun, as described in **178**.

## 231 Agreement

Ordinal numerals agree like other adjectives in number and gender with the noun to which they pertain.

> *la tercera observación*     the third observation
> *los primeros comentarios*   the first comments

In the compound ordinals from 13th to 19th inclusive, agreement of the first part is optional:

> *Se ha olvidado usted de la Décimo Octava Enmienda de la Constitución* (A. Carpentier, 1976: 283)
> You have forgotten the Eighteenth Amendment of the Constitution
> (One could also say ... *la décima octava* ...

It has been suggested[25] that when the ordinal is written as one word, only the second part agrees, and that when it is written as two (not very common today) both parts should agree.

## 232 Elliptical Use of some Ordinals

*Primera*, etc., is often used on its own as an ellipsis for *primera clase*:

> *Una actriz de tercera* (C. Martín Gaite, 1980: 67)
> A third-rate actress
> (Implies *de tercera clase, categoría* as opposed, for example, to *una actriz de primera*)

# Fractions, Multiples and Collectives

**233** The following have special forms:

> ½      *una mitad* (noun); *medio* (adjective)
> ⅓      *un tercio*

When *medio* means 'half' it precedes the noun (see also **173**), e.g. *medio (kilo)* 'half a kilo', *medio (pan)* 'a half(-size) loaf'. In this sense, it can also be used as an adjectival noun (so in an appropriate context *un medio* can itself mean 'a half-size (loaf)').

*Note:* The noun *medio* means 'middle, mean; medium'.

*Mitad* carries the idea of 'half part', and is generally used with an article, e.g. *la mitad de sus bienes* 'half his goods'. The forms *en mitad de* and *en medio de* 'in the middle of' are synonymous.[26]

In mathematics, *un medio* is sometimes used for *la mitad*, though this is strictly incorrect.[27]

**234** From 1/4 to 1/10 the ordinal numeral is used:

| | |
|---|---|
| 1/4 | *un cuarto* |
| 1/5 | *un quinto* |
| 2/8 | *dos octavos* |
| 4/10 | *cuatro décimos* |

From 1/11 to 1/199 the fractions are formed from the cardinal numeral and the suffix *-avo*.

| | |
|---|---|
| 1/11 | *un onceavo* or *un onzavo* (also, exceptionally, *un undécimo*) |
| 4/12 | *cuatro doceavos* or *cuatro dozavos* (also, exceptionally, *cuatro duodécimos*)[28] |
| 5/30 | *cinco treintavos* |
| 8/100 | *ocho centavos* |
| 23/183 | *veintitrés ciento ochenta y tresavos* |

From 1/200 the form of the corresponding ordinal numeral can be used (or *-avo* can be added to the cardinal numeral).

| | |
|---|---|
| 3/524 | *tres quingentésimo vigésimo cuartos* or *tres quinientos veinticuatroavos* |

1/1000 and 1/1.000.000 (and their compounds) are however *un milésimo* and *un milionésimo*.

| | |
|---|---|
| 1/200 | *un ducentésimo* or *un doscientosavo* |
| 1/10.000 | *un diezmilésimo* |

*A cada cienmillonésimo de segundo* (E. Sábato, 1981: 41)
Every hundred millionth of a second

Fractions can also be rendered by an ordinal numeral + *parte*.

| | |
|---|---|
| *una sexta parte* or *un sexto* | a sixth (part) |
| *la décima parte de su fortuna* (from Alcina Franch and Blecua, 668) | the tenth part of his fortune |
| *una dozava parte* | a twelfth part |
| *cuatro quintas partes* (R. Garriga, 1980: 221) | four fifths |

## 235 Multiples

| | |
|---|---|
| *simple* | single |
| *doble* | double |

| | |
|---|---|
| *triple* | triple |
| *cuádruple* | quadruple |
| *quíntuple* | quintuple |
| *múltiple* | multiple |

*Simple, doble* and *múltiple* are the only terms in common use. An alternative construction with *veces* is generally used to express other multiples, and is even used for *doble*, eg:

*La población de España es el doble (*or: *dos veces más) de la que era en el siglo XIX*
The population of Spain is double what it was in the nineteenth century

*Londres es el doble de grande (*or: *dos veces mayor) de lo que era*
London is twice as big as it was

Exceptionally, and only in the written language, forms ending in *-o* are encountered (*duplo, triplo, cuádruplo, quíntuplo, séxtuplo, séptuplo*).[29]

## 236 Collectives

| | |
|---|---|
| *una decena* | about ten |
| *una docena* | a dozen, about twelve |
| *una veintena* | a score, about twenty |
| *una treintena* | about thirty |
| *una cuarentena* | about forty |

(and note that *cuarentena* has the special meaning of 'quarantine')

| | |
|---|---|
| *una cincuentena* | about fifty |
| *una centena, un centenar,* | |
| *una centenada* | about a hundred |
| *un millar, una millarada* | about a thousand |
| *una millonada* | about a million |

(*costar una millonada* 'to cost a packet')

These are also used in the plural:

*No tiene más de dos docenas de libros (DUE, I, 1028)*
He doesn't have more than two dozen books

## 237 Twins, etc.

| | |
|---|---|
| *mellizos/as* or *gemelos/as* | twins |
| *trillizos/as* | triplets |
| *cuatrillizos/as* | quadruplets |
| *quintillizos/as* | quintuplets |
| *sextillizos/as* | sextuplets[30] |

# Personal Pronouns

## Forms

**238** Spanish personal pronouns have different forms according to the function they fulfil.

| Person | Subject pronoun | | Direct or indirect object pronoun (no preposition) | | Prepositional object pronoun | |
|---|---|---|---|---|---|---|
| 1 sg | *yo* | I | *me* | me | *mí* | me |
| 2 sg | *tú* | you (fam) | *te* | you (fam) | *ti* | you (fam) |
| | *usted* | you (pol) | *le* | you (pol) | *usted* | you (pol) |
| | (Note that *usted* takes a third person verb) | | | | | |
| 3 sg | | | Direct object: | | | |
| | *él* | he, it | *le, lo* | him | *él* | him, it |
| | | | *lo* | it | | |
| | | | Direct object: | | | |
| | *ella* | her, it | *la* | her, it | *ella* | her, it |
| | | | Indirect object: | | | |
| | | | *le* | him, her, it | | |
| | (For *ello,* see **257**) | | (Note that *le* → *se* before another pronoun, see **274**) | | | |
| 1 pl | *nosotros/as* we | | *nos* | us | *nosotros/as* us | |
| 2 pl | *vosotros/as* you (fam) (almost never used in Latin America, see **249**) | | *os* | you (fam) | *vosotros/as* you (fam) | |

| | ustedes | you (pol) | les | you (pol) | ustedes | you (pol) |
|---|---|---|---|---|---|---|
| 3 pl | | | Direct object: | | | |
| | ellos | they (masc) | los | them | | |
| | | | Direct object: | | | |
| | ellas | they (fem) | las | them | ellas | them |
| | | | Indirect object: | | | |
| | | | les | them | | |
| | | | (Note that les → se before another pronoun see **274**) | | | |
| Reflexive sg/pl | | | se | -self, -selves | sí | -self, selves |

The subject and prepositional object pronouns are sometimes called stressed, tonic or disjunctive pronouns; the direct and indirect object pronouns are sometimes called unstressed, atonic or clitic pronouns.

## 239 Remarks

The written accent is used on some forms to avoid confusion with similar words:

> tú as opposed to tu (possessive adjective)
> él as opposed to el (definite article)
> mí as opposed to mi (possessive adjective)

No such confusion is possible with ti, and therefore this word does not have an accent (though using an accent is a common spelling mistake among Spanish speakers).

## Meaning and Usage

Subject Forms

### 240 Optional and Obligatory Use

The subject of a verb in Spanish is generally implicit in the form of the verb ending, and the use of a subject pronoun is therefore strictly speaking superfluous, e.g. *hablamos* 'we speak, we spoke', *habláis* 'you (plural familiar) speak'. However, the subject pronouns are used in certain cases.[1]

## 241 For Clarity

Forms like *hablaba, hablaría, hablara, hablase*, etc. are ambiguous between first and third person singular. The third person is always ambiguous, since it may represent masculine or feminine (*él* or *ella, ellos* or *ellas*) third person or the polite second person (*usted, ustedes*). In such cases a pronoun is often used when the overall context does not make the identity of the subject clear.[2]

> *Yo me figuraba que ella querría cambiar de vida* (P. Baroja, 1946-51: I, 1092)
> I imagined that she would want to change her life
> (Here *ella* indicates that the subject of *querría* is third person and feminine. Otherwise, it would be construed as *yo*, as for the first verb *me figuraba*)

> *Cuando iba a casa, ella me esperaba a la puerta* (A. M. Matute, 1977: 20)
> When I went home, she was waiting for me at the door

As in the above examples, the feminine third person form is especially likely to be used when there might be doubt about the gender of the subject. However, there are other means of indicating gender, as the next example shows:

> *Comía lenta los restos que encontraba* (J. C. Onetti, 1979: 45)
> She was slowly eating the scraps that she found
> (The adjective *lenta*, used adverbially (see **199–203**), identifies the subject as feminine)

## 242 To Stress the Subject or to Mark a Contrast

In Spanish the use of a subject pronoun often has a stylistic value indicating stress or contrast. This is not the case in English, where the pronoun cannot be omitted. Its emphatic nature is intensified when it is repeated or placed after the verb. In the written language, italics or capitals are sometimes used, although these devices are not typical of Spanish. Note also the author's own comment in the fourth example.[3]

*No sé si será verdad pero yo estoy segura* (J. Cortázar, 1973:49)
I don't know if it's true, but I'm sure

*¿Ve usted que yo tenía razón?* (J. Icaza, 1980: 80)
Do you see that I was right?

*Él mismo me ponía el azúcar en la taza para que no cogiera yo demasiado* (P. Baroja, 1946–51: VII, 901)
He himself put the sugar in my cup so that I wouldn't take too much

*«Vas a ver»* ... *«Tú vas a ver», añadiendo el pronombre para individualizarme* (G. Cabrera Infante, 1979: 229)
(This might be translated: 'You'll see ... You'll see, stressing the pronoun to mean "me" particularly')

*Yo las maté y le prendí fuego a la casa. Yo.* (R. J. Sender, 1965–66: II, 252)
It was me that killed them and set fire to the house. Me

*¡Qué pena que no sea yo la novia!* (M. Mihura, 1981: 151)
What a pity it's not me who's the bride!

*Yo creo que no hay otra solución*
I don't think there's any other solution
(Here the emphatic use of *yo* has a different psychological motivation. It can be used contrastively to imply a superior opinion ('My opinion is better'), or it can imply modesty ('What I am saying is nothing more than my own personal opinion'))

The use of a (strictly speaking superfluous) *yo* appears to be gaining in frequency, especially with verbs of thinking (*yo creo, yo digo, yo afirmo, yo estimo,* etc.), and characterizes the speech of many politicians.[4]

**243** The emphasis referred to in **242** is also found in advertising language and political slogans. The personal pronoun, which strictly speaking is unnecessary for the clarity of the message, lays emphasis on a possible personal advantage or interest and/or panders to the vanity of those concerned.

*La España que tú quieres conocer* (*Ronda Iberia* (an advertising magazine issued on Iberia flights), February 1978)
The Spain you want to get to know

*Trabajador*
*EN MARCHA*
*Hacia la consolidación del sindicalismo que tú necesitas* (an advertisement seen in Spain in February 1978)
Worker
FORWARD
Towards the establishment of the union you need

**244** In the spoken language, *tú*, placed at the end of the sentence, may have an affective value. The usage is not so regionalized as the first example suggests.

> *No hay duda, tú – dijo ella empleando esa forma familiar habanera de colocar el pronombre al final de la oración* (G. Cabrera Infante, 1979: 270)
> 'There's no doubt, you know', she said . . .

> *¿Qué hora es, tú?* (C. Martín Gaite, 1980: 181)
> What time is it, eh?

**245 Remark**

It has already been noted (**35**) that *nosotros* and *vosotros* are often omitted before a noun. Indeed, there can be no doubt about the meaning of sentences like the following. where the use of the subject pronouns would have an emphatic effect.

> *Por otra parte, los médicos ya sabes que estamos de vuelta de muchas cosas* (S. Lorén, 1962: 75)
> On the other hand, you well know that we doctors are blasé about a lot of things

> *Los hombres creéis todo lo malo que se dice de las mujeres* (R. del Valle-Inclán, 1963: 78)
> You men believe anything bad that is said about women

Use of *usted, ustedes* (and contrast with *tú*), *don, doña*

**246** *Usted* and *ustedes* are the polite second person singular and plural respectively. They may be abbreviated in writing as *Vd.*, *Vds.*, *Ud.*, *Uds* (also *U.*, *Us.*, *V.*, *Vs.* or *VV.*).

When written out in full. a capital letter is not normally used.[5] Just as *Vd.* and *Vds*. require a third person verb, so pronouns and adjectives which refer to them are also third person:

> *Si usted me permite, le recordaré su promesa*
> If you don't mind. I'll remind you of your promise

**247** Perhaps because of the possibility of confusion with third person pronouns. as well as its use as a courtesy form, *usted(es)* is omitted less often than the other subject pronouns.[6] As a rule, *usted(es)* is not repeated in the same sentence, although there are exceptions (see the second example below).

> *Vd. puede acompañarme, si quiere*
> You can come with me if you like

> *Cuando usted se case con la niña, usted no podrá ser tan desordenado en el vivir* (M. Mihura. 1981: 136)
> When you marry the girl, you won't be able to lead such a disorderly life

In Latin-American Spanish there is a tendency to omit *usted(es)* more frequently than in the Peninsula.[7]

**248** Spanish speakers readily use the familiar forms *tú* and *vosotros/as*. especially with people of similar age and social standing.[8] Women use the familiar forms more easily than men.[9] and among children the formal forms are practically never used (see the third and fourth examples below). Age difference is an important factor in the use of the formal forms, as is evident from contexts where stress is laid on this fact (explicitly in the first example, indirectly in the second).

> *A usted le tiene sin cuidado quien gane, don Fidel. Vicente le habla de usted por la edad* (M. Aub, 1963: 18)
> You don't care who wins. don Fidel. Vicente uses *usted* to him because of his age. (The characters are sixty and twenty-three respectively)

> *Al volver de Francia me chocó que ahora todo el mundo tutee incluso a las personas de noventa años* (J. Carabias, *Vestimenta y tuteo*, in *Heraldo de Aragón*, 1 February 1978: 26)
> When I returned from France it shocked me that everyone now uses *tú*. even to people of ninety
> (The author had lived in France for a long time without returning to Spain)

*Resulta raro tratarse de usted; es cosa de viejos* (M. Vargas Llosa, 1973: 106)
It's odd calling each other *usted*; that's what old folk do

*Nos daba risa que nos hubieran llamado de usted* (C. Martín Gaite, 1981: 112)
It amused us that they should have called us *usted*
(They are twelve-year-old girls)

But *tú* can still be a mark of disrespect if *usted* would normally be expected:

*Y te voy a decir, te tuteo porque ya te has caído de usted, ya te has caído de cualquier posible respeto, hijo de puta . . .* (M. Vázquez Montalbán, 1990: 220)
And I'll tell you, I'm calling you *tú* because you've fallen from being *usted*, you've fallen from any possible respect, you bastard.

See also **309**, fourth example.

In recent years there has been a clear preference for the use of *tú* and *vosotros*. Young people nowadays use *tú* to one another from the start;[10] when a middle-aged man bumped into JdeB in the street in Zaragoza in 1983 he said *¡Perdona!* A recent circular from the Barcelona Instituto de Idiomas read as follows:

*Estimados colegas: Os enviamos información . . . si tenéis cualquier tipo de sugerencia . . .*
Dear Colleagues: We send you information . . . if you have suggestions of any kind . . .

Max Aub corrected himself at an international conference in 1972 in the following way:

*No se les escapará o no se os escapará, para hablar como se habla ahora aquí . . .* (J. F. Botrel and S. Salaün, 1974: 249)
It won't escape you . . .

**249** In Latin America, and sometimes in Andalusia and the Canary Isles, *ustedes* is used instead of *vosotros/as*. In these regions of Spain, it is generally used in this function with the *vosotros/as* verb form (e.g. *ustedes tenéis* for *vosotros/as tenéis* 'you have', *ustedes os sentáis* for *vosotros/as os sentáis* 'you sit down') but in Latin America it almost always takes the third person plural verb form (e.g. *ustedes tienen*).[11]

**250** *Don* and *doña* are used with Christian names (in Latin American sometimes with a surname);[12] *señor, señora, señorita* are normally used with surnames. The following examples give the flavour of the difference between the two:

> *«Buenas tardes, señor Castro». ¿Señor Castro o don Paulino? Con dos motoras el tratamiento. Don Paulino. Paulino Castro era don Paulino* (I. Aldecoa, 1969: 88)
> 'Good afternoon, Señor Castro. Señor Castro or Don Paulino? A person with two motorboats had to be shown respect. Don Paulino. Paulino Castro was Don Paulino

> *Dudaba si visitar primero a don Salvador Pérez del Molino o a Luis Rodríguez Malo, este último sin don, por socialista* (M. Aub, 1970: 163)
> He hesitated between visiting Don Salvador Pérez del Molino first or Luis Rodríguez Molino: no *Don* for the latter, because he was a socialist

*Don* can be used to convey an attitude: the right-wing newspaper *El Alcázar* referred to the leader of the failed military coup of 23 February 1981 as *don Antonio Tejero* (16 February 1983: 3), which implied a certain admiration. *Don* is also used to 'personalize' abstract ideas, e.g. *don balón* 'King Football', *un don nadie* 'a nobody', *doña melindres* 'a fusspot',[13] *Don Tacañete* 'Mr Mean' (Spanish translation of the children's book by Roger Hargreaves).

## 251 Remarks

The polite form is sometimes used in circumstances where the familiar form would normally be used. In this way the speaker can indicate that there is a distance, for one reason or another, from the person being spoken to. This change in tone is explained by feelings of anger, outrage, etc., as for example when a mother suddenly uses *usted* to her child in order to scold, or when someone uses *usted* to a friend whom he feels is deceiving him.

> *Cuando en mi casa me hablan de usted, cerca anda el palo* (Berschin, 1987: 200)
> When they use *usted* to me at home, the stick isn't far away

Although *usted* is widely used in a similar way in Latin America, there are also areas and registers in which the change from *tú* to *usted* has the opposite meaning of affection.[14]

**252** In Peninsular usage *ustedes* is used to a group of people when some would normally be addressed as *tú* and some as *usted*. In the following example, a youngster is mistakenly flattered that someone apparently uses the adult form to him:

> – *¿Por quién preguntan ustedes?*
> *Entonces no advertía yo lo raro que hubiese sido que la mujer dijera: ¿Por quién preguntan usted y el niño?* (M. Delibes, 1948: 15)
> 'Who are you asking for?'
> 'I didn't notice at that time how odd it would have been if the woman had said, "Who are you and the child asking for?"'

**253** The form *usía(s)* is sometimes found as an alternative to *usted(es)*, especially in official language (to judges and members of the Spanish Parliament, and in the army, for example); it is also still occasionally used by older people, but is gradually falling out of the spoken language.[15]

> *¿Da usía su permiso? – preguntó un escribiente* (P. Baroja, 1946–51: I, 498).
> 'Do you give your permission, your honour?' asked a clerk (addressing a judge)

> *Yo quisiera que usías – dijo la vieja – la metieran a esta chica en un asilo* (P. Baroja, ibid., 437).
> 'I want you to put this girl in a charitable institution', said the old woman

**254** The archaic form *nos* (= *nosotros/as*) is today found only in official documents issued by the King, the Pope, a provincial governor, an archbishop, etc.[16] It can be used as a subject, an object or a prepositional object.[17]

> *Nos pensamos que los hombres...* (Spanish translation of the Papal Encyclical *Humanae Vitae*, 31)
> We think that people ...

> *Nos el Presidente de la República, hemos resuelto ...* (A. Bello, 1972: 76)
> We, the President of the Republic, have resolved ...

Agreeing adjectives are in the singular:

> *Nos somos consciente ...* (*DD*, 271)
> We are conscious ...

However, *nosotros/as* is used by writers, scientists, etc.

## 255 *Voseo*

In many areas of Latin America, especially Argentina and Uruguay,[18] *vos* is used instead of *tú* (subject pronoun form) and *ti* (prepositional pronoun form),[19] although *te* is still used as the direct and indirect object pronoun form, and the possessive forms are still *tu, tuyo*. This phenomenon is called *voseo*. *Vos* often has a special set of verb-forms, although there is much diversity in this respect. The best-known *voseante* area is the River Plate, where the following representative verb-forms are found:[20]

> Present Indicative: *cantás, tenés, venís*
> Imperative: *cantá, tené, vení*
> Present Subjunctive: *cantés, tengás, vengás*
> Preterite: *cantastes, tuvistes, vinistes*

Other forms correspond to the *tú* forms found elsewhere.
   The present indicative of *ser* is *sos*.

Examples:

> *¿Vos no sentís a veces como si adentro tuyo tuvieras un inquilino que te dice cosas?* (*DD*, 378)
> Don't you feel at times as if you had a lodger inside you telling you things?
> (On the construction *adentro tuyo*, see **340**)

> *Ahora nos tuteamos. Vos lo provocaste* (J. Cortázar, 1974: 209)
> Now we're talking to each other familiarly. You provoked it

> *Yo no te conozco, vos venís acá y esta pobre gitana te dice todo, por un peso* (M. Puig, 1989: 90)
> I don't know you, you come here and this poor gipsy tells you everything, for a peso

> *Sos un puto* (I. Malinow, 1983: 62)
> You're a bugger

> *No hablemos de mí, hablemos de vos, de tus trabajos, de tus preocupaciones. Pensé constantemente en tu pintura, en lo que me dijiste ... Quiero saber qué hacés ahora, si has pintado o no* (E. Sábato, 1983, quoted in Berschin: 1987, 193)

Don't let's talk about me, let's talk about you, about your work, about your concerns. I've thought constantly about your painting, about what you said to me ... I want to know what you're doing now, whether you've done any painting or not

## 256 *Che*

The use of *che* in the River Plate area is such that it may now be thought of as a personal pronoun of address corresponding to *vos*.[21]

> *¡Che, decime!*
> Hey you, tell me!

> *¡Che, vení!*
> Come on, you!

> *Buenos Aires ha vuelto a ser lo que era, ché, una ciudad de tres millones, chic, despejada* (A. Posse, 1990: 17)
> Buenos Aires has returned to being what it was, man, a city of three millions, chic and lively

## 257 Use of *ello*

*Ello* is a neuter form which refers to something which is not further qualified. This pronoun refers to something previously mentioned, and its meaning is close to that of the demonstrative *esto*. *Ello* is less and less common in speech.[22]

*Ello* may be used as a subject or a prepositional object. The expression *todo ello* 'all this') may also be a direct object.

> *... ello es delito* (M. Vargas Llosa, 1983a: 385)
> ... it is a crime

> *En México, y no es ello excepción, se disipa la vida a Pedro Garfias* (C. Blanco Aguinaga et al., 1979–81: III, 136)
> In Mexico – and this is no exception – Pedro Garfias's life dissolved into nothing

> *Veía que con ello hacía feliz a Carmen Elgazu* (J. M. Gironella, 1966a: 546)
> He saw that he was making Carmen Elgazu happy in this way

*Entregaba todo ello a la admiración del extranjero* (A. Palacio Valdés, quoted in Fernández, 1951: 213–14)
She exposed all this to the foreigner's admiring gaze

*Y en ello estamos* (Marsá, 1986: 113)
And there we are

## 258 Replacement of the Personal Pronoun

A personal pronoun, especially the first person singular, may sometimes be avoided by the use of another expression.

**259** The first person can be expressed by the noun *(un(a)) servidor(a) (de ustedes)* (also *su servidor, este servidor* and even *servidorcito*)[23] to indicate modesty, politeness, or sometimes cheekiness. The verb is in the third person.

*Le juro a usted que un servidor no tiene nada que ver con todo esto* (C. J. Cela, 1969: 253)
I swear to you that I have nothing to do with all this

*Y por eso un servidor de ustedes se revuelve ahora contra su suerte* (S. Lorén, 1962: 67)
And so now I'm turning against my fate

*Bueno, este servidor se echa a dormir* (J. García Hortelano, 1979: 318)
Well, I'm going to bed

*Descuide señorito: servidora es muy considerada* (C. J. Cela, 1979b: 345)
Don't worry, young sir: I'm very discreet

The form may also be used as a direct or indirect object, or after a preposition:

*Un día invitaron a un servidor de ustedes en una casa* (M. Delibes, 1979a: 237)
One day they invited me into a house

**260** Although there is a tendency today to simplify the convoluted formulae in letter-writing, the following may still be found:

*Saluda(n) a Vd(s).S.S.S.* = ... *su(s) seguro(s) servidor(es)*

*S.S.Q.E.S.M.* = *Seguro(s) servidor(es) que estrecha(n) sus manos*

They may be preceded by *Quedamos de Vd(s).*, *Nos repetimos de Vd(s).*, etc.

**261** Another way of expressing the first person, quite frequent today in popular speech, is by using the word *menda (lerenda)* (a borrowing from gipsy language), again followed by the verb in the third person. *Menda* can also be used with a possessive or demonstrative adjective and after a preposition.

> *¡Amigo Vega! Está demostrado que menda hubiera podido servir en infantería* (J. M. Gironella, 1971: I, 89)
> Friend Vega, it's clear that I could have served in the infantry
>
> *¡Pues, si vas de machista, te has equivocado con mi menda!* (E. Parra, 1981: 111)
> Now if you're going to be a chauvinist, you've picked on the wrong one with me![24]
>
> *Había una, de buena familia, que estaba encaprichada con menda lerenda* (J. Goytisolo, 1981a: 17)
> There was one girl, from a good family, who was bewitched by yours truly

The association with the first person idea is clear in the following example:

> *A menda, que no soy general, me dan aquello* (J. M. Gironella, 1986: 127)
> They give me that, even though I'm not a general

*Menda* is also found today with the value of a third person singular or as a synonym for *individuo*. In this meaning, *menda* is preceded by an article or numeral and can also be plural: e.g. *dos mendas* (C. Pérez Merinero, 1982: 20, 36 and passim). In the same work (p. 186), *la menda lerenda* is used as a third person.

**262** The expression *el hijo/la hija de su madre* may also be used as a substitute for the first person singular:

> *Ya es hora que el hijo de su madre vuelva a hacer algo* (J. Izcaray, 1961: 144)
> It's time yours truly went back to work

For the (frequent) use of *uno* with first person value, see **380**ff.

**263** In place of the third person (singular or plural) pronoun, *el andova*, plural *los andovas*, another borrowing from gipsy language, is occasionally used.

> *Pero el andova no se quería marchar* (T. Salvador, 1968b: 200)
> But the guy didn't want to go

> *Los andovas se me acercan y se atreven a decirme lo que piensan sobre vosotros* (R. J. Sender, 1967: 74)
> These characters come up to me and dare to tell me what they think of you

## Clitic Pronouns

### 264 Order of Unstressed Object Pronouns with the Verb

The direct or indirect object (unstressed, clitic) personal pronouns of Spanish precede the finite verb to which they pertain.

| | |
|---|---|
| *Lo veo* | I see it |
| *Le regalamos un libro* | We gave him a book |

**265** Unstressed pronouns follow the verb when the verb is

an infinitive
a gerund (but see **269**)
a positive imperative (or a subjunctive used as a positive imperative).

> *Es fácil contármelo, pero ¿lo has hecho de verdad?*
> It's easy to say so, but have you really done it?

> *Casi todos los indianos venís de allí, echándooslas de espíritus fuertes* (J. A. de Zunzunegui, 1959b: 61)
> Almost all you *indianos* (Spaniards who have been in Latin America and have returned home wealthy, a term used especially in the north of Spain) come back from there posing as freethinkers

> *Metámonos en la cama, hace mucho frío* (R. Montero, 1979: 53)
> Let's go to bed, it's very cold

> *Búsquesemelo* (*Esbozo*, 427)
> Look for it for me

*¡Soltadlo, dejádnoslo! ¡Asesino!* (F. García Pavón, 1980b: 148)
Let him go! Hand him over to us! Murderer!

But:

*¡No se lo explique(s)!*
Don't explain to him!
(This is a negative imperative)

## 266 Remarks

When unstressed pronouns follow the verb, the stress pattern of
the verb remains unchanged, and so it is sometimes necessary to
add a written accent. The rules given in **273** for the order of pronouns apply just the same.

**267** Forms like *siéntesen* (for *siéntense*) and *dígamen* (for *díganme*),
in which the *-n* of the third person of the verb is added to the *me* or
*se*, are common in popular speech.[25]

**268** The placing of pronouns after a finite verb, especially when
the verb is first in the sentence, is a feature of Old Spanish, and
may still be found in dialects, or, in the written language, when an
author wishes to imitate an older style. Some Latin-American
authors also favour postposition of pronouns.[26]

*Díjomelo ayer* (for *me lo dijo ayer*) (Beinhauer, 1968: 338,
n.30)
He told me yesterday

*¿Hay naranjas? – Haylas* (for *las hay*) (*ibid.*)
'Are there any oranges?' 'There are'

*Le dije que sí y hame respondido* . . . (T. Salvador, 1968b: 36)
I said 'yes' and he answered me . . .

This feature should not be imitated by foreigners.

**269** When the infinitive or gerund is dependent on an auxiliary
or semi-auxiliary (see **1171** and **1197**), the pronouns may be
placed after the infinitive or gerund or before the auxiliary or
semi-auxiliary verb.[27]

*¿No me quieres ver mañana?* (J. Rulfo, 1981: 68)
Don't you want to see me tomorrow?
(Or: *¿No quieres verme . . .?*)

*Sus amigos lo tuvieron que traer en taxi, por la noche* (C. J. Cela, 1963a: 230)
His friends had to bring him in a taxi, at night
(Or: *Sus amigos tuvieron que traerlo en taxi ...*)

*¿Qué haces tú en la vida, me lo quieres decir?* (R. J. Sender, 1967: 73)
How do you earn your living, can you tell me?
(Or: *¿Quieres decírmelo?*)

*Me voy poniendo viejo – pensó* (A. Carpentier, 1976: 123)
'I'm getting old,' he thought
(Or: *Voy poniéndome viejo ...*)

Placing the pronoun(s) before the auxiliary appears to be increasingly common in modern Spanish, especially in speech. Variation may be for stylistic reasons: in the same half page of text we find both

*sólo te podría reprochar*
I could only reproach you

and

*yo no puedo recomendarte* (J. Arreola, 1986: 174)
I cannot recommend you

**270** The final *-s* of the first person plural of the present subjunctive falls when used as an imperative and followed by the pronoun *nos*.

*Unamos + nos* → *unámonos*
Let us unite

The *-s* is also lost in other tenses of the verb when *nos* follows the verb:

*Íbamos + nos* → *íbamonos*
We were going away

**271** When a first or second person plural form is followed by *se*, only one *s* is written.

*Hagamos + se + lo* → *hagámoselo*
Let us do it

and the old-fashioned

*¿Disteis + se + la?* → *¿dísteisela?* (*Esbozo*, 427)
Did you give it him/her?

**272** The *-d* of the second person plural of the imperative falls before *os*:

*¡Sentad!* + *os* → *¡sentaos!*
Sit down!

## 273 Sequences of Unstressed Object Pronouns

Two, and sometimes even three, unstressed object pronouns may be used in sequence. Their order is governed by the following rules:

(1)   *Se*, whatever its function (reflexive or as the equivalent of *le*, *les*) precedes all other pronouns.
(2)   Second person pronouns precede first person pronouns.[28]
(3)   First and second person pronouns precede third person pronouns.

*En cuanto vi su carta, se la devolví sin abrirla* (Marsá, 1986: 142)
As soon as I saw her letter I gave it her back without opening it
(*Se* [= *le*, see **274**], is the first pronoun in the sequence)

*Te me recomendaron* (A. Bello, 1972: 265)
They recommended you to me (or: They recommended me to you)
(Second person precedes first person. Bello observes that such constructions are generally avoided, and that only the context makes the identity of the direct and indirect object clear. *Me han recomendado a ti* would be an alternative construction)

*Ruego que se me lo busque* (*Esbozo*, 427)
I'm asking you to look for it for me
(*Se* in its impersonal function, see **537**, stands first; first person pronoun precedes third person)

Constructions of this kind, with three unstressed object pronouns, are not common, however,[29] and are better avoided: alternative constructions would be *Ruego que Vd./alguien me lo busque*.

Rule (1) is sometimes broken in popular speech:[30]

*¿Te se ofrece algo?* (M. Delibes, 1980: 11)
Can I offer you anything?
(The normal construction is *¿Se te ofrece algo?*)

## 274 Use of *se* instead of *le* or *les*

If a pronoun sequence consists of two third person pronouns, the indirect object pronoun *le* or *les* becomes *se*. *Se* thus represents masculine and feminine singular and plural.

> *Los demás se lo agradecen* (M. Aub, 1963: 44)
> The others thank him for it
> (One CANNOT say: \**los demás le lo agradecen*. Only from the context in the book do we know that *se* is masculine singular here)

Sometimes the value of *se* is clarified, usually by another pronoun. A sentence like *se lo entregué* is in itself unclear. If there is no disambiguating context, the value of *se* must be explained in the following way:

| | |
|---|---|
| *Se lo entregué a él* | I gave it to him |
| *Se lo entregué a ella* | I gave it to her |
| *Se lo entregué a ellos* | I gave it to them (masculine) |
| *Se lo entregué a ellas* | I gave it to them (feminine) |
| *Se lo entregué a usted* | I gave it to you (singular) |
| *Se lo entregué a ustedes* | I gave it to you (plural) |
| *Se lo entregué a Juan* | I gave it to Juan[31] |

## 275 Leísmo, loísmo, laísmo

There is considerable variation in unstressed third person pronoun usage in the Spanish-speaking world.

*Leísmo* is the most common phenomenon, especially in Madrid and the surrounding area. By this is meant the replacement of *lo, la* (or, less frequently, *los* and *las*) by *le* (*les*). See **276**(i)–(iv).

*Laísmo* is when *le* (and sometimes *les*) as feminine indirect object is replaced by *la* (and *las*). See **276**(v) and (vi).

*Loísmo* is when *le* and (less often) *les* as masculine indirect object is replaced by *lo* (*los*). See **276**(vii) and (viii).[32]

In all three cases, the reason is the same: the desire to make a distinction between persons and things (or animals), or between masculine and feminine.

The result does not always have the desired effect of avoiding ambiguity, however. For *leísta* speakers, *le conozco* can mean both

'I know him' and 'I know her' (strictly only the first meaning is correct). These speakers choose *le* to indicate that the object is a person rather than a thing or an animal; but in avoiding one misunderstanding another is created: is *le* masculine or feminine?[33]

**276** As in other areas of Spanish grammar, there is a vast difference between theory and practice. The *Esbozo* recalls the Academia's unambiguous point of view: as far as *leísmo* is concerned, only the use of *le* as a direct object, as a substitute for *lo* when it refers to a person, is acceptable.[34] *Laísmo* and *loísmo* are always regarded as incorrect.

In practice examples of the forms censured or considered inadmissible by the Academia are regularly found, though they often come from representations of the spoken language.

In modern Spanish *le* is seldom used, especially in the written language, as a direct object form referring to a thing.[35] The plural is used still less often in such cases.[36]

(1)   *le* for *la*

   – *Vamos a llamarle.*
   – *¿A la camarera? Eso está hecho* (C. Pérez Merinero, 1982: 122)
   'Let's call her.'
   'The waitress? It's already been done'

(2)   *le* for *la* or *lo*

   *Y se le* (= *la fe*) *llama del carbonero* (M. de Unamuno, quoted in De Kock & Gómez Molina, 1982: 116)
   And it is called a miner's faith
   (*Lo* is never replaced by *le* when it refers to a 'neuter' idea)

(3)   *les* for *los*

   *Vaya, les dejo* . . . (J. A. de Zunzunegui, 1956a: 133)
   Well now, I'll leave you . . .

(4)   *les* for *las*

   *El tiempo se les* (= *las tejas*) *va comiendo* (R. Gómez de la Serna, quoted in Fernández, 1951: 203)
   The weather is eating them (the tiles) away

(5)   *la* for *le*

> *La dio un beso en la mejilla* (J. A. de Zunzunegui, 1956a: 224)
> He gave her a kiss on the cheek
> (See also **848**, fifth example)

(6)   *las* for *les*

> *Si se encontrase la manera de abordarlas sin darlas miedo* (R. Gómez de la Serna, 1959: 26)
> If a way of approaching them without frightening them could be found
> (*-las* of *darlas* is an indirect object)

(7)   *lo* for *le*

> *Lo pegaron una bofetada* (Gili Gaya, 1964: 235)
> They gave him a slap

(8)   *los* for *les*

> *Llaman y no los hacen caso* (Marsá, 1986: 140)
> They call and they do not notice them[37]

## 277 The 'Ethical' Dative

The so-called 'ethical dative' or 'dative of interest', where the use of an indirect object pronoun expresses the involvement of the subject in the action of the verb, intensifies such feelings as sadness, happiness and mockery.

> *Ten cuidado, y no te me cortes un dedo* (F. Monge, in a lecture given at the University of Antwerp, 11 March 1983)
> Be careful you don't cut one of your fingers
> (By using *me* the speaker indicates that he is involved, that he will be sorry if it happens)

> *El marido empezó con unos comentarios imbéciles, y me le reí en la cara* (M. Puig, 1980: 61)
> Her husband began with some stupid remarks, and I laughed in his face

> *La semana pasada se nos suicidó un parroquiano* (E. Mendoza, 1985: 44)
> Last week one of our parishioners committed suicide

*¿Y si soy un monstruo? ¿Y si me la violo?* (A. Bryce Echenique,
1981: 85)
And if I'm a monster? And if I rape her?

## 278 Pleonastic Pronouns

A direct or indirect object pronoun is often used pleonastically
(i.e., when a full direct or indirect object is also present). *Esbozo*,
423, suggests that the pronoun 'announces' the following object in
some way. This pleonastic use is more frequent in Latin
America.[38]

> *Dígale usted al señor Yarza que . . .* (P. Baroja, 1951: 142)
> Tell Señor Yarza that . . .
> (*Le* here 'announces' al señor Yarza)
>
> *Lo engañaron a Juan* (*Esbozo*, 424)
> They deceived Juan
>
> *Escribo para avisarles a los amigos que no me esperen*
> (*Esbozo*, 423)
> I am writing to tell my friends not to wait for me
>
> *No se lo dijo a nadie* (G. García Márquez, 1977: 228)
> He did not tell anyone
>
> *Yo le hablaba a Carlos y tú le decías a Carlos: «Dile a Umbral que
> . . .»* (F. Umbral, 1985: 152)
> I was talking to Carlos and you said to Carlos, 'Tell Umbral
> that . . .'

*Le* is sometimes found for *les* in such examples:[39]

> *Tengo que comprarle un poco turrón a mis mujeres* (F. García
> Pavón, 1980b:138)
> I must buy a little *turrón* for my ladies
> (*Tengo que comprarles un poco de turrón* would be considered
> more correct)

**279** The following example shows just how frequent the use of
expressive and pleonastic pronouns is in Spanish:

> *¡Cuánto le agradecería, Irene, si consigue que «el noruego» se dé
> una vuelta por mi casa a echarle un vistazo al fogón que no me
> tira!* (J. A. de Zunzunegui, 1956a: 19)

I'd be very grateful, Irene, if you would get 'the Norwegian' to slip round to my house and have a look at my fire; it won't draw!

## 280 Remarks

For the use of *lo* with *todo*, see **443**.

**281** The use of a pleonastic pronoun is obligatory when an indirect object or direct object introduced by *a* stands before the verb. It is also obligatory when a direct object which is determined by a definite article, a demonstrative or possessive pronoun or a numeral precedes the verb.

> *A su familia la mataron* (M. Puig, 1980: 87)
> They killed his family

> *A José Hierro lo había leído* (F. Umbral, 1977: 9)
> I had read José Hierro('s work)

> *¿A ella le gustaban mucho los hombres?* (F. García Pavón, 1980b: 33)
> Did she like men much?

> *Este libro lo has leído ya*
> You've already read this book

But:

> *Algún pedazo de hielo tengo* (J. C. Onetti, 1979: 150)
> I have a piece of ice

> *Leche no quiero*
> I don't want any milk

## 282 Fixed Use of Pronouns with some Verbs

Some verbs combine with a personal pronoun or pronouns to give fixed expressions in which it is not always easy to see to what the pronoun refers. Such expressions are typical of the spoken language. The direct object pronoun concerned is generally feminine (the first example being an exception).

| | |
|---|---|
| *pasarlo bien/mal* | to have a good/bad time |
| *arreglárselas para* | to manage to |

*dárselas/echárselas de* + adj          to make oneself out to be adj

*Se las dan de graciosos, mi teniente* (M. Vargas Llosa, 1973: 48)
They think they're being funny, sir.

*diñarla/entregarla*                     to snuff it, kick the bucket
(*la* here = *la vida*)

*no tenerlas todas consigo*              to have one's doubts

*pasarlas muy mal*                       to go through hell

*pintarla*                               to put on airs and graces

*prometérselas muy felices*             to have high hopes

*El autor del referido artículo se las promete muy felices* (M. Delibes, 1968b: 78).
The author of the article referred to has a rosy view of the future.

*me la pagarás*                          you'll pay for it
*vas a pagármelas*

*así las gasta él*                       that's how he behaves

*Sabían lo bruto que era Agapito y cómo las gastaba* (J. A. de Zunzunegui, 1954: 577)
They knew what a lout Agapito was and how he behaved

## 283  *Me, te, le, nos, os, les* in the Sense of 'from me', 'from you', etc.

The indirect object pronouns sometimes have the meaning, in English terms, of 'from' rather than 'to'.

> *¿Me aceptas una copita?* (C. J. Cela, 1976b: 68)
> Would you accept a drink from me?

> *Le aceptó incluso dinero* (J. M. Gironella, 1966b: 707)
> He even accepted money from him

With a verb like *aceptar* there is no ambiguity, since any indirect object associated with such verbs cannot mean 'to'. But in a sentence like *nos han comprado un cuadro viejo* is ambiguous between 'they bought an old picture for us' and 'they bought an old picture from us': only the context will make the meaning clear.[40]

## Personal Pronouns after a Preposition: Special Forms

### 284 *Con*

*Mí, ti* and *sí* become *-migo*, *-tigo* and *-sigo* after *con*:

> *Puedes ir conmigo, si quieres*
> You can come with me if you like
> *Me quedo contigo*
> I'll stay with you
> *Estaban decididos a llevarme consigo, de grado o por fuerza* (R. J. Sender, 1965–6: II, 322)
> They were determined to take me with them whether I went willingly or by force
> *Es lo de la copla: «Ni contigo ni sin ti»* (F. Umbral, 1985: 134)
> As the song has it, 'Neither with you nor without you'

### 285 *De*

Note the following expression:

> *... en una conversación de tú a tú* (*Conversaciones con Monseñor Escrivá de Balaguer*, 152)
> ... in a man to man conversation

**286** For pronouns following the preposition *de* in its intensifying function, see **702**.

### 287 *Entre*

After *entre* 'among, between', the subject form is used if the preposition is followed by two pronouns or by a noun and a pronoun; if there is just one pronoun, the normal prepositional form is used.

> *Usted sabe muy bien que nunca hubo nada entre ella y yo* (C. Fuentes, 1979: 14)
> You know very well that there has never been anything between her and me
> *Entre el muchacho y yo lo devoramos hasta los huesos* (P. Baroja, 1946–51: VI, 192)
> Between us, the boy and I devoured even the bones (of a chicken)

But:

> *Dije entre mí*                I said to myself
>
> *Tal pensaba entre sí*         So she thought to herself
>
> *Tres nombres que tienen poco que ver entre sí* (J. Alcocer, 1978: 123)
>
> Three names which have little to do with one another

## 288 *Excepto, menos, salvo, hasta, incluso*

After *excepto, menos, salvo* 'except' and *hasta, incluso* 'even', the form of the pronoun is determined by the function of the noun or pronoun to which it relates in the main part of the sentence. It may therefore be in the subject case.

> *Todos estaban presentes excepto yo*
> *menos yo*
> *salvo yo*
>
> Everyone was there except me
>
> *Todos habían venido, ¡incluso tú!*
> *¡hasta tú!*
>
> Everyone had come, even you!

But:

> *Os debo mucho a todos vosotros, menos a ti*
>
> I owe a great deal to you all, except for you

## 289 *Según*

After the preposition *según* 'according to', a subject pronoun form is used.

> *¿Según tú, una mujer, si no puede casarse, no tiene más remedio que entrar en el convento?* (C. Laforet, 1966: 101)
>
> According to you, a woman, if she cannot marry, has no alternative but to go to a convent?

## Reflexive and Reciprocal Pronouns

## 290 Third Person Reflexive Forms

*Sí* is used when the object refers back to the subject of the sentence (= '-self, -selves', 'each other').

*José Luis había rodeado con sus brazos el cuello de María Victoria, y la apretaba contra sí* (J. M. Gironella, 1966c: 396)
José Luis had put his arms around María Victoria's neck, and was hugging her against himself

*Victoriano Terraza habla para sí, seguro de que los demás se lo agradecen* (M. Aub, 1963: 44)
Victoriano Terraza is talking to himself, certain that the others are grateful to him for it

*Conozco espíritus consecuentes consigo mismos* (M. de Unamuno, quoted in Fernández, 1951: 221)
I know spirits who are consistent with each other

**291** *Habla siempre de sí* 'He is always talking about himself' and *Habla siempre de él* 'He is always talking about him (i.e. another person)' are thus in principle quite distinct in meaning. However, the non-reflexive form is sometimes encountered in speech,[41] and even in the written language. especially where, as in the following example, the structure is a complex one:

*Lo invitó a tomarse un café. . ., y él se lo tomó encantado, en contra de su costumbre, oyéndola hablar de ella misma* (G. García Márquez, 1985: 352)
She invited him to have coffee . . . and he was delighted to do so, against his custom, when he heard her talking about herself

## 292 Intensive Use of the Reflexive

Some uses of reflexive pronouns in Spanish have no exact equivalent in English, and are often untranslatable, or translatable only by paraphrase. Such pronouns generally add a slight emphatic nuance to the verb, or else they indicate that the subject has a special involvement in, or benefits from, the action.

*Nadie se sabía la lección* (I. Agustí, 1944: 38)
No one knew their lesson
(Here the pronoun effectively replaces a possessive adjective: see also **323**)

*No estoy loca; sé muy bien lo que me digo* (J. A. de Zunzunegui, 1959a: 69)
I'm not mad; I know what I'm talking about

*A los tres años, Nilo, el joven, aún no se andaba* (M. Delibes, 1967: 122)
At the age of three, Nilo, the little one, still could not walk

(See also **341**, sixth example.)

– *Y también lo has pasado bien, ¿verdad?*
– *¡Hay que ver cómo te reías!* (J. M. Gironella, 1966b: 79).
'And you've had a good time too, have you?'
'You should see how you were laughing!'

*Se durmió, y de repente soñó que había dado con la isla* (J. A. de Zunzunegui, 1952b: 217)
He went to sleep, and suddenly dreamed that he had found the island
(*Dormirse* has the specific translation 'to go to sleep')

*¡Muérete, cabrón!* – *dijo* (A. Carpentier, 1976: 137)
'Die, you bastard!' he said

*¡Vete, Ramón, córrete . . . larga eso y vente!* (F. Aínsa, 1984: 45)
Go on, Ramón, run . . . leave that and come on!

*¿Qué te pensabas?* (M. Delibes, 1987:69)
What were you thinking?

Other verbs commonly used in this way are *beber* 'to drink' (*beberse* 'to drink up'), *comer* 'to eat' (*comerse* 'to eat up'), *llevar* 'to carry' (*llevarse* 'to carry off'), *salir* 'to go out' (*salirse* 'to get out'). The usage is more frequent in speech and in Latin-American Spanish.[42]

**293** Some transitive verbs have an 'intensive' reflexive form followed by *con*. There may also be a reciprocal value present, since verbs like those illustrated necessarily involve two participants.

*Yo tenía una novia y la he encontrado a las dos de la madrugada besándose con otro* (M. Delibes, 1967: 191)
I had a girl-friend and I found her kissing someone else at two in the morning

*Don José se escribía con Espronceda* (F. Umbral, 1980: 219)
Don José used to correspond with Espronceda

Similar verbs are *encontrarse con* 'to meet' and *hablarse con* 'to converse with'.

**294** It is worth noting that *ser* and *estar* can also be used in the reflexive with an 'intensive' meaning:

> *Yo me soy hombre pacífico* (*Esbozo*, 368)
> I am (by nature) a peaceful man
> *¡Estáte quieto!*
> Be quiet!

Note also the formula *Érase una vez* ... 'once upon a time'.

## 295 'Mediopassive' Use of the Reflexive

The Spanish reflexive often renders the English idea of 'getting something done' or 'having something done'.

> *Acudimos al dentista para extraernos una muela* (M. Delibes, 1948: 111)
> We went to the dentist to have a tooth out
> *Mi madre siempre fue enemiga de retratarse* (J. Rulfo, 1981: 11)
> My mother was always opposed to having her picture taken
> *Su único acto democrático consistía en ir a afeitarse de tarde en tarde en la barbería de Raimundo* (J. M. Gironella, 1966a: 195)
> His only democratic act was to go and have himself shaved from time to time at Raimundo's, the barber's
> *Fui a Madrid a operarme* (C. J. Cela, 1967d: 115)
> I went to Madrid to have an operation

The above examples could parallel English more closely by the use of *hacer*: ... *para hacernos extraer* ..., ... *para hacerse afeitar* ... etc.

## 296 Verbs which are Always Reflexive

A number of Spanish verbs are always reflexive: *atreverse a* 'to dare', *confesarse con* 'to confess to', *negarse a* 'to refuse', *sentarse* 'to sit down'. This may lead to the presence of two reflexive pronouns in the same verb group:

> *No me atrevo a asomarme* (C. Martín Gaite, 1981:168)
> I daren't look out

## 297 'Passive' Use of *se*

The 'passive' use of *se* is discussed in **536**ff and **1022**ff.

# Demonstrative Pronouns and Adjectives

## Forms

**298**

|    | masculine | feminine | neuter |
|----|-----------|----------|--------|
| sg | *éste*    | *ésta*   | *esto* |
| pl | *éstos*   | *éstas*  |        |
| sg | *ése*     | *ésa*    | *eso*  |
| pl | *ésos*    | *ésas*   |        |
| sg | *aquél*   | *aquélla* | *aquello* |
| pl | *aquéllos* | *aquéllas* |      |

The masculine and feminine forms serve as both adjectives and pronouns: when they are used as adjectives, they are written without the accent: *este, ese, aquel,* etc.; when they are used as pronouns, the accent is usual, though not obligatory, except in case of ambiguity.[1] Note that the neuter forms are used only as pronouns, and never take a written accent.

**299** The masculine forms *este* and *ese* are sometimes found before a feminine noun beginning in a stressed *a-,* e.g. *este ave* 'this bird', *este agua* 'this water', *ese alma* 'this soul'.[2]

### 300 Position of the Demonstratives

*Este, ese, aquel* normally precede the noun to which they relate. But they may follow, especially in the spoken language, and the noun is then preceded by another determiner, usually a definite article. A pejorative or ironic meaning is often associated with this usage.[3]

> *este muchacho*                  this boy
>
> *en aquella época*              at that time
>
> *¡Qué mujer esta! Debe ser temible* (J. Benavente, quoted in Fernández, 1951: 261)
> What a woman! She must be fearsome
>
> *El doctor ese del perrito* (J. M. Gironella, 1966b: 520)
> That doctor who has the little dog
>
> *¿Cómo estaba la mar la tarde aquella?* (C. J. Cela, 1963b: 229)
> What was the sea like that afternoon?

## 301 Agreement

The demonstrative adjective generally agrees with the noun to which it relates; however, in the spoken language, the use of a neuter form is not uncommon, especially when the demonstrative functions as a subject, or, less frequently, as the nominal part of a predicate.[4]

> *Ésa es la taberna . . . esto es un chaleco* (S. J. Álvarez Quintero, quoted in Fernández, 1951: 262)
> That is the inn . . . and this is a waistcoat
>
> *Esto es la civilización* (A. Uslar Pietri, 1983:79)
> This is civilization

# Meaning and Use

## 302 General Meaning

Whereas English distinguishes only two demonstrative positions ('this' and 'that'), Spanish distinguishes three. The most helpful way of summarizing the general meaning of the Spanish demonstratives is to say that *este, ese, aquel* relate respectively to the first, second and third person:

> *este libro (cerca de mí)*        this book (near to me, here)
>
> *ese libro (cerca de ti)*          that book (near to you, there)

*aquel libro (cerca de él)*      that book (near a third
person, over there).

*Lo he tocado con estas manos* (Beinhauer, 1968: 177) (*con estas
manos = con mis propias manos*)
I touched it with these (= my own) hands

*Y tu clarinete, papá, ¿cómo va ese clarinete?* (J. A. de Zunzunegui, 1954: 50)
And your clarinet, Daddy, how's that clarinet (of yours)?

*Mire usted: aquella señora lleva un palmo de tacón en medio del
pie* (Alcina Franch and Blecua. 1975: 622)
Just look: that lady's got heels the size of fists on her feet

The form *ese* is also used for preference in numerous constructions
where it has to do with something known by the (real or fictitious)
hearer (as in the next example) or in cases where a noun already
mentioned is referred to again (literally or through another word,
as in the example following):

*Al ver una gallina desplumada, nos acordamos de esas brujas que
vuelan en una escoba* (R. Gómez de la Serna, quoted in Coste
and Redondo, 1965: 225)
When we see a plucked hen, we think of those witches who
fly on a broomstick

*Me convendría perfeccionar mi inglés. Papá dice que dominando
ese idioma tengo bastante para ganarme la vida* (A. M. de Lera,
quoted in Coste and Redondo, 1965: 224)
I should improve my English. Father says that if I master that
language I will have enough to earn my livelihood

In Latin-American Spanish, there is a tendency for *aquel* to be
used systematically for *ese*. In the spoken language, *este* often
functions as a hesitation, rather like *pues*; and it also has a usage as
a vocative, to address an unknown person (*¡Esta chica! = I* say,
miss!).[5]

*Señorita, este... dispénseme, pero ¿usted no sabe, por casualidad,
dónde vive la familia Rodríguez?* (Díaz-Solís, quoted in Kany,
1951: 137)
Señorita, er ... excuse me, but you don't happen to know
where the Rodríguez family live, do you?

**303** In correspondence, *está* refers to the town where the writer is,
*ésa* to the addressee's town, and *aquélla* to the town of a third

person referred to in the letter. The forms are feminine since the word *ciudad* is understood.

> *Permaneceré en ésta dos semanas* (quoted by M. Alvar Ezquerra, 1982: 199)
> I shall stay here (i.e. in this town) two weeks

> *Llegaré a esa*(sic) *el lunes próximo* (*DUE*, I, 1191)
> I will arrive there (i.e. where you are) next Monday

## 304 'Former' and 'Latter'

Used after two nouns, *este* refers to the last mentioned, *aquel* to the noun furthest away, that is to say, the first mentioned.

> *Juan y Pedro son mis amigos; éste* (= *Pedro*) *estudia filosofía, aquél* (= *Juan*) *trabaja en Iberia*
> Juan and Pedro are my friends: the latter studies philosophy, the former works at Iberia

> *Teníamos un coche y una moto: ésta* (= *la moto*) *estropeada y aquél* (= *el coche*) *sin gasolina* (*DUE*, I, 227)
> We had a car and a motorbike: the latter was broken and the former had no petrol

## 305 Demonstratives in Time Expressions

*Este* appears chiefly in expressions which refer to the present (*Esbozo*, 214). To indicate that a moment in the past or future is not far removed from the present, or that it is being thought of as such (see the second and third examples), *este* or *ese* may be used.[6] *Aquel* refers principally to the remoter past (fifth example), although it may occasionally refer to the future (sixth example).

> *Este año* (*Esbozo*, 214)      This year

> *El nivel de la enseñanza, en estos años, era bajo* (V. Pozuelo Escudero, 1980: 88)
> The level of teaching was low during these years (seen from a past perspective)

> *Ese día murieron heroicamente el teniente y los soldados* (E. Líster, 1977: I, 181)
> That day the lieutenant and soldiers died heroically

*Ese día, el indiano no tendrá más remedio que cederte la plaza* (J. A. de Zunzunegui, 1959b: 94)
That day, the *indiano* [see **265**] will have no alternative but to give you his place

*Una canción me recuerda aquel ayer*, from *La Paloma*, a song by Julio Iglesias
A song reminds me of that yesterday (long ago)

*En aquellos tiempos, las reservas de petróleo se han agotado* (*El Norte de Castilla*, 12 August 1989: 48)
Then the reserves of oil will have been exhausted

The expression *a eso de* has the meaning of 'about, approximately':

*Voy por ahí a eso de las nueve* (F. García Pavón, 1980b: 77)
I'll go over there about nine

## 306 Special Meanings: Demonstrative Pronoun for Personal Pronoun

In Spanish, a demonstrative pronoun is sometimes used where English would use a personal pronoun. Care should be taken with this usage, since the demonstrative may have a pejorative meaning or at the very least can seem disrespectful, especially when the person referred to is present (*Esbozo*, 431–2).

*Dale también un paquete de rubio a ésta* (C. J. Cela, 1963a: 183)
Give her a packet of fags as well

*¿No le has visto a ése por ahí?* (J. A. de Zunzunegui, 1958: 265)
Haven't you seen him around here?

## 307 Possible Perjorative Meaning of *ese*

*Ese* (and, less frequently, *este*)[7] may be used with a pejorative meaning, and as such may appear before or after the noun.[8]

*¿Qué quiere ese hombre?* (E. Martínez Amador, 1961:571)
What does that dreadful man want?

*El mejicano ese* (*Esbozo*, 432)
That damn Mexican

*Y también me mortificaba que dijeran despectivamente: «Ese no, ése es de pueblo»* (M. Delibes, 1979a: 114)
And I was also mortified when they said disparagingly: 'Not him, he's only a village lad'

**308** This value of *ese* can be further strengthened by another word with unfavourable meaning.

*¿Habrán abandonado el bote esos granujas?* (P. Baroja, 1960: 74)
Will those rascals have left the boat?

## 309 The Neuter Demonstrative: *esto, eso, aquello* + *de* + Noun

This construction with a neuter demonstrative pronoun, chiefly used in the spoken language, corresponds to English 'the business, matter of'. It sometimes refers to a fact or situation already mentioned and/or suggests a feeling of doubt, indignation, reproach, etc.[9]

*Anda con ojo en esto de los precios* (J. A. de Zunzunegui, 1958: 305)
Be wary in this matter of prices

*No sé cómo está ahora eso de los inquilinos* (ibid., 314)
I don't know how this business of the tenants stands at the moment

*Aquello de pasarme cuatro a cinco años seguidos en el mar me parecía muy duro* (P. Baroja, 1958: 131)
That business of spending four or five years continuously at sea seemed very hard to me

*Esto de que delante de todo el mundo te tutee tu criado ...* (S. J. lvarez Quintero, quoted in Fernández, 1951: 255)
The fact that your servant addresses you as *tú* in front of everyone ...

**310** The neuter article could be used instead of the demonstrative in the foregoing examples: *en lo de los precios, lo de los inquilinos, lo de pasarme, lo (de) que.*

**311** The neuter forms *esto, eso* and especially *aquello* are sometimes used with euphemistic meaning in cases where there is a need for discretion, decency or delicacy. These affective forms, which have roughly the same meaning as *lo*, often imply something like 'you know what I'm talking about'. It is sometimes difficult to give a precise translation of the neuter form.

> *Para pintar a dos personas en «eso» hacía falta un dominio del dibujo* (A. Carpentier, 1976: 300)
> (The erotic allusion is clear from the context)
> To paint two people doing you know what, you had to have a command of drawing

> *Es necesario que vuelvas a tu casa y que busques un poco de aquello* (I. Agustí, 1957: 399)
> You must go home and get a bit of that stuff

> *Después de todo, esto vuestro se arreglará en cuanto su madre se mejore* (J. A. de Zunzunegui, 1952b: 190)
> After all, this problem of yours will clear up as soon as their mother gets better

> – *¿Se le arregló aquello?*
> – *¿Cuál?*
>  *Lo de . . .*
> – *No, salió mal* (C. J. Cela, 1963a: 32)
> 'Did that business of his get sorted out?'
> 'Which?'
> 'The business of . . .'
> 'No, it turned out badly'

## 312 Stereotyped use of *eso*

The neuter form *eso* often appears in expressions which can be considered as clichés, e.g. *eso sí* (see **317**, second example), *eso no* 'yes indeed, no indeed', *eso sí que no* 'certainly not', *por eso* 'that's (precisely) why'.[10]

**313** Used alone, *eso* can have an affirmative meaning and is then approximately synonymous with *sí* 'yes'. It is possible to repeat it with an intensified meaning.

> *Eso es.*                Agreed.

> *Los adelantos técnicos son la llave del progreso. Eso, eso.* (C. J. Cela, 1971: 163)
> Technical advances are the key to progress. Sure, sure

Compare also the concessive use of *y eso que*:

> *Y eso que las portuguesas tienen fama de feas* (C. Martín Gaite, 1980: 38)
> In spite of the fact that Portuguese women are said to be ugly

## Constructions Involving Demonstratives

### 314 Demonstrative + Possessive

This combination is not impossible in Spanish, although, with the exception of the affective use of the neuter form (see **311**, third example), it is restricted to the written language.

> *De esta su manera de «ir tirando» se contaban sucedidos graciosos* (J. A. de Zunzunegui, 1959b: 46)
> People told amusing tales about this way of his of 'getting by'
>
> *El título de estos mis artículos . . .* (J. Casares, 1961: 207)
> The title of these articles of mine
>
> *Intentaba recordar aquella su otra cara* (F. García Pavón, 1980b: 85)
> He tried to recall that other face of his
> (Here *aquella su* is followed by a third adjective)
>
> *Esta su casa . . .* is a set expression by which a Spanish speaker places his/her home at the disposal of a visitor

### 315 Remark

Another such combination involving a demonstrative is the (now old-fashioned-sounding) *estotro* (= *este* + *otro*, i.e. demonstrative indefinite).

> *Dispusieron dónde habría de ir esta lámpara y estotro mueble* (J. A. de Zunzunegui, 1956a: 143).
> They arranged where this lamp and this other piece of furniture were to go.

### 316 Other Uses: Special Uses of *este* and *ese*

The feminine forms of *este* and *ese*, usually in the plural, are found in expressions like *ésas tenemos, en éstas andamos, ni por ésas*, etc., where it is impossible to say exactly what noun is being referred to.

> *¡Vaya, vaya, muchacha! . . . ¿Ésas tenemos?* (D. Medio, 1958: 193)
> Well, well, miss . . . So that's how things are?

> *El padre le dijo: ¿Conque en éstas andamos?* (I. Aldecoa, 1969: 89)
> Father said to him, 'So that's it, is it?'

> *Ni por ésas* has the meaning of 'even so, not at all'

## 317 *Aquel* as a Noun

*Aquel* is sometimes used as a noun, when it means 'attractiveness', 'charm', 'elegance', 'a certain something'. It is also used in the expression *por el aquel de* (synonymous with *por lo de, a causa de* 'because of'). This usage belongs to the spoken language.[11]

> *Era esbelto y de buen ver, y con aquel de la leyenda más de un corazón quedó prendido en sus encantos* (J. A. de Zunzunegui, 1959b: 40)
> He was slim and good-looking, and as a result of that legendary attractiveness more than one heart was ensnared in his charms

> *Eso sí, con doña Carmen tiene mucha confianza y mucho aquél* (J. A. de Zunzunegui, 1956a: 71)
> Yes indeed, he's on very intimate terms with Doña Carmen; there's a special something between them

> *Piden dos coca-colas por el aquel de la higiene* (R. Montero, 1979: 89)
> They order two cokes for the sake of hygiene

**318** It is even possible for *aquel* to appear twice in sequence (with different meanings):

> *Daba gusto mirar al señorito manejar el dinero con aquel aquél* (T. Salvador, 1966: 150)
> It was lovely to see the young master handle money in that elegant way of his

## 319 *Aquí* and *acá* Replacing Demonstratives

In the spoken language the adverbs of place *aquí* and *acá* (literally 'here') are sometimes heard to indicate a person or thing close to the speaker. *Aquí* and *acá* then replace *este, esta* used adjectivally.[12] See also **614** on the relationship between demonstratives and certain adverbs of place.

> *Sí, es la madre de aquí, de mi marido* (F. García Pavón, 1972: 183)
> Yes, it's this chap's mother, my husband's
>
> *Cuando acá y yo nos casamos* ... (Kany, 1951: 269)
> When she and I got married ...

# Possessive Pronouns and Adjectives

## Forms

**320** Two series of possessives are to be distinguished:

| Series I | | Series II | |
|---|---|---|---|
| *mi* (m/f sg)<br>*mis* (m/f pl) | my | *mío* (m sg)<br>*mía* (f sg)<br>*míos* (m pl)<br>*mías* (f pl) | of mine |
| *tu* (m/f sg)<br>*tus* (m/f pl) | your (sg) | *tuyo* (m sg)<br>*tuya* (f sg)<br>*tuyos* (m pl)<br>*tuyas* (f pl) | of yours (sg) |
| *su* (m/f sg)<br>*sus* (m/f pl) | his, her,<br>its, their,<br>your (sg/pl) | *suyo* (m sg)<br>*suya* (f sg)<br>*suyos* (m pl)<br>*suyas* (f pl) | of his, of hers,<br>of its, of theirs,<br>of yours (sg/pl) |
| *nuestro* (m sg)<br>*nuestra* (f sg)<br>*nuestros* (m pl)<br>*nuestras* (f pl) | | our; of ours | |
| *vuestro* (m sg)<br>*vuestra* (f sg)<br>*vuestros* (m pl)<br>*vuestras* (f pl) | | your (pl); of yours (pl) | |

## Usage

### Series I Forms (Adjectives)

**321** These forms precede the noun. *Mi(s)*, *tu(s)*, *su(s)* can be masculine or feminine.

| | |
|---|---|
| *mi coche* | my car |
| *mi abuela* | my grandmother |
| *tus amigos* | your friends |
| *tus cartas* | your letters |
| *nuestra casa* | our house |

As in English, an adjective may come between the possessive and the noun.

| | |
|---|---|
| *mi mejor amigo* | my best friend |
| *tu querida amiga María* | your dear friend María |

**322** The form *su(s)* has a variety of meanings: masculine, feminine, neuter, singular and plural. It renders a number of different English possessive forms, as can be seen from the table in **320** and the first example below. The correct interpretation is usually clear from the context. If not, a clarifying phrase is added, as in the second example.[1]

| | |
|---|---|
| *su casa de él* | his house |
| *su casa de ella* | her house |
| *su casa de usted* | your (sg) house |
| *su casa de ellos* | their (m) house |
| *su casa de ellas* | their (f) house |
| *su casa de ustedes* | your (pl) house |

*También su mano de él estaba sudorosa y helada* (G. García Márquez, 1977: 262)
His hand also was cold and sweaty

*La/Su señora de usted* 'your wife' is sometimes used to convey politeness or respect.

**323** The possessives are used less in Spanish than in English. Possession is often expressed by an indirect object pronoun, the noun possessed being used with the definite article (second to fourth examples). When the identity of the possessor is obvious, the definite article alone is used (first example).

*He dejado el gabán en casa* (*Esbozo*, 428)
I've left my mac at home (implies the mac belongs to the subject of the sentence)

But:

*He dejado tu gabán en casa*
I've left your mac at home

*Nunca le vi la cara* (J. Cortázar, 1973: 101)
I've never seen his face

*Los ojos se le llenaron de lágrimas* (*Esbozo*, 428)
His/her eyes filled with tears

*Ganarse la vida* (*DUE*, II, 1524)
To earn one's living

The use of a possessive adjective in such cases, though increasing,[2] is considered an anglicism:

*Le costó la amputación de «su» pierna* (*MEU*, 152, considered incorrect)
It cost him the amputation of his leg

The two constructions are combined in:

*El sacerdote bendijo los anillos de oro y en seguida Esteban puso uno a su novia y se colocó el otro a su dedo* (I. Allende, 1984: 86)
The priest blessed the gold rings and Esteban immediately put one on his fiancée's finger and placed the other on his own

### 324 Series I Forms in 'Vocative' Expressions

The Series II adjectives are normally used in forms of address (see **355**). However, the Series I adjectives are used in some special contexts.

**325** The possessive *mi* is used when a member of the armed forces is addressing a higher-ranking officer:

*Venimos a cargar la pieza, mi teniente* (J. Ibargüengoitia, 1981: 37)
We've come to load the gun, sir (= lieutenant)

*Sí, mi coronel* (T. Salvador, 1968b: 191)
Yes, sir (= colonel)

*Sí, mi cabo ... no, mi cabo* (M. Delibes, 1987: 293)
Yes, corporal ... no, corporal
(But in other instances in this book *cabo* is used without a
possessive (pp. 361 and 370))

The possessive is omitted when the speaker ranks higher than the
person addressed or sometimes when the speaker is a civilian: in
F. Umbral's interview of General Gutiérrez Mellado (1985: 262-3),
he oscillates between *mi general* and *general*.

**326** *Mi* is also found, optionally, before other words which imply
a hierarchical relation, sometimes in an ironic context, where *mi*
stands before a proper noun. The meaning is affective rather
than possessive.

> *¡No va a cenar nada, mi ama!* (A. Casona, 1968: 58)
> You're not going to have anything for dinner, mistress!

> *Yo le ayudaré, mi señor* (M. Alvar, 1982: 47 - words of an old
> man from a remote village in Santander province)
> I'll help you, sir

> *A sus órdenes, mi Ortega* (C. Pérez Merinero, 1982: 117 - a
> young villain says in opposition to the leader of the gang)
> As you say, Ortega, sir

Such use of *mi* in Spain is chiefly found in rural areas and in
archaic language. In Latin America, however, this construction is
very common in the spoken language and even compound forms
like *mija* (<*mi hija* 'my daughter'), the diminutive *mijita* (<*mi
hijita*), *mijo* (<*mi hijo* 'my son') and *miamigo* 'my friend', are found
as forms of address, where today in Spain *hija mía, hijo mío*, etc.,
would be heard exclusively:[3]

> *Lo felicito, mi amigo* (A. Roa Bastos, 1977: 83)
> I congratulate you, my friend

> *El Premio Nobel de Literatura, mijo* (A. Skármeta, 1986: 20
> and passim)
> The Nobel Prize for Literature, my son

## 327 Series I Adjectives with More than one Noun

When there is more than one noun, the possessive is generally
repeated before each one. However, this is not the case when the

nouns are considered by the speaker to be a single concept or where they relate to the same person, animal or thing.

Instead of *mis padres* (the usual translation of 'my parents'), one could say – considering them as individuals – *mi padre y mi madre*

*Tu padre y tu madre son tus mejores amigos* (Marsá, 1986: 133)
Your father and mother are your best friends

*Todos mis actos y mis pensamientos los mueves tú* (I. Agustí, 1944: 91)
You are the force behind all my actions and thoughts
(One could also say *todos mis actos y pensamientos*, in which case *actos y pensamientos* would be considered a unitary concept)

But:

*Mis oficiales, suboficiales y soldados*
My officers, warrant officers and men (implying: all my men)

*Mi colega y amigo*
My friend and colleague (referring to the same person)

## 328 Definite or Indefinite Article + Series I Possessive

In older or archaistic language, and in some contemporary varieties of Spanish, including Latin-American Spanish, a possessive adjective may be preceded by a definite or indefinite article.

*Santificado sea el tu nombre*
Hallowed be thy name

*Aquel sobrino de quien he hablado era hijo de una mi hermana* (M. J. de Larra, 1966: 16 – the text dates from 1832)
That nephew of whom I spoke was the son of one of my sisters
(A Series II adjective would preferably be used here: *era hijo de una hermana mía*)

*Tengo una mi amiga poetisa* (M. A. Carrera, 1986: 115)
I have amongst my friends a poetess

## Series II Forms

### 329 As Pronouns

The Series II forms are preceded by an article:

| | |
|---|---|
| *el mío, la mía, los míos, las mías* | mine |
| *el tuyo, la tuya, los tuyos, las tuyas* | yours (sg) |
| *el suyo, la suya, los suyos, las suyas* | his, hers, yours, theirs |
| *el nuestro, la nuestra, los nuestros,* | ours |
| *las nuestras* | |
| *el vuestro, la vuestra, los vuestros,* | yours (pl) |
| *las vuestras* | |

*Creo que para ti el único problema es el de despreocuparte. Y el mío es a la inversa* (I. Agustí, quoted in Coste and Redondo, 1965: 246)
I think that the only problem for you is to stop worrying. And mine is the opposite

*Su mundo no es el nuestro* (*Esbozo*, 211)
His world is not ours

*Unos, amigos o enemigos, sin nombre en la historia nacional, en la memoria comunal, y que son, en parte los más míos, los más pedazos de mi alma* (M. de Unamuno, 1967b: 12)
Some, friends or enemies, nameless in our national history, in our common memory, and who are, partly, those who belong to me the most, those who are the most pieces of my soul

*Lo mío, lo tuyo*, etc., are dealt with below (**337**), since they are, properly speaking, adjectives.

**330** A Series II possessive pronoun is sometimes replaced by the definite article + *de* + personal pronoun: this construction is chiefly found in the written language and is restricted to the third person.[4]

*Posó su cabeza contra la de él, fatigada de tanta emoción* (J. A. de Zunzunegui, 1954: 304)
Exhausted by such emotion, she rested her head against his (The use of *de él* here avoids the potential ambiguity of *suya*)

## 331 As Adjectives

As attributive adjectives, these possessives always follow the noun. The meaning is different from that of the Series I adjectives: the English translation of the Series II adjectives is normally 'of mine'.

> *Una hermana mía*
> A sister of mine; one of my sisters
> (This notion could also be expressed, but less commonly, by *una de mis hermanas*)

> *Ninguno de los dos era amigo mío* (G. Cabrera Infante, 1979: 656)
> Neither of the two was a friend of mine

Sometimes the Series II adjective has an emphatic or affective value by comparison with the Series I adjective which is difficult to translate in English:

> *Ella decía: «Eloy, no es lo mismo decirle a una mujer vida mía que mi vida»* (Coste and Redondo, 1965: 245)
> She said, 'Eloy, it is not the same thing saying *vida mía* to a woman as saying *mi vida*'

**332** These forms also function as predicative adjectives with *ser*, etc.

> *¿De quién es esta casa? Es nuestra*
> Whose is this house? It's ours

> *Larry, no es mía la culpa* (M. Puig, 1980: 171)
> Larry, the fault isn't mine

**333** Note that the adjective or pronoun always agrees in Spanish with the noun to which it relates (i.e. the noun 'possessed'). The distinction made in English between 'his', 'her' and 'their' in the third person often confuses English-speaking learners of Spanish: in Spanish, *suyo, suya, suyos, suyas*, agree with the nouns they qualify, not with the possessor.

> *Pedro se ha marchado a América donde vive una hermana suya*
> Pedro has gone off to America where a sister of *his* lives

*¿Conoces a Carmen Martín Gaite? Sí. Tengo vari<u>os</u> libr<u>os</u> suy<u>os</u>*
Do you know Carmen Martín Gaite? Yes, I have several of
her books

**334**  The series II possessive adjectives may be qualified by adverbs:
*La ciudad parece más suya* (C. J. Cela, 1963a: 202)
The city seems more his own
*Ese hombre es mío, muy mío y sólo mío* (J. A. de Zunzunegui,
1954: 98)
That man is mine, very much mine and mine alone

## 335 Meanings

The Series II possessive adjective are used in forms of address (but
see **324** above):
*Muy señor mío . . .*
Dear Sir . . .
*¡Ay, hijo mío!* (*DUE*, II, 421)
Ah, my son!

**336**  They may also be used in prepositional phrases: sometimes,
there is practically no difference in meaning between a Series I
and a Series II form in this context.[5]
*por su cuenta* or *por cuenta suya*
on his/her/your/their account
*en mi presencia* or *en presencia mía*
in my presence
*de su parte* or *de parte suya*
on his/her/your/their behalf
*Un desequilibrio a su favor* (*El Alcázar*, 16 February 1983: 15)
An imbalance in his favour
*Estamos a favor suyo* (*El País*, 16 February 1983: 15)
We are in favour of him

**337**  Just like other adjectives, Series II possessives can be used
with the neuter article *lo*.
*Lo mío mío y lo tuyo de entrambos* (Spanish saying)
My things belong to me and your things belong to both
of us

**338** Forms like *lo mío, lo tuyo, lo nuestro*, etc., can nevertheless also have a completely different, figurative meaning. These expressions may allude to behaviour or a state of affairs of which the person addressed is assumed to be informed. These neuter (hence vague, general) terms are also used euphemistically and avoid more precise words or expressions which might call up unpleasant memories or allude to difficulties.

> *Lo mío debió de hacerla sufrir mucho, ¿no?* (J. A. de Zunzunegui, 1958: 302)
> My behaviour must have made her suffer a lot, mustn't it? (Here a girl who had run away from home years before meets her brother and is talking of their mother)

> *Te quiero con toda mi alma y nadie ni nada podrá oponerse a lo nuestro* (J. M. Gironella, 1966b: 538)
> I love you with all my heart and no one and nothing can get in the way of our happiness

> *Mira, Bea, esto nuestro no tiene más que una solución: que nos casemos* (J. A. de Zunzunegui, 1952b: 187)
> Look here, Bea, in our position there's only one way out: to get married

In such constructions the use of the neuter forms can include a quantitative nuance ('too much', 'too long'), or may refer to a typical or characteristic aspect of someone's attitude or lifestyle:

> *Anda hija, ya has tardado lo tuyo* (J. García Hortelano, 1979: 77)
> Come on, girl, you've been doing it long enough

> *He leído lo mío, de religiones orientales sobre todo* (J. García Hortelano, ibid., 99)
> I've read quite a lot, especially about eastern religions

> *Tras la fiesta, el escritor se retira a trabajar. Es lo suyo.* (M. Tudela, 1970: I, 90)
> After the party, the writer retires to work. That is his way

> *Lo tuyo se sabe en todo el barrio*
> *– ¿Y cuál es lo mío?*
> *Lo tuyo con María Antonieta* (F. Umbral, 1976b: 122)
> All the neighbourhood knows about your behaviour
> What behaviour?
> Your behaviour with María Antonieta.

> – *Dorotea te había dicho que «aquello» se movía ya.*
> – *¿Aquello?*
> – *Sí, tonto, «lo nuestro»* (S. Lorén, 1960: 70).
> 'Dorotea had told you "that business" was moving.'
> 'That business?'
> 'Yes, stupid, "our business".'

**339** Note also the meaning of the possessive in:

> *No seas tuya, mujer* (J. García Hortelano, 1979: 159)
> Don't be so self-opinionated, woman

> *Ella era muy simpática, pero muy suya* (F. García Pavón, 1980b: 143)
> She was very nice, but very self-centred

## 340 *Mío* = *de mí*, etc.

Series II possessives can appear with prepositions of place, such as *delante mío*, *delante tuyo*, *delante suyo*, etc. ('before me, you, him/her/you/them'), *en torno mío*, *en torno tuyo*, etc. ('about me, you'), *detrás mío*, *detrás tuyo*, etc. ('behind me, you'), *encima mío*, etc. ('on top of me'), although such constructions are generally considered incorrect.[6] They are frequent in Latin America and in some areas of Spain (notably Asturias and Andalusia), but unusual in the literary language in Spain.[7] However, examples are to be found among present-day Peninsular writers.[8]

> *Sentí una presencia, detrás mío* (M. Puig, 1980: 71–2)
> I felt a presence behind me

> *«Guárdame dentro tuyo», balbucea con voz rota* (R. Montero, 1979: 116).
> 'Hold me in your heart,' stammers a broken voice

> *Estaba justamente detrás suyo* (J. Goytisolo, 1960: 77)
> He stood just behind him

> *María sólo había sentido repugnancia por esas bestias que temblaban encima suyo como atacados del mal de San Vito* (M. Vargas Llosa, 1981: 50)
> María had felt only repugnance towards those creatures which trembled above her as if they had Saint Vitus' dance

*Ella era la advenediza en un ambiente predispuesto en contra
suya hacía trescientos años* (G. García Márquez, 1985: 346)
She was the parvenue in an atmosphere that had been pre-
judiced against her for three hundred years

A feminine form of the possessive sometimes appears in these
constructions when the possessive refers to a feminine noun or a
noun ending in *-a* (e.g. *encima mía, delante suya*), and in some
Latin-American countries *en/por su delante* is a more frequently
used variant of *delante suyo*.[9]

### 341 Idioms with Series II Possessives

The forms of the third person *suyo* appear in a number of set
phrases, such as:

| | |
|---|---|
| *ir a lo suyo* | to go one's own way, look after number one |
| *hacer de la(s) suya(s)* | to be up to one's tricks |
| *salir(se) con la suya* | to get one's own way |
| *de suyo* (invariable, see next example) | in itself, intrinsically |

*La madre de Marta era de suyo poco cariñosa* (J. M. Gironella,
1986: 237)
Marta's mother was not affectionate by nature

*De suyo* has a corresponding first-person form:

*Yo de mío me soy tranquilo y pacífico* (J. Goytisolo, 1981a: 44)
I am by nature calm and peace-loving

# Relatives

## Forms

**342** Spanish has the following relatives:

*que*

*el que/la que/los que/las que; lo que*
(*El que* is also used as an ellipsis for *el hecho de que* to introduce a noun clause, see **1039**)
*quien(es)*
*el cual/la cual/los cuales/las cuales; lo cual*
*cuyo/cuya/cuyos/cuyas*
*cuanto/cuanta/cuantos/cuantas*

### Que, el que, etc.

**343** *Que* is undoubtedly the most frequent of the relative pronouns. It is invariable, and may refer to any kind of noun. *Que* can function as subject or object:

| | |
|---|---|
| *La muchacha que canta* | The girl who sings |
| *El niño que veo* | The boy I see |

*Que* can also be preceded by a monosyllabic preposition, although other prepositions are occasionally to be found:[1]

*Fíjese en el modo tímido con que se le acerca* (M. Puig, 1980: 166–7).
Notice how timidly he approaches him
(*con el que* is also possible)

In careful speech prepositions are followed by *el que/la que/los que/las que* or, when the antecedent denotes a person or persons, by *quien(es)* (see **350**).

> *¿Quién era el tipo al que miraste todo el tiempo?* (A. Bryce Echenique, 1981: 156)
> Who was the guy you were looking at all the time?

> *¿Era el primer hombre con el que te acostabas?* (C. Martín Gaite, 1980: 166)
> Was he the first man you slept with?

> *España es uno de los países de los que estoy más orgulloso* (O. Caballero, 1980: 11)
> Spain is one of the countries I am most proud of

Constructions like the following are hence far from usual:

> *La persona a que enviaste recado* (E. Alarcos Llorach, 1982: 264)
> The person to whom you sent a message

> *Aquella chica de que tú me hablaste* (S. J. Álvarez Quintero, quoted in Fernández, 1951: 374)
> That girl of whom you spoke to me

With the 'personal *a*' (**658**ff) the use of the 'compound relative' is obligatory. It is not possible to say \**el niño a que veo*: instead, *el niño al que veo* or, more simply, *el niño que veo* must be used.

**344** In adverbial phrases, *que* must be preceded by a preposition corresponding to the type of phrase (time, place, etc.).[2]

> *Se pasaron quince días en que no la vimos* (Cervantes, quoted in *Esbozo*, 529)
> A fortnight went by during which we did not see her
> (*Se pasaron quince días que no la vimos* would be strictly incorrect)

In practice this rule is often broken, especially in phrases of time and place. A typical example is the title of a book by F. Umbral:

> *La noche que llegué al café Gijón*
> The night I arrived at the Cafe Gijón
> (More 'correctly': *la noche en (la) que llegué . . .*)[3]

However, if the antecedent belongs to a prepositional phrase, the preposition before *que* may be omitted to avoid repetition:

> *En el lugar (en) que estaba instalada la fábrica, hay ahora . . .* (*MEU*, 45).
> In the place where the factory was situated, there is now
> . . .

The preposition *a* is also often omitted, especially in the spoken language,[4] when it introduces an indirect object or when it is the 'personal *a*':

> *Para mí una mujer que no le gustan los niños es como un árbol sin hojas* (C. Martín Gaite, 1980: 146)
> For me, a woman who does not like children is like a tree without leaves

> *Uno que le llaman el Chato* (*Esbozo*, 530)
> Someone called 'El Chato'

Note the presence of the pronoun *le* in these examples, which makes clear the function of *que*.

## 345 Special Meaning of *la que*

*La que* may have a special elliptical meaning:

> *¿Dónde vas con la que cae?* (M. Delibes, 1968a: 59)
> Where are you going in this blizzard (lit. 'with the amount of snow that is falling')?

(Compare *la de*, **62**.)

## 346 *Lo que/lo cual*

*Lo que* (or *lo cual*, see **359**) is the equivalent of English 'what', 'which'. It refers to a preceding clause.

> *Recuerda lo que te dije ayer*
> Remember what I said to you yesterday

> *Sostenía que el hombre es pariente del mono, lo que regocijaba a doña Bernarda* (V. Blasco Ibáñez, quoted in Fernández, 1951: 358)
> He maintained that men are related to monkeys, which delighted Doña Bernarda

## 347 Special Meaning of *lo que*

In popular speech, *en lo que* or even simply *lo que* is heard with the meaning of *mientras* 'while'.

> *En lo que tú te arreglas, yo tomo un café* (Lapesa, 1980: 473)
> While you're getting ready, I'll have a cup of coffee

Note also the idiom *en lo que va de mes/año/siglo*, etc. 'so far this month, year, century', etc.

> *En lo que va de año, 3.665 personas han perdido la vida en las carreteras* (*ABC*, 17 August 1989: 40)
> 3665 people have lost their lives on the roads so far this year

## 348 *Que* with No Antecedent

The relative *que* is sometimes used after a preposition with no overt antecedent. It then takes a written accent (*qué*).[5]

> *Si el maíz este año se da bien, tendré con qué pagarte* (J. Rulfo, 1981: 65)
> If the corn does well this year, I'll have something to pay you with
> (*Qué* may here be thought of as standing for *dinero* 'money')

> *– Gracias – dijo.*
> *– ¡Oh! no hay de qué* (E. Parra, 1981: 66).
> 'Thank you,' he said.
> 'Oh, don't mention it.'

## 349 *Todo el que*, etc.

English 'all who', besides a literal Spanish equivalent *todos/as los/las que*, also has an equivalent in which the singular relative pronoun *que* (with a corresponding singular verb) is used.

> *«El niño» proponía a todo el que pasaba por el mostrador hacerse de la peña* (J. A. de Zunzunegui, 1954: 76)
> 'El Niño' would invite all those who passed by the counter to join the group

## Other Relatives

### 350 *Quien(es)*

*Quien(es)* is only used for persons or personified animals or things.[6]

The word does not vary according to gender. The use of the plural *quienes* is optional: *quienes* is not so frequently used in the spoken language.[7]

With an antecedent. *quien(es)* can function as subject or object, or as the object of a preposition. However, *quien* cannot be the subject of a restrictive relative clause. Contrast:

*Los obreros que estaban cansados no quisieron trabajar más*
The workers who were tired would not work any more

*Los obreros, quienes* (or *que*) *estaban cansados, no quisieron trabajar más*
The workers, who were tired, would not work any more

Other examples of the use of *quien(es)*:

*Fue Fernanda quien impuso el rigor de aquel duelo* (G. García Márquez, 1977: 247)
It was Fernanda who imposed such strict mourning

*Fue ella quien le empezó a besar* (C. Martín Gaite, 1980: 70)
It was she who began to kiss him

*Ella era la mujer con quien había soñado desde niño* (R. J. Sender, 1964: 149)
She was the woman he had dreamed of since he was a child

*El hombre interesante es el hombre de quien las mujeres se enamoran* (J. Ortega y Gasset, 1959: 32)
An interesting man is one with whom women fall in love

*Sostenía que es mejor ser varón, porque hasta el más mísero tiene su propia mujer a quien mandar* (I. Allende, 1987: 46)
He maintained that it is better to be a man, because even the most lowly has his own wife to order around

*El cuerpo es quien nos individualiza* (E. Sábato, 1981: 145)
The body is what makes us individuals
(*Cuerpo* is here thought of as something personified)

In the six above examples the definite article + *que* or *que* alone
(see **343**) could equally well be used:[8] *Fue Fernanda (la) que . . ., A
mí es al que . . .*, etc.

**351** *Quien(es)* can also be used without an antecedent, the antecedent then being implicit in *quien(es)* itself. The meaning is then 'he/
she/they who, anyone who'. In the following examples (except the
third, which is a fixed expression) *quien(es)* could be replaced by a
compound relative (*el que*, etc.).

> *Entregaré este objeto a quien me lo pida* (Alcina Franch and
> Blecua, 1975: 1083)
> I'll give this object to anyone who asks me for it
>
> *Quienes no quisieron escribir le dieron recados verbales* (G.
> García Márquez, 1977: 257)
> Those who would not write gave her verbal messages
>
> *Quien va a Sevilla, pierde la silla* (proverb)
> (Also: *El que se fue a Sevilla, perdió la silla*)[9]
> He who goes to the fair loses his chair
>
> *Siento asco por quienes manejan la necesidad ajena*
> (M. Alvar, 1982: 110)
> I am disgusted by those who exploit other people's need

See also **111**, second example.

**352** The use of *quien(es)* can be a means of effectively stressing a
pronoun: *yo soy quien* 'I'm the one who', *tú eres quien* 'You're the
one who', etc. The *el que*, etc., form may replace *quien(es)*.

> *¡Nosotros somos quien(es)/los que vencimos/vencieron!*
> We're the ones who won!
> (Note that the verb in the relative clause may agree with the
> subject (first, second or third person) or with the relative pro-
> noun (third person))[10]

## 353 Remarks

*Quien* is losing ground to *el que*, etc., in present-day Spanish,
especially in the spoken language.[11] *Quien* is felt to be less definite
and more general than *el que*.[12] The following example shows that
the two forms can alternate for stylistic reasons (the avoidance
of repetition):

*Nunca quedó claro si fue ella quien abandonó al esposo, o si fue éste el que la abandonó a ella* (G. García Márquez, 1985: 258-9)
It was never clear whether it was she who left her husband or he who left her

**354** Another common use of *quien(es)* is in the expression *hay quien(es)* 'there are those who'.
The verb following *quien(es)* is in the third person.

*Hay quien cree en los fantasmas, hay quien duda y hay quien los niega* (P. Baroja, 1946-51: V, 1054)
There are those who believe in ghosts, those who doubt whether they exist and those who deny that they exist

*Hay quien opina que los ingleses no son extraordinariamente inteligentes* (J. Camba, 1964: 56)
There are those who think that the English are not extraordinarily bright

*Hay quienes afirman que el publicitario nace y no se hace* (El País, 27 May 1980: 34)
There are those who say that one is born an adman rather than becoming one

A similar expression is *no falta quien* 'there is always someone who':

*No falta quien supone que deshacemos sus bodas* (Fernández, 1951: 363)
There is always someone who thinks we are spoiling their wedding

*No hay quien* means 'there is no one who' (followed by the subjunctive, see **1049**).

*Y aquí no hay quien se permita el más ligero derroche* (*Estafeta literaria*, 620, 15 September 1977: 15)
There is no one here who allows themselves the slightest waste

*¿No habrá quien haga justicia en este pueblo?* (J. A. de Zunzunegui, 1959b: 204)
Is there no one who will do justice in this village?

**355** The construction *ser* + *quien* (with or without a written accent) + *para* means 'not to be suitable for':

*No soy quién para opinar al respecto* (**P**. Gimferrer, quoted in *DD*, 317)
My opinion doesn't count in this matter

*(Yo) no soy quien para intervenir enérgicamente* (Van Dam, 1967: 982)
I'm not the person to make an energetic intervention

*Nosotros creemos que el padre no es quién para educar a su hijo* (**P**. Baroja, *Artículos*, in *Obras Completas*, V, 1131)
We believe that a father is not the right person to educate his son

**356** *Quien ... quien* may also have a distributive use, meaning 'one ... one'. This expression occurs mainly in the spoken language.[13]
*Quien más, quien menos* has the meaning of 'one somewhat more than the other' (see also **654**).
The use of the written accent on *quien* is optional in both cases.

*Quien dijo que había pasado a Extremadura, quien aseguró que estaba casada* (R. León, quoted in Duviols and Villegier, 1960: 108)
One said she had gone to Extremadura, another was certain she was married

*Los vecinos de la casa del crimen, que eran todos españoles, pronunciaron quién más, quién menos, su frase lapidaria* (C. J. Cela, 1963a: 113)
The neighbours of the house where the crime took place, who were all Spaniards, each had their choice comment to make

**357** *El que más y el que menos* is also used with the same meaning, chiefly in the spoken language (see **654** for examples).

## 358 *El cual/la cual/los cuales/las cuales*

These forms function as subject or object and as the object of prepositions. They belong primarily to the written language.

As a relative pronoun, *cual* is always preceded by a definite article. In restrictive relative clauses, *que* can always be replaced by *el cual*, etc. *El cual*, etc., is preferred when the relative pronoun is separated from the antecedent or when the use of the invariable *que* could give rise to ambiguity. *El cual*, etc., is used rather than *que* after a preposition.[14]

(See also on *cualo*, etc. **374**.)

> *Se aproximó <u>al boquete</u> de la obstruida escalera de la torre, <u>el cual</u> los sitiados habían tapado con cascote y maderas* (B. Pérez Galdós, *Zumalacárregui*, 308, quoted in Alcina Franch and Blecua, 1975: 1093)
> He went up to the breach in the blocked staircase of the tower, which the people under siege had sealed off with rubble and planks

> *La madre y <u>su hijo</u>, <u>el cual</u> había nacido en Roma, pensaban pasar sus vacaciones en Italia*
> The mother and her son, who ( = the son) had been born in Rome, intended to spend their holidays in Italy
> (Use of *el cual* makes the reference to *hijo* clear)

**359** The neuter form *lo cual* is equivalent to *lo que* (see **346**), and refers to a preceding clause.

> *Es algo a lo cual no está acostumbrado* (J. Casalduero, quoted in Fernández, 1951: 357)
> It is something he is not accustomed to

> *El guarda le reiteró que sería enviado a prisión, ante lo cual el joven cobró miedo* (*ABC*, 10 February 1980: 46)
> The guard repeated that he would be sent to prison, which frightened the youngster

In the spoken language *cosa que* is similarly used, although never as a prepositional object.

> *Cuando se enfurecía, cosa que le ocurría con frecuencia...* (C. J. Cela, quoted in Fernández, 1951: 359)
> When he got annoyed, which happened to him frequently . . .

> *Ignacio se manifestaba muy patriota, cosa que yo entonces no comprendía* (P. Baroja, 1946–51:III, 123)
> Ignacio showed himself very patriotic, which I did not then understand

(Note that in American Spanish *cosa que* may be used in the sense of *para que*, *de modo que*.)[15]

## 360 *Cuyo, cuya, cuyos, cuyas*

*Cuyo* is the equivalent of English 'whose', 'of which'.[16] It agrees in number and gender with the following noun, not with the antecedent.

> *El árbol a cuya sombra estábamos sentados* (A. Bello, 1972: 108)
> The tree in whose shadow we sat
> *El árbol cuyas flores perfumaban el aire* (ibid.)
> The tree whose flowers perfumed the air
> *Ha iniciado las conversaciones con el Gobierno, con cuyo presidente y vicepresidente se ha entrevistado hoy* (*MEU*, 44–5)
> He has begun conversations with the Government, with whose President and Vice-president he has had talks today

**361** *Cuyo* is used less and less in contemporary Spanish, especially in the spoken language. where alternative means of expressing the possessive idea (*del cual*, etc., *de quien*, *que ... su*) have emerged.[17]

> *Roma, sujeta a una tiranía de que nadie podía prever el término* (instead of ... *cuyo término nadie podía prever*) (Alcina Franch and Blecua, 1975: 1035)
> Rome, subject to a tyranny the end of which nobody could foresee

Often in the spoken language, and occasionally even in higher register (see last example below), *cuyo* is replaced by *que + su*, though this is considered incorrect.[18] *Que* and *su* may be separated, as in the third example below.

> *Una vecina que su marido está empleado en el gas* (for *Una vecina cuyo marido...*) (Beinhauer, 1968: 344)
> A citizen whose husband is an employee of the gas company
> *Ese niño que su padre es carpintero* (for *Ese niño cuyo padre...*) (R. Seco, 1960: 217)
> That boy whose father is a carpenter
> *En el hotel Eden cenaban las mujeres más bellas pero que no se conocían sus medios de vida* (R. Garriga, 1980: 157)
> In the Eden Hotel, there dined the most beautiful women, but their means of livelihood were not known

*Hay autores que no escriben para niños pero que sus poesías pueden ser dadas a los niños* (G. de Mello, 1992: 67)
There are authors who do not write for children but whose poems can be given to children (from the text of a University lecture)

**362** *Cuyo* is also used with a demonstrative value. Although the Spanish Academy censures this usage,[19] examples can be found in well-known modern authors.[20]

*Disponía de cincuenta destructores que el presidente Roosevelt le había vendido, con cuyo acto los Estados Unidos habían dejado prácticamente de ser neutrales* (J. M. Gironella, 1966b: 431)
He had fifty destroyers at his disposal which President Roosevelt had sold him. an act by which the United States had effectively ceased to be neutral

*Podría no aparecer su verdadero amo, en cuyo caso...* (J. A. de Zunzunegui, 1956b: 26)
His true master might well not appear, in which case ...

A number of expressions in which *cuyo* appears with this demonstrative meaning are established by usage,[21] e.g.:

| | |
|---|---|
| *con cuyo fin* | to which (this) end |
| *en cuyo caso* | in which (that) case |
| *por cuya razón* | for which (this/that) reason |

## 363 *Cuanto*

'All who', 'all that/which' can also be translated in the written language[22] by *todos/as cuantos/as* or simply *cuantos/as*, or *cuanto/a* in the singular (see **145–146** above). *Todo cuanto* or *cuanto* on their own function as neuter forms.[23] Note that the relative *que* is not used after *cuanto*.

*Se enamora de todas cuantas ve* (*DUE*, I, 818)
He falls in love with all the girls he sees

*Atendió a cuantos caprichos le pasaron por la mente* (M. Aub, 1971: 101)
He attended to all the whims that passed through her mind

*Estaba suscrita a cuanta revista de modas se publicaba en Europa* (G. García Márquez, 1977: 348)
She subscribed to all the fashion magazines published in Europe

*Vendieron cuanto tenían* (C. Rojas, 1982: 53)
They sold all they had

## 364 Use of Adverbs in Place of Relative Pronouns

The so-called relative adverbs *donde* (*en donde, a donde, por donde*,[24] *como, cuanto*, and sometimes *cuando*) may be used instead of the relative pronouns *que* and *el cual*, etc., if an adverbial subordinate clause relates to a noun that is in the main clause.

*La casa donde pasé mi niñez no existe ya...* (*Esbozo*, 533)
The house where I spent my childhood no longer exists...
(Alternatively: *la casa en (la) que* (see **343**) or *la casa en donde...*)

*Estaban de acuerdo sobre la manera como había de entablarse la demanda* (*Esbozo*, 534)
They were agreed as to the way in which the petition should be lodged
(Alternatively: ... *la manera según (la) que...*)

*Que coman y beban cuanto quieran* (*Esbozo*, 534)
Let them eat and drink as much as they want
(In the meaning of 'anything (that)', *cuanto* may be preceded by *todo* (see **349**))

*Todo cuanto decía le parecía gracioso* (*Esbozo*, 534)
Everything he said appeared witty
(Alternatively: *Todo lo que decía...*)

*Recordábamos los años cuando íbamos juntos a la escuela* (*Esbozo*, 534)
We remembered the years (when) we went to school together
(Alternatively: ... *los años en que...* The use of *cuando* in this way is not very common.[25]

Sometimes a relative adverb is used without a main clause antecedent:

*Aquí no hay donde acostarse* (J. Rulfo, 1981: 17)
There is nowhere to sleep here

# Interrogative and Exclamatory Pronouns and Adjectives

## Forms

**365** The interrogative pronouns and adjectives are similar in form to the relatives, except that they bear a written accent (*¿qué?/ ¡qué!*, etc.). *¿Cuál?* is not preceded by the definite article. *¡Qué!*, *¡quién!* and *¡cuánto!* also have an exclamatory function.

### 366 ¿Qué?/¡Qué!

Interrogative *¿qué?* has an adjectival and pronominal use. In speech, *qué* is sometimes used for *cuántos* (see the third example).

> *¿En qué ciudad vives?*    Which town do you live in?

> *¿Qué ideas son las de usted?* (Azorín, quoted in Fernández, 1951: 369)
> What are your views?

> *¿Qué años tienes tú, Azarías?* (M. Delibes, 1981: 166)
> How old are you, Azarías?

> *¿Qué quieres?*    What do you want?

> *Es una calle en que pasea mucho el que no tiene nada que hacer, el que busca algo, no sabe bien qué* (F. Umbral, 1977: 96)
> It is a street where people often go who have nothing to do, people who are searching for something, they do not know what

*¿Qué?* may also be an interjection:

*¿Qué, mala la comida, no?* (G. Cabrera Infante, 1978: 89)
Well, the food's bad, isn't it?

**367** Exclamatory *¡qué!* is only used adjectivally. Its force is sometimes strengthened by the addition of a demonstrative after the noun (third example).

*¡Qué tío!*                    What a guy!

*¡Qué catástrofe!*            What a disaster!

*¡Qué Elenita ésta!* (J. A. de Zunzunegui, 1956b: 242)
What an Elenita!

**368** *¡Qué!* also often has the value of a degree adverb, in both direct and indirect exclamations.

*¡Qué romántico!* (R. J. Sender, 1969d: 238)
How romantic!

*Mira qué fea estoy* (M. Vázquez Montalbán, 1979b: 202)
Look how ugly I am!

*Ya verás qué a gusto duermes* (J. Ibargüengoitia, 1981: 48)
You'll see how comfortably you sleep

*– Qué caras son las mujeres – dijo* (G. García Márquez, 1985: 484)
'How dear women are,' he said

*¡Cuán!* is sometimes found as an alternative to *¡qué!* in the written language:

*¡Cuán felices son!* (*Esbozo*, 358)
How happy they are!

In Latin-American Spanish, *¡qué!* appears in elliptical constructions where *hace* (or *ha*, see **1261**) is omitted:

*¡Qué años!* (Kany, 1951: 224)
What a long time ago!
(= *¡Cuántos años hace!*)

See also *lo* (**69**).

**369** When the exclamatory *¡qué!* (with the value of an adverb of degree) precedes a noun followed by an adjective (or, as in the third example below, an adjectival phrase), *más* or *tan* is normally placed before the adjective, although exceptions to this rule are found (e.g. fourth example).[1]

*¡Qué país tan desierto, qué hombres tan solitarios, qué pesadilla tan larga!* (F. Arrabal, 1972a: 116)
What a deserted country, what lonely men, what a long nightmare!

*Un poco brusca . . ., pero es una mujer guapísima. ¡Qué cintura tan ideal!* (F. García Lorca, 1955: 928)
A little abrupt . . ., but she's a very pretty woman. What a fine waist!

*¡Qué vida más sin sentido esta nuestra!* (J. A. de Zunzunegui, 1952b: 180)
How senseless this life of ours is!

*¡Qué noche triste, Señor, qué noche triste!* (I. Agustí, 1945: 138)
What a sad night, Lord, what a sad night!

**370** But if the adjective is placed before the noun, the use of *más* or *tan* is impossible.

*¡Ah, qué bello país Francia!* (J. M. Gironella, 1966b: 131)
What a beautiful country France is!

*¡Qué precioso vestido!* (J. Donoso, 1980: 87)
What a pretty dress!

**371** *Lo que* can also appear in exclamatory sentences.[2]

*¡Lo que le habrá enseñado!* (M. de Unamuno, quoted in *Esbozo*, 225)
What he must have taught him!

## 372 ¿Quién?, ¡Quién!

*¿Quién?* is the equivalent of English 'who?'; as a direct object ('who(m)') it must be preceded by the personal *a*. When referring to a plural notion, the plural form *¿quiénes?*, while often avoided (see third example), is strictly more correct.[3]

| | |
|---|---|
| *¿Quién me ha llamado?* | Who's called me? |
| *¿A quién has llamado?* | Who(m) have you called? |

*¿Quién serán aquellas tres?* (F. García Lorca, quoted in Fernández, 1951: 336)
Who can those three women be?
(The preferred form is *¿Quiénes serán aquellas tres?*)

*¿Sabes quiénes llegaron anoche?* (F. Marsá, 1986: 144)
Do you know who arrived last night?

**373** For a special use of *¡quién!* in exclamatory sentences, see **1028.**

### 374 ¿Cuál?, ¡Cuál!

*¿Cuál?* (plural *¿cuáles?*) strictly has only a pronoun function (first example). It may also replace an adjectivally used *¿qué?* (third and fourth examples), especially in Latin America, although *qué* is still much more frequent in this function in the Peninsula.[4]
  Unlike the relative pronoun (*el cual*), the interrogative *¿cuál?* is not preceded by the definite article.

> *¿Cuál es el más loco de los dos?* (*DD*, 124)
> Which is the madder of the two?

> *¿En cuál* (more usually *qué*) *ciudad vives?*
> In which town do you live?

> *¿Cuáles* (or *¿qué?*) *libros has comprado?*
> Which books have you bought?

> – *¿Y las leyes?* – *¿Cuáles leyes, Fulgor?* (J. Rulfo, 1981: 60)
> 'And the laws?' 'What laws, Fulgor?'

In popular speech, forms such as *¿cuálo?, ¿cuálos?, ¿cuála?, ¿cuálas?* are found.

> – *Bueno, ponme un blanco en aquella mesa.*
> – *¿En cuála?* (C. J. Cela, 1971: 170)
> 'Right, put me a glass of white wine on that table over there.'
> 'Which table?'

### 375 ¿Cúyo?

*¿Cúyo?* is largely obsolete in modern Spanish. Thus *¿De quién es esta casa?, ¿De quién son estos coches?* are to be preferred to *¿Cúya es esta casa?, ¿Cúyos son estos coches?*[5]

### 376 ¿Cuánto?, ¡Cuánto!

*Cuánto* agrees with the noun to which it relates in number and gender.

*¿Cuánto le debo a Vd.?*　　　How much do I owe you?

*- He comprado muchos libros.*
*- ¿Cuántos?*
'I've bought a lot of books.'
'How many?'

*¿Cuánta gente había en el teatro?*
How many people were there at the theatre?

*Cuánto* also has an adverbial function:

*¡Cuánto ha trabajado este hombre!*
How hard this man has worked!

*¡Cuánto lo siento, señora!*
I'm terribly sorry, madam

**377** A somewhat more expressive alternative in the spoken language to *¡cuánto!*, etc. is *¡qué de* + noun*!*,[6] which expresses quantity or intensity.

*¡Qué de tonterías dices!* (M. Delibes, 1948: 77)
What foolish things you say!

# Indefinite Pronouns and Adjectives

## *Uno*

**378** *Uno* is dealt with above as an article (**71-85**) and as a numeral (**204** ff).

For *uno* in combination with *otro*, see **459-460**. As the equivalent of English 'one' (impersonal subject), see **543-544**. For *uno que otro*, see **388**.

### 379 Adjectival Use of *uno*

The plural *unos, unas* means 'some, a few'. It is often followed by *pocos* or *cuantos*.

> *Unas mujeres ayudaron a la señorita Teresa* (A. Roa Bastos, 1977: 154)
> Some women helped Miss Teresa

> *En unas pocas semanas habían conquistado un verdadero imperio* (R. Garriga, 1980: 224)
> Within a few weeks they had conquered a veritable empire

> *Tenía unas cuantas cajas* (Fernández, 1951: 412)
> He had a few boxes

When followed by a numeral, *unos, unas* has the meaning of 'some, approximately':

> *En los hogares españoles hay instalados unos 2,5 millones de teléfonos pirata* (*El Periódico*, 17 February 1989: 1)
> There are 2.5 million illegal telephones installed in Spanish homes

*Las tres parecían tener la misma edad – unos veinte años* (J. Ibargüengoitia, 1981: 93)
The three girls seemed to be the same age – about twenty

The two meanings of *unos, unas* can be seen in the following example:

*Al cabo de unos instantes bajó Pilar. Le echó unos cincuenta años* (J. Fernández Santos, 1977: 80)
After a few moments, Pilar came down. He reckoned she must be about fifty

## 380 *Uno* as a Pronoun Substituting *yo*, etc.

There is a tendency, chiefly in colloquial usage, for the indefinite (impersonal) pronoun *uno, una* to be 'personalized'. It then denotes a first person singular.[1]

In certain cases the equivalence of *uno* and *yo* follows from the context; in others it is unambiguously evident from a grammatical element appearing in the sentence (as in the second and third examples). In English it is sometimes appropriate to render this use of *uno, una* by 'you'.

*¿La música?. . . ¡La adoro! – grita uno* (J. Camba, 1964: 64)
'Music?. . . I love it!' I/you shout

*– ¿Por qué no se arregla con don Pablo?*
*– Porque no quiero. Una también tiene su orgullo, doña Rosa* (C. J. Cela, 1963a: 32)
'Why don't you make it up with Don Pablo?'
'Because I don't want to. I've got my pride as well, Doña Rosa'
(The feminine form *una* is usual when it refers to a woman, but the masculine *uno* can also be found, at least when no ambiguity can arise)[2]

*Porque uno tiene su bachillerato completo, para que nadie me tutee ni se dirija a mí de esa manera* (R. Sánchez Ferlosio, 1971: 67)
No one's going to be rude to me or address me in that way when I've done all my school exams

The following example shows the subtle way in which *uno* can be identified with the first person idea:

*– Te quería preguntar si le gusta que las mujeres te lo digan.*
*– Bueno, claro que a uno le gusta – dijo Felipe, empleando el*
*«uno» después de vacilar imperceptiblemente* (J. Cortázar, 1981:
304)
'I wanted to ask you if you like women to say that to you'
'Well, of course one likes it,' said Felipe, using 'one' after an
imperceptible hesitation

In the following examples, *uno* has a first person plural
meaning:

*Pietro Crespi pidió que se casara con él.*
*– Por supuesto, Crespi – dijo –, pero cuando uno se conozca mejor*
(G. García Márquez, 1977: 90)
Pietro Crespi asked her to marry him.
'Of course, Crespi', she said, 'but when we know each
other better.'

*Los hombres hacen todo lo posible por acostarse con una y*
*cuando lo consiguen nos desprecian* (I. Allende, 1987: 210)
Men do everything they can to go to bed with you/us
(women), and when they've done it they despise you/us

**381** When *uno* denotes the first person singular, it can express a
nuance of modesty which cannot be rendered by *yo*.

*Uno no tiene competencia ni talla para hacer la gran historia de*
*la División Azul* (T. Salvador, 1968b: 26)
I do not have the competence or the ability to write the history of the División Azul (a group of Spanish volunteers who
fought with the German army on the Eastern Front in the
Second World War)

**382** The use of *yo* is also avoided in a sentence like the following
for the sake of modesty. A singular stylistic effect, not directly
translatable into English, is given by the contrast between the
impersonal *uno* and the third person pronoun *él*:

*Una es una señora y él es un tipo impresentable* (J. A. de Zunzunegui, 1952b: 168)
I am a lady and he is an unpresentable character

**383** *De uno* can also be used instead of a possessive pronoun,
as in:

*La historia de las culturas que no son de uno tiene, inevitablemente, mucho de silueta y de esquema abstracto* (A. Castro, 1970: 96)
The history of other people's cultures is, inevitably, fairly vague and abstract

*El hogar de uno es sagrado* (S. Lorén, 1967a: 58)
One's home is sacred[3]

## Alguno, ninguno, alguien, algo, nadie, nada

**384** *Alguno* and *ninguno* ('someone'/'no one', 'some'/'no') can be used, like *uno*, as pronouns or as adjectives, and vary according to number and gender:

*alguno, alguna, algunos, algunas*
*ninguno, ninguna, ningunos, ningunas*

### 385 *Alguno*

As a pronoun, *alguno* has the meaning of 'someone', or, in the plural, 'some (people)'. In the singular it is losing ground in modern Spanish to *alguien*.[4]

*Dale la carta a alguno que vaya para allá* (*DUE*, I, 132)
Give the letter to somebody who is going there

*Algunos no quieren creérselo* (*DUE*, I, 132)
Some don't want to believe it

See also **392**.

**386** As an adjective, *alguno* (*alguna*) in the singular is merely a variant of *uno*, sometimes with the nuance 'one or other'. Like *uno*, *alguno* is apocopated (to *algún*) before a masculine noun (sometimes even when the noun is preceded by an adjective: see fourth example) and sometimes before a feminine noun beginning in a stressed *a* or *ha*, e.g. *algún arma* 'some weapon'.[5]

*Algún sacerdote amigo* (V. Blasco Ibáñez, quoted in Fernández, 1951: 393)
Some friendly priest

*En algún rincón de mi calabozo* (P. Baroja, quoted ibid.)
In some corner of my cell

*Podría amasar algún dinero para la vejez* (ibid., 401)
I could amass some money for my old age

*Algún desagradable contratiempo* (*DD*, 29)
Some disagreeable setback

The plural *algunos, algunas* is equivalent to *unos, unas* (see **379**).

*Tengo algunos libros* (*Esbozo*, 412)
I have some books

**387** *Algunos, algunas,* like *unos, unas,* may be followed by *pocos, pocas*

*Lezama Lima, Nicanor Parra y algunos pocos más* (O. Paz, 1971: 38)
L.L., N.P. and a few others besides

## 388 (Alg)uno que otro

The compound form *alguno/a que otro/a* is only used in the singular. However, it has a plural meaning: 'some (but a few)', 'the occasional'. When a masculine noun follows, *alguno* is frequently, though not always,[6] apocopated (to *algún que otro*).

*Hasta entonces apenas si conocía algún que otro detalle sobre su vida y sus actividades* (R. Fernández de la Reguera, quoted in Coste and Redondo, 1965: 86)
Until then he scarcely knew any details about their life and activities

*Alguno que otro curioso se veía en lo alto de una azotea o en un balcón abierto pero pocos* (P. Baroja. 1946–51: II, 1339)
The odd busybody was seen on a rooftop or at an open balcony, but they were few and far between
(Note here how *pocos* refers to *alguno que otro curioso*, demonstrating its plural meaning. This construction should not, however, be imitated)

An alternative construction is *uno que otro*.

*Hemos hecho uno que otro viaje* (A. Bryce Echenique, 1981: 139)
We have made the occasional journey

Less commonly, the noun may follow *alguno* (or *uno*), in which case apocopation to *algún*, *un*, before a masculine noun is obligatory.[7]

> *Me como algún bomboncillo que otro* (F. García Pavón, 1980a: 15)
> I eat a small sweet now and again

> *Un alfiler que otro* (F. García Lorca, quoted in Fernández, 1951: 403)
> A pin or two

## 389 *Alguno* as a Negative

When *alguno* is used in negative sentences, it has the same meaning as *ninguno* 'no, not one'. It then follows the noun to which it relates. In this usage, *alguno* is almost always in the singular.[8]

> *Nicolás no formuló comentario alguno* (R. Garriga, 1980: 266)
> Nicolás did not utter a single comment

> *No creemos que 'El País' haya desatado campaña alguna contra el Gobierno socialista* (from a reader's letter in *El País*, 12 February 1983: 10)
> We do not believe that *El País* has waged any campaign against the socialist government

Equally possible would be ... *no formuló ningún comentario,* ... *haya desatado ninguna campaña* ... The construction with *alguno* is generally considered a stronger negative than *ninguno*.[9]

**390** *Alguno* also has a negative meaning in the expressions *en parte alguna* 'nowhere', *en modo alguno* 'not at all'.[10] *En ninguna parte*, *de ningún modo* would also be possible.

> – *Puedo sentarme allí perfectamente.*
> – *En modo alguno – dijo Elósegui* (J. Goytisolo, 1960: 48)
> 'I can perfectly well sit here.'
> 'No way,' said Elósegui

## 391 *Alguien*

*Alguien* is invariable and is used exclusively as a pronoun. Like its English equivalent 'someone', it can refer only to people.

*Alguien ha preguntado por usted*
Someone has been asking for you
*¿Ha llamado alguien?*
Has anyone called?

**392** According to some authorities,[11] *alguien* cannot be followed by *de* + noun or pronoun, and *alguno* must be used:

> *Hay alguno de ustedes que se atreve a gritar* ... (R. del Valle-Inclán, 1981: 69)
> There is one of you who dares shout ...
> *Alguna de esas princesas de teatro* (E. Benavente, quoted in *DD*, 30)
> One of those theatre princesses

## 393 *Algo*

*Algo* is invariable (but see **398**, third example). It practically always denotes things rather than people. It can be used in various functions.

## 394 *Algo* as a Pronoun

*Algo* 'something, anything', may be followed immediately by an adjective. An alternative to *algo* in this sense is *alguna cosa*.

> *Voy a ver si encuentro algo que comer* (alternatively *algo de comer*) (P. Baroja, 1946–51: I, 450)
> I'm going to see if I can find anything to eat
> *Nunca antes había visto algo igual* (C. Fuentes, 1979: 55)
> Never before had I seen anything like it
> *Le habrá dicho alguna cosa ofensiva* (R. Pérez de Ayala, quoted in Fernández, 1951: 387)
> He must have said something offensive to him

## 395 *Algo* + Adjective

| | |
|---|---|
| *algo caliente* | something hot |
| *algo malo* | something bad |

*Algo de* + adjective (not recommended, and considered by some purists as a Gallicism) is nevertheless found frequently in modern Spanish):[12]

*Ese pobre viejo podía haber cenado algo de caliente en el pueblo* (S. Lorén, n.d.: 245)
That poor old man could have had something hot for supper in the village

*¿Hay algo de malo en eso?* (R. J. Sender, 1967: 161)
Is there anything bad in that?

## 396  *Algo de* + Noun

The construction *algo de* + noun has the meaning of 'a little', 'some':

*Deseó, por un instante, tener algo de vino para ofrecerlo a las mujeres, cantar con ellas una canción alegre* (J. Goytisolo, 1960: 183)
For a moment, he wanted to have a drop of wine to offer the women and to sing a jolly song with them

*Su marido le enviaba algo de dinero* (A. Bryce Echenique, 1981: 206)
Her husband envied her some money

## 397  *Algo* as an Adverb

With a verb or an adjective (sometimes preceded by an adverb, as in the third example below), *algo* has an adverbial value. It then has the meaning of *un poco* or *un tanto* 'a little', 'rather'.

– *¿Conoces la potentación?*
– *Algo, señor* (M. Delibes, 1948: 31)
'Do you know about involution?'
'A little, sir'
(*algo* here implicitly qualifies a verb: *la conozco algo*)

*La señora se encuentra algo indispuesta* (A. Bryce Echenique, 1981: 207)
Madam is a little indisposed

*Paco Fernández encontraba un Desiderio algo muy cambiado* (I. Agustí, 1957: 14)
Paco Fernández found a very changed Desiderio

## 398 *Algo* as a Noun

*Algo* can also be used as a noun, and may be qualified by an adjective, as in the second example. Sometimes even the plural *algos* is found.

> *Un algo como la nostalgia de una infancia bruscamente rota se removía en mi interior* (M. Delibes, 1967: 85)
> Something like a feeling of nostalgia for a suddenly interrupted childhood stirred within me

> *Tenían en su aspecto un algo interesante* (C. Laforet, 1966: 32)
> They had something interesting in their appearance

> *Los historiadores sabemos algo y aun algos de las dificultades . . .* (C. Sánchez Albornoz, 1975: 72)
> We historians know something, and even more than something, of the difficulties . . .

## 399 *Ninguno*

See remarks on the syntax of negatives, **1291**ff.
*Ninguno . . .* is felt to be slightly stronger than *No . . . ninguno*.

## 400 *Ninguno* as a Pronoun

As a pronoun *ninguno* means 'no one' (though with this meaning *nadie* is more common[13] – (see **411**), 'none', 'not one', and has no plural.

> *Ninguno lo sabía/No lo sabía ninguno*
> No one knew

> *No me gusta ninguna de estas casas/Ninguna de estas casas me gusta*
> I don't like any of these houses

**401** *Ninguno* referring to persons may be used with a first or second person plural verb in the sense of 'none of us', 'none of you':

> *Todo el mundo tiene sus defectos. Ninguno somos una obra de arte* (C. J. Cela, 1971: 178–9)
> Everyone has their faults. None of us is a work of art

*Ninguno salís a tu padre* (M. Delibes, 1981: 146)
None of you takes after your father

## 402 *Ninguno* as an Adjective

*Ninguno* is apocopated to *ningún* in the same circumstances as *uno* and *alguno* (see **72** and **386**).[14]

*Ningún buen escritor usaría esta expresión*
No good author would use this expression

*Aquí no se puede traer ningún arma*
No weapons may be brought here

**403** As an adjective, *ninguno* means 'no', 'not one', '(not) . . . a(n)', '(not) . . . any'. Its use is sometimes strictly speaking superfluous and it simply reinforces the meaning of *no*. When a negative element (e.g. *no*, *sin*) precedes the verb (see **1293–1294**), *ninguno* may come before or after the noun to which it relates, the preceding position being more common.[15]

*No puede haber ninguna duda al respecto*
There can be no doubt about it

*– Probablemente – me decía con humor – ella no tiene alma ninguna* (R. J. Sender, 1969b: 121)
'Probably', I said laughingly to myself, 'she has no soul'.

**404** Before a noun complement, *ninguno* is stronger than *uno*.

*Ya no era ninguna niña* (C. J. Cela, 1963a: 270)
She was no child any more

*Casilda, por lo visto, no era ninguna tonta* (J. Donoso, 1980: 50)
Casilda was obviously no fool

**405** Another way of strengthening the negative meaning is to use a definite article or a possessive with *ninguno*.

*Iba a decir algo referente a la ninguna vergüenza de su padre, pero se contuvo* (J. A. de Zunzunegui, 1954: 283)
He was going to say something about his father's total lack of shame, but he contained himself

*Fleming y su ninguna esquivez ante el retrato* (E. d'Ors, quoted in Fernández, 1951: 414)
Fleming and his complete lack of bashfulness over the portrait

**406** *Ninguno* is nowadays generally used only in the singular. Use of *ninguno* in the plural, though on the decline and not to be imitated,[16] can still be found in modern writers: as in the singular, it may appear before or after the noun to which it relates.

*No podía hundirse en las pupilas negras del pintor ni en ningunas otras* (J. Donoso, 1980: 166)
She could not sink into the black pupils of the painter, nor any others

*Victorita no sentía deseos ningunos de golfear* (C. J. Cela, 1963a: 188)
Victorita had no desire to lead a loose life

## 407 Remark

The neologism *ningunear*, meaning 'ignore', 'belittle', originating in Mexico, is also found in Spain.[17]

*Mis obras eran «ninguneadas» en España* (J. Goytisolo, 1978: 32)
My works were ignored in Spain. (Goytisolo uses the noun *ninguneo* (1978: 138), and it also appears in *El País*, 30 September 1988:12)

## 408 *Nadie*

See remarks on the syntax of negatives, **1291**ff.

**409** Like *ninguno* (**401**), *nadie* may also be used with a first or second person plural verb:

*Comenzó a funcionar una consigna que no la sentíamos nadie como novedad* (J. L. Alcocer, 1978: 103)
An order which none of us felt was new came into operation

**410** *Nadie* 'no one' is invariable. It refers exclusively to persons and is only used as a pronoun.

**411** When *de* + noun follows, *ninguno* is preferred to *nadie* (as *alguno* is preferred to *alguien* – see **392**):[18]

> *Ninguno de Vds. ha protestado*
> None of you has protested

> *Ninguno de los oyentes ha protestado*
> None of the listeners has protested

**412** A humorous, stronger alternative to *nadie* is *ni Dios* (literally 'not even God').[19]

> *Plantaba el brazo en la mesa, y no se le doblaba ni Dios* (J. Goytisolo, 1981a: 59)
> He would plant his arm on the table, and no one at all could bend it

**413** The ironical combination *don Nadie* (with or without a capital letter) (see also **250**) has the meaning of 'a nobody'.

> *Quico no es nadie; un don nadie, un pobre diablo sin nombre* (M. Delibes, 1974: 73)
> Quico is no one; a nobody, a poor devil with no name

**414** Occasionally the plural *nadies* is found, in both the spoken and written language.

> *No tenemos que pedir favor a nadies. A nadies* (J. Icaza, 1980: 81)
> We do not have to ask any one a favour. Anyone (at all)

## 415 *Nada*

See remarks on the syntax of negatives, **1291**ff. The force of *nada* is stronger when it is in initial position:

> *El Curador, en fin, nada desembolsaría* (A. Carpentier, 1971: 20)
> The Curator, in short, would not give anything

**416** *Nada* is invariable (though see the unusual plural in **428**, fourth example).

## 417 *Nada* as a Pronoun

(As *algo* + adjective, see **395**). *Nada de* + adjective is similarly to be found, though is not recommended:

> *No ocurrió nada de particular* (**P.** Baroja, 1959: 176)
> Nothing in particular happened
> (More correctly: *No ocurrió nada particular*)

**418** In popular speech *nada* is sometimes shortened to *na*:

> *Pues no sabía na* (J. Goytisolo, 1981a: 57 and passim)
> No, he didn't know anything

**419** In colloquial Spanish, *nada* may be replaced by nouns denoting small things like *pepino* 'cucumber', *pelo* or *cabello* 'hair', or by *cosa* 'thing', to reinforce the negative idea:[20]

> *Esto no importa un pepino*
> This doesn't matter a jot

> *Me importa un bledo/No se me da un bledo* (*DUE*, I, 385)
> I don't care two hoots

## 420 *Nada* as an Adverb

*Nada* may qualify an adjective or an adverb and then has the adverbial meaning 'not at all'. It is a strong negative, and can also bring to the utterance a subjective vision which is absent from the neutral *no*.

> *Silvestre abría descomunalmente su nada pequeña boca* (S. Lorén, 1955: 282)
> Silvestre opened his far from small mouth gaping wide

> *Eliacim, ya nada me importa absolutamente nada* (C. J. Cela, 1958: 209)
> Eliacim, nothing is the slightest bit important to me now
> (The first *nada* is a pronoun, the second an adverb)

> *No me llevo nada bien con él* (*DD*, 267)
> I don't get on at all well with him
> (Seco notes that in popular speech *de* is sometimes found between *nada* and the element modified: *nada de bien*)

**421** *Nada* is used on its own in the spoken language to negate a verb, an adjective or a whole sentence.

> – *¿No te es simpático el capitalismo?*
> – *Nada* (J. A. de Zunzunegui, 1956b: 162)
> 'Is capitalism agreeable to you?'
> 'Not at all'

> *De embarazo, nada* (F. García Pavón, 1980b: 110)
> No question of being pregnant

**422** *Nada* in this sense is sometimes repeated to make the negative meaning even stronger.

> – *¿Para qué vamos a hablar con ellos?*
> – *¡Nada! ¡Nada! No hay que hacerles caso* (M. Aub, 1963: 144)
> 'Why should we talk to them?'
> 'No question of it: we don't have to take any notice of them'

**423** Note the common idioms *pues nada* and *y nada* 'right, OK'.

> *Pues nada, me voy*
> OK, I'm off

**424** *Nada de nada* in the spoken language (*na de na* (see **417**) in popular speech) has the meaning of 'absolutely not'. It often appears at the end of a sentence as a reinforcement of a preceding negative.

> *Toda su vida había andado buscando un poco de atención literaria sin conseguirla ... Nada, nada de nada* (R. J. Sender, 1972: 162)
> All his life he had gone around looking for a bit of literary attention but without getting it ... Nothing, nothing at all

> *El dialectólogo ya no encuentra ni cíclopes, ni sirenas ni nada de nada* (M. Alvar, 1982: 71)
> The dialectologist does not find cyclops nor sirens nor anything at all any more

**425** *De nada* is used as a standard reply to *¡gracias!* 'thank you' with the meaning of 'don't mention it', 'you're welcome'.

**426**  Note the adverbial expressions of time *dentro de nada* and *(a) cada nada*.

> *Al fin y al cabo esto se ha acabao* ( = *acabado*, see **2**) *y dentro de nada habrá de todo* (M. Aub, 1971: 239)
> After all, this business (= the war) is over and in no time everything will be available

> *Cada nada hacían nuevas obras* (F. García Pavón, 1971: 161)
> At every touch and turn they were doing new things

**427**  For *nada más* + infinitive see **1102**.

## 428  *Nada* as a Noun

*Nada* as a noun is feminine; it may be further qualified by an adjective, and is occasionally found in the plural (*nadas*).

The meaning varies according to whether *nada* is used with a definite or an indefinite article: *la nada* = 'nothingness' (cf. *la Nada* = 'oblivion'); *una nada* = 'something of little worth', 'a trifle'.

> *Nicolás montó su academia de iluminados. La llamó Instituto de Unión con la Nada* (I. Allende, 1984: 264–5)
> Nicolás set up his academy of the enlightened. He called it the Institute of Union with Oblivion

> *La vida tal como la presenta Kafka es la nada activa y burbujeante* (M. Peñuelas, 1969: 133)
> Life as Kafka presents it is active, bubbling nothingness

> *No tenía ni un marco, ni un kopec, ni una nada* (T. Salvador, 1968b: 365)
> He did not have a mark, a kopek, or anything at all

> *La vida para él era un paréntesis entre dos nadas* (A. Castro, 1973: 147)
> Life for him was an interval between two nothings

**429**  A noun derived from *nada* is *nadería* 'mere trifle'.

> *Papa Telmo le preguntó otras tres o cuatro naderías* (M. Delibes, 1987: 142)
> Papa Telmo asked him another three or four trifling things

## *Cualquiera*

**430** *Cualquiera* can be used as an adjective or a pronoun and may refer to people, animals or things.

It does not vary for gender, but does have a plural *cualesquiera* which is optional and is chiefly used in the written language.[21] *Cualesquiera* is also used as a singular in spoken Latin-American and Peninsular Spanish.[22]

In adjectival usage, *cualquiera* generally drops the *-a* (*cualquier*) before a singular noun (masculine or feminine) even when there is an intervening adjective[23] – but the form with *-a* is often used before a feminine noun (see second example below).

> – *¿Qué deseas comer?*
> – *Cualquier cosa* (A. Bryce Echenique, 1981: 205)
> 'What would you like to eat?'
> 'Anything'

> *De cualquiera manera, no son independientes* (C. Fuentes, 1979: 129)
> Anyway, they are not independent

> *Cualquier otro hombre* (*DD*, 125)
> Any other man

> *A golpes cualquiera entiende – agregó mi Madrina* (I. Allende, 1987: 66)
> 'Anyone understands with a beating'. added my godmother

> *Nosotros, quizá más que cualesquiera hombres en el mundo, nos sentimos identificados con nuestras respectivas naciones* (S. Lorén, 1971: 250)
> We, perhaps more than anyone in the world. feel identified with our respective nations

> *Vecinos de cualesquiera edad y condición* (E. Tierno Galván, 1984: 62)
> Residents of any age and social standing
> (This example is archaic in tone)

**431** *Cualquiera* can also follow a noun. In this case, the noun is always preceded by the indefinite article and *cualquiera* is never apocopated.

> *Un libro cualquiera* (*DUE*, I, 816)
> Any book

*Ése es el problema como diría un Hamlet cualquiera* (I. Malinow, 1983: 13)
That is the question, as any Hamlet would say

**432** *Cualquiera* sometimes has a negative (ironic) meaning, especially in exclamatory sentences.

*Si mi mujer viera aquello, ¡cualquiera la hacía regresar!* (J. M. Gironella, 1966a: 174)
If my wife were to see that, no one would make her go back!
(Note the conditional value of the imperfect tense *hacía* here – see **1013** and **1061**.)

*¡Cualquiera entiende a las mujeres!* (E. Jardiel Poncela, 1973: 68)
Who (i.e. no one) understands women!

**433** *Cualquiera* can also be used as a noun. It then has a pejorative meaning and is preceded by an indefinite article; its plural as a noun is *cualquieras*.[24]

*Y ahora un cualquiera, lo que se llama de veras cualquiera, se atrevía a quererse llevar a su hija mayor* (M. Aub, 1970: 53)
And now a nobody, a real nobody, was daring to want to take his elder daughter away

*No es un cualquiera* (C. J. Cela, 1963a: 42)
He's not just anybody

*Son dos cualquieras* (*DD*, 125)
They are two people of no account

The feminine *una cualquiera* is a euphemism for 'prostitute'.[25]

### 434 Remark

In concessive subordinate clauses (see **1065–1069**) a subjunctive is used after *cualquiera que*.

*Cualquiera que lo desee puede acompañarnos*
Anyone who wants can go with us

*Me encontrarás en casa, cualquiera que sea la hora*
You'll find me at home, whatever the time

## 435 *Quienquiera*

*Quienquiera* 'whoever' is an invariable pronoun in present-day Spanish, the older plural form *quienesquiera* and the apocopated form *quienquier* being hardly used today.[26] Its only use is with a following *que*.

Like *cualquiera que*, *quienquiera que* is followed by the subjunctive.

> *Quienquiera que sea, es un miserable* (*DD*, 317)
> Whoever he is, he is a poor thing

# *Todo*

**436** *Todo* varies in number and gender: *todo*, *toda*, *todos*, *todas*. Like *nada* (*na*), it has a reduced form (*to*) in popular speech.

## 437 Adjectival Use

When followed by an article or a demonstrative, *todo* has the meaning 'all', 'whole'.

> *¡Tráeme toda la información!*
> Bring me all the information!
>
> *La niña ha comido todo un pan*
> The child has eaten a whole loaf

> *Todos estos libros son míos*
> All these books are mine

*Todo el mundo* (or sometimes in Latin America *todo mundo*,[27] without the article) has the meaning of 'everyone'.

## 438 Remarks

In the written language, *todo* may be given emphasis by being placed after the noun to which it relates.

> *Lo exigía su hombría y la historia toda de España* (F. Díaz-Plaja, 1966: 186)
> His sense of honour and the whole history of Spain demanded it

*El vicario había recomendado particularmente esta oración porque juzgaba que en su estructura estaban contenidos los elemen tos todos de la vida humana* (J. M. Gironella, 1966a: 579)

The curate had particularly recommended this prayer because he considered that every single element of human life was contained in its structure

**439** The expressions *el todo París, el todo Londres, el todo Madrid,* etc.,[28] denote a social event made up of prominent people in the town.

*Entre el auditorio abundan también los rostros, bien conocidos, del «todo Madrid» de las letras, la economía y la política* (L. Carandell, 1970: 132)

Amongst the audience there was an abundance of well-known faces, the Madrid of letters, business and politics.

## 440 *Todo* 'Any', 'Every'

When *todo* immediately precedes a noun or noun phrase, it generally has the meaning 'any, every'.

*Puedes tomar contacto conmigo en todo momento*
You can contact me at any time

*Casi toda mujer tiene un sentido más que el hombre* (F. Umbral, 1981: 145)
Almost every woman has (or all women have) one sense more than a man

*Todo buen ciudadano debe ayudar a la justicia* (*DUE*, II, 1330)
Every good citizen should assist justice

It appears in the plural in a few set expressions, e.g. *de todos modos* 'in any case', *en todas partes* 'everywhere'.[29]

## 441 *Todo un, toda una*

This very frequent expression has a superlative value.

*Era todo un economista* (J. Camba, 1964: 75)
He was a complete economist

*No cabe duda de que (su madre) era toda una mujer* (J. M. Gironella, 1966a: 156)
There is no doubt that (his mother) was a fine woman

*Nada menos que todo un hombre* (title of a work by M. de
Unamuno)
Nothing less than a real man

## 442 *Todo* as a Pronoun

In the singular, *todo* has the indefinite meaning of 'everything'; in
the plural (*todos, todas*), it has the meaning of 'all' (people, animals
or things).

| | |
|---|---|
| *Todo le interesaba* | Everything interested him |
| *Todos lo habían visto* | They had all seen it |

## 443 Remark

*Todo* as an object requires the unstressed pronoun *lo* with the
verb.

*Todo era materia y la materia lo era todo* (R. J. Sender,
1969a: 179)
Everything was matter and matter was everything

*Lo sé todo* (M. Vargas Llosa, 1973: 257)
I know everything

*De Vicente Aleixandre lo había leído todo, lo sabía todo*
(F. Umbral, 1977: 109)
I had read everything, knew everything, about Vicente
Aleixandre

*Discutiéndolo y criticándolo todo soltaban a veces datos que se
referían a hechos verdaderos* (E. Líster, 1977: I, 143)
In discussing and criticising everything, they sometimes let
out things which related to real facts

There is a tendency today to omit the *lo*, as in the first part of the
following example, though this is strictly incorrect:

*Husmeó todo, lo miró todo, lo curioseó todo* (J. A. de Zunzunegui, 1956b: 308)
He sniffed everything, looked at everything and stuck his
nose in everything

**444** For *todos los que*, etc., see **349**.

## 445 *Todo* as an Adverb

*Todo* as an adverb is invariable and has the meaning of 'completely', 'very', etc.

> *Y se paseaban por delante de mis ojos hombres con las caras alargadas y serias, y otros de caras muy anchas; unos todo boca y otros todo orejas* (P. Baroja, *Vidas sombrías*, in *Obras completas*, VI, 1035)
> And there passed in front of my eyes men with long, serious faces, and others with very broad faces; some were all mouth and others all ears

> *Todo ojos la Juana, todo nervios el capataz* (A. Grosso, 1978: 210)
> Juana was all eyes, the foreman all nerves

**446** However, *todo* qualifying an adjective agrees in number and gender.[30]

> *Y Esther, toda roja, empezó a chillarme* (M. Delibes, 1969a: 168)
> And Esther, quite red, started to scream at me

> *Aquí tienes a tu madre, toda preocupada por tu tardanza* (*DUE*, II, 1330)
> Here's your mother, dreadfully worried because you're so late
> (*Todo* here has the value of *completamente, muy*)

**447** The adverbial expression *(no)* ... *del todo* has the meaning '(not) ... completely'.

> *Y me casaré con Chelo en cuanto esté restablecido del todo* (J. M. Gironella, 1966b: 546)
> And I will marry Chelo as soon as I am completely better

> *Cuando uno no se ha despertado del todo* (M. Puig, 1980: 36)
> When you haven't fully woken up

## 448 *Todo lo* + Adverb, *a todo* + Infinitive

The adverbial expressions *todo* + *lo* + adverb (or adverbial expression) *que* and *a* + *todo* + infinitive have a superlative meaning.

*La mujer comenzó a vestirse todo lo de prisa que su corpulencia le permitía* (J. Fernández Santos, 1977: 72)
The woman began to dress as fast as her stoutness allowed

*A todo meter bajó las escaleras* (C. Pérez Merinero, 1982: 115)
He went downstairs at full speed

### 449 *Todo* as a Noun

*El todo, un todo* mean 'the whole', 'a whole'. As a noun, *todo* can also be used in the plural.

*El todo es mayor que cualquiera de las partes que lo componen* (A. Bello, 1972: 115)
The whole is greater than any of the parts which comprise it

*La imaginación construye todos de cada una de sus partes* (M. Menéndez Pelayo, *Ideas estéticas*, quoted in *Esbozo*, 232)
The imagination constructs wholes from each one of its parts

## *Más* and *menos*

**450** *Más* and *menos* are invariable and correspond to English 'more' and 'less'.

*En tu jardín hay más árboles que en el mío*
In your garden there are more trees than in mine

*En Andalucía hay menos agua que en el País Vasco*
In Andalusia there is less water than in the Basque Country

**451** *Los (las) más de* means 'the majority', 'most'. The preposition *de* is sometimes omitted.

*Las más de las familias pagan los primeros meses* (R. del Valle-Inclán, 1981: 132)
The majority of families pay for the first few months

*Las más veces* (Fernández, 1951:445)
Mostly
(Or: *las más de las veces*)

*Los (las) más* can also be used as a pronoun in the sense of *la mayoría*:

> *Había mucha gente que gritaba sin parar; otros lloraban. Los más cantaban* (V. Pozuelo Escudero, 1980: 40)
> There were a lot of people who shouted ceaselessly; others wept. The majority sang

## *Mucho* and *poco*

**452** As adjectives and pronouns, *mucho* and *poco* vary in number and gender.

> *A causa de su mucha edad (Bernardo) había sido enviado a veranear...* (I. Agustí, 1944: 94)
> Because of his advanced age, Bernardo had been sent to take his summer holiday ...

> *Perdió la poca sangre que le quedaba* (*Esbozo*, 234)
> He lost the small amount of blood he had left

> *Tus muchas ocupaciones no te permiten atenderme* (J. A. de Zunzunegui, 1952b: 105)
> Your many jobs do not allow you to attend to me

> *Son ustedes muchos* (I. Agustí, 1944: 102)
> There are a lot of you

As an indefinite pronoun, *mucho* is invariable:

> *Mucho se espera de su prudencia* (A. Bello, 1972: 114, no. 355)
> We expect a lot of his discretion

### 453 Remarks

Besides the very frequent use of *un poco* + adjective 'a little', there is also the expression *un mucho* + adjective, which has the meaning of 'very', 'rather'. 'fairly' ('more than usual').

> *Empolló a Encarna con una mirada un mucho cínica* (J. A. de Zunzunegui, 1954: 61)
> He gave Encarna a very hard look

> *Bea piensa en este hombre, un poco irónico, un mucho reservón* (J. A. de Zunzunegui, 1952b: 48)
> Bea is thinking of this man with his touch of irony and his decided reserve

**454** *Mucho* and *poco* may give a 'mass' meaning to the noun, or may have a superlative meaning.

> *Mucho cuello* and *poca nariz* can respectively mean 'a long neck' and 'a (very) small nose' (both examples from Fernández, 1951: 387, n. 1)

> *Mire, don Pedro, que está usted equivocado. Que esa mujer es mucha mujer* (S. Lorén, 1975: 79)
> Look here, Don Pedro, you're mistaken. This woman is a terrific woman

> *Hay mucha España todavía por delante* (words of King Juan Carlos in Santiago de Compostela on 25 July 1983, taken from *Ya*, 26 July 1983: 1)
> There is a lot still to be done in Spain.[31]

G. Cabrera Infante plays on the different meanings of *mucho* in:

> *Mucha Margarita. Mucha mujer. Muchas mujeres* (1979: 645)
> Margarita, a woman of character. A real woman. Lots of women

**455** Similarly, *poco* used adjectivally can emphasize inadequacy or lack of quality.

> *El Opel-4 es poco coche para mí* (M. Delibes, 1969b: 162)
> The Opel-4 is not the car for me (i.e. is not good enough for me)

**456** *Mucho* and *poco* have no comparative forms with *más*. *Muy poco* exists (second example below) but *muy mucho* is rare.[32] The forms *muchísimo* and *poquísimo* exist, and can be used adjectivally, adverbially, or as pronouns; they can occur before *más* and *menos* with the meaning of 'very many more/less'.

> *Me pesan terriblemente los años, mis muchísimos años* (C. Sánchez Albornoz, 1977: 23)
> The years, my very many years, weigh terribly upon me

> – *Diga usted que me quiere un poco*
> – *Pero muy poco, muy poquísimo* (F. Arrabal, 1972b: 59).
> 'Say that you love me a bit.'
> 'A little bit, then, a very little bit.'

*Con decirte que Australia es mayor que Europa y tenía entonces muchísimos menos habitantes que España* (J. A. de Zunzunegui, 1958: 204)
And telling you that Australia is bigger than Europe and then had far fewer inhabitants than Spain

In the following example, *poquísimo* is preceded by the 'neuter' *lo*:

*Lo poquísimo que yo he presenciado aquí esta tarde* (R. Sánchez Ferlosio, 1971: 325)
The very little I've seen here this afternoon

**457** As well as *un poco de* + noun, the following constructions are also encountered in speech:[33] *una poca de* + feminine noun, *un poco* + noun, *una poca* + feminine noun.

*Sólo tomó a mediodía una poca de leche* (J. A. de Zunzunegui, 1959a: 53)
He only had a little milk at midday

*Que una poca de tinto levanta (un hombre)* (E. Quiroga, 1950: 202)
Because a drop of red wine picks you up
(The use of a feminine form *poca* before a masculine noun is strange. Perhaps the construction can be explained by understanding a feminine noun such as *cantidad* to be implied)

*He hecho ebullir en un tubo una poca orina* (S. Lorén, 1955: 370)
I have boiled a little urine in a tube

*Poco* may also take a diminutive suffix (see also **Affective Suffixes**) in such expressions:

*Con una poquilla leche* (F. García Pavón, 1980b: 47)
With a little drop of milk

Perhaps by analogy with *un poco de* the less common sequence *un mucho de* has been formed:

*Hay un mucho de magia en el lenguaje* (A. de Miguel, 1985: 132)
There is a good deal of magic in language

## Otro

**458** *Otro* varies in number and gender (*otro, otra, otros, otras*). It can be used as a pronoun or as an adjective and combines with *lo* to form a 'neuter' (see **64**, third example).

*Otro* cannot be preceded by an indefinite article: thus Spanish *otro* is the equivalent of English 'other' or 'another' (see **74**).

| | |
|---|---|
| *Me lo ha dicho otro amigo* | Another friend told me |
| *No veo otras posibilidades* | I cannot see any other possibilities |
| *Se fue con otro* | She went off with somebody else |

### 459 Uno(s) . . . otro(s), (el) uno y (el) otro

*Uno(s) . . . otro(s)* – with or without the definite article[34] has the meaning of 'one . . . another', 'some . . . others'.
The neuter *lo uno . . . lo otro* is also possible (as in the third example below).

> *Unos cantaban, otros bailaban* (A. Bello, 1972: 331)
> Some sang, others danced

> *De sus dos hijos el uno se dedicó a las armas y el otro a las letras* (ibid., 333)
> Of his two sons, one chose a military career and the other a literary one

> *Me ha sorprendido más lo uno que lo otro* (D. Ridruejo. 1976: 21)
> The one surprised me more than the other

*Unos . . . otros* – with or without an article – sometimes has the reciprocal meaning 'each other':

> *Amaos los unos a los otros* (*El Imparcial*, 19 August 1979: 5)
> Love one another

*(El) uno y (el) otro* has the meaning of 'both':

> *La una y el otro habían transformado rápidamente a la muchacha* (D. Ridruejo. 1976: 46)
> The two of them (one female, one male) had quickly changed the girl

*El peligro ronda siempre a uno y otro interesados* (F. Umbral, 1979: 117)
Danger always attends both those concerned

Note that genders can be mixed as appropriate in these constructions, as in the last but one above.

Other possibilities for the rendering of 'both' are *los dos* and (predominantly in the written language) *ambos, ambas,* together with the less frequently used alternatives *ambos a dos, entrambos, entrambos a dos.*[35]

*Salieron los dos*　　　　They both went out

*En ambas (telas) figura la cabeza ruda y obstinada de Cézanne* (E. d'Ors, quoted in Fernández, 1951: 460)
In both canvases Cézanne's rough, obstinate head appears

*Se les escapó (la cesta) de las manos y ambos a dos se precipitaron para detenerla* (A. M. de Lera, quoted in Coste and Redondo, 1965: 251)
The basket slipped from their hands and both of them rushed to stop it

*Entrambos extraen su energía y vitalidad de su imperioso egoísmo* (J. Goytisolo, 1977: 32)
Both drew their energy and vitality from their overriding egoism

*Ambos* is very rarely used with a definite article:[36]

*Los ambos detalles ...* (C. J. Cela, 1989: 8)
Both details ...

**460** The expression *una y otra vez* (or *una vez y otra*) has the meaning 'repeatedly', 'time after time'.

*Llegan a la conclusión de que teléfono es una palabra muy hermosa y la repiten una y otra vez* (F. Umbral, 1977: 133–4)
They reach the conclusion that 'telephone' is a very beautiful word and they repeat it time after time

**461** Expressions like *el otro día* 'the other day', *la otra noche* 'the other night' refer to a recent past (but further back than yesterday).[37] In some Latin-American countries *otro* refers to the future and means 'the following': *el otro domingo* 'the following Sunday'.[38]

## 462 Remarks

In some cases *otro* is close in meaning to *segundo* 'second':[39] *otra vez* 'again' = *una segunda vez*. In such expressions, *otro* can be replaced by *más*: *otra vez* = *una vez más*; *sin otra preocupación* = *sin más preocupación* 'with no other worry'.

**463** *Otro* is used pleonastically in a number of compound expressions involving demonstratives and numerals.

> *La señorita Elvira devolvió los dos tritones al cerillero: Y este otro para ti* (C. J. Cela, 1963a:55)
> Señorita Elvira gave the two cigars back to the match-seller. 'And this one here is for you'

> *Los precios del petróleo bajarán otros cinco dólares* (*Cinco días*, 7 May 1983: 25)
> Oil prices will drop another five dollars
> (*Otros cinco dólares* = *cinco dólares más*, with the implication of 'another five dollars')

**464** English speakers should bear in mind that another way of expressing the notion *de (los) otros* (chiefly in the written language) is by using the adjective *ajeno*.

> *El miedo ajeno ayuda a superar el propio* (C. Martín Gaite, 1981: 209)
> Other people's fear helps you to overcome your own

> *Estábamos en manos ajenas* (C. Pérez Merinero, 1982: 147)
> We were in the hands of others

(*Ajeno a* also has the meaning 'foreign to', 'beyond':

> *Por razones ajenas a mi voluntad*
> For reasons beyond my control)

## 465 Word Order with *otro*: With *tanto(s)*

Note the order of *otro tanto* 'such a thing' and *otros tantos* 'as many':

> *Carlos Murciano, en quince años de vida literaria, ha lanzado otros tantos libros* (*Estafeta literaria*, 15 May 1977: 16)
> Carlos Murciano, in fifteen years of literary activity, has launched as many books

*No puedes tú decir otro tanto de tu hijo* (R. J. Sender, 1967: 28)

You cannot say such a thing about your son

*Tantos otros* means 'so many others'

*Era también la hora de los odiadores, cuando venían el anti-Buero y el anti-Cela, y tantos otros antis* (F. Umbral, 1977: 123)

It was also the time of the 'haters', when the anti-Bueros and anti-Celas and so many other antis came along. (Refers to the modern Spanish writers A. Buero Vallejo and C. J. Cela)

### 466 Word Order with *otro*: With a Numeral

*Otro* (with or without an article) usually precedes a numeral.

*Los otros dos* (Fernández, 1951: 463)

The other two/the two others

*Otras dos mujeres brillantes del café eran María Antonia Dans y Eugenia Serrano* (F. Umbral, 1977: 126)

Two other brilliant women in the cafe were María Antonia Dans and Eugenia Serrano

*El español ha resistido a la autoridad en otras mil cosas* (F. Díaz-Plaja, 1966: 126)

The Spanish have resisted authority in a thousand other things

**467** The same order is possible when *otro* combines with *cualquiera*, *poco* and *mucho*.

*Fue día de trabajo como otro cualquiera* (F. Franco Araujo-Salgado, 1977: 96)

It was a working day like any other

*¿No quieres otro poco?* (J. Goytisolo, 1960: 200)

Would you like a little more?

*Las golondrinas y otras muchas aves inmigran en bandadas desde regiones más cálidas* (J. Valera, quoted in Coste and Redondo, 1965: 271)

Swallows and many other birds migrate in flocks from warmer regions

But note *otros muchos* or *muchos otros* 'many others', *otros pocos* or *pocos otros* 'few others', *otros algunos* or *algunos otros* 'some others'.[40]

*Otro(s)* always follows *alguno* and *ninguno*, except when *alguno* has a negative meaning (see **389**).

### 468 *Otro* in Comparisons

In comparative structures, *otro que* or *otro del que* 'other than' are used.[41]

> *El cura tiene otro invento que nosotros* (R. del Valle-Inclán, quoted in Fernández, 1951: 450)
> The priest has a different invention from ours

> *Aunque de otro orden del que enseñábamos* (*Boletín de la Real Sociedad Española de Historia Natural*, quoted in Fernández, 1951: 450)
> Though of a different order from the one we showed

## Démas

**469** *Demás* is an alternative to *otros* in the sense of 'others'. It can be used as an adjective or a noun and does not vary in number or gender.

> *Lo malo de la primera cana es que los demás pelos se contagian* (R. Gómez de la Serna, 1979: 252)
> The bad thing about the first grey hair is that the other hairs are affected

> *Un buen hombre es un hombre bueno para los demás* (M. de Unamuno, *Ensayos*. quoted in *Esbozo*. 235)
> A good man is a man who is good for others

> *Toda la demás gente lo vio* (M. Puig, 1980: 11)
> All the other people saw it

**470** *Demás* may appear without an article, but only at the end of a list, in the summarizing expression *y demás. . .*:[42]

> *. . . y demás camelos estúpidos* (A. D. Canabate, quoted in *Esbozo*, 235)
> . . . and all other stupid cock-and-bull stories

**471** The 'neuter' *lo demás* means 'the rest'.

*No me importa lo demás* (*DUE*, I, 884)
The rest is not important

**472** *Demás* may also be used adverbially in the sense of *además*:

*Tal interpretación plantea problemas y, demás, resulta ambigua* (E. de Bustos Gisbert, 1986: 232)
Such an interpretation poses problems and furthermore is ambiguous.

**473** *Demás* should not be confused with *de más* (see **584**).

## *Cada*

**474** *Cada* 'each, every' is invariable. It is normally only used adjectivally, although in the spoken language elliptical constructions like *cien pesetas cada* for *cien pesetas cada corbata* 'ties, a hundred pesetas each', may be heard.[43]

*Cada niño recibió su juguete* (*DUE*, I, 449)
Each child received his/her toy

*Cada oveja con su pareja*
Birds of a feather flock together
(lit. Each sheep with its mate)

*Cada otra contestación sería errónea*
Any other answer would be wrong

*Cada* is used before a numeral or expression of quantity to indicate frequency:

*Sólo llega una vez cada cien años* (G. García Márquez, 1977: 323)
It only happens once every hundred years

*Subieron despacio, parándose cada pocos pasos, pues el compañero se encontraba aún flojo* (J. A. de Zunzunegui, 1958: 125)
They went up slowly, stopping every few steps, because their companion was still weak

*Se subía cada poco las gafas con su dedo grueso* (F. Umbral, 1977: 118)
Every so often he pushed his glasses up with his thumb

*Alguien comentó que los pronunciamientos militares deberían hacerse cada cierto número de años* (J. Edwards, 1985: 92)
Someone commented that military risings should take place every certain number of years

*Note:* The use of *cada* as a synonym for *todos* is considered incorrect by purists. Thus *¿Tú vienes todos los días?* is to be preferred to *¿Tú vienes cada día?*[44]

*Cada* need not be repeated before each noun in a list:

*Cada hombre, mujer, anciano y niño fue empleado* (I. Allende, 1984: 59)
Each man, woman, old person and child was an employee

**475** *Cada uno (cada una)* and *cada cual* (also *cada quien* in Latin-American Spanish) have the meaning 'each (one)'.[45] A humorous alternative is *cada quisque*, or *quisqui*.[46]

*Ya desde el segundo domingo que se hizo baile cada uno tenía echado el ojo a cada cual* (S. Lorén, n.d.: 314)
From the second Sunday on which there was a dance each one had got his eye on a partner

*Cada quien tenía una explicación* (G. García Márquez, 1985: 458)
Each had an explanation

*Bermudo, que, si bien poseyendo como cada quisque, la palabra hablada, parecía haber enajenado el usufructo de ella* (R. Pérez de Ayala, quoted in Coste and Redondo, 1965: 268)
Bermudo, who, even though he had the use of speech like anyone else, seemed to find its use foreign to him

## 476 Remarks

*Cada* sometimes, especially in colloquial language, carries an implication of quantity.

*Que Dios te oiga, porque hay por el mundo cada granuja suelto* (J. A. de Zunzunegui, 1956b: 112)
May God hear you, for there are thousands of rogues about in the world

**477** In popular speech, and texts representing it, *cada* is sometimes shortened to *ca*.

> *En estos pueblos hay a lo mejor ca veterinario* (Beinhauer, 1968: 107)
> In these villages there is sometimes a vet (here in the meaning 'bad doctor')

## Bastante, demasiado, tanto, varios

### 478 Bastante

*Bastante* does not vary for gender. Its plural is *bastantes*. Its meaning is 'enough' or 'quite a lot'.

> *No tenemos bastante tiempo para hacer este trabajo*
> We haven't enough time to do this work

> *Había leído bastantes cosas mías* (P. Baroja, 1946–51: VII, 800)
> He had read quite a few things of mine

> – *¿Dispones de muchos datos?*
> – *Tengo bastantes.*
> 'Have you got much information?'
> 'I've got quite a lot (or enough)'

*Bastante* may also be used adverbially – see **572**.

**479** Although *bastante* normally precedes the noun, as in **478**, it may exceptionally follow:

### 480 Demasiado

*Demasiado* 'too much, too many' varies in number and gender (*demasiado, demasiada, demasiados, demasiadas*). It can be used as an adjective or as a pronoun.

> *Respiró profundamente y siguió diciendo: Hay ya demasiadas ruinas, demasiados muertos, demasiada hambre, demasiados sufrimientos* (A. M. de Lera, 1970: 192)
> He breathed deeply and went on to say, 'There are already too many ruins, too many dead, too much hunger, too much suffering'

*Los manifestantes son muchos, son demasiados* (C. J. Cela, 1967: 207)

There are a lot of demonstrators, too many

*Demasiado* can also be used as an adverb – see **577**.

## 481 Remarks

*Demasiado* sometimes has a weakened meaning which is little more than an alternative to *mucho*. It is regularly used in this way in Latin America.[47]

*Es curioso; no tenía demasiada sed, pero el agua me sabe buena* (S. Lorén, n.d.: 184)

It's funny; I wasn't very thirsty, but water tastes good

*Pío García no es muchacho de demasiada salud* (C. J. Cela, 1969: 314)

Pío García is not a very healthy boy

**482** In some cases, *demasiado* is preceded by a definite article. It then has the meaning 'excessive'.

*Si he sido duro contigo fue a causa de la demasiada tirantez de mis nervios* (C. Laforet, 1966: 262)

If I have been hard on you it was due to my nerves being over-tense

*Los demasiados cigarrillos . . .* (R. Montero, 1979: 130)

The excessive number of cigarettes . . .

**483** *Demasiado* may also give a 'mass' meaning to the noun it qualifies (cf. the use of *mucho* and *poco* in **454**):

*«Demasiada mujer para un solo hombre» había dicho de ella el capitán Jáuregui* (D. Medio. 1958: 38)

'This woman is too much for one man,' Captain Jáuregui had said of her

**484** The placing of *demasiado* after the noun in unusual, though may sometimes be found:

*En sus ojeras hay algo de cristal y en ellas sufre ella la transparentación de los amores demasiados* (R. Gómez de la Serna, 1979: 220)

The rings under her eyes are rather glass-like and through them she suffers her excesses in love being made transparent (The normal construction would be *los demasiados amores*. Through putting *demasiados* after the noun, the author is aiming at a special stylistic effect: *demasiados* has the meaning 'excessive in number and intensity')

**485** Note a particular use of *demasiado* (and *demasié*)[48] in recent Madrid slang:

– *Eres demasiado, oye* (F. Umbral, 1981: 13)
'You're a bit over the top, aren't you?'

## 486 *Tanto*

*Tanto* 'so much, so many' varies in number and gender (*tanto, tanta, tantos, tantas*). It can be used as an adjective or as a pronoun.

*No podíamos prever que iba a venir tanta gente*
We could not foresee that so many people would come

*Pero, ¿han venido tantos?*
But, have as many come?

*No tengo tanta suerte como él*
I am not as lucky as him

**487** For the use of *otro tanto* see **465**.

**488** *Tanto* can also be used as an adverb – see **574–576**.

## 489 Remarks

In certain cases *tanto* has a meaning similar to *mucho*.[49]

*Cada noche estudia hasta las tantas* (J. M. Gironella, 1966b: 222)
Every night he studies until very late
(*horas* is to be understood)

**490** After a numeral denoting a multiple of ten, *y tantos* indicates a greater number, the number and *y tantos* sometimes being written as one word.

*El regente tenía unos treinta y tantos años* (P. Baroja, 1946–51: I, 568)
The foreman (here, in a printing house) was thirty-odd

*Todos los años se van a veranear a Lequeitio hacia el veintitantos de junio* (C. J. Cela, 1969: 327)
Every year they go and take their summer holiday in Lequeitio about the twenty-something of June

*Muchos, pocos* or *más* may be used instead of *tantos*, especially in the expression of age:

*Con sus cuarenta y muchos años* (F. García Pavón, 1980a: 21)
With his being well over forty

*Un señor de unos cuarenta y más años* (C. Tellado, 1984: 76)
A man of forty-odd

*Tantos* also expresses an indefinite number in expressions like:

*Página tantas* (Fernández, 1951: 454)
Page such-and-such

**491** *Tanto* has a superlative *tantísimo*:[50]

*Hacía tantísimo tiempo que no se hablaba de aquello que hasta se había olvidado* (S. Lorén, n.d.: 12)
It was such a very long time since they had spoken of it that it had been almost forgotten

*Además, no hay derecho a pagar tantísimo por un interior* (A. Buero Vallejo, 1966: 48)
Besides, it's not right to pay such a lot for a room that doesn't look on to the street

**492** *Un tanto* has the value of an adverbial expression meaning 'a little', 'somewhat', synonymous with *algo* or *un poco*.

*Hoy me encuentro un tanto cansado*
Today I feel a bit tired

*Es un tanto gandul* (*DUE*, II, 1261)
He's just a little idle
(*DUE* comments that with a pejorative adjective like *gandul*, *un tanto* is ironic in meaning)

## 493 Varios

*Varios, varias* in its indefinite sense of 'several' can be used as an adjective or as a pronoun.

*Te lo he dicho varias veces*
I have told you several times

*Varios se marcharon antes del final de la función*
Several people left before the end of the function

**494** In the singular *vario* has the meaning of 'varying':

*Sucesos de varia fortuna* (*DUE*, II, 1442)
Events of varying fortune

This meaning extends to the plural in the written language; but *varios* in this sense appears after the noun:

*Gentes muy varias* (C. J. Cela, 1967b: 283)
Very various (i.e. differing) people

**495** *Varios, varias* may be replaced by *diversos, diversas* or *diferentes*. In the meaning of 'several' they appear before the noun:

*Hay diferentes/diversas soluciones*
There are several solutions

and in the meaning of 'different' they appear after the noun:

*Son dos soluciones diferentes/diversas*
They are two different solutions[51]

## Mismo

**496** *Mismo* varies in number and gender (*mismo, misma, mismos, mismas*).

### 497 *Mismo* as an Adjective: 'Same'

*Mismo* 'same' must be preceded by an article.

*Este cuadro es del mismo pintor* (*Esbozo*, 412)
This picture is by the same painter

*Eran mozos de una misma edad* (*Esbozo*, 412–13)
They were boys of the same age

The usage with the definite article is preferred today.[52]

### 498 *Lo mismo*

The adjective *mismo* can also be used with *lo*: *lo mismo* 'the same (thing)'. *Propio* can be used in the written language instead of *mismo*.[53]

> *Todos han dicho lo mismo/propio*
> They have all said the same

**499** *Lo mismo* is used adverbially in popular speech with the meaning of 'perhaps':

> *Lo mismo me toca el gordo* (Lapesa, 1980: 473)
> Perhaps I'll win the jackpot

### 500 *Lo mismo que*

*Lo mismo que* (or *lo mismo . . . que*) has the meaning of 'both . . . and' (compare *tanto(. . .) como*, **657**).

> *Después del verbo esperar se puede encontrar el indicativo lo mismo que el subjuntivo*
> After the verb *esperar* both the indicative and the subjunctive can be found

*Lo mismo que* also has an adverbial usage:

> *El plural del adjetivo se forma lo mismo que el del substantivo* (*Esbozo*, 180, n. 1)
> The plural of the adjective is formed in the same way as that of the noun

### 501 'Own'

*Mismo* can also have the meaning 'own' and as such is a synonym for *propio* (which is used for preference in the written language).[54]

> *Sería muy triste, tan triste como su misma historia* (C. J. Cela, 1963b: 238)
> It would be very sad, as sad as his own story
> (Or . . . *como su propia historia*)

### 502 '-self, -selves', 'Very'

*Mismo* may be used with an intensifying value after a personal, reflexive or demonstrative pronoun.

*Él mismo me lo dio esta mañana* (R. H. Moreno-Durán, 1981: 251)
He himself gave it me this morning

*Los solteros somos hombres que nos hemos casado con nosotros mismos* (M. Mihura, in F. Vizcaíno Casas, 1976a: 208)
We bachelors are men who have married ourselves

*En Roma, la mujer inicia la lenta reconquista de sí misma* (O. Paz, 1971: 14)
In Rome, women began the slow reconquest of themselves

– *¿Sabe quién le digo, verdad?*
– *¡Pues claro!, la morenita de gafas*
– *Esa misma* (E. Parra, 1981: 118)
'You know who I mean, don't you?'
'Of course! The little dark girl in glasses'
'Exactly: her'

**503** *Mismo* may also be used in this intensifying sense with nouns. It may precede or follow the noun, though the preceding position is preferred. *Propio* (preceding the noun) may also be found as an alternative to *mismo* in the written language and in affected speech.[55] An adverbial equivalent is often used in English translation.

*La RAE misma dice: ...* (A. Rabanales, 1984: 51)
The Real Academia Española itself says ...

*Los propios vecinos de Madrid se han hecho desidiosos* (E. Tierno Galván, 1984: 1)
The inhabitants of Madrid themselves have become slovenly

*En la misma Valencia no hay melón mejor que este* (*Esbozo*, 412)
In Valencia itself/Even in Valencia there is no better melon than this

(Note the alternative construction *En Valencia mismo ...* (ibid.). When *mismo* follows a place-name, it may be masculine even if the place-name is feminine, although modern usage tends to favour agreement in gender[56] – see **98**)

*En los propios Estados Unidos, en todas partes, se integran las familias judías* (C. Fuentes, 1979: 131)
Even in the United States, Jewish families are integrated everywhere

*Cuando un amor es verdadero ni la misma muerte puede nada contra él* (A. Casona, 1968: 100)
When love is true, not even death itself can have power against it

*Los mismos Reyes presenciaron la función*
The King and Queen themselves attended the function
(*Los Reyes mismos* ... is however possible)[57]
Note that *mismo* preceding the noun is ambiguous out of context, since it may also have the meaning of 'same'

*Pero en nuestros días mismos, un eminente lingüista ha escrito* ...
(F. Lázaro Carreter, 1980: 208)
But even in our own day, an eminent linguist has written . . .

**504** *Mismo* can also make an adverb of time, place or manner more precise: it is then invariable. In this meaning it follows the adverb:

*¿Por qué no lo dijiste ayer mismo?* (A. Casona, 1968: 106)
Why didn't you tell me *yesterday*?

*Aquí mismo os espero* (*Esbozo*, 412)
I'll wait for you right here

Note that if *mismo* precedes the adverb, it has the sense of 'even':

*Y además, mismo aquí, donde estamos ahora, ya no puede ir usted de la forma que va* (R. Sánchez Ferlosio, 1971: 154)
And besides, even here, where we are now, you can't go around dressed like that

## 505 Remarks

*Mismo* as an adjective has a (frequent) superlative form *mismísimo*.

*¿Pero si ha sido el mismísimo don Ventura el que me lo ha mandado?* (S. Lorén, n.d.: 164)
But is it Don Ventura in person who has sent it me?

*¡Este destino es el mimísimo demonio!* (C. J. Cela, 1967b: 118)
This destiny is the very devil!

*De esa manera Pilar podría visitar el piso en que vivió Mateo y tal vez pudiera trabajar en su mismísimo despacho* (J. M. Gironella, 1966c: 468)

In this way Pilar would be able to visit the apartment where Mateo lived and could perhaps even work in his study

*Este «desvelar», como habrán advertido mis lectores, es el mismísimo «dévoiler» francés* (J. Casares, 1961: 149)

This *desvelar*, as my readers will have noticed, is the very same as French *dévoiler*

**506** In the sense of '-self', *mismo* may take the suffix *-ito* to give a more emphatic meaning:

*Va todas las semanas una y dos veces hasta la mismita Francia con el tren* (J. A. de Zunzunegui, 1954: 497)

He goes at least once a week all the way to France by train

**507** The idea of 'even' is expressed twice (by *hasta* and *mismo*) in the following example:

*Hasta el mismo jefe de ellos, Trujillo, pide algo de comer* (A. M. de Lera, 1970: 167)

Even their chief, Trujillo, is asking for something to eat

**508** In popular speech, the form *mismamente* is sometimes encountered.

*Tú, una mujer casada con el hombre más bueno y honrado del barrio, porque el señor Benito es mismamente un ángel . . .* (J. A. de Zunzunegui, 1954: 158)

You, a woman married to the nicest and most honest man in the area, because Señor Benito is a real angel . . .

## 509 *Mismo* as an Adverb

*Mismo* is freely used as an adverb in Latin-American Spanish.[58] Here it can be found as an equivalent for *precisamente* 'precisely', *es cierto* 'it is certain', etc. Thus a sentence like *¿Ella mismo se va mañana?* has the meaning 'Is she really going tomorrow?'

**510** The phrase *ya mismo* is discussed in **610**.

## 511 *Mismo* in Comparisons

In comparative sentences, *(el) mismo* is normally followed by *que*. However, *de* and even *como* are sometimes found, though the latter (no doubt formed by analogy with *tan, tanto . . . como*) is censured by purists.[59]

> *Digerir es lo mismo que hacer la digestión* (*DUE*, I, 426)
> 'Digerir' is the same thing as 'hacer la digestión'

> *Los síntomas del amor son los mismos del cólera* (G. García Márquez, 1985: 98)
> The symptoms of love are the same as those of cholera

> *Ella es de la misma pasta como las demás mujeres* (*DD*, 262)
> She's made of the same stuff as other women

## 512 *El mismo*, etc, as a Pronoun

*El mismo, la misma, los mismos, las mismas* correspond to English 'the same (ones, etc.)'.

> *No siempre pueden ganar los mismos*
> The same people cannot win all the time

**513** In modern Spanish, *mismo* is increasingly used in expressions where strictly speaking a demonstrative, possessive, relative or personal pronoun ought to be used.[60]

> *En Madrid ha pronunciado una conferencia el embajador inglés. Al final de la misma el embajador afirmó que . . .* (J. M. Gironella, 1966b: 591)
> In Madrid, the British ambassador has given a lecture. At the end of it, the ambassador stated that . . .
> (More correctly: *Al final de la cual . . .* or *Al final de ella . . .*)

> *Le dije que tenía en mi poder las críticas, pero que, dado su poco interés y el carácter negativo de las mismas, no había considerado oportuno enviárselas* (F. Díaz-Plaja, 1966: 231)
> I told him that I had the criticisms to hand, but that in view of their being of small interest and negative in nature, I had not thought it opportune to send him them
> (More correctly: *. . . y su carácter negativo. . .*)

*Respecto a la ley de Peligrosidad Social recordó que la homosex-*
*ualidad ha desaparecido de la misma* (*El País*, 12 February
1983: 22)
With regard to the law of Social Perils, he recalled that
homosexuality has disappeared from it

## Tal

**514** *Tal* varies only in number (*tales*).

### 515 *Tal* as an Adjective

*Tal* with no article before a noun corresponds to English 'such a':
> *No quiero nada con tal individuo* (*DUE*. II, 1252)
> I don't want anything to do with such a character
> *Yo no he dicho tal cosa* (*Esbozo*, 217)
> I have not said such a thing

**516** *Un(a) tal* before a personal name has the meaning of 'a certain', 'one':
> *Los indios mataron a un tal Molina* (R. J. Sender, 1964: 178)
> The Indians killed a certain/one Molina

**517** *El tal* means 'in question':
> *El tal león es mayor que una montaña* (M. de Cervantes,
> 1960: 430)
> The lion in question is bigger than a mountain

**518** *Cual ... tal ...* corresponds to English 'like ... like ...':
> *Cual la madre, tal la hija* (*Esbozo*, 530)
> Like mother, like daughter
> (Also: *Tal la hija cual la madre*)

**519** *Tal cual* is similar in meaning to *alguno que otro* (see **388**)
'one or two, a few'. The usage belongs to the literary language.[61]
> *Valleruela es pueblo pobre, con algún que otro prado y tal cual*
> *viñedo* (C. J. Cela, quoted in Coste and Redondo, 1965: 271)
> Valleruela is a poor village with one or two fields and the
> odd vineyard

**520** After a noun, *tal cual* has the meaning of *pasadero*, *mediano* 'average'.

> *Es un muchacho tal cual* (*DD*, 5th edn, 322)
> He's an average boy

## 521 *Tal* as a Pronoun

*Tal* is sometimes used as a synonym for *tal cosa*, *esto*, *eso* 'such a thing'; but this use is now exclusively literary and is even considered archaic.[62]

> *No haré tal* (E. Martínez Amador, 1961: 1392)
> I will not do such a thing

> *No digo yo tal* (R. Pérez de Ayala, quoted in Fernández, 1951: 266 and *Esbozo*, 217)
> I do not say that

**522** After a definite article, *tal* may mean 'in question':

> *El tal, o la tal, se acercó a mí* (*DRAE*, 1371)
> The man (the lady) in question came up to me[63]

*Note: Una tal* can also mean 'prostitute'.[64]

**523** *Tal ... cual ...* has an indefinite meaning in the following sentence:

> *Habían clasificado al mundo. Tal era admirable; cual detestable* (P. Baroja, 1946–51: I, 381)
> They had classified the world. Such-and-such was admirable; such-and-such detestable

**524** *Y tal* has a rather vague meaning like English 'and so on', 'and that'.

An alternative to *y tal* is *y todo*. Both expressions belong to popular speech.

> *Es un chico alegre. ¡Vamos! Quiero decir amable y tal* (J. M. Gironella, 1966a: 123)
> He's a happy boy. Come on, I mean friendly and so on
> (Also: *... amable y todo*)

## 525 *Tal* as an Adverb

The interrogative adverbial expression *¿qué tal?* is especially common in speech; it has the meaning of 'how?', 'how are you?', 'what do you think?', or may be a general greeting (more informal than *¿cómo está(s)?*).[65]

> *¿Qué tal tolera usted la leche?* (J. A. de Zunzunegui, 1959b: 162)
> How do you stand milk?

> *No te había visto. ¿Qué tal?* (J. García Hortelano, 1967: 106)
> I hadn't seen you. How are you?

> *¿Qué tal ese libro?* (Beinhauer, 1968: 139, n. 27)
> What do you think of that book?

In popular modern Spanish, *¿qué tal?* is also used adjectivally:

> *¿Y tú qué tal persona eres, Adolfo?* (F. Umbral, 1985: 126)
> And what kind of person are you, Adolfo?

*Note: ¿Qué tal?* does not render English 'how' when this indicates manner; thus 'How did he die?' is NOT *¿Qué tal ha muerto?* but *¿Cómo ha muerto?*

**526** *Tal de* + adjective has the same value as *tan* + adjective 'so'. *Tal* may be omitted in this construction. The adjective agrees with the noun or pronoun to which it refers.

> *Tal estaba de nerviosa que no supo contestar*
> She was so nervous that she could not reply
> (Also: *Estaba de nerviosa que . . .* or *Estaba tan nerviosa que . . .*)

**527** *Tal como* or (more recently) *tal y como* reinforce the meaning of *como* 'as'. In *tal y como*, *tal* sometimes varies for number.[66]

> *El viaje iba saliendo tal y como lo imaginó* (J. M. Gironella, 1966b: 188)
> The journey was turning out just as he had imagined

**528** The colloquial formula *como si tal cosa* (or *como si nada*) has the meaning 'just like that', 'as if nothing had happened'.

For the adverbial expressions *con (tal) de que* 'provided that' and *tal vez* 'perhaps', see **1070** and **1027**.

## 529 Remark

The adverb *talmente* is only used in popular speech, and is synonymous with *como*.

> *Tienen ya un niño que es talmente un sol* (C. J. Cela, 1967b: 159)
> They now have a child who is a real treasure

## *Fulano*

**530** *Fulano* together with *Mengano*, *Zutano* and *Perengano* (feminine forms: *Fulana*, *Mengana*, *Zutana*, *Perengana*) are used instead of the name of a person which is unknown or which the speaker does not wish to use. They are always used as nouns. They are generally used in the above order, though this is not an invariable rule (see the third example).

> *Fulano, dicen, aparenta creer, pero es hipocresía* (J. Balmes, 1959: 63)
> They say that such-and-such a person appears to believe, but it is hypocrisy

> *Debían haberle dado el premio a Fulana y no a Mengana* (J. A. de Zunzunegui, 1959b: 30)
> They should have given the prize to so-and-so rather than to so-and-so

> – *¿Cuáles son los escritores favoritos de usted?*
> – *Zutano, Mengano y Perengano* (W. Fernández Flórez, 1967: 44)
> 'Who are your favourite writers?'
> 'What's-his-name, so-and-so and thingumybob'

**531** *Fulano de Tal* (*Fulana de Tal*) is sometimes used instead of *Fulano* (*Fulana*). This compound form may be combined with other (less usual) alternatives, as in the second and third examples.

> *Fulano de Tal os conseguirá una colocación* (J. M. Gironella, 1966a: 511)
> So-and-so will get you a post

*Desde tal día no sabemos nada de Fulano de Tal. Quisiéramos saber el paradero de Zutano de Cual* (J. L. Castillo Puche, 1956: 234)
We have no knowledge of so-and-so from that day. We want to know the whereabouts of such-and-such

*Fulano de Tal se negó a recibir los auxilios de la religión y murió desesperado, mientras Mengano de Cual confesó y comulgó con gran fervor, muriendo feliz y resignado* (C. J. Cela, 1983: 144)
Such-and-such refused to receive the comforts of the faith and died without hope, while such-and-such confessed and made his communion very fervently, dying in a state of content resignation

**532** *Fulano* is sometimes used as a noun. It can then be accompanied by a definite or indefinite article and/or an adjective, and it may be pluralized. The meaning is often pejorative,[67] or at least ironical. It is written without a capital letter.

*Sebastián tardó un par de minutos en comprender que le había insultado el fulano del volante* (S. Lorén, 1967b: 152)
It took Sebastián a couple of minutes to realize that the guy behind the steering wheel had insulted him

*Es indudable que estos fulanos tan conocidos se equivocaban* (S. Lorén, 1955: 117)
There is no doubt that these very well-known characters were wrong

*Una casa de fulanas* is a euphemism for *burdel* 'brothel', and *fulana* a euphemism for *puta* 'prostitute'[68]

*No es novia, eso; es una fulana* (M. Delibes, 1967: 191)
She's no fiancée, that one; she's a tart

## 533 Remark

A diminutive suffix (usually *-ito*) may be added to the above words.

*¡Qué guapetona está usted, Fulanita!* (C. J. Cela, 1963a: 26)
You're looking pretty, darling!

*Me había conocido cuando la Fulanita y la Zutanita llamaban la atención en Madrid por su elegancia y por sus joyas* (P. Baroja, 1952: 7–8)
He had got to know me when A—— and B—— were causing a stir in Madrid with their fine clothes and jewels

## Sendos

**534** *Sendos* (feminine: *sendas*) is used only in the plural (but see **535**), and has the distributive meaning 'each'. It is used most frequently in the literary language.[69] pronominal constructions with *cada uno* or *cada cual* being preferred in the spoken language.

*Don Antonio y Alvaro, en el despacho, beben sendos vasos de vino* (E. Quiroga, 1950: 224)
Don Antonio and Alvaro drink a glass of wine each in the office
(Or: . . . *beben cada uno un vaso de vino*)

*Rogelio se pegó sendas palmadas en las rodillas* (J. M. Gironella, 1971: I, 288)
Rogelio slapped both hands on his knees

*Pasó un sacerdote y luego tres monjas con sendas carteras de mano* (J. A. de Zunzunegui, 1959a: 166)
A priest and then three nuns passed by, each with their briefcase

## 535 Remark

*Sendos* is used today as a synonym for *repetidos* 'repeated' or *descomunales* 'enormous' though this usage is considered incorrect.[70]

*Le dio sendas bofetadas* (Alcina Franch and Blecua, 1975: 669)
He gave him some great blows
(According to the authors, the meaning of *sendos* here is *fuertes* 'strong', 'hard')

*Alguien se bebió un sendo vaso de vino* (Alonso and Henríquez Ureña, 1955: 77)
Someone drank down a prodigious glass of wine

# Impersonal Expressions

536 Introduction

## 536 Introduction

Spanish has various devices for rendering the idea of 'one', 'somebody', 'you', 'they', 'people', etc.

## Use of the Reflexive Pronoun *se*

**537** *Se* followed by a third person singular verb avoids the need for the explicit mention of a subject.

> *Se quiere colgar una escultura de Chillida en la Universidad* (*ABC*, 16 May 1978: 34)
> They want to hang a carving of Chillida in the University

> *Cuando se sueña se está completamente solo* (M. Puig, 1980: 11)
> When you dream you are completely alone

> *¿Se es consejero de Estado para siempre?* (F. Umbral, 1985: 161)
> Is one a counsellor of state for ever?

> *Se ve a las alumnas desde el despacho* (Alcina Franch and Blecua, 1975: 918)
> The pupils can be seen from the office

> *Son sitios donde se bebe, se charla, y siempre se encuentra algo que celebrar* (*Cambio 16*, 21 May 1978: 83)
> They are places where people drink and chat and always find something to celebrate

The rule for the position of *se* given in **273** (i.e., that *se* precedes all other pronouns) continues to hold:

> *No se os puede dejar solos* (F. Vizcaíno Casas, 1978: title page)
> You cannot be left alone

**538** The verb may be plural when there is a plural direct object – see also the remarks on the 'reflexive passive' (**1022**).

> *Se edifican muchas casas en este barrio* (Alcina Franch and Blecua, 1975: 918)
> A lot of houses are being built in this area

However, a singular verb is also possible in this case (*se edifica casas*). The construction with the plural verb is felt to be equivalent to a passive whereas that with the singular verb is felt primarily to imply an unspecified subject. Thus, appropriate translations might be:

| | |
|---|---|
| *Se venden botellas* | Bottles (are) for sale |
| *Se vende botellas* | People are selling bottles |
| | |
| *Se alquilan coches* | Cars (are) for hire |
| *Se alquila coches* | People are hiring out cars |

There is also a difference in register: the plural construction is recognized as more correct and is preferred in the literary language,[1] whereas the singular construction is widely considered incorrect by many linguists. However, the latter has now become so common in the spoken language and in advertising that it must be accepted as equivalent to the plural construction.[2]

The preference for the singular is noticeable in Latin America, where the influence of the written language is less significant than in Spain. Compare:

> *En muchos países se conocen mis filmes* (F. Arrabal, in *El País*, 4 December 1980: 56) (Spain)
> My films are known in many countries

> *En el Ejército no se puede cometer errores* (M. Vargas Llosa, 1973: 264) (Latin America)
> In the Army you can't make mistakes

## Use of the Third Person Plural

**539**  When the third person plural is used to render the idea of the indefinite subject *se* is not used and the verb has no subject pronoun. Often a plural subject is implied.[3]

> *Anuncian la caída del Ministerio* (A. Bello, 1972: 226)
> The fall of the Ministry is being announced

> *Cuentan pormenores alarmantes de lo ocurrido* (*Esbozo*, 382)
> Alarming details of the incident are being related

In English a literal translation is usually possible and sometimes more appropriate:

> *Dicen que llueve*
> They say it's raining

> *Dicen que a todas las suegras las van a tirar al mar* (Carrascal, popular song in *Canciones populares españolas*, 35)
> They say they'll throw all mothers-in-law into the sea

**540**  The verb can be in the plural even if it is known that the subject is really singular.

> *Dispararon un tiro* (*Esbozo*, 382)
> A shot was fired (only one person could have fired it)

> *Llamaron al teléfono y Gloria lo cogió con presteza* (C. Martín Gaite, 1980: 116)
> The telephone rang (presumably only one person was ringing) and Gloria picked it up quickly

## Use of a Second Person Singular

**541**  The *tú* form in Spanish (usually only the verb-form, without the subject pronoun) is used in colloquial Spanish rather like English 'you'.

> *No te das cuenta. Y de pronto te encuentras con que te han engañado. Luego te convences de que es inútil* (Beinhauer, 1968: 142, n. 31a)
> You don't realise. And suddenly you find out they've fooled you. Then you persuade yourself it's useless

This construction is unusual in Latin-American Spanish, however, where such sentences would be interpreted as referring literally to the familiar second person singular.[4]

## Use of the First Person Plural

**542** The first person plural form is used rather like English 'we'.

> *Vemos vagamente la catedral a través de una cortina de agua* (Azorín, quoted in Lapesa, 1970: 142)
> We see the cathedral vaguely through a curtain of water

The connection between the impersonal *se* and the first person plural is illustrated in the following example, where the two alternate:

> *Se cantaba y se gritaba. Otras veces, se iba en silencio, como si todos cantásemos por lo bajo* (J. García Hortelano, 1979: 15)
> Folk were singing and shouting. At other times, one went along in silence as if singing to oneself

## Use of *uno*

**543** See also **378**.

*Uno* corresponds to English 'one'. It is often used to express an indefinite subject when the verb is reflexive, since the impersonal *se* cannot be used in this case:

> *Con esos cordones no puede ahorcarse uno* (R. J. Sender, 1970: 240)
> You couldn't hang yourself with these laces
> (*\*No se puede ahorcarse* is impossible)

**544** In many cases where *uno* is used, it appears to be 'personalized' in that it implies an involvement of the speaker in the situation (see also **380–383**).

Spanish *uno* is extremely versatile: it optionally varies for gender (feminine: *una*); it may be the second term of a comparison; it can be a complement, a direct or indirect object; it can be followed by *mismo*, and it can (exceptionally) follow the verb as a subject (see eighth example).

*La vida es más corta de lo que uno cree* (G. García Márquez, 1977: 322)
Life is shorter than one thinks

*Una nunca sabe en primavera . . . , en realidad, una jamás sabe nada* (J. Donoso, 1980: 185)
One never knows in springtime . . . actually, one never knows anything
(The speaker is female)

*Siempre se cree que los demás soportan las enfermedades y las desgracias con más facilidad que uno* (P. Baroja, 1946–51: I, 1368)
One always thinks that others bear illnesses and misfortunes more easily than oneself

*El hogar de uno es sagrado* (S. Lorén, 1967a: 58)
One's home is sacred

*Así, en la vida, muchas veces no se sabe si es uno que empuja los acontecimientos, o si son los acontecimientos los que le arrastran a uno* (P. Baroja, 1946–51: I, 552)
So, in life, you often do not know whether it is you who are pushing events or whether it is events that are dragging you along with them

*A uno nunca se le hubiera ocurrido pensar que . . .* (M. Delibes, 1968b: 187)
It would never have occurred to you to think that . . .

*El orden familiar, el respeto a uno mismo, y a los demás, quedaba a salvo* (G. García-Badell, 1971: 227)
Domestic order, respect for oneself and for others, remained safe

*Dichoso pueblo este, donde ni dormir puede una* (J. Fernández Santos, 1977: 37)
This damned village, where one can't even sleep
(The speaker is female)

*Uno va a besar a una. Los dos guapos y bien peinados* (R. J. Sender, 1970: 140)
Boy is going to kiss girl. Both attractive and well-groomed

*El gran negocio consiste en que trabajan otros para uno* (J. A. de Zunzunegui, 1954: 530)
The great thing is to have other people working for you

## El personal

**545** *El personal* is currently sometimes found as a slang equivalent to *uno* or other impersonal expressions such as *la gente*.[5] It is used in various ways.

> *En una época donde el personal no respeta nada...* (*Cambio 16*, 4 April 1983: 121)
> At a time when people respect nothing...

> *El candidato de AP machaca al personal* (*Cambio 16*, 9 May 1983: 162)
> The Alianza Popular (a right-wing Spanish party) candidate crushes people

F. Umbral notes that *el personal* is used in *cheli* speech (a young people's slang) to mean *amigos íntimos* 'intimate friends':

> *Saca el whisky para el personal* (F. Umbral, 1983: 81 and 235)
> Get the whisky out for my mates

But it can even be found in higher registers:

> *La costumbre, muy arraigada en el personal, de leer a los costumbristas* (A. Mingote, 1988: 11)
> The custom, which is very deep-rooted amongst my colleagues, of reading the *costumbristas*
> (From an entrance speech to the Real Academia Española)

*Note: El personal* is otherwise used in the standard language with the meaning of 'staff': *el personal docente* 'teaching staff', *personal subalterno* 'auxiliary staff'.

# The Adverb

## Forms

**546** From the formal point of view, there are two kinds of adverb in Spanish:

(1)  Adverbs regularly derived from adjectives, characterized by the ending *-mente*.
(2)  Uninflected adverbs (i.e. with no characteristic ending).

Spanish adverbs are invariable (apart from diminutive and augmentative suffixation, e.g. *lejos* – *lejitos*: see **1323**).

## Adverbs Derived from Adjectives

**547** Adverbs can be formed from most adjectives in Spanish by adding *-mente* to the feminine singular (though it must be remembered that many adjectives have the same form in the feminine as in the masculine). Such adverbs preserve any written accent that the adjective may bear (see the second and third examples).

| | | | | |
|---|---|---|---|---|
| *claro*<br>'clear' | → | *clara* | → | *claramente* |
| *rápido*<br>'fast' | → | *rápida* | → | *rápidamente* |
| *fácil*<br>'easy' | → | *fácil* | → | *fácilmente* |
| *inteligente*<br>'intelligent' | → | *inteligente* | → | *inteligentemente* |

## 548 *Mayormente*, etc.

Adverbs in *-mente* can also be formed from comparative adjectives.

| | | |
|---|---|---|
| *mayor* 'bigger' | → | *mayormente* 'chiefly' |
| *superior* 'higher' | → | *superiormente* 'in the best way' |

## 549 Adjective + *-ísimo* + *-mente*

*-Mente* can also be added to superlative adjectives in *-ísimo*. Prudence is advised in the handling of these forms which are nevertheless used by many Spanish authors. M. Aub has *firmísimamente* 'very firmly' (1971: 101); G. Diego talks of *un amigo buenísimamente intencionado* 'a very well-intentioned friend' in *El soneto de ochenta, Estafeta literaria*, 620, 15 September 1977: 7, and the eight-syllable form *matizadísimamente* 'very finely nuanced' is to be found in D. Alonso, 1974: Introduction, p. 20.

**550** Adverbs in *-mente* are sometimes formed from personal names: *joseantonianamente* < *José Antonio (Primo de Rivera)*, founder of the Falange (example in F. Umbral, 1980: 70), *d'orsianamente* < *Eugenio d'Ors*, Catalan author (example in G. Díaz-Plaja, 1981: 135), *verlenianamente* < *Paul Verlaine*, French poet (example in F. Umbral, 1977: 121), *dostoievskianamente* < *Dostoievsky*, Russian novelist (example in J. Cortázar, 1974: 208).

These adverbs chiefly have the meaning of 'in the style of . . .' and are similar to the expression *a lo* . . . (see **66**).

Note that such adverbs, like the corresponding adjectives, are written with a small letter.

## 551 *Buenamente* and *malamente*

Although *bien* and *mal* are the normal adverbs associated with the adjectives *bueno* and *malo*, the relatively infrequent *buenamente* and *malamente* also exist. They generally have a special meaning, implying respectively 'easily', 'without much difficulty', 'voluntarily', and 'wrongly', 'poor', 'difficult'. They are almost always placed before the verb.

> *Anselmo estiró las piernas por donde buenamente pudo* (T. Salvador, 1968b: 34)
> Anselmo stretched his legs wherever he conveniently could

*Has estado acostumbrado a recibir lo que buenamente te man-*
*dan tus administradores* (J. Icaza, 1980: 9)
You have been used to getting what your administrators
choose to send you

*Un cuadro malamente atribuido a Velázquez* (Van Dam,
1967: 311)
A picture erroneously attributed to Velázquez

*Recordó lo malamente que había sacado dinero* (J. Marsé,
1982: 191)
He remembered with what difficulty he had got money

*Una comedia de Lope malamente traducida al francés* (R. J. Sender, 1972: 159)
A play of Lope's poorly translated into French

However, *malamente* can occasionally be found with the meaning
of 'badly' normally expressed by *mal*:[1]

*Y acabó malamente* (F. Quiñones, 1979: 202)
And it turned out badly (concerning a woman who died after
an operation)

## 552 Recién

The abbreviated form *recién* is used in the sense of *recientemente*
before adjectives and past participles.

| | |
|---|---|
| *recién afeitado* | clean shaven |
| *recién casado* | newly wed |
| *recién libre* | just freed |
| *recién llegado* | newly arrived |
| *recién muerto* | recently died |
| *recién nacido* | newborn |
| *recién limpio* | recently cleaned |

(On the use of *limpio* for *limpiado*, see **1225–1226**.)

*¿Qué cosa no estaba recién limpia, recién doblada, recién guar-*
*dada en su sitio?* (C. Martín Gaite, 1981: 87)
What was not recently cleaned, recently folded and recently
put away in its place?

In Latin America, *recién* is often used alone[2] to indicate a recent
past or a close future moment, with meanings like 'a short time
ago', 'just', etc.

*Recientito*, the diminutive form, is also sometimes found.

*Recién* is sometimes used pleonastically with other expressions which have approximately the same meaning.

> *Recién salía Prestes en libertad* (P. Neruda, 1976: 427)
> Prestes was recently set free

> *Recuerdo que se lo trajeron recién, apenas ayer* (J. Rulfo, 1981: 95)
> I remember that they brought it him recently, only yesterday

> *Beatriz recién me va a llamar dentro de dos horas* (A. Bryce Echenique, 1981: 156)
> Beatriz is going to ring me shortly, in the next two hours

**553** The apocopated form *recién* is also occasionally found before nouns which denote a state.

> *La recién viuda no está en casa, no ha vuelto* (M. Aub, 1970: 89)
> The widow is not at home, she has not returned

## Adjectives as Adverbs

**554** Some adjectives are regularly used as adverbs (see **199–203**).

### 555 *Medio*

*Medio* is a special case; it is used adverbially (and hence is invariable) before adjectives, nouns, past participles and gerunds:

> *Frieda estaba medio desnuda en el diván* (J. C. Onetti, 1979: 109)
> Frieda was lying half-naked on the couch

> *Mi mujer está medio convencida* (J. Fernández Santos, 1977: 61)
> My wife is half-convinced

> *Habrán sido medio novios* (C. Martín Gaite, 1981: 144)
> They must have been half-engaged

> *La medio novia de Gerard Ospino se llamaba Carlos* (C. J. Cela, 1988: 200)
> The name of the half-fiancée of Gerard Ospino was Carlos

In the spoken language, especially in Latin-America, *medio* often agrees in such cases, e.g. *media muerta* 'half-dead'.[3]

## Sequences of Adverbs

**556** As a rule, a sequence of adverbs in -*mente* in the same sentence is avoided, especially in the written language.[4] Only the last adverb of the sequence has the full form, and the feminine singular adjective is used for the preceding adverbs. Such sequences of adverbs can be separated by commas or by short conjunctions (*o*, *y*, *pero*, *como*, etc.).

> *Lo vio avanzar en la sombra, ridícula, minuciosamente vestido de blanco* (J. C. Onetti, 1979: 149)
> He saw him moving forward in the shadow, ridiculously, meticulously dressed in white

> *Impensada pero providencialmente, recibió una carta de Manuel* (C. Rojas, 1982: 81–2)
> Unexpectedly, but providentially, he received a letter from Manuel

> *Por todo ello, la manifestación era, inevitable, lógica, fatalmente, una convocatoria destinada a despertar cada año menos entusiasmos* (F. Vizcaíno Casas, 1978: 198)
> Because of all this, every year the demonstration was inevitably, but naturally and irrevocably, doomed to excite less enthusiasm

> *España entera se descomponía política, social, moral y territorialmente* (J. L. Comellas, 1967: 567)
> The whole of Spain was decomposing politically, socially, morally and territorially

## 557 Remark

It has already been noted (**203**) that some adjectives also function as adverbs (e.g. *hablar alto* 'to talk loudly', *hablar claro* 'to talk clearly', etc.). Hence in the following example, the masculine adjective is in fact an adverb in its own right:

*Hablemos claro y fraternalmente* (*El Imparcial*, 10 May
1980: 1)
Let us speak clearly and in a brotherly way
(One could of course also say: *Hablemos clara y fraternalmente*)

Similarly, in the following example, the adverb in *-mente* combines with an uninflected adverb:

*Camilo entra despacio y solemnemente* (M. Tudela, 1970: 42)
Camilo came in slowly and solemnly

Two adverbs ending in *-mente* may not stand together even when
one might modify the other: thus *\*lo hiciste extraordinariamente
hábilmente* ('you did it extraordinarily cleverly') is unacceptable.
(But *lo hiciste muy hábilmente*, where the modifying adverb *muy*
does not end in *-mente*, is acceptable.)

**558** In practice, the rule given in **556** is not always adhered to. In
the written language especially, authors may use a sequence of
adverbs in *-mente* for greater clarity (first example below), or to
achieve a more emphatic or other stylistic effect (second and third
examples). A sequence of forms in *-mente* can lead to a 'heavy' style
and give a monotonous acoustic effect, as in the fourth and fifth
examples (a feature no doubt intended by the author and characteristic of him).

*Un gran número de ejemplos que fonéticamente, formal y semán-
ticamente parecen compuestos deberían ser excluidos del estudio*
(E. de Bustos Gisbert, 1986: 19)
A large number of examples that phonetically, formally and
semantically seem to be compounds ought to be excluded.

*Dijo Tim tenuemente, sumisamente* ... (M. Delibes, 1967: 170)
Tim said weakly and submissively ...

*Todo se decía a gritos, impacientemente, nerviosamente, colérica-
mente* (J. L. Castillo Puche, 1956: 93)
People were shouting everything they said, impatiently
and nervously

*La vida nos da la mejor oportunidad de transformarla
humanamente, estéticamente, socialmente, literariamente* (F.
Umbral, 1972: 12)
Life itself gives us the best opportunity of changing it in a
humane, aesthetic, social and literary way

> *Los niños habían escuchado aquellos párrafos miles de veces rutinariamente, aburridamente, cotidianamente* (F. Umbral, 1980: 144)
> The children had heard those paragraphs thousand of times, routinely, boringly, daily

The pursuit of a stylistic effect is clear in the following sentence, where both the meaning of the word and its repetition make the gradualness of the process apparent:

> *La torre se inclinaba progresivamente, progresivamente, progresivamente* ... (E. Jardiel Poncela, 1946–51: IV, 537)
> The tower began to lean more and more and more ...

## Uninflected Adverbs

**559** Adverbs in *-mente* are generally adverbs of manner, denoting the way in which something is done, whereas uninflected adverbs are more varied in function.

Some uninflected adverbs have an interrogative usage (e.g. *¿cuándo?, ¿dónde?, ¿cómo?*): when used in direct or indirect questions these adverbs, like other interrogatives, bear a written accent (see **12**). Many of the same uninflected adverbs may also have a relative function.

Some inflected adverbs belong to more than one meaning category: *ya*, for example, can be an adverb of time or an adverb of confirmation.

## Adverbs of Manner

### 560 Forms

Besides the adverbs in *-mente*, the following common adverbs of manner may be mentioned:

| | |
|---|---|
| *así* | thus, so |
| *bien* | well |
| *¿cómo?* | how? |
| *despacio* | slowly |
| *mal* | badly |
| *pronto* | soon |
| *según* | accordingly; it depends |

## Special Uses of some Adverbs of Manner

### 561 *Así*

*Así* is sometimes used as an adjective, in both the spoken and the written language. It then follows the noun and is invariable, whatever the number and gender of the noun.

> *Con un hombre así dentro de la casa, ¿qué va a ser de mí?* (J. A. de Zunzunegui, 1959a: 130)
> With such a man in the house, what will become of me?

> *La cuadratura del círculo y cosas así* (M. de Unamuno, 1967b: 30)
> The squaring of the circle and things like that

A popular variant of *así* is *asín*. *Ansí* is an older form of *así* (cf. *El mundo es ansí*, the title of a novel by P. Baroja), which can still be heard in popular speech and in rural dialects.[5]

### 562 *Bien*

*Bien* can be used adjectivally after a noun (in the spoken language):

> *Con su risa de señora bien*
> With her fine lady's laugh

> *Una chica bien*
> A well-off, privileged girl

Note that *bien* is used with *estar*:

> *Estos coches están muy bien*
> These cars are very good

> *Mi padre está bien*
> My father is well

Contrast the following example, where *bien* has the value of an adverb of degree:

> *Ha cazado unas perdices bien hermosas* (*DD*, 71)
> He has shot some very fine partridge

## 563 *Cómo*

*Cómo*, with a written accent, can be used in exclamatory sentences.

> *¡Cómo nos hemos divertido!*
> How we've enjoyed ourselves!
> (Also: *¡Cuánto nos hemos divertido!*)

*Cómo* may be used as a synonym of *por qué* 'why':

> *No sé cómo madrugamos tanto* (J. Fernández Santos, 1977: 37)
> I don't know why we get up so early

Without an accent, it may have the meaning 'approximately':

> *Paso a cambiarme como a las ocho* (C. Fuentes, 1979: 22)
> I go and change about eight

**564**  *Cómo no*[6] is a very common expression in the spoken language, used especially in Latin America, but more recently in Spain, as an alternative to *sí, naturalmente* 'of course', 'that goes without saying'. *Cómo no* can be written with or without question or exclamation marks:

> – *¿Puedo mirarlo?*
> – *Cómo no* (Kany, 1951: 413)
> 'May I see?'
> 'Sure.'

> *El periódico publicaba, cómo no, la carta del presi (= presidente)*
> (C. Pérez Merinero, 1982: 138)
> The paper published, needless to say, the president's letter

**565**  An expression which is castigated by purists but very fashionable at present is *como muy* + adjective,[7] which has a meaning between 'rather' and 'very':[8]

> *Este señor había sido como muy antifranquista* (F. Umbral, 1987: 149)
> This gentleman had been a strong opponent of Franco

> – *¿Qué le parece este chico?*
> – *Lo encuentro como muy estúpido* (Quoted ironically by F. Lázaro Carreter in a lecture *El español hoy: problemas y tendencias*, given in Antwerp on 31 January 1987)
> 'What do you think of this lad?'
> 'I think he's really stupid'

*No sabemos si a alguien estas cuestiones gramaticales le parecen como muy baladíes* (Marsá, 1986: 114)
We don't know whether these grammatical questions will seem extremely trivial to some people
(The example is described as odd by Marsá)

**566** Note also *como un poco*:

*La madre encontraba a aquel brigada como un poco demasiado mayor para novio de su niña* (F. Umbral, 1989: 87)
The mother found that warrant officer a bit too old to be her child's fiancé

## 567 Despacio

*Despacio* is equivalent to *lentamente* 'slowly'.

In Latin America and sometimes also in popular speech in Spain[9] *despacio* is used with the meaning of 'quietly': *hablar despacio* 'to speak softly' (i.e., *hablar en voz baja*). Speakers who use *despacio* in this way sometimes use *despaciosamente* for the notion 'slowly'.[10]

## 568 Mal

*Mal*, like *bien*, is used with *estar*.

*Estas casas no están mal*        These houses aren't bad

*Mal* is used in a series of compound verbs (all with pejorative meaning), e.g. *malcriar* 'to bring up badly, spoil', *maldecir* 'to damn', *malherir* 'to wound badly', *malquerer* 'to dislike, hate', *maltratar*, 'to treat badly, maltreat', *malvender* 'to sell off cheap'.

*Algunos jóvenes malvendían el patrimonio de sus abuelos* (J. M. Gironella, 1986: 23)
Some youngsters were selling off the legacy of their ancestors cheaply

## 569 Según

*Según* as an adverb expresses a possibility dependent on a circumstance:

*– ¿Vas a ir mañana?*
*– Según (DD, 337)*
'Are you going tomorrow?'
'It depends'

## Adverbs of Degree and Quantity

### 570 Forms

| | |
|---|---|
| *algo* (see also **397**) | rather, somewhat |
| *apenas* | scarcely |
| *bastante* | rather, enough |
| *casi* | almost |
| *cuanto* | as (with *tanto*) |
| *¿cuánto?* | how much? |
| *¡cuánto! (¡cuán!, ¡qué!)* | how (much)! |
| *demasiado* | too much |
| *más* | more |
| *menos* | less |
| *mucho, muy* | very (much) |
| *nada* (see also **420–426**) | not at all |
| *poco* | little |
| *sólo* | only |
| *también* | also |
| *tanto (tan)* | as much, as |

Special Uses of some of these Adverbs

### 571 *Apenas*

*Apenas* has the meaning 'hardly', 'scarcely'. When it follows the verb, the verb is preceded by a negative.

*No le he visto apenas (DUE, I, 211)*
I have scarcely seen him

*Apenas llega a la mesa (ibid.)*
It scarcely reaches the table

In literary Spanish *apenas* is often followed by *si*.[11] *Apenas si* always precedes the verb:

*El coronel Buendía apenas si comprendió que el secreto de una buena vejez no es otra cosa que un pacto honrado con la soledad* (G. García Márquez, 1977: 185)
Colonel Buendía found it difficult to understand that the secret of a comfortable old age is nothing more than an honourable pact with solitude

*Apenas si quedan un par de días* (J. M. Pemán, quoted in *DD*, 44)
They stayed a bare couple of days

## 572 Bastante

*Bastante* can be used both as an adjective and an adverb. As an adjective it agrees in number with the noun to which it relates (see **478**).

In the language of young people today, *bastante* tends to have the meaning of *mucho* 'a lot'.[12]

## 573 Casi

*Casi casi* (with or without commas) has the meaning 'almost', 'more or less':

*Se levanta casi casi cuando yo me acuesto* (J. A. de Zunzunegui, 1959a: 156)
He gets up more or less when I go to bed

*Se enfurecía contra sí mismo por lo que estimaba una flaqueza y casi, casi, una deserción* (M. Delibes, 1969b: 102)
He was cross with himself for what he considered weakness and very nearly desertion

Examples of the following type are found in the spoken language:

*Casi lo escribo* (example quoted by A. Quilis in a lecture in Antwerp, 6 December 1980)
It's better if I write it down

The form *casimente* is found in US and Santo Domingo Spanish.[13]

## 574 *Cuanto, (cuánto), tanto*

*Cuanto* and *tanto* may be used with verbs:
*No tendrías que trabajar tanto*
You should not have to work so much
*Dime cuánto vale*
Tell me how much it is

**575** The apocopated forms *cuan (cuán)* and *tan* are used before adjectives, past participles, adverbs and adverbial expressions.
*¡Cuán felices son!* (*Esbozo*, 358)
How happy they are!
(Cuán is used in literary language; *¡Qué felices son!* is the preferred form in speech, see **368**.)
*Nunca le había visto tan agradecido*
I had never seen him so grateful
*¡No articules tan mal!*
Don't speak so indistinctly!
... *detalles tan sin importancia como los caprichos del azar* (S. Lorén, n.d.: 175)
... details as unimportant as the whims of chance
*El Oriente no es tan otra cosa como pretenden los orientalistas* (J. Cortázar, 1974: 189)
The East is not so different as orientalists claim

**576** There is no apocopation before comparative adjectives or adverbs, or when an adjective, though understood, is not stated (fourth example below):
*Él es tanto más tranquilo que tú*
He is so much quieter than you
*¡Tanto mejor!*          So much the better!
*¡Tanto peor!*           So much the worse!
– *Estoy borracho.*
– *No tanto como crees* (A. Bryce Echenique, 1981: 214 (also quoted in **650**))
'I'm drunk.'
'Not as much as you think'
But:
*Él es tan tranquilo como tú*
He is as quiet as you

*Tanto* may be omitted before *mejor* and *peor*:

> *Si podemos coger al rey vivo, mejor* (P. Baroja, 1946–51: I, 637)
> If we can capture the king alive, so much the better

> *María exclamó: «Peor para él!»* (J. M. Gironella, 1966b: 111)
> María exclaimed, 'So much the worse for him!'

## 577 Demasiado

*Demasiado* may also be used as an adjective – see **480**. As an adverb, *demasiado* is invariable. In popular speech, however, agreement of *demasiado* with a following adjective, though considered incorrect,[14] is sometimes heard (*\*eres demasiada buena*).

It is considered a vulgarism to introduce *de* between *demasiado* and the adjective it qualifies:

> *Es usted demasiado de bueno para estos tiempos* (M. Delibes, quoted in *DD*, 139–40)
> You are too good for these times

The form *demasiadamente* is very occasionally found:[15]

> *Sus dientes eran pequeños, oscuros y el enseñarlos demasiadamente era su Waterloo* (J. A. de Zunzunegui, 1952b: 124)
> Her teeth were small and dark, and showing them too much was the cause of her downfall

**578** *Demasiado* is not used as much as English 'too'; the idea is often implicit in Spanish, especially where a construction with *para* follows on.

> *«Tarde. . . Es tarde para ti» Creía escuchar carcajadas burlonas: «es tarde amigo, es tarde. . .»* (E. Quiroga, 1950: 115)
> 'Too late . . . It's too late for you.' He thought he could hear derisory laughter: 'it's too late, my friend, it's too late . . .'

> *Se marchó hace ya rato y todavía es pronto para que vuelva* (C. J. Cela, 1963a: 219)
> He went some time ago and it is still too early for him to be back

> *Nunca es tarde* (J. A. Vallejo-Nágera, 1980: 149)
> It is never too late

**579** *Mucho* and *muy* may also be used with a sense close to that of *demasiado*:

> *La junta decide acudir en su ayuda; tal vez muy tarde: su muerte sobrevino en seguida* (F. Lázaro. 1972: 94)
> The junta decides to come to his aid; perhaps much too late: immediately after that he was dead

> *Estimaba mucho lo que él llamaba su hombría para volverse atrás* (M. Delibes, 1969b: 194)
> He thought too much of what he called his manhood to go back

In the spoken language, *demasiado mucho* and *demasiado menos* are found, though they are not considered to be correct.

> *Bueno, hijo, que trabajes no demasiado mucho* (A. M. Vigara Tauste, 1992: 155)
> Hey, kid, don't work too hard
> (More correctly: *que no trabajes demasiado*)

**580** The idea of 'too much' can also be rendered by an augmentative suffix.

> *¿Para qué nacemos, Dios mío, si nuestra vida es brevísima para explicárnoslo?* (C. J. Cela, 1967c: 187)
> Why are we born, my God, if our life is much too short to explain it all to us?

> *Ya estoy grandullona para andar saltando* (C. Martín Gaite, 1968: 143)
> I'm too big now to go jumping about

or even a diminutive suffix:

> *(Tú) eres jovencito para esto*
> You're very (= too) young for this

**581** *Demasiado* cannot be omitted where there would be room for ambiguity without it.

> *¿Es que no bebo, o es que bebo demasiado?* (I. Agustí, 1945: 101)
> Don't I drink, or do I drink too much?
> (*¿... bebo mucho?* alone would mean '... do I drink a lot?')

> *Me encuentro muy mal, demasiado mal* (C. J. Cela, 1967c: 156)
> I feel very ill, too ill

**582** *Demasiado* can also be used to highlight a particular part of the sentence.

> – *Ahora ya es tarde*
> – *Demasiado tarde* (A. Casona, 1968: 148–9)
> 'It's too late now'
> 'Far too late'

**583** In Latin America, *demasiado* is used as a synonym for *mucho* and *muy*[16] – see also **481**.

> *Su conversación me era demasiado agradable* (Kany, 1951: 297)
> Their conversation was very agreeable to me

> *El despacho de Sergio Ramírez es más austero y vacío, empezando porque Sergio no está demasiado en él* (J. Cortázar, 1984: 33)
> Sergio Ramírez's study is more austere and emptier, to start with because Sergio is not in it very much

## 584 Más

*De más* (two words, not to be confused with *demás*, see **469–473**) has the meaning of 'too much'.

> *Haber bebido un poco de más* (Van Dam, 1969: I, 758)
> To have drunk a bit too much

> *De más está decir*... (G. Cabrera Infante, 1978: 112)
> It is excessive to say ...

**585** In Latin America (and also in some areas of Spain), *más* is used for *nada*, *nadie* and *nunca*; and instead of the usual combinations *nada más*, *nadie más*, *nunca más*, the expressions *más nada*, *más nadie*, *más nunca* are used ...[17]

> *¿No se le ofrece más nada, mamá?* (Kany, 1951: 310)
> Can I do anything else for you, Mum?
> (More usually: ... *nada más* ...)

> *Se metió en la isla para no salir más nunca* (A. Uslar Pietri, 1983: 13)
> He went to the island, never again to leave it

**586** *No más* (or *nomás*) is very common in Latin America. It has a number of meanings: it can be synonymous with *sólo* 'only' or with *nada más* in its temporal meaning 'immediately after', 'scarcely'; or it can be used as a reinforcing element after verbs, especially imperatives.[18]

> *Voy a mironear un poco nomás* (A. Roa Bastos, 1977: 59)
> I'm just going to nose around a bit

> *No más que llegue, lo haré* (Kany, 1951: 316)
> I'll do it immediately I arrive

> *Una invitación del Señor Presidente nomás se rechaza* (C. Fuentes, 1979: 12)
> You don't just refuse an invitation from the President

> *Llámame Chunga, nomás* (M. Vargas Llosa, 1986: 26)
> Just call me Chunga

## 587 *Mucho* and *muy*

*Mucho* qualifies a verb.

> *Este hombre trabaja mucho*     This man works a lot/hard

**588** *Mucho* is used before comparatives and before the adverbs *antes* and *después*.

> *Tienes que dar una explicación mucho más clara*
> You must give a much clearer explanation

> *Este trabajo es mucho mejor que el anterior*
> This work is much better than the last

> *Esto ocurrió mucho antes*
> This happened long before

**589** *Mucho* has the meaning 'well' rather than 'much' when used with *conocer*:

> *Hablábamos de los poetas de postguerra que el duque había conocido mucho* (F. Umbral, 1981: 114)
> We were speaking of the postwar poets whom the Duke had known well

## 590 *Muy*

*Muy* qualifies an adjective, a past participle, an adverb or adverbial expression.

| | |
|---|---|
| *Una muchacha muy inteligente* | A very intelligent girl |
| *Un hombre muy agradecido* | A very grateful man |
| *Lo hizo muy rápidamente* | He did it very quickly |
| *El director viene muy de tarde en tarde* | The director comes only from time to time |
| *Saldremos muy de mañana* | We shall leave very early in the morning |

**591** *Muy* is also used with comparative forms when these do not have a comparative meaning:

*Mayor* 'old'

> *Tu padre murió muy mayor* (C. Alonso de los Ríos, 1971: 85)
> Your father died when he was very old

*Muy* may also be found with *menor* in the sense of 'young', although the usage is not generally accepted:

> *Y la verdad es que Valentina era 'muy menor', como me dijo un día Isabelita* (R. J. Sender, 1965–6: II, 413)
> And the truth is that Valentina was 'very little', as Isabelita told me one day

*Superior/inferior* 'superior/inferior'

> *Un producto muy superior/inferior*
> A very superior/inferior product

**592** *Muy* may be found before a noun used as an adjective:

> *Pilar era una muchacha hermosa, muy mujer* (J. M. Gironella, 1966b: 49)
> Pilar was a beautiful girl, very feminine

> *Aquello es para los muy hombres* (R. J. Sender, 1969a: 16)
> That is for real men

**593** *Muy* may precede an adjectival phrase consisting of *de* + noun:

> *El ron es una bebida muy de hombres* (C. J. Cela, 1958: 28)
> Rum is very much a man's drink

> *María llevaba una vida muy de sociedad* (P. Baroja, 1946–51: VII, 383)
> María led a very social life

## 594 Translation of English 'Very'

Note that English 'very' + adjective corresponds in certain expressions to *mucho* + noun in Spanish: *hace mucho frío/calor* 'it's very cold/hot'.

> *Hace mucho aire* (C. Martín Gaite, 1981: 120)
> It's very draughty

**595** *Muy* cannot be used in isolation or without a following element which it qualifies; *mucho* is used in such cases.

> *Estoy cansado y mucho*
> I'm really tired

> *Ha llegado tarde pero no mucho*
> He arrived late, but not very

> *Es muy bella Jara, mucho* (R. Montero, 1979: 220)
> Jara is very beautiful, very beautiful

> – *¿Estás contento?*
> – *Mucho*
> 'Are you happy?'
> 'Very'

> – *¿Saldrás temprano?*
> – *Mucho*
> 'Will you leave early?'
> 'Very'

## 596 *Sólo*

*Sólo* bears an accent only when used adverbially (i.e. when it is equivalent to *solamente*), and the accent is even then not obligatory, except when ambiguity might result (see third example).[19] In its adjectival usage it has no accent. Thus:

| | |
|---|---|
| *Sólo tres chicos* | Only three boys |
| *Tres chicos solos* | Three boys on their own |

> *Tomo café solo sólo los domingos*
> I only have black coffee on Sundays

# Adverbs of Time

## 597 Forms

| | |
|---|---|
| *ahora* | now |
| *anoche* | last night |
| *anteayer* | the day before yesterday |
| *antes* | before(hand) |
| *aún* | still, yet |
| *ayer* | yesterday |
| *¿cuándo?* | when? |
| *después* | after(wards) |
| *entonces* | then |
| *hoy* | today |
| *jamás* | never |
| *luego* | then |
| *mañana* | tomorrow |
| *nunca* | never |
| *pronto* | soon |
| *siempre* | always |
| *tarde* | late |
| *temprano* | early |
| *todavía* | still, yet |
| *ya* | already |

Details of Usage of some Adverbs of Time

## 598 *Aún, aun*

*Aún* (with a written accent) is an alternative to *todavía*; *aun* (without a written accent) is similar in meaning to *hasta*, *incluso* 'even'.[20]

Contrast:

> *No han llegado aún los comensales* (F. Marsá, 1986: 75)
> The dinner guests have not yet arrived

> *Aun en la indigencia conservaba toda su dignidad* (A. Bello, 1972: 342, no. 1216)
> Even in poverty he preserved all his dignity
> (Also: *Hasta/incluso en la indigencia. . .*)

## 599 *Cuando*

*Cuando* is often used elliptically in modern Spanish with no verb; it then stands immediately before a noun (sometimes even a proper noun as in the fourth example below) and is hence more properly a preposition than an adverb.[21]

> *Cuando la guerra (= en el tiempo de la guerra)* (A. Bello, 1972: 336)
> During the war

> *Púsose a fumar, sentado frente a la chimenea, como cuando soltero (= cuando era soltero)* (E. Quiroga, 1950: 179)
> He sat down to smoke in front of the hearth, just as when he was a bachelor

> *Era una marcha alemana de cuando los nazis (= de la época de los nazis)* (R. Sánchez Ferlosio, 1971: 227)
> It was a German march from the time of the Nazis

> *Hacía tanto frío como cuando Possad y Olensky (= como cuando combatían en Possad y Olensky)* (T. Salvador, 1968b: 321)
> It was as cold as it had been during the Possad and Olensky offensives

**600** In Latin-American Spanish, *¡cuándo!* is sometimes used as an interjection in the sense of *¡imposible!* 'Impossible!' or *¡nunca!* 'never!'.[22]

> – *Me dicen, Elvira, que te casas, con él.*
> – *¿Yo? ¡Cuándo!* (Kany, 1951: 415)
> 'I'm told that you're marrying him, Elvira.'
> 'Me? Never!'

## 601 *Hoy = ahora*

In Latin-American Spanish *hoy* is sometimes used in the sense of *ahora* 'now': *hoy son las once* 'it's eleven o'clock now'. *Hoy día* (which normally has the meaning of 'nowadays') is then used for *hoy* 'today'.[23]

> *Hoy día estamos a siete de mayo* (Kany, 1951: 277)
> Today is the seventh of May

> *¿No tienes colegio, hoy día?* (J. Edwards, 1971: 10)
> Haven't you got school today?

## 602 *Jamás, nunca*

*Jamás* and *nunca* follow the rules for negatives (see **Syntax of Negative Elements**).

> *Casi nunca lloro* (J. Cortázar, 1974: 294)
> I almost never cry

> *Jamás se volvió a saber de ella* (G. García Márquez, 1977: 33)
> Nothing more was heard of her

But:

> *No te cases nunca* (M. Mihura, 1981: 130)
> Don't ever get married

**603** *Jamás* has a somewhat stronger negative meaning than *nunca*:

> – *¿No te cansas?*...
> – *¡Nunca!*
> – *¿No?*
> – *¡Jamás!* (E. Jardiel Poncela, 1969: IV, 1255)
> 'Don't you get tired?'
> 'Never!'
> 'What, never?'
> 'Never!'

*En mi vida* is also used in the sense of 'never' (see **727**). *Nunca más* has the meaning of 'never again':

> In his song *Momentos* Julio Iglesias sings of *momentos que no vuelven nunca más* 'moments which will never come again'

**604** *Nunca* and *jamás* can even appear together to reinforce the idea of 'never'.

> *Se va para no volver nunca jamás* (J. García Hortelano, 1979: 88)
> He is going away, never to return

> *Y ella contestó que jamás, nunca* (J. Edwards, 1985: 210)
> And she answered, never, ever

**605** An even stronger alternative to *nunca jamás* is *(en) jamás de los jamases*, in which the second *jamás* is turned into a noun.

*Don Pedro hizo unos visajes tan pronunciados que Régula pensó que jamás de los jamases se le volvería a poner derecha la cara* (M. Delibes, 1981: 157)
Don Pedro pulled such extraordinary faces that Régula thought his face would never go right again

## 606 Translation of *nunca* and *jamás*

*Nunca* and *jamás* are translated by English 'ever' in negative contexts. The main instances are:

(a) when there is another negative word in the sentence:

*Ninguna novela ha probado nunca nada* (F. Umbral, 1981: 47)
No novel has ever proved anything

(b) after a comparative:

*No me gusta mentir y en este momento menos que nunca* (J. Cortázar, 1973: 148)
I do not like lying and less than ever at this moment

(c) in some questions where a negative answer is expected:

*¿Quién jamás se puso en armas contra Dios?* (A. Bello, 1972: 324)
Who ever took up arms against God?

(See also **1291**ff.)

**607** Note also the expression *por/para siempre jamás*:

*Por siempre jamás* (or *para siempre jamás*) *me acordaré* (*Esbozo*, 356)
I will remember for ever

– *Quiero que me ames para siempre.*
– *Siempre es un tiempo algo largo.*
– *Para siempre jamás y eternamente* (G. Cabrera Infante, 1979: 611)
'I want you to love me always.'
'Always is rather a long time.'
'For ever and ever and eternally'

## 608 *Siempre*

In addition to its general meaning of 'always', *siempre* can also have the value of *en todo caso* 'in any case'.

In Latin-American Spanish, *siempre* is also sometimes used as an equivalent to *todavía*,[24] *decididamente* 'definitely', *al fin* 'finally' and *sí* 'yes'.[25]

## 609 Ya

Besides the usual meaning of 'already', *ya* is also used in the expressions *ya no (no ... ya)* 'no more', 'no longer'.

*Ya no llevas el vendaje – dijo* (J. Marsé, 1982: 216)
'You've not got the bandage on any more,' he said

*No estoy segura ya de nada* (F. Umbral, 1981:78)
I'm no longer sure of anything

The same notion can also be expressed by *ya no ... más* or simply by *no ... más*:

*Ya no llora más* (J. Cortázar, 1974: 100)
She is not crying any more

*No quiero verte más* (J. Rulfo, 1981: 68)
I don't want to see you again

*No la aburro más, gracias por todo* (C. Martín Gaite, 1981: 172)
I won't bore you any longer; thank you for everything

However, the use of *no ... más* in the sense of 'no more, not any more' for *ya no* is censured by purists: thus *costumbres seculares, que la gente no entiende más* ('age-old customs, which people no longer understand') should be *costumbres seculares que la gente ya no entiende*.[26]

**610** The expression *ya mismo*, used in popular speech in Latin America, has the meaning 'immediately'.[27]

*No hay nadie. Acaban de salir. Comencemos ya mismo* (M. Vargas Llosa, 1973: 369)
There's nobody there. They've just gone out. Let's start right away

See also **629**.

# Adverbs of Place

## 611 Forms

| | |
|---|---|
| *abajo* | below |
| *acá* | here |
| *ahí* | there |
| *allá* | (over) there |
| *allí* | there |
| *aquí* | here |
| *arriba* | above |
| *cerca* | near |
| *delante* | in front |
| *detrás* | behind |
| *dentro* | inside, within |
| *donde* | where |
| *encima* | on top |
| *fuera* | outside |

### Details of the Use of some Adverbs of Place

### 612 *Abajo, arriba*

These adverbs can immediately follow a noun and form an adverbial phrase which concisely expresses the notion of direction.

| | |
|---|---|
| *río abajo* | downstream |
| *río arriba* | upstream |

*(Marchó) escaleras abajo (DUE, I, 3)*
He went downstairs

*Adentro* can be used in the same way: *ir tierra adentro* 'to go inland'.

**613** In Latin-American Spanish, there is a tendency to use *abajo* where in Spain *debajo* would be used:

*Con el gato abajo del brazo* (J. Cortázar, quoted in *DD*, 8)
With the cat under his arm

*Arriba* is similarly used for *encima*.[28]

## 614 *Aquí, ahí, allí*

These three adverbs are used according to the distance that separates the speaker from the person, animal or thing in question. Broadly speaking, they correspond to the demonstratives *este, ese, aquel* (see **302**).

> *Te veo mañana, aquí en mi despacho*
> I'll see you tomorrow, here in my study

> *Creo que ahí no os llegan los periódicos* (*DUE*, I, 99)
> I believe the papers don't reach you there

> *Allí arriba hay otra tienda*
> Up there there is another shop

## 615 *Acá, allá*

In the Peninsula, *acá* often has the meaning 'to here, hither':

> *¡Ven acá!*
> Come here!

> *De ayer acá*
> Since yesterday (i.e. from yesterday until now)

*Allá* 'over there' sometimes appears (to English speakers at least) to have approximately the same meaning as *allí*, although it is used to refer to less precise and more remote locations. *Allá*, immediately followed by a second or third person personal pronoun or by a noun, expresses the speaker's indifference to what others do or think.

> *Allá tú* (Van Dam, 1969: I, 61)
> That's your affair

> *Había unas monjas que no llevaban hábito. Allá ellas* (M. Alvar, 1982: 34)
> There were some nuns not wearing habits. That was up to them

Both adverbs are used in the construction *más acá/allá de* 'nearer/further than' (*aquí* and *allí* are impossible here), and are also used contrastively, e.g. *acá y allá* (also *acá y acullá*) 'here and there', *de acá para allá* 'to and fro'.

In some parts of Latin America (especially Argentina), *acá* is systematically used for Peninsular *aquí*.[29] In J. Cortázar's book

*Rayuela*, two of the three parts are called *Del lado de allá* (p. 13) and *Del lado de acá* (p. 257) respectively. In the former (*allá*) the author, an Argentine, is referring to events in Paris; in the latter (*acá*) the characters are in his own country.

**616** On the use of *aquí* as a demonstrative pronoun, see **319**.

## 617 *Donde*

In both Spain and Latin America *(en) donde* is sometimes used as a time expression, and has the same meaning as *cuando*.[30]

> *Luego vino la época romántica, en donde la mujer prefería presentar un aspecto lánguido* (A. Llorente, 1980: 35)
> Then came the Romantic era, when Woman preferred to present a languid aspect

**618** With verbs of motion, *adonde* (or as two words, *a donde*) is used (with a written accent if in a direct or indirect question). The use of the preposition *a* is, however, optional.

> *Aquélla es la casa adonde vamos* (*Esbozo*, 538, n. 1)
> That is the house we are going to
> (Or: . . . *la casa donde vamos*)

> *¿Dónde vamos, Manuel?* (F. García Pavón, 1980b: 69)
> Where are we going, Manuel?

*Adonde* may also be found, especially in questions, with verbs whose principal meaning is not motion, but which may be understood as such.

> *¿Adónde estaba Beatrice?* (A. Bryce Echenique, 1981: 169)
> Where was Beatrice?
> (Implies: *¿Adónde se habrá metido Beatrice?* 'Where can Beatrice have got to?')

**619** *Donde* is found in the spoken language as an equivalent to English 'at . . .'s'. In the following sentences, a verb like *estar* or *vivir* is implied.

> *¿Hay mucha gente donde Paulina? – preguntó Alberto* (M. Vargas Llosa, 1973: 129)
> 'Are there a lot of people at Pauline's?' asked Alberto

*Se tiró de la cama y fue donde ella* (J. A. de Zunzunegui, 1954: 424)
He jumped out of bed and went over to her

**620** In Latin-American Spanish *lo de* is used in much the same way as *donde* with a noun.

*En lo de Habeb compraron dos litros de tinto* (J. Cortázar, 1974: 245)
At Habeb's they bought two litres of red wine

*Ir a lo del médico* (Kany, 1951: 129)[31]
To go to the doctor

## Adverbs of Confirmation and Negation

### 621 Forms

| | |
|---|---|
| *no* | not, not |
| *sí* | yes |
| *también* | also, as well |
| *tampoco* | neither |
| *ya* | indeed, surely, yes |

### Details of the Use of some of these Adverbs

### 622 *No*

*No* precedes the verb; in verbal groups its placing may be crucial to the meaning of the sentence: *puede no ser verdad* 'It may not be true' versus *no puede ser verdad* 'it cannot be true'.

**623** *¿No?* is often used at the end of a sentence to form a 'tag question' (cf. English 'isn't it?'), especially in Latin-American Spanish,[32] as an equivalent to *¿eh?*, *¿(no es) verdad?*, *¿no es cierto?*

*Es muy serio, ¿no?* (Beinhauer, 1968: 327)
It's very serious, isn't it?

## 624 With *hasta*

Note that the order may also be *hasta . . . no*:

> *No nos volveremos a ver hasta el verano/Hasta el verano no nos volveremos a ver*
> We shall not see each other again until the summer

In Latin America, the *no* of *no . . . hasta* is often omitted when *hasta* is followed by a time expression, especially when this is followed by a verb.

> *Hasta las tres iré*
> I won't go until three
> (In standard Spanish: *No iré hasta las tres/Hasta las tres no iré*)

## 625 Pleonastic *no* with *hasta*

A second (pleonastic) *no* is sometimes used in negative sentences with *hasta*, especially in Latin-American Spanish:

> *No saldré hasta que él no llegue*
> I won't leave until he comes
> (In standard Spanish: *No saldré hasta que él llegue*)

although examples can now also be found in the Peninsula:

> *Yo pido que no se publiquen estos papeles hasta que no hayan muerto todos* (C. J. Cela, 1988: 238)
> I ask that these papers should not be published until everyone has died

Indeed, the use of a redundant *no* is so frequent that it even appears after *hasta* in positive sentences:

> *A tu lado me tendrás hasta que no nos muramos*[33]
> You will have me at your side until we die

(For the use of pleonastic *no* in comparative sentences, see **639**.)

## 626 *Sí*

*Sí*, in addition to its meaning of 'yes', may be used to deny a negative in a preceding sentence, and is the equivalent of an English contrastive stress or 'indeed, sure, right'. Note also the apparently logically contradictory expression *eso sí que no* 'certainly not'.

> *Yo no sé si el progreso es útil o no – dijo Antonio –. Lo que sí sé es que el pueblo tiene derecho a vivir mejor* (P. Baroja, *El mayorazgo de Labraz*, 1964a: 102).
> 'I do not know if progress is useful or not,' said Antonio. 'What I do know is that people have the right to live better'

> *Ahora, sí que voy a San Francisco* (J. Cortázar, 1973: 51)
> Now I'm certainly going to San Francisco

> *¿Rindiéndonos? Eso sí que no – y Federico dio un puñetazo en la mesa* (A. M. de Lera, 1970: 28)
> 'Surrender? Certainly not!', and Federico brought his fist down on the table

## 627 *Bueno*

*Bueno* is sometimes used for *sí* to show acknowledgement of a request:

> *¿Quieres agua?*
> – *Bueno* (overheard by JdeB in the Instituto de Cooperación Iberoamericana, 1989)
> 'Do you want water?'
> 'Yes'

*Bueno* is also used in Mexican Spanish when answering the telephone (corresponding to Peninsular *¡diga!*).

## 628 *Tampoco*

*Tampoco* may come before or after the verb, and if the latter, the verb must be preceded by *no* or another negative word.

> *Yo tampoco quiero morir como una rata* (M. Vargas Llosa, 1981: 419)
> I don't want to die like a rat either
> (Or: *Yo no quiero morir como una rata tampoco*)

## 629 *Ya*

Besides the meaning discussed in **609–610**, *ya* can also be used in an affirmative sense, even as an equivalent for 'yes'.

*Ya sabes que mi tío vive en Barcelona*
You know of course that my uncle lives in Barcelona

*«La vida, chico», fue la respuesta del murciano.*
*«Ya», hizo el otro* (J. Marsé, 1982: 214)
'Life, my lad', was the man from Murcia's reply.
'Right', said the other

**630** *Ya* also has a ponderative usage:

*Al jardinero le están echando una fama que ya, ya . . .* (*La Codorniz*, 1941–4)
The gardener is getting a reputation that, well . . .

## Adverbs of Doubt

**631**

| | |
|---|---|
| *acaso* | perhaps |
| *quizá(s)* | perhaps |
| *tal vez* | perhaps |

See **1027** for the use of indicative and subjunctive after these words.

## Adverbial Expressions

**632** Some important adverbial expressions are:

| | |
|---|---|
| *a gusto* | at ease |
| *a medias* | half |
| *a menudo* | often |
| *a tiempo* | in time |
| *a veces* | sometimes |
| *de repente* | suddenly |
| *de vez en cuando* | from time to time |
| *en general* | generally |
| *en seguida* | immediately |
| *muchas veces* | frequently |
| *no . . . hasta* | not until |
| *por cierto* | certainly |
| *por poco* | almost |

## 633 Remark: *Cosa de*

In the spoken language, the expression *cosa de* is used in the sense of 'about':

> *He recorrido cosa de dos kilómetros y medio* (L. Ricardo Alonso, 1981: 177).
> I have covered about two and a half kilometres

> *Quedó en venir aquí en cosa de hora y media* (E. Parra, 1981: 187)
> He agreed to come here in about an hour and a half

## Degrees of Comparison

(See remarks on comparison of adjectives, **181**ff.)

**634** Most adverbs form comparatives in the same way as adjectives:

| *lentamente* | → | *más lentamente* |
| slowly | | more, most slowly |

**635** The following common adverbs have irregular comparative forms:

| *bien* | *mejor* |
| well | better, best |
| *mal* | *peor* |
| badly | worse, worst |
| *poco* | *menos* |
| little | less, least |
| *muy, mucho* | *más* |
| very, a lot | more, most |

Sometimes the forms *óptimamente* (as a superlative of *bien*) and *pésimamente* (as a superlative of *mal*) are used, with the respective meanings 'very good' and 'very bad'.

**636** See also **57** on the omission of the definite article with the superlatives of adverbs.

# Special Constructions in Spanish

## 637 An Adverb in English Corresponds to a Verbal Construction in Spanish

A number of commonly used verbs in Spanish have adverbial equivalents in English.

| | |
|---|---|
| *acabar de* | ... just |
| *acaba de llegar* | he has just arrived |
| *acabar por* | ... finally |
| *acabará por confesar* | He will finally confess |
| *soler* | ... usually |
| *solemos comer aquí* | We usually eat here |
| *volver a* | ... again |
| *¡Vuelve a escribirle!* | Write to her again! |
| *¡Vuelve a leer esta frase!* | Read this sentence again! |

*No he vuelto a saber de él* (A. M. Matute, 1977: 54)
I have never heard of him again

# Comparative Constructions

## More . . . than, Less . . . than

**638** Comparison of like terms with *más* and *menos* requires *que* as the conjunction:

> *Yo tengo más/menos libros que tú*
> I have more/fewer books than you

> *Tengo más libros que discos*
> I have more books than records

**639** A pleonastic *no* is sometimes used in comparative sentences which express a contrast of ideas.[1]

> *Más vale ayunar que no enfermar* (*DRAE*, 1022)
> It is better to fast than to be ill

**640** Where the comparative expression expresses a number or quantity, *de* must be used; here *más de*, for example, may be thought of as having the meaning 'in excess of':

> *Tengo más de doscientos libros*
> I have more than (in excess of) two hundred books

> *Estoy convencido de que tiene menos de treinta años*
> I'm sure he's less than (under) thirty

> *Gastaron en dos meses más de la mitad del presupuesto anual* (*Esbozo*, 418)
> In two months they spent more than (over) half the annual budget

Compare also the expression *más de la cuenta* 'too much' (typical of the spoken language).

| | |
|---|---|
| *haber bebido más de la cuenta* | to have had one [drink] too many |
| *hablar más de la cuenta* | to talk too much |
| *castigar más de la cuenta* | to overdo the punishment |

The use of *más que* before a numeral indicates a genuine comparison of a like term with the whole noun phrase; distinguish carefully between:

*Hemos perdido más de dos años*
We've lost more than two years (i.e. in excess of two: three or four, for example)

*Hemos perdido más que dos años*
We've lost more than two years (i.e., other things besides: our business and our house too, for example)

### 641 *Más de dos, más de cuatro*

The expressions *más de dos* and *más de cuatro* mean respectively 'a few' and 'many'.

*Uno, que de joven fue pegón . . . en la Casa de Socorro del callejón de la Ternera a uno le zurcieron más de dos veces* (C. J. Cela, 1979b: 184)
One who was a young tough was sewn up a number of times in the First Aid post on the Callejón de la Ternera

*Luchando contra el muro de la censura, más de cuatro trataron de inventar unas tremendas burradas* (M. Tudela, 1970: 40)
In the fight against the barrier of censorship, quite a few people tried to invent tremendously stupid things

**642** The combination *no . . . más que* is synonymous with *sólo*, *solamente* 'only'.

*Manolita no se vestía más que de verde* (F. Quiñones, 1979: 185)
Manolita dressed only in green

There is a similar difference between *no . . . más que* and *no . . . más de* to that noted in **640** for *más . . . que* and *más . . . de* when used before a numeral. Compare:

*No gastamos más de <u>doscientos</u> pesos*
We spent no more than <u>two hundred</u> pesos (i.e. not in excess
of two hundred pesos; we may well have spent a lot less)

*No gastamos más que <u>doscientos pesos</u>*
We only spent <u>two hundred pesos</u> (implying, for example,
that we consider that a trifling amount)
(Examples from *Esbozo*, 418)

### 643 Comparisons Involving a Clause

*Más* or *menos* + noun is here followed by *del que, de la que, de los
que, de las que* according to the number and gender of the
noun.

*Tenía más <u>dinero</u> <u>del</u> que le hacía falta* (Fernández, 1951: 138)
She had more money than she needed

*Se veía obligado a expresarse con más <u>rapidez</u> de <u>la</u> que tenía cos-
tumbre* (P. Baroja, 1964a: 23)
He found himself obliged to express himself more quickly
than he was used to

*Oyéndote, todo el mundo diría que tienes veinte <u>años</u> más de <u>los</u>
que aparentas* (J. Goytisolo, 1960: 203)
To hear you, anyone would say that you were twenty years
older than you looked

Sometimes *que* on its own or *de lo que* are used instead of *del que, de
la que*, etc.

*Sueles hacerlo con más frecuencia de lo que piensas* (Fernández, 1951: 138)
You usually do it more often than you think[2]

### 644 *Mucho* and *poco* with *más* and *menos*

When qualifying *más* and *menos*, *mucho* and *poco* agree in number
and gender with the noun (see also **452**). Thus, using the examples
already given in **643**:

*Tenía <u>mucho</u> más <u>dinero</u> del que . . .*
*Se veía obligado a expresarse con <u>mucha</u> más <u>rapidez</u>. . .*
*Tienes <u>pocos</u> <u>años</u> más de los que aparentas*

The same is also true of the superlatives *muchísimo* 'very much, very many' and *poquísimo* 'very little, very few':

> *Ha hecho muchísimas menos fotografías de las que el director había pedido*
> He has taken very many fewer photographs than the director asked him to

**645** When *más* and *menos*, etc., are not followed by a noun in comparisons involving a clause, the pattern *más/menos de lo que* is used:

> *No temamos, pues, este escollo del egoísmo – evitable y menos peligroso de lo que se cree* (G. Marañón, 1952: 60)
> Let us therefore not be afraid of this stumbling-block of selfishness, which is avoidable and less dangerous than is thought

> *Somos mucho peores de lo que suponíamos* (J. Goytisolo, 1986: 216)
> We are much worse than we supposed

> *Yo parezco mayor de lo que soy* (J.Cortázar, 1974: 137)
> I seem older than I am

> *Nos hemos encontrado más tarde de lo que habíamos pensado*
> We have met later than we had thought

#### 646 *Más de lo* + Adjective

A construction similar to that in **645** involves a nominalized adjective with *lo* instead of a clause:

> *Se aprovechaban de su ignorancia cobrándole más de lo justo* (P. de Ayala, quoted in Fernández, 1951: 138)
> They took advantage of his ignorance by charging him more than what was fair

#### 647 *Cuanto más/menos . . . (tanto) más/menos*

*Tanto* is often omitted from this construction, which is rendered in English by 'the more/less . . . the more/less'. *Cuanto* and *tanto* agree with any nouns they may qualify:

*Cuantos más juguetes este niño tiene, (tantos) más querría tener*
The more toys this child has, the more he would like to have

*Cuanto más se tiene, más se quiere* (F. Arrabal, 1972b: 21)
The more one has, the more one wants
(One could also say: ... *tanto más se quiere*)

*Y cuanto más la miraba, menos había cambiado* (A. Bryce Echenique, 1981: 211)
And the more he looked at her, the less she had changed

*Cuanto más viejo más amigo*: an advertisement for jeans seen in Zaragoza in 1980
The older they are, the better friends they are

*(Tanto) más/menos* and *cuanto más/menos* may appear in reverse order:

*La imagen vale tanto más cuanto más absurda es* (E. Sábato, 1981: 119)
The more absurd the image is, the more it is worth

*La gente parece más feliz cuanto más primitiva e ignorante* (P. Baroja, 1959: 210)
The more primitive and ignorant people are, the happier they seem

*Cuanto* is even omitted in the following example:

*Nada nuevo: a más muertos, más peticiones de negociación* (*El Alcázar*, 16 February 1983: 40)
Nothing new: the more dead, the more demands for negotiation

The construction *tanto más ... cuanto que* 'all the more ... since' belongs exclusively to the literary register:

*Tanto más lo compadecemos cuanto más y mejor sentimos su semejanza con nosotros* (M. de Unamuno, *Del sentimiento trágico de la vida*, quoted *Esbozo*, 546)
The more we pity him the more and the better we feel his similarity to ourselves

## 648  *Cada vez más/menos, cada día más/menos, más y más, menos y menos*

These expressions add a progressive nuance to the comparative. The construction with *cada vez* is in fact the most usual equivalent of English 'more and more . . .', 'less and less . . .'. *Cada vez* is also used with *mejor* and *peor*.

> *Se hacía cada día más perezoso*
> He got lazier by the day

> *Te comprendo cada vez menos*
> I understand you less and less

> *El corazón me marcha cada vez peor* (E. Jardiel Poncela, 1973: 169)
> My heart is getting worse and worse

> *A medida que se aproximaba la fiesta, Mariona se iba sintiendo más y más importante* (I. Agustí, 1944: 61)
> As the festival approached, Mariona felt increasingly important

## 649  *A cuál más*

The comparative expression *a cuál* (with or without the accent) *más* + adjective or adverb means 'each as much as the other'. The adjective should strictly speaking be in the singular (as in the first example below), but it is also found in the plural (as in the second example).[3]

> *Aminta Dechamps y sus siete hijas a cuál más diligente, lo habían previsto* (G. García Márquez, 1985: 57)
> A.D. and her seven daughters, each as diligent as the other, had foreseen it

> *Las muchachas, a cual más feas, se dedicaban a hacer encaje* (P. Baroja, 1946–51: I, 531)
> The girls, each as ugly as the other, would devote themselves to lace-making

## Comparison of Equality

**650**  The constructions *tan* + adjective + *como* and *tanto* + noun + *como* express equality. *Tanto* agrees with the noun it modifies.

*Su proyecto es tan interesante como el tuyo*
Her plan is as interesting as yours

*No tengo tantos libros como tú*
I don't have as many books as you

*Tan* + adjective may be replaced by *tanto* when the adjective is understood, or to avoid repetition:

– *Estoy borracho.*
– *No tanto como crees* (A. Bryce Echenique, 1981: 214)
'I'm drunk.'
'Not as drunk as you think'

## 651 *Tanto ... cuanto*

If the second term of the comparison of equality is a clause, *tanto ... cuanto* is used. This construction is limited to the written language.

*Tanto*, like *cuanto*, must agree with the noun it modifies.

*Dios cuenta tantos adoradores cuantos son los hombres que piensan* (J. Balmes, 1959: 125)
God has as many worshippers as there are thinking people

## 652 *Tanto ... que*

*Tanto ... que* is used to express a consequence:

*Tiene tanto dinero que no tiene tiempo para contarlo* (Marcos Marín, 1978: 102)
He has so much money that he has no time to count it

**653** When two different comparatives are used in the same sentence, the conjunction is determined, as in English, by the second comparative.

*El gato estaba tan feliz, más feliz, que sus dueños* (G. Cabrera Infante, 1978: 113)
The cat was as happy – happier – than its owners
The sentence could also be expressed as follows: *El gato estaba más feliz o al menos tan feliz como sus dueños* (but in isolation *más feliz que, tan feliz como*)

## 654 *El/la que más y el/la que menos*

The frequently used formula *el/la que más y el/la que menos* is a way of expressing the idea of 'everyone', but with the additional notion of 'some more than others'. An alternative, *quien más, quien menos* is used in literary language (see **356**).[4]

*Lo que más y lo que menos* similarly means 'everything'.

> *El que más y el que menos pasó cariciadera la mano por la cabeza del animal* (J. A. de Zunzunegui, 1958: 290)
> Everyone stroked the animal's head

> *Hoy día, la que más y la que menos hace lo que puede* (C. J. Cela, 1963a: 248)
> Today, everyone does as much as they can

> *Lo que más y lo que menos todo está ya en orden, señor, me había respondido* (M. Delibes, 1948: 268)
> Everything is more or less in order, sir, she replied

> *En Sacedón no es como en otros pueblos; aquí, quien más, quien menos, todos se van a dormir con la panza llena* (C. J. Cela, 1967d: 134)
> In Sacedón, it is not like in other villages; here, everyone goes to bed with their bellies more or less full

**655** *El que más* . . . , etc. alone means 'he, etc. especially'.

> *A él, como el que más, se le podía condenar por ser culpable de «ayuda a la rebelión»* (R. Garriga, 1980: 115)
> He above all could be condemned for being guilty of 'aid to the rebellion'

## 656 Remarks

If there is a finite verb in the second part of a comparison, then *que* is replaced by *de lo que*, as for adjectives (see **645**).

> *Nos hemos encontrado más tarde de lo que habíamos pensado*
> We met later than we had thought

**657** *Tanto . . . como* has the meaning of 'both . . . and' (cf. *lo mismo . . . que*, **500**).

*Tanto en éste como en el tercero hay pasajes* ... (L. Cernuda, in correspondence with E. Wilson, in *Ínsula*, 432, November 1982: 1)
Both in this and in the third there are passages ...

Note, however, that *tanto* ... *que* must be used for a consequence:

*Tiene tanto dinero que no tiene tiempo para contarlo* (Marcos Marín, 1978: 102)
He has so much money that he has no time to count it

# Prepositions

## A

### 658 'Personal a'

*A* is often used in Spanish before a direct object which refers to human beings or animals, a phenomenon which is known as the 'personal *a*'. However, the principles governing the use of the 'personal *a*' are more complex than this name suggests:[1] register[2] and even personal preference play an important role in its usage.

**659** *A* precedes the direct object when it is:

*The Name of a Person or Animal*

> *Estimo a Pedro* (*Esbozo*, 372)
> I hold Pedro in esteem

> *Don Quijote cabalgaba a Rocinante* (*Esbozo*, 372)
> Don Quixote was riding Rocinante

> *Mi madre me había preguntado: ¿Qué estás dibujando? Y yo:*
> *– A Dios* (A. Posse, 1990: 23)
> My mother had asked me, 'What are you drawing?', and I replied, 'God'

> *He leído a Virgilio* (A. Bello, 1972: 253, no. 890)
> I have read Virgil
> (The 'personal *a*' is used here even though the name refers not to the actual person but to his works)

*Nouns (or Collective Nouns) or Pronouns*[3] *Denoting People*

*Abandonas a tu marido y huyes conmigo* (A. Bryce Echenique, 1981: 221)
You leave your husband and run away with me

*Se fusiló a treinta de sus miembros* (R. Garriga, 1980: 122)
Thirty of its members (of a masonic lodge) were shot

*Empezábamos a conocer al pueblo de España* (J. L. Alcocer, 1978: 171)
We were getting to know the Spanish people

*Nancy escandalizó a Londres escapándose con un negro* (P. Neruda, 1976: 66)
Nancy scandalized London by running off with a negro

*Te dejé a ti para seguirlo a él* (C. Fuentes, 1979: 281)
I left you in order to follow him

*No conozco a nadie* (*Esbozo*, 373)
I don't know anyone

*Ese a quien tú has visto* (*Esbozo*, 373)
The man you have seen

*A* is often used before nouns denoting animals where the animal is a pet, or otherwise personally involves the subject:

*No quise degollar a mi perro favorito* (F. García Lorca, quoted in Coste and Redondo, 1965: 326)
I did not want to cut my favourite dog's throat

*Los últimos cinco años los pasó estudiando a los leopardos de Shaba* (*El País*, 5 January 1980: 32)
He spent the last five years studying the leopards of Shaba

But:

*He visto pocos elefantes en mi vida* (*DUE*, I, 695)
I have seen few elephants in my life

The *a* also tends to be used after a verb which is normally associated with a personal object:

In the summer of 1982, notices about a meeting of conservationists in Jaca in northern Spain read:
*¡Salvemos al quebrantahuesos!*
Save the osprey!

*Nouns Denoting Things Used Personally*

The objects of verbs normally associated with personal objects tend to take the personal *a*:

> *Queremos comprender al mar* (P. Baroja, 1958: 12)
> We want to understand the sea

> *Los griegos mataron entonces a la poesía* (M. Alvar, 1982: 71)
> The Greeks killed poetry

> *Llamar a la Muerte* (*Esbozo*, 373)
> To call on Death

> *Yo bendigo a la técnica* (G. Marañón, 1952: 28)
> I bless technology

> *¿Conoce usted a España?* (used by the Spanish Ministry of Tourism throughout Spain in 1977 and 1978)
> Do you know Spain?

The purist position on the use of *a* with names of towns and countries is that *a* is used when the town or country has no article, and indeed this was formerly the custom. However, *a* is generally not used today:[4]

> *¿Conoces Windsor?* (A. Bryce Echenique, 1981: 223)
> Do you know Windsor?

There is a general tendency in Latin-American Spanish (mostly in the spoken language, but also in the written language) for *a* to be used with nouns denoting things to a much greater extent than in Spain.[5]

> *Esos cambios mejoran al habla* (Kany, 1951: 2)
> Those changes improve the language

> *Vio a las sierras* (Kany, 1951: 2)
> He saw the mountains

**660** The 'personal *a*' is sometimes used with non-personal objects when ambiguity might otherwise result. This is particularly the case with verbs which express a relation of precedence or status, such as *preceder* 'to precede', *seguir* 'to follow', *exceder* 'to exceed', *igualar* 'to equal', *superar* 'to overcome', *sustituir* 'to substitute', *vencer* 'to conquer', etc.

*Era la hora quieta que precede al alba* (J. M. Mendiola, quoted in Coste and Redondo, 1965: 330)
It was the quiet hour which comes before dawn

*El deseo ha vencido a la pereza* (*DUE*, I, 696)
Desire has conquered sloth
(See also **1305**)

See also **29**, first example (*perjudicar*).

**661** The use of *a* is in certain cases due in part to stylistic considerations. It is clear that in sentences like the following it is used to achieve balance in the sentence structure:

*Corazón, corazón mío – balbució –, tu madre te quiere más que a nadie y a nada* (J. Goytisolo. 1960: 145)
'My love, my love,' she stammered, 'your mother loves you more than anyone or anything'

*Registraban a los peatones y a los coches* (*MEU*, 67)
They were searching pedestrians and cars

Conversely, the preposition may be omitted in a long list:

*Taboada caricaturizaba a la clase media, los cursis, los veraneantes* ... (A. Mingote, 1988: 11)
Taboada caricatured the middle class, people with poor taste, holidaymakers ...

But in other cases, the rules for the use of *a* are more strictly applied, and the preposition is used only for the appropriate direct object.

*Cruzaba por el salón como buscando algo o a alguien* (C. Martín Gaite, 1981: 51)
He went through the room as if looking for something or someone

*Tzará llegó a París muy dispuesto a devorar a Bretón y el surrealismo* (F. Umbral. 1987: 70)
Tzará arrived in Paris ready to devour Breton and surrealism

**662** *A* is not used:

*Where the Construction with the Verb Involves a Second Noun with A*

*Prefiero el discreto al valiente* (A. Bello, 1972: 255, no. 900)
I prefer a cautious man to a bold man

*Prefiero Barcelona a Madrid* (*Esbozo*, 374)
I prefer Barcelona to Madrid

*(La mujer) prefiere el militar al civil y el guerrero al militar de Academia* (F. Umbral, 1989: 46)
Women prefer soldiers to civilians and fighting men to Academy soldiers

Indeed, the use of *a* before both a direct and an indirect object can give rise to ambiguity, as in the following sentence:

*Soledad presentó a Pepita y a Larrañaga a Silvia* (P. Baroja, 1964b: 136)
Soledad introduced Pepita and Larrañaga to Silvia
(This could be understood the other way round. *Esbozo* recommends the use of an alternative construction in such a case)[6]

*When the Noun does not Denote a Specific Person (or Persons)*

*Busco una secretaria* (*DD*, 5)
I am looking for a secretary (i.e., I am looking for someone to be my secretary, but I do not yet know who)
(Contrast: *Busco a mi secretaria*, where the reference is to a specific person)

*El niño requiere un maestro severo* (A. Bello, 1972: 253)
The child requires a strict master (whose identity is as yet unknown)

*Para esta misión he contratado a dos personas que hablan ruso*
For this mission I have hired two people who speak Russian (the reference is to two specific people)

*Para esta misión busco dos personas que hablen ruso*
For this mission I am looking for two people who speak Russian (I do not yet know who they will be)[7]

Note the connection with the choice between indicative and subjunctive in such sentences (see **1048**).

**663** As already stated, the rules given are not always strictly adhered to, and authors may get tangled up in the difficulties that the use of *a* can present, as the following sentence shows:

*Y el historiador, que a lo que más teme siempre es a perder la atención del curioso invisible* (S. Lorén, 1967a: 11)
And what the historian always fears most is losing the attention of the invisible seeker of knowledge
(It would be simpler to say: *Lo que más teme el historiador es perder la atención...*)

**664** The English equivalents of some verbs vary according to whether *a* is used or not.

| | | | |
|---|---|---|---|
| *afectar a* | to have an effect on | *afectar* | to affect |

*La situación política afectó a la economía*
The political situation had an effect on the economy

| | | | |
|---|---|---|---|
| *ayudar a* | to contribute to | *ayudar* | to help |
| *dejar a* | to leave in the lurch | *dejar* | to leave |
| *obedecer a* | to respond to | *obedecer* | to obey |

*La enfermedad obedeció a los medicamentos*
The illness responded to the medicine

| | | | |
|---|---|---|---|
| *perder a* | to be the ruination of, to lose (figuratively) | *perder* | to lose |

*Perdió a su mujer a los dos años de boda* (I. Agustí, 1944: 24)
He lost his wife two years after they were married

| | | | |
|---|---|---|---|
| *querer a* | to love | *querer* | to want |
| *robar a* | to rob | *robar* | to steal |
| *tener a* | to keep, hold, have in one's house, consider | *tener* | to have |

*María tiene tres hijos*
María has three children

*María tenía a su hijo mayor en brazos*
María was holding her eldest child in her arms

*El verano pasado María tenía a su suegro en casa*
Last summer María had her father-in-law at home

*Tengo al presidente por un hombre honrado*
I consider the president an honourable man


## Other Meanings Associated with *a*

### 665 Direction

The preposition *a* is almost always used after verbs which express
the idea of direction or in constructions in which a similar verb
can be understood (see, however, *en* with a directional meaning,
**720–721**)

> *¡A casa!*
> Home!

> *La atrajo de nuevo a sí* (J. Izcaray, 1961: 147)
> He pulled her towards him again

> *Ahora, ven a mis brazos* (W. Fernández Flórez, 1967: 114)
> Now, come to my arms

> *Llegué a Madrid el martes* (*DUE*, II, 273)
> I got to Madrid on Tuesday

> *Llegar a la conclusión* (*DUE*, II, 274)
> I reached the conclusion

> *Tenía don Fausto que ir a la frontera a reunirse con su hija* (P.
> Baroja, 1951: 116)
> Don Fausto had to go to the border to meet his daughter
> (Note the double use of *a* here: *ir a la frontera/ir . . . a
> reunirse . . .*)

> *¿A qué vienes tú?* (C. Fuentes, 1979: 112)
> What have you come for?

> – *Usted quiere casarse conmigo? – preguntó Clara.*
> – *Sí, Clara, a eso he venido* (I. Allende, 1984: 84–5)
> 'You want to marry me?' asked Clara.
> 'Yes, Clara, that's what I've come for'


**666** Verbs like the following which suggest the idea of direction
(at least in a figurative sense), are also constructed with *a*:

|  |  |
|---|---|
| *comenzar a* | to begin to |
| *disponerse a* | to prepare to |

| | |
|---|---|
| *empezar a* | to begin to |
| *enseñar a* | to teach how to |
| *invitar a* | to invite to |

(Note that in some areas of Latin America *a* is not used with *invitar*: *te invito otra copa* for *te invito a otra copa*)[8]

| | |
|---|---|
| *obligar a* | to oblige to |
| *romper a* | to break out . . .ing |

(On the use of *a* in expressions like *total a* (or *por*) *pagar*, see **1116**.)

## 667 Remark

On the use of *a* + *por* see **778**.

## 668 Time

*A* is used in the following time expressions:

| | |
|---|---|
| *a las cinco* | at five o'clock |
| *al día siguiente* | on the following day |
| *a los veinte años* | at twenty (years old) |

*Manolo pensó que llovería a la noche* (J. Fernández Santos, 1977: 66–7)
Manolo thought that it would rain that night

*A la noche, a la mañana*, etc., are equivalent to *por la noche, por la mañana*, etc.[9]

**669** *A* can also be used in the sense of 'after':

*Murió a los tres meses y seis días de haber llegado a Italia* (A. Bryce Echenique, 1981: 181)
He died three months and six days after reaching Italy

*A poco mi tío estrechó la mano de aquel hombre* (M. Delibes, 1948: 16)
After a short while, my uncle shook that man's hand

*Al poco* is an alternative to *a poco*:

*Al poco llegó el alcalde* (F. García Pavón, 1980b: 160)
After a short time, the mayor arrived

*Al momento* has the same meaning as *en seguida* 'immediately':
- *Sírvame un vermú.*
- *Al momento, señorita* (C. J. Cela, 1991b: 173)
'Bring me a vermouth.'
'Immediately, miss'

## 670 Place

*A* is used in a number of set expressions of place, for example:

*Nos sentamos a la mesa* (C. Pérez Merinero, 1982: 44)
We sat down at the table

*La señora estaba sentada a la puerta* (A. Bello, 1972: 94)
The lady was sitting by the door

*A la sombra de un árbol*
In the shade of a tree

*A la entrada de la casa*
At the entrance to the house

*A la orilla del río*
On the bank of the river

*A bordo*
On board

*A la izquierda/derecha*
On the left/right

## 671 Manner

*A lo* + adjective (e.g. *a lo inglés* 'in the English way') has been mentioned in **66**.

*A la* + adjective, an ellipsis for *a la manera* + adjective, is also used with the same meaning (e.g. *a la inglesa*). It is common in culinary terminology: *a la andorrana* 'in the Andorran style', *a la gerundense* 'in the style of Gerona', *a la jardinera* 'à la jardinière', etc.

*A la*, like *a lo*, may be used with a noun or proper name:

*Era el último de los matrimonios a la antigua usanza* (J. Edwards, 1985: 92)
It was the last of the old-style marriages

*Una melena a la Paul MacCartney* (A. Skármeta, 1986: 132)
Long hair like Paul McCartney's

**672** *A* is also used in manner expressions such as:

> *Hecho a mano*                    Made by hand
>
> *Carmen Elgazu tenía su cara entre las manos y le comía a besos*
> (J. M. Gironella, 1966a: 688)
> Carmen Elgazu held his head in her hands and covered him
> in kisses
>
> *Retrato a lápiz de Pablo Jiménez* (A. Skármeta, 1986: 174)
> A pencil portrait of Pablo Jiménez

**673** Before a noun denoting a means of transport, *en* is generally
used, however, except with *pie* and *caballo*, which take *a*.

> *ir en avión*                      to go by plane
> *ir en coche*                      to go by car
> *ir en taxi*                       to go by taxi
> *ir en tren*                       to go by train

But:

> *ir a pie*                         to go on foot
> *Iremos a caballo*                 We'll go on horseback

**674** *A* is used in expressions indicating price or rate.

> *Compré este vino a cien pesetas el litro*
> I bought this one at 100 pesetas a litre
>
> *Al cinco por ciento*             At five per cent
>
> *Dos a dos*                        Two by two
>
> *El santo más santo peca siete veces al día* (A. M. Matute,
> 1977: 23)
> The greatest saint sins seven times a day
>
> *Historias de este tipo se publicaron a cientos* (A. Mingote,
> 1988: 33)
> Stories of this kind were published by the hundred

### 675 A after Verbs of Perception

*A* is used after verbs of perception such as *oler* 'to smell', *saber* 'to
taste', *sonar* 'to sound', etc.

> *Aquí huele a algo sofocante, que no es perfume* (P. Baroja, 1946–
> 51: I, 1218)
> It smells of something overpowering, and it is not perfume

*Esta medicina sabe a naranja* (*DUE*, II, 1074)
This medicine tastes of orange

*Suena a falso, ¿verdad?* (J. M. Gironella, 1966b: 286)
It sounds wrong, doesn't it?

## 676 *A* with the Meaning 'If'

Before an infinitive *a* may be used with the value of *si* 'if' – see
**1098–1099**.

## 677 *A* with an Indirect Object

Although English often uses 'to' to render Spanish *a* when it marks
the indirect object, other English prepositions are sometimes used.
Spanish *aceptar a una persona alguna cosa* is 'to accept something
from a person'; *le he comprado a mi primo un libro* is 'I've bought a
book from my cousin'.

> *Era para ver las piernas a la moza que traía las cartas* (M. Alvar,
> 1982: 32)
> It was in order to see the legs of the girl who brought the
> letters
> (Or: . . . *las piernas de la moza* . . .)

See also the last example of **278**.

## 678 Adverbial Expressions

*A* is used in a large number of adverbial expressions and idioms,
for example:

| | |
|---|---|
| *a tientas* | gropingly, feeling one's way |
| *a bulto* | roughly, approximately |
| *a manos llenas* | generously |
| *a oscuras* | in the dark |
| *a todo correr* | at full speed |
| *a regañadientes* | grudgingly |
| *a tontas y a locas* | haphazardly, any old how |
| *a diario* | daily[10] |

## *Ante*

### 679 Place

*Ante* can be used instead of *delante de*.

> *Se detuvo Martina ante un portal de miserable aspecto* (M. Delibes, 1948: 206)
> Martina stopped in front of a miserable-looking doorway

> *Decenas de polacos hacen cola ante una lechería* (*El País*, 4 December 1980: 3)
> Many Poles are queuing outside a dairy

### 680 *Ante* = 'in the Presence of'

> *Compareció ante el juez* (*Esbozo*, 439)
> He appeared before the magistrate

> *Firmar ante dos notarios*
> Signing before two notaries

> *Pedro era el hombre con quien soñó ante sus compañeras de colegio* (A. Bryce Echenique, 1981: 137)
> Pedro was the man she dreamed of with her school friends

### 681 Precedence

> *ante todas cosas/todo* (*Esbozo*, 439)
> in the first place, above all

**682** As a prefix, *ante-* expresses precedence of time or place:

| | |
|---|---|
| *anteayer* | the day before yesterday |
| *anteanoche* | the night before last |
| *los antepasados* | ancestors, forefathers |
| *la antesala* | anteroom |
| *el antebrazo* | forearm |

### 683 Cause

*Ante* may have the meaning 'because of', 'as a result of', a use which is favoured today in journalistic writing.

*Ante esta grosera impertinencia, el alcalde le puso una multa de 100 pesetas* (J. A. de Zunzunegui, 1959b: 184)

As a result of this gross impertinence, the mayor imposed a fine of 100 pesetas on him

*El guardia le reiteró que sería enviado a prisión ante lo cual el joven cobró miedo* (*ABC*, 10 February 1980: 46)

The policeman told him again that he would be sent to prison, which made the young man afraid

## Bajo

**684** *Bajo*, like *debajo de*, has the meaning 'under'.

*Tres grados bajo cero* (*Esbozo*, 439)

Three degrees below zero

*Bajo un montón de arena* (Marsá, 1986: 160)

Under a pile of sand

*Bajo de* is sometimes found in literary register, but is restricted in meaning to the literal indication of place:

*Y he venido a vivir mis días aquí, bajo de tus pies blancos* (*DD*, 67)

And I have come to live out my days here, beneath your white feet

**685** *Bajo*, unlike *debajo de*, can be used figuratively:

*Lena vivió algunas días bajo el temor de que iban a internarla en un Reformatorio* (D. Medio, 1958: 102)

For some days, Lena lived in fear that they would put her in a Reformatory

*Se prohibe jugar a la pelota, bajo la multa de dos pesetas* (P. Baroja, 1946–51: VI, 249)

It is forbidden to play ball games, on penalty of a fine of two pesetas

*Estar bajo tutela* (*Esbozo*, 439)

To be under guardianship

## Cabe

**686** *Cabe* is occasionally found in deliberately archaistic literary texts with the meaning of 'near' (= *junto a, cerca de*):

*Vive en la plaza mayor, cabe la iglesia* (Marsá, 1986: 160)
He lives in the main square, next to the church

## Con

### 687 *Con* = 'With'

*Con* almost always corresponds to English 'with': not only in the meaning of 'in the company of', but also indicating an instrument or means.

> *Vino con mi padre* (*Esbozo*, 439)
> He came with my father
>
> *Le hirió con la espada* (*Esbozo*, 439)
> He wounded him with the sword
>
> *Le recibió con los brazos abiertos*
> She received him with open arms
>
> *Café con leche* (*Esbozo*, 439)
> Coffee with milk ('white coffee')

### 688 *Con* = 'Although'

One of the values of *con* with an infinitive is that of 'although' (see also **1097**).

> *Con ser Álvaro tan sagaz, no evitó que le engañasen* (*Esbozo*, 440)
> Although Álvaro is so shrewd, he did not avoid being deceived
> (Also: *Aunque Álvaro es tan sagaz ...*)

### 689 Cause

*Con* has the meaning of 'because of', 'through' in an example such as:

> *Con la emoción no podía decir nada*
> She could not say anything for emotion

Similarly, *con* is sometimes used in reflexive passive sentences to introduce an instrumental agent:[11]

*La pared se hundió con el peso de la techumbre* (Gili Gaya, 1964: 127)
The wall collapsed with the weight of the roof
(= *la pared fue hundida por el peso de la techumbre*)

## 690 *Con* = 'Against'

*Y el día que perdamos con Portugal aquí habrá que matar a alguien* (E. Romero, 1963: 310)
And the day we lose against Portugal someone will get killed here

This usage is no doubt by analogy with *jugar con* 'to play with', *un partido con* 'a match with'.

## 691 Latin-American Usages of *con*[12]

*Pedro jamás regresó con ella* (J. Rulfo, 1981: 23)
Pedro never went back to her house
(Standard Spanish has no simple preposition for this notion; it would have to be expressed by *a su casa*)

*¿Me puedes presentar con él?* (Kany, 1951: 348)
Can you introduce me to him?
(Standard Spanish *a*)

# *De*

## 692 Possession

*La casa de mi padre* (*Esbozo*, 440)
My father's house

*El amigo de todos* (*Esbozo*, 440)
Everyone's friend

*El agua del río*
The river water

## 693 Origin, Provenance, Starting-point, Cause

*El alumno nuevo es de Londres*
The new student is from London

*Procede de buena familia* (*DD*, 133)
She comes from a good family

*Iremos de Barcelona a Sevilla*
We shall go from Barcelona to Seville

*Lo hice de miedo* (*Esbozo*, 441)
I did it out of fear

*Un hombre muere de risa* (O. Caballero, 1980: 113)
A man dies of laughter

*Se casó o amancebó con una mujer de la que tuvo una hija* (J. Goytisolo, 1985: 223)
He married or shacked up with a woman by whom he had a daughter

*De* + infinitive can be the equivalent of a causal subordinate clause (see **1099**).

## 694 Material

*La estatua de mármol* (*Esbozo*, 440)
The marble statue

| | |
|---|---|
| *Un tenedor de plata* | A silver fork |
| *Un jersey de lana* | A woollen jersey |

## 695 Conditional

*De*, like *a*, can form a conditional structure with a following infinitive (see **1098**).

## 696 *De* = 'As'

*De* sometimes corresponds to English 'as' in the sense of 'in the function of':

*Vístete de peregrino* (C. Rojas, 1982: 34)
Dress as a pilgrim

*De joven soñó con la jubilación, y ahora, de jubilado, soñaba con la juventud* (M. Delibes, quoted in Coste and Redondo, 1965: 346)
As a young man he dreamed of retirement, and as a retired man he dreamed of youth

*Chimista hacía de médico en el país* (P. Baroja, 1959: 204)
Chimista acted as a doctor in the country

### 697 *De* in Adjectival Phrases

*De* often corresponds to English 'with' in such expressions:

*Un hombre de dinero* (J. A. de Zunzunegui, 1952b: 68)
A man with money

*Un chiquillo de ojos azules* (P. Baroja, 1959: 36)
A little boy with blue eyes

*¿Ves la casa de la chimenea alta?*
Can you see the house with the tall chimney?

*Una silla de ruedas*          A wheelchair

**698** *De* may also express function in adjectival phrases.

*una sala de espera*          a waiting-room
*un coche de alquiler*          a hired car

### 699 Manner

*De* can express the manner in which something is done or the use
that is made of something.

*Almuerza de pie* (*Esbozo*, 440)
He has his lunch standing up

*Me ha mirado de dar miedo* (J. A. de Zunzunegui, 1952a: 228)
He has looked at me in a way that makes me afraid

*Lo hizo de mala gana* (*Esbozo*, 441)
He did it unwillingly

*¿Quieres que nos hablemos de tú?* (M. Mihura, 1981: 128)
Would you like us to call each other *tú*?

Compare the following with the second example:

*Pero los precios son de miedo* (J. A. de Zunzunegui, 1952a: 149)
But prices are frightful

Expressions of this kind involving the numeral *uno, una* indicate
that an action is carried out quickly:

*De un trago se bebió la tisana* (*Esbozo*, 441)
He drank the infusion down with one gulp

*Acabemos de una vez* (*Esbozo*, 441)
Let's get it over with in one go

**700** Some common Spanish verbs are constructed with a follow
ing *de* which does not have a regular equivalent in English.

| | |
|---|---|
| *coger de* | to take by |
| *coger a alguien del brazo* | to take someone by the arm |
| *colgar de* | to hang on |
| *colgar su sombrero* | to hang one's hat on the peg |
| *de la percha* | |
| *ir(se) de* | |
| *irse de copeo* | to go drinking |

*Por la noche Boris Karloff se va de cementerios* (*La Codorniz*, 1941–4: 272)
At night Boris Karloff goes round the cemeteries

| | |
|---|---|
| *tirar de* | to pull (on) |
| *¡No me tires del pelo!* | Don't pull my hair! |

Some verbs which are in the standard language constructed with a following *a* are constructed with *de* in Latin-American Spanish. Kany (1951: 352–3) mentions *atreverse de* 'to dare to' for standard *atreverse a*, *comenzar de* and *empezar de* 'to begin to' for standard *comenzar a* and *empezar a*.[13] He also mentions the use of *olvidar de* 'to forget to' for standard *olvidar* or *olvidarse de*.

## 701 Time

*De* is used in some expressions of time.

*Viajaremos de noche y descansaremos de día*
We'll travel by night and rest by day

*Las galerías de arte no abren de mañana* (M. Puig, 1980: 30)
Art galleries are not open in the morning

## 702 *De* with Emphatic Meaning

*De* has an emphatic value in constructions which express an element of pity, irony, disparagement, threat, etc. They always have to do with feelings or opinions which imply negative or unpleasant states of affairs or information. *De* stresses the preceding word (a noun or adjective or interjection expressing pain or threat). In the examples given, it is clear that the word following *de* is the real subject of the sentence.[14]

*Las pobrecitas de las mujeres se quedan abandonadas* (P. Baroja, 1946–51: VI, 20)
The poor women were left behind

*¡Tontos de nosotros!* (J. A. de Zunzunegui, 1959b: 182)
How silly we are!

*Hasta la imbécil de tu mujer se burla ya de ti* (C. Laforet, 1966: 34)
Even your stupid wife laughs at you now

*¡Ay de ellos si pierden!* (J. Izcaray, 1961: 100)
Woe betide them if they lose!

But:

*¡Feliz tú!*                 Lucky old you!
(The adjective has a positive affective value)

**703** When the preposition *de* is used after words which generally have a favourable meaning, an ironic nuance is given to the sentence.[15] There is thus a difference between:

*Feliz él, que cree que no morirá nunca* (L. Ricardo Alonso, 1981: 224)
Lucky the person who believes that he will never die

and

*Feliz de ella que podía creer sin ver* (J. Cortázar, 1974: 35)
Fortunately for her, she was able to believe without seeing

**704** *De* + adjective sometimes expresses cause or consequence, and here too *de* has an emphatic, almost superlative, value. The adjective agrees with the noun or pronoun (which may be implicit) to which it relates. *Puro* used adverbially (hence invariably) before the adjective gives further reinforcement.

*Ahora de puro impaciente me he puesto a escribir este cuento* (A. Bryce Echenique, 1981: 247)
Now, through sheer impatience, I have sat down to write this tale

*Estoy de nervioso que no sé cómo no he degollado a este hombre* (C. Arniches, quoted in Fernández, 1951: 106)
I'm so nervous I don't know how I've avoided cutting this man's throat

*Hay zapatos que recuerdo con ternura: así de suaves y flexibles eran* (J. J. Arreola, 1986: 187)
There are some shoes that I remember with affection, (because they were) so soft and pliable

## 705 *De* in Expressions of Quantity

*De*, like English 'of', is normally used in expressions of quantity (*medio kilo de queso* 'half a kilo of cheese', etc.). *Un poco* normally takes *de*:

*Un poco de carne*          A little meat/a bit of meat

but in the spoken language, *de* is sometimes omitted:

*Ahora nos traen un poco vino* (R. Sánchez Ferlosio, 1971: 209)
Bring us a drop of wine now

*Por Dios, Sergio, un poquito caldo de gallina para entonar el estómago* (J. A. de Zunzunegui, 1956b: 207)
For heaven's sake, Sergio, a drop of chicken broth to settle the stomach

Compare also:

*Tengo yo aquí un cachito queso* (ibid., 217)
I've got a bit of cheese here

(See also the examples in **457**.)

## 706 *De* in Dates

A date such as the '21st of November 1985' is read and written in full in Spanish as *el veintiuno de noviembre de 1985*. In correspondence there are various ways of representing the date. The form generally favoured by older people is, for example, *Madrid, 21 de noviembre de 1985*; but it is usual nowadays to use only numerals, e.g. *21-XI-(19)85*, and many people use commas instead of *de*, e.g. *Madrid, 27, agosto, 75* (C. Martín Gaite, 1980: 101), *Jaca, 25 de julio, 1987* (letter to JdeB from R. Lapesa).

## 707 *De* in Expressions of Place

*De* is used, as is English 'of', in geographical names such as

*La provincia de Málaga*          The province of Malaga
*La isla de Tenerife*          The island of Tenerife

**708** Formerly, *de* was also used with names of streets, e.g. *la avenida de José Antonio*, *la plaza de Colón*, *la calle de Génova*, etc., although today *de* is often omitted.[16] JdeB noticed (August 1983) a street in Valladolid which had the sign *Calle de Tudela* on one side and *Calle Tudela* on the other. Streets, etc. are also frequently referred to simply by their distinctive names, omitting *calle de*, etc.

> *Era la una y media y la plaza bullía de gentes que venían de Sol por Romanones, que subían de Atocha por Magdalena y del Rastro por Duque de Alba* (J. A. de Zunzunegui, 1954: 130)
> It was half past one and the square was seething with people coming from the Puerta del Sol along the Calle de Romanones, from Atocha along the Calle de Magdalena and from the Rastro along the Calle del Duque de Alba
> (See also the first examples in **736** and **1204**.)

This usage can give rise to ambiguity and hence humour:

> *Otra vez entró un señor de aspecto sólido a comprarse una capa. Dijo que la enviasen al general Perón. Como general Perón es una calle madrileña, insistieron en preguntarle su nombre propio. Era el general Perón* (F. Umbral, 1972: 95)
> On another occasion a solidly built gentleman came in to buy a cape. He told them to send it to General Perón. Since General Perón is the name of a street in Madrid, they insisted on asking him his own name. It was General Perón

> *Y Mario apenas tuvo tiempo ya de saltar a un taxi rugiendo:*
> *– ¡Don Ramón de la Cruz!*
> *A lo que contestó el chófer:*
> *– Encantado de conocerle, caballero* (E. Jardiel Poncela, *¡Espérame en Siberia, vida mía!*, 92)
> And Mario hardly had time to jump into a taxi yelling, 'Don Ramón de la Cruz!'
> To which the driver replied, 'Pleased to meet you, sir'.

## 709 Remark

With names of banks, the full title is generally used, although occasionally *de* is omitted:

> *Estaba empleado en el Banco Bilbao* (J. A. de Zunzunegui, 1956b: 76)
> He worked in the Banco de Bilbao

## 710 *De* as a Partitive

This usage, in which *de* expresses an indefinite quantity, is generally associated with the verb *dar* 'to give' (also in Latin-American Spanish with *pegar*):[17]

> *Dar de bofetadas (cuchilladas, palos, puñaladas) a una persona*
> To slap (knife, club, stab) someone
> *Oímos que alguien daba de cabezazos contra nuestra pared*
> (J. Rulfo, 1981: 70)
> We could hear someone hitting their head against our wall

**711** *De* is used before a husband's surname by his wife (*la señora de Sánchez* 'Mrs Sánchez') or by a married couple (*los señores de Sánchez* 'Mr and Mrs Sánchez').

**712** *De* may form part of a Spanish surname (often a noble family name), but it is omitted when reference to the surname only is made: thus *Miguel de Unamuno* but *Unamuno murió en 1936* 'Unamuno died in 1936'. This principle also applies to foreign surnames, which should be borne in mind when consulting alphabetical lists in the Spanish-speaking world.

## 713 Superfluous Use of *de*

*De* is nowadays often found before *que*, a phenomenon known as *dequeísmo*.[18] It is considered incorrect.

> *Pienso de que la orden no es justa* (*DD*, 134)
> I don't think the order is fair
> (*Pienso que la orden no es justa* is the correct form)
> *No creo de que vaya a dimitir nadie* (Marsá, 1986: 154)
> I don't think anyone's going to resign
> (*No creo que vaya a dimitir nadie* is the correct form)
> *Se queja el escritor de que muchos periodistas dicen «es preciso DE QUE»* (A. Mingote, 1988: 16)
> The writer complains that many journalists say . . .

## 714 Omission of *de*

In Latin-American Spanish, *de* is sometimes omitted in cases where it is required in the standard language:

... *zapatos tenis* ... (C. Fuentes, 1979: 17)
... tennis shoes ...
(Standard Spanish *zapatos de tenis*)

... *agua Colonia* ... (J. Cortázar, 1974: 202)
... eau-de-Cologne ...
(Standard Spanish *agua de Colonia*)

## Desde

### 715 Place

*Desde* has the meaning 'from'.

> *Desde la finca a donde llegan por igual el repiqueteo de las campanas de Amurrio y Respaldiza, se divisan los picachos verdes de las montañas* (M. Vázquez Montalbán, 1990: 11)
> From the estate to where the sound of the bells of Amurrio and Respaldiza reaches, you can see the green peaks of the mountains

### 716 Time

It is used in time expressions corresponding to English constructions with 'since' and 'for', e.g.

> *La conozco desde el año pasado*
> I have known her since last year

> *La conozco desde hace quince años*
> I have known her for fifteen years

It is often used in combination with *hasta*, e.g.

> *Desde las tres hasta las cinco*
> From three o'clock till five
> I have known her for fifteen years

In Latin-American Spanish *desde* is sometimes used to indicate a point in time (English 'on', 'at'):

> *Desde el lunes llegó* (Lapesa, 1980: 592)
> She arrived on Monday

Compare the parallel use of *hasta* in **624**.

## 717 Remark

When a state of affairs continues from a past starting-point indicated by *desde* or *desde hace* up to the present, a present tense is used in Spanish by contrast with the perfect which is used in English:

> *Te parece hablar con ese extraño compañero enquistado que desde hace años llevas dentro de ti* (M. Vázquez Montalbán, 1990b: 9)
> It seems to you that you are talking with that strange, closed person that you have carried inside you for years

Similarly, in past time a Spanish imperfect corresponds to the English pluperfect:

> *La conocía desde el año anterior*
> I had known her since the year before

> *La conocía desde hacía quince años*
> I had known her for fifteen years

> *No podía ser verdadera porque nos conocíamos con Huxley desde hacía años* (P. Neruda, 1976: 227)
> It could not be true, because we had known Huxley for years

## *En*

## 718 Place

*En* is used to indicate location.

> *El libro está en la mesa*
> The book is on the table

> *Mañana no estaremos en casa*
> Tomorrow we shall not be at home

> *Jugar en la calle*
> Playing in the street

> *Mi amigo Juan está en España*
> My friend Juan is in Spain

However, if a notion of direction is involved, *a* is mostly used (but see **720**); *a* often corresponds in such cases to English 'in' or 'at' with verbs of motion:

> *Don Fausto fue a vivir a la calle Galande* (P. Baroja, 1951: 78)
> Don Fausto went to live in the Calle Galande
>
> *¿Qué vienes a buscar a esta casa?*
> What have you come to look for in this house?
>
> *Velasco convenció a Sacha de que debían ir a concluir el verano a Biarritz* (P. Baroja, 1946–51: II, 99)
> Velasco convinced Sacha that they should go and finish the summer at Biarritz
>
> *Quiero invitarte a dormir a mi casa* (J. Rulfo, 1981: 49)
> I would like to invite you to sleep at my house

The use of *a* rather than *en* in the four above examples depends upon the presence of verbs of motion (*ir, venir, invitar*) rather than on the verb immediately preceding the preposition: without such a verb one would say *vivir en una calle, buscar algo en una casa, concluir el verano en Biarritz, dormir en la casa de alguien*. When the notion of location is uppermost, and when the prepositional phrase is separated from the verb of motion, *en* can be used:

> *Mira, vamos a terminar de discutir esto en mi cuarto* (C. Laforet, 1966: 207)
> Look, let's go and finish talking about this in my room
> (But note that only *Vamos a mi cuarto a terminar de discutir esto* would be possible)
>
> *Casilda se marchó a vivir definitivamente en París* (J. Donoso, 1980: 196)
> Casilda went off to live in Paris for ever

### 719 *En* in Elliptical Expressions

> *Ya se ve que no ha estudiado usted en los jesuitas* (P. Baroja, 1961: 98)
> One can see that you have not studied with the Jesuits
> (*en los jesuitas = en una escuela de los jesuitas*)
>
> *Estaba medio pensionista en las monjas del Sagrado Corazón* (J. A. de Zunzunegui, 1952b: 100)
> She was a half-boarder with the nuns of the Sacred Heart
> (*en las monjas = en una escuela de las monjas*)

*Cenamos con los hermanos Peña y sus mujeres en Juanito Kojúa*
(M. Delibes, 1972: 165)
We dined with the Peña brothers and their wives at
Juanito Kojúa's
(*en Juanito Kojúa* = *en el restaurante de Juanito Kojúa*)

*Estuve en los toros* (M. Delibes, 1972: 52)
I was at the bullfight
(but *fui a los toros*)

## 720 *En* Indicating Direction

*En* is used to indicate direction with verbs which carry the implication of 'going inside', such as *entrar*, *penetrar*, etc.

*Entró en la iglesia* (*Esbozo*, 441)
She went into the church

*Los soldados penetraron en la ciudad*
The soldiers penetrated the town

However, *a* is used with *entrar* when it denotes the beginning of a process.[19]

*El reconocimiento médico es al viejo estilo: tocar timbre, entrar a una sala de espera y someterse a cinco horas de exámenes médicos* (*Cambio 16*, 21 May 1978: 109)
Medical appraisal is in the old style: a bell rings, you go into a waiting-room and submit yourself to five hours of medical exams

*A* is also regularly, though not invariably, used with *entrar*, *penetrar*, etc. in Latin-American Spanish:

*Cuando los nazis entraron a París* (P. Neruda, 1976: 66)
When the Nazis entered Paris
(See also **1163**, second example)

**721**  *En* is also used with verbs which denote only a limited movement.

*Me sentaré en un banco*
I will sit down on a bench

*El niño se acostará en la cama de sus padres*
The boy will sleep in his parents' bed

*Tumbarse en un sillón*
To lounge in an armchair

## 722 Time

*En* is also used to indicate a point in time or within a period of time:

| | |
|---|---|
| *En aquel momento* | At that moment |
| *Esto ocurrió en invierno* | This happened in winter |

In Latin-American Spanish, *en* is often omitted in popular speech with words like *ocasión* (= *vez*), *instante* and *momento*. Thus *aquel momento* may have the meaning *en aquel momento*, as in the first example above.[20]

*En* is increasingly found with the meaning of *dentro de* 'within' or *antes de* 'before', although examples like *\*vuelvo en quince minutos*[21] for 'I'll be back in fifteen minutes' are regarded as anglicisms and criticized by purists:

*En minutos serán ya las cinco* (*DD*, 170)
In minutes it will be five o'clock

(Seco recommends avoidance of this construction, and comments that it is more widespread in Latin America than in Spain.)

*Regreso en diez minutos* (sign read by JdeB in the University of Granada, March 1989)
Back in ten minutes

## 723 Manner

A number of adverbial expressions of manner are formed with *en*:

| | |
|---|---|
| *Estar en huelga* | To be on strike |
| *En mangas de camisa* | In one's shirtsleeves |
| *Viajar en avión/tren* | To travel by plane/train |
| (See also **673**) | |
| *Permanecer en pie* | To remain standing |
| *Ponerse en pie* | To stand up |

(Note, however, that *de pie* can also be used in the last two examples)

*Lo dijo en broma* (*Esbozo*, 441)
He said it in jest

> *Es maravillosa la facilidad y la hondura con que reacciona una mujer en madre, pensó* (J. A. de Zunzunegui, 1956b: 292)
> How easily and how deeply a woman reacts as a mother, he thought

*En* is also used with *hacer bien/mal*:

> *Qué bien hizo Baudelaire en morirse joven* (F. Umbral, 1979: 67)
> How well Baudelaire did to die young

**724** *En* is used elliptically for *en el papel de* 'in the role of':

> *Lucía Bosé en George Sand*
> Lucía Bosé as George Sand
>
> *Christopher Sandhorst en Frédéric Chopin*
> Christopher Sandhorst as Frédéric Chopin

## 725 With Ordinal Numbers

*En* + infinitive is used after *primero, último*, etc. ('the first, last, etc. to . . .').

> *El último país americano en abolir la esclavitud sería Brasil, el trece de mayo de 1888* (*Cuadernos Hispanoamericanos*, 451-2, January–February 1988: 42)
> The last American country to abolish slavery was to be Brazil, on 13 May 1888

## 726 Price

*En* may be used instead of *por* in expressions of price:

> *Déjemelo en cinco mil pesetas y me lo llevo* (J. A. de Zunzunegui, 1952b: 240)
> Let me have it for 5,000 pesetas and I'll take it away with me
>
> *Le vendí mi cronómetro en ciento noventa pesos* (P. Baroja, 1959: 171)
> I sold him my chronometer for 190 pesos

## 727 *En* in Negative Expressions

When, before the verb, *en* is followed by (*todo* +) a noun denoting a period of time such as *mañana* 'morning', *día* 'day', *noche* 'night', *año* 'year', etc., the expression always has a negative meaning.

*En toda mi vida tuve otra idea de mis padres* (M. Delibes, 1948: 14)
I had no other idea of my parents for the whole of my life

*En tu vida has trabajado, Pedro* (A. Bryce Echenique, 1981: 134)
You've never worked in your life, Pedro

*En toda la tarde agarró una rata* (M. Delibes, 1968a: 73)
He did not catch a single rat in the whole afternoon

If *en* + noun phrase follows the verb, the verb must be preceded by a negative, just as if it were a negative like *nunca, ninguno*, etc. Thus the first example above might be recast as *No tuve otra idea de mis padres en toda la vida*. See **1292**.

**728** There are expressions of place which behave in the same way.

*En parte alguna se le pudo encontrar* (A. Bello, 1972: 322, no. 1134)
Nowhere could it be found

*En el mundo se ha visto una criatura más perversa* (ibid.)
Nowhere in the world has a more perverse creature been seen

Again, the first example in this paragraph might be re-expressed *No se le pudo encontrar en parte alguna* and the second *No se ha visto una criatura más perversa en el mundo*.

**729** The adverbial expression *en absoluto* (and the Latin-American *absolutamente* and - especially in the spoken language - *todavía*) are also often used with negative meaning, 'not at all' and 'not yet' respectively.

*Dices, por ejemplo, que soy perezoso. En absoluto* (L. Buñuel, 1982: 75)
You say, for instance, that I am lazy. Not at all

– *¿Tienes veinte pesos que prestarme?*
– *Absolutamente* (Kany, 1951: 268)
'Have you got twenty pesos to lend me?'
'Certainly not'

– *¿Ya vino tu padre?*
– *Todavía* (Kany, 1951: 269)
'Has your father come yet?'
'Not yet'

## *Entre*

### 730 *Entre* = 'Between', 'Among'

See **287** for the forms of the pronoun following *entre*.

**731**   *Vivo entre Leeds y Bradford*
I live between Leeds and Bradford

*Estoy entre dos fuegos*
I'm caught in the crossfire

*Ésta era la costumbre entre los romanos*
This was the custom among the Romans

### 732 Collaboration

*Entre* can also be used in expressions which suggest an idea of cooperation among a number of people. Sometimes there is a problem of number agreement between verb and subject, as in the fourth example below.

*Y entre los cinco no pudimos levantar al animal* (P. Baroja, 1955: 67)
And the five of us could not lift the animal

*Entre Dagobert y don Fausto le tranquilizaron* (P. Baroja, 1951: 138)
Dagobert and Don Fausto calmed him down between the two of them

*Entre todos me arrastraron hacia el molino de trigo* (J. Goytisolo, 1960: 136)
Together they all dragged me towards the mill

*Entre ella, tú y Juana haríais el trabajo* (A. Grosso, 1978: 153)
She, you and Juana together would do the work
(See also **1277**.)

## 733 *Entre semana*

*Entre semana* has the meaning 'during the week':

> *Entre semana podría ir todas las tardes, una vez terminadas las clases* (J. M. Gironella, 1966b: 279)
> During the week he could go every evening, once classes were over

## 734 *Entre* + Noun + *y* + Noun (Repeated)

This is equivalent to English 'between two', 'between one and the next':

> *La suegra suspiraba profundamente entre sorbo y sorbo de Vichy* (C. J. Cela, 1967b: 41)
> Mother-in-law gave a deep sigh between one sip of her Vichy and the next

> *Casi siempre entre amor y amor, comían desnudos en la cama* (G. García Márquez, 1977: 356)
> Between one lovemaking session and the next they almost always ate naked in bed

# *Hacia*

## 735 Direction

The notion of direction expressed by *hacia* may be literal or figurative.

> *Mira hacia el Norte* (*Esbozo*, 441)
> Look towards the north

> *Tomó en sus manos la barbilla de Marta y, atrayendo a la muchacha hacia sí, le dio un beso* (J. M. Gironella, 1966b: 61)
> He took Marta's chin in his hands and, pulling the girl towards him, gave her a kiss

> *El camino de España hacia Europa pasa por Iberoamérica* (*Cambio 16*, 21 May 1978: 117)
> Spain's way towards Europe passes through Spanish America

*La muchacha siente hacia Pablo un agradecimiento profundo*
(C. J. Cela, 1963a: 206)
The girl feels a deep sense of gratitude towards Pablo

## 736 Approximate Place and Time

The use of *hacia* for the notion of place gives a vaguer impression than *en*.

*Yo creo que vive hacia Antón Martín, pero no sé más* (C. J. Cela, 1969: 341)
I think he lives around the Calle Antón Martín, but more than that I don't know
(For *Antón Martín*, see **708**.)

*Hacia* can similarly express approximate time or age.

*Nos veremos hacia las cinco de la tarde*
We'll see each other about five in the afternoon

*Hacia San Segundo caían todos los años por el pueblo los extremeños* (M. Delibes, 1968a: 77)
The men from Extremadura appeared in the village every year around the feast of San Segundo

*Hacia los treinta años se marchó a América*
When he was about thirty he went off to America

## Hasta

**737** *Hasta* is used in the sense of 'until, up to':

*La patrulla llegó hasta las líneas enemigas* (Marsá, 1986: 165)
The patrol reached the enemy lines

**738** It also has the meaning 'even' and is an alternative to *aun, incluso*:

*Gritó, lloró y hasta pataleó* (*DD*, 219)
He shouted, wept and even kicked

*Hasta los niños lo comprenden* (*DUE*, II, 22)
Even children understand

(In this usage, *hasta* is usually considered to be adverbial in nature.)

**739** In Central America and Colombia,[22] it has the meaning 'not before' when used with a point in time:

> *Hasta las tres iré (DD, 219)*
> I won't go before three
> (Standard: *No iré hasta las tres*)

## Para

**740** The correct use of *por* and *para* is one of the delicate points of Spanish grammar for English speakers, since both are frequently rendered in English by 'for', and both can be used in the same contexts without the difference in meaning between them always being clear in English terms. Thus both *por* and *para* can be used in place and time expressions, and both can express purpose.

However, *por* and *para* are rarely completely interchangeable (but see **754**): there is usually some difference in meaning between them.

### 741 Destination, Purpose

*Para* is the equivalent of English 'for' in the sense of destination and purpose 'in order to'.

> *Esta carta es para el correo (Esbozo, 442).*
> This letter is for the post

> *Tela buena para camisas (Esbozo, 442)*
> Good cloth for (making) shirts

> *El gobierno ha realizado gastos enormes para la construcción de sus bases (La Vanguardia, 20 January 1963: 5)*
> The government has spent an enormous amount of money on constructing its bases

> *Pues eso era, me dije para mí (E. Romero, 1963: 56)*
> 'So that was it', I said to myself

> *En las calles madrileñas cada vez hay menos sitio para aparcar (ABC, 16 May 1978: 3)*
> In the streets of Madrid there is increasingly little space to park

**742** *Para* is used with *bastante, suficiente*:

> *Esta temperatura no es bastante para fundir el vidrio* (*DUE*, I, 355)
> This temperature is not enough to melt glass

Note the alternative construction *(lo) bastante como para*:

> *No fueron lo bastante discretos y misteriosos como para impedir una ampliación de la sociedad* (C. J. Cela, 1963b: 105)
> They were not sufficiently prudent and secretive to prevent a broadening of the society

**743** After a verb of motion, destination is generally expressed by *a* (see **665**).

**744** *Para que*, followed by the subjunctive, forms an adverbial clause of purpose:

> *Repito mi mandato para que no lo olvides* (*Esbozo*, 442)
> I will repeat my order so that you do not forget it

## 745 Movement

*Para* has the meaning of 'in the direction of', 'to':

> *Tshombe salió hoy para Kolwezi* (*La Vanguardia*, 20 January 1963: 10)
> Tshombe left today for Kolwezi

> – *¡Pero siéntense y tomen algo!*
> – *No, no, que es tardísimo, vamos para casa* (J. A. de Zunzunegui, 1954: 540)
> 'But sit down and have a drink.'
> 'No, no, it's very late; we're going home'

> *El hombre del puro mira para el viajero* (C. J. Cela, 1967d: 29)
> The man with the cigar looked at the traveller

Compared with *a*, *para* denotes a less concrete direction:

> *Este tren va para el Norte* (Berschin, 1987: 253)
> This train is bound for the north

> *Este tren va al Norte* (ibid.)
> This train is going to the north

## 746 Time

Both *por* and *para* can be used to indicate time. *Para* indicates a limit, a time by which something is due to happen. It is often the equivalent of English 'until', 'by'.

*Lo dejaremos para mañana* (*Esbozo*, 442)
We'll leave it for (= until) tomorrow

*Miraba también los árboles y pensaba: «Para setiembre se les caerán las hojas y yo no lo veré»* (R. J. Sender, 1970: 230)
He also looked at the trees and thought, 'By September their leaves will fall and I shall not see it'

*– ¿Cuántos años tienes tú?*
*– Voy para dieciocho* (J. A. de Zunzunegui, 1952a: 198)
'How old are you?'
'I'm coming up to eighteen'

## 747 Relation

*Para* may express a relationship in which an expected consequence does not take place:

*Para principiante no lo ha hecho mal* (*Esbozo*, 442)
For a beginner he has not done it badly
(Note the absence of the indefinite article in Spanish –see **83ff.**)

*Para el tiempo que hace no está atrasado el campo* (*Esbozo*, 442)
In view of the weather things are not being slow on the land

## 748 *Para con*

*Para con* has the meaning of 'towards' when used of a feeling:

*En nada disminuyó su amistad para con López* (M. de Unamuno, 1967a: 66)
His friendship towards López did not at all diminish

*Pido al lector cierta indulgencia para conmigo* (C. J. Cela, 1958: 14)
I ask the reader to have a certain indulgence towards me

*Hace unos años una reunión de solidaridad para con el pueblo de Chile se celebró en Polonia* (J. Cortázar, 1984: 83)
Some years ago a solidarity meeting for the people of Chile was held in Poland

**749** *Para con* may also have the meaning of 'compared with':

*Para con mi padre soy bastante alto* (Van Dam, 1967: 341)
I am tall compared with my father

## 750 Estar para

*Estar para* indicates the imminence of a future action:

*Está para llover* (*Esbozo*, 442)
It is about to rain

*Estás para ascender a capitán* (*Esbozo*, 442)
You're on the point of becoming a captain

**751** *Estar para* also has the meaning of 'to feel like':

*Pensábamos hacerlo en seguida porque ni yo ni ella estamos para perder el tiempo* (J. A. de Zunzunegui, 1956b: 108)
We intended to do it straightaway because neither she nor I are people to waste time

*Hay años en que no está uno para nada* (F. Díaz-Plaja, 1966: 249)
There are years when you're fit for nothing

*Ser para* has the meaning 'to be of use to':

*Yo no soy para esto* (Van Dam, 1969: I, 1092)
I'm not the person for this

*No soy quién para ella* (ibid., 982)
I'm not the man for her

## 752 Remark

In popular speech and in songs *para* is often shortened to *pa*, or even to *p'* when the following word begins with *a*.

*El agua, 'pa' las ranas – interrumpió Chomín* (J. A. de Zunzunegui, 1952a: 34)
'Water for the frogs,' interrupted Chomín

*¡Voto 'pa' los dieciséis!* (F. Vizcaíno Casas, 1978: 115)
I'm voting for the age of majority being sixteen!
*Tu hijo ya me han dicho que va p'alante* (J. A. de Zunzunegui, 1954: 595)
Your son is getting on well, they tell me
(*alante = adelante*)

## Por

### 753 *Por* Introducing an Agent

*Por* introduces the agent of a passive sentence and as such is the equivalent of English 'by'.[23]

> *¿Por qué dejarse dominar por los caprichos meteorológicos?* (*ABC*, 16 May 1978: last page)
> Why let ourselves be dominated by the weather's whims?

> *El presidente Adolfo Suárez se vio de repente increpado por una moza* (*Cambio 16*, 21 May 1978: 124)
> President Adolfo Suárez suddenly found himself scolded by a young girl

Note also the expressions *es doctor por la universidad de Madrid* 'he has a doctorate from the University of Madrid', *es diputado por Barcelona* 'he is a deputy for Barcelona', which carry the idea of *su doctorado fue concedido por la universidad de Madrid, ha sido elegido diputado por los barceloneses* respectively.

### 754 Purpose

The meaning of *por* is here very close to that of *para* in **741**.[24] In the following examples, *para* could equally be used.

> *Hay veces que una ríe por no llorar* (M. Delibes, 1969a: 262)
> There are times when you laugh in order not to cry
> (The speaker is a woman)
> (More literally, this could be translated as '. . . for the sake of not crying')

> *Es necesario un esfuerzo por desarrollar la organización del Partido en Madrid* (J. Izcaray, 1961: 84)
> An effort is necessary to develop the organization of the Party in Madrid

(Verbs of 'effort', e.g. *esforzarse, luchar, pugnar*, etc., take *por* with an infinitive)

*Ir por* (see also *a por*, **778**) has the meaning of 'to go for':

> *Espere, voy por la llave* (J. Fernández Santos, 1977: 109)
> Wait, I'll go for the key

Even Spanish speakers may hesitate between *por* and *para* denoting purpose, as can be seen from the following example:

> – *Se han formado ya las comisiones.*
> – *¿Quiénes son?*
> – *Presiden Rius, por los tejidos; Marín para las sedas, y Moixó, para el yute y derivados* (I. Agustí. 1945: 90)
> 'The commissions have been formed already.'
> 'Who are they?'
> 'The chairmen are: Rius, for textiles, Marín for silks and Moixó for jute and derivatives'

Indeed, *por* + infinitive sometimes expresses both cause and purpose simultaneously:

> *(Metí el periódico en la chaqueta.) Para leerlo en el viaje, me dije mentalmente, por justificarme a mí mismo el gesto* (F. Umbral, 1976b: 246–7)
> (I put the paper in my jacket.) To read on the journey, I told myself mentally, to justify my action to myself

### 755 Duration, Time

*Por* introduces adverbial phrases which signify duration or a period of time.

> *Un amor pleno va inserto por siempre en el alma sensible* (J. Ortega y Gasset, 1959: 76)
> A complete love is enshrined for ever in the feeling soul

> *Se quedaría aquí por cinco días* (*DUE*, II, 804)[25]
> He would stay here for five days

It is also used in phrases involving *vez* 'time, occasion':

> *Por primera vez tuve una visión directa, rica, importante y variada de la gloria literaria* (F. Umbral, 1977: 47)
> I had for the first time a direct, rich, important and varied vision of literary glory

**756** *Por* also indicates an approximate time:

> *(Era una) zarzuela que invadió por entonces toda España* (M.
> Aub, 1963: 45)
> It was a zarzuela (operetta) which swept the whole of Spain
> about that time

There is a clear difference between *por* and *para* when they are
used with points in time such as dates or festivals: *por* indicates a
period AROUND the date whereas *para* (see **746**) indicates that
the date is a LIMIT.

> *Vendré por Navidad*
> I'll come around Christmas time

> *Vendré para Navidad*
> I'll come in time for Christmas

The following examples from M. Delibes are instructive:

> *Por San Severo se fue la cellisca y bajaron las nieblas... Para San*
> *Andrés Corsino el tiempo despejó* (M. Delibes, 1968a: 61)
> Around San Severo's Day the sleet went and the clouds came
> down ...   By San Andrés Corsino's Day the weather
> cleared up

> *El Centenario le dijo por el Santo Ángel, que la nieve estaba próx-*
> *ima y para San Victoriano, o sea, cinco días más tarde, los copos*
> *empezaron a descolgarse* (ibid., 71)
> About the Holy Angel's Day, the Hundred-Year-Old told
> him that snow was not far off, and by San Victoriano's Day,
> that is, five days later, the first flakes fell

Either *por* or *para* may be used in the phrase *por/para siempre*
*jamás* 'for ever more' (cf. **607**).

## 757 Place

*Por* may have the meaning of 'along':

> *Quiero decir que la política no consiste en dar gritos por las calles*
> (F. Vizcaíno Casas, 1978: 195)
> I mean that politics doesn't consist of shouting in the streets

*Por la otra acera iba el padre Cristo-Teodorito* (F. Umbral, 1976b: 232)
Father Cristo-Teodorito was going along the other side of the street

As in time expressions, *por* often indicates vagueness:

*Le veo a usted poco por clase* (S. Lorén, 1955: 139)
I don't see you very often in class

*Busqué por otro sitio* (F. Umbral, 1977: 41)
I looked elsewhere

*A Román no se le veía por casa* (C. Laforet, 1966: 63)
Román was not to be seen around the house
(Contrast **745**, second example; *por* implies no sense of direction or movement)

## 758 Reason, Motive

*Se cerró el aeródromo por la nevada* (*Esbozo*, 442)
The aerodrome shut because of the snowstorm

*Había entrado de institutriz por orgullo* (P. Baroja, 1951: 18)
She became a schoolmistress out of pride

*El Rey no ha sido nunca fumador empedernido, en parte por el Protocolo y, sobre todo, por su afición a los deportes* (*Cambio 16*, 21 May 1978: 125)
The King has never been a hardened smoker, partly because of protocol and above all because of his love of sport

*Cerrado por vacaciones*
Closed for (= on account of) holidays
(But note the following witty notice, modelled on the standard *CERRADO POR DESCANSO DEL PERSONAL* 'closed for (= on account of) staff break', which was observed by JdeB in Granada in March 1987: *CERRAMOS LOS MIÉRCOLES PARA DESCANSO DE LOS CLIENTES* 'we close on Wednesdays so that customers can have a break')

*Por su seguridad no exceda esta velocidad* (road sign seen in Puerto Rico, September 1987)
For your safety do not exceed this speed

*Por* has essentially the same meaning in the expressions *porque* 'because', *¿por qué?* 'why?', *por ello* and *por esto* 'therefore', and in *preguntar por* 'to ask after, enquire about'.

*Lo primero que haré al llegar será preguntar por él* (G. García Márquez, 1977: 257)
The first thing I shall do when I arrive will be to ask after him

**759** *Por* in this sense often participates in elliptical constructions from which *ser* or *estar* are absent:

*Claro es que Kafka estaba enfermo, tuberculoso, había sido perseguido por judío* (M. Peñuelas, 1969: 133)
Of course, Kafka was ill, he had tuberculosis, he had been persecuted for being a Jew
(*por judío = por ser judío, porque era judío*)

*Ella lo miraba sin comprender:*
*– Me gustas por romántico* (R. J. Sender, 1969a:103)
She looked at it uncomprehendingly.
'I like you because you're a romantic'

*Todos le querían por servicial, por atento y cumplidor de sus deberes* (J. A. de Zunzunegui, 1952b: 161)
Everyone loved him because he was obliging, attentive and performed his duties well

A similar ellipsis also occurs in the stereotyped expression *no por* + adjective ... *menos* + adjective, which emphasises that the qualities represented by two adjectives are not mutually exclusive.

*La metáfora, no por repetida es menos cierta. Los árboles no dejan ver el bosque* (F. Díaz-Plaja, 1966: 11)
The metaphor is no less true for being repeated. You cannot see the wood for the trees
(The meaning is: *La metáfora, no por ser repetida...*)

In questions *¿por?* can be used on its own in popular speech as an equivalent to *¿por qué?*

*– Hoy no salgo.*
*– ¿Por?*
*– Porque está enfermo mi hermano* (Beinhauer, 1968: 338, n. 29: the author observes that *¿por?* instead of *¿pues?* is common today)
'I'm not going out today.'
'Because?'
'Because my brother is ill'

**760** Closely connected with the idea of cause or reason is the use of *por* in expressions denoting feeling (sympathy, love, admiration, interest, hatred, etc.).

> *Está loca por usted a su manera* (R. J. Sender, 1969b: 127)
> She is mad about you in her way

> *Mira, no quiero que sufras por ella* (A. Buero Vallejo, 1966: 42)
> Look, I don't want you to suffer for her

> *¡Qué cosas no haré por ti!* (M. Aub, 1963: 67)
> What I wouldn't do for you!

> *Nunca has tenido la menor consideración por mí* (M. Delibes, 1969a: 81)
> You've never had the slightest consideration for me

> *El horror que sentís por las ratas* (F. Grande, 1985: 59)
> The horror you feel for rats

**761** The frequent *por* + infinitive construction is discussed in **1103–1104** and **1115**.

### 762 Means, Manner

> *Llamar por teléfono* (*Esbozo*, 442)
> To telephone (literally, to call someone by using the phone)

> *Se casaron en Zürich por lo civil en 1907* (C. J. Cela, 1969: 69)
> They had a civil wedding in Zürich in 1907

> *Tenía que casarse por la iglesia* (ibid., 125)
> She had to get married in church

> *Vende por mayor* (*Esbozo*, 442)
> He sells wholesale
> (also *al por mayor*)

Note also the expressions *de por sí* 'on one's own' (*el lugar es agradable de por sí* 'the place is pleasant in itself'), *por (un) igual* 'equally', *por lo general* 'in general'.

**763** The elliptical expression *conocido por* 'known as' (for *conocido por el nombre de*) may also be mentioned under this heading.

*En toda Villachica, las tres solteronas – Rosario, Purificación y Dolorcitas – son conocidas generalmente, por «las niñas», a secas* (J. M. Pemán, 1972: 70)
In the whole of Vilachica, the three old maids – Rosario, Purificación and Dolorcitas – are generally known simply as 'the girls'

*José Gómez Ortega, conocido por Joselito* (a pen-and-ink drawing seen by JdeB in a taberna in Madrid)
José Gómez Ortega, known as Joselito

## 764 Price, Quantity

*Venderá la casa por dinero* (*Esbozo*, 442)
He will sell the house for a lot of money

*El cuadro «La bañista» de Renoir, vendido por 86 millones de pesetas* (*El País*, 4 December 1980: 30)
Renoir's picture *The bather*, sold for 86 million pesetas

*¡¡¡Y la vida entera por un abrigo de piel!!!* (M. Mihura, 1981: 115)
And a whole life for a fur coat!

*Estornudó Paulina por dos veces* (R. Sánchez Ferlosio, 1971: 295)
Paulina sneezed twice
(*Por* is optional here: it perhaps suggests repetition)

**765** The use of *por* in expressions of price and quantity is connected with its use in the sense of exchange:

*Doy mi gabán por el tuyo* (*Esbozo*, 442)
I'll swop my coat for yours

**766** *Por* is the equivalent of English 'per' in the expression of rate:

*Pocos españoles podían gastarse las trescientas pesetas por barba que costaba el cine* (F. Vizcaíno Casas, 1978: 59)
Few Spaniards could afford the 300 pesetas per person that the cinema cost

*Tiene un diez por ciento de comisión* (Marsá, 1986: 169)
He has a ten per cent commission

**767** *Por* is the equivalent of English 'times' in multiplication (see **219**):

> *Tres por cuatro, doce* (Marsá, 1986: 169)
> Three times four is twelve

## 768 Substitution

*Por* sometimes means 'instead of':

> *Si no paga, yo pagaré por él* (*Esbozo*, 442)
> If he doesn't pay, I'll pay for (= instead of) him
>
> *Actuar por su padre* (Van Dam, 1967: 343)
> To act for his father

**769** The meaning 'for the benefit of', 'in support of', is another related value of *por*.

> *Hay que tomar partido por los Cadillacs, o por la gente sin zapatos* (P. Neruda, 1976: 236)
> You have to be on the side of the Cadillacs or on the side of the barefoot people
>
> *Tenemos que trabajar por la lengua* (Alonso, 1978: 426)
> We must work for the language
>
> – *¿Por quién votó el señor Stuart en las elecciones de junio?*
> – *¿Y usted?*
> – *Voté a Esquerra Republicana de Catalunya* (M. Vázquez Montalbán, 1979b: 56)
> 'Who did Señor Stuart vote for in the June elections?
> 'And you?'
> 'I voted Esquerra Republicana de Catalunya'
> (Note the use of *votar a* as well as *votar por*)

## 770 Equivalence

Under this heading come usages like the following:

> *Pocos soldados buenos valen por un ejército* (*Esbozo*, 442)
> A few good soldiers are worth an army
> (But note that the object of *valer* normally has no preposition: *vale un dineral* 'it's worth a fortune')
>
> *Pasa por rico* (*Esbozo*, 442)
> He passes for a rich man

**771** The value of *por* in *darse por* 'to be considered', and *tener por* 'to consider', is similar:

> *Parece haber dado por zanjada la cuestión* (C. Martín Gaite, 1981: 101)
> He seems to consider the matter settled
>
> *Recibo cartas de sujetos a quienes no conozco, dándose por aludidos personalmente en algo de lo que escribo* (M. de Unamuno, 1967b: 29)
> I receive letters from folk I do not know, who consider that they have been personally referred to in something I write
>
> *Le tengo por una persona inteligente* (Marsá, 1986: 169)
> I consider him an intelligent person

**772** *Por* also has the meaning of *en calidad de* 'as':

> *Le tomé por criado* (*Esbozo*, 443)
> I took him for a servant
>
> *Me adoptó por hijo* (*Esbozo*, 443)
> She adopted me as a son

**773** Followed by a personal pronoun or by a noun referring to a person, *por* may have the meaning of 'as far as . . . is concerned', 'with . . . in mind'.

> – *Si le molesta hablar de eso, no he dicho nada.*
> – *¿Por qué? Por mí, encantado* (J. M. Gironella, 1966a: 136)
> 'If it annoys you talking about this, I've said nothing.'
> 'Why? It's O.K. by me'
>
> *Esto, ¿lo dices por mi hermano Pedro?*
> Are you saying this with my brother Pedro in mind?

## 774 *Estar por*

*Por* can be used before an infinitive with approximately the same meaning as *sin*. Both constructions imply that an action has not (yet) taken place. (See **1110–1116**.)

**775** *Estar por* can also mean 'to be in favour of':

> *La gente nueva está por la píldora, el aborto, el amor libre y punto* (M. Delibes, 1978a: 69)
> Modern people are in favour of the pill, abortion, free love and that's all

With a following infinitive it has by extension the meaning 'to be inclined to':

> *Estoy por decir que se trata aquí de un caso de plagio* (Van Dam, 1967: 344)
> I would almost say that we have to do here with a case of plagiarism

> *Estuvo por no ir pensando que Gálvez le recibiría con Contreras* (R. J. Sender, 1969c: 96)
> He was inclined not to go away, since he thought that Gálvez would receive him with Contreras

This meaning is very close to that of *estar para* 'to be on the point of' (see **750**) and *estar por* is also used in this sense, especially among Latin-American writers:

> *Ella estaba por morirse* (J. Rulfo, 1981: 7)
> She lay dying

### 776 *Por* in Concessive Clauses

*Por* + an adjective, adverb or adverbial expression + *que* has a concessive meaning. (On the use of the subjunctive or indicative in such clauses, see **1065**.)

> *Señores; por doloroso que nos resulte a todos, reconozcamos que el Real Madrid siempre llena los estadios* (F. Vizcaíno Casas, 1978: 50)
> Gentlemen: painful though it may be for us all, we must recognize that Real Madrid always fills the stands

> *Por más que traté de hacer ver al hijo cuáles eran sus obligaciones, nada conseguí* (J. A. de Zunzunegui, 1958: 311)
> However much I tried to make my boy see what his obligations were, I achieved nothing

### 777 *Por* in Oaths

> *Es lo que acostumbra a hacer siempre con las cosas importantes, y ésta sí que lo es, ¡por Cristo!* (S. Lorén, 1967a: 11)
> That is what he usually does with important things, and this is certainly important, by God!
> (Also: *¡por Dios!*)

*¡Por mi madre que lo vi, padre!* (F. Vizcaíno Casas, 1978: 211)
I swear by my mother that I saw it, father!

## 778 *A por*

*Ir a por* has the meaning 'to go for', 'to go and get'. The idea can equally be rendered by *ir por*, and *ir a por* is sometimes considered incorrect[26] or typical of colloquial usage. Nevertheless, *a por* is well attested in literature:

> – *¿Qué, ya está usted por aquí?*
> – *Vengo a por unas truchas* (M. Delibes, 1968b: 122)
> 'What, are you still here?'
> 'I've come for some trout'

> *Doña Consuelo iba a la barra a por su tacita de café* (F. Umbral, 1977: 127)
> Doña Consuelo would go to the bar to get her cup of coffee

> *¡A por los trescientos diputados!* (E. Romero, 1963: 56)
> Now for the three hundred deputies!

> *Me voy a por el abrigo* (R. H. Moreno-Durán, 1981: 65)
> I'm going to get my coat

But note:

> *La muchacha iba por agua* (J. Arreola, 1986: 184)
> The girl was going for water

> *Va por leña/va por pan* (*Esbozo*, 442)
> He is going for wood/for bread

The use of *a por* may prevent ambiguity. *Vine a por ti* can only mean 'I came for (= to get) you', whereas *vine por ti* may mean either 'I came for (= to get) you' or 'I came for (= because of, instead of) you'.[27]

## 779 *Por* and *para* together

*Por* and *para* may be used in the same sentence and even next to each other. Spanish authors sometimes make a play on words in this way which is difficult to render in English.

*Pero él sí estaba dispuesto a seguirla a donde fuera, a vivir por ella y para ella* (P. Baroja, 1946–51: VI, 958)
But he was certainly ready to follow her wherever she went, to live because of her and at her disposal

*En él había un cierto conocimiento tanto del por qué como del para qué de la ceremonia* (L. Martín Santos, 1972: 194)
He had a certain knowledge of the why and wherefore of the ceremony (i.e. the reason for the ceremony and its purpose)

*Vivir para las mujeres era morir por las mujeres* (E. Jardiel Poncela, 1969: IV, 867)
Living for women meant dying (with desire) for women

*A Nietzsche lo deja para por el día* (C. J. Cela, 1963a: 184)
He leaves Nietzsche for the daytime

## Sin

**780** *Sin* is equivalent to English 'without':

*Estoy sin empleo* (*Esbozo*, 443)
I am without work

*Trabaja sin cesar* (*Esbozo*, 443)
He works without stopping

See **1110–1114** for *sin* + infinitive.

**781** *Sin* can sometimes render an English negative idea: *sin problema* 'no problem', *vuelo sin escala* 'non-stop flight'.

## So

**782** *So* has the same meaning as *bajo*, *debajo de* 'under', but it appears only in set expressions in the modern language, e.g. *so capa de* 'under the cloak of', 'on the pretext of', *so pena de* 'on pain of', *so pretexto de* 'on the pretext of'.[28]

**783** The preposition *so* is not to be confused with *so* as a form of address (see **889**, last example).

## Sobre

**784** *Sobre* has the literal meaning 'on', though in a figurative sense it can mean '(over and) above'.

> *Dejé el libro sobre la mesa* (*Esbozo*, 443)
> I left the book on the table

> *El bien común está sobre los intereses particulares* (*Esbozo*, 443)
> The common good is above private interest

> *Las hermanastras, sobre estar gordas, tenían más barbas que un melocotón maduro* (C. J. Cela, 1963b: 30)
> The stepsisters, as well as being fat, had chins which were hairier than a ripe peach

**785** *Sobre* can also introduce a subject which is being dealt with, and corresponds in this sense to English 'on', 'about'.

> *Gabriel de Herrera escribió sobre Agricultura* (*Esbozo*, 443)
> Gabriel de Herrera wrote on agriculture

> *Hablamos sobre las noticias del día* (*Esbozo*, 443)
> We spoke about the day's news

**786** *Sobre* may also mean 'approximately':

> *Francisco tendrá sobre cincuenta años* (*Esbozo*, 443)
> Francisco must be about fifty
> (See also *unos*. **379**.)

> *Se presentaba los domingos sobre las once* (M. Delibes, 1968a: 83)
> He came on Sundays about eleven o'clock

See also **1084**, fourth example.

**787** Lastly, note the expressions *tomar sobre sí* 'to take upon oneself' and *estar sobre sí* 'to be above oneself' (*Esbozo*, 443).

## Tras

**788** *Tras* (also *tras de*) 'after' is used to denote both place and time. Both forms belong to written style: in speech, *detrás de* (place) and *después de* (time) are preferred.[29]

*Voy tras ti* (*Esbozo*, 443)
I'll come after you

*¡Con el tiempo que hacía que andaba tras ellas!* (J. M. Gironella, 1966b: 516)
And considering how long I had been in search of them!

*Tras dar secamente las buenas noches iba la muchacha a entrar en la cueva pero Pascual la detuvo* (J. Izcaray, 1961: 47)
After wishing them a curt good night, the girl was about to go into the cave, but Pascual stopped her
(Also: *Después de dar . . .*)

*He estado tras de ti más de dos años* (M. Vargas Llosa, 1973: 242)
I've been after you for more than two years

**789** *Tras* can also have the meaning of 'besides':

*Tras de venir tarde, no me dice la verdad* (Van Dam, 1969: I, 1191)
Besides coming late, he doesn't tell me the truth

## Other Prepositions

**790** Other prepositions offer few problems in usage; the chief ones are *contra* 'against', *según* 'according to, depending on' (see **289**) and the infrequent *pro* 'pro, in favour of'.

*1959, año en el que usted participó en una manifestación contra el gobierno Eisenhower* (M. Vázquez Montalbán, 1990: 35)
1959, the year in which you took part in a demonstration against the Eisenhower government

*Según el mapa, la ciudad no queda lejos*
According to the map, the town is not far away

*Iremos a un sitio o a otro según el dinero que tengamos* (*DUE*, II, 1126)
We'll go to one place or another depending on how much money we have

*Asociación pro ciegos* (*DUE*, II, 847)
Blind association

## 791 Groups of Prepositions

A group consisting of adverb + preposition may form a complex preposition and render a simple preposition in English:

| | |
|---|---|
| *acerca de* | concerning |
| *alrededor de* | around |
| *antes de* | before |
| *debajo de* | under |
| *delante de* | before |
| *después de* | after |
| *detrás de* | behind |
| *dentro de* | inside |
| *en contra de* | against |
| *enfrente de* | opposite |
| *frente a* | opposite |
| *junto a* | beside |

Differences in meaning between simple and complex prepositions are sometimes difficult to perceive for English speakers:

| | |
|---|---|
| *ante* | 'before', sometimes in a literal spatial sense (i), but often used in a more abstract sense (ii). |
| *antes de* | 'before', in a temporal sense (iii) |
| *delante de* | 'before', in a literal spatial sense (iv) |

(i) *Puso la bandeja ante la puerta cerrada* (I. Allende, 1990: 41)
   She placed the tray in front of the closed door

(ii) *Una misma comunión ante el peligro los une a todos* (J. Goytisolo, 1988: 113)
   Fellowship in the face of danger unites everyone

(iii) *Antes de la cena*
   Before the dinner

(iv) *Pon la silla delante de la ventana*
   Put the chair in front of the window

| | |
|---|---|
| *bajo* | 'under', sometimes in a literal spatial sense (v), but often used in a more abstract sense (vi) |
| *debajo de* | 'under', in a literal spatial sense (vii) |

(v)   *Elena escondió los libros y los zapatos bajo unas mantas* (I. Allende, 1990: 29)
Elena hid the books and the shoes underneath some blankets

(vi)  *Numerosos pueblos de la frontera se colocaron bajo su custodia* (A. Gala, 1993: 252)
Many border villages placed themselves in his custody

(vii) *El perro se escondió debajo de la mesa*
The dog hid under the table

| | |
|---|---|
| *tras* | 'after' in a literal temporal sense, especially linking two nouns (viii), 'behind' in a literal spatial sense, especially where there is an idea of 'hidden behind' (ix);[30] also 'after' with a verb of motion (x) |
| *detrás de* | 'behind' in a literal spatial sense (xi, xii) |

(viii) *Día tras día*
Day after day

(ix)  *Tras esa sonrisa oculta una gran crueldad* (*DUE*, II, 1369)
Behind that smile he hides great cruelty

(x)   *Los perros corren tras la liebre* (ibid.)
The dogs run after the hare

(xi)  *Una mirada vieja, detrás de cristales oscurecidos en contacto con la luz* (M. Vázquez Montalbán, 1990a: 11)
An old look, behind glasses which had darkened in contact with the light

(xii) *Yo me escondí detrás de un ciprés grueso* (A. Gala, 1993: 56)
I hid behind a thick cypress tree

| | |
|---|---|
| *contra* | 'against' in a literal (xiii) or more abstract sense (xiv) |
| *en contra de* | 'against' in a more abstract sense (xv) |

(xiii) *La escalera está apoyada contra la pared*
The ladder is leaning against the wall

(xiv) *Estuvo contra la tiranía por tierras y gentes que no eran suyas* (M. Vázquez Montalbán, 1990b: 13)
He was against tyranny by countries and peoples who were not his own

(xv) *En contra de nuestra costumbre cuando nos desplazábamos a la ciudad vecina, habíamos regresado en el mismo tren* (J. Marías, 1989: 34)
Contrary to our custom when we went to the next town, we had returned in the same train.

*frente a*        'opposite' in a literal (xvii) or more abstract (xvi) sense

*enfrente de*    'opposite' in a literal spatial sense (xvii)

(xvi) *Tengo frente a mí tu carta* (M. Puig, 1989: 109)
I have your letter in front of me

(xvii) *Frente a/enfrente de mi casa hay una panadería*
Opposite my house there is a baker's shop

**792** Two or even three prepositions may appear together in Spanish. Such groups may be understood 'hierarchically', e.g.

| | |
|---|---|
| *entre los árboles* | among the trees |
| *por (entre los árboles)* | somewhere (among the trees) |
| *desde (por (entre los árboles))* | from (somewhere (among the trees)) |

Note especially in this connection the use of *por* to indicate motion:

| | |
|---|---|
| *por delante de* | in front of |
| *por detrás de* | behind |
| *por debajo de* | under |
| *por encima de* | over |
| *por entre* | between |

*Para con* (**748–749**) and *a por* (**778**) have special meanings.

– *¿Es usted de por aquí?*
– *Más bien de un poco más allá – dije finalmente* (W. Fernández Flórez, 1967: 109)
'Are you from around here?'
'From a bit further on, really', I said nicely

*Tuvimos que dejar la calle a unos soldados de a caballo* (R. del Valle-Inclán, 1963: 100)
We had to abandon the street to some soldiers on horseback

*Desde por entre los árboles nos espiaban sin ser vistos* (Van Dam, 1967: 357)
From among the trees they could spy on us without being seen

*Seguía (yo) los esguinces que hacían los niños correteando por delante de ellas, por detrás, alrededor* (C. Martín Gaite, 1978: 119)
I followed the children's movements as they served in front of them, behind them and around them

## 793 Compound Prepositions

Preposition + noun + preposition sequences have always been possible in Spanish (e.g. *al lado de* 'by the side of, beside', *por parte de* 'on behalf of', etc.) but seem to be on the increase nowadays. Note also the following:

| | |
|---|---|
| *a la altura de* | abreast of |
| *en aras de* | for the sake of |
| *en calidad de* | as, in the capacity of |
| *en ciernes de* | in the grip of |
| *en función de* | in line with |
| *a lo largo de* | during, throughout |
| *en el marco de* | within the framework of |
| *a nivel de* | on the level of |
| *a raíz de* | as a consequence of |
| *en razón de* | by reason of |
| *en torno a* | concerning |
| *en el transcurso de* | in the course of |
| *a través de* | across |

*Podemos afirmarlo en base a los datos de que disponemos* (*MEU*, 39)
We can say so on the basis of the facts at our disposal. (*MEU* recommends instead *según los datos* or *basándonos en los datos*)

*El asunto será tratado a nivel de ministros económicos* (*MEU*, 39)
The matter will be dealt with at finance minister level. (*MEU* reommends *por los ministros económicos*)

*Te lo digo a nivel de secreto* (F. Lázaro Carreter, lecture in Antwerp, 31 January 1987)
I am telling you this as a secret
(*En* or *como* are to be preferred to *a nivel de*)

**794** The same preposition may be used more than once in the same sentence with different meanings:

> *Te daré dos decilitros por el mismo precio y por ser para ti* (J. Rulfo, 1981: 174)
> I'll give you half a pint (of alcohol) for the same price and because it's for you

# Constructions with Verbs and Nouns

## Verbs with a Dependent Infinitive

### No Preposition between Verb and Dependent Infinitive

### 795 The Subject of the Main Verb is the Same as the Implied Subject of the Dependent Infinitive

*Non-reflexive Verbs*

> *Juan consiguió encontrar el libro*
> Juan managed to find the book
> (Juan is also the implied subject of *encontrar*)

This group also includes a number of verbs of saying or thinking which in English have a full clause complement and which may also take a full clause complement in Spanish:

> *María cree haberlo hecho/que lo ha hecho*
> María thinks that she has done it

Note that in this example *María* is necessarily the implied subject of *haberlo hecho*, while *María cree que lo ha hecho* allows for a different third person subject for *lo ha hecho*, e.g. 'María thinks that he has done it.'

There are also a number of verbs in this group which require a *que* + subjunctive construction (see **Use of the Moods**) if the subject of the main verb and the subject of the subordinate verb are not the same, e.g.:

> *Evitaré hacerlo*
> I will avoid doing it
> (*Yo* is the subject of *evitar* and the implied subject of *hacerlo*)

But:

> *Evitaré que Pedro lo sepa*
> I will avoid Pedro getting to know
> (*Yo* is the subject of *evitaré*; *Pedro* is the subject of *sepa*)

The principal verbs in this class are:

| | |
|---|---|
| *aceptar* | to undertake to |
| *acordar* | to agree to |
| *acostumbrar* | usually to |
| | (see next example below) |
| *afirmar* | to affirm (that) |
| *ambicionar* | to have the ambition of -ing |
| *amenazar* | to threaten to |
| (also with *con*) | |
| *anhelar* | to long to |
| *ansiar* | to long to |
| *aparentar* | to make as if to |
| *buscar* | to seek to |
| *codiciar* | to covet -ing |
| *comunicar* | to communicate (that) |
| *concertar* | to agree to |
| *confesar* | to confess -ing/(that) |
| *conseguir* | to manage to. to succeed in -ing |
| *creer* | to think (that) |
| *deber* | to have to (see **1270–1272**) |
| *decidir* | to decide to |
| *decir* | to say (that) |
| *declarar* | to declare (that) |
| *demostrar* | to show (that) |
| *deplorar* | to regret -ing |
| *descuidar* | to neglect -ing |
| *desear* | to want to |
| *determinar* | to decide to |
| *dudar* | to doubt (if, whether, that) |
| *escoger* | to choose to |
| *esperar* | to hope to (see also **1037**) |
| *evitar* | to avoid -ing |
| *fingir* | to pretend to |
| *idear* | to plan to |
| *imaginar* | to imagine -ing |
| *intentar* | to try to |

| | |
|---|---|
| *jurar* | to swear to |
| *juzgar* | to judge (that) |
| *lamentar* | to regret to |
| *lograr* | to succeed in -ing |
| *manifestar* | to state (that) |
| *merecer* | to deserve -ing |
| *necesitar* | to need to |
| *negar* | to deny -ing |
| *ofrecer* | to offer to |
| *olvidar* | to forget -ing |
| *osar* | to dare to |
| *parecer* | to seem to |
| *pedir* | to ask to (see second example below) |
| *pensar* | to think (that) |
| *pensar* | to intend to |
| *planear* | to plan to |
| *poder* | to be able to (see **1273–1275**) |
| *preferir* | to prefer to/-ing |
| *pretender* | to want to, to try to, to claim to |
| *pretextar* | to claim (that) |
| *prever* | to foresee -ing |
| *procurar* | to try to |
| *prometer* | to promise to |
| *proyectar* | to plan to |
| *querer* | to want to |
| *recelar* | to be afraid to |
| *reconocer* | to recognize (that) |
| *recordar* | to remember -ing |
| *rehuir* | to avoid -ing |
| *rehusar* | to refuse to |
| *resolver* | to resolve to |
| *resultar* | to prove to, to turn out to (usually with *ser*, see third example below) |
| *saber* | to know how to |
| *sentir* | to regret to/-ing |
| *simular* | to simulate -ing |
| *soler* | usually to (see **637**) |
| *solicitar* | to ask to |
| *temer* | to fear to/-ing |

Examples:

> *Acostumbro salir sobre las nueve*
> I usually go out around nine

> *Pidió saber qué había ocurrido*
> He/she asked to know what had happened

> *Resultó ser el autor del folleto*
> He turned out to be the author of the pamphlet

*Reflexive Verbs*

Example:

> *Me propongo estudiar varios aspectos del problema*
> I propose to study several aspects of the problem

Some verbs in this class are:

| | |
|---|---|
| *dignarse* | to deign to |
| *figurarse* | to imagine -ing |
| *proponerse* | to propose to/-ing |

## 796 Remark

*Dudar*

*Dudar* + infinitive is the equivalent of *dudar si* + indicative (see **1040**) or *dudar que* + subjunctive:

> *Dudo estar en condiciones para ir*
> I doubt I am fit to go
> (= *Dudo si estoy en condiciones para ir*)

*Dudar en* + infinitive has the meaning 'to hesitate to' (see **809**):

> *¡No dudes en preguntar!*
> Don't hesitate to ask!

## 797 The Subject of the Main Verb is not Identical with the Implied Subject of the Dependent Infinitive

To this group belong several verbs of ordering, e.g.

> *Te prohíbo salir*
> I forbid you to go out

and verbs of perception, e.g.

> *Oí cantar a María*
> I heard María sing(ing)
> (See also **798** below)

The principal verbs of this category are:

| | |
|---|---|
| *aconsejar* | to advise to |
| *consentir* | to allow to |
| *dejar* | to let |
| *hacer* | to make |
| *impedir* | to prevent from -ing |
| *mandar* | to order to |
| *oir* | to hear (see second example above and **798**) |
| *ordenar* | to order to |
| *permitir* | to allow to |
| *prohibir* | to forbid to |
| *vedar* | to forbid |
| *ver* | to see (see **798**) |

## 798 Remarks

The verbs of perception in **797** may also have a gerund complement if the ongoing nature of the action is to be stressed (see **1145**).

**799** The dependent infinitive of *hacer, oir* and *ver* may also sometimes be understood passively, e.g.:

> *Oí cantar una melodía popular*
> I heard a popular tune being sung
>
> *Hicimos construir una pared*
> We had a wall built

**800** In the constructions of **799**, the main verb is usually followed immediately by the infinitive, in contrast to the corresponding English construction:

> *Hice comer a Juan* (Schroten, 1978: 9)
> I made Juan eat
>
> *Hice comer las patatas a Juan* (ibid.)
> I made Juan eat the potatoes

*Hice entregar los diplomas a las alumnas por Juan* (ibid.)
I made Juan deliver the diplomas to the students

*El hombre oyó crecer el silencio en su interior* (I. Allende, 1990: 127)
The man heard the silence growing within him

## 801 Impersonal Verbs

A number of verbs have infinitives as their subjects (see **1083**, fourth example). The normal order is for the infinitive to follow the verb, and so superficially these constructions resemble those in **795** and **797**, e.g.:

*Conviene rendir homenaje al maestro*
It's proper to pay tribute to the master

*Non-reflexive Verbs*

In the following list, the translations given are as literal as possible, although English often renders the Spanish rather differently, as shown in the next five examples.

| | |
|---|---|
| *agradar* | to please |
| *alegrar* | to gladden |
| *apasionar* | to arouse passion in |
| *apetecer* | to appeal to |
| *atraer* | to attract |
| *bastar* | to be enough |
| *caber* | to be appropriate, fitting |
| *convenir* | to be fitting, proper |
| *corresponder* | to be up to |
| *costar* | to cost effort |
| *cumplir* | to behove |
| *encantar* | to please, delight |
| *entusiasmar* | to arouse enthusiasm in |
| *extrañar* | to surprise |
| *hacer falta* | to be lacking |
| *fascinar* | to fascinate |
| *fastidiar* | to annoy |
| *gustar* | to be pleasing |
| *importar* | to be important, to matter to |
| *incumbir* | to be incumbent upon |

| | |
|---|---|
| *interesar* | to interest |
| *molestar* | to be a nuisance to |
| *quedar* | to remain for |
| *sobrar* | to be superfluous |
| *tocar* | to fall to |

*¿Te gustaría bailar?*
Would you like to dance?

*¿Te importaría dejarme las notas?*
Would you mind lending me the notes?

*Me toca contestar*
It's my turn to answer

*Hace falta pasar por recepción*
You must go through reception

*Molesta tener que salir con este tiempo*
It's a nuisance to have to go out in this weather

## Reflexive Verbs

The following verbs both offer difficulties of translation:

*Antojarse:*

> *Se me antoja ir a Sevilla*
> I feel like going to Seville

*Ocurrirse:*

> *Se me ocurrió ir a verle.*
> I made up my mind to come and see you

## Verbs Taking *a* with a Dependent Infinitive

## 802 The Subject of the Main Verb is the Same as the Implied Subject of the Dependent Infinitive

*Non-reflexive Verbs*

Example:

> *Manolo aspira a dar clases de japonés*
> Manolo aspires to give Japanese classes

This group includes a number of verbs of movement which correspond to English constructions involving *and*, e.g.:

*Corrimos a verlo*
We ran to see it/we ran and saw it
(Note that *ir y* + verb and *coger y* + verb are used in the colloquial language with an intensifying meaning, especially in Latin America, where, however, since *coger* often has obscene connotations, *agarrar y* + verb is often preferred to *coger y* + verb.)[1]

The other principal verbs of this group are:

| | |
|---|---|
| *acceder* | to agree to |
| *acertar* | to manage to; to happen to |
| *acudir* | to come to/and, turn up to/and |
| *aguardar* | to wait to/and |
| *alcanzar* | to manage to |
| *andar* | to go to/and |
| *aprender* | to learn how to |
| *arrancar* | to burst out -ing |
| *aspirar* | to aspire to |
| *atinar* | to manage to |
| *bajar* | to go down to/and |
| *bastar* | to be enough to |
| *coadyuvar* | to help to |
| *comenzar* | to begin to |
| *concurrir* | to gather to |
| *contribuir* | to contribute towards -ing |
| *correr* | to run to/and |
| *echar* | to begin to |
| *empezar* | to begin to |
| *entrar* | to go in to/and |
| *huir* | to flee to |
| *ir* | to go to |
| *llegar* | to succeed in -ing, to end up -ing |
| *marchar* | to go to/and |
| *parar* | to stop to/and |
| *partir* | to leave to |
| *pasar* | to go on to |
| *principiar* | to begin to |
| *probar* | to try to |
| *proceder* | to proceed to -ing |

| *propender* | to tend to |
| *renunciar* | to renounce -ing |
| *romper* | to burst out -ing |
| *salir* | to go out to/and |
| *subir* | to go up to/and |
| *tender* | to tend to |
| *tornar* | to —— again (like *volver*) |
| *venir* | to come to |
| *volar* | to fly to/and |
| *volver* | to —— again (see **637**) |

*Reflexive Verbs*

Examples:

> *Pedro se aplicó a estudiar*
> Pedro devoted himself to studying

> *Me acomodé a leer*
> I settled down to read/I settled down and read

Other verbs in this category:

| *acercarse* | to get near to/and |
| *acomodarse* | to settle down to |
| *adelantarse* | to get ahead to/and |
| *aplicarse* | to devote oneself to -ing |
| *aprestarse* | to get ready to |
| *apresurarse* | to hasten to |
| *arriesgarse* | to risk -ing |
| *arrojarse* | to rush into -ing |
| *asomarse* | to show up to/and |
| *atreverse* | to dare to |
| *avenirse* | to agree to |
| *aventurarse* | to venture to |
| *brindarse* | to offer to |
| *comprometerse* | to undertake to |
| *consagrarse* | to devote oneself to -ing |
| *darse* | to dedicate oneself to |
| *decidirse* | to decide to |
| *dedicarse* | to dedicate oneself to -ing |
| *detenerse* | to stop to/and |
| *determinarse* | to make up one's mind to |
| *dirigirse* | to head towards -ing |

| *disponerse* | to prepare to |
| *echarse* | to begin to |
| *encaminarse* | to set out to |
| *ensayarse* | to practise -ing |
| *entregarse* | to devote oneself to -ing |
| *entremeterse* | to meddle in -ing |
| *exponerse* | to expose oneself to -ing |
| *extenderse* | to stretch oneself to |
| *hacerse* | to get used to -ing |
| *lanzarse* | to rush into -ing |
| *levantarse* | to get up to/and |
| *limitarse* | only to |
| *matarse* | to kill onself -ing |
| *mentalizarse* | to make up one's mind to |
| *meterse* | to begin to |
| *negarse* | to refuse to |
| *ofrecerse* | to offer to |
| *pararse* | to stop to/and |
| *ponerse* | to begin to |
| *precipitarse* | to hasten to |
| *prepararse* | to prepare to |
| *presentarse* | to turn up to/and |
| *prestarse* | to lend oneself to -ing |
| *quedarse* | to stay to/and |
| *rebajarse* | to stoop to |
| *recogerse* | to go off to/and |
| *resignarse* | to resign oneself to -ing |
| *resistirse* | to resist -ing |
| *resolverse* | to resolve to |
| *retirarse* | to go off to/and |
| *sentarse* | to sit down to |

## 803 The Object of the Main Verb is the Same as the Implied Subject of the Dependent Infinitive

Verbs of this category express a form of command or other influence by the subject of the main verb. A subjunctive construction (see **Use of the Moods**) is also possible in some cases, especially with more complex complements:

*Me animaron a salir/Me animaron a que saliese*
They encouraged me to go out

The principal verbs of this group are:

| | |
|---|---|
| *acostumbrar* | to accustom to |
| *animar* | to encourage to |
| *autorizar* | to authorize to |
| *ayudar* | to help to |
| *condenar* | to condemn to |
| *conducir* | to lead to |
| *convidar* | to invite to |
| *desafiar* | to challenge to |
| *determinar* | to determine to |
| *empujar* | to push into -ing |
| *enseñar* | to teach to |
| *enviar* | to send to |
| *excitar* | to urge to |
| *exhortar* | to exhort to |
| *forzar* | to force to |
| *habituar* | to accustom to |
| *impeler* | to drive to |
| *impulsar* | to impel to |
| *incitar* | to incite to |
| *inclinar* | to incline to |
| *inducir* | to lead to |
| *instar* | to urge to |
| *invitar* | to invite to |
| *llamar* | to call to |
| *llevar* | to lead to |
| *mandar* | to send to |
| *mover* | to move to |
| *obligar* | to oblige to |
| *persuadir* | to persuade to |
| *reducir* | to reduce to |
| *sentenciar* | to sentence to |
| *tentar* | to tempt to |
| *traer* | to bring to |

## 804 Remark

Not all verbs of ordering and influence behave in this way. Some (see **797**) take no preposition before the dependent infinitive. Others (e.g. *influir*, *pedir*) always take a full clause complement:

*Influyó con el ministro para que se entrevistara con los terroristas*
He influenced the minister to grant an interview to the terrorists

*Juan me pidió que le contara la verdad*
Juan asked me to tell him the truth

Verbs Taking *de* with a Dependent Infinitive

## 805 The Subject of the Main Verb is the Same as the Implied Subject of the Dependent Infinitive

*Non-reflexive Verbs*

Example:

*¡Deje de cantar!*
Stop singing

The principal verbs of this category are:

| | |
|---|---|
| *acabar* | to have just; to finish -ing (see **806**) |
| *cesar* | to stop -ing |
| *cuidar* | to take care to |
| *dejar* | to stop -ing |
| *desconfiar* | to doubt (whether) |
| *desesperar* | to despair of -ing |
| *desistir* | to desist from -ing |
| *distar* | to be a long way from -ing |
| *gustar* | to like to (see **807**) |
| *parar* | to stop -ing |
| *terminar* | to stop -ing |
| *tratar* | to try to |
| *ver* | to try to |

*Reflexive Verbs*

Example:

*Me arrepentí de decírtelo*
I repented telling you

The principal verbs of this category are:

| | |
|---|---|
| *abstenerse* | to abstain from -ing |
| *acordarse* | to remember to |
| *alegrarse* | to be glad about |
| *arrepentirse* | to repent of -ing |
| *avergonzarse* | to be ashamed of -ing |
| *cansarse* | to tire of -ing |
| *desdeñarse* | to scorn to |
| *desesperarse* | to despair of -ing |
| *desinteresarse* | to lose interest in -ing |
| *echarse* | to begin to |
| *encargarse* | to see about -ing, attend to -ing |
| *excusarse* | to apologize for -ing |
| *fatigarse* | to get tired of -ing |
| *gloriarse* | to be proud of -ing |
| *guardarse* | to be careful not to |
| *hartarse* | to be fed up with -ing |
| *jactarse* | to boast of -ing |
| *librarse* | to escape from -ing |
| *lisonjearse* | to be flattered by -ing |
| *maravillarse* | to marvel at -ing |
| *olvidarse* | to forget to |
| *preciarse* | to boast of -ing |
| *saciarse* | to be fed up with -ing |
| *ufanarse* | to be proud of -ing |
| *vanagloriarse* | to boast of -ing |

### 806 Remarks

*Acabar de* + infinitive corresponds to English 'to have just' when used in the Present and Imperfect tenses (see **637**). It has the meaning 'to finish -ing' in other tenses.

**807** With *gustar*, the impersonal verb construction listed in **801** is more common, and is always used in the spoken language.

### 808 The Object of the Main Verb is the Same as the Implied Subject of the Dependent Infinitive

Example:

*Juan me disuadió de entrar*
Juan dissuaded me from going in

The principal verbs in this group are:

| | |
|---|---|
| *acusar* | to accuse of -ing |
| *consolar* | to console for -ing |
| *culpar* | to blame for -ing |
| *dispensar* | to forgive for -ing |
| *disuadir* | to dissuade from -ing |

### Verbs Taking *en* with a Dependent Infinitive

## 809 The Subject of the Main Verb is the Same as the Implied Subject of the Dependent Infinitive

*Non-reflexive Verbs*

Example:

> *El tren tardó veinte minutos en llegar*
> The train took twenty minutes to get there

The principal verbs in this category are:

| | |
|---|---|
| *coincidir* | to coincide in -ing |
| *condescender* | to agree to |
| *consentir* | to consent to -ing |
| *convenir* | to agree to |
| *dudar* | to hesitate in -ing |
| *hacer bien/mal* | to do well, badly in -ing |
| *insistir* | to insist on -ing |
| *perseverar* | to persevere in -ing |
| *persistir* | to persist in -ing |
| *porfiar* | to persist in -ing |
| *quedar* | to agree to |
| *reincidir* | to fall back into -ing |
| *tardar* | to take time to |
| *titubear* | to hesitate in -ing |
| *vacilar* | to hesitate in -ing |

*Reflexive Verbs*

Example:

> *Nos complacemos en informarle que . . .*
> We are pleased to tell you that . . .

The principal verbs in this category are:

| | |
|---|---|
| *complacerse* | to take pleasure in -ing |
| *concentrarse* | to concentrate on -ing |
| *deleitarse* | to delight in -ing |
| *divertirse* | to enjoy -ing |
| *ejercitarse* | to practise -ing |
| *embebecerse* | to be lost in wonder at -ing |
| *embelesarse* | to be enraptured by -ing |
| *empeñarse* | to insist on -ing |
| *enconarse* | to get angry -ing |
| *ensañarse* | to vent one's anger -ing |
| *entretenerse* | to pass the time (in) -ing |
| *esforzarse* | to strive to |
| *esmerarse* | to take pains to |
| *fatigarse* | to get tired in -ing |
| *gozarse* | to enjoy -ing |
| *interesarse* | to be interested in -ing |
| *obstinarse* | to persist in -ing |
| *ocuparse* | to spend one's time -ing |
| *quedarse* | to be reduced to -ing |
| *recatarse* | to fight shy of -ing |
| *recrearse* | to enjoy -ing |
| *solazarse* | to relax -ing |

## Verbs Taking *con* with a Dependent Infinitive

### 810  The Subject of the Main Verb is the Same as the Implied Subject of the Dependent Infinitive

*Non-reflexive Verbs*
Example:
> *Amenazó con denunciar el delito*
> He/she threatened to report the crime

Verbs in this category are:

| | |
|---|---|
| *amenazar* | to threaten to |
| *soñar* | to dream of -ing |

*Reflexive Verbs*
*Contentarse* 'to content oneself with -ing' appears to be the only common verb in this category:

*Me contento con gritar insultos*
I contented myself with shouting insults

Verbs Taking *para* with a Dependent Infinitive

## 811 The Subject of the Main Verb is the Same as the Implied Subject of the Dependent Infinitive

*Prepararse* 'to prepare oneself for -ing' is such a verb.

**812** The object of the main verb is the same as the implied subject of the dependent infinitive.
Example:

*Me autorizaron para consultar el archivo*
I was authorized to consult the archive

The verbs in this category are:

| | |
|---|---|
| *autorizar* | to authorize to |
| *imposibilitar* | to make it impossible to |

## 813 The Indirect Object of the Intransitive Main Verb is the Same as the Implied Subject of the Dependent Infinitive

*Me falta una semana para liquidar el trabajo*
I need a week to finish off the work

Other verbs of this category are:

| | |
|---|---|
| *bastar* | to be enough |
| *sobrar* | to be too much |

These usages must be distinguished from those in **801**.

Verbs Taking *por* with a Dependent Infinitive

## 814 The Subject of the Main Verb is the Same as the Implied Subject of the Dependent Infinitive

*Non-reflexive Verbs*
Example:

*Voy a comenzar por leer el texto*
I'll begin by reading the text

The principal verbs belonging to this category are:

| | |
|---|---|
| *acabar* | to end up -ing |
| *comenzar* | to begin by -ing |
| *concluir* | to end up -ing |
| *empezar* | to begin by -ing |
| *hacer* | to try to |
| *luchar* | to fight to |
| *optar* | to opt for -ing |
| *pugnar* | to fight to |
| *quedar* | to be left to |
| *rabiar* | to be dying to |
| *reventar* | to be bursting to |
| *suspirar* | to long to |
| *terminar* | to end up -ing |
| *votar* | to vote for -ing |

*Reflexive Verbs*

Example:

> *Nos apresuramos por llegar con tiempo*
> We hastened to arrive on time

The principal verbs belonging to this category are:

| | |
|---|---|
| *afanarse* | to strive to |
| *apresurarse* | to hasten to |
| *apurarse* | to worry about -ing; to hasten to |
| *desvivirse* | to yearn to |
| *entusiasmarse* | to get enthusiastic about -ing |
| *esforzarse* | to strive to |
| *morirse* | to be dying to |

# Verbs with a Dependent Gerund

## 815 The Subject of the Main Verb is the Same as the Implied Subject of the Gerund

Example:

> *Seguí leyendo*
> I carried on reading

The verbs of this category are:

| | |
|---|---|
| *continuar* | to continue to /-ing |
| *llevar* | to spend time -ing |
| *seguir* | to continue to /-ing |

## Nouns with a Dependent Infinitive

**816** Nouns always have a preposition before a dependent infinitive. Most often, the preposition is the one used for the corresponding verb, e.g.:

*Lucharon por conseguir la democracia*
They fought to achieve democracy

*La lucha por conseguir la democracia*
The fight to achieve democracy

Where the corresponding verb is one which has no preposition with a dependent infinitive (**795–800**), then *de* is usually used:

*Deseamos establecer la verdad*
We wish to establish the truth

*El deseo de establecer la verdad*
The desire to establish the truth

In a few cases, however, a preposition other than *de* is used in accordance with the general meaning of the preposition itself:

*Un anhelo por marcharse*
A longing to go away

## Verbs with a Prepositional Object

### 817 Verbs Taking *a* with an Object

For verbs taking *a* with an object, see **659** (the inanimate objects of verbs normally associated with personal objects), **675** (verbs of smell and taste), and **677** (*a* with indirect objects).

### 818 Verbs Taking *de* with an Object

Verbs denoting change take *de* with an object which is used in a categorial sense:

> *Vamos a mudar de casa*
> We're going to move house

Contrast:

> *Vamos a mudar esta casa por otra*
> We're going to change this house (specific) for another

*Cambiar* 'to change' belongs to this category, as does *variar* 'to vary'.

## 819 *Gozar* and *disfrutar*

The objects of *gozar* and *disfrutar* 'to enjoy' may be preceded by *de* when these verbs are used in the sense of 'to possess':

> *Goza de excelente salud*
> He enjoys excellent health

## 820 *Vestir(se)*

See also *vestirse* (**696**).

## 821 Reflexive Verbs Taking *de*

A prepositional phrase with *de* is used with a large number of reflexive verbs to denote an agent or cause, e.g.:

> *Me asombré de su audacia*
> I was amazed at/by his audacity

> *Nos beneficiamos de su generosidad*
> We benefited by her generosity

Similar verbs are:

| | |
|---|---|
| *aburrirse* | to be bored |
| *admirarse* | to admire |
| *aprovecharse* | to benefit (from) |
| *enamorarse* | to fall in love (with) |
| *escandalizarse* | to be scandalized |
| *espantarse* | to be frightened |
| *extrañarse* | to be surprised |
| *gloriarse* | to be proud (of) |
| *maravillarse* | to marvel (at) |

| | |
|---|---|
| *pagarse* | to be satisfied |
| *preocuparse* | to be worried |
| *reírse* | to laugh (at) |
| *sonreírse* | to smile (at) |
| *ufanarse* | to be proud (of) |

## 822 Verbs Taking *en* with an Object

*En* often corresponds to English 'in' and 'on': *creer en Dios* 'to believe in God', *insistir en sus derechos* 'to insist on one's rights'. It is also used with verbs of motion carrying the implication of 'going inside' (see **720**). Other verbs requiring *en* with a noun are:

| | |
|---|---|
| *consentir* | to consent to |
| *fijarse* | to notice |
| *influir* | to influence (see also **804**) |
| *reparar* | to notice |

# Conjunctions

## Forms

**823** The most frequently used conjunctions in Spanish are listed below:

Coordinating conjunctions:

| | |
|---|---|
| *ni* | nor (or) |
| *ni ... ni* | neither ... nor |
| *o* | or |
| *pero* | but |
| *sino* | but |
| *y* | and |

Subordinating conjunctions:

Cause:

| | |
|---|---|
| *como* | because |
| *porque* | because |
| *pues* | because, for |
| *puesto que* | since |
| *que* | that; because |
| *ya que* | since |

Consequence:

| | |
|---|---|
| *conque* | so |
| *de manera que* | so |
| *de modo que* | so |

Condition:

| | |
|---|---|
| *a condición de que* | on condition that |
| *con tal (de) que* | provided that |
| *si* | if |
| *siempre que* | provided that |

Concession:

| | |
|---|---|
| *aunque* | although |
| *bien que* | although |
| *aun cuando* | even though |

Purpose:

| | |
|---|---|
| *a fin de que* | |
| *de forma que* | |
| *de manera que* | in order that |
| *de modo que* | |
| *para que* | |

Time:

| | |
|---|---|
| *antes de que* | before |
| *apenas* | scarcely |
| *cuando* | when |
| *después de que* | after |
| *hasta que* | until |
| *mientras* | while |

Many of these conjunctions are discussed in **1051–1075** in connection with the mood used after them.

## Details of the Use of Some Conjunctions

### 824 *Conque*

*Conque* introduces a consequence:

    (i)   *Está de muy mal humor, conque trátale con cuidado* (*DD*, 115)

         He's in a very bad mood, so treat him carefully

It also frequently introduces an ironical question reminding someone of an unfulfilled promise, for example:

(ii)   *¿Conque ibas a venir a las seis?* (*DD*, 115)
You were going to come at six, were you (implying that the person has forgotten)?

Distinguish *conque* from the relative *con que* (example iii), *con que* introducing a noun clause (example iv) and the indirect question *con qué* (example v):

(iii)   *Éstos son los medios con que cuento* (*DD*, 115)
These are the means I am counting on

(iv)   *Me amenazó con que avisaría a la policía* (Marsá, 1986: 90)
She threatened me that she would tell the police

(v)   *Nunca he sabido con qué pagó sus deudas* (Marsá, 1986: 90)
I have never known what he paid his debts with

## 825 *Ni* and *ni . . . ni*

*Ni* may be used on its own or in conjunction with another *ni*. As with other negative elements, the verb must be preceded by *no* or another negative when it follows the verb (see **1292**).

*¡Pero ella no huía de nada ni de nadie!* (J. Donoso, 1980: 59)
But she was not fleeing from anything or anybody!

*Nunca piensa, ordena, dispone ni manda cosa contraria al bien público* (*Esbozo*, 506)[1]
Never think, order, arrange or order anything which is contrary to the public good

But:

*Ni teníamos descanso, ni nos daban educación* (F. Vizcaíno Casas, 1978: 129)
We had no rest, nor were we given any education

**826** *Ni* may also have an intensifying negative value: 'not one', 'not even'.

– *¿Entiende usted el vasco?*
– *Ni palabra* (P. Baroja, 1946–51: VIII, 385)
'Do you understand Basque?'
'Not a word'

*Cuando a los pocos días le adjudicaron la obra ya ni se acordaba de ella* (J. A. de Zunzunegui, 1956b: 142)
When a few days later they awarded him the work he could not even remember it

Note also the expression *ni que decir tiene*:

*El viaje era largo, ni que decir tiene* (R. J. Sender, 1972: 9)
The journey was long, needless to say

**827** *Ni siquiera* (and *ni tan siquiera* in the spoken language) also have the meaning 'not one', 'not even'.

*A ninguno de ellos le creía capaz de estrangular ni tan siquiera a un canario* (E. Parra, 1981: 55)
He didn't think that any of them was capable of strangling even a canary

*Ni aun* (*aun* has no accent) has the same meaning, and is used especially before the gerund:

*Ni aun pagándolo a peso de oro se consigue* (*DUE*, I, 303)
You cannot even get it by paying its weight in gold

**828** *Ni* + infinitive has a strong affective value, indicating indignation, disappointment, etc. *Ni hablar* is especially common.

*¿Queréis que se las entreguemos al enemigo así, por las buenas? ¡Ni hablar!* (A. M. de Lera, 1970: 189)
Do you want us to hand them over to the enemy just like that, voluntarily? No chance!

*Macario Martín se quejó a gritos: Ni comer. Ni comer* (I. Aldecoa, 1969: 100)
Macario Martín complained loudly, 'Nothing to eat. Nothing to eat'.

*¡Pero con esa zarabanda de millones – pensó –, ni intentarlo!* (J. A. de Zunzunegui, 1952b: 201)
'But with those seething millions', he thought, 'I won't even try it!'

– *¿No permitirán todavía tocar sardanas?*
– *¡Qué pregunta! Ni soñarlo. . .* (J. M. Gironella, 1966b: 254)
'Won't they allow sardanas (Catalan popular dance) to be played yet?'
'What a question! You mustn't even think of it . . .'

**829** *Ni* can also be used in elliptical expressions which make ironical reference to some well-known person or object:

> *Rodeados de unas medidas de seguridad que ni la cárcel de Span-dau, los muy mamelucos permanecían en Valencia* (C. Pérez Merinero, 1982: 144)
> Surrounded by security measures which would have put even Spandau prison in the shade, the clots stayed in Valencia

**830 *O***

*O* is the equivalent of English 'or'.

> *Vendrá él o su hermano* (*DUE*, II, 537)
> He or his brother will come

**831** *U* is used for *o* if the following word begins with *o* or *ho*.

> *Uno u otro lo dirá* (*Esbozo*, 509)
> One or the other will say

> *¡Alto, u os quedáis fritos!* (M. Vázquez Montalbán, 1979b: 12)
> Halt, or you're done for!

> *No sé si es belga u holandesa*
> I don't know whether she's Belgian or Dutch

This rule is followed even for numerals:

> *El 70 u 80 por ciento* (M. Delibes, 1977: 79)
> 70 or 80 per cent
> (Read: . . . *u ochenta* . . .)

**832** The force of the alternative can be strengthened by the use of *o* before both elements:

> *O te callas o me marcho* (*DUE*, II, 537)
> Either you shut up or I go

**833** When *o* follows a numeral or is used between two numerals, it is often written with an accent to avoid confusion with zero.

| | |
|---|---|
| *Faltan 2 ó más palabras* | Two or more words are missing |
| *Todavía tengo 8 ó 9 dólares* | I still have 8 or 9 dollars |

## 834 *Pero, (mas)* and *sino*

*Sino* must be used to express a mutually exclusive contrast:

> *No lo hizo él, sino ella* (*DD*, 345)
> It wasn't him that did it, but her
> (*Él* and *ella* are mutually exclusive)

Contrast:

> *Eres pobre, pero decente* (*Esbozo*, 510)
> You are poor but respectable
> (*Pobre* and *decente* are not mutually exclusive)

*Sino* thus usually follows a negative, as in the first example above. Compare also:

> *Imagínese si, a pesar nuestro, se oficializara la cuestión y empiezan a aparecer no amigos, sino amigas, muchas amigas* (M. Vázquez Montalbán, 1979b: 36)
> Just imagine if, despite us, the matter became official and there begin to appear not just friends, but girlfriends, lots of girlfriends

However, it is quite possible for *pero* to be used after a negative when the contrasted ideas are not mutually exclusive:

> *Una mañana gris. No fría; pero gris* (J. Rulfo, 1981: 168)
> A grey morning. Not cold; but grey
> (*Fría* and *gris* are not mutually exclusive; indeed, it would normally be expected that a grey morning was cold)

> *La mujer no ha estado nunca marginada, pero sí privada de cultura* (*Heraldo de Aragón*, 9 February 1978: 30)
> Women have never been outsiders, but they have been deprived of culture

> *No era bella, pero en cambio era simpática* (G. García Márquez, 1977: 250)
> She wasn't beautiful, but on the other hand she was a nice person
> (*Simpática* does not contradict *bella*)

The word *mas* (no accent) is an archaic form occasionally used in literary register as an equivalent of *pero*:

> *Quise reunir más dinero, mas no pude* (Marsá, 1986: 75)
> I wanted to get more money together, but I couldn't

**835** Some examples of *pero* and *sino* in the same sentence:

*Era como si estuviera el mar a la vuelta de la esquina, pero no un mar grande sino pequeño y privado* (R. J. Sender, 1969b: 94)
It was as if the sea was round the corner, though not a big sea but a small, private one

*Los impertinentes de doña Virtudes no eran de oro sino de plata, pero de una plata muy limpia* (C. J. Cela, 1971: 58)
Doña Virtudes's lorgnette was not gold but silver, but a very pure silver

**836** *Sino* is not to be confused with *si no* 'if not':
*No come si no trabaja* (*DD*, 346)
He doesn't eat if he doesn't work

## 837 *Sino que*

Before a clause, *sino que* is used. Note that a comma is usual before *sino que*.

*No sólo se piensa, sino que se siente con palabras* (M. de Unamuno, 1967b: 25)
Not only does one think, but one feels with words

*– Me han despedido de la imprenta – dijo al entrar.*
*– Habrás ido tarde – saltó la Salvadora.*
*– No, sino que Ortiz me dijo ayer que esta tarde tenía que ir con él* (P. Baroja, 1946–51: I, 503)
'They've fired me from the press,' he asaid as he came in.
'You must have been late,' la Salvadora exploded.
'No, but Ortiz told me yesterday that I was to go with him this afternoon'

## 838 *No . . . sino*

*No . . . sino*, like *no . . . más que*, has the meaning 'only'.

*No se oía sino el rumor de las hojas* (A. Bello, 1972: 355)
Only the sound of the leaves could be heard

*No se hablaba sino de él* (A. Uslar Pietri, 1983: 78)
They spoke only of him

## 839  Other Uses of *pero*

*Pero* (sometimes followed by *y*) may introduce a question; it adds an overtone of astonishment, anxiety or reproach. As the first word in a sentence, *pero* has an emphatic value.

> *Pero ¿y Cristo-Teodorito?* (F. Umbral, 1976b: 141)
> What about Cristo-Teodorito, then?

> *Pero ¿la Medicina? argüirán los optimistas* (M. Delibes, 1979b: 34)
> 'What about medicine?' optimists will argue

> *Pero ¡qué maravilla!* (*Esbozo*, 511)
> How absolutely wonderful!

**840**  In the spoken language *pero que* strengthens the force of a following adjective or adverb.

> *Estás pero que mucho más guapa cuando te sonríes* (J. A. de Zunzunegui, 1954: 18)
> You're very much prettier when you smile
> (For the reflexive use of *sonreír*, see **292**)

> *Ignacio, eso está pero que muy mal* (J. M. Gironella, 1966b: 714)
> That is really terrible, Ignacio

**841**  *Pero* can also function as a noun with the meaning of 'objection'.

> – *Tú mandas. Pero . . .*
> – *No hay peros* (M. Aub, 1970: 95)
> 'You're the boss. But . . .'
> 'No buts'

> – *Es verdad. Pero . . .*
> – *No hay pero que valga* (J. Icaza, 1980: 107)
> 'That's true. But . . .'
> 'There are no buts about it'

## 842  *Pues*

*Pues* is very frequently used in the spoken language. Often it is simply a hesitation word which allows speakers to organise their thoughts or fill pauses.

*Bueno, pues yo estoy conforme hasta cierto punto* (*DD*, 310)
Well, I agree up to a certain point

– *¿Cómo sigue el enfermo?*
– *Pues está algo mejor* (*DUE*, II, 881)
'How's the patient?'
'Well, a bit better'

– *¿Qué tal el examen?*
– *Pues* ... (conversation between two students overheard by
JdeB, 20 August 1988)
'How did the exam go?'
'Well ...'
(The second speaker had failed)

The expression *pues nada* can preface a farewell:

*Bueno, pues nada, Mariano, hasta luego y gracias por todo*
(Beinhauer, 1968: 102)[2]
OK then, Mariano, so long and thanks for everything

**843** *Pues* may also have the fuller meaning 'because'. In the
spoken language, it is nowadays replaced in this meaning by *porque* or *que*.

*Me iré, pues os molesta mi presencia* (*DUE*, II, 881)
I'll go, since my presence annoys you

**844** *Pues* also has a related meaning in a sentence like the following, where it expresses a relation of consequence:

*Parece un símbolo, pues, la muerte de Joy Adamson* (*El País*, 5
January 1980: 32)
The death of Joy Adamson thus seemed a symbol

**845** *Pos* (also, in Latin-American Spanish *pus, pes, pis, pu*, etc.)[3] is
a regional variant of *pues*.

## 846 Que

Of all the conjunctions, *que* has the greatest range of different
meanings, the most common of which[4] are:

*que* = 'that' (introducing a subordinate clause)

*Se puede demostrar que Dios existe o no existe* (C. J. Cela, *El País,
edición internacional*, 6 June 1983: 10)
It can be shown that God exists or does not exist

In the written language, *que* is usually used only before the first of a
series of subordinate clauses (as in the above example).
  Repetition of *que* before each subordinate clause is more typical
of popular speech.[5]

*que* = *para que* 'in order that' (with the subjunctive)

*Dio voces a los criados, que le ensillasen el caballo* (Marsá,
1986: 153)
He shouted to the servants to saddle his horse

*que* = 'instead of'

*Yo que tú, me casaba* (F. Umbral, 1973a: 96)
If I were you, I'd get married

*que* = 'because'

*Dale limosna mujer, que no hay en la vida nada como la pena de
ser ciego en Granada* (a favourite text on souvenirs from
Granada)
Give him alms, lady, for there is nothing worse in this life
than the sadness of being blind in Granada

*que* = 'than' (in comparative sentences)

*Eres más alto que yo*
You are taller than me

*que* = 'as far as' (with the subjunctive)

*Que yo sepa, todavía no ha llegado*
As far as I know, he hasn't arrived yet[6]

*que* = 'or' (to render a concessive idea, with the subjunctive)

*Tendrán que venir, quieran que no*
They must come, whether they want to or not
(See also the examples in **776**)

*Que ría o que llore, se lo tengo que decir* (*DUE*: II, 1076).
Whether he laughs or cries, I've got to tell him
(*DUE* comments that one *que* may be omitted)

*que* = 'still'

*Anda, Conchi. Que estamos todos reunidos. Que todos te queremos* (J. M. Gironella, 1966b: 236)
Come on, Conchi. We're still all together. We still all love you

**847** *Que* has an intensifying meaning when used between two identical verbs or adjectives. Such constructions appear exclusively in popular speech.

*Allí permanecía, lava que te lava, de la mañana a la noche la pobre viuda* (J. A. de Zunzunegui, 1959b: 35)
There stayed the poor widow, washing, washing, from morning till night

*Muerto que muerto* and *vivo que vivo* have the respective meanings 'stone dead' and 'alive and kicking'.

*Que* also has an emphatic meaning in a sentence such as

*Bea, por Dios, que son las tres* (J. A. de Zunzunegui, 1952b: 58)
For goodness' sake, Bea, it's three o'clock

On *estar que* + verb, see **1243**.
  *Que* can also combine with *pero* to give an intensifying meaning – see **840**.

**848** *Que* is sometimes omitted in the written language when it introduces a subordinate clause, after verbs of willing, wishing or fearing, e.g., *rogar* 'to ask', *temer* 'to fear', etc.[7] (see **1038**).

*Temieron se perdiese la ocasión* (*Esbozo*, 517)
They feared the opportunity would be missed

It is sometimes omitted before other verbs to give an impression of 'elegance'.[8]

*Supo vivía en casa de una amiga* (J. A. de Zunzunegui, 1956b: 104)
He knew that she was living with a friend

*¿Te parece comamos juntos?* (J. A. de Zunzunegui, 1956b: 266)
OK if we eat together?
(*¿Te parece?* = *¿te parece bien?*)

*Espero os encontréis bien* (letter to JdeB from J. Domínguez, Zaragoza, 3 September 1985)
I hope you are well

In popular speech, *que* or *que si* are sometimes used elliptically to suggest a main clause verb.

> *Y en estas, el Bisa se cabreó, la puso la punta del machete en la barriga y que una habitación para el general, y ella entonces, que bien, que la segunda puerta a la derecha* (M. Delibes, 1975: 22)
> And then Bisa got cross, stuck the end of his machete into her belly and demanded a room for the general, and then she said fine, the second door on the right
> (Possible main clause verbs would be: *y que una habitación* = *y que hacía falta una habitación; ella entonces, que bien* = *ella entonces decía que estaba bien; que la segunda puerta* = *que podían entrar por la segunda puerta*)
> (The use of *la* with *puso* is an example of *laísmo* – see **275–276** and **894**, first example)

**849** In the spoken language of lower registers, *que* is sometimes used superfluously:

> *El primer día de curso me había preguntado que si yo era pariente de un violinista célebre* (C. Laforet, 1966: 60)
> On the first day of lectures he had asked me if I was any relation of a famous violinist

> – *¿Me da tres cuartos de tomates?*
> – *¿Eh?*
> *La verdulera es sorda como una tapia.*
> – *¡Que si me da tres cuartos de tomates!* (C. J. Cela, 1967d: 34)
> 'Could I have a pound and a half of tomatoes?'
> 'What?'
> The lady greengrocer is as deaf as a post.
> 'Could I have a pound and a half of tomatoes?'

Another strictly superfluous use of *que*, again in the spoken language, occurs when the subordinate clause has within it another, usually fairly long, subordinate clause:

> *Dijo que como era ya muy tarde para ir a clase, que no le esperaran* (*DD*, 5th edn, 284)[9]
> He said that, as it was now too late to go to the class, they shouldn't wait for him

**850** In some indirect questions in popular speech a superfluous *que* is sometimes used before the interrogative pronoun *qué*.[10]

> *Sé lo que piensa ... que qué va a decir la gente* (J. A. de Zunzunegui, 1956a: 13)
> I know what you're thinking: 'What will people say?'

> *Ella decía que era así y que qué le haremos, añadía* (title of a short story by J. Vilallonga in *Ínsula*, no. 422, January 1982, p. 16)
> She said that that's how it was and what could we do about it, she added

> *Le pregunté que qué hora era* (*DUE*, II, 901)
> I asked her what the time was

## 851 *Si*

*Si* is the equivalent of both the indirect question and conditional uses of English 'if', 'whether'.

> *No sé si vendrá*
> I don't know whether he will come

> *Si vienes mañana te daré el libro*
> If you come tomorrow I'll give you the book

**852** After verbs of saying or thinking, *si* can sometimes be found where *que* would be expected. The explanation for this is probably that there is always a feeling of doubt, the verb actually having the meaning *preguntar* 'to ask' or *preguntarse* 'to wonder'.

> *Don Nicolás se marchó de España el año 39, porque decían si era masón* (C. J. Cela, 1963a: 270)
> Don Nicolás left Spain in 1939, because people were saying he was a mason

> *Murmuraban si la chica tendría hecho algún pacto con el Malo* (V. Blasco Ibáñez, 1963: 28)
> There was gossip that the girl might have made some pact with the devil

> *Pitusa pensó si había hecho bien dándole el libro* (C. Tellado, 1984: 69)
> Pitusa wondered if she been right to give him the book

**853** *Si* can also express an overtone of shock.[11]

> *Si está descalzoncillado* (F. García Pavón, 1980a: 37)
> But he's got no underpants (shorts) on!

> – *¿No estás ya con el marqués?*
> – *Pero hombre, si se arruinó* (quoted by A. Mingote, 1988: 19)
> 'Aren't you with the marquis now?'
> 'But surely you know he's ruined'

## 854 Y

*Y* is the equivalent of English 'and'. Like 'and', it is used only before the last of a series of items. unless a subgrouping is intended.

> *Ha trabajado mucho y está cansado* (Marsá, 1986: 152)
> He has worked hard and he is tired

> *El padre, la madre y los niños* (R. Seco, 1960: 200)
> The father. the mother and the children

> *Eran todos jóvenes y estaban bebiendo y comiendo y riendo y discutiendo* (J. Donoso, 1980: 125)
> They were all young and they were eating and drinking and laughing and talking

Used between the same verbs. *y* has a durative and/or intensifying value:

> *Peleamos y peleamos y peleamos* (M. Puig. 1980: 101)
> We quarrelled and quarrelled and quarrelled

**855** *E* is used instead of *y* before a word beginning with *i* or *hi* (even if before a comma, as in the third example, unless the *i* is part of a diphthong (see **9**)).

> – *Lástima, porque es simpático.*
> – *E inteligente* (M. Aub, 1970: 117)
> 'A pity, because he's nice.'
> 'And clever'

> *Enamoramiento, éxtasis e hipnotismo* (J. Ortega y Gasset, 1959: 101)
> Falling in love, ecstasy and hypnotism

*¡E, inopinadamente, reaparece el espectro de la bohemia!* (R. del Valle-Inclán, 1981: 81)
And unexpectedly, the spectre of Bohemian life reappears

but:

*Matan y hieren sin piedad* (*Esbozo*, 506)
They kill and wound without mercy
(*Hieren* begins with a diphthong [*ie*])

The rule is not without exceptions: either *e* or *y* can be used before a proper noun:

*Sisí se esforzó en mostrarse amable.*
*– ¿Y Hipolitín? dijo* (M. Delibes, 1969b: 296)
Sisí did his best to appear friendly.
'And little Hipólito?' he said

*E Ignacio le había contestado: «sí»* (J. M. Gironella, 1966a: 776)
And Ignacio had answered, 'Yes'

**856** In several areas of Latin America, an independent *¿y?* is used instead of questions like *¿de qué se trata?* 'what's it about?', *¿qué pasó?* 'what happened?' and *¿y qué?* 'and what now?'.[12]

# The Verb: Conjugation

## Differences between Peninsular and Latin-American Spanish

**857** Forms of the verb other than those given in the following sections may be used with *vos* in Latin-American Spanish. The second person plural forms given in this chapter are generally totally absent in Latin America. For the forms used with *vos*, see **255**.

## Regular Verbs

**858** In Spanish there are three groups of regular verbs. Their respective infinitives end in *-ar*, *-er*, *-ir*. By far the majority of verbs belong to the first group and nearly all new forms take the ending *-ar*.[1]

The conjugation of these verbs is as follows.

### Simple Tenses of the Indicative

### 859 Present Indicative

|        | *CANTAR*<br>'to sing' | *COMER*<br>'to eat' | *VIVIR*<br>'to live' |
|--------|-----------|-----------|-----------|
| 1 sg   | cant/o    | com/o     | viv/o     |
| 2 sg   | cant/as   | com/es    | viv/es    |
| 3 sg   | cant/a    | com/e     | viv/e     |
| 1 pl   | cant/amos | com/emos  | viv/imos  |
| 2 pl   | cant/áis  | com/éis   | viv/ís    |
| 3 pl   | cant/an   | com/en    | viv/en    |

**860** Note that:

(1)   The first person singular ending is always -*o* except in the case of the irregular verbs *estar (estoy)*, *dar (doy)*, *haber (he)*, *ir (voy)*, *saber (sé)* and *ser (soy)* (see **936**).

(2)   -*Er* and -*ir* verbs differ only in the first and second persons plural.

(3)   The second person plural ending has a written accent.

## 861 Imperfect Indicative

|        | CANTAR       | COMER       | VIVIR      |
|--------|--------------|-------------|------------|
| 1 sg   | cant/aba     | com/ía      | viv/ía     |
| 2 sg   | cant/abas    | com/ías     | viv/ías    |
| 3 sg   | cant/aba     | com/ía      | viv/ía     |
| 1 pl   | cant/ábamos  | com/íamos   | viv/íamos  |
| 2 pl   | cant/abais   | com/íais    | viv/íais   |
| 3 pl   | cant/aban    | com/ían     | viv/ían    |

There are only three verbs which forms their imperfect irregularly in Spanish: *ir* 'to go' (see **939**), *ser* 'to be' (see **910**) and *ver* 'to see' (see **939**).

**862** Note that:

(1)   The imperfect indicative of verbs in -*er* and -*ir* is formed in the same way.

(2)   There is a written accent in *cantábamos* and no written accent in *cantabais*.

## 863 Preterite[2]

|        | CANTAR       | COMER       | VIVIR      |
|--------|--------------|-------------|------------|
| 1 sg   | cant/é       | com/í       | viv/í      |
| 2 sg   | cant/aste    | com/iste    | viv/iste   |
| 3 sg   | cant/ó       | com/ió      | viv/ió     |
| 1 pl   | cant/amos    | com/imos    | viv/imos   |
| 2 pl   | cant/asteis  | com/isteis  | viv/isteis |
| 3 pl   | cant/aron    | com/ieron   | viv/ieron  |

**864** Note:

(1)   Here too there is only one series of endings for -*er* and -*ir* verbs.

(2)  The importance of the written accent: *canto* (1 sg present indicative) contrasts with *cantó* (3 sg preterite); *cante* (1 and 3 sg present subjunctive) contrasts with *canté* (1 sg preterite).

(3)  The first person plural of regular *-ar* and *-ir* verbs (*cantamos, vivimos*) is identical in the present and the preterite.

## 865  Future Indicative

|       | *CANTAR*      | *COMER*      | *VIVIR*      |
|-------|---------------|--------------|--------------|
| 1 sg  | *cantar/é*    | *comer/é*    | *vivir/é*    |
| 2 sg  | *cantar/ás*   | *comer/ás*   | *vivir/ás*   |
| 3 sg  | *cantar/á*    | *comer/ás*   | *vivir/ás*   |
| 1 pl  | *cantar/emos* | *comer/emos* | *vivir/emos* |
| 2 pl  | *cantar/éis*  | *comer/éis*  | *vivir/éis*  |
| 3 pl  | *cantar/án*   | *comer/án*   | *vivir/án*   |

**866**  The future is formed in the same way for all regular *-ar*, *-er* and *-ir* verbs, the same endings being added to the infinitive of the verb.

## 867  Conditional

|       | *CANTAR*        | *COMER*        | *VIVIR*        |
|-------|-----------------|----------------|----------------|
| 1 sg  | *cantar/ía*     | *comer/ía*     | *vivir/ía*     |
| 2 sg  | *cantar/ía*     | *comer/ía*     | *vivir/ía*     |
| 3 sg  | *cantar/ía*     | *comer/ía*     | *vivir/ía*     |
| 1 pl  | *cantar/íamos*  | *comer/íamos*  | *vivir/íamos*  |
| 2 pl  | *cantar/íais*   | *comer/íais*   | *vivir/íais*   |
| 3 pl  | *cantar/ían*    | *comer/ían*    | *vivir/ían*    |

**868**  Like the future, the conditional is formed in the same way for all regular *-ar*, *-er* and *-ir* verbs. the imperfect endings of *-er* and *-ir* verbs being added to the infinitive of the verb.

## Simple Tenses of the Subjunctive

## 869  Present

|       | *CANTAR*   | *COMER*   | *VIVIR*   |
|-------|------------|-----------|-----------|
| 1 sg  | *cant/e*   | *com/a*   | *viv/a*   |
| 2 sg  | *cant/es*  | *com/as*  | *viv/as*  |
| 3 sg  | *cant/e*   | *com/a*   | *viv/a*   |

| 1 pl | *cant/emos* | *com/amos* | *viv/amos* |
| 2 pl | *cant/éis* | *com/áis* | *viv/áis* |
| 3 pl | *cant/en* | *com/an* | *viv/an* |

**870** Note that:

(1) In the formation of the present subjunctive, a kind of 'exchange' of vowels takes place: -*ar* verbs take endings in *e*, which is the characteristic vowel of the -*er* verbs, and verbs in -*er* and -*ir* take endings in *a*, which is the characteristic vowel of the -*ar* verbs.

(2) The present subjunctive of nearly all verbs (for exceptions, see **946**) is formed from the first person singular of the present indicative, the -*o* being replaced by the endings in **869**. This rule holds even when the first person singular of the indicative is the only irregular form: compare the present indicative of *caber* 'to fit, be contained', which is *quepo* (irregular), *cabes, cabe, cabemos, cabéis, caben*, and the present subjunctive of the same verb, which is *quepa, quepas, quepa, quepamos, quepáis, quepan* (all based on *quepo*).

(3) There is a written accent on the second person plural forms: *cantéis, comáis, viváis*.

## 871 Imperfect Subjunctive

The imperfect subjunctive has two forms, both of which are used extensively in both written and spoken Spanish. Once again there is no difference between -*er* and -*ir* verbs as regards endings.

| **872** | *CANTAR* | *COMER* | *VIVIR* |
|---|---|---|---|
| 1 sg | *cant/ara* | *com/iera* | *viv/iera* |
| 2 sg | *cant/aras* | *com/ieras* | *viv/ieras* |
| 3 sg | *cant/ara* | *com/iera* | *viv/iera* |
| 1 pl | *cant/áramos* | *com/iéramos* | *viv/iéramos* |
| 2 pl | *cant/arais* | *com/ierais* | *viv/ierais* |
| 3 pl | *cant/aran* | *com/ieran* | *viv/ieran* |
| 1 sg | *cant/ase* | *com/iese* | *viv/iese* |
| 2 sg | *cant/ases* | *com/ieses* | *viv/ieses* |
| 3 sg | *cant/ase* | *com/iese* | *viv/iese* |
| 1 pl | *cant/ásemos* | *com/iésemos* | *viv/iésemos* |
| 2 pl | *cant/aseis* | *com/ieseis* | *viv/ieseis* |
| 3 pl | *cant/asen* | *com/iesen* | *viv/iesen* |

**873** Both forms of the imperfect subjunctive are formed from the third person plural of the preterite by substituting the endings *-ra*, *-ras*, etc. or *-se*, *-ses*, etc. for the final *-ron*. This rule holds for all verbs, including irregular ones; thus:

> from *canta–ron*: *canta–ra*, *canta–ras*, etc.
> from *comie–ron*: *comie–se*, *comie–ses*, etc.
> from *fue–ron*: *fue–ra*, *fue–ras*, etc.

Note the written accent in the first person plural forms (*cantáramos*, *cantásemos*).

**874** On the possible difference in usage between the *-ra* and *-se* forms of the imperfect subjunctive, see **1011–1012**.

### 875 Future Subjunctive

This form is scarcely if ever used in modern Spanish (see **1017**), but is included here for the sake of completeness.

   It is like the imperfect subjunctive in the manner of its formation, *-re* being used in place of *-ra* (*-se*).

**876**

|  | *CANTAR* | *COMER* | *VIVIR* |
|---|---|---|---|
| 1 sg | *cant/are* | *com/iere* | *viv/iere* |
| 2 sg | *cant/ares* | *com/ieres* | *viv/ieres* |
| 3 sg | *cant/are* | *com/iere* | *viv/iere* |
| 1 pl | *cant/áremos* | *com/iéremos* | *viv/iéremos* |
| 2 pl | *cant/areis* | *com/iereis* | *viv/iereis* |
| 3 pl | *cant/aren* | *com/ieren* | *viv/ieren* |

### Compound Tenses of the Indicative

**877** The compound tenses are formed from the auxiliary verb *haber* + past participle (see **900–902**).

### 878 Perfect

The perfect of every Spanish verb is formed from the present tense of *haber* + past participle.

|      | CANTAR         | COMER         | VIVIR         |
|------|----------------|---------------|---------------|
| 1 sg | he cantado     | he comido     | he vivido     |
| 2 sg | has cantado    | has comido    | has vivido    |
| 3 sg | ha cantado     | ha comido     | ha vivido     |
| 1 pl | hemos cantado  | hemos comido  | hemos vivido  |
| 2 pl | habéis cantado | habéis comido | habéis vivido |
| 3 pl | han cantado    | han comido    | han vivido    |

## 879 Pluperfect Tenses (Pluperfect and Past Anterior)

The pluperfect is formed from the imperfect tense of *haber* + past participle.

|      | CANTAR           | COMER           | VIVIR           |
|------|------------------|-----------------|-----------------|
| 1 sg | había cantado    | había comido    | había vivido    |
| 2 sg | habías cantado   | habías comido   | habías vivido   |
| 3 sg | había cantado    | había comido    | había vivido    |
| 1 pl | habíamos cantado | habíamos comido | habíamos vivido |
| 2 pl | habíais cantado  | habíais comido  | habíais vivido  |
| 3 pl | habían cantado   | habían comido   | habían vivido   |

**880** The past anterior is formed from the preterite tense of *haber* + past participle.

|      | CANTAR           | COMER           | VIVIR           |
|------|------------------|-----------------|-----------------|
| 1 sg | hube cantado     | hube comido     | hube vivido     |
| 2 sg | hubiste cantado  | hubiste comido  | hubiste vivido  |
| 3 sg | hubo cantado     | hubo comido     | hubo vivido     |
| 1 pl | hubimos cantado  | hubimos comido  | hubimos vivido  |
| 2 pl | hubisteis cantado| hubisteis comido| hubisteis vivido|
| 3 pl | hubieron cantado | hubieron comido | hubieron vivido |

## 881 Future Perfect

The future perfect is formed from the future tense of *haber* + past participle.

|      | CANTAR         | COMER         | VIVIR         |
|------|----------------|---------------|---------------|
| 1 sg | habré cantado  | habré comido  | habré vivido  |
| 2 sg | habrás cantado | habrás comido | habrás vivido |
| 3 sg | habrá cantado  | habrá comido  | habrá vivido  |

| 1 pl | *habremos cantado* | *habremos comido* | *habremos vivido* |
| 2 pl | *habréis cantado* | *habréis comido* | *habréis vivido* |
| 3 pl | *habrán cantado* | *habrán comido* | *habrán vivido* |

## 882 Conditional Perfect

The conditional perfect is formed from the conditional of *haber* + past participle.

| | *CANTAR* | *COMER* | *VIVIR* |
|---|---|---|---|
| 1 sg | *habría cantado* | *habría comido* | *habría vivido* |
| 2 sg | *habrías cantado* | *habrías comido* | *habrías vivido* |
| 3 sg | *habría cantado* | *habría comido* | *habría vivido* |
| 1 pl | *habríamos cantado* | *habríamos comido* | *habríamos vivido* |
| 2 pl | *habríais cantado* | *habríais comido* | *habríais vivido* |
| 3 pl | *habrían cantado* | *habrían comido* | *habrían vivido* |

## Compound Tenses of the Subjunctive

## 883 Perfect Subjunctive

This tense is formed from the present subjunctive of *haber* + past participle.

| | *CANTAR* | *COMER* | *VIVIR* |
|---|---|---|---|
| 1 sg | *haya cantado* | *haya comido* | *haya vivido* |
| 2 sg | *hayas cantado* | *hayas comido* | *hayas vivido* |
| 3 sg | *haya cantado* | *haya comido* | *haya vivido* |
| 1 pl | *hayamos cantado* | *hayamos comido* | *hayamos vivido* |
| 2 pl | *hayáis cantado* | *hayáis comido* | *hayáis vivido* |
| 3 pl | *hayan cantado* | *hayan comido* | *hayan vivido* |

## 884 Pluperfect Subjunctive

This tense is formed from the imperfect subjunctive of *haber* + past participle.

| | *CANTAR* | *COMER* | *VIVIR* |
|---|---|---|---|
| 1 sg | *hubiera cantado* | *hubiera comido* | *hubiera vivido* |
| 2 sg | *hubieras cantado* | *hubieras comido* | *hubieras vivido* |
| 3 sg | *hubiera cantado* | *hubiera comido* | *hubiera vivido* |
| 1 pl | *hubiéramos cantado* | *hubiéramos comido* | *hubiéramos vivido* |
| 2 pl | *hubierais cantado* | *hubierais comido* | *hubierais vivido* |
| 3 pl | *hubieran cantado* | *hubieran comido* | *hubieran vivido* |

| 1 sg | hubiese cantado | hubiese comido | hubiese vivido |
| 2 sg | hubieses cantado | hubieses comido | hubieses vivido |
| 3 sg | hubiese cantado | hubiese comido | hubiese vivido |
| 1 pl | hubiésemos cantado | hubiésemos comido | hubiésemos vivido |
| 2 pl | hubieseis cantado | hubieseis comido | hubieseis vivido |
| 3 pl | hubiesen cantado | hubiesen comido | hubiesen vivido |

**885** The future perfect subjunctive, formed from the future subjunctive of *haber* + past participle (*hubiere cantado, hubieres cantado, hubiere cantado, hubiéremos cantado, hubieseis cantado, hubieren cantado*, etc.) is found occasionally in legal documents in modern Spanish, but is otherwise no longer used (see **1017**).

### Perfect Infinitive

**886** The perfect infinitive is formed from the infinitive *haber* + past participle (*haber cantado*, etc.). See **1084** and **1118**.

### The Imperative

**887** Strictly speaking, the imperative has distinct forms only in the second person singular and plural. However, several other verb forms act as imperatives in Spanish: the subjunctive, the future indicative, the infinitive and the gerund are commonly used in this way (see **890, 889, 1003, 1122-1136** and **1153-1155**).

|  | CANTAR | COMER | VIVIR |
| 2 sg | ¡canta! | ¡come! | ¡vive! |
| 2 pl | ¡cantad! | ¡comed! | ¡vivid! |

For regular verbs, the second person singular of the imperative is identical to the third person singular of the present indicative.

### 888 Remarks

Clitic pronouns follow positive imperative forms and the combination of imperative clitic is written as one word:

| ¡Lávate! | Wash yourself! |
| ¡Míralo! | Look at it! |

Note that the written accent reflects the preservation of stress on the verb form.

**889** In the second person plural imperative, the final *-d* falls before the reflexive clitic pronoun *-os*.

> *¡Lavaos!*          Wash yourselves!
>
> *¡Acercaos!*          Come over here!

> *Ahora, disolveos pacíficamente y que nadie se preocupe* (F. Vizcaíno Casas, 1978: 202)
> Now break up peacefully and don't anyone worry

> *¡Proletarios de todos los países, uníos!* (A. Carpentier, 1976: 225)
> Workers of the world, unite!

*Id*, from *ir*, is an exception to this rule:

> *Idos y dejadme en paz, ¡so cretinos!* (A. Roa Bastos, 1977: 213)
> Go away and leave me in peace, you idiots!

As will also be seen from the last example, the final *-d* of the second person plural imperative does not fall before other clitic pronouns (*dejadme*).

**890** The present subjunctive is used to render the imperative in the following cases:

(1)    With *usted, ustedes* (which take 'third person' verb forms):

|  | *CANTAR* | *COMER* | *VIVIR* |
|---|---|---|---|
| 2 sg (polite) | *¡cante (Vd.)!* | *¡coma (Vd.)!* | *¡viva (Vd.)!* |
| 2 pl (polite) | *¡canten (Vds.)!* | *¡coman (Vds.)!* | *¡vivan (Vds.)!* |

A sign in the Madrid metro (seen in February 1985) reads:
*EN BENEFICIO DE TODOS:*
*ENTREN Y SALGAN RAPIDAMENTE*
*NO OBSTRUYAN LAS PUERTAS*
For everyone's benefit: enter and leave quickly; do not obstruct the doors

(2)    In the first person plural:

|  | *CANTAR* | *COMER* | *VIVIR* |
|---|---|---|---|
|  | *¡cantemos!* | *¡comamos!* | *¡vivamos!* |

Note that the final -*s* falls before the reflexive clitic pronoun:

> *¡Lavémonos!*                    Let's get washed!
>
> *Abracémonos, hermanos* (R. del Valle-Inclán, 1981: 58)
> Let us embrace each other, brothers

But:

> *Ejemplifiquémoslo* (Alarcos Llorach, 1982: 261)
> Let us give an example of it
> (*Lo* is not reflexive)

(3)    When the imperative is in the negative:

|        | CANTAR        | COMER         | VIVIR         |
|--------|---------------|---------------|---------------|
| 2 sg   | *¡no cantes!*   | *¡no comas!*    | *¡no vivas!*    |
| 2 pl   | *¡no cantéis!*  | *¡no comáis!*   | *¡no viváis!*   |

> *No te cases con Leticia* (E. Jardiel Poncela, 1973: 170)
> Don't marry Leticia

Note that with the negative imperative the clitic pronoun precedes the verb and is written separately from it. thus *¡levántate!* 'get up!' but *¡no te levantes!* 'don't get up!'. Compare the forms in the following example:

> *Hijos, manteneos unidos y no os ocupéis de cuestiones de política*
> (L. Ricardo Alonso, 1981: 74)
> Children. keep together and do not concern yourselves with political matters

**891**  The writing of a double -*s*- is avoided with clitic forms, thus *¡digámoselo!* (< *digamos* + *se* + *lo*).[3]

**892**  In popular speech, especially in reflexive constructions. the third person plural -*n* is sometimes attached to the clitic pronoun rather than to the verb, e.g. *¡Márchesen Vds.!* for *¡Márchense Vds.!* 'Go away!'; sometimes the -*n* appears twice. e.g. *¡Márchensen Vds.!*.[4] Such forms are to be avoided by foreign learners.

**893**  Imperative forms with the pronoun before the verb may be heard in the spoken language, especially in Castilla la Vieja and Aragón.

> *¡Se sienten!* (words of Lieutenant-Colonel Tejero on the occasion of the abortive military coup of 23 February 1981)
> Sit down!

*¡Me ponga un kilo de arroz!*
Give me a kilo of rice!

(Both the above examples are taken from a lecture by J. Mondéjar given in Antwerp on 26 April 1986.)

**894** The rule given in **890** does not always hold in popular speech and texts which represent speech. The imperative may sometimes be used in the negative where a subjunctive is strictly needed, especially in the plural.

*No hacedla caso* (J. García Hortelano, 1979:100)
Don't take any notice of her
(Note also the use of *la* for *le* (*laísmo*) – see **275–276**.)

*¡No abrid a desconocidos!* (*Heraldo de Aragón*, 13 August 1982)
Don't open the door to strangers!

In the following examples, the imperative is similarly used, though the correct subjunctive is also present:

*Ni fía ni porfía, ni entres en cofradía* (*Esbozo*, 362, n. 3)
Trust no one and quarrel with no one, and mind your own business

*No aceptéis la mano tendida, no caed en la trampa* (J. Goytisolo, 1986: 143)
Do not accept the outstretched hand, do not fall into the trap

The converse situation is also found, especially with the forms *sepas*, *sepáis* and (less commonly) *digas*, *digáis*:

*Sepáis que no os necesito para nada* (*DUE*, II, 1474)
You should know that I don't need you for anything

*Digas que no quieres hacerlo* (ibid.)
Say that you don't want to do it

(The correct forms are respectively *sabed* and *di*.)[5]

**895** The third person present subjunctive, used reflexively, may be regarded as a kind of 'impersonal' imperative.

*UTILÍCESE COMO RECIPIENTE EN CASO DE MAREO*
(on sick-bags on Iberia planes)
To be used in case of air sickness

**896** As in English, Spanish imperatives can be used with a subject.

> *Bebe tú primero*
> You drink first
>
> *Entrad vosotros antes*
> You go in first
>
> *Deja en paz a tu tío Jairo y tú da gracias a Dios por haber nacido cristiano* (M. Delibes, 1987: 131)
> Leave your uncle Jairo in peace and you give thanks to God that you were born a Christian

**897** In the written language, the imperative may be reinforced by the use of double and even treble exclamation marks (see **19**).

## The Gerund and Past Participle

**898** The gerund of *-ar* verbs ends in *-ando*, and that of *-er* and *-ir* verbs in *-iendo*:

| CANTAR | COMER | VIVIR |
|--------|-------|-------|
| cantando | comiendo | viviendo |

**899** The gerund is invariable. Its use is dealt with in **1137–1174**.

**900** The past participle of *-ar* verbs ends in *-ado*, and that of *-er* and *-ir* verbs in *-ido*:

| CANTAR | COMER | VIVIR |
|--------|-------|-------|
| cantado | comido | vivido |

**901** When used with the auxiliary *haber*, the past participle is invariable. When used as part of a passive after *ser* or *estar*, it agrees in number and gender with the subject of the verb, and as an adjective it agrees in number and gender with the noun to which it refers. When used with *tener, dejar, llevar* and *traer* (see **1197**), it agrees with the direct object of the verb. On the use of the past participle, see **1175–1230**.

**902** Irregular forms of the gerund and the past participle are given in **950** and **951**.

# Irregular Verbs

**903** In the following tables, the future subjunctive forms are not given: they can easily be constructed from the imperfect subjunctive (see **873**).

Irregular Verbs which do not Form a Class with any Other Verb: *haber, tener, ser, estar*

**904** *Haber*

|       | Indicative Present | Imperfect | Preterite |
|-------|-----------|-----------|-----------|
| 1 sg  | *he*      | *había*   | *hube*    |
| 2 sg  | *has*     | *habías*  | *hubiste* |
| 3 sg  | *ha (hay)* | *había*  | *hubo*    |
| 1 pl  | *hemos*   | *habíamos* | *hubimos* |
| 2 pl  | *habéis*  | *habíais* | *hubisteis* |
| 3 pl  | *han*     | *habían*  | *hubieron* |

|       | Future    | Conditional |
|-------|-----------|-----------|
| 1 sg  | *habré*   | *habría*  |
| 2 sg  | *habrás*  | *habrías* |
| 3 sg  | *habrá*   | *habría*  |
| 1 pl  | *habremos* | *habríamos* |
| 2 pl  | *habréis* | *habríais* |
| 3 pl  | *habrán*  | *habrían*  |

|       | Subjunctive Present | Imperfect | |
|-------|-----------|-----------|-----------|
| 1 sg  | *haya*    | *hubiera* | *hubiese* |
| 2 sg  | *hayas*   | *hubieras* | *hubieses* |
| 3 sg  | *haya*    | *hubiera* | *hubiese* |
| 1 pl  | *hayamos* | *hubiéramos* | *hubiésemos* |
| 2 pl  | *hayáis*  | *hubierais* | *hubieseis* |
| 3 pl  | *hayan*   | *hubieran* | *hubiesen* |

The imperative of *haber* is never needed today. *Habed* is generally reckoned to be the plural imperative; *he* is often thought of as the singular imperative (see also **1260**), though the form *habe* is also proposed.[6]

Gerund: *habiendo*
Past participle: *habido*

## 905 Remarks

*Habemos* is sometimes found for *hemos* – see **1259**, third example.

**906** The existential 'there is', 'there are' is rendered by the third person singular of *haber* except in the present tense, where the special form *hay* is used. (The past anterior is practically never used).[7]

> *A veces hay alguna choza* (M. Alvar, 1982: 110)
> Sometimes there is a hut

> *No hay malentendidos entre Europa y España* (*El País*, 16 February 1983: 15)
> There are no misunderstandings between Europe and Spain

> *Hubo un error, es todo lo que sé* (M. Puig, 1980: 70)
> There was a mistake, that's all I know

> *Para Róbinson no habría habido mujeres* (A. Uslar Pietri, 1983: 27)
> There would have been no women for Robinson

The use of the third person plural is considered incorrect,[8] although constructions like *hubieron fiestas* for *hubo fiestas* 'there were festivities' and *habían muchos soldados* for *hubo muchos soldados* 'there were a lot of soldiers' are frequently found today, especially in Latin-American Spanish.[9]

**907** *Ha* is occasionally found for *hay* in some set phrases, e.g. *no ha lugar* 'there's no room'.[10]
For *ha . . .* in the sense of *hace . . .* '. . . ago', see **1261**.

**908** In popular speech, *haiga* is sometimes found for *haya*, but is considered incorrect.

## 909 *Tener*

|        | Indicative Present | Imperfect | Preterite |
|--------|---------|-----------|-----------|
| 1 sg   | *tengo* | *tenía*   | *tuve*    |
| 2 sg   | *tienes* | *tenías* | *tuviste* |
| 3 sg   | *tiene* | *tenía*   | *tuvo*    |

| | | | |
|---|---|---|---|
| 1 pl | *tenemos* | *teníamos* | *tuvimos* |
| 2 pl | *tenéis* | *teníais* | *tuvisteis* |
| 3 pl | *tienen* | *tenían* | *tuvieron* |

| | Future | Conditional | |
|---|---|---|---|
| 1 sg | *tendré* | *tendría* | |
| 2 sg | *tendrás* | *tendrías* | |
| 3 sg | *tendrá* | *tendría* | |
| 1 pl | *tendremos* | *tendríamos* | |
| 2 pl | *tendréis* | *tendríais* | |
| 3 pl | *tendrán* | *tendrían* | |

Subjunctive

| | Present | Imperfect | |
|---|---|---|---|
| 1 sg | *tenga* | *tuviera* | *tuviese* |
| 2 sg | *tengas* | *tuvieras* | *tuvieses* |
| 3 sg | *tenga* | *tuviera* | *tuviese* |
| 1 pl | *tengamos* | *tuviéramos* | *tuviésemos* |
| 2 pl | *tengáis* | *tuvierais* | *tuvieseis* |
| 3 pl | *tengan* | *tuvieran* | *tuviesen* |

Imperative

| | |
|---|---|
| 2 sg | *¡ten!* |
| 2 pl | *¡tened!* |

Gerund: *teniendo*
Past participle: *tenido*

## 910 Ser

Indicative

| | Present | Imperfect | Preterite |
|---|---|---|---|
| 1 sg | *soy* | *era* | *fui* |
| 2 sg | *eres* | *eras* | *fuiste* |
| 3 sg | *es* | *era* | *fue* |
| 1 pl | *somos* | *éramos* | *fuimos* |
| 2 pl | *sois* | *erais* | *fuisteis* |
| 3 pl | *son* | *eran* | *fueron* |

| | Future | Conditional | |
|---|---|---|---|
| 1 sg | *seré* | *sería* | |
| 2 sg | *serás* | *serías* | |
| 3 sg | *será* | *sería* | |
| 1 pl | *seremos* | *seríamos* | |
| 2 pl | *seréis* | *seríais* | |
| 3 pl | *serán* | *serían* | |

### Subjunctive

|       | Present | Imperfect |         |
|-------|---------|-----------|---------|
| 1 sg  | *sea*    | *fuera*    | *fuese*   |
| 2 sg  | *seas*   | *fueras*   | *fueses*  |
| 3 sg  | *sea*    | *fuera*    | *fuese*   |
| 1 pl  | *seamos* | *fuéramos* | *fuésemos* |
| 2 pl  | *seáis*  | *fuerais*  | *fueseis* |
| 3 pl  | *sean*   | *fueran*   | *fuesen*  |

### Imperative

| 2 sg | *¡sé!*  |
|------|------|
| 2 pl | *¡sed!* |

Gerund: *siendo*
Past participle: *sido*

## 911 Remarks

*So* is occasionally found for *soy* in Latin-American Spanish.

**912** *Ser* and *ir* have the same preterite (and imperfect subjunctive) forms: thus *fui*, for example, can mean either 'I was' or 'I went', according to context.

**913** The second person singular imperative, *¡sé!*, is written with an accent to distinguish it from the reflexive pronoun *se*. Nevertheless, it is identical to the first person singular present of *saber*.
   Note that the accent is maintained even if *¡sé!* is followed by a clitic pronoun, e.g. *¡séme fiel!* 'be faithful to me.'[11]

## 914 *Estar*

### Indicative

|       | Present | Imperfect | Preterite |
|-------|---------|-----------|-----------|
| 1 sg  | *estoy*   | *estaba*    | *estuve*     |
| 2 sg  | *estás*   | *estabas*   | *estuviste*  |
| 3 sg  | *está*    | *estaba*    | *estuvo*     |
| 1 pl  | *estamos* | *estábamos* | *estuvimos*  |
| 2 pl  | *estáis*  | *estabais*  | *estuvisteis* |
| 3 pl  | *están*   | *estaban*   | *estuvieron* |

|      | Future     | Conditional |
|------|-----------|-------------|
| 1 sg | *estaré*   | *estaría*   |
| 2 sg | *estarás*  | *estarías*  |
| 3 sg | *estará*   | *estaría*   |
| 1 pl | *estaremos*| *estaríamos*|
| 2 pl | *estaréis* | *estaríais* |
| 3 pl | *estarán*  | *estarían*  |

Subjunctive

|      | Present   | Imperfect     |              |
|------|-----------|---------------|--------------|
| 1 sg | *esté*    | *estuviera*   | *estuviese*  |
| 2 sg | *estés*   | *estuvieras*  | *estuvieses* |
| 3 sg | *esté*    | *estuviera*   | *estuviese*  |
| 1 pl | *estemos* | *estuviéramos*| *estuviésemos*|
| 2 pl | *estéis*  | *estuvierais* | *estuvieseis*|
| 3 pl | *estén*   | *estuvieran*  | *estuviesen* |

|      | Imperative |
|------|-----------|
| 2 sg | *¡está!*  |
| 2 pl | *¡estad!* |

Gerund: *estando*
Past participle: *estado*

## Irregular Verb Types

**915** Under this heading are a number of classes of verbs which have systematic irregularities in their endings.

### 916 'Radical-changing Verbs': *e* → *ie* and *o* → *ue*

In a number of verbs, the stem vowel *e* changes to *ie* and the stem vowel *o* changes to *ue* when the stem is stressed, that is, in the first, second and third person singular and the third person plural of the present indicative and the present subjunctive, and in the second person imperative. For example:

*Pensar*

|      | Present indicative | Present subjunctive | Imperative |
|------|--------------------|---------------------|------------|
| 1 sg | *pienso*           | *piense*            |            |
| 2 sg | *piensas*          | *pienses*           | *¡piensa!* |
| 3 sg | *piensa*           | *piense*            |            |

| | | |
|---|---|---|
| 1 pl | *(pensamos)* | *(pensemos)* | |
| 2 pl | *(pensáis)* | *(penséis)* | *(¡pensad!)* |
| 3 pl | piensan | piensen | |

*Contar*

| | | |
|---|---|---|
| 1 sg | cuento | cuente | |
| 2 sg | cuentas | cuentes | ¡cuenta! |
| 3 sg | cuenta | cuente | |
| 1 pl | *(contamos)* | *(contemos)* | |
| 2 pl | *(contáis)* | *(contéis)* | *(¡contad!)* |
| 3 pl | cuentan | cuenten | |

All other forms of such verbs are regular.

**917** However, not all verbs with a stem vowel in *e* and *o* behave in this way. Those that do are usually indicated as such in dictionaries.

**918** There follows a list (not exhaustive)[12] of the commoner verbs which do undergo change of this kind in the stem vowel.

*e → ie*

Verbs in -*ar*:

| | |
|---|---|
| acertar | to hit; to get right |
| acrecentar | to increase |
| alentar | to breathe; to encourage |
| apretar | to squeeze, grip |
| arrendar | to lease |
| atravesar | to cross |
| calentar | to heat |
| cegar | to blind |
| cerrar | to close |
| comenzar | to begin |
| concertar | to arrange, fix |
| confesar | to confess |
| desconcertar | to disconcert |
| desherbar | to weed |
| desmembrar | to dismember |
| despertar | to wake |
| desterrar | to exile |
| empezar | to begin |
| encomendar | to commend |

| | |
|---|---|
| *enmendar* | to amend |
| *enterrar* | to bury |
| *errar* | to wander |
| *fregar* | to rub |
| *gobernar* | to govern |
| *helar* | to freeze |
| *invernar* | to spend the winter |
| *manifestar* | to demonstrate |
| *mentar* | to mention |
| *merendar* | to picnic; to have tea |
| *negar* | to deny |
| *nevar* | to snow |
| *pensar* | to think |
| *plegar* | to fold |
| *quebrar* | to break |
| *recomendar* | to recommend |
| *regar* | to water |
| *renegar* | to deny; to be a renegade |
| *segar* | to mow |
| *sembrar* | to sow |
| *sentar* | to seat |
| *serrar* | to saw |
| *temblar* | to tremble |
| *tentar* | to touch; to tempt |
| *tropezar* | to stumble |

Verbs in *-er*:

| | |
|---|---|
| *ascender* | to ascend |
| *atender* | to attend to |
| *defender* | to defend |
| *descender* | to descend |
| *encender* | to light, switch on |
| *entender* | to understand |
| *heder* | to stink |
| *hender* | to split |
| *perder* | to lose |
| *querer* | to wish, want |
| *tender* | to spread; to tend |
| *verter* | to pour |

*o → ue*:

Verbs in *-ar*:

| | |
|---|---|
| *acordar* | to agree; to remind |
| *acostar* | to put to bed |
| *almorzar* | to lunch |
| *apostar* | to bet |
| *avergonzar* | to put to shame |
| *colar* | to strain |
| *colgar* | to hang |
| *concordar* | to reconcile; to agree |
| *consolar* | to console |
| *contar* | to count; to tell |
| *costar* | to cost |
| *degollar* | to cut the throat of |
| *denostar* | to insult |
| *derrocar* | to knock down |
| *encontrar* | to find |
| *forzar* | to force |
| *holgar* | to rest, be idle |
| *mostrar* | to show |
| *poblar* | to populate |
| *probar* | to prove |
| (and derivatives) | |
| *recordar* | to remind of; to remember |
| *regoldar* | to belch |
| *renovar* | to renovate |
| *rodar* | to roll, run |
| *rogar* | to ask |
| *soldar* | to weld, solder |
| *soltar* | to release |
| *sonar* | to sound |
| *soñar* | to dream |
| *tostar* | to toast |
| *trocar* | to exchange |
| *tronar* | to thunder |
| *volar* | to fly |
| *volcar* | to overturn |

Verbs in *-er*:

| | |
|---|---|
| *absolver* | to absolve |

| | |
|---|---|
| *cocer* (see **938**) | to cook |
| *demoler* | to demolish |
| *disolver* | to dissolve |
| *doler* | to hurt |
| *llover* | to rain |
| *moler* | to grind |
| *morder* | to bite |
| *mover* | to move |
| *oler* | to smell |
| *poder* | to be able |
| *resolver* | to resolve |
| *soler* | usually to (see **637**) |
| *torcer* | to twist |
| *volver* | to turn; to return (see **637**) |

## 919 Remarks

In *adquirir* 'to acquire' and *inquirir* 'to enquire', the *i* of the stem changes to *ie*: thus

> *adquiero, adquieres, adquiere,* (*adquirimos*), (*adquirís*), *adquieren*

Similarly, in *jugar* 'to play', the *u* of the stem changes to *ue*: thus

> *juego, juegas, juega,* (*jugamos*), (*jugáis*), *juegan*

**920** There is some variation in the behaviour of these verbs according to region and register. For example, *apretar* is often regularized in popular speech to *apreto*, etc.,[13] there is variation in the forms of *mentar* (*miento* ~ *mento*, etc.),[14] *denostar* (*denuesto* ~ *denosto*, etc.)[15] and *derrocar* (*derroco* ~ *derrueco*, etc.)[16] and *errar* does not diphthongize in parts of Latin America.[17]

Conversely, *templar* 'to temper, tune' diphthongizes in parts of Latin America though not in Spain.[18]

Both *amoblar* and *amueblar* (with diphthongization in all forms) 'to furnish' are found.[19] *Innovar* 'to innovate' does not diphthongize whereas *renovar* 'to renovate' does.[20]

Sometimes in popular speech a diphthong generalizes to other forms, e.g. *juegar* for *jugar*, etc. 'to play'.[21]

**921** The same change in stem vowel may be found in other related parts of speech:

| | | | |
|---|---|---|---|
| *cegar* | → | *ciego* | 'blind' |
| *helar* | → | *hielo* | 'ice' |
| *gobernar* | → | *gobierno* | 'government' |
| *invernar* | → | *invierno* | 'winter' |
| *almorzar* | → | *almuerzo* | 'lunch' |
| *contar* | → | *cuento* | 'story' |
| *probar* | → | *prueba* | 'test' |
| *jugar* | → | *juego* | 'game' |

**922** Changes in spelling may also affect some of the above verbs – see **956**ff. Note especially:

   (1)   That in the *o* → *ue* verbs the *u* must be written with a diaeresis (*ü*) after a *g* to preserve the pronunciation *ue*: thus *avergonzamos* but *avergüenzo*, etc.

   (2)   That there are no words in Spanish beginning with *ie* or *ue*; thus an initial *e* changing to *ie* is written *ye* and an initial *o* changing to *ue* is written *hue*: *erramos* but *yerro*, etc., *olemos* but *huelo*, etc.

### 923 'Radical-changing Verbs': *e* → *i*

In this group of verbs, *e* changes to *i* in the present indicative and imperative where the stem is stressed, in the whole of the present subjunctive, and in all forms where the ending begins with *i* as a semivowel (the third persons singular and plural of the preterite and the whole of the imperfect subjunctive). The phenomenon is often referred to in Spanish as *debilitación vocálica* (vocalic weakening). For example:

*Pedir*

| | Present indicative | Present subjunctive | Imperative |
|---|---|---|---|
| 1 sg | *pido* | *pida* | |
| 2 sg | *pides* | *pidas* | *¡pide!* |
| 3 sg | *pide* | *pida* | |
| 1 pl | *(pedimos)* | *pidamos* | |
| 2 pl | *(pedís)* | *pidáis* | *(¡pedid!)* |
| 3 pl | *piden* | *pidan* | |

| | Preterite | Imperfect Subjunctive | |
|---|---|---|---|
| 1 sg | *(pedí)* | *pidiera* | *pidiese* |
| 2 sg | *(pediste)* | *pidieras* | *pidieses* |
| 3 sg | *pidió* | *pidiera* | *pidiese* |

| 1 pl | *(pedimos)* | *pidiéramos* | *pidiésemos* |
|------|-------------|--------------|--------------|
| 2 pl | *(pedisteis)* | *pidierais* | *pidieseis* |
| 3 pl | *pidieron* | *pidieran* | *pidiesen* |

Gerund: *pidiendo*

**924** Again, not all verbs with stems in *e* belong to this category, and a dictionary should be consulted to ascertain to which class a given verb belongs. The following is a list of the commonest:[22] all belong to the *-ir* conjugation.

| | |
|---|---|
| *ceñir* | to gird |
| *colegir* | to collect |
| *competir* | to compete |
| *concebir* | to conceive |
| *conseguir* | to achieve |
| *corregir* (see **962**) | to correct |
| *derretir* | to melt |
| *despedir* | to dismiss |
| *elegir* | to choose |
| *embestir* | to assault, attack |
| *expedir* | to dispatch |
| *freír* (see **951**) | to fry |
| *gemir* | to moan |
| *henchir* | to fill up |
| *impedir* | to prevent |
| *investir* | to invest |
| *medir* | to measure |
| *pedir* | to ask for |
| *perseguir* | to pursue, persecute |
| *proseguir* | to pursue, carry on with |
| *regir* (see **962**) | to rule |
| *reír* (see **925**) | to laugh |
| *rendir* | to yield |
| *reñir* (see **967**) | to quarrel |
| *repetir* | to repeat |
| *seguir* | to follow |
| *servir* | to serve |
| *sonreír* (see **925**) | to smile |
| *teñir* (see **967**) | to stain |
| *vestir* | to dress |

**925** Note the spelling of verbs in *-eír*:

*Reír*

|       | Present indicative | Present subjunctive | Imperative |
|-------|--------------------|---------------------|------------|
| 1 sg  | *río*              | *ría*               |            |
| 2 sg  | *ríes*             | *rías*              | *¡ríe!*    |
| 3 sg  | *ríe*              | *ría*               |            |
| 1 pl  | *(reímos)*         | *riamos*            |            |
| 2 pl  | *(reís)*           | *riáis*             | *(¡reíd!)* |
| 3 pl  | *ríen*             | *rían*              |            |

|       | Preterite    | Imperfect Subjunctive |            |
|-------|--------------|-----------------------|------------|
| 1 sg  | *(reí)*      | *riera*               | *riese*    |
| 2 sg  | *(reíste)*   | *rieras*              | *rieses*   |
| 3 sg  | *rio*        | *riera*               | *riese*    |
| 1 pl  | *(reímos)*   | *riéramos*            | *riésemos* |
| 2 pl  | *(reísteis)* | *rierais*             | *rieseis*  |
| 3 pl  | *rieron*     | *rieran*              | *riesen*   |

Gerund: *riendo*

## 926 'Radical-changing Verbs' Combining Dipthongization and *e* → *i* or *o* → *u*

In this group of verbs, diphthongization occurs when the stem is stressed in the present indicative, the present subjunctive and the imperative, and the change of *e* to *i* or *o* to *u* occurs in the first and second persons plural of the present subjunctive and in all forms where the ending begins with *i* as a semivowel (the third persons singular and plural of the preterite and the whole of the imperfect subjunctive). For example:

*Preferir*

|       | Present indicative | Present subjunctive | Imperative    |
|-------|--------------------|---------------------|---------------|
| 1 sg  | *prefiero*         | *prefiera*          |               |
| 2 sg  | *prefieres*        | *prefieras*         | *¡prefiere!*  |
| 3 sg  | *prefiere*         | *prefiera*          |               |
| 1 pl  | *(preferimos)*     | *prefiramos*        |               |
| 2 pl  | *(preferís)*       | *prefiráis*         | *(¡preferid!)* |
| 3 pl  | *prefieren*        | *prefieran*         |               |

|       | Preterite       | Imperfect Subjunctive |                |
| ----- | --------------- | --------------------- | -------------- |
| 1 sg  | *(preferí)*     | *prefiriera*          | *prefiriese*   |
| 2 sg  | *(preferiste)*  | *prefirieras*         | *prefirieses*  |
| 3 sg  | *prefirió*      | *prefiriera*          | *prefiriese*   |
| 1 pl  | *(preferimos)*  | *prefiriéramos*       | *prefiriésemos*|
| 2 pl  | *(preferisteis)*| *prefirierais*        | *prefirieseis* |
| 3 pl  | *prefirieron*   | *prefirieran*         | *prefiriesen*  |

Gerund: *prefiriendo*

*Morir*

|       | Present indicative | Present subjunctive | Imperative  |
| ----- | ------------------ | ------------------- | ----------- |
| 1 sg  | *muero*            | *muera*             |             |
| 2 sg  | *mueres*           | *mueras*            | *¡muere!*   |
| 3 sg  | *muere*            | *muera*             |             |
| 1 pl  | *(morimos)*        | *muramos*           |             |
| 2 pl  | *(morís)*          | *muráis*            | *(¡morid!)* |
| 3 pl  | *mueren*           | *mueran*            |             |

|       | Preterite       | Imperfect Subjunctive |              |
| ----- | --------------- | --------------------- | ------------ |
| 1 sg  | *(morí)*        | *muriera*             | *muriese*    |
| 2 sg  | *(moriste)*     | *murieras*            | *murieses*   |
| 3 sg  | *murió*         | *muriera*             | *muriese*    |
| 1 pl  | *(morimos)*     | *muriéramos*          | *muriésemos* |
| 2 pl  | *(moristeis)*   | *murierais*           | *murieseis*  |
| 3 pl  | *murieron*      | *murieran*            | *muriesen*   |

Gerund: *muriendo*

**927** The verbs which belong to this category are not very numerous: all are of the *-ir* class. The commonest are:[23]

Verbs ending in *-ferir*, e.g.:

| *diferir*  | to differ |
| ---------- | --------- |
| *preferir* | to prefer |
| *referir*  | to refer  |

Verbs ending in *-vertir*, e.g.:

| *advertir*      | to warn          |
| --------------- | ---------------- |
| *controvertir*  | to debate, argue |
| *convertir*     | to convert       |

| | |
|---|---|
| *divertir* | to entertain |
| *invertir* | to invest (e.g. money) |
| *pervertir* | to pervert |

The verbs

| | |
|---|---|
| *adherir* | to stick on |
| *arrepentirse* | to repent |
| *concernir* | to concern |
| *digerir* | to digest |
| *discernir* | to discern |
| *erguir* | to raise |
| *herir* (and compounds) | to wound |
| *hervir* | to boil |
| *injerir* | to insert |
| *mentir* (and compounds) | to lie |
| *requerir* | to beg; to require |
| *sugerir* | to suggest |
| *sentir* (and compounds) | to regret |

Two verbs only of the $o \to u$ type:

| | |
|---|---|
| *dormir* | to sleep |
| *morir* | to die |

## 928 Remarks

The verb *pudrir* 'to rot', which is generally regular in standard Spanish apart from the past participle *podrido*, sometimes has the infinitive form *podrir* and even (the rarely used!) *podrimos, podrís*, especially in Latin America.[24]

> *El agua del lago parece podrida. Pero mi carne se pudrirá mucho antes que él expire* (M. A. Carrera, 1986: 141)
> The water of the lake seems rotten. But my flesh will rot a long time before it expires

**929** *Erguir* may also, less commonly, be conjugated as a straightforward $e \to i$ radical changing verb (i.e. like *pedir*).[25] Notice the spellings of the various forms.

*Erguir*

|  | Present indicative | Present subjunctive | Imperative |
|---|---|---|---|
| 1 sg | *irgue/yergo* | *irga/yerga* | |
| 2 sg | *irgues/yergues* | *irgas/yergas* | *¡yergue!* |
| 3 sg | *irgue/yergue* | *irga/yerga* | |
| 1 pl | *(erguimos)* | *irgamos/yergamos* | |
| 2 pl | *(erguís)* | *irgáis/yergáis* | *(¡erguid!)* |
| 3 pl | *irguen/yerguen* | *irgan/yergan* | |

|  | Preterite | Imperfect Subjunctive | |
|---|---|---|---|
| 1 sg | *(erguí)* | *irguiera* | *irguiese* |
| 2 sg | *(erguiste)* | *irguieras* | *irguieses* |
| 3 sg | *irguió* | *irguiera* | *irguiese* |
| 1 pl | *(erguimos)* | *irguiéramos* | *irguiésemos* |
| 2 pl | *(erguisteis)* | *irguierais* | *irguieseis* |
| 3 pl | *irguieron* | *irguieran* | *irguiesen* |

Gerund: *irguiendo*

## 930 Verbs in *-iar* and *-uar*

In some verbs which end in *-iar* and *-uar*, the *i* or *u* is stressed in the first, second and third persons singular and third person plural of the present indicative and subjunctive and the second person singular of the imperative; in other forms it is a semivowel as in the infinitive. Thus:

*Confiar*

|  | Present Indicative | Present Subjunctive | Imperative |
|---|---|---|---|
| 1 sg | *confío* | *confíe* | |
| 2 sg | *confías* | *confíes* | *¡confía!* |
| 3 sg | *confía* | *confíe* | |
| 1 pl | *(confiamos)* | *(confiemos)* | |
| 2 pl | *(confiáis)* | *(confiéis)* | *(¡confiad!)* |
| 3 pl | *confían* | *confíen* | |

*Continuar*

|  | Present Indicative | Present Subjunctive | Imperative |
|---|---|---|---|
| 1 sg | *continúo* | *continúe* | |
| 2 sg | *continúas* | *continúes* | *¡continúa!* |
| 3 sg | *continúa* | *continúe* | |

| | | |
|---|---|---|
| 1 pl | *(continuamos)* | *(continuemos)* |
| 2 pl | *(continuáis)* | *(continuéis)* | *(¡continuad!)* |
| 3 pl | *continúan* | *continúen* |

**931** Some verbs like *confiar*[26] are:

| | |
|---|---|
| *aliar* | to combine, ally |
| *amnistiar* | to grant an amnesty to |
| *ampliar* | to enlarge |
| *averiarse* | to break down |
| *cinematografiar* | to film |
| *confiar* | to entrust |
| *contrariar* | to upset |
| *criar* | to rear |
| *chirriar* | to creak; to cheep |
| *desafiar* | to challenge |
| *desconfiar* | to distrust |
| *desviar* | to divert |
| *enfriar* | to cool |
| *enviar* | to send |
| *espiar* | to spy |
| *esquiar* | to ski |
| *estenografiar* | to take down in shorthand |
| *expiar* | to expiate |
| *extasiar* | to send into raptures |
| *extraviar* | to mislead |
| *fiar* | to trust |
| *fotografiar* | to photograph |
| *guiar* | to guide |
| *hastiar* | to weary, bore |
| *inventariar* | to take stock of |
| *mecanografiar* | to type |
| *porfiar* | to persist |
| *radiar* | to radiate |
| *resfriar* | to cool |
| *rociar* | to sprinkle |
| *telegrafiar* | to telegraph |
| *vaciar* | to empty |
| *variar* | to vary |

**932** Some verbs like *continuar*[27] are:

| | |
|---|---|
| *acentuar* | to accentuate |

| | |
|---|---|
| *actuar* | to act |
| *atenuar* | to lessen |
| *desvirtuar* | to impair |
| *efectuar* | to carry out |
| *evaluar* | to evaluate |
| *exceptuar* | to except |
| *fluctuar* | to fluctuate |
| *graduar* | to graduate |
| *habituar* | to accustom |
| *insinuar* | to insinuate |
| *perpetuar* | to perpetuate |
| *situar* | to situate |
| *tatuar* | to tattoo |

**933** There are, however, many verbs in *-iar* and *-uar* which do not undergo the above changes, for example *cambiar* 'to change', *limpiar* 'to clean', *saciar* 'to satiate', *santiguar* 'to make the sign of the cross', etc.[28]

In some verbs there is variation: *(re)conciliar* 'to reconcile' has the forms *(re)concilio* and *(re)concilío* (with preference given to the former);[29] both *evacuo* and *evacúo* from *evacuar* 'to evacuate, to defecate' are found.[30]

> *Debo volver al retrete donde por fin evacuo normalmente* (S. Dalí, 1983: 63)
>
> I have to go back to the lavatory, where at last I pass a normal motion

*Vacio* is sometimes heard in popular speech for *vacío*.[31]

### 934 Verbs with a Diphthong in the Stem

The diphthong in the stem of some infinitives becomes two syllables with the stress on the second syllable when the stem of the verb is stressed:

*Reunir*

| | Present Indicative | Present Subjunctive | Imperative |
|---|---|---|---|
| 1 sg | *reúno* | *reúna* | |
| 2 sg | *reúnes* | *reúnas* | *¡reúne!* |
| 3 sg | *reúne* | *reúna* | |
| 1 pl | *(reunimos)* | *(reunamos)* | |
| 2 pl | *(reunís)* | *(reunáis)* | *(¡reunid!)* |
| 3 pl | *reúnen* | *reúnan* | |

Other such verbs are:

| | |
|---|---|
| *ahumar* | to smoke (transitive) |
| *aullar* | to howl |
| *rehusar* | to refuse |

Note that according to the latest spelling convention *ahumar* and *rehusar* carry accents in the same way as *reunir*, despite the intervening *h* between the two vowels: thus *rehúso*, etc.

### Irregular Forms

**935** In the following sections are discussed verbs which do not exhibit systematic irregularity.

### 936 Present Indicative

A number of verbs are irregular only in the first person singular. It should be remembered, however, that this form is also usually the basis for the Present Subjunctive (**870**).

| | | |
|---|---|---|
| *asir* | *asgo* | to seize (infrequent) |
| *caber* | *quepo* | to be contained |
| *caer* | *caigo* | to fall |
| *dar* | *doy* | to give (but Present Subjunctive *dé*, etc.) |
| *decir* | *digo* | to say |
| *hacer* | *hago* | to do, make |
| *ir* | *voy* (and *vas, va, vamos, vais, van*) | to go (but Present Subjunctive *vaya*, etc.) |
| *oír* | *oigo* (and *oyes, oye, oímos, oís, oyen*) | to hear |
| *poner* | *pongo* | to put |
| *saber* | *sé* | to know (but Present Subjunctive *sepa*, etc.) |
| *salir* | *salgo* | to leave |

| | | |
|---|---|---|
| *satisfacer* | *satisfago* | to satisfy |
| *traer* | *traigo* | to bring |
| *valer* | *valgo* | to be worth |
| *venir* | *vengo* (and otherwise *e* → *ie*) | to come |
| *ver* | *veo* | to see |

(*prever* 'to foresee' is conjugated like *ver*, athough a puristically castigated variant *preveer* (with *preveyó, preveyendo*, etc.) is also found, perhaps as a result of analogy with *proveer* 'to provide' and *leer* 'to read')[32]

Note also the irregular present tenses of *estar* (**914**), *haber* (**904**), *ser* (**910**) and *tener* (**909**).

**937** *Roer* 'to gnaw' has three attested first person singular forms: *roo, roigo* and *royo* (the first being preferred). The derivative *corroer* 'to corrode, rust', on the other hand, is regular.[33]

**938** Most verbs ending in *-cer* and *-cir* form their first person singulars in *-zco*, although other persons are regular:

| | *NACER* 'to be born' | *CONOCER* 'to know' | *TRADUCIR* 'to translate' | *MERECER* 'to merit' |
|---|---|---|---|---|
| 1 sg | *nazco* | *conozco* | *traduzco* | *merezco* |
| 2 sg | *naces* | *conoces* | *traduces* | *mereces* |
| 3 sg | *nace* | *conoce* | *traduce* | *merece* |
| 1 pl | *nacemos* | *conocemos* | *traducimos* | *merecemos* |
| 2 pl | *nacéis* | *conocéis* | *traducís* | *merecéis* |
| 3 pl | *nacen* | *conocen* | *traducen* | *merecen* |

Important exceptions to this rule are *cocer* (*cuezo*) 'to cook', *hacer* (see **936**) and *mecer* (*mezo*) 'to rock' (the subjunctive forms *mezca*, etc., are sometimes found in older texts and in Latin-American Spanish.[34]

*Yacer* 'to lie' (literary only) has three variants: *yazgo, yago* and *yazco*.[35]

Other verbs like *merecer* are:

| | |
|---|---|
| *acontecer* | to happen |
| *agradecer* | to thank |
| *amanecer* | to dawn |
| *anochecer* | to get dark |

Note that *amanecer* and *anochecer* also have the meaning of 'to find oneself, be found in the morning/at nightfall':[36]

> *Al día siguiente el comisario amaneció muerto en su casa* (A. Roa Bastos, 1977: 231)
> The following morning the commissioner was found dead in his house

| | |
|---|---|
| *aparecer* | to appear |
| *apetecer* | to crave; to appeal |
| *carecer* | to lack |
| *compadecer* | to pity |
| *comparecer* | to appear (in a court of law, etc.) |
| *embellecer* | to beautify |
| *enflaquecer* | to weaken |
| *ennoblecer* | to ennoble |
| *enriquecer* | to enrich |
| *envejecer* | to get old |
| *establecer* | to establish |
| *fallecer* | to die |
| *favorecer* | to favour |
| *florecer* | to flourish |
| *fortalecer* | to fortify |
| *humedecer* | to dampen |
| *obedecer* | to obey |
| *ofrecer* | to offer |
| *oscurecer* | to get dark |
| *padecer* | to suffer |
| *parecer* | to seem |
| *permanecer* | to stay |
| *pertenecer* | to belong |
| *rejuvenecer* | to rejuvenate |
| *restablecer* | to reestablish |

## 939  Imperfect Indicative

Three verbs have irregular imperfects:

> *ir: iba, ibas, iba, íbamos, ibais, iban*
> *ser:* see **910**
> *ver: veía, veías, veía, veíamos, veíais, veían*

## 940 Preterite

Several verbs are irregular in the preterite. An important feature of irregular preterites is that in the first and third persons singular the stress falls on the stem rather than on the ending: thus *dijo* 'he said' but *cantó* 'he sang'.

The monosyllabic preterite forms *fui*, *dio*, *fue*, *rio* and *vio* are in older usage sometimes written with an accent (*fuí*, *dió*, *fué*, *rió*, *vió*).

*Ir* and *ser* have the same preterite form (*fui*, etc.). *Ver* is not exactly irregular, but the absence of a written accent in modern Spanish should be noted. *Dar* forms its preterite like *ver*.

|        | *IR* and *SER* | *VER*   | *DAR*   |
|--------|----------------|---------|---------|
| 1 sg   | *fui*          | *vi*    | *di*    |
| 2 sg   | *fuiste*       | *viste* | *diste* |
| 3 sg   | *fue*          | *vio*   | *dio*   |
| 1 pl   | *fuimos*       | *vimos* | *dimos* |
| 2 pl   | *fuisteis*     | *visteis* | *disteis* |
| 3 pl   | *fueron*       | *vieron* | *dieron* |

Other irregular preterites are listed below. They follow the pattern:

|        | *ANDAR*      | *QUERER*     |
|--------|--------------|--------------|
| 1 sg   | *anduve*     | *quise*      |
| 2 sg   | *anduviste*  | *quisiste*   |
| 3 sg   | *anduvo*     | *quiso*      |
| 1 pl   | *anduvimos*  | *quisimos*   |
| 2 pl   | *anduvisteis*| *quisisteis* |
| 3 pl   | *anduvieron* | *quisieron*  |

| *andar*      | *anduve*    | to go            |
|--------------|-------------|------------------|
| *caber*      | *cupe*      | to be contained  |
| *decir*      | *dije*      | to say           |
| *haber*      | *hube*      | Perfect auxiliary and existential |
| *hacer*      | *hice*      | to do, make      |
| *poder*      | *pude*      | to be able       |
| *poner*      | *puse*      | to put           |
| *querer*     | *quise*     | to wish, want    |
| *saber*      | *supe*      | to know          |
| *satisfacer* | *satisfice* | to satisfy       |
| *tener*      | *tuve*      | to have          |

| *traer* | *traje* | to bring |
| *venir* | *vine* | to come |

To these may be added verbs which end in the element *-ducir*:

| *conducir* | *conduje* | to drive |
| *deducir* | *deduje* | to deduce |
| *introducir* | *introduje* | to introduce |
| *producir* | *produje* | to produce |
| *reducir* | *reduje* | to reduce |
| *reproducir* | *reproduje* | to reproduce |
| *seducir* | *seduje* | to seduce |
| *traducir* | *traduje* | to translate |

For verbs with a preterite stem in *-j-* (e.g. *decir* (*dije*)), the third person plural ending is *-eron* instead of *-ieron*; thus:

> *decir: dije, dijiste, dijo, dijimos, dijisteis, dijeron*
> *conducir: conduje, condujiste, condujo, condujimos, condujisteis, condujeron*

**941** The imperfect subjunctive of these verbs is, as usual, formed on the third person plural of the preterite (e.g. *supieron* → *supiera*, *supiese*, etc.). For verbs with a preterite stem in *-j-* (e.g. *decir* (*dije*)) and a third person plural in *-eron*, the imperfect subjunctives similarly have the endings *-era*, *-ese*; thus:

> *decir: dijera, dijeras, dijera, dijéramos, dijerais, dijeran*
> *dijese, dijeses, dijese, dijésemos, dijeseis, dijesen*

## 942 Remarks

*Responder* 'to reply', in addition to the regular preterite *respondí*, etc., sometimes has the earlier irregular preterite *repuse*, etc., which is also the preterite of *reponer* 'to replace'. A consequence of this is that in the literary language other forms of *reponer* are used with the meaning of *responder*.[37]

**943** There is a tendency in popular speech to regularize some irregular preterites. *Andé* is sometimes used for *anduve*[38] and *decí* for *dije*.[39] This is not to be imitated by foreign learners.

**944** In the spoken language, *cantastes, dijistes, vinistes*, etc. are occasionally used instead of *cantaste, dijiste, viniste*, the addition of -s no doubt being felt to be characteristic of the second person singular.[40] These forms are considered incorrect, however, in standard usage.

## 945 Future Indicative and Conditional

All futures and conditionals have the same endings, but some have irregular stems. They are:

| caber | cabré, etc. | to be contained |
|---|---|---|
| | cabría, etc. | |
| decir | diré | to say |
| haber | habré | to have (auxiliary) |
| hacer | haré | to do, make |
| (and compounds of *hacer*, e.g. *contrahacer. rehacer*) | | |
| poder | podré | to be able |
| poner | pondré | to put |
| querer | querré | to wish, want |
| saber | sabré | to know |
| salir | saldré | to leave |
| satisfacer | satisfaré | to satisfy |
| tener | tendré | to have |
| valer | valdré | to be worth |
| venir | vendré | to come |

*Bendecir* 'to bless' and *maldecir* 'to damn', have regular futures and conditionals (*bendeciré, maldeciré*); *contradecir* 'to contradict' does have an irregular future (*contradiré*). although *contradeciré* is also frequently used.[41]

## 946 Tenses of the Subjunctive

Many irregularities in the present subjunctive and all irregularities in the imperfect (and future) subjunctive directly relate to those in the present indicative and preterite which have been dealt with above.

Other irregular present subjunctives are:

*caber:* quepa, quepas, quepa, quepamos, quepáis, quepan
*dar:* dé, dés, dé, demos, deis, den
*estar:* esté, estés, esté, estemos, estéis, estén
*haber:* haya, hayas, haya, hayamos, hayáis, hayan

*ir:* vaya, vayas, vaya, vayamos, vayáis, vayan (also in popular speech *vaiga*)[42]
*saber:* sepa, sepas, sepa, sepamos, sepáis, sepan
*ser:* sea, seas, sea, seamos, seáis, sean

## 947 Remark

*¡Vaya!* (*<ir*) and *¡venga!* (*<venir*) are often used as interjections, their original verbal value being practically lost. They reinforce what follows. In this function they are invariable, as is clear from the third example, where *venga* is used in conjunction with *vosotros*:

> *El Príncipe me dijo: «Vaya tarde que has pasado»* (V. Pozuelo Escudero, 1980: 190)
> The Prince said to me, 'What an afternoon you've had'

> *Ahí van los García; vaya par de locos* (M. Delibes, 1987: 160)
> There are the Garcías: what a pair of madcaps!

> *¡Venga, vosotros, ya es hora!* (Van Dam, 1967:376)
> Hey, you lot, it's time!

> *¡Venga gastar dinero!* (*DUE*, II. 1468)
> Talk about spending money!

## 948 The Imperative

All second person plural forms are regular: *decir →¡decid!*, *hacer →¡haced!*, *ser →¡sed!*, etc.

Second person singulars which are not identical with the third person singular of the present indicative are:

| | |
|---|---|
| *decir* | *¡di!* |
| *hacer* | *¡haz!* |
| *ir* | *¡ve!* (*¡ves!* is very common in speech)[43] |
| *poner* | *¡pon!* |
| *salir* | *¡sal!* |
| *satisfacer* | *¡satisfaz!* or *¡satisface!* |
| *ser* | *¡sé!* |
| *tener* | *¡ten!* |
| *valer* | *¡val!* or. preferably, *¡vale!*[44] |
| *venir* | *¡ven!* |

**949**   In areas of Latin America where *voseo* is used (see **255**), the following second person singular imperatives are found: *decí* (for *di*), *salí* (for *sal*), *vení* (for *ven*), *cantá* for *canta*, *tené* for *ten*.[45]

## 950 Gerund

The gerunds of *e → i* and *o → u* radical-changing verbs change their stem vowel; thus *pedir → pidiendo*, *preferir → prefiriendo*, *dormir → durmiendo*. Otherwise there are only three verbs which have irregular gerunds:

| | |
|---|---|
| *decir* | *diciendo* |
| *poder* | *pudiendo* |
| *venir* | *viniendo* |

(See also **928** concerning *pudrir* (*podrir*), the gerund of which is always *pudriendo*.)

The gerund of *ir* is *yendo*.

## 951 Past Participle

The following verbs have an irregular past participle, not formed with *-ado* or *-ido*:

| | | |
|---|---|---|
| *abrir* | *abierto* | to open |
| *absolver* | *absuelto* | to absolve |
| *cubrir* | *cubierto* | to cover |
| *decir* | *dicho* | to say |
| *escribir* | *escrito* | to write |
| *freír* | *frito* | to fry |
| *hacer* | *hecho* | to do, make |
| *imprimir* | *impreso* | to print |
| *morir* | *muerto* | to die |
| *poner* | *puesto* | to put |
| *prender* | *preso* | to arrest, imprison |
| | (but *prendido* in the sense of 'fastened' and, in Latin America, 'lit') | |
| *resolver* | *resuelto* | to resolve |
| *romper* | *roto* | to break |
| *satisfacer* | *satisfecho* | to satisfy |
| *ver* | *visto* | to see |
| *volver* | *vuelto* | to turn, return |

## 952 Remarks

In the written language, *muerto* is sometimes used instead of *matado* in non-compound tenses of the passive when the subject is a person.[46]

> *Tres guerilleros fueron muertos por los soldados* (*DD*, 256)
> Three guerrilleros were killed by the soldiers

and it is not impossible to find *muerto* also used for *matado* in an active sense in this register:

> *José Marco ha muerto siete perdices* (Azorín, quoted in *DD*, 256)
> José Marco has killed seven partridge

**953** The past participle of *pudrir* (*podrir*) is *podrido* (see **928**).

**954** A number of verbs have a regular past participle form which is used with the auxiliary to form the perfect tenses but also an irregular past participle which is used adjectivally:

| | | |
|---|---|---|
| *absorber* | *absorbido* | absorbed |
| | *absorto* | absorbed (adjective) |
| *corromper* | *corrompido* | corrupted |
| | *corrupto* | corrupt (adjective) |
| *obseder* | *obsedido* | obsessed |
| | *obseso* | obsessed (adjective) |

## 955 Defective Verbs

Some verbs are not used in all persons and tenses: the impersonal verbs *llover* 'to rain', *nevar* 'to snow', *concernir* 'to concern', etc., are only used in the third person, as in English. *Abolir* 'to abolish' and *agredir* 'to attack', exist only with endings which begin in *i*: thus *agredimos, agredía, agredirá, agredió, agrediera*, etc., but not \**agrede*, \**agreda*, etc.[47]

## Orthographic-changing Verbs

### 956 Verbs in *-ar*

In a number of verbs, spelling of the stems ending in *c, g, gu* and *z* has to change before endings beginning with *e* in order for the pronunciation of the stem to be preserved.

### 957

*Secar* 'to dry'

|       | Present subjunctive | Preterite    |
|-------|---------------------|--------------|
| 1 sg  | *seque*             | *sequé*      |
| 2 sg  | *seques*            | *(secaste)*  |
| 3 sg  | *seque*             | *(secó)*     |
| 1 pl  | *sequemos*          | *(secamos)*  |
| 2 pl  | *sequéis*           | *(secasteis)*|
| 3 pl  | *sequen*            | *(secaron)*  |

### 958

*Negar* 'to deny'

|       | Present subjunctive | Preterite    |
|-------|---------------------|--------------|
| 1 sg  | *niegue*            | *negué*      |
| 2 sg  | *niegues*           | *(negaste)*  |
| 3 sg  | *niegue*            | *(negó)*     |
| 1 pl  | *neguemos*          | *(negamos)*  |
| 2 pl  | *neguéis*           | *(negasteis)*|
| 3 pl  | *nieguen*           | *(negaron)*  |

### 959

*Averiguar* 'to verify'

|       | Present subjunctive | Preterite       |
|-------|---------------------|-----------------|
| 1 sg  | *averigüe*          | *averigüé*      |
| 2 sg  | *averigües*         | *(averiguaste)* |
| 3 sg  | *averigüe*          | *(averiguó)*    |
| 1 pl  | *averigüemos*       | *(averiguamos)* |
| 2 pl  | *averigüéis*        | *(averiguasteis)*|
| 3 pl  | *averigüen*         | *(averiguaron)* |

**960**

*Empezar* 'to begin'

|       | Present subjunctive | Preterite |
|-------|---------------------|-----------|
| 1 sg  | *empiece*           | *empecé*  |
| 2 sg  | *empieces*          | *(empezaste)* |
| 3 sg  | *empiece*           | *(empezó)* |
| 1 pl  | *empecemos*         | *(empezamos)* |
| 2 pl  | *empecéis*          | *(empezasteis)* |
| 3 pl  | *empiecen*          | *(empezaron)* |

### 961 Verbs in *er* and *-ir*

Spelling changes affect stems ending in *g, gu, c* and *qu*.

**962**

*Coger* 'to take, pick'

|       | Present indicative | Present subjunctive |
|-------|--------------------|---------------------|
| 1 sg  | *cojo*             | *coja*              |
| 2 sg  | *(coges)*          | *cojas*             |
| 3 sg  | *(coge)*           | *coja*              |
| 1 pl  | *(cogemos)*        | *cojamos*           |
| 2 pl  | *(cogéis)*         | *cojáis*            |
| 3 pl  | *(cogen)*          | *cojan*             |

*Corregir* 'to correct'

|       | Present indicative | Present subjunctive |
|-------|--------------------|---------------------|
| 1 sg  | *corrijo*          | *corrija*           |
| 2 sg  | *(corriges)*       | *corrijas*          |
| 3 sg  | *(corrige)*        | *corrija*           |
| 1 pl  | *(corregimos)*     | *corrijamos*        |
| 2 pl  | *(corregís)*       | *corrijáis*         |
| 3 pl  | *(corrigen)*       | *corrijan*          |

**963**

*Distinguir* 'to distinguish'

|       | Present indicative | Present subjunctive |
|-------|--------------------|---------------------|
| 1 sg  | *distingo*         | *distinga*          |
| 2 sg  | *(distingues)*     | *distingas*         |
| 3 sg  | *(distingue)*      | *distinga*          |

| 1 pl | *(distinguimos)* | distingamos |
|---|---|---|
| 2 pl | *(distinguís)* | distingáis |
| 3 pl | *(distinguen)* | distingan |

**964**

*Delinquir* 'to break the law'

| | Present indicative | Present subjunctive |
|---|---|---|
| 1 sg | *delinco* | *delinca* |
| 2 sg | *(delinques)* | *delincas* |
| 3 sg | *(delinque)* | *delinca* |
| 1 pl | *(delinquimos)* | *delincamos* |
| 2 pl | *(delinquís)* | *delincáis* |
| 3 pl | *(delinquen)* | *delincan* |

**965**

*Vencer* 'to conquer, beat'

| | Present indicative | Present subjunctive |
|---|---|---|
| 1 sg | *venzo* | *venza* |
| 2 sg | *(vences)* | *venzas* |
| 3 sg | *(vence)* | *venza* |
| 1 pl | *(vencemos)* | *venzamos* |
| 2 pl | *(vencéis)* | *venzáis* |
| 3 pl | *(vencen)* | *venzan* |

**966** In verbs ending in *-uir, y* is inserted before an ending beginning with *a, e* or *o* in order to avoid hiatus. (*U + i* forms a diphthong.)

*Huir* 'to flee'

| | Present indicative | Present subjunctive | Preterite |
|---|---|---|---|
| 1 sg | *huyo* | *huya* | *(hui)* |
| 2 sg | *huyes* | *huyas* | *(huiste)* |
| 3 sg | *huye* | *huya* | *huyó* |
| 1 pl | *(huimos)* | *huyamos* | *(huimos)* |
| 2 pl | *(huís)* | *huyáis* | *(huisteis)* |
| 3 pl | *huyen* | *huyan* | *huyeron* |

| | Imperfect subjunctive | Imperative | Gerund |
|---|---|---|---|
| 1 sg | *huyera/huyese* | | *huyendo* |
| 2 sg | *huyeras/huyeses* | *¡huye!* | |
| 3 sg | *huyera/huyese* | | |

| 1 pl | *huyéramos/huyésemos* | |
|---|---|---|
| 2 pl | *huyerais/huyeseis* | *(¡huid!)* |
| 3 pl | *huyeran/huyesen* | |

**967**  Verbs ending in *-llir, -ñer* and *-ñir* drop the *i* of the gerund, the third person singular and plural of the preterite and the imperfect subjunctive. This does not affect the pronunciation. For example:

*Bullir* 'to boil'

Gerund: *bullendo*

| | Preterite | Imperfect subjunctive |
|---|---|---|
| 1 sg | *(bullí)* | *bullera/bullese* |
| 2 sg | *(bulliste)* | *bulleras/bulleses* |
| 3 sg | *bulló* | *bullera/bullese* |
| 1 pl | *(bullimos)* | *bulléramos/bullésemos* |
| 2 pl | *(bullisteis)* | *bullerais/bulleseis* |
| 3 pl | *bulleron* | *bulleran/bullesen* |

**968**  *Henchir* 'to fill up' may also behave like the verbs in **925**: the forms *hinchó* and *hinchió, hincheron* and *hinchieron* are found. However, there is a corresponding change in pronunciation in this case.

**969**  In verbs ending in *-aer, -eer, -oer. -oír* and *-uir*, the *i* of the gerund, the third person singular and plural preterite and the imperfect subjunctive endings is replaced by *y*:

*Caer* 'to fall'

Gerund: *cayendo*

| | Preterite | Imperfect subjunctive |
|---|---|---|
| 1 sg | *(caí)* | *cayera/cayese* |
| 2 sg | *(caíste)* | *cayeras/cayeses* |
| 3 sg | *cayó* | *cayera/cayese* |
| 1 pl | *(caímos)* | *cayéramos/cayésemos* |
| 2 pl | *(caísteis)* | *cayerais/cayeseis* |
| 3 pl | *cayeron* | *cayeran/cayesen* |

*Oír* 'to hear'

Gerund: *oyendo*

| | Preterite | Imperfect subjunctive |
|---|---|---|
| 1 sg | *(oí)* | *oyera/oyese* |

| 2 sg | (oíste)    | oyeras/oyeses       |
|------|------------|---------------------|
| 3 sg | oyó        | oyera/oyese         |
| 1 pl | (oímos)    | oyéramos/oyésemos   |
| 2 pl | (oísteis)  | oyerais/oyeseis     |
| 3 pl | oyeron     | oyeran/oyesen       |

## Formation of the Passive

**970** The passive is formed from the auxiliary verb *ser* + past participle:

*Invitar* 'to invite'

|      | Present indicative | Imperfect indicative |
|------|--------------------|----------------------|
| 1 sg | soy invitado/a     | era invitado/a       |
| 2 sg | eres invitado/a    | eras invitado/a      |
| 3 sg | es invitado/a      | era invitado/a       |
| 1 pl | somos invitados/as | éramos invitados/as  |
| 2 pl | sois invitados/as  | erais invitados/as   |
| 3 pl | son invitados/as   | eran invitados/as    |

All other tenses are formed in the same way. The past participle agrees in number and gender with the subject:

> *fuimos invitados/as*      we were invited

> *Esta mujer no ha sido invitada*
> This woman has not been invited

The auxiliary and the past participle are not necessarily adjacent but see **1192–1193**:

> *Los cómplices fueron también condenados a muerte* (Marsá, 1968: 222)
> The accomplices were also condemned to death

Although the *ser* + past participle form is traditionally labelled the passive, it must be remembered that it is not the only equivalent of the English passive (see **1018**). Spanish has other ways of rendering the passive idea, in particular by the use of a reflexive form of the verb (see **1022–1023**). *Estar* + past participle may also have the value of a passive – see **1020–1021**.

The agent of a passive is normally introduced by *por*, although *de* is also used in literary texts and in archaic language.

*Ya no tendría valor para dejarse ver desnuda ni de él ni de nadie*
(G. García Márquez, 1985: 417)
She wouldn't have been brave enough to allow herself to be
seen naked by him or by anyone

*De* is also used when *estar* is the auxiliary, and when the past participle is used adjectivally. e.g. *ahogado de trabajo* 'submerged in
work', *comido de ratones* 'eaten by mice', etc.[48]

# Use of the Tenses

## Present Indicative[1]

### 971 With Present Meaning

The Spanish present indicative (*hablo*) when referring to a period of time including the present corresponds to both the English simple present ('I speak') and present continuous ('I am speaking').

> *Lo deseo tanto como tú*
> I want it as much as you

> *El carillón de la catedral da las doce* (Marsá, 1986: 188)
> The cathedral bell is striking twelve

> *Yo duermo siempre profundamente* (Marsá, 1986: 188)
> I always sleep deeply

### 972 With Future Meaning

Like the English present, the Spanish present can function as a future. It usually carries the overtone of obligation or dueness.

> *Mañana te mueres* (J. Ibargüengoitia, 1981: 140)
> Tomorrow you die
> – *Silencio, puta, o te despacho de un solo corte – la amenazó* (I. Allende, 1990: 37)
> 'Quiet, you whore, or I'll finish you off with one stroke', he threatened her.

### 973 With Past Meaning

The Spanish present may be used in place of a past tense to make past actions and events more vivid.

(i)   *La guerra estalla en setiembre y la invasión de Bélgica tiene lugar en . . . (DUE*, II, 1470)
      The war broke out in September and the invasion of Belgium took place in . . .

This usage is especially common in conditional sentences in the spoken language:[2]

(ii)  *¿Qué hubiera pasado si Martín no llega a tiempo?* (A. Casona, 1968: 95)
      What would have happened if Martín hadn't arrived in time?

(iii) *De haberlo sabido, salgo esta mañana a dar un paseo* (J. A. de Zunzunegui, 1952a: 217)
      If I had known, I would have gone out for a walk this morning
      (See **1098** on the use of *de* + infinitive here)

(iv)  *Si no llega a tener la úlcera, no muere* (P. Baroja, 1946-51: VIII, 391)
      If he had not developed the ulcer, he would not have died

(v)   *Si lo sé antes, no me acuesto contigo* (M. Aub, 1971: 242)
      If I'd known before, I wouldn't have gone to bed with you

(vi)  *Reconoció a su hijo y casi se desmaya* (Alvar and Pottier, 1983: 213)
      He recognized his son and nearly fainted

## 974 As an Imperative

*Vas a la farmacia y me traes un calmante* (Marsá, 1986: 189)
Go to the chemist's and get me a tranquillizer

## 975 Simple and Continuous Forms in Spanish and English

The Spanish continuous constructions (*estar, andar*, etc. + gerund) often do correspond to the English present continuous:

*Sara Montiel está teniendo un gran éxito en Barcelona* (F. Umbral, *Noche de famosos*, in *Heraldo de Aragón*, 12 May 1974: 30)
Sara Montiel is making a great hit (at the moment) in Barcelona

*Siempre anda buscando quien le preste dinero* (Marsá, 1986: 209)
He's always looking for someone to lend him money

However, the Spanish *estar* + gerund is much more restricted in use than its English counterpart:

(1) It is only used to emphasize that an action is in progress: thus the normal equivalent of the English 'What are you doing?' would be *¿Qué haces? ¿Qué estás haciendo?* would imply 'What are you in the process of doing at the moment?'. Note also *¡Ya voy!* 'I'm coming!' (which really means 'I'm about to come'). *Estudio español* 'I'm studying Spanish' (which implies a general situation rather than active study at the moment).

(2) It can never act as a future: 'What are you doing tomorrow?' is *¿Qué haces mañana?*

(3) It cannot represent a state of affairs: 'You're looking very lovely' is *Pareces muy guapa.*

## 976 With *por poco*

The present tense is very commonly used with *por poco* 'nearly, almost' with past meaning:

*Por poco le pilla un auto* (*DUE*, II, 788)
He nearly stole a car from him

*Por poco me atropellan* (*DD*, 291)
I was nearly run over

## 977 'Since' Expressions

There are a number of ways of expressing 'time since when' in Spanish. The present tense is used in such constructions when a state of affairs continues from a moment in the past up to the present (see also **717**):

*Estudio aquí desde hace cinco años/Hace cinco años que estudio aquí*
I've been studying here for five years
(Note also the increasingly popular construction *Llevo cinco años estudiando aquí*, see **1171**)

*Espero aquí desde que oí las noticias*
I've been waiting here since I heard the news

*Desde hace años veo pasar los días con la sensación de descenso que todos los hombres sienten más pronto o más tarde* (J. Marías, 1989: 161)

For years I've watched the days go by with the feeling of decline which everyone feels sooner or later

However, an event which took place between the moment in the past referred to and the present requires, as in English, the Perfect:

*Le he visto desde que se marchó*
I've seen him since he went away

and when *hace ... que* marks a point in the past at which something happened (also rendered by English 'ago'), a Preterite is normally used:

*Hace cinco años que se casó*
He got married five years ago/It's five years since he got married

*Hace un año que sobre estas colinas se celebró el ritual de descubrir el monolito* (M. Vázquez Montalbán, 1990b:9)
It's a year ago since the ritual of discovering the monolith was celebrated on these hills

## Imperfect and Preterite Indicative

**978** This distinction has no straightforward equivalent in English, and so is particularly problematic for English speakers.[3] The basic distinction between imperfect and preterite is that the imperfect relates to an open period of time whereas the preterite relates to a single point in time or a defined period of time. Thus the typical functions of these tenses are as follows:

| IMPERFECT | PRETERITE |
| --- | --- |
| Descriptions | Events, single or in sequence; states of affairs which are treated as events |
| Habitual actions not limited to a particular period of time | Repeated actions taking place within a defined period of time |

| Actions or states of affairs which are in progress | Actions or states of affairs which last for a defined period of time; the beginning point of a state of affairs |
|---|---|

## 979 Events, Single or in Sequence (Preterite)

*La «cápsula robot» soviética «Progress I» se desintegró ayer sobre el océano Pacífico (Informaciones,* 9 February 1978: 5)
The Soviet 'robot capsule' Progress I disintegrated yesterday over the Pacific

*Me armé, apunté y disparé y la perdiz se desplomó como un trapo* (M. Delibes, 1977: 45)
I raised my gun, took aim and fired, and the partridge fell like a rag

## 980 States of Affairs Treated as Events

A particularly difficult usage for English speakers to master is the use of the preterite to represent a state which is in fact being treated in Spanish as a sequential event:

> – *¿No creía que estaba en los mares del Sur?*
> – *En cierta ocasión estuve por allí* (M. Vázquez Montalbán, 1979b: 85)
> 'Didn't you think he was in the South Seas?'
> 'I was there once'
> (*Estaba* refers to a state of affairs, *estuve* to a particular event)
>
> *Los días siguientes fueron agitados* (E. Sábato. 1983: 99)
> The following days were hectic

## 981 Repeated Actions

*Habitual actions not limited to a particular period of time (imperfect)*

In this usage, the Spanish imperfect is sometimes rendered by English 'would' + verb. (Note that the Spanish conditional is NOT used in this way.)

*Además, se presentaba generalmente la familia entera: padre, madre, hijos* (*Cambio 16*, 21 May 1978: 102)

Furthermore, the whole family usually appeared: father, mother and children

*Félix asistía todas las mañanas a un desayuno político* (C. Fuentes, 1979: 11)

Félix attended a political breakfast every morning

*Llegábamos, nos saludábamos, nos sentábamos, pedíamos de beber y se iniciaba una conversación errabunda* (L. Buñuel, 1982: 62)

We would arrive, greet one another, sit down, order something to drink and a conversation about nothing in particular would begin

*Non-habitual actions repeated within a defined period of time (preterite)*

*El presidente repitió varias veces que . . .* (*Informaciones*, 6 February 1978: 1)

Several times the chairman repeated that . . .

(*Varias veces* defines the period of time. *El presidente repetía . . .* would imply '. . . on a number of (different) occasions')

## 982 Actions or States of Affairs in Progress (Imperfect)

In this usage, the Spanish imperfect is often rendered by the English past continuous.

*Transcribía, mientras en los oídos le iban resonando unos versos de sus tiempos de estudiante* (M. Alvar. 1975: 25)

He sat writing, and in his ears there rang some lines from his student days

A combination of preterite and imperfect is often used in complex sentences when an event (preterite) takes place during an action or state of affairs already in progress (imperfect):

*Cuando llegué, ya estaba el tío* (F. García Pavón, 1977: 143)

When I arrived. my uncle was already there

The two verbs may be represented graphically as follows:

*Llegué* is an event; *estaba* refers to a state of affairs which holds before this event and continues after it.[4]

The following examples are similar:

*Mi hermana murió cuando yo tenía 12 años* (J. Rulfo, 1981: 63)
My sister died when I was twelve

*Al monarca Felipe III le sorprendió la muerte de su mujer cuando cazaba en La Ventosilla* (M. Delibes, 1977: 36)
Philip III received the news of the death of his wife unexpectedly while he was out hunting in La Ventosilla

*Más tarde miss Mary llamó a Clarita y le explicó la discusión. Rosi, tumbada encima de la cama, lloraba* (J. A. de Zunzunegui, 1971: 289)
Later. Miss Mary called Clarita and explained what had been discussed. Rosi was lying on the bed crying

*Ahora se dice pastelería, antes se decía confitería y aún antes se dijo dulcería* (C. J. Cela, 1991b: 204)
Nowadays one says *pastelería*, before that one used to say *confitería* and even before that one said *dulcería*.
(With *se decía*, the writer has in mind an ongoing situation; with *se dijo* a closed period of time)

**983** A special case of this usage is the so-called *imperfecto de conato*, an action which is just beginning to be in progress:

*Salía cuando llegó una visita* (*Esbozo*, 467)
I was just going out when a visitor arrived

*Le dio un dolor tan fuerte, que se moría; hoy está mejor* (*Esbozo*, 467)
It caused him such great pain that he almost died: (but) today he is better
(See **292**ff. on use of *morirse*)

### 984  Actions or States of Affairs which Last for a Defined Period of Time (Preterite)

*Durante semanas o meses anduvieron por París* (J. Cortázar, 1974: 39)
They wandered round Paris for weeks or months

## 985 The Beginning Point of a State of Affairs (Preterite)

The preterite is used with verbs of mental state to represent the beginning of that state. English usually renders the difference between the Spanish preterite and imperfect in such cases by using a different verb altogether:

> *No sabía cómo explicar el fenómeno*
> I didn't know how to explain the phenomenon

> *Meses más tarde supe que sí guardaba algunas* (A. Muñoz Molina, 1990: 13)
> Months later I found out that he had indeed kept some

> *Conocía a muchos italianos*
> I knew many Italians

> *Aquel verano conocí a muchos italianos*
> That summer I got to know many Italians

## 986 Imperfect and Preterite with Modal Auxiliaries

Although from the Spanish point of view the choice of tense with modal auxiliaries follows exactly the same principles as those already outlined, this is an area which gives English speakers considerable difficulty. The guiding principle is once again that the imperfect represents an ongoing state of affairs in the past while the preterite refers to an action or state that is seen as complete in itself.

*Deber*

> *Debías haberlo hecho ayer*
> You should have done it yesterday
> (The imperfect represents the moral state of obligation)

> *Debiste hacerlo entonces*
> You should have done it then
> (The speaker focuses on the action itself)

*Deber* is especially difficult because of its translation into English by 'ought' and other modal expressions:

> *Tales actuaciones recuerdan épocas que debían estar superadas* (*El País*, 5 September 1987)
> Such actions recall times which ought to be behind us

*Debía ir*
I was (due) to go

## Poder

*Estaba encarcelado y no podía escapar*
I was imprisoned and couldn't escape
(The imperfect represents a state of inability)

*Por más que me esforcé, no pude salir*
However hard I tried, I couldn't get out
(Refers to a particular attempt)

## Querer

*Al llegar a la valla, el caballo no quiso saltar*
When it got to the fence, the horse would not jump

*No quería salir de noche porque tenía miedo*
She didn't want to go out at night because she was frightened

## 987 Spanish Continuous Tenses in the Imperfect and Preterite

Exactly the same considerations govern the choice of imperfect and preterite of *estar* + gerund:

*Durante algo más de media hora bebí cerveza oscura y helada y lo estuve observando* (A. Muñoz Molina, 1990: 10)
During somewhat more than half an hour I drank dark, chilled beer and kept watching him

*– ¿Y qué estabas haciendo? ¿Rezando?*
*– No, abuela, solamente estaba viendo llover* (J. Rulfo, 1981: 77)
'And what were you doing? Praying?'
'No, grandma, only watching it raining'

### Other Uses of the Imperfect and Preterite

## 988 Imperfect as a Polite Form

The imperfect may be used instead of the present for politeness:[5]

*Quería pedirle un favor* (*Esbozo*, 467)
I want(ed) to ask you a favour

*Me proponía hablar contigo* (*Esbozo*, 467)
I was proposing to talk to you

In the above examples the imperfect expresses the wish more gently than the present.

## 989 'Hypochoristic' Imperfect

The imperfect is frequently used in children's language to represent imaginary situations:

*Yo era un caballito y tú eras el tío Jairo, ¿quieres?* (M. Delibes, 1987: 135)
I'll be a little horse and you be old Jairo, OK?

## 990 *Se acabó*

The form *se acabó* (from *acabar* 'to finish'), with the variant form *sanseacabó*, is often used as a set phrase with the meaning 'that's it', 'that's all'.[6] The absence of any past temporal value is clearly seen in the second example below, where the expression is used in a future context.

*Hablando de Rusia, se dice: ¡Entrega de los hijos al Estado! Y se acabó* (J. M. Gironella, 1966a:110)
When there is talk of Russia, they say 'Children handed over to the State!'. That is all

– *¿Cuándo empezará el campeonato?*
– *¿Cuándo va a empezar? En octubre ...*
– *¡Se acabó la siesta de los domingos por la tarde!* (J. M. Gironella, 1966b: 148)
'When does the championship begin?'
'When does it begin? In October ...'
'No more Sunday afternoon naps, then!'

*Antes de autorizar un guión o comprar un filme europeo, se los cuento a Fidel y, si le gustan, sanseacabó* (J. Goytisolo, 1986: 174)
Before authorizing a script or buying a European film, I gave Fidel the story, and if he liked them, that was it

Note also the noun *el acabose*,[7] with the same meaning as *el colmo* 'the limit'.

### 991 Imperfect and Preterite with Conditional Value; Preterite with Pluperfect Value

See **1013** and **997** respectively.

## Perfect and Preterite[8]

**992** In general, the uses of the Spanish preterite and perfect correspond to those of the English simple past and perfect. The perfect is used when the action is considered to take place in a period of time which includes the present, and thus occurs with adverbs like *ahora* 'now', *hoy* 'today', *esta mañana* 'this morning', *estos días* 'these days', *todavía no* 'not yet', etc.; the preterite is used when the action is considered to take place in a period of time which has passed, and thus occurs with adverbs like *ayer* 'yesterday', *anoche* 'last night', *un día* 'one day', *hace años* 'years ago', etc.[9] There is a clear difference in Spanish, as in English, therefore, between

> *En ocho días no he dormido*
> I haven't slept for a week (i.e. from a week ago today)

and

> *En ocho días no dormí*
> I didn't sleep for a week (i.e. for a week some time in the past)

and between

> *Mi padre ha muerto hace tres años*
> My father has been dead for three years
>
> *Mi padre murió hace tres años* (both examples from *Esbozo*, 466)
> My father died three years ago

**993** The distinction between perfect and preterite can be exploited for special effect:

> *Sólo Dios sabe cuánto te quise* (G. García Márquez, 1985: 72)
> God only knows how much I loved you (the words of a dying man to his wife, implying that the time of loving is over)

G. Colón (professor of Spanish at Basle) told JdeB the story of an exchange between a speaker and a member of his audience which went as follows:

*– ¿Le ha gustado la conferencia?*
*– Me gustó*
'Have you enjoyed the lecture?'
'I did enjoy it' (implying that it had been heard before and that he enjoyed it on a previous occasion)

**994** In some areas of the Spanish-speaking world, there is a preference for one of these tenses at the expense of the other, although in general spoken as well as written Spanish employs both. In Galicia and Asturias, as well as in much of Latin America, there is a marked preference for the preterite:

*Esta mañana encontré a Juan* (*Esbozo*, 466)
I met Juan this morning (quoted as being typical of the usage of Galicia and Asturias)
*– Toma, te traje algo caliente* (I. Allende, 1987: 231)
'Here, I've brought you something hot' (Latin American usage)
*Me contaron que tu madre murió esta tarde* (J. Edwards, 1971: 113)
They have told me that your mother has died this afternoon

The spoken language of Madrid, on the other hand, favours the perfect.[10]

*Ayer he ido a verlo* (Kany, 1951:161)
I went to see him yesterday (quoted as being typical of Madrid speech, with the observation that the usage is rare in Latin-American Spanish)

**995** In some areas of Latin America the preterite is used to express an imminent action: *me fui, nos fuimos* can mean 'I'm going, we're going'.[11]

## Pluperfect and Past Anterior

**996** These tenses correspond to the English pluperfect, indicating an action or state of affairs which takes place before another action or state of affairs in the past. The past anterior is increasingly rarely used in modern Spanish; when it is, the action it denotes takes place immediately before another (which is always expressed by a preterite).[12]

Pluperfect:

> *Recordó la tarde que le había llevado al «Olivar» de don Daniel*
> (G. Miró, *El obispo leproso*, 212, quoted in Alcina Franch and
> Blecua, 1975: 803)
> He recalled the evening he had taken him to Don Daniel's
> 'olive grove'

Past Anterior:

> *Confundí sus nombres y sus fisonomías apenas hube besado con-*
> *vencionalmente sus manos* (E. Mendoza, 1985: 116)
> I confused their names and faces as soon as I had conven-
> tionally kissed their hands

**997** The preterite is often used instead of the pluperfect or
past anterior:

> *Solita frisaba los treinta años y nunca la sedujo la idea de*
> *quedarse soltera* (J. M. Gironella, 1966b: 607)
> Solita was getting on for thirty and the idea of remaining a
> spinster had never appealed to her

> *Tenía 24 años y lo conoció todo* (G. Cabrera Infante, 1978:
> 167)
> He was twenty-four and had got to know everything

In some areas of Latin America, the imperfect may have the value
of a pluperfect, especially with *todavía* and *aún* 'still':

> *El capitán todavía no se vestía* (Kany, 1951: 156)
> The captain had still not got dressed

**998** The *-ra* imperfect subjunctive also sometimes has the value
of a pluperfect (see **1015**).

## Future and Future Perfect Indicative

**999** These tenses correspond to their English counterparts as far
as the expression of time is concerned:

> *El domingo comeremos en el campo* (*DD*, 202)
> We'll eat in the country on Sunday

> *Mañana ya habrán olvidado lo ocurrido* (Marsá, 1986: 192)
> Tomorrow they will have forgotten what has happened

However, the future is used infrequently in the spoken language with a purely temporal meaning, and the notion is often expressed by the present tense (see **972**) or by *ir a* + infinitive. In Latin America *haber de* + infinitive is also commonly used.[13] There is a difference in meaning between the simple future and the *ir a* + infinitive paraphrase, the latter implying a greater immediacy.[14]

> *Mejor he de ir yo (= iré yo) a sorprenderlos* (Kany, 1951: 153)
> Better still, I'll go and surprise them
> (Kany also points out that the *de* is sometimes omitted)

**1000** The future and future perfect can express a modal meaning of possibility, probability or supposition;[15] the third example below makes the supposition explicit.

> *Serán las ocho* (*Esbozo*, 471)
> It must be eight o'clock

> *Cosas que todos habréis experimentado, leyendo, alguna vez* (*Esbozo*, 471)
> Things which you all must have experienced sometimes when reading

> *Serán las nueve y media, por ahí – contestó Pura* (C. Martín Gaite, 1980: 13)
> 'It must be half past nine, or thereabouts,' replied Pura

**1001** The future can be used in speech with a polite value, like the imperfect (see **988**), though this is less common.

> *¿Me dejará usted pasar, por favor?* (Marsá, 1986: 191)
> Would you let me through, please?

**1002** In interrogative and exclamatory sentences the future can express surprise:

> *¿Te pasa algo. Azarías. no estarás enfermo?* (M. Delibes, 1981: 63)
> Is something the matter with you, Azarías? You're not ill, are you?

> *¡Qué desvergonzado será ese sujeto!* (*Esbozo*, 471)
> What a cheeky character!

**1003** As in English, the future can be used in Spanish as an imperative:

*No matarás* (*Esbozo*, 362)
Thou shalt not kill

*Irá usted* (*Esbozo*, 362)
You will go

*¡Te callarás!* (Marsá, 1986: 191)
Be quiet!

**1004** Note that, as in English, the present tense, NOT the future, is used after the conditional conjunction *si* (see **1059**ff.):

*Si vienes te veré*
If you come I'll see you
(Not \**si vendrás.* . . .)

## Conditional and Conditional Perfect

**1005** These tenses are the past equivalents of the future and future perfect:

| | | |
|---|---|---|
| *No sé si vendrá* | → | *No sabía si vendría* |
| I don't know if he will come | | I didn't know if he would come |
| *No sé si habrá venido* | → | *No sabía si habría venido* |
| I don't know if he will have come | | I didn't know if he would have come |

**1006** The conditional can express a possibility, probability or supposition about the past, in parallel with the future (see **1000**).

– *Asún no me ha invitado*
– *No sabría tus señas* (J. A. de Zunzunegui, 1952a: 149)
'Asún hasn't invited me.'
'She couldn't have known your address.'

*Tendría entonces 50 años* (*Esbozo*, 474)
He must have been fifty then

*Tu proyecto sería aceptado en seguida* (*Esbozo*, 358)
Your plan must have been accepted immediately
(Out of context this could also mean 'Your plan would be accepted (in the future) immediately')

**1007** The conditional is used in the main clause of a conditional sentence (see **1059**ff.) where the condition, expressed by the imperfect or pluperfect subjunctive, is unlikely or impossible:

> *Qué hermosa sería Suiza si no existiera el franco suizo* (*Heraldo de Aragón*, 1 August 1977: 28)
> How beautiful Switzerland would be if the Swiss franc did not exist
>
> *Si tuviese dinero, compraría esta casa* (*Esbozo*, 473)
> If I had money, I would buy this house
>
> *Si se hubiera marchado el día anterior, habría llegado a tiempo* (*DUE*, II, 1486)
> If he had gone the day before, he would have arrived in time

## 1008 Remarks

The conditional, like the future, cannot normally be used after *si* in a conditional sentence (see **1004**), although there is some regional use of it (in the Basque country, the north of Castile and in parts of Latin America):[16]

> *Si trabajarías más, ganarías mejor jornal* (*Esbozo*, 473)
> If you worked more, you would earn a better wage
> (This example is represented as typical of the Basque area and neighbouring parts of Burgos and Santander provinces)
>
> *Si tendría tiempo, iría* (Kany, 1951: 159)
> If I had time, I'd go
> (This example is an Argentinism)

(The conditional can of course be used after *si* in an indirect question – see **1005**, first example.)

**1009** The conditional can be used to express politeness, as in English:

> *Le ofrecieron una taza de café.*
> *– Gracias, pero preferiría algún licor dulce.*
> *– ¿Anís? ¿Calisay?*
> *– Preferiría Calisay* (J. M. Gironella, 1966b: 49)
> They offered him a cup of coffee.
> 'Thanks. but I'd prefer a sweet liqueur.'
> 'Aniseed? Calisay?'
> 'I'd prefer Calisay'

**1010** A recent use of the conditional is the so-called *condicional de rumor*, which indicates something doubtful or only possible, and the truth of which is not guaranteed:

> *El gobierno estaría dispuesto a entablar negociaciones con ETA* (*MEU*, 53)
> The government is thought to be ready to enter into negotiations with ETA

> *Se calcula que unas veinte personas habrían sido detenidas* (ibid.)
> It is estimated that some twenty people may have been arrested

Although this usage is condemned as a Gallicism,[17] the same meaning can be expressed only by using an introducing *parece que, se dice que, es posible que*, etc.

**1011** The *-ra* form of the imperfect subjunctive is sometimes used as an alternative to the conditional. The substitution is most common with the verbs *poder* 'to be able', *deber* 'to have to'. *saber* 'to know', *querer* 'to want' and the auxiliary *haber*, but is otherwise considered archaic or pedantic.[18] There is some regional variation in usage (in the fourth and fifth examples below).

(i)    *– ¿Y tus negocios? ¿Qué tal van?*
   *– No tan bien como yo quisiera* (P. Baroja, 1946–51: I, 632)
   'And your business? How is it going?'
   'Not as well as I could wish'

(ii)    *A aquellos tiempos debiéramos volver* (F. Umbral. 1975: 124)
   We ought to go back to those times

(iii)    *Si hubiese hecho buen tiempo hubiera salido* (*Esbozo.* 481)
   If the weather had been fine I would have gone out

(iv)    *¿Cómo se lo explicara?* (A. Skármeta, 1986: 25)
   How should I explain it?
   (A Latin-American example: in standard Spanish *¿Cómo se lo explicaría?*)

(v)    *– Antonio Roa está en La Chanca.*
   *– Pues por ahí, desde luego, no, o yo lo conociera* (J. Goytisolo, 1981a: 32)
   'Antonio Roa is in La Chanca.'
   'No, no, he isn't, not here, or I'd know him'
   (The second speaker is from a poor village in Almería)[19]

**1012** The *–se* form of the imperfect subjunctive is also occasionally found as an alternative to the conditional, though is generally only considered admissible with the auxiliary verb *haber*.[20]

> *Nuestros «marines» hubiesen liquidado ya el asunto* (A. Carpentier, 1976: 81)
> Our 'marines' would already have dealt with the matter

> *Si hubieses querido te hubiesen pagado en el acto* (*Esbozo*. 475)
> If you had wanted, they would have paid you immediately
> (But a sentence such as *\*Si quisieses, te pagasen en el acto*, where *pagasen* is used instead of *pagarían*, would be considered incorrect)[21]

**1013** The imperfect indicative is also regularly found, chiefly in the spoken language, but occasionally in the written language too, with conditional meaning, especially with *poder*, *deber*, *saber* and *querer*.[22]

> *Lo que podíamos hacer es comer aquí* (P. Baroja, 1951: 99)
> What we could do is eat here
> (Also *Lo que podríamos hacer...*)

> *El cuadro es como es; pero lo mismo podía haber sido de otra manera* (J. Ortega y Gasset, 1959: 67)
> The picture is as it is; but it could equally well have been otherwise

The preterite is also sometimes found with the same value:

> *Los efectos del atentado pudieron ser mucho más graves si los terroristas hubieran colocado la bomba en la casa de al lado* (*La Vanguardia*, 14 February 1978: 20)
> The effects of the attack could have been much more serious if the terrorists had planted the bomb in the next house

## Sequence of Tense with the Subjunctive

**1014** Not as many distinctions among tense forms are available in the subjunctive mood as in the indicative. The present subjunctive may be seen as the equivalent of both the present and the future indicative, the perfect subjunctive as the equivalent of both the perfect and future perfect indicative, the imperfect subjunctive as the equivalent of the imperfect, the conditional and the preterite indicative, and the pluperfect subjunctive as the equivalent of the pluperfect, the conditional perfect and the past anterior indicative. This *No creo que venga Juan* may have the meaning of 'I don't think John is coming' or 'I don't think John will come'.

The following examples[23] show these equivalences:

| | | |
|---|---|---|
| *Creo que viene/vendrá Juan* | → | *No creo que venga Juan* |
| *Creo que ha/habrá venido Juan* | → | *No creo que haya venido Juan* |
| *Creí/creía/creo que llegaba/llegaría/llegó Juan* | → | *No creí/creía/creo que llegara/llegase Juan* |
| *Creía que había/habría llegado Juan* | → | *No creía que hubiera/hubiese llegado Juan* |

Note that according to the meaning, a present or future tense in the main clause may be used with a present, perfect, imperfect or pluperfect subjunctive in the subordinate clause.

(i)   *No creen* (or *no creerán*) *que haya habido* (or *que haya/que hubiera/que hubiera habido*) *tales caballeros en el mundo*
They do not think (they will not think) that there have ever been (that there were/that there had been) such knights in the world

A past tense in the main clause, however, may strictly be followed only by an imperfect, perfect or pluperfect subjunctive in the subordinate clause, although when the meaning requires a present subjunctive, this is increasingly used (examples v and vi):

(ii)  *No creyeron que hubiera* (or *hubiese/haya habido/hubiera habido/hubiera habido/hubiese habido*) *tales caballeros en el mundo*
BUT NOT *No creyeron que haya* ...[24]
They did not think that there ever had been/have been/were such knights in the world

(iii) *Ignoraba que Silvia, su hija mayor, la casada con el diplomático, residiera en Ginebra* (M. Delibes, 1983: 65)
He did not know that his eldest daughter Silvia, the one who was married to the diplomat, was living in Geneva

(iv)    *Unos que estaban allí nos dijeron que no pasáramos* (*DUE*, II, 1420)
Some who were there told us not to go through

(v)    *Felipe González pidió que la IS supere sus tradicionales principios e intente sofocar los problemas actuales desde prismas nuevos* (*El País*, 12 February 1983: 3).
Felipe González asked the Socialist International to overcome its traditional principles and to attempt to suppress the present problems from new perspectives

(vi)    *No sabemos qué escritores «sociales» hubo en la época de Tolstoi, porque si los hubo no tuvieron la suficiente importancia como para que transcendieran y los conozcamos* (E. Sábato, 1981: 17)
We do not know what 'social' writers there were in the time of Tolstoy, because if there were any they were not sufficiently important to survive the years and for us to know about them

In Latin-American Spanish, however, the breaking of the strict sequence of tense rule is especially common:

(vii)    *Fui a verla para que me preste un libro* (Kany, 1951: 181)
I went to see her so she could lend me a book
(In standard Spanish: . . . *para que me prestara/prestase un libro*)

With a conditional in the main clause, the situation is not so clear-cut. Strictly speaking, the sequence of tense rule demands that the subordinate clause form is an Imperfect or Pluperfect Subjunctive; but there is much variation, with the Present or Perfect Subjunctive especially frequent in the spoken language and in Latin-American Spanish.

## 1015 Imperfect Subjunctive: *-ra* and *-se* Forms

The two forms of the imperfect subjunctive (*cantara*, *cantase*) are not completely equivalent, the main differences between them being:

(1)    The *-ra* form is increasingly used in the written language as a pluperfect indicative:[25]

*Como prometiera la tortuga, no pesaba nada* (Fabiola, 1960: 1)
As the tortoise had promised, it did not weigh anything

*¡Cómo deploraba él lo que hiciera!* (J. A. de Zunzunegui, 1959a: 177)
How he deplored what he had done!

*Quedaba incumplida la promesa que en París le hiciera* (A. Carpentier, 1976: 140)
The promise which he had made to her (= the Virgin) in Paris remained unfulfilled

*Esa criatura sería el vivo retrato de ese hombre ejemplar que fuera el notario don Mamerto* (J. Donoso, 1980: 70)
That little child would be the living image of the exemplary man that Don Mamerto the lawyer had been

The *-se* form is found only exceptionally with this meaning:

*(Fue) como si hubieran transcurrido años desde que en su somnolencia lo oyese* (J. García Hortelano, 1979: 301)
It was as if years had passed since he had heard it (= the shriek) in his somnolent state[26]

Sometimes the *-ra* form is used with the value of a preterite or an imperfect:[27]

*Se comenta el discurso que anoche pronunciara el Presidente* (*Esbozo*, 480)
The speech that the President made last night is being discussed
(*Pronunciara = pronunció*)

(2)   The *-ra* form may also have the value of a conditional (see **1011**), though here too the *-se* form may occasionally be found.

**1016** Elsewhere, either the *–ra* or the *–se* form can be used,[28] although some authors[29] avoid using the same form twice in close proximity.

*Era muy frecuente que, al acercarse al canal de la isla Formosa, cambiara el tiempo y comenzase a hacer frío* (P. Baroja, 1955: 183)
It was very common, on approaching the Formosa channel that the weather changed and it began to be cold

– *Podía ser alguien lo hubiera empujado.*
– *¿Cómo?*
– *Que lo hubiese empujado alguien* (R. J. Sender, 1967: 162)
'It could be that somebody had pushed it?'
'Pardon?'
'That somebody had pushed it'

*La señorita me ha dicho que cuando llegase usted la esperara* (M.
Vázquez Montalbán, 1979b)
The girl told me that when you arrived you were to wait
for her

## Future and Future Perfect Subjunctive

**1017** These forms, especially the future, survive in the conservative language of legal texts and set expressions; the future subjunctive is also still found in some dialects.[30]

*El que hiriere, golpeare o maltratare* ... (Código penal de
España, Artículo 420)
Anyone who wounds, strikes or mistreats ...

*Valga lo que valiere*
Whatever it may be worth

*Sea lo que fuere*
Be that as it may

*Pase lo que pasare*
Come what may

*Si así no fuere*
If it were not so

*A donde fueres haz como vieres* (J. M. Iribarren, 1974: 557)
When in Rome, do as Rome does

*Algunas palabras al que leyere* (C. J. Cela, 1958: 9)
Some words to the reader

*Si el rey se inhabilitare para el ejercicio de su autoridad y la
imposibilidad fuere reconocida por las Cortes generales, entraría
a ejercer inmediatamente la Regencia el príncipe heredero de la
Corona, si fuere mayor de edad* (*Constitución española*, article
59, paragraph 2)

If the king should become incapable of exercising his authority and his incapacity is recognized by the Cortes, the hereditary Crown Prince would immediately undertake the Regency, provided he has attained his majority.

*Después se anunciarán los asuntos para premios, se publicarán los que se hubieren adjudicado, y un Académico leerá un discurso (Estatutos y Reglamento de la Real Academia Española*, article XXVIII)
Then the subjects for prize competitions shall be announced, the winners of those that have been judged shall be announced, and one of the Academicians shall read a paper.

# The Passive

## The Passive Idea

**1018** English and Spanish show important differences in rendering the passive idea, which is characterized by (1) the object of an active verb changing its function to that of the subject of the corresponding passive verb and hence being brought into greater prominence, and (2) the possibility of omitting mention of the subject (or 'agent') of the active verb, which becomes part of a prepositional phrase in the corresponding passive construction. The English passive ('be' + past participle) may accordingly be rendered in Spanish in a number of ways, among which are:

(i) *Ser* + past participle (the closest formal parallel to English, and the form traditionally referred to as the passive in Spanish)

(ii) *Estar* + past participle

(iii) A reflexive form of the verb (increasingly nowadays referred to as the *pasiva refleja*)[2]

(iv) A reflexive form of the verb in the third person singular and with no grammatical subject, often termed the 'impersonal reflexive'

(v) An active verb in the third person plural

(vi) An active verb with an indefinite subject, such as *la gente* 'people'

(vii) An active sentence in which the direct object is placed first.

In constructions (i) to (iii) the object of the corresponding active verb becomes the grammatical subject of the passive form, e.g.:

(i)   *La prensa criticó al escritor*
      The press criticized the writer

      *El escritor fue criticado por la prensa*
      The writer was criticized by the press

(ii)  *El primer ministro dirigía la delegación*
      The prime minister headed the delegation

      *La delegación estaba dirigida por el primer ministro*
      The delegation was headed by the prime minister

(iii) *La nueva editorial publicó el libro*
      The new publishing house published the book

      *El libro se publicó por la nueva editorial*
      The book was published by the new publishing house

Construction (iv) is simply a way of avoiding the expression of a specific subject or agent, e.g.:

(iv)  *Se ha roto el vaso*
      The glass has got broken

(On the differences between (iii) and (iv) see **538**.) Constructions (v), (vi) and (vii) remain active sentences in Spanish terms, though (v) and (vi) allow vague reference to a subject and (vii) simply gives some prominence to the object. All have literal active sentence equivalents in English:

(v)   *Me han pedido una carta*
      I've been asked for a letter/They've asked me for a letter

(vi)  *La gente siempre critica a los políticos*
      Politicians are always being criticized/People are always criticizing politicians

(vii) *Ese coche lo compró ayer mi hermano*
      That car was bought by my brother yesterday/My brother bought that car yesterday

Types (i), (ii) and (iii) are all subject to different kinds of limitations, and are further discussed and exemplified below.

## *Ser* + **Past Participle**

**1019** *Ser* + past participle can be quite freely used in all tenses except the Present and the Imperfect, and with non-finite forms of the verb, although it is perhaps more usual in literary and journalistic styles. The agent is introduced by the preposition *por*:

(i)   *El agresor fue detenido por la policía* (*Esbozo*, 452)
      The attacker was arrested by the police

(ii)  *El Conde había sido visto por el Cholo Mendoza pocos días antes* (A. Carpentier, 1976: 307)
      The Count had been seen by 'Cholo Mendoza' a few days previously

(iii) *Javier (es) un hombre acostumbrado a ser servido por mujeres* (R. Montero, 1979: 59)
      Javier is a man who is used to being waited on by women

The *ser* + past participle form of the passive implies the involvement of an agent, even if this is not expressed;[3] when no specific agent can be involved, it is preferable to use the reflexive:

(iv)  *Se produjeron incidentes* (Gómez Torrego, 1988: 186)
      rather than
      *\*Fueron producidos incidentes*
      There were incidents

Care must be exercised in using the *ser* + past participle passive in the Present and Imperfect tenses. There is no problem with verbs which denote a state of affairs, e.g.:

(v)   *Ese médico es respetado por todos* (Porroche Ballesteros, 1988: 69)
      That doctor is respected by everyone

but with verbs which denote an action a repetitive meaning normally results:

(vi)  *Después de cenar, era rezado el rosario* (I. Agustí, 1944: 10)
      After dinner, the rosary was (regularly) said

However, the use of the *ser* + past participle passive appears to be increasing its range in modern Spanish. In the Present, it is often used in newspapers and to make a commentary or to provide a photograph caption:

(vii) *El féretro con los restos de Josu Muguruza es llevado a hombros por sus compañeros y amigos* (photo caption, *El País Internacional*, 27 November 1989)
The coffin with the remains of Josu Muguruza is carried on the shoulders of his colleagues and friends

and it is often used in the 'historic present' (see **973**):

(viii) *En aquel momento el gol es anulado por el árbitro sin motivo aparente* (Gómez Torrego, 1988: 187)
At that moment the goal was disallowed by the referee for no apparent reason

The Imperfect is increasingly found as an equivalent to the English Past Continuous:

(ix) *Había bajado a la capital para convencer a sus jefes sobre la necesidad de cambiar de estrategia, porque sus muchachos eran diezmados por el Ejército* (I. Allende, 1987: 202)
He had come down to the capital to persuade his bosses of the necessity of changing strategy, because his lads were being decimated by the Army

(x) *Las llamadas a casa del escritor eran respondidas por un contestador automático* (*El País Internacional*, 20 February 1989)
Calls to the writer's house were being answered by an answering machine[4]

## *Estar* + Past Participle

**1020** The passive with *ser* has essentially the same meaning as the corresponding active verb, and the time at which the action takes place is the same as that denoted by the auxiliary verb. The passive with *estar*, on the other hand, denotes a resultant state.

*Las casas eran edificadas con mucho cuidado* (*Esbozo*, 452)
The houses were being built with great care

But:

*Las casas estaban edificadas con mucho cuidado* (ibid., 452)
The houses had been built with great care

*El problema ha sido resuelto* (Gili Gaya, 1964: 125)
The problem has been solved

But:

> *El problema está resuelto* (ibid.)
> The problem is solved

*Estar* + past participle is often very similar in meaning to *haber sido* + past participle:

> *Los bolsos están diseñados para proporcionar una mayor co-modidad en los viajes* (advert in *Tiempo*, July 1984)
> The bags are (= have been) designed to afford greater comfort on journeys

Sometimes the difference in meaning between the *ser* passive and the *estar* passive is elusive, and certainly difficult to render in English:

> *Las casas fueron/estuvieron edificadas con mucho cuidado* (Gili Gaya, 1964: 110)
> The houses were built with great care

although Spanish speakers will perceive a difference between the two constructions.[5]

**1021** The *estar*-passive only admits an agentive phrase when the agent is necessarily involved in the 'resultant state':

> *España está representada por el vicepresidente del Gobierno* (Pountain, 1993: 176)
> Spain is represented by the Vice-president of the Government

The agentive phrase in such cases is sometimes introduced by *de*:

> *La joven está acompañada de su madre*
> The young girl is accompanied by her mother

## The Reflexive

**1022** As we have seen, the reflexive passive does not imply the involvement of an agent. The difference between

> *Se ha descubierto/Ha sido descubierto un arsenal de armas en un piso* (*MEU*, 48)
> An arsenal of arms has been discovered in a flat

is precisely that *Ha sido descubierto* ... implies the involvement of

an agent (e.g. ... *por la policía*), whereas *Se ha decubierto* ...
does not.

The reflexive passive is accordingly most normally found
without an agent:

> *La paz se aceptó* (*Esbozo*, 383)
> The peace was accepted

> *Se alquilan coches* (*Esbozo*, 383)
> Cars for hire (lit. Cars are hired)

> *El domingo se celebraron dos manifestaciones en Madrid* (*La
> Vanguardia*, 14 November 1978: 13)
> On Sunday two demonstrations were held in Madrid

It can often be the equivalent of English *get* + past participle:

> *Se rompió el cristal*
> The window got broken

However, the reflexive passive is increasingly being used with
agentive phrases, despite purist strictures to the contrary:[6]

> *En cambio, se han escrito por La Rochefoucauld cosas acertad-
> ísimas* (S. Ramón y Cajal, 1966: 95)
> On the other hand, very clever things have been written by La
> Rochefoucauld

> *Don Ramón del Valle-Inclán, «don Ramón», como se le llamaba
> por sus amigos y admiradores* (P. Salinas, *Literatura española
> siglo XX*, 115)
> Don Ramón del Valle-Inclán, or 'Don Ramón', as he used to
> be called by his friends and admirers

> *La primera fase de la «operación piloto» se firmará en el próximo
> mes de septiembre por todos los organismos implicados* (*Casa
> grande, periódico del Ayuntamiento de Salamanca*, no. 117, 29
> July 1983: 1)
> The first phase of the pilot scheme will be signed in Septem-
> ber next by all the bodies concerned

> *Se me ha propuesto su reimpresión por algunas editoriales* (F.
> Lázaro Carreter, 1985: 35)
> Reprinting it has been suggested to me by some publishers

and there is even an example in the Statutes of the Real
Academia Española:

> *El escrutinio y resumen de los votos se harán por el Secretario y el Censor (Estatutos de la Real Academia Española, artículo XXVI)*
> The scrutiny and declaration of the votes will be made by the Secretary and the Auditor

Again we find the construction with the meaning of English *get* + past participle:

> *A veces ocurre que un jugador se va a operar por otro médico (Heraldo de Aragón, 22 September 1977: 17)*
> Sometimes it happens that a player gets operated on by another doctor

**1023** The reflexive passive is not normally used if the verb involved can have a literal passive or intransitive interpretation:

> *Mario se despidió sin motivos (Porroche Ballesteros, 1988: 68)*
> Mario took his leave without reason

cannot be the equivalent of

> *Mario fue despedido sin motivos*
> Mario was dismissed without reason

> *La bola era alejada de su itinerario (Fernández, 1986b: 421)*
> The ball was being sent off course

cannot be the equivalent of

> *La bola se alejaba de su itinerario*
> The ball was going off course

# Use of the Moods

## General

**1024** Although it is impossible to give a very general rule for the use of the subjunctive, it may be helpful to bear in mind that the subjunctive:

(1)  Is often used in contexts which express unreality or a subjective view or feeling. Thus:

| | |
|---|---|
| *La puerta está cerrada* | The door is shut (objective fact) |
| *Temo que la puerta esté cerrada* | I fear the door may be shut (a subjective view is involved; the door may or may not be shut) |
| *Tiene mucho dinero* | He has a lot of money (presented as a fact) |
| *Dudo que tenga mucho dinero* | It's very unlikely that he has a lot of money (presented as doubtful) |

(2)  Is associated with the expression of a command or influence

| | |
|---|---|
| *Quiere que le escriba* | She wants me to write to her |

## Use of the Subjunctive

### The Subjunctive in Independent or Main Clauses

**1025** The forms of the present subjunctive can be used with imperative value, e.g. *¡Huyamos!* 'Let's run away'; *¡Empecemos!* 'Let's start!' (see **890**).

The present subjunctive is normally used in negative imperative sentences (see **890** and **894**).

**1026** The subjunctive, sometimes introduced by *que* or *ojalá*. is used to express a command or a wish in the third person:

> *La verdad sea dicha* (*Estafeta literaria*, no. 620, 15 September 1977: 35)
> Let the truth be told

> *La paella, nadie lo olvide, es un plato de arroz* (C. J. Cela, 1979b: 329)
> Paella, let nobody forget, is a plate of rice

> *Adiós señorito, que siga usted bien* (C. Martín Gaite, 1980: 31)
> Goodbye, young sir, and keep well

> *Que el hombre, todo hombre, el alto y el bajo, trabaje* (G. Marañón, 1952: 32)
> Man, any man, high or low, should work

> *El dinero no importa. Que se lo meta tu abuela por el culo* (J. L. Alonso de Santos, 1987: 25)
> Money doesn't matter. Your grandma can shove it up her arse

> *¡Ojalá llueva!* (*Esbozo*, 455)
> I wish it would rain!
> Note also *¡Ojalá lloviera!*, which suggests that it is extremely unlikely that it will rain.
> (*Ojalá que* and *ojalá que y* are also found in popular speech)[1]

> *¡Viva la muerte!*
> Long live Death! (title of a film by F. Arrabal)

> *Vivan las muchachas cariñosas* (M. Mihura, 1981: 118)
> Hurray for loving girls

Note that *viva* is sometimes treated as invariable:

> *Viva los fachas muertos* (F. Gan Bustos, 1978: 128)
> Up with dead fascists

It is helpful to think of the sentences in the first four examples of this paragraph as elliptical; the verb in the subjunctive might be considered to depend on another verb or expression such as *quiero* 'I want', *deseo* 'I wish', *es necesario* 'it is necessary', etc.

**1027** After *acaso* (now found chiefly in the written language), *quizá(s)*,[2] *tal vez* (also written *talvez* in Latin America) and *posiblemente*, which are all possible equivalents of English 'perhaps',[3] both indicative and subjunctive are found, according to the degree of certainty involved.

The same rule applies to *quien sabe*, represented as one or two words (literally 'who knows'), which occurs with the same meaning in some areas of Latin America.[4]

When *acaso*, etc. follow the verb, however, the verb is always in the indicative.[5]

After *a lo mejor* (a spoken equivalent of *acaso*, etc.) only the indicative is used.[6]

> – *¿Acaso es usted de la Policía?* – *preguntó el hombre.*
> – *No; no señor.*
> – *Pues lo parece* (P. Baroja, 1946–51: I, 504)[7]
> 'Perhaps you are from the Police?' asked the man.
> 'No, not at all.'
> 'Well you look like it'

| | |
|---|---|
| *Quizá lo sabes* | Perhaps you know |
| *Quizá lo sepas* | Perhaps you may know |
| (*Esbozo*, 456) | |

*Tal vez que el pueblo español se parecía sustancialmente al italiano* (J. M. Gironella, 1966b: 204–5)
Perhaps Spanish people were substantially similar to Italians

*Tal vez nos quedemos encerrados hasta fin de año* (M. Vargas Llosa, 1973: 140)
Perhaps we might stay shut up until the end of the year

> – *¿Dónde está mi sombrero?*
> – *Quien sabe Juan lo haya cogido* (Kany, 1951: 322)
> 'Where's my hat?'
> 'Perhaps Juan's picked it up'

*Posiblemente llegue antes que tú*
Perhaps I may arrive before you

*Posiblemente llegaré antes que tú*
Perhaps I'll arrive before you
(*DUE*, II, 1467)

*A lo mejor se muere* (Lorenzo, 1971: 160)
Perhaps he'll die

Note also:

*Seguramente el único personaje poco conocido de todos los citados sea Francisco de Benavides* (L. Vázquez:100)
Surely (= perhaps) the only person out of all those referred to who is not well known is F. de B.[8]

The imperfect subjunctive may be used similarly as an equivalent to the conditional of supposition (see **1006**) when the verb refers to the past:[9]

*Quizá le conocerías/conocieras/conocieses en Valparaíso* (*Esbozo*, 359)
Perhaps you met him in Valparaíso

**1028** The imperfect subjunctive (usually the *-ra* form, though this is not an absolute rule)[10] is also used in exclamatory sentences beginning with *¡Quién!* which express a wish on the part of the speaker.[11]

*¡Quién pudiera ir de vacaciones! ¡Quién fuera la novia del marqués!* (E. Jardiel Poncela, 1969: IV, 1056)
If only I could go on holiday! If only the Marquis were in love with me!

*¡Quién ganase los duros que se embolsa ése al año!* (S. Lorén, 1955: 185)
If only I earned the money that that character pockets each year!

*¡Ah, Francia! – dicen –. ¡Quién estuviera allí!* (J. Goytisolo, 1981a: 62)
'Ah, France,' they say. 'What I wouldn't give to be there!'
(The plural verb *dicen* shows that the 'I' refers collectively)

**1029** For the use of the imperfect subjunctive (generally the *-ra* form) as a conditional in main clauses, see **1011** and **1015**.

## The Subjunctive in Subordinate Clauses

### 1030 Subject Clauses

The subjunctive is used in subordinate clauses which are the subject of a verb or an impersonal expression expressing an opinion, possibility or impossibility, need, etc. (Such clauses usually follow the verb or impersonal expression, both in Spanish and the equivalent English sentences.)

> *No se preocupe, a mí me es igual que el «tailleur» me esté estrecho* (C. J. Cela, 1958: 193)
> Don't worry, it doesn't matter to me if the suit is tight

> *La primera noche que entré en el café Gijón puede que fuese una noche de sábado* (F. Umbral, 1977: 9)
> The first night I went into the Café Gijón was probably a Saturday
> (Note the sequence of tense in the past: *entré, fuese*)

> *No es lícito que se mate tan impunemente* (*El Alcázar*, 16 February 1983: 40)
> It is not right for people to kill with such impunity

> *Que ahora los chicos quieran ser futbolistas, es normal* (F. Vizcaíno Casas, 1977a: 38)
> It is natural that boys should want to become footballers now

> *Pero la cuestión es que don Joaquín no me eche* (J. Edwards, 1985: 89)
> But the (important) thing is that Don Joaquín shouldn't throw me out

When a fact is presented as certain (e.g. after *es cierto que* 'it is certain that', *es evidente que* 'it is evident that', *es indudable que* 'there is no doubt that', *es manifiesto que* 'it is obvious that', *es seguro que* 'it is sure that'), the indicative is used; when negated, these expressions normally take the subjunctive, since the certainty is denied. Contrast:

> *Es cierto que hay un «problema regional»* (J. Marías, 1976: 36)
> It is certain that there is a 'regional problem'

> *No es cierto que España no sea país de inventores* (F. Umbral, 1975: 77)
> It is not certain that Spain is not a country of inventors

Similarly, if *es cierto que*, etc., are modified so as to change the degree of certainty, they normally take the subjunctive. Thus *lo más seguro es que* (equivalent to *lo más probable es que*, see **1031**) 'the most likely thing is that' and *es casi seguro que* 'it is almost certain that' both take the subjunctive:

> *Me dijo el médico que el hombre estaba muy mal, que lo más seguro era que se muriera* (F. Quiñones, 1979: 177)
> The doctor told me that the man was very ill, that the most likely thing was that he would die

> *Si está usted vestido, es casi seguro que no vea sus pies* (G. Cabrera Infante, 1982: 230)
> If you are dressed, it's almost certain that you won't see your feet

**1031** After the expressions *es (muy) probable que* 'it is (very) possible that', *lo (más) probable es que* 'the (most) likely thing is that', etc., the subjunctive is always used.

> *Es probable que tengas algo de fiebre* (*DUE*, II, 847)
> It's likely that you've got a slight temperature

> *Lo más probable es que vaya a la Coruña o a Pontevedra* (*Estafeta literaria*, no. 613, 1 June 1977: 16)
> The most likely thing is that I shall go to Corunna or Pontevedra

*Probablemente* may be used for *es probable que*:

> *Probablemente hayamos pagado muy cara aquella ignorancia* (J. L. Alcocer, 1978)
> We have probably paid very dearly for not knowing that

However, the subjunctive is not used when *probablemente* follows the verb and is treated as a kind of afterthought to a statement of something presented as a fact:

> *Le encontrarás probablemente en casa* (*DUE*, II, 848)
> You'll probably find him at home
> (cf. You'll find him at home – probably)

After *parece que* 'it seems that', expressing something the speaker accepts as a fact, the indicative is usually used, as with other verbs of thinking, although the subjunctive is also sometimes encountered (and is felt to be typical of some regions).[12] However, when *parece que* is an ellipsis for *parece (bien) que*, expressing a judgement by the speaker, the subjunctive is used:

> *¿Te parece que nos marchemos?* (Fernández. 1986b: 319)
> Do you think it's a good idea for us to go?

After *es de suponer que* 'it is to be supposed that', 'presumably'. the indicative or subjunctive can be used according to whether the hypothetical nature of the supposition is dominant or whether it is felt as being 'real' (the indicative is more frequent):

> *Es de suponer que ya le habrán avisado* (*DUE*, II, 1237)
> Of course she will already have been told

> *Es de suponer que viaje gratis* (Van Dam, 1967: 445)
> He will presumably travel free

**1032** The subjunctive is used after expressions which denote or imply frequency (or infrequency).

> *Era muy frecuente que, al acercarse al canal de la isla Formosa, cambiara el tiempo* (P. Baroja, 1955: 152)
> It was very common on approaching the Formosa channel, that the weather changed

> *Era muy raro que salieran sin sus respectivas esposas* (J. M. Gironella, 1966b: 558)
> It was very unusual for them to go out without their respective 7ives

> *Lo normal era que los esposos se ignoraran* (I. Allende, 1984: 224)
> The normal thing was for the couple to ignore one another
> (See **140** on *los esposos*)

### 1033 Object Clauses: After Verbs Expressing a Feeling

The subjunctive is almost always used in clauses which depend on a verb which expresses a wish or a request. an order or prohibition, approval or disapproval, advice or a feeling of fear, pleasure, doubt, gratitude, supposition, surprise, etc. (see, however, **1037** for verbs like *confiar*, *temer*, etc. which take both indicative and subjunctive).

*El sindicato hizo ayer público un comunicado pidiendo que no se fuera a la huelga (Diario 16.* 11 February 1978: 24)
Yesterday the union made public a communiqué which asked that no one should go on strike

*Mandaré que le cuelguen a usted de una verga* (P. Baroja, 1959: 147)
I will order them to hang you from a yardarm

*¿Sabías que la Iglesia se opuso durante años y años a que los médicos practicásemos autopsias?* (J. M. Gironella, 1966b: 609)
Did you know that for years and years the Church was opposed to us doctors carrying out post-mortems?

*No obstante, se permitía aconsejar al Gobernador que meditara con calma* (J. M. Gironella. 1966b: 83)
Nevertheless, he allowed himself to advise the Governor to think it over calmly

*Temo que me hayan visto* (*Esbozo*, 457)
I'm afraid they've seen me

*– ¿Se acuerda que le dije que algún día yo sería rica?*
*– Me alegro de que lo hayas conseguido* (I. Allende, 1984: 365)
'Do you remember I told you that one day I would be rich?'
'I'm glad you've made it'

*Le agradezco que haya venido a avisarme* (J. C. Onetti. 1979: 165)
I am grateful that you have come to warn me

Some verbs of ordering, allowing, prohibiting and asking take infinitive as well as subjunctive constructions (e.g. *mandar, ordenar, prohibir, permitir, dejar* and *rogar*).[13]

*Le prohibían escuchar la radio* (Haverkate, 1989: 119)
They did not allow him to listen to the radio

*Me rogó que le ayudara a subir la maleta* (ibid., 119)
She asked me to help her carry the case upstairs

The use of the infinitive construction is perhaps more typical of the spoken language.[14]
If the subject of the main verb and the subordinate verb is the same, then the infinitive is always used:

*Quiero ir a París*
I want to go to Paris

But:

*Quiero que vayas a París*
I want you to go to Paris

*Quieren asustarnos y que nos entreguemos, claro* (J. L. Alonso de
Santos, 1987: 63)
They want to frighten us and they want us to give ourselves
up, of course

**1034** Sometimes the main verb expressing a reaction, a feeling or
a mental state is omitted[15] (see also **1038**). The subordinate clause
verb remains in the subjunctive.

*La pobre Concha enjugó sus lágrimas: – ¡Que la tía Soledad me
escriba así, cuando yo la quiero y la respeto tanto! ¡Que me odie,
que me maldiga, cuando yo no tendría goce mayor que cuidarla y
servirla como si fuera su hija!* (R. del Valle-Inclán, 1963: 66)
Poor Concha wiped away her tears: 'That Aunt Soledad
should write to me like this, when I love and respect her so
much! That she should hate me and curse me, when I would
enjoy nothing more than to look after her and wait on her as
if I were her daughter!'
(The subjunctives can be considered as dependent on un-
expressed verbs such as *no comprendo que* 'I don't understand
how', *siento que* 'I regret that')

– *Oye, a ver si me localizan a Eladio Cabañero, el poeta.*
– *¿Y que se lo traigan?* (F. García Pavón, 1980b: 77)
'Hey, can you find me Eladio Cabañero, the poet?'
'And bring him to you?'
(*Quiere que* 'Do you want' can be understood here)

**1035** The subjunctive is also used in clauses dependent on
nouns, adjectives and other expressions which have the types of
meaning listed in **1033**.

Feelings:

*Tengo miedo de que me hayan visto* (*Esbozo*, 457)
I am afraid they have seen me

*Estaba harta de que mi madre me tratara como una niña* (A. M. Matute, 1977: 81)

I was fed up with my mother treating me like a child

Desire:

*Nuestro deseo es que nuestra existencia no acabe* (M. de Unamuno, 1967b: 23)

Our desire is that our existence should not come to an end

Command:

*Él le había dado orden de que no se le interrumpiese para nada* (J. A. de Zunzunegui, 1956a: 93)

He had given orders that he was not to be interrupted for anything

*Pinole, es hora de que vayas a confesar a la señora de Ochoa* (J. Ibargüengoitia, 1981: 50)

Pinole, it's time you went to hear Señora de Ochoa's confession

## 1036 Verbs Taking both Subjunctive and Indicative

When *decir* 'to say' and *escribir* 'to write' are used in the sense of obligation, advice or command, they are followed by the subjunctive:

*El confesor me dice*
*que no te quiera*
*y yo le digo: ¡ay, padre!,*
*si usted la viera* (F. Díaz-Plaja, 1966:38)

The confessor tells me that I should not love you, and I say to him, 'Ah, Father, if only you saw her!'

*Me dijiste anoche que te despertara* (J. Rulfo, 1981: 71)

Last night you told me to wake you up

*Mis padres me escribieron que me fuera pronto* (Haverkate, 1989: 114)

My parents wrote to me (to say) that I should go soon

Similarly, *decidir* can be used with the subjunctive to indicate an instruction:

*Luego, decide que nos tuteemos* (F. Vizcaíno Casas, 1976a: 127)

Then he decided that we should call each other 'tú'

**1037** After verbs like *confiar* 'to trust', *esperar* 'to hope', *temer* 'to fear', *quejarse* 'to complain', etc., which appear to fall into the subjunctive-requiring category of **1033**, either subjunctive or indicative can be used, according to the degree of certainty implied:

Contrast the fifth example in **1033** with:

> *Me temo que este hombre no nos va a llevar a la victoria* (P. Baroja, 1960: 46)
> I am afraid that this man will not carry us to victory
> (Implying the conviction that he almost certainly will not)

The English translation of *esperar* may vary according to the choice of mood;[16] contrast:

> *Espero que ustedes sabrán agradecer mi sacrificio* (E. Jardiel Poncela, 1977: 47)
> I hope (= trust) that you will appreciate my sacrifice
> (Implying expectation)

> *Espero que lo pases bien en Mallorca*
> I hope you'll have a good time in Majorca

> *Esperé que no lloviera*
> I hoped it wouldn't rain (but it did)
> *De todos modos, esperó que se le acostumbrara la vista a la penumbra y que aparecieran los contornos de los muebles* (I. Allende, 1990: 29)
> Anyway, she waited until her eyes were used to the half-light and she could see the outline of the furniture

> *Esperaremos a que vengas para comer* (*DUE*, I, 1205)
> We shall wait for you to come before we eat
> (*A* is optional here, though note that *esperar a que* will always require the subjunctive)
> (*Esperar hasta que* follows the rules for *hasta que* – see **1051**)

The difference between subjunctive and indicative may also depend on whether a verb is used with its 'full' meaning or not; contrast:

> *Se queja de que no hayas venido*
> He complains that you haven't come

*Juan se quejaba a su vecino (de) que el periódico había llegado tarde*
Juan complained to his neighbour that the paper had arrived late
(Here there is no genuine complaint; *se quejaba* really has the meaning of *comunicaba, decía*)[17]

*Sentir* only takes the subjunctive in its meaning of 'regret'; in its meanings of 'feel', 'perceive', 'notice', where it is essentially functioning as a verb of perception, it takes the indicative:

*El dialectólogo siente que ya no encuentra cíclopes* (M. Alvar, 1982: 71)
The dialectologist is aware that there are no more cyclops
(*... siente que ya no encuentre ...* would have the meaning of '... regrets that there are no ...')

**1038** *Que* is sometimes omitted in the written language[18] after verbs of asking, wishing or fearing, especially *rogar* 'to ask'. but also after *demandar* 'to demand', *desear* 'to wish', *querer* 'to want', *suplicar* 'to beg', etc.

*El soberano le rogó humildemente se compadeciese de ellos.* (Fabiola, 1960: 16)
The sovereign humbly asked him to have pity on them

*La conferencia internacional de los sindicatos libres ha demandado prosigan las negociaciones* (*La Vanguardia*, 20 June 1963)
The free unions' international conference has demanded that the negotiations are carried forward

*Los usuarios de la piscina piden se amplíe el horario del bar* (*El Norte de Castilla*, 7 August 1989: 9)
The swimming pool users ask for the opening hours of the bar to be extended

See also **848**.

### 1039 *El que, el hecho de que*

Both subject and object clauses can be introduced by *el que* or in more formal language *el hecho de que*. Subject clauses introduced in this way often precede the main clause, and in this position usually take the subjunctive, despite the apparently factual nature of *el (hecho de) que* (first three examples). If the subject clause introduced by *el (hecho de) que* is in postverbal position (fourth example) it is more likely that the verb will be in the indicative, especially when it is clear that a fact is being asserted.[19]

> *El hecho de que los cristianos fueran mayoría era un fenómeno en gran parte sociológico* (*El País*, 23 September 1985)
> The fact that the Christians were in the majority was for the most part a sociological phenomenon
>
> *La mujer es muy agradecida; el que le hagan un poco de caso la llena de alegría* (C. J. Cela, 1963a: 209)
> The woman is very grateful; taking a bit of notice of her fills her with joy
>
> *El hecho de que venga a vernos significa que nos tiene afecto* (Haverkate, 1969: 167)
> The fact that he is coming to see us means that he has affection for us
>
> *Y todo ha surgido del hecho de que Juan II el Gordo engulló en aquel lugar unos manjares hace 569 años* (ibid., 167)
> And it all arose from the fact that Juan II the Fat gobbled down some provisions in that spot 569 years ago

## 1040 *Dudar*

After *dudar* 'to doubt', *si* may be used instead of *(de) que*, in which case the verb is in the indicative.

> *Sería prudente dudar si tienen algo de común* (J. Ortega y Gasset, 1959: 86)
> It would be prudent to doubt whether they have anything in common

**1041** If *dudar* is used in the negative, then the indicative is used in the dependent clause (since *no dudar* expresses a certainty).

> *No dudo que con estas reflexiones se quedará usted convencido* (J. Balmes, 1959: 166)
> I do not doubt that with these thoughts you will be convinced

## 1042 After Verbs of Influence

The subjunctive is used in clauses which depend on verbs of achievement or influence on others:

*Algo tendré yo . . . – se decía la mujer – cuando he conseguido que un hombre como el doctor Chaos me bese* (J. M. Gironella, 1966b: 611)
'I must have something', the woman said to herself, 'when I've got a man like Doctor Chaos to kiss me.'

*El trato diario con la muerte hace que cada momento la tema más* (J. A. de Zunzunegui, 1958: 270)
Daily dealing with death makes him fear it more every moment

### 1043 After Verbs of Saying, Thinking, Observing and Knowing

Verbs in these categories, when used in the affirmative, normally take the indicative:[20]

*Creo que está en casa*
I think he's at home

*Sabemos que se han marchado ayer*
We know they went away yesterday

*Se ve que está enferma*
It can be seen that she is ill

**1044** If the verb is in the negative, the subjunctive is normally used:[21]

*No creo que ningún tipo de régimen dé la felicidad; pero estoy seguro de que algunos la quitan* (J. Marías, 1976: 15)
I do not think that any kind of régime gives happiness; but I am sure that some take it away
(Contrast subjunctive *dé* after *no creo* and indicative *quitan* after *estoy seguro*)

*No digo que esté lloviendo* (*DUE*, II, 1496)
I don't say that it is raining

Note also:

*No parece que tenga muchas ganas de trabajar* (*DUE*, II, 1497)
He doesn't seem to be very keen on working

However, verbs in this category in the negative imperative or in the interrogative normally take the indicative:

*No creas que será tan fácil* (*DUE*, II, 1496).
Don't think that it will be so easy

*¿Cree usted que la empresa es peligrosa?*
Do you think the enterprise is dangerous?
(But compare **1076**, first example)

But negative interrogatives usually take the subjunctive, perhaps because some element of doubt is usually implicit:

*¿No crees tú que esté enferma?*
Don't *you* think she's ill?[22]

**1045** When verbs of thinking or saying are followed by *si* rather than *que*, they always take the indicative – see **852** and the examples given there.

But note the use by some Latin-American writers of *no saber si* with the subjunctive, where the subjunctive expresses suggestion or hypothesis:[23]

*No sé si pueda – le dije* (G. Cabrera Infante, 1979: 603)
'I don't know if I could,' I said to him

*No sé si estas ideas sean aplicables al arte* (O. Paz, 1971: 20)
I don't know if these ideas could be applicable to art

### 1046 *Ignorar, negar*

Since *ignorar* 'not to know' has a negative meaning as a synonym of *no saber*, it is usually followed by the subjunctive.[24]

*Ignoraba que el muchacho tuviese problemas* (M. Delibes, 1987: 227)
He did not know that the boy had problems

But *no ignorar* takes the indicative:

*No ignoraba que el muchacho tenía problemas*
He was not unaware that the boy had problems

Similar considerations apply to *negar* 'to deny' (i.e. 'to say . . . not') and similar verbs:

*Niego rotundamente que en nuestras penitenciarias haya tortura* (*ABC*, 10 February 1980: 8)
I roundly deny that there is torture in our prisons

*Solchaga desmiente que participe en la lucha por el poder*
(headline in *El Independiente*, 2 March 1990: 1)
Solchaga denies part in power struggle

## 1047 Relative Clauses: 'Unidentified' Antecedent

The indicative is used in a relative clause when the antecedent is
identified or known. The subjunctive is used when the antecedent
is unidentified, vague or unknown. Hence the subjunctive often
follows a main verb in the future or imperative, since in such cases
the antecedent is vague or unknown.

Indicative:

*Haré lo que usted manda* (*Esbozo*, 456)
I will do what you tell me
(Implying that I know what you have told me)

Subjunctive:

*Haré lo que usted mande* (*Esbozo*, 456)
I will do what (= anything) you (may) tell me
(Implying that I do not yet know what you will tell me)

*Dame todo lo que encuentres* (J. Rulfo, 1981: 132)
Give me what (= anything) you find
(It is not yet known what will be found)

– *Pero ¿los conejos se cazan o se pescan?*
– *Eso depende de la borrachera que tenga uno, señorita* (M.
Mihura, 1981: 109)
'But do you hunt or fish for rabbits?'
'It depends how drunk you are, miss'
(The state of drunkenness is unknown and variable!)

**1048** 'Unknown' antecedents are often associated with a condition, a wish or a required quality.

*Los obreros en paro buscaron en el interior un sitio donde moles-
taran lo menos posible* (J. M. Gironella, 1966a: 90)
The unemployed workers sought a place inside where they
would be as little of a nuisance as possible
(The location of the place is still unknown. Contrast: *Los
obreros habían encontrado un sitio donde molestaban lo menos*

*posible* 'The workers had found a place where they were as little of a nuisance as possible' – the location of the place is now known)

Contrast also:

*Ella quiere casarse con un hombre que tiene mucho dinero*
She wants to marry a man (a particular man, already known) who has a lot of money

*Ella quiere casarse con un hombre que tenga mucho dinero*
She wants to marry a man (as yet unknown) who has a lot of money
(Examples from Schroten, 1972: 73.)

*Convocamos a quienes no deseen que España desaparezca* (*ABC*, 16 May 1978: 13)
We are calling together those who do not wish (i.e. anyone who does not wish) Spain to disappear
(But *Aquí están reunidos los que no desean* ... 'Here assembled are those (now identified) who do not wish ...')

*Dígame algo que me alivie el dolor* (M. Puig, 1980: 71)
Tell me something (= anything) which will relieve my pain

## 1049 Non-existent or Indefinite Antecedent

The subjunctive is also used in relative clauses whose antecedent is non-existent or indefinite. The main clauses of such sentences are negative and express lack, impossibility or unreality. The antecedent cannot refer to an individual.

*No se cruzó con alma ni vio nada especial que llamara su atención* (C. J. Cela, 1967d: 148)
He did not meet a soul, nor did he see anything special that attracted his notice

*Y aquí no hay quien se permita el más ligero derroche* (*Estafeta literaria*, no. 620, 15 September 1977: 35)
And here there is no one who allows themselves the slightest waste

*No hay tranvías ni coches que entorpezcan la circulación* (J. Camba, 1964: 78)
There are no trams or cars to delay the traffic

*Sin vino no hay comida que valga la pena* (O. Paz, 1971: 108)
Without wine, there is no food that is worthwhile

Contrast:

*Cruzó con una persona que llamaba su atención*
He met a person who attracted his notice
(This relates to a definite individual)

**1050** The idea of lack or non-existence can however be expressed or suggested in a less absolute way than by the use of the negative *no*.

*Hay pocos españoles que no pidan confesor al sentirse cerca del fin* (F. Díaz-Plaja, 1966: 43)
There a few Spaniards who do not ask for a confessor when they feel that they are near their end
(*Hay pocos españoles* = *no hay muchos españoles*)

*Falta un líder que ilusione al país* (*El Imparcial*, 10 May 1980: 12).
What is lacking is a leader who will inspire the country
(*Falta* = *no hay*)

## 1051 Adverbial Clauses of Time

The subjunctive is used in adverbial clauses of time which refer to the future.

It is not essential that the main clause verb is in a future tense; it is sufficient that the subordinate clause verb refers to the future from the point of view of the main clause.[25] The main verb can thus equally be in a past tense, as in the third example below, where, following the sequence of tense rule (**1014**), the subordinate clause verb is in the imperfect subjunctive.

*Anda, prepárate para cuando venga tu novio* (J. A. de Zunzunegui, 1971: 459)
Go on, get ready for when your fiancé comes

*Cuando el agua hierva de nuevo se le incorporan los langostinos y gambas* (C. J. Cela, 1979b: 330)
When the water boils again add the prawns

*En esa reunión se estudiaron medidas a tomar cuando se implantara la República* (E. Líster, 1977: I, 34)

At that meeting measures to take when the Republic was established were considered
(On *medidas a tomar*, see **1116**)

*En cuanto que dividamos el dinero me iré a Galicia* (C. Pérez Merinero, 1982: 75)
As soon as we divide up the money I'm going to Galicia
(*En cuanto que* is a popular variant of *en cuanto*)[26]

*Mientras dure su memoria, recordará un Viernes Santo que trabajaba en el Ayuntamiento* (M. Alvar, 1975: 41)
As long as his memory lasts he will remember one Good Friday that he worked in the Town Hall

If the subordinate clause expresses a present or past fact, or a repeated action in the present or the past, then the indicative is used: compare the first example in this paragraph with

*Cuando vino su novio ella ya estaba preparada*
When her fiancé came she was ready
(Her fiancé did come; and the action is not seen as future from any point of view)

*Siempre llevaba muchos libros cuando viajaba*
He always took a lot of books when he travelled

The indicative is also used when *cuándo* is used interrogatively (in a direct or indirect question):

*¿Cuándo iremos a España?*
When shall we go to Spain?

*Dime cuándo vas a venir* (*DD*, 126)
Tell me when you are coming

**1052** The subjunctive is always used after *antes (de) que* 'before', whatever the status of the subordinate clause action.

*Antes de que nos metamos en tratos les advierto a ustedes que un burro viejo no es una ballena* (J. A. de Zunzunegui, 1959b: 95)
Before we get down to business I warn you that an old donkey is not a whale

*Antes que te cases, mira lo que haces* (*DD*, 40)
Look before you leap (lit. Before you marry, look what you are doing)

**1053** The indicative is in principle used after *después (de) que* when the clause does not refer to the future as described in **1051**. However, there is a tendency in modern written Spanish to use the *-ra* form of the subjunctive after *después (de) que* when the clause refers to past time.

> *Después que supo la noticia, no volvió a escribirnos* (*DD*, 146)
> After he found out the news, he did not write to us again
>
> *Delibes me contrató unos años después de que le dieran el Nadal* (F. Umbral, 1987: 156)
> Delibes hired me some years after he was awarded the Nadal prize

## 1054 Adverbial Clauses of Purpose

Expressions of purpose, usually involving the conjunctions *a que*, *a fin (de) que*, *para que* 'in order that' and *no sea que* 'lest', take the subjunctive.

> *Será necesario cierto tiempo para que los distintos servicios se adapten a los nuevos métodos de trabajo* (*Diario 16*, 11 February 1978: 15)
> A certain time is necessary for the different services to adapt to the new work methods
>
> *Quítate el frac, ¡no sea que lo manches!* (M. J. de Larra, 1966: 25)
> Take your coat off, in case you stain it!

## 1055 Remarks

*Porque* may sometimes be used to introduce an adverbial clause of purpose, in which case it takes the subjunctive, although in its more usual causal use it takes the indicative.[27]

> – *Bien. Brindemos.*
> – *Porque la guerra concluya pronto* – dijo Adela (M. Delibes, 1969b: 26)
> 'Good. Let's drink a toast.'
> 'That the war may end soon', said Adela
> (*brindar por algo* = 'to drink to something')
>
> *A veces daría cualquier cosa porque me gustaran las tías, de verdad, cualquier cosa* (A. Grandes, 1990: 173)
> At times I would give anything if I liked girls, really, anything

**1056** The notion of purpose may be expressed elliptically, without a conjunction: this construction almost always involves a negative clause.

> *- Vigila - dijo Martín -. No vayas a enfriarte* (J. Goytisolo, 1960: 49)
> 'Watch out', said Martín, 'don't get cold'

> *Carmen Elgazu se cubrió las piernas con la servilleta, no fuera el viento a levantarle la falda* (J. M. Gironella, 1966c: 492)
> Carmen Elgazu covered her legs with her serviette in case the wind should raise her skirt

**1057** As in other cases, if the subject of the main clause is the same as the subject of the subordinate clause, an infinitive construction is used.

> *Levantaba, a pesar suyo, la cabeza a mirar a Juan* (*Esbozo*, 548)
> In spite of himself, he raised his head to look at Juan

## 1058 Conjunctions Taking Both Indicative and Subjunctive

Some conjunctions may express consequence or purpose according to whether they are followed by indicative (consequence) or subjunctive (purpose). Such conjunctions are *de (tal) manera que*, *de (tal) modo que*, *de suerte que* 'so that' (now obsolescent),[28] *tan* 'so' + adverb, *tanto que* 'as much as', etc. Contrast:

> *Hágalo de manera que no se entere nadie* (Van Dam, 1967: 469)
> Do it in such a way that no one gets to know.
> (Expression of purpose)

> *Te lo advertí a tiempo, de manera que no puedes echarme a mí la culpa* (*DUE*, II, 335)
> I warned you in time, so (= consequently) you can't blame me

## 1059 Conditional Sentences

In conditional sentences in which the subordinate clause is introduced by *si*, the use of the subjunctive in the *si*-clause (protasis) depends on whether the condition has been or can be fulfilled.

If the fulfilment of the condition is an open possibility (i.e. if the action in the main clause simply depends on the action in the *si*-clause taking place), then the verb in the *si*-clause is in the indicative, NEVER in the subjunctive, and the verb in the main clause is in the indicative or the imperative. Note that the *si*-clause verb is NEVER a future or a conditional, even if it refers to future time.

> *Si alguien te pide dinero, niégaselo* (*DD*, 342)
> If anyone asks you for money, refuse
> (Someone may or may not ask for money)
> *Si tienes miedo, te acompañaré hasta la esquina* (F. García Lorca, *Yerma*, III, I, quoted in *Esbozo*, 555)
> If you are afraid, I'll go as far as the corner with you
> (The following are IMPOSSIBLE:
> *Si alguien te pedirá/pida/pediría dinero* . . .
> *Si tendrás/tengas/tendrías miedo* . . .)

The English translation possibilities of sentences like the above may sometimes lead to difficulty: thus the first may be rendered 'if anyone should ask you for money . . .', 'should anyone ask you for money . . .' In old-fashioned and archaic English, a subjunctive is sometimes used: 'if the room be empty . . .' (*si el cuarto está vacío* . . .). The Spanish pattern remains the same for all these cases.

**1060** A subjunctive form is used after *si* when the condition is not fulfilled in the past (pluperfect subjunctive)

> *Si lo hubiera/hubiese sabido, te lo habría dicho*
> If I had known, I would have told you
> (Implies that I did not know)

or is not able to be fulfilled in the present (imperfect subjunctive)

> *Si lo supiera/supiese, te lo diría*
> If I knew, I would tell you
> (Implies that I do not know)

or is improbable in the future (imperfect subjunctive)

> *Pero si algún día tuviera suegra, se lo disculparía todo* (E. Jardiel Poncela, 1977: 50)
> But if ever I had a mother-in-law, I would forgive her everything
> (Implies that it is unlikely the speaker will have a mother-in-law)

**1061** The imperfect indicative is commonly used in the spoken language[29] for either the imperfect subjunctive, or conditional, or both.

> *Si se casaban Blanca y Luis se iban a reunir el hambre y la necesidad* (P. Baroja, 1951: 20)
> If Blanca and Luis married, hunger and need would be united

> *Si le ocurría algo, el enlace quedaría roto* (J. M. Gironella, 1966a: 768)
> If anything happened to him, the link would be broken

> *Si yo estuviese seguro de que los vecinos de Villaespesantes no me tiraban a un pozo, yo abría una barbería en Villaespesantes y me casaba aquí* (C. J. Cela, 1967b: 155)
> If I were sure that the inhabitants of Villaespesantes wouldn't throw me down a well, I'd open a barber's shop in Villaespesantes and get married there

**1062** The imperfect subjunctive may be used instead of the conditional (see **1011** (i), (ii), (iv), (v)), and the pluperfect subjunctive instead of the conditional perfect (**1011** (iii)).

The present indicative may be used with past time reference in a *si*-clause (**973** (ii), (iv), (v)).

### 1063 Other Conditional Sentences

*Como, (en el) caso (de) que* and *siempre que* also have conditional meaning. However, these conjunctions are always followed by the subjunctive, even when they represent 'open' conditions, and unlike *si* they may, when the sequence of tense demands, be followed by the present subjunctive:

> *Como esto siga así – dijo –, no me quedará más remedio que traerme aquí un contable* (J. M. Gironella, 1966b: 310)
> 'If it goes on like this', she said, 'there'll be nothing for it but to bring in an accountant'

> *Siempre que tú también estés conforme, acepto la propuesta* (*DD*, 344)
> If you are in agreement, I will accept the proposal

## 1064 *Como si* and *como que*

*Si* also appears in the expressions *como si* (and less commonly *cual si*) 'as if', which is followed by the imperfect or pluperfect subjunctive.

> *Y Soledad sintió como si le atravesasen el corazón con una espada de hielo* (M. de Unamuno, 1967a: 78)
> And Soledad felt as if an icy sword were going through her heart

> *Los guardias civiles tenían que vigilar – cual si de malhechores se tratase – a cuantos españolitos no cumplían el rito de taparse con el albornoz* (E. Acevedo, 1969: 177)
> The civil guards had to watch out – as if they were criminals – for any little Spaniards who did not cover themselves with a bath robe

Note, however, that *como que*, with the same meaning, and the elliptical *hacer que* take the indicative:

> *Yo hago como que cumplo con mi deber* (J. Ibargüengoitia, 1981: 114)
> I am acting as if I am carrying out my duty

> *Sacó el periódico e hizo como que leía* (P. Baroja, 1951: 136)
> He took out the newspaper and pretended to read

> *Y se volvió de espaldas haciendo que miraba los libros* (J. A. de Zunzunegui, 1954: 624)
> And he turned round as if to look at the books

## 1065 Concessive Adverbial Clauses

Clauses introduced by *aunque* 'although' have traditionally been considered to take the indicative or subjunctive according to whether the obstacle or difficulty in the subordinate clause is considered real or hypothetical,[30] though this principle needs refining.[31]

Use of the indicative always implies the reality of the difficulty or obstacle, though the subjunctive may equally be used in such a case:

With indicative:

*Es feliz aunque nada tiene* (Marsá, 1986: 273)
He is happy even though he has nothing

*Aunque no lo crees, esto es la pura verdad* (*DUE*, I, 304)
Although you don't believe it, this is the pure truth

*Aunque es español, no le gustan los toros* (*DUE*, I, 304)
Even though he is Spanish, he doesn't like bullfighting

With subjunctive:

*Aunque sea mi hijo, le castigaré* (Hernández, 1979: 271).
Even though he is my son, I will punish him

Choice between indicative and subjunctive depends on the meaning the speaker attributes to *aunque*. If it has a contrastive meaning, it is followed by the indicative: the construction then essentially consists of two coordinate sentences in which the sentence introduced by *aunque* is presented as more important, or at least as important, as the main clause.

*Aunque me ha ofendido profundamente, sabré perdonarle* (*Esbozo*, 557)
Even though he has deeply offended me, I will be able to forgive him
(The idea of offence is paramount (intensified by *profundamente*); the meaning is 'I will forgive him, but that doesn't alter the fact that he has deeply offended me')

When *aunque* has a genuinely concessive value, in a subordinate clause which expresses a possibility, it is followed by the subjunctive. There is often a clear parallel between this type of concessive sentence and conditional sentences, especially where the obstacle is presented as hypothetical.

*Aunque te quedes solo en el mundo, siempre tendrás a tu madre para hacerle confidencias* (C. Fuentes, *La región más transparente*, quoted in *Esbozo*, 558)
Even if you are left alone in the world, you will always have your mother to confide in
(Here the *aunque* clause is of less importance than the main clause. It has approximately the same meaning as a *si* clause: *(incluso) si te quedas solo* ...)

## 1066 *Así, bien que, si bien, a pesar de que, siquiera,* etc.

The above considerations on *aunque* also hold for *así* 'even if', *bien que, si bien* 'although', *a pesar de que* 'in spite of', *siquiera* 'although' and a few other relatively uncommon conjunctions:[32]

> *Nunca en la vida he presenciado un hecho semejante ni creo vuelva a presenciarlo así llegue a los cien* (M. Delibes, 1977: 67)
> Never in my life have I witnessed such a thing, nor do I think I will witness it again even if I reach a hundred

> *Madariaga, en ocasiones, no estuvo lejos del relativismo, si bien su humanidad le preservó de convertirlo en indiferencia* (Haver-kate, 1989: 133)
> Madariaga, on occasions, was not far away from relativism, even though his humanity saved him from changing it into indifference

> *A pesar de que estábamos prevenidos, hubo un sobresalto* (*DD*, 288)
> In spite of the fact that we were forewarned, there was a shock (Seco observes that the *de* cannot be omitted here)

> *La marquesa, bien que no hubiera entendido, aprobó con vehemencia* (R. Pérez de Ayala. quoted in *DD*. 71)
> Even though the marquesa had not understood, she signalled her approval vehemently

## 1067 *Por . . . que*

There is a similar distinction in the meaning of the subjunctive and the indicative with the expressions *por . . . que* 'however . . .', *por más (. . .) que, por muy (. . .) que. por mucho (. . .) que* 'however (much) . . .', *por poco (. . .) que* 'however little . . .'

> *Por mucho que la llames, no te va a hacer caso* (C. Martín Gaite, quoted in Coste and Redondo, 1965: 448)
> However much you call her, she won't take any notice of you

But:

> *Por más que busqué, no pude encontrar la figurita de marfil* (C. J. Cela, 1958: 177)
> However much I searched, I could not find the little ivory figure

## 1068 *-quiera* Expressions

After *cual(es)quiera que* 'whoever, whatever', *dondequiera que* 'wherever' and *quien(es)quiera que* 'whoever', the subjunctive is always used.

> *Los tiempos pasados, para don Eustoquio, cualesquiera que hayan sido, fueron mejores* (C. J. Cela, 1967d: 159)
> Times past, whatever they may have been, were better for Don Eustoquio

> *Dondequiera que uno se encuentre, de Belleville a Auteuil, no debe temer que le falte una mesa a la que sentarse* (L. Buñuel, 1982: 45)
> Wherever you are, from Belleville to Auteuil, you are never afraid of not having a table to sit at

**1069** A concessive clause may not be introduced by a conjunction at all. The verb is always in the subjunctive. There are a number of possible patterns, the commonest of which are exemplified below:

A single verb:

> *Se tratara de Filosofía, de Ciencias o de Derecho, estaba siempre dispuesto a examinarse* (P. Baroja, 1951: 90)
> He was always ready to take an examination, whether in Arts, Science or Law

A repeated verb, or two verbs, the second of which is part of a relative clause:

> *Los hombres se defienden mejor en la vida, y hagan lo que hagan, siempre son personas decentes* (J. A. de Zunzunegui, 1952a: 29)
> Men get on better in life, and, whatever they do, they are always decent people

> ... *dígase lo que se quiera* (*Esbozo*, 559)
> ... say what they like

The formula (*que*) + verb + *o no*:

> *Queramos o no, Barcelona ya es capital de muchas cosas* (F. Umbral, 1975: 36)
> Whether we like it or not, Barcelona is now the capital of many things
> (Alternatively: *que queramos o no* ...)

The formula (*que*) + verb + *que no*:

> *Los lunes se discutía de fútbol con todo el que entrara por la puerta, que quisiera que no* (C. Martín Gaite, 1968: 110)
> On Mondays football was discussed with everyone who came through the door, whether they wanted to or not

## 1070 Adverbial Clauses of Limitation

The subjunctive is used in clauses introduced by the limiting conjunctions *a menos que* and *a no ser que* 'unless', *con tal (de) que* (an ellipsis for *con tal condición (de) que*) and *siempre que* 'provided that' (see also **1063**), and *sin que* 'without'.

> *¡Pero si no lo sabe nadie! A menos que tú vayas por ahí pregonándolo* (J. M. Gironella, 1966b: 619)
> But nobody knows! Unless of course you go around spouting it

> *Consiéntele se case con quien quiera, siempre que sea un hombre decoroso* (J. A. de Zunzunegui, 1956b: 103)
> Allow her to marry who she wants, provided it's a respectable man

> *Las nuevas «Sopas para Uno» Maggi son las buenas sopas que cada uno se prepara sin que las tenga que hacer mamá* (*Cambio 16*, 21 May 1978: 131)
> The new Maggi 'Soup for One' is a lovely soup that anyone can make without Mummy having to do it

**1071** The subjunctive is used after *que* in clauses of the type *que yo sepa* 'as far as I know', *que yo recuerde* 'as far as I remember', etc.

Note also the colloquial expression *que digamos* or *que se diga*, with approximately the same meaning as *precisamente*:

> *La autora no ha vuelto, que sepamos, a producir otras obras* (quoted by Cartagena and Gauger, 1989: I, 386)
> The authoress has not produced any other works, as far as we know

> *No es muy blanda, que digamos* (Beinhauer, 1968: 60)
> It's not exactly very soft

## 1072 *Ni que*

*Los hombres españoles son insufribles. ¡Ni que fueran pachás!*
(C. J. Cela, 1979b: 240)
Spanish men are insufferable. They're worse than pashas

*Ni que fuera uno mudo* (Beinhauer, 1968: 187)
Do you think I'm going to keep quiet?

## 1073 Causal Subordinate Clauses

*Porque* as a causal conjunction 'because' takes the indicative (but see **1055**); but when negated it takes the subjunctive (compare the use of the subjunctive after negative verbs of saying and thinking, **1044**).

*Él se sentó, no porque ella se lo ordenase, sino porque tenía hambre* (J. A. de Zunzunegui, 1959a: 140)
He sat down, not because she told him to, but because he was hungry

*No era solamente porque Dizzy sintiese la muerte del ser más querido del mundo* (A. Maurois, 1968: 180)
It was not just because Dizzy regretted the death of the dearest person in the world

But:

*La mató porque la odiaba* (Marsá, 1986: 89)
He killed her because he hated her

## 1074 *Es que, no (es) que*

A causal clause can also be introduced by *no (es) que no*; here too the subjunctive is used:

*No es que no me parezca divertida la cosa, pero preferiría que fuera la risa a costa de otros* (S. Lorén, n.d.: 334)
It's not that I don't think it's funny, but I'd prefer the joke to be at the expense of other people

*Quedóse absorto nuestro joven. No que no hubiese tenido sus aventuras* (M. Aub, 1971: 13)
Our young friend was absorbed. Not that he had not had his adventures

## 1075 *Como, como quiera que*

Causal clauses introduced by *como* or *como que* 'as, since' always take the indicative, never the subjunctive.[33]

> *Como se hacía tarde, hemos empezado a comer sin ti* (*DUE*, II, 1497)
> As it was getting late, we've started to eat without you

*Como quiera que* 'however' also generally takes an indicative or a conditional, although in modern Spanish, a subjunctive is sometimes also used.

## 1076 Conclusion

The foregoing account covers the main areas of subjunctive use, but cannot possibly be exhaustive. Spanish is full of possibilities for exploiting the indicative/subjunctive contrast, and it would be impossible to deal with all of these without obscuring the general principles on which subjunctive usage is based.

Using subjunctive for indicative or vice versa may depend on the speaker's point of view. Use of subjunctive where indicative is usual distances the speaker from the view expressed:

(i)    *¿Cree usted que la empresa sea peligrosa?*
       Do you think the enterprise is dangerous (implying: as other people seem to think, though I don't)?[34]

(ii)   *Parece que tenga mucho dinero* (Lleó, 1979: 4)
       It seems he has a lot of money (but I know he hasn't)

Moliner quotes the following subjunctive usages as typical of emphatic popular speech:

(iii)  *Entiendo de eso tanto como pueda entender él* (*DUE*, II, 1467)
       I understand as much of this as he can
       (The indicative is normally used in comparative sentences)

(iv)   *¡Pueda ser!* (*DUE*, II, 1467: considered incorrect)
       That could be so!

In both cases the use of the subjunctive distances the speaker from the view expressed: example (iii) implies 'he doesn't understand very much'; example (iv) 'but I don't think it is'.

Use of indicative where the subjunctive is usual implies that the speaker accepts what is being denied (example (v)) or is asserting what might otherwise be a subjective view (example (vi)):

(v)   *Max no cree que la CIA participó en el golpe chileno* (Lleó, 1979: 4)

Max doesn't think that the CIA played a role in the Chilean coup[35]

(vi)  *Me alegro de que conseguiste empleo* (Berschin, 1986: 244)

I'm pleased you have (finally) found work

# The Impersonal Forms of the Verb

## Introduction

**1077** This chapter deals with the use of the infinitive, the gerund, and the participle, which may be regarded as a verbal noun, a verbal adverb and a verbal adjective respectively.[1] These forms carry in themselves no indication of person or tense.

Although at first sight these forms appear not to be related, they sometimes participate in similar functions, for example

> *Ahí está la clave. Iñigo lo ha dicho sin querer o queriendo: son demasiados* (F. Umbral, *Salir en la tele*, in *Heraldo de Aragón*, 6 February 1976: 26)
>
> Here is the explanation. Iñigo has said so advertently or inadvertently: there are too many

These forms appear to be growing in importance in the language, in both its spoken and written forms.[2]

## The Infinitive

### 1078 Definition

The infinitive may be considered as a verbal noun, which means that it can be used in the same contexts as other nouns. It often corresponds to an English form in '-ing' and like the English form is a kind of abstract noun which denotes an action:[3] contrast

| | | | |
|---|---|---|---|
| *amar* | loving | *amor* | love |
| *jugar* | playing | *juego* | game |
| *vivir* | living | *vida* | life |

Examples:

*Era trabajo duro que exigía un vivir alerta, sujeto a frecuentes desplazamientos* (J. A. de Zunzunegui. 1956b: 115)
It was hard work which demanded constantly being on the alert and necessitated moving around frequently
(*Un vivir* has a more active, dynamic meaning than *una vida* 'a life')

*Me acostumbré a tu querer* (from *Después de ti*, a song by Julio Iglesias)
I got used to your loving
(*Tu querer* suggests the amorous behaviour of a particular person. In another song, the line *Que nadie sepa mi sufrir* 'Nobody must know my suffering' appears, which again produces a more vivid, continuous effect than would *mi sufrimiento*)

## The Infinitive as a Noun

The infinitive may be qualified in much the same way as a noun. It is always treated as masculine.

### 1079 Presence of an Article (Definite or Indefinite)

*No valía la pena perder el tiempo para cosa de tan leve importancia como era el comer* (M. Delibes, 1948: 21)
It was not worth losing time for something of such slight importance as eating

*¿No oyes un crepitar, como de leña seca?* (D. Medio, 1958: 320)
Can't you hear a crackling, like dry wood?

### 1080 Infinitive + Adjective

Placing of the adjective before or after the infinitive is governed by the same considerations as placing of the adjective with nouns (see **171**).

*Por la ventana abierta entraba la vida, el ruido de los insectos en la noche, el gotear persistente de la lluvia* (E. Quiroga. 1950: 171)
Through the open window there came in life, the sound of insects in the night, the persistent dripping of rain

*¿Y nuestra vida correrá así toda, en un constante fluctuar?* (M. Delibes, 1948: 249)
And will all our life go by like that, in a constant ebb and flow?

*Pagarás mis palabras. Pagarás mi mirarte* (D. Fernández Flórez, 1973: 72)
You'll pay for my words. You'll pay for my looking at you

## 1081 *Esto, eso, aquello* + *de* + Infinitive

This construction is found chiefly in popular speech, and corresponds to English 'the fact, matter, business of' (see also **309**):

*En eso del morir interviene más o menos la voluntad del interesado* (R. J. Sender, 1979: 56)
The wishes of the person concerned play a more or less important role in the matter of dying

## 1082 Full Nouns

Some infinitives have become 'full' nouns,[4] as can be seen from the fact that they have plural forms. In some cases the meaning of the nominalized infinitive is slightly different from that of the verb:

| | | |
|---|---|---|
| *acontecer* 'to happen' | *el acontecer* 'event' | *los aconteceres* |
| *amanecer* 'to dawn' | *el amanecer* 'daybreak' | *los amaneceres* |
| *andar* 'to walk, go' | *el andar* 'walk, gait' | *los andares* 'way of walking' |
| *anochecer* 'to get dark' | *el anochecer* 'nightfall' | *los anocheceres* |
| *atardecer* 'to get late, grow dark' | *el atardecer* 'dusk' | *los atardeceres* |
| *deber* 'to have to' | *el deber* 'duty' | *los deberes* 'homework' |

| | | |
|---|---|---|
| *decir* 'to say' | *el decir* 'saying' | *los decires* 'rumours' |
| *despertar* 'to wake up' | *el despertar* 'awakening' | *los despertares* |
| *haber* 'have' (auxiliary) | *el haber* 'credit' (see **1256–1257**) | *los haberes* 'assets' |
| *hablar* 'to speak' | *el hablar* 'speech' | *los hablares* |
| *parecer* 'to seem' | *el parecer* 'opinion' | *los pareceres* |
| *pesar* 'to grieve, weigh' | *el pesar* 'sorrow, grief' | *los pesares* |
| *placer* 'to please' | *el placer* 'pleasure' | *los placeres* |
| *provenir* 'to come from' | | *los provenires* 'origins' |
| *querer* 'to want, love' | *el querer* 'affection' | *los quereres* |
| *saber* 'to know' | *el saber* 'knowledge' | *los saberes* |
| *sentir* 'to feel, regret' | *el sentir* 'sentiment' | *los sentires* |
| *ser* 'to be' | *el ser* 'being' | *los seres* |

Note also the set phrases *andar en dares y tomares* 'to bicker', *los decires y haceres* 'words and deeds', *los ires y venires* 'comings and goings'. Further examples of usage are:

> *Cuando nos vio se levantó y vino con andares poco seguros* (R. J. Sender, 1970: 152)
> When he saw us he stood up and came towards us with an unsteady gait

> *Fermina había soportado de mal corazón, durante años, los amaneceres jubilosos del marido* (G. García Márquez, 1985: 48)
> For years Fermina had put up under sufferance with her husband's jubilant early mornings

> *Siempre hay envidias, malos quereres, ya sabe usted* (C. J. Cela, 1963a: 151)
> There is always envy and bad feeling, as you well know

The nominal nature of these infinitives is clear from examples like the following, where they are conjoined with other nouns:

> *Uno, aparte los saberes y prendas que adornan al padre Martín Descalzo, dispone de otras razones para estimarle* (M. Delibes, 1968b: 73)

I have other reasons to hold Father Martín Descalzo in high regard apart from his great knowledge and talents
(On this use of *uno* see **380**ff.)

*Otras gentes me echan risas y decires* (F. García Pavón, 1980a: 193)
Other people laugh and talk about me

## 1083 Functions of the Infinitive

The infinitive can function as subject, complement or object of the verb or as the object of a preposition.

*Subject*

> *Pero el repetir siempre la misma cosa, le producía la impresión de aquella paletada de tierra que no servía para nada* (D. Medio, 1958: 187)
> But always repeating the same thing gave him the impression of that useless shovelful of earth

*Object*

See **1084**, third example.

*Complement*

> *Eso es sufrir y lo demás son cuentos* (M. Delibes, 1969a: 164)
> That's really suffering; everything else is child's play

*Prepositional Object*

> *Primero tuvo que dejar de odiar a Tomás Arroyo por enseñarle lo que pudo ser* (C. Fuentes, 1985: 11)
> First she had to stop hating Tomás Arroyo for showing her what she might have been

The infinitive acts as the subject, object or oblique (i.e. prepositional object) complement of many verbs:

*Subject Complement*

> *Me gusta salir de noche*
> I like going out at night
> (*Salir* is the subject of *gustar*)

*Object Complement*

> *¿Qué piensas hacer?*
> What do you intend to do?
> (*Hacer* is the object of *pensar*)

*Oblique Complement*

> *Amenaza con llover*
> It's threatening to rain
> (*Llover* is the object of the preposition *con*)

## The Infinitive as a Verb

### 1084 General

An infinitive which acts as a noun in the ways described in the foregoing sections nevertheless continues to behave as a verb with regard to the formation of the perfect, the passive and the continuous, the position of enclitic pronouns and the form of negation:

> *Pero la principal causa de aquel haber reaccionado de Lorenzo era Lucía* (R. Gómez de la Serna, 1959: 46)
> But the chief cause of Lorenzo's having reacted in that way was Lucía

> *L. Howard, al ser preguntado sobre qué le parecía Madrid, respondió con su mejor sonrisa* (C. J. Cela, 1963b: 62)
> When he was asked how Madrid seemed to him, L. Howard replied with his broadest smile

> *¿Quién les podría impedir el estar jugando sobre los montones de hojas secas?* (I. Aldecoa, 1970: 94)
> Who could prevent them from playing on the piles of dead leaves?

> *Tenía escritas don Fidel sobre la docena de obras de teatro, y el no estrenarlas no le producía el más ligero malhumor* (C. J. Cela, 1967b: 84)
> Don Fidel had written about a dozen works for the theatre, and the fact that not one of them had been staged did not cause him the slightest ill humour

> *El beber, el emborracharse es cosa de viejos* (M. Aub, 1963: 31)
> Drinking and getting drunk are for old folk

> *Es el no discutir, los largos silencios, lo que arruina la conversación* (A. de Miguel, 1985: 131)
> It is not saying anything, long silences, that ruin conversation

## 1085 The Infinitive with a Subject

The subject is normally placed after the infinitive:

*Al entrar yo, algunas damas se pusieron de pie* (R. del Valle-Inclán, 1963: 170)
When I went in, some ladies stood up

*Saltar él, asustado, y disparar yo fueron dos movimientos simultáneos* (M. Delibes, 1977: 57)
His (a fox's) springing up in fright and my firing a shot were two simultaneous movements

The common expression *sin yo saber* is an exception to this:

*Se fijó en mí sin yo saber* (F. Quiñones, 1979: 241)
He stared at me without me knowing

and other sequences of preposition + subject + infinitive are not impossible, especially in the spoken language:[5]

*Por yo no saber nada me sorprendieron* (Gili Gaya, 1964: 189)
They surprised me because I knew nothing

Note also the exceptional

*El pelo le brillaba con unos brillos tan lozanos que daba por pensar que hubiera resucitado al él morir* (C. J. Cela, 1967a: 61)
His hair shone with such vigour that you would have thought he had come to life again when he died

## 1086 Infinitive with Direct and/or Indirect Object

*¡Qué naturalidad! Y lo mismo al saludar a Manolo* (J. M. Gironella, 1966b: 585)
What simplicity! And the same when you say hello to Manolo

*Llegó alguno con retraso en el quitarse la boina* (I. Aldecoa, 1969: 98)
One of them was late in taking his beret off

## 1087 Infinitive with Adverbial Phrase

*Lo único que no puede llevar el viajero en la maleta al venir a Madrid es el billete de regreso* (I. Agustí, 1945: 92)
The only thing the traveller cannot bring in his suitcase when coming to Madrid is his return ticket.

## 1088 Infinitive + Adverb

An infinitive functioning as a noun may be qualified by either an adverb or an adjective, there being a choice between

    (i)    *ese protestar constantemente*
           that continual protesting

and

    (ii)   *ese protestar constante* (*Esbozo*, 485)
           that continual protest

There is, however, a difference in meaning between the two constructions.[6] The adverb and adjective respectively express a dynamic or static aspect; in particular, as in example (iv), use of the adjective may make the infinitive interpretable as a full noun (see **1082**).

    (iii)  *Contemplaba el desnudarse lentamente de los plátanos del jardín* (I. Agustí, 1944: 135)
          He was watching how the plane trees in the garden were slowly getting bare
          (This presents the action as ongoing and perceptible. Using . . . *el lento desnudarse* . . . would also be possible: this would present the action as a whole, as not perceptible)

    (iv)  *– No te entiendo una palabra – le dije.*
          *Era ese juego de siempre. Ese hablar cabalísticamente, como si las palabras corrieran, como pájaros, en medio de los árboles* (J. Asenjo Sedano, 1978: 111–12)
          'I don't understand a word you're saying.' I said to him. It was the same old game. That cryptic way of speaking, as if the words were running, like birds, among the trees
          (. . . *ese hablar cabalístico* . . . would mean rather 'that cryptic language')

    (v)   *Las etapas de este firme e intermitente enseñarse no habrían de ser difíciles de marcar* (C. J. Cela, 1957: 51)
          The stages of this solid and intermittent self-tuition would not be difficult to chart

**1089** The dual status of the infinitive as noun and verb is shown clearly in the construction *al caer (de) la tarde* 'as darkness falls/

fell'. With the preposition *de*, the infinitive *caer* has primarily a nominal value (literally 'at the fall of the evening'); without the preposition, *la tarde* functions as the subject of *caer* as in the examples in **1085**.

> *Al caer de la tarde la andaluza viste su casa de limpio* (J. M. Pemán, 1972: 35)
> At nightfall the Andalusian woman makes her house clean

> *Al caer la tarde se sentaban todos y hablaban de cosas hermosas y tranquilas* (A. Casona. 1968: 93)
> As night fell they all sat down and spoke of beautiful, peaceful things

The choice between the two constructions is not always free. When an adjective is used with the infinitive, it must be construed as a noun, and the construction with *de* is therefore obligatory. Thus P. Neruda writes *el prolongado correr de los años* (1976: 84) 'the long passing of the years' and *\*el prolongado correr los años* would be impossible.

On the construction *al* + infinitive, see **1092**.

**1090 Remark**

Nouns and adjectives are often linked to the infinitive by *de*:

> *Tengo el honor de invitarle*
> I have the honour to invite you/of inviting you

> *No eres capaz de hacerlo*
> You are not capable of doing it

> *Tendréis el derecho de despreciarlas* (*DD*, 141)
> You will have the right to despise them

## Special Constructions

**1091** The majority of the following constructions have no direct equivalent in English and must be translated by paraphrases.

Constructions which have the Value of a Subordinate Clause

## 1092 *Al* + **Infinitive**

This has the value of an adverbial clause of time in which the infinitive generally (but see **1149**) indicates a precise moment. Simultaneity of the actions expressed by the infinitive and the main verb is almost always implied. In some cases, the action of the infinitive takes place immediately before the action represented by the main verb. Like the majority of the other constructions described below, *al* + infinitive does not have an intrinsic temporal value: it is clear from the form of the main verb whether the action expressed by the infinitive is to be viewed as past, present or future.

*Fidel Muñoz abre los ojos al oir algún disparo* (M. Aub, 1963: 123-4)
Fidel Muñoz opens his eyes when he hears a shot
(*Abre los ojos* and *oir algún disparo* are practically simultaneous)

*El primero que tuvieron se murió al nacer* (S. Lorén, 1962: 50)
The first one they had died at birth

**1093** This construction may also be used with an overtone of cause (especially in Latin America),[7] condition[8] or manner, the temporal value being weakened especially when the infinitive is negated.

*La Sagrario, la Gitana y el Mamés se consideraron afortunados al poder cambiar su cueva por una de las casitas* (M. Delibes, 1968a: 61)
Sagrario, the Gipsy and Mamés considered themselves fortunate that they could exchange their cave for one of the cottages

*Al no conseguirlo se preguntan: ¿Para qué estamos en el mundo?* (*Conversaciones con Monseñor Escrivá de Balaguer*, 158)
When they do not get it, they wonder 'Why are we in the world?'

*¿No cree usted que al desnudarse pretenden ... animarnos?* (S. Lorén, 1971: 221)
Don't you think they're trying to cheer us up when they strip off?

## 1094 Remarks

The construction *estar al* + infinitive expresses the imminence of the action represented by the infinitive.

> *Los exámenes estaban al caer* (J. M. Gironella, 1966a: 176)
> The exams were at hand

> *Ahora vámonos, que mi hermana está al regresar con su marido* (G. Cabrera Infante, 1979: 609)
> Let's go now, because my sister will be back in a moment with her husband

**1095** The expressions *al parecer* and *al decir* are set phrases, meaning respectively 'it seems', 'according to . . .'

> *El caso es que fueron al parecer dos individuos* (R. J. Sender, 1970: 129)
> The fact of the matter is that there were apparently two people

> *Al decir de su padre, iba a acabar muy mal* (C. J. Cela, 1967b: 93)
> According to his father, he would come to a bad end

## 1096 *Con* + Infinitive

In the majority of instances, *con* + infinitive has the value of a concessive adverbial clause which corresponds to *aunque* + finite verb.

> *Quiero dar a entender con esto que el hecho de querer ser escritor, con ser importante, no lo es todo* (M. Delibes, 1968b: 150)
> By this I wish to imply that the fact of being a writer, though important, is not everything

> *¡No me han arruinado las mujeres, con haberlas amado tanto!* (R. del Valle-Inclán, 1981: 134)
> Women have not ruined me, even though I loved them so fervently!

With the same meaning, *a pesar de*, *pese a*, *sin embargo de* (less commonly) and *no obstante*[9] + infinitive (also *no obstante a/de*, though these are considered incorrect) are also found:

*Había grupos en el «hall», a pesar de ser las dos de la mañana* (J. A. de Zunzunegui, 1956b: 314)
There were groups in the 'hall', in spite of it being two in the morning

*Pese a tener la edad de João Meninho, João Grande parecía llevarle varios años* (M. Vargas Llosa, 1981: 37)
In spite of being the same age as João Meninho, João Grande seemed to be several years older

**1097** *Con* + infinitive may also have a conditional value.

*Ángel me decía: «Come; con no comer no arreglas nada»* (M. Delibes, 1969a:18)
Ángel said to me, 'Eat; if you don't eat you'll not sort anything out'

When the idea of time is added to the above conditional value, the combination *con* + infinitive takes on a restrictive sense. In the following sentence, it has the nuance 'it is enough to', 'you only have to':

*Con dar la vuelta a la esquina, verá usted la zapatería* (P. Baroja, quoted in Coste and Redondo, 1965: 476)
If you go round the corner, you'll see the cobbler's

In such cases, *con sólo* (or, less frequently, *sólo con* or just *sólo*) can be used as a reinforcing element:

*Desde el primer momento, con sólo ver el aspecto de la habitación, se había sentido un extraño* (J. M. Gironella, 1966a: 217)
From the very first moment, just by seeing how the room looked, he had felt an outsider

## 1098 *A* or *de* + Infinitive

*A* and *de* + infinitive (*de* is more common in modern Spanish)[10] have the value of a conditional adverbial clause: a simple way of avoiding the use of *si* and the often difficult subsequent choice of tense and mood.

*A ser cierta la noticia, el gobierno tomará medidas urgentes* (*Esbozo*, 487)
If the news is true, the government will take urgent measures (Or: *Si es cierta la noticia . . .*)

*Hubiera llegado a meterle en un puño a no haberse muerto* (P. Baroja, 1951: 33)
She would eventually have had him under her thumb if she had not died
(Or: *. . . si no se hubiera/hubiese muerto*)

*De no ser así prefiero que no me conteste* (C. J. Cela, 1967c: 99)
If that is not so, I prefer you not to answer
(Or: *Si no es así. . .*)

*De no temer lo que pensaron los camaradas, se hubiera escondido detrás de una roca hasta que la batalla terminara* (J. M. Gironella, 1966c: 543)
If he had not been afraid of what his comrades might think, he would have hidden behind a rock until the battle was over
(*Temer* here has the value of the perfect infinitive *haber temido*, a phenomenon which is common in Spanish. Expressions like *después de comer* with the meaning of *después de haber comido* 'after having eaten' are regularly encountered. See also **1107** and **1182** (vi))

Note, however, the following set phrases with *a*:

| | |
|---|---|
| *a no ser por mí* | if it were not for me |
| *a decir verdad* | to tell the truth |
| *a juzgar por lo que dicen* | going by what people say |
| *a no ser posible* | if that is impossible[11] |

**1099** *De* + infinitive may also replace a causal subordinate clause.

*Pues eso, a la cama, a descansar de no hacer nada, como yo digo* (M. Delibes, 1969a: 249)
So go to bed, have a rest when (= since) you're not doing anything, I always say

In this meaning, *de* may be reinforced by *sólo*:

*Me reía de sólo pensarlo* (J. L. Castillo Puche, 1951: 132)
I laughed just thinking it

**1100** *A* + infinitive may form set phrases with no conditional meaning. *A no dudarlo* has the meaning 'undoubtedly'. The constructions *a todo* + infinitive and *a más (no)* + infinitive are adverbial phrases of manner: *a todo correr* 'at full speed', *a todo gritar* 'at the top of one's voice', *a todo meter* 'with all one's might', *a más tardar* 'at the latest'.

> *Es que estamos a todo meter . . . ¡Figúrate qué redada!* (A. M. de Lera, 1970: 313)
> We're pulling with all our might . . . Just imagine what a catch!

> *La besa a más no poder* (M. Aub, 1963: 71)
> He's kissing her like mad

## 1101 *En* + Infinitive

This (not very common)[12] construction, can have the value of a time or manner adverbial (or sometimes the two together, as in the second example):

> *. . . y en verlas llegar huía* (*DUE*, II, 1468)
> . . . and when he saw them coming he would run

> *Entre las gentes hay, quizás, algún niño pálido que goza en ver como el perro no acaba de morir* (C. J. Cela, 1963a: 284)
> Amongst the people there is, perhaps, some pale child who enjoys it when he sees how the dog has not died
> (. . . *en ver* . . . has here the same sense as . . . *al ver* . . .)

## 1102 *Nada más* (or *sólo*, *no más*) + Infinitive

In modern Spanish, the constructions *nada más* + infinitive and *sólo* + infinitive are very common, especially in the spoken language. *No más* (or *nomás*) + infinitive and *al no más* (or *nomás*) + infinitive[13] are also used with the same meaning, especially in Latin America. These expressions have the value of a temporal adverbial clause introduced by *en seguida*, *en cuanto*, *apenas* 'immediately after', 'hardly', where the action expressed by the infinitive takes place immediately before that of the main verb.

> *Doña Matilde y doña Asunción se reúnen todas las tardes, nada más comer, en una lechería de la calle de Fuencarral* (C. J. Cela, 1963a: 121)
> Doña Matilde and Doña Asunción meet every afternoon, straight after lunch, in a milk shop on the Calle Fuencarral

*Chica, estás hecha un brazo de mar – le dijo Bea sólo entrar* (J. A. de Zunzunegui, 1952b: 151)
'Child, you're dressed to kill,' said Bea to her as soon as she had come in
*Al no más llegar a la tumba se inclinó* (Kany, 1951: 316)
He came to the grave and immediately bowed his head

## 1103 *Por* + Infinitive

*Por* + infinitive may replace a causal subordinate clause.
*Un día el reuma te roerá los huesos por vivir bajo tierra* (M. Delibes, 1968a: 109)
One day your bones will be gnawed by rheumatism through having lived underground
See also **759**.

**1104** See also **1115** on *por* + infinitive as an equivalent to *sin* + infinitive.

**1105** For *estar por* + infinitive see **775**.

## 1106 Other Prepositional Expressions + Infinitive

The prepositional expressions *a(l) poco de* 'shortly after', *antes de* 'before', *después de* 'after', *en seguida de* and *inmediatamente de* 'immediately after', and *luego de* 'after' combine with an infinitive with the value of a temporal subordinate clause. So do a number of noun expressions with temporal value (e.g. *al día siguiente de* 'the following day', *el primer día de* 'the first day', etc.).
*Inmediatamente de leer esto se me ocurrió la idea* (P. Baroja, 1960: 18)
Immediately after reading this the idea occurred to me
*El dinero lo ingresé en tu cuenta corriente al día siguiente de recibir tu carta* (J. A. de Zunzunegui, 1952a: 19)
I put the money in your current account the day after receiving your letter
*Se casó con Julio días antes de cumplir los dicisiete años, a poco de volver él de Barcelona* (A. M. de Lera, 1970: 110)
She married Julio a few days before her seventeenth birthday, shortly after he returned from Barcelona

Such constructions can sometimes be quite complex and difficult to translate economically into English:

*El marido había muerto en un sanatorio después de algún tiempo de no trabajar* (S. Lorén, 1960: 206)
The husband had died in a clinic after a period of being unable to work

Note also the formula *a* + time expression + *de* + infinitive (see **669**).

*Roncaba a los cinco minutos de tumbarse en la cama* (M. Delibes, 1948: 61)
He was snoring five minutes after lying down in bed

## 1107 Remark

The simple infinitive is frequently used in Spanish with the value of a perfect infinitive, especially after *después de*.

*Salí a la calle después de comer unas costillas asadas* (J.L. Castillo Puche, 1956: 85)
I went out into the street after eating some roasted chops

See also **1098**, fourth example.

## 1108 *Además de, aparte* and *sobre* + Infinitive

*Además de* and *sobre* + infinitive have the meaning 'besides, as well as'. *Aparte* + infinitive (and *sobre de* + infinitive in the written language, though this is not considered correct)[14] have the restrictive meaning 'except'.

*Organizaron funeral y misas, además de dirigir por turno el rezo de los rosarios, en casa de Benigno, los días subsiguientes* (S. Lorén, 1960: 122)
The following days, in Benigno's house, they organized the funeral and masses, besides leading in turn the saying of the rosaries

*Se necesita, sobre ser torero, ser un gran actor* (C. J. Cela, 1972: 55–6)
In addition to being a bullfighter, you need to be a great actor

*Aparte mover el estiércol, nadie tenía entonces nada que hacer en el campo* (M. Delibes, 1968a: 53)
Apart from moving manure, no one then had anything to do in the country

## 1109 *A medio* + Infinitive

This common construction corresponds to English 'half' + past participle and is used adjectivally: in Spanish, the infinitive of a transitive verb has a passive sense.

> *Al observar el vasito de vodka que Santiago tenía a medio consumir, le comentó* ... (F. Vizcaíno Casas, 1978: 27)
> Observing the glass of vodka that Santiago had half consumed, he observed ...
> (*a medio consumir* = *que había consumido a medias*)

> *Pidió permiso para acabar de servir a los clientes a medio enjabonar y luego salió a la calle* (S. Lorén, 1962: 32)
> He asked permission to finish serving the half-soaped customers and then went out into the street

> *Jeannine estaba ante la puerta abierta. a medio arreglarse* (I. Agustí, 1957: 104)
> Jeannine stood half-dressed before the open door

## 1110 *Sin* + Infinitive: With Adjectival Value

*Sin* + infinitive may have the function of an adjective, indicating that an action has (still) not taken place. Again, a transitive infinitive has a passive value.[15]

> *Déjame decirte que le encontré sin afeitar, cosa rarísima en él* (M. Aub, 1963: 233)
> Let me tell you that I found him unshaven, something very unusual with him

> *La escalera sigue sucia y pobre, los cristales de las ventanas, sin lavar* (A. Buero Vallejo, 1966: 29)
> The staircase is still dirty and miserable, the window panes still unwashed

English translation is often by a past participle beginning with 'un', although this is sometimes impossible:

> *El sol primero llenó de luz unos cuerpos, algunos todavía sin morir* (E. Romero, 1963:9)
> The first rays of sunlight filled some bodies with light, some of which were still not dead

It is not necessary to repeat *sin* if it is followed by more than one infinitive.

*Fue a ponérselo y estaba sin planchar y cepillar* (J. A. de Zunzunegui, 1956b: 106)
He went to put it on and it was (still) unironed and unbrushed

**1111** With an intransitive or reflexive infinitive, *sin* + infinitive is often used elliptically to render a negative. The expression carries an affective overtone.

*Y Carmina sin venir* (A. Buero Vallejo, 1966: 25)
And Carmina hasn't come
(In such sentences there is an overtone, according to context, of indignation, unease, etc.)

*Durante la guerra don Juan entró en España bajo el nombre de Juan López y yo sin enterarme* (J. M. Gironella, 1966b: 505)
During the war, Don Juan entered Spain under the name of Juan López and I didn't even know

## 1112 As an Adverb

*Sin* + infinitive may also correspond to English 'without' + gerund:

*Trabaja sin cesar* (*Esbozo*, 443)
She works without ceasing

*Se tumbaban en cualquier parte, sin importarles mucho que ...* (A. Roa Bastos, 1977: 230)
They lay down anywhere, without it mattering to them much ...

**1113** The adverbial expression *sin querer* has the meaning 'involuntarily, unintentionally':

*El gobernador miró sin querer el retrato de su mujer* (J. M. Gironella, 1966b: 625)
The governor looked involuntarily at his wife's portrait

## 1114 As an Imperative

*Sin* + infinitive is used in the spoken language as an invariable negative imperative, with a polite value.

- *¿A quién vas a agarrar tú, idiota?*
- *Sin insultar* (S. Lorén, 1960: 131)
'Who do you think you're grabbing, you idiot?'
'Don't insult me'
(*Sin insultar* = *¡no me insultes!*)

*¡Pero, hombre, señor director, sin empujar!* (C. J. Cela, 1979b: 244)
Come on now, sir, no pushing!
(*Sin empujar* = *¡no empuje usted!*)

## 1115 *Por* + Infinitive

Besides the meanings already mentioned in **1103**, *por* + infinitive may also be used adjectivally to indicate an action which has (still) not taken place. Its meaning is therefore sometimes comparable to that of *sin* + infinitive in **1110**[16] and a transitive infinitive again has a passive value.

> *Puede decirse que está todo por decir; mejor, que está todo por pensar* (J. Ortega y Gasset, 1959: 33)
> It can be said that everything remains to be said; rather, that everything remains to be thought

> *Fechas conmemoradas o por conmemorar* (title of an article by J. Gallego in *Ínsula*, nos. 428–9, 19)
> Dates which have been or are to be commemorated

## 1116 *A* + Infinitive

Although the construction *a* + infinitive (used adjectivally with the same value as *por* + infinitive) is often censured as a Gallicism,[17] it is found in both spoken and written Spanish so commonly today that it cannot now be considered incorrect.[18]

> *Hay dos aspectos a considerar* (M. Delibes, 1968b: 139)
> There are two aspects to consider

> *Macario explicaba la táctica a seguir* (I. Aldecoa, 1969: 112)
> Macario explained the tactic to follow

> *En la Costa Atlántica se habla además el inglés: otro problema a enfrentar* (J. Cortázar, 1984:40)
> On the Atlantic Coast, English is spoken as well: another problem to be faced

*Total a pagar* is a common formula as the equivalent of 'Total to pay' (see also **1051**, third example).

## Infinitives with the Value of an Independent or Coordinate Clause

**1117** In all these cases the infinitive has a clear verbal value.

### 1118 A Special Use of the Perfect Infinitive

The perfect infinitive (affirmative or negative) is used elliptically in the spoken language to express an idea of obligation.

> *Habérmelo dicho, hombre; parecía buen muchacho* (C. J. Cela, 1963a: 46)
> You should have told me, old chap; he seemed a nice lad
> (*Habérmelo dicho = debías/deberías habérmelo dicho*)

> *Haberlo pensado antes, que a esta situación no te he llevado yo* (J. A. de Zunzunegui, 1952a: 22)
> You should have thought of that before; it's not my fault you're in this mess
> (*Haberlo pensado antes = debías/deberías haberlo pensado antes*)

> *¿Figuraría Mateo entre los heridos? ¡Ay, no haberle cosido en el pecho un detente!* (J. M. Gironella, 1966b: 730)
> Could Mateo be among the wounded? Ah, I should have sewn a lucky badge on his chest!
> (*No haberle cosido = debía/debería haberle cosido*)

### 1119 Infinitive + Finite Form of the Same Verb

The infinitive, generally followed by a comma (though note example (ii)), may appear separately in front of a finite form of the same verb: the effect is to call special attention to the action or quality expressed by the verb. The meaning is really 'where ... is concerned'. The construction is chiefly found in popular speech.

The reinforcing element expressed in Spanish by the repetition of the verb may be rendered in English by an adverb or an adverbial phrase such as 'not at all', 'of course', 'in point of fact', etc., or by the English emphatic form of the verb with 'do'. The force of the

construction may be heightened by the use of introductory for
mulae such as *claro (que)* or *como*, or by the insertion of a confirmatory *sí que*, or even by repeating the infinitive, as in example (v).

(i)    *¿Yo? No, señorita. Rezar, rezo, pero no pido nada a Dios*
       (R. J. Sender, 1969d: 64)
       Me? No, miss. I do indeed pray. but I don't ask God
       for anything

(ii)   *Claro que ayudar ayudaba, hasta el punto que algunos
       días igualaba el jornal del padre* (J. Izcaray, 1961: 72)
       Of course he really did help, to such an extent that some
       days he worked as long as his father

(iii)  – *Dime qué ocurre en tu casa.*
       – *Como ocurrir, no ocurre nada por ahora* (S. Lorén,
       n.d.: 305)
       'Tell me what goes on in your house.'
       'Well absolutely nothing goes on at the moment.'

(iv)   *Cenar, sí que cenó Fortunato* (S. Lorén, 1967b: 305)
       Fortunato really did dine well

(v)    *Pero saber Joaquín, lo que es saber, ése sabe muchas cosas*
       (F. Quiñones, 1979: 206)
       But Joaquín really does know a lot

Compare the following construction with nouns:

(vi)   *Pero naranjas, lo que se dice naranjas, yo no tengo naran-
       jas, Paco* (F. Umbral, 1985: 14)
       But as for *real* oranges – I haven't got any, Paco

## 1120 *Ni* + Infinitive (*¡ni hablar!*)

*¡Ni hablar!* 'Don't mention it!' (for examples, see **828**) is by far the
commonest construction of this type. *Ni* + infinitive expresses
feelings of disapproval, disappointment, indignation, etc., and is
most common in the spoken language.

## 1121 The Historic Infinitive

The infinitive, sometimes preceded by the preposition *a*, is
occasionally used instead of a preterite. Although this usage is
associated mainly with the language of classical authors, it is not
impossible to find examples in present-day Spanish.[19]

*Y por fin, romperme mis cueros y derramarme mi vino* (*Don Qui-jote*, quoted by Martínez Amador, 1961: 763)
And then he broke open my wineskins and spilled my wine

*Esa conferencia fue la última y ya con eso, a tomar el avión y regresar a Méjico* (Luna Trail, 1980: 83)
That lecture was the last one, and so with that I caught the plane back to Mexico

For a number of years,[20] the infinitive has been used in radio and television headlines where normally an inflected verb-form would be expected:

*Ya en la información internacional destacar que el Parlamento iraní ha anulado hoy el mandato parlamentario del almirante X* (*DD*, 232)
International news: the Iranian Parliament has today cancelled the parliamentary mandate given to Admiral X

## Use of the Infinitive as an Imperative

**1122** The imperative forms are often replaced, especially in colloquial language,[21] by an infinitive, sometimes reinforced by a preceding *a*.[22] It is sometimes suggested that the infinitive corresponds in this usage to the second person plural[23] (see **1124**), but this is not necessarily the case. In fact the infinitive is used in place of all imperative forms.

## 1123 Infinitive as a Second Person Singular Imperative

*Seguir* (a lady speaking to her dog, overheard by JdeB)
Come on!

*¡Tú a sujetarte los pantalones y a callar!* – *dijo Román* (C. Laforet, 1966: 29)
'Fasten your trousers and shut up!' said Román

## 1124 Infinitive as a Second Person Plural Imperative

*Oir, niñas, ¿este pueblo es Casasana?* (C. J. Cela, 1967d: 127)[24]
Hey, girls, is this village Casasana?

*Ahora, vosotros a estudiar, y esta niña a la cama* (P. Baroja,
1946–51: 656)
You're going to study now, and this girl's going to bed

## 1125 Infinitive as a Polite Imperative

*Adiós, señorita Elvira, descansar* (C. J. Cela, 1963a: 86)
Goodbye, Señorita Elvira, sleep well

*Que ustedes sigan bien, y divertirse – les gritó el hombre* (P.
Baroja, 1946–51: II, 143)
'All the best, and enjoy yourselves,' the man shouted to them

## 1126 Infinitive as a 'First Person' Imperative

*Es bien triste que en toda una vida sólo se pueda recordar un día
de vacaciones ... en una casa que no era nuestra. Y ahora a
empezar otra vez* (A. Casona, 1968: 93-4)
It's very sad when out of a whole life you can only remember
one day of your holidays ... in a house which wasn't ours.
Now I/we have to begin it all over again

*A* + infinitive clearly has the value of a first person imperative in
an example such as:

*¡A trabajar!*
(Let's go) to work!

*¡A desalambrar! ¡A desalambrar!*
*Que la tierra es nuestra, es tuya y de aquel,*
*de Pedro y María, de Juan y José* (Daniel Viglietti, Uruguayan
protest song)
Let's tear down the wires! Let's tear down the wires!
For the land belongs to us, to you, to others,
It's Pedro's and María's, Juan's and José's

## 1127 Infinitive in Negative Imperative Sentences

Here the infinitive cannot be preceded by *a*.

*¡Por Dios! No hablar de Kirkegaard – dijo la señorita Nord* (P.
Baroja, 1946–51: I, 1123)
'For goodness' sake! Don't talk about Kirkegaard,' said
Señorita Nord

*No* + infinitive is common in public notices, e.g.:

> *No apoyarse en las puertas*
> Do not lean on the doors
>
> *No sujetar las puertas* (signs in the Barcelona Metro)
> Do not force the doors
>
> *No fumar* (sign in Madrid buses)
> No smoking

**1128** The use of *sin* + infinitive with negative imperative value has been dealt with in **1114**.

### 1129 Imperative Infinitive with Clitic Pronoun(s)

Purists rule that only a third person pronoun (*se*) may be added to the infinitive with imperative value,[25] but there is greater freedom in practice.

> *Buenas noches . . . Conservarse* (*DD*, 231)
> Good night . . . Take care
>
> *Guardároslas en el bolsillo – murmuró* (J. Goytisolo, 1960: 235)
> 'Keep them in your pocket,' he murmured
> (*Guardáoslas* would be the 'correct' imperative form)[26]

See also **1130**, second example.

### 1130 Infinitive of *ir* + Gerund

> *Hale, niños – les decía – ir saliendo* (R. Sánchez Ferlosio, 1971: 239)
> 'Come on, kids,' he said to them, 'out you go'
>
> *Iros duchando – dijo a sus ayudantes* (M. Delibes, 1978b: 62)
> 'Go and take a shower', he said to his assistants

### 1131 Remarks

The imperative and the infinitive with imperative value often occur together.

> *Hay que tener calma . . . cuidaros, cuidaos, cuidaos* (I. Aldecoa, 1970: 89)
> You must keep calm . . . take care of yourselves, take care, take care

*Venir, no os separéis* (C. Martín Gaite, 1981: 61–2)
Come along, don't get separated
*Ahora, acuéstate, y desde mañana a estudiar* (M. Vargas Llosa,
1973: 246)
Go to bed now, and tomorrow start working

**1132** The subject of an infinitive used as an imperative may be
mentioned explicitly.
> *Bien. Déjales la comida a ésos y veniros tú y Cubas hacia la
> puerta* (A. M. de Lera, 1970: 186)
> Fine. Leave them the food and you and Cubas come over to
> the door

The subject may also be expressed in the *a* + infinitive construction. Here it is always placed before the verb (see **1123** and **1124**,
second example).[27]

**1133** The use of the infinitive may 'soften' the impact of the
imperative.
> *Ser formales, ¿eh? – aconsejó Bea* (J. A. de Zunzunegui,
> 1952b: 152)
> 'Let's behave ourselves, shall we?' advised Bea
> (The interrogative *¿eh?* and the verb *aconsejar* show that this
> is not a full imperative)

**1134** Note the grammatical oddity (but see in this connection
**1129**) of the following examples, where an infinitive apparently
referring to a *vosotros* form is used with a third person reflexive
pronoun:
> *Andad, niños, a levantarse* (I. Agustí, 1944: 35)
> Come along, children, get up
>
> *Zurdo les amenazaba: – Callarse, cerdos* (R. J. Sender, 1969a: 125)
> Zurdo threatened them: 'Shut up, you pigs'

**1135** Especially frequent in colloquial language is the use of the
expressions *a ver, a ver si*, which can have various meanings.[28]
> *Bueno, Carmen, a ver si mandas a la nena a las monjitas y tomas
> una criada* (J. A. de Zunzunegui, 1952a: 131)
> Well, Carmen, why don't you send the girl to school with the
> nuns and take a maid?
> (*A ver si* here has the value of a polite imperative)

*Nunca has tenido la menor consideración por mí, a ver si no* (M. Delibes, 1969a: 81)
You've never had the slightest consideration for me, have you?
(*A ver si* here stresses what has been previously said)

*¡A ver qué vida!* (I. Aldecoa, 1969: 142)
What a life!
('How hard and disagreeable life is!' is the implication here)

*A ver si nos vemos* (C. J. Cela, 1967d: 74)
Perhaps we'll see each other
(*A ver si* here suggests 'hopefully', 'if possible')

**1136** Although statistical information is lacking, we have the impression that the infinitive is being increasingly used with imperative value in modern Spanish, and that its use is gradually infiltrating the higher registers of the language.[29]

# The Gerund

## 1137 General Remarks

Use of the gerund is currently undergoing a great deal of change, and the contrast between prescriptive rule and actual usage is striking.[30] Although the gerund is traditionally said to be adverbial in nature, it is clear that it is being construed increasingly as an adjective. It remains an invariable element, however.

**1138** Like the infinitive, the gerund has a simple and a compound form, the latter being formed from the gerund of the auxiliary verb *haber* + past participle:

*cantando*                    *habiendo cantado*

The simple form generally denotes a durative process which is simultaneous with or immediately prior to the action of the main verb with which it occurs. The compound form refers to a process which has been completed before the action of the main verb.[31]

*Llegué temblando hasta el umbral de su alcoba* (R. del Valle-Inclán, 1963: 81)
I reached the threshold of her bedroom trembling

*El notario me ha dicho que habiendo habido fuerza mayor, no le obligan a nada* (P. Baroja. 1961: 148)
The lawyer has told me that due to *force majeure*, he is not obliged to do anything

## 1139 The Gerund as an Adverb with the Verb

The gerund can be used as an adverbial expression of manner, answering the question 'how?'.[32] It generally follows the verb to which it relates, although for stylistic reasons it may precede it.[33]

*¡Papá, papá! ¡Ven corriendo!* (S. Lorén, 1962: 263)
Daddy, Daddy! Come quickly! (lit. 'come running')
(*Corriendo* denotes the manner of coming; it could be replaced by an adverb such as *rápidamente*)

*Y corriendo fue Ofelia a sus escaparates* (A. Carpentier, 1976: 12)
And Ofelia ran off to her wardrobe
(In the Peninsula *escaparate* = 'shop window'. The effect of *corriendo* preceding the verb is strengthened by the introductory *y*.)

*Y matando he de morir* (C. J. Cela. 1988: 222)
And I am to die by killing

The adverbial nature of the gerund is clearly shown in the following example, where it is qualified by *tan* (with verbs, *tanto* is used):

*¿Y adónde ibas tan corriendo?* (A. M. de Lera, 1970: 18)
And where were you running off to?
(Cf. *tan rápidamente, tan de prisa*)

## 1140 The Gerund as an Adjective

Only *ardiendo* and *hirviendo* are regularly acknowledged as adjectives. They are always invariable, however.

| | |
|---|---|
| *un horno ardiendo* | a burning hot oven |
| *agua hirviendo*[34] | boiling water |

*Frente a la iglesia ardiendo rodeaba el talle de una mujer madura* (I. Agustí, 1945: 238)

Opposite the burning church he put his arms round the figure of a mature woman

*Lo que más terror producía a los negros era el agua hirviendo* (P. Baroja, 1959: 89)
What frightened the negroes most was boiling water

Note that as an adjective the gerund never precedes the noun.

**1141** Some authorities add *colgando* to the list of gerunds permitted as adjectives.

*Conchi se entendió de maravilla con el patrón del Cocodrilo al que tenían sin cuidado los moños grasientos y las horquillas colgando* (J. M. Gironella, 1966b: 241)
Conchi got on marvellously with the boss of the 'Cocodrilo', who did not mind her greasy knots of hair and her hairpins hanging out

Beinhauer (1968: 146) mentions the expression *me deja usted con las piernas colgando* as a colloquial, humorous equivalent to *me deja usted perplejo* 'you astonish me'

Increasingly common is the adjectival usage of the gerund with a noun following the existential verb *haber*:

*En una de las escaleras de la iglesia había una mujer gimiendo* (I. Agustí, 1945: 133)
On one of the church's flights of steps there was a woman wailing

*Arribó a la mantequería con el mejor ánimo. No había gente comprando* (S. Lorén, 1960: 143)
He arrived at the dairy in the best of spirits. There was no one buying

*No había niños jugando* (J. Rulfo, 1981: 14)
There were no children playing

The adjectival usage can sometimes give rise to ambiguity:

*El portero se marchaba con su nieta refunfuñando* (P. Baroja, 1946–51: II, 56)
The porter went off with his grumbling granddaughter
(As a result of the lack of punctuation, the meaning of the sentence is not clear: who is grumbling, the porter or his

granddaughter? If the latter, the construction should be ...
*con su nieta que refunfuñaba* (... *con su nieta, refunfuñando*,
with a comma, would imply that it was the porter who was
grumbling, cf. **1144**).)

Another kind of adjectival usage is to be found in legal register.

*Decreto nombrando gobernador* (*Esbozo*, 491)
A decree to appoint a governor

*Ley reformando las tarifas aduaneras* (*Esbozo*, 491)
A law to reform customs tariffs

(See also **1033**, first example.)

This usage is sometimes referred to as the *gerundio del Boletín Oficial*, the official state gazette in Spain.[35] In all the above examples,
the 'correct' form would be a relative clause: *las horquillas que
colgaban* (though note that *colgando* has been considered to have a
regular adjectival usage), *una mujer que gemía, con su nieta que
refunfuñaba, decreto que nombra, ley que reforma*, etc.

**1142** A syntactic indication of the adjectival nature of the gerund
is found in cases where the form is used in conjunction with a 'real'
adjective, adjectival past participle or adjectival phrase.

*Atravesaban la penumbra del hall riendo y apresuradas* (S.
Lorén, 1971: 189)
They hurried laughing across the half-light of the hall

*La Venus de Milo, con brazos y sabiendo taquigrafía, puede hacer
tanto por la prosperidad de una industria como la más acertada
reglamentación laboral* (E. Acevedo, 1972: 31)
A Venus de Milo, if she has arms and knows shorthand, can
do as much for the prosperity of an industry as the most successful labour laws

**1143** The dividing line between the adjectival usage of the gerund and its use with verbs of perception is a hazy one: the latter
usage is dealt with immediately below (**1145-1147**).

### 1144 The Subject of the Gerund is the Subject of the Main Clause

Here the gerund has the value of a non-restrictive relative clause, and should be placed between commas (or after a comma if at the end of the sentence).[36]

> *Benigno, suspirando, cerró la puerta* (S. Lorén, 1960: 124)
> Sighing, Benigno shut the door
> (Here, *suspirando* has the force of *que suspiraba*; it is another action carried out by Benigno, the subject, and it complements the meaning of the main verb *cerró*)

> *¿Qué le trae por aquí, requetepreciosa? – le preguntó, disimulando* (J. A. de Zunzunegui, 1954: 150)
> 'What brings you here, my beauty', he asked her, as if he did not know

## 1145 The Subject of the Gerund is the Direct Object of the Main Clause

The subject of the action expressed by the gerund may be the object of the main verb when the main verb is a verb of sensory or intellectual perception (e.g. *mirar* 'to watch', *oir* 'to hear', *ver* 'to see', *conocer* 'to know', *distinguir* 'to distinguish', *recordar* 'to remember', etc.) or a verb of description or representation (e.g. *describir* 'to describe', *dibujar* 'to draw', *pintar* 'to paint', *representar* 'to represent', etc.).[37]

> *Te conocí cogiendo margaritas en las praderas de Carolina del Sur* (C. J. Cela, 1963b: 355)
> I got to know you when you were picking daisies in the meadows of South Carolina

> *Había visto al vascofrancés bailando con la Ignacia* (P. Baroja, 1946–51: 188)
> He had seen the French Basque dancing with Ignacia

> *Docenas de fotógrafos retrataban a los cardenales entrando en el cónclave* (*MEU*, 49)
> Dozens of photographers were taking pictures of the cardinals going into the conclave

and

> *En los balcones se veían hombres fumando* (J. M. Gironella, 1966c: 58)
> On the balconies men could be seen smoking
> (*Hombres* is strictly the grammatical subject of *se veían*, but the construction is parallel to those in the three examples above)

*Al ver que llegaban tres soldados discutiendo les preguntó de qué trataban* (R. J. Sender, 1964: 259)

When he saw three soldiers coming along chatting he asked them what they were talking about

(*Tres soldados* is not strictly the object of *ver*, but this usage is no doubt modelled on *al ver a tres soldados discutiendo. . .*)

Although the purist view[38] is that in such cases the gerund must denote an action or observable change and not a quality or state of affairs (i.e. it can be paraphrased by the continuous form of the verb, cf. the first example of this paragraph *te conocí cuando estabas cogiendo maragaritas . . .*), the usage is in fact becoming more widespread:

*En verano se la había visto en el jardín llevando pantalones* (J. M. Gironella, 1966a: 246)

In summer she had been seen wearing trousers in the garden

(. . . *con pantalones* . . . would be more 'correct', but not *\*cuando estaba llevando pantalones* . . .)

*A veces se le veía en el café fumando y oliendo a éter* (P. Baroja, 1946-51: II, 975)

Sometimes they saw him in the cafe, smoking and smelling of ether

(But not *\*cuando estaba oliendo a éter*)

**1146** However, the gerund is being used increasingly in modern Spanish when neither of the conditions in **1144** or **1145** are met:

*(Clara) puso ante el hombre el plato conteniendo una fritura de pimientos y tomates* (A. M. de Lera, 1970: 109)

Clara set a plate of fried peppers and tomatoes in front of the man

. . . *que contenía* . . . would be more 'correct'

*Al chico mayor lo tienen educándose en Londres* (J. A. de Zunzunegui, 1952b: 71)

They have their eldest son being educated in London

(Other solutions would be: *El chico mayor es educado en Londres*, or *El chico mayor se educa en Londres*)

## 1147 Gerund Relating to Another Part of Speech

Furthermore, despite the prohibitions of purists,[39] the gerund can nowadays even be found with an indirect or oblique object, with a predicate noun, or with an adjectival adjunct.

> *Aquel día yo no entendía el entusiasmo de Raquel por un cuarto oliendo a sudor humano* (R. J. Sender, 1969b: 19)
> That day I did not understand Raquel's enthusiasm for a room which smelt of human sweat
> (Or: ... *un cuarto que olía a sudor humano*)

> *Y mi soberbia fue castigada por Dios, condenándome a tenerte presente, hijo mío* (C. J. Cela, 1958: 61)
> And my pride was punished by God, who condemned me to have you always in my mind, my son
> (Or: ... *que me condenó a tenerte* ...)

> *Era una mujer diferente de la que solía tener en mis brazos, siendo la misma* (R. J. Sender, 1969b: 143)
> It was a different woman from the one I used to hold in my arms, although she was the same
> (Or: ... *aunque era la misma*)

> *Se acordaba ella de los indios, del incendio en el bosque, de sí misma huyendo* (R. J. Sender, 1969a: 30)
> She remembered the Indians, the fire in the wood, herself running away
> (Or: ... *y de su propia huida*)

## 1148 Remark

Sometimes a number of gerunds, with different functions, can be used in the same sentence.

> *Estábamos en una antesala, mirando la Puerta del Sol, desierta, viendo alguno que otro corriendo pegado a las paredes* (M. Aub, 1963: 225)
> We were in an anteroom, looking at the Puerta del Sol, which was deserted. Now and then we saw someone running close up against the walls
> (The subject of *mirando* and *viendo* is *nosotros* (see **1144**); the subject of *corriendo* is *alguno que otro* (see **1145**).)

*Se estaba colocando en una posición ridícula ante sus camaradas. Primero, dejándose sorprender robando* . . . (D. Medio, 1958: 310)
He was getting into a ridiculous position with his colleagues. First, because he had allowed himself to be caught stealing . . .

(*Colocando* forms the continuous imperfect with *estar* (see **1171**); the subject of *dejándose* and *robando* is that of the main verb of the first sentence (see **1144**).)

## 1149 The Gerund in 'Absolute' Constructions

Here, by contrast with the preceding examples, the subject of the gerund is not represented by a noun in the main clause. When the subject of the gerund is expressed (whenever it is not understood or is impersonal), it follows the gerund. The absolute construction may have the value of an adverbial clause of cause, condition, manner, time, concession, purpose or contrast. These are also the meanings associated with the gerund uses in **1144** and **1145**.

CAUSE
*No habiendo firmado mi nombramiento el Presidente de la República, es anticonstitucional* (M. Aub, 1963: 11)
Since the President of the Republic has not signed my appointment, it is unconstitutional

CONDITION
*¿Si escampa nos deja ir, mamá?*
*Concha respondió: Escampando, sí* (R. del Valle-Inclán, 1963:74)
'If it clears up, can we go out, Mummy?'
Concha answered, 'Yes, if it clears up'

MANNER
*Me siguió envuelta en la sábana y castañeteándole los dientes* (C. Laforet, 1966: 130)
She followed me wrapped in the sheet and with her teeth chattering

TIME
*Necesitó esperar bastante tiempo, porque quería llegar de noche, o anocheciendo* (T. Salvador, 1966: 38)
He had to wait some time, because he wanted to arrive at night, or as it was getting dark

(Some authorities[40] claim that the gerund typically expresses duration, whereas *al* + infinitive does not. However, in modern Spanish, there are examples of *al* + infinitive expressing duration, e.g.:

> *De este modo al finalizar diciembre, el Nini divisaba desde la cueva el antiguo potro* (M. Delibes, 1968a: 57)
> So in the last days of December, Nini could make out the old shoeing-frame from the cave)

CONCESSION
*Pudiendo ser un buen amante las cosas habían sucedido de una manera mediocre* (R. J. Sender, 1969b: 20)
Although he might have been a good lover, things had gone in a mediocre way

PURPOSE
*Le escribí una larguísima carta pidiéndole explicaciones detalladas* (J. M. Gironella, cited in Coste and Redondo, 1965: 463)
I wrote him a very long letter asking him for detailed explanations

CONTRAST
Sign seen at the Rubén Darío metro station in Madrid in February 1985:

*ESTE ACCESO SE CIERRA A LAS 22 PERMANECIENDO ABIERTOS ALMAGRO Y MIGUEL ÁNGEL*
This entrance closes at 11 p.m. but Almagro and Miguel Ángel will remain open

## 1150 Remarks

The difference in meaning amongst all these adverbial nuances is not always very sharp. In the following sentence, the gerunds *viviendo*, etc., could be considered to be an answer to a question introduced by *¿Cómo?* (MANNER), but could also have the value *a condición de que* (*vivamos*, etc.) (CONDITION):

> *Todos sabemos por experiencia que podemos ser castos, viviendo vigilantes, frecuentando los sacramentos y apagando los primeros chispazos de la pasión sin dejar que tome cuerpo la hoguera* (J. M. Escrivá de Balaguer, 1965: no. 124)

All of us know through experience that we can be chaste, by living/if we live vigilantly, by receiving/if we receive the sacraments regularly and by extinguishing/if we extinguish the first sparks of passion without letting the blaze take hold

**1151** *¡Deseando!* has a half-concessive, half-contrastive use in the following sentence:

... *«para la señorita, yo no quiero nada», no vas a querer, ¡deseando! como que te crees que él no lo notaba* (M. Delibes, 1969a: 225)

...'It's for the young lady; I don't want anything'. Like hell you didn't want anything! And you thought he didn't realize

**1152** The action denoted by the gerund when in absolute usage or when referring to the subject of a main verb must be **simultaneous** with that of the main verb or be completed **shortly before** or **immediately after** it, at least in the standard language.[41] Thus the first example below is acceptable while the second is not:

*Volvió a marcharse Augusto, encontrándose al poco rato en el paseo de la Alameda* (M. de Unamuno, cited in *Esbozo*, 488)

Augusto started to walk again and found himself a little later in the Paseo de la Alameda

But:

*\*A los sesenta años (1607) emigró a América, muriendo en Méjico, en 1614* (*DD*, 208)

At the age of sixty (1607) he emigrated to America and died in Mexico in 1614

### 1153 The Gerund as an Imperative

The gerund, like the infinitive, can be used as an imperative in colloquial style. As the following examples show, this value of the gerund is especially frequent with verbs of motion (sometimes in a figurative meaning, as in the fourth example below). Exclamation marks are not usually used.

*Romualdo consultó el reloj:* – *Bueno, andando* (J. A. de Zun-zunegui, 1952a:52)
Romualdo consulted his watch. 'Right, let's go'

*Bueno, ahuecando* – *dijo el pequeño* (P. Baroja, 1946–51: II, 287)
'OK, let's beat it,' said the little one

*Saliendo, saliendo, que es la una* (heard by JdeB in Spain: a mother to her children who were swimming)
Come on, out you get, it's one o'clock

*Volviendo al día anterior* (T. Salvador, 1968b: 355)
Let's go back to the previous day

The imperative value of the gerund is clear in the following example, where it occurs with the imperative proper:

*Circulen, circulen, andando...* (R. Sánchez Ferlosio, 1971: 286)
Move along, move along there

**1154** When the gerund is used as an imperative, the confirmatory phrase *que es gerundio* is sometimes added. The usage seems to date from quite recently (see the third example below). This combination, which is found only in familiar colloquial usage, seems paradoxical, but it suggests a possible equivalence between the gerund and the imperative in the linguistic consciousness of Spanish speakers.

*Compañeros, andando que es gerundio* (M. Aub, 1971: 212)
Let's go, comrades

*Rectificando, que es gerundio* (C. J. Cela, 1979b: 239)
Put it right

*Váyase. Venga. Largo. Marchando que es gerundio. Marchando que es gerundio. Desenvoltura de los años cuarenta o cincuenta* (M. Vázquez Montalbán, 1983: 63)
Get out. Come on. Clear off. Get on. Get on. Currency of the forties or fifties

**1155** The gerund also has an imperative value with *estar*, e.g. *¡Ya te estás callando!* 'Just you shut up!'. This is a stronger form of the imperative, chiefly found in popular speech.[42]

## 1156 The Gerund as a Noun

Some gerunds function as 'permanent nouns' (as do some infinitives – see **1082**). These words have a plural, and sometimes also (when referring to people) a feminine form. They are mostly 'technical' words: *el bautizando* 'person about to be baptized', *el doctorando* 'person about to receive a doctorate', *el examinando* 'examinee', *el considerando* 'consideration (legal)', etc.[43]

> ... *las educandas:   niñas de hasta diez años* (C. J. Cela, 1979a:122)
> ... the pupil-teachers: girls up to ten years old

> ... *sus antiguos confesandos* (F. Vizcaíno Casas, 1979a: 80)
> ... those whose confession he formerly heard

## Special Constructions

## 1157 *En* + Gerund[44]

*En* is the only preposition that can be used with the gerund.

## 1158 Expressing Time

Nowadays, *en* + gerund indicates an action taking place immediately before that of the main verb[45] (= *en cuanto* 'as soon as' or *(inmediatamente) después de* 'immediately after', introducing a subordinate clause of time), though in older Spanish it could indicate simultaneity. In the modern language,[46] the construction is chiefly used in popular speech.

> *En llegando el verano, don Evaristo se ponía una chaqueta blanca* (J. M. Pemán, 1972: 129)
> When the summer came, Don Evaristo would don a white jacket

> *Plinio y don Lotario marcharon a casa, mayormente con la intención de echar una siesta en comiendo* (F. García Pavón, 1972: 103)
> Plinio and Don Lotario went off home, mainly with the intention of taking a nap after lunch

(Note that Spanish *en* + gerund is NOT the equivalent of French *en* + present participle.)

## 1159 Expressing Condition or Cause

Examples:

> *En teniendo con qué alimentarnos y con qué cubrirnos, estemos contentos* (M. Delibes, 1969a: 47)
> If we've got food and clothing, let's be content

> *Lo único que tengo es gaseosa para los jóvenes, en no queriendo vino* (R. Sánchez Ferlosio, 1971: 22)
> The only thing I've got is lemonade for the youngsters, if they don't want wine

> *(El matrimonio) es cosa de quererse. Y, en habiendo esto, todo lo demás sale sobrando* (J. Rulfo, 1981: 58)
> (Marriage) is a matter of loving each other. And, if there's love, all the rest is superfluous

## 1160 *Como* + Gerund

Purists[47] say that this has the value of *como si*:

> *Trujillo hizo un gesto como queriendo dar a entender a Encarna que la respuesta era obvia* (A. M. de Lera, 1970: 172)
> Trujillo made a face as if wanting to give Encarna to understand that the reply was obvious
> (Here *como queriendo* = *como si quisiese*)

*Como siendo* in the following sentences, where it means 'as', is regarded as a Gallicism:

> *El rey ha declarado nulas las resoluciones adoptadas por los diputados como siendo ilegales* (*GRAE*, 417)
> The king has declared null and void the resolutions adopted by the deputies, as being illegal

> *El fiscal ha rechazado los argumentos de la defensa como siendo carentes de razón* (*MEU*, 50, where this example is deemed unacceptable)
> The prosecutor has rejected the defence's arguments as being unreasonable

## 1161 Gerund + *Como* + Finite Form of the Same Verb

This usually expresses emphatically a cause:

> *Doña Carmen es incapaz de hacerme esa jugada sabiendo como sabe que estoy embrujada por ti* (J. A. de Zunzunegui, 1956a: 139)
> Doña Carmen is incapable of playing that dirty trick on me knowing as she does that I am bewitched by you

> *Una de las cosas que dijo Mungía, ignorando como ignoraba las últimas novedades trágicas fue lo siguiente*: ... (R. J. Sender, 1964: 322)
> One of the things Mungía said, ignorant as he was of the latest tragic news, was the following ...

## 1162 Repetition of the Gerund

This is another way of stressing the ongoing, durative or systematic nature of the action denoted by the gerund. *Y* may be used, as in the third example below, to link the two gerunds.

> *Y, corriendo, corriendo se trasladaron a Berlín* (J. Camba, 1964: 41)
> And on, on they went until they got to Berlin

> *Subía por una escalerita al cementerio del Padre La Chaise, y andando, andando, se encontraba ante el Panteón* (Azorín, 1964: 42)
> He went up a short flight of steps to the Père La Chaise cemetery, and after walking about a good deal, he found himself in front of the Pantheon

> *Creo que vino a parar aquí rodando y rodando sobre las palabras que querían evitar la pregunta* (G. Cabrera Infante, quoted in J. Goytisolo, 1977: 209)
> I think that he ended up here in a torrent of words which sought to avoid the question

> *Sólo rodeado por su guardia sería capaz de seguir viviendo, viviendo, viviendo eternamente* (M. Mujica Lainez, 1983: 173)
> Only when surrounded by his guard would he be capable of living, really living, living eternally

## 1163 'Sentence Gerunds'

Despite the fact that the use of several gerunds in the same sentence is discouraged by purists,[48] long groups of gerunds may be found in modern Spanish prose. In some cases, there is no finite verb, and the sentence is constructed completely of gerunds, so that one can almost speak of a 'sentence gerund'.[49]

> *Y el «¡no pasarán!» repitiéndose, saltando, quebrándose, arremolinándose y desbordándose después, como una ola cimera convertida en espuma, por encima de las cabezas y llegando hasta un cielo de nubes bajas y sombrías* (A. M. de Lera, 1970: 263)
> And the cry of *¡no pasarán!* was repeated, rising, breaking, eddying and then spilling over, like the crest of a wave turning into spray, above our heads, and reaching up into a sky of low, dark clouds

When referring to past time, this use of the gerund bears a certain similarity to the imperfect indicative;[50] both are durative in nature, and the gerund, like the imperfect, is often used in descriptions:

> *El señor Presidente de la República entró al salón. Avanzó entre los invitados, saludando afablemente, seguramente haciendo bromas, apretando ciertos brazos, evitando otros, dando la mano efusivamente a unos, fríamente a otros, reconociendo a éste, ignorando a aquél, iluminado por la luz pareja y cortante de los reflectores, despojado intermitentemente de sombra por los flashes fotográficos. Reconociendo, ignorando* (C. Fuentes, 1979: 59)
> The President of the Republic came into the room. He moved forward among the guests, giving friendly greetings, making self-confident jokes, gripping some arms and avoiding others, shaking some effusively by the hand, others coolly, recognizing one person and not another, lit by the sharp, uniform light of the spotlights and stripped of shadow from time to time by the flashguns. Sometimes acknowledging, sometimes unseeing

## 1164 The Gerund with Diminutive Suffixes

Diminutive suffixes are sometimes added to the gerund – even when it has the value of an imperative.

*Delante de Santiago, con la cruz, silbandillo* (C. J. Cela, 1967a: 65)
Santiago went in front with the cross, gently whistling

*Hizo Pacheco un lío con estas prendas y dijo:*
*– Andandito; primero iré yo* (P. Baroja, 1946–51:I, 757)
Pacheco made these clothes into a bundle and said, 'Let's go carefully; I'll go first'

## 1165 Position of the Gerund with respect to its Subject

The 'rule' is that the gerund should stand as close as possible to its subject, whether this is the subject or the object of the main verb,[51] thereby preventing the ambiguity of reference that might otherwise result, e.g.:

*Vi ayer a Juana paseando por el jardín*
Yesterday I saw Juana walking in the garden
(*Juana*, the object of *vi*. stands immediately next to *paseando*, of which it is the subject. The sentence cannot therefore be read as 'Yesterday I saw Juana as I was walking in the garden')

**1166** In practice this rule is not observed. When additionally punctuation is defective or completely lacking, inelegant and obscure sentences result:

*Prosista es aquel a quien se le ocurren las cosas escribiendo* (F. Umbral, 1977: 143)
A prose writer is a person to whom things occur as he is writing
(*Prosista*, the subject of *escribiendo*, could not be further away from it! The gerund could be avoided by using *mientras escribe*)

*Manuel podía estar después de comer algún día charlando* (P. Baroja, 1946–51: I, 568)
Manuel might stay chatting one day after eating
(Better: *Después de comer, Manuel podía estar charlando algún día*)

*Era un plan madurado durante muchas noches calurosas, sentado en el cenador del jardín, a oscuras, para evitar los mosquitos y fumando* (S. Lorén, 1962: 137)

It was a plan which had been brought to maturity over many hot nights, sitting in the summerhouse in the garden smoking, in the dark to avoid the mosquitoes
(The subject of *fumando* (*yo*) is not even present in this sentence)

Sometimes, however, the separation of gerund and subject can be turned to stylistic advantage:

*Fue la época más feliz de la vida de Agustín. Pilar le cuidaba como a un hijo, y él se dejaba querer queriendo* (M. Aub, 1971: 196)
It was the happiest period of Agustín's life. Pilar looked after him like a child, and he allowed himself to be loved whilst himself loving
(The author produces a neat stylistic effect: Agustín is simultaneously the object of *querer* and the subject of *queriendo*)

## 1167 The Gerund in Elliptical Constructions

The gerund is often used without a finite verb in a commentary on a painting or photograph, in titles of stories, in descriptions, etc. The usage presents an action in progress or makes a situation realistic.[52]

*Aníbal pasando los Alpes* (*Esbozo*, 490)
Hannibal crossing the Alps

*La actriz X recibiendo los aplausos del público* (*Esbozo*, 490)
The actress X receiving the audience's applause

*Máscaras bailando* (title of a picture by Goya in the Prado Museum, Madrid)
Dancing masks

**1168** The omission of *estar* is common in a conversational exchange:[53]

| TRINI | – *¿Y Carmina?* |
|---|---|
| GENEROSA | – *Aviando la casa* (A. Buero Vallejo, 1966: 13) |
| TRINI | Where's Carmina? |
| GENEROSA | Getting the house ready |

*¿Qué diría Clara si viese cómo está la casa?. . . Su casa. ¡Tantos años pagándola!* (M. Aub, 1963: 15)
'What would Clara say if she could see what a state the house was in?' 'Her house. That she's been paying for for so many years!'
(*Pagándola = la había estado pagándo*)

**1169** Ellipsis of *estar* can also be imagined in constructions with an affective meaning which are introduced by *y* or *conque*. Such sentences often have an emphatic or ironical meaning.

*El tenientajo ese tiene su cuarto abarrotado de víveres. Y mis chavales pasando hambre* (A. M. de Lera, 1970: 152)
That bloody lieutenant has got his room stuffed full of provisions. And my lads feel hungry

*Conque espiándonos, ¿eh?* (J. Goytisolo, 1960: 225)
Well, well, spying on us, are you?

**1170** In some Latin-American countries the gerund is used with the verbs *hacer* and *decir*, with the meanings, respectively, of 'why?' and 'how?':

*¿Qué haciendo viniste?* (= *¿Por qué viniste?*)
Why have you come?

*¿Qué haciendo se cayó el niño?* (= *¿Cómo se cayó el niño?*)
How did the child fall?

*¿Qué diciendo?* (= *¿Qué razón hay para ello?*)
Why?
(All examples from Kany, 1951: 239.)

## 1171 The Gerund in Verbal Phrases

The gerund is used with the verbs *andar, continuar, estar, ir, llevar, seguir*, etc. The durative nature of the action is emphasized, though each auxiliary has its own special meaning.

*Estar* + Gerund

This is often referred to as the 'progressive' or 'continuous' form of the verb, and indicates that an action is in progress. Durative aspect is particularly stressed here, and may be made explicit by an adverb (as in the second example).[54]

*Jorge Fiestas, viejo amigo, me cuenta que Sara Montiel está teniendo un gran éxito en Barcelona* (F. Umbral, *Noche de famosos*, in *Heraldo de Aragón*, 12 May 74: 28)
Jorge Fiestas, an old friend, tells me that Sara Montiel is having great success in Barcelona
(Use of *estar* + gerund makes reference to the present moment clear, implying *actualmente*)

*Y un día y otro había estado temiendo, durante cuarenta años seguidos, que apareciera un día un enviado de Firouz* (I. Agustí, 1957: 369)
And day after day, for forty years, he had been afraid that someone sent by Firouz would come

*La cena estaba concluyendo y se notaba, por fin, tranquilo* (I. Agustí, 1945: 105)
Dinner was coming to an end and at last he felt calm
(See also **1208** on *estar siendo* past participle)

*Hasta pasado un tiempo no sabemos que estamos habitando nuestro propio cadáver* (F. Aguirre, 1972: 46)
Until a time has gone by we do not know that we are inhabiting our own corpses

In some areas of Latin America, *estar* + gerund is used as the equivalent of the simple present form: *estás pudiendo* = *puedes*, *estar teniendo* = *tener*, etc. Sometimes it has the meaning of 'to begin to . . .', or implies *aún, todavía* (*estoy teniendo* = *todavía tengo* 'I still have').[55]

*Andar* + Gerund

generally carries the idea of motion, though often without precise direction, and lays emphasis on the repeated nature of the action.

*A las chicas les es más cómodo escupir que andarse lavando* (C. J. Cela, 1969: 23)
It is easier for the girls to spit than to be washing all the time

*Luego no andes viniendo, que Luisa se va a acostar - intervino Pura* (C. Martín Gaite, 1980: 27)
'So stay away, because Luisa is going to bed,' interposed Pura

*Ir* + Gerund

is chiefly used to indicate a gradual action and may stress the slowness of an action or process.[56] The progressive nature of the event may be intensified by the use of an adverb or by the repetition of either the gerund or the whole verbal phrase.

> *En la lejanía, el mar iba siendo de un azul profundo* (R. J. Sender, 1969a: 137)
> In the distance, the sea gradually became deep blue

> *Su número va aumentando progresivamente* (M. Delibes, 1948: 154)
> Their number steadily increased

> *El indiano se iba apagando, apagando* (J. A. de Zunzunegui, 1959b: 203)
> The *indiano* (see **265**) was gradually fading away

> *El hombre del hongo y del guardapolvo va subiendo, va subiendo* (E. Jardiel Poncela, 1969: IV, 633)
> The man in the bowler hat and overalls climbs higher and higher

Sometimes *ir* + gerund indicates that an action is nearing its end, as in *voy terminando* (= *estoy a punto de terminar*).[57] It may also have an imperative value, as in *vete cerrando las puertas* 'shut the doors', *id comiendo* 'eat up', etc.[58]

The combination *ir* + *yendo*, though criticized,[59] is sometimes found in Spanish writers, and is more widely used in Latin America.[60]

> *Oiga, ¿nos vamos yendo? Es ya muy tarde* (C. J. Cela, 1963b: 27)
> Look here, shall we be going? It's very late

> – *¿Nos vamos?*
> – *Sí, lo mejor será que nos vayamos yendo* (C. J. Cela, 1991a: 145)
> 'Shall we go?'
> 'Yes, it'll be best if we get going'

*Ir* + gerund can be used in combination with *ir a* + infinitive:

> *No se lo voy a ir diciendo a todo el barco* (I. Aldecoa, 1969: 131)
> I'm not going to go telling all the ship

*Venir* + Gerund

This often corresponds to the English perfect progressive and indicates an action taking place up to the moment of speech or a moment in the past:[61]

> *Eso lo vengo oyendo desde hace cuarenta años* (J. M. Carrascal, 1973: 95)
> I've been hearing that for forty years

(*Ir* + gerund, by contrast, indicates that the action still continues.)

*Llevar* + Gerund

This is similar to *venir* + gerund, but lays stress on the continuity of the action:

> *Llevo casi cuarenta años predicando* (*Conversaciones con Monseñor Escrivá de Balaguer*, 1968: 135)
> I have been preaching (constantly) for forty years

> In the Café Novelty in the Plaza Mayor in Salamanca, there is a metal plaque by the entrance which reads:

> *ESTE ESTABLECIMIENTO LLEVA ATENDIENDO AL PÚBLICO DESDE 1905* (seen in August 1984)
> This establishment has been serving the public since 1905

*Seguir* (or *continuar*) + Gerund

This indicates that an action is still in progress.

> *Siguen dando nombres a todas las entradas y salidas del lago* (P. Baroja, 1960: 153)
> They carry on giving names to all the entrances and exits of the lake

> *Muchas iglesias continuaban ardiendo* (F. Franco Salgado-Araujo, 1977: 135)
> Many churches continued to burn

## 1172 Remarks

Enclitic pronouns can be placed after the gerund or before the auxiliary verb:

> *Estaba mirándola* or *La estaba mirando* (DUE, I, 1393)
> He was looking at her
> (See also **269**)

**1173** Two gerunds together. though grammatically possible. are usually considered stylistically infelicitous, and the following example is therefore not to be imitated:

> *En 1955, estando terminando la carrera de Derecho en Madrid, hube de presentarme a esos exámenes* (F. Arrabal. 1972a: 145)
> In 1955, as I was finishing my law course in Madrid, I had to take those exams

### 1174 Final Remark

The gerund is used increasingly in modern Spanish. This can sometimes give rise to ambiguity and even incomprehensibility, as the following example shows:

> . . . *la expulsión de Diarte fue por dar este jugador un codazo a Ribera en la nariz, produciéndose esta agresión a mis espaldas consultando con el juez de línea explicándome dicha incidencia* (*Heraldo de Aragón*, sports supplement, 30 September 1975)
> Diarte's explusion was due to this player's elbowing Ribera on the nose; this act of aggression happened behind my back while I was consulting with the linesman, who described the incident to me

It is perhaps the most delicate problem of grammar for Spanish speakers, and many writers comment on it, even though their own usage is not immune. Francisco Umbral (1977: 210) denounces the 'incorrect' use of the gerund by Pío Baroja, though, as we have seen (**1166**) his own usage is not flawless.

## The Past Participle

### 1175 Terminology, Forms, Double Meaning of some Past Participles

Irregular forms of the past participle are given in **951**.

**1176** Some verbs have two past participles: one regular and the other irregular. In such cases, the irregular forms are used exclusively as adjectives and do not combine with the auxiliary *haber* to form the Perfect. The commonest of these are:

| Verb | Past Participle | Adjective |
|------|----------------|-----------|
| *absorber*<br>to absorb | *absorbido* | *absorto* |

> *La esponja ha absorbido el agua*
> The sponge has absorbed the water

> *Quedó absorta en su libro*
> She was absorbed in her book

| *bendecir*<br>to bless | *bendecido* | *bendito* |
|------|----------------|-----------|
| *confundir*<br>to confuse | *confundido* | *confuso* |

> *Hemos confundido las dos formas*
> We have confused the two forms

> *Es una historia muy confusa*
> It is a very confused story

| *corregir*<br>to correct | *corregido*<br>corrected | *correcto*<br>correct |
|------|----------------|-----------|
| *despertar*<br>to awaken | *despertado*<br>awakened | *despierto*<br>awake; intelligent, bright |
| *hartar*<br>to satisfy | *hartado*<br>satisfied | *harto*<br>fed up |

> *Se ha hartado en poco tiempo*
> He satisfied his hunger in a short time

> *Estoy harto*
> I'm fed up

| *juntar*<br>to join | *juntado*<br>joined | *junto*<br>together |
|------|----------------|-----------|

> *Han juntado las manos*
> They have joined hands

> *Fuimos juntos a París*
> We went to Paris together

| *maldecir*<br>to damn | *maldecido*<br>damned | *maldito*<br>damned, accursed |
|------|----------------|-----------|

| *nacer* | *nacido* | *nato* |
|---------|----------|--------|
| to be born | born | born |

*Tú has nacido en la ciudad*
You were born in the town

*Era un criminal nato*
He was a hardened criminal

| *presumir* | *presumido* | *presunto* |
|------------|-------------|------------|
| to presume | | presumed |

*Presumido* as an adjective has the meaning 'presumptuous'

*Todos hemos presumido que es inocente*
We have all presumed that he is innocent

*Es muy presumido*
He's a show-off

*El presunto autor del crimen*
The presumed author of the crime

| *soltar* | *soltado* | *suelto* |
|----------|-----------|----------|
| to release | released | loose, separate |

*Han soltado el ancla*
They have dropped anchor

*Estos libros se venden sueltos*
These books are sold separately

**1177** The past participle of a transitive verb is characteristically passive in meaning.[62] However, several past participles have both a passive and an active value: *aburrido*, for instance, can mean either 'bored' (passive) or 'boring' (active):

*¡Qué historia más aburrida!*
What a boring story!

*Estaba muy aburrido*
He was very bored

**1178** Such past participles are:

| *aburrido* | bored | boring |
|------------|-------|--------|
| *agradecido* | thanked | thankful, grateful |

| | | |
|---|---|---|
| *almorzado* | having had for lunch | having lunched |
| *bebido* | having been drunk | drunk, inebriated |
| *callado* | kept quiet, concealed | quiet, taciturn |
| *cansado* | tired | tiring, tiresome |
| *cenado* | having had for dinner | having had dinner |
| *comido* | having been eaten | having eaten |
| *confiado* | trusted | trusting |
| *considerado* | considered | considerate |
| *desayunado* | having had for breakfast | having had breakfast |
| *desconfiado* | distrusted | distrustful |
| *descreído* | not believed | not believing |
| *desesperado* | despaired of | in despair, desperate |
| *divertido* | entertained | entertaining |
| *entendido* | understood | knowledgeable |
| *fingido* | feigned | dissimulating |
| *(bien) hablado* | spoken (well) | well spoken |
| *leído* | read | having read a lot |
| *mirado* | looked at | careful |
| *necesitado* | needed | needy |
| *osado* | dared | daring |
| *(mal) pensado* | (badly) thought of | suspicious |
| *pesado* | weighed | heavy, tedious |
| *resuelto* | resolved | having resolved |
| *sabido* | known | knowing |
| *sentido* | (deeply) felt | sensitive |
| *sufrido* | suffered | (long-)suffering |

*Todos venían recién comidos, eufóricos, liberados de sus oficinas, ministerios, empleos* (F. Umbral, 1973b: 24)
They all came recently fed and euphoric, freed from their offices, ministries and jobs

*Comer con gente importante es lo más cansado de este mundo* (C. Martín Gaite, 1980: 169)
Eating with important people is the most tiring thing in this world

*El boticario era muy bien hablado y un hombre, según lenguas, leído* (C. J. Cela, 1971: 19)
The apothecary was very well spoken and, according to the gossip, a well-read man

*Eran las tres de la tarde y su hijo no volvería sino ya cenado* (M. Aub, 1971: 11)
It was three o'clock in the afternoon and her son would not return without having dined

*Tú que eres un sabido* (M. Vargas Llosa, 1973: 213)
You who are a learned person

*La Marujita era muy mirada y correcta de expresión* (C. J. Cela, 1979b: 178)
Marujita was very cautious and proper in what she said

When used as adjectives, past participles agree in number and gender with the nouns to which they refer, and may, like adjectives, be used as nouns (as in the penultimate example above).

## 1179 The Past Participle in Absolute Usage

The past participle *has* may have the function of an adverbial clause and have a different subject from that of the main verb. This is known as the 'absolute' usage. The subject generally follows the participle, except in the four following cases:

(1)   In short set phrases and *refranes* (proverbs) (although there is a preference for the subject following, especially when it is a pronoun.[63]

   *esto admitido* or *admitido esto*
   admittedly

   *esto dicho* or *dicho esto*
   this being said

   *esto hecho* or *hecho esto*
   thereupon

*esto sentado* or *sentado esto*
having established this

*comida hecha, compañía deshecha*
When the meal is over, the company is parted

(2) When the subject is a personal pronoun.

*Después de yo muerto or después de muerto yo* (*Esbozo*, 498)
After I am dead ...

(3) When the past participle has a modal value (see **1183**).

(4) When the past participle has an impersonal subject.

*A Burgos llegaron ya anochecido* (J. M. Gironella, 1966c: 613)
They reached Burgos when it was already dark

**1180** The absolute past participle construction precedes the main clause, except when it has a modal meaning, when it may alternatively follow the main clause (see **1183**).[64]

**1181** The absolute past participle construction is generally rendered in English by an adverbial clause. It has various kinds of meaning. The past participle agrees in number and gender with the noun to which it relates.

## 1182 Time

The past participle denotes an action or state of affairs which is prior to that of the main verb. It can be reinforced by an adverb, an adverbial expression or a preposition (e.g. *después de, luego de, hasta, al año de, recién, ya,* etc.).

(i) *Pasada la luna de miel, Martín volvió a las andadas* (P. Baroja, 1946–51: I, 244)
After the honeymoon, Martín returned to his old ways

(ii) *Después de muerto su padre, ganada la beca del Ayuntamiento, empezó a asistir al Instituto* (J. A. de Zunzunegui, 1956a: 29)
When he won the Council scholarship after his father died, he began to attend the Instituto

(iii)  *Al año de comenzada la lucha, tuvo la desgracia de ser alcanzado por la metralla en la parte baja del cuerpo* (J. Goytisolo, 1960: 237)
A year after the fight began, he had the misfortune to be hit by shrapnel in the lower part of his body

(iv)  *Cuando deja de llover antes de la noche, las tardes, recién puesto el sol, se quedan melancólicas y despejadas* (C. Martín Gaite, 1968: 74)
When it stops raining before it is dark, the evenings become melancholy and brighter just after the sun has set

(v)  *Terminada la misa, un fraile subió al púlpito, y predicó ante los tercios vizcaínos que acabados de llegar, daban por primera vez escolta al Rey* (R. del Valle-Inclán, 1963: 91)
When the mass had ended, a brother went up into the pulpit and preached to the Biscayan regiments who, newly arrived, were escorting the King for the first time

The similarity of the preposition + past participle and the preposition + infinitive constructions may be seen from the following example (see also **1098**):

(vi)  *Salí a la calle después de comer unas costillas asadas y bebido un buen trago de vino* (J. L. Castillo Puche, 1956: 85)
I went out into the street after eating roast cutlets and drinking a fair amount of wine

## 1183 Manner

Here the absolute past participle construction may follow the main clause.

*En esta gruta se veían figuras de ninfas, hechas de piedra, los cabellos esparcidos sobre la espalda* (J. Valera, quoted in *Esbozo*, 498)
In this cave there could be seen figures of stone nymphs with their hair spread over their backs

*Carmen Elgazu, enrojecidos los ojos y con un rosario colgándole de las manos, presenció incluso cómo los albañiles se apoderaban de aquel cuerpo* (J. M. Gironella, 1966b: 139)

Carmen Elgazu, her eyes red and a rosary hanging from her hands, even witnessed the masons taking charge of that body

## 1184 Concession

*La obra, si bien retocadas algunas escenas, podría representarse con éxito* (*Esbozo*, 498)
The work could be put on successfully, even with a few scenes revised

## 1185 Condition

As is shown by the *hubieras* form in the main clause, the past participle construction has the value of a conditional clause introduced by *si* in the following sentence:

*Además, casada conmigo, no hubieras sabido apreciar las pequeñas condiciones espirituales que tengo* (P. Baroja, 1946–51: I, 1333)
Besides, if you had been married to me, you would not have been able to appreciate the little spiritual characteristics I have

## 1186 Cause

The past participle construction is the equivalent of a causal clause in:

*El pánico es terrible. Despertados bruscamente, nadie se da cuenta de lo que pasa* (P. Baroja, 1946–51: II, 180)
The panic is terrible. Rudely awakened, no one realizes what is happening

## 1187 Place

*¿El local?. . . Eso está pasados los cuarteles de Artillería, un barrio extremo* (J. M. Gironella, 1966a: 115)
Where is it? Past the artillery barracks, in an outlying district

**1188** See also the construction past participle + *que* + finite verb, described in **1209**.

The Past Participle with *haber*

## 1189 Agreement

The past participle is invariable with the auxiliary *haber* in modern Spanish.

> *Hemos cogido flores/Las flores que hemos cogido*
> We have picked flowers/The flowers we have picked

> *La Miguela se había sentado en el extremo de un estupendo diván*
> (S. Lorén, 1955: 274)
> Miguela had sat down at the end of a splendid divan
> (*Se había sentado* is a pluperfect)

**1190** However, when *haber* is used in its impersonal form (*hay*, *había*, etc.) and is therefore not an auxiliary, the past participle functions as an adjective, and agrees with the noun to which it relates:

> *No hay escrita una vida popular de este caudillo* (P. Baroja, 1946-51: V, 1133)
> There is no popular biography written about this leader

> *En los balcones hay colgadas muchas jaulas rústicas con pájaros* (J. Gutiérrez Solana, 1972: 87)
> On the balconies hang many rustic cages with birds in them

> *Es en la vesícula – decía una guapa señora, hablando con otras dos que había sentadas en aquella salita* (S. Lorén, 1955: 273)
> 'It's in the gall-bladder,' said one fine lady, speaking to two others who were sitting (lit. who there were sitting) in the small room
> (*Había* is the impersonal imperfect)

**1191** In compound forms of the impersonal *haber*, the past participle *habido* is of course invariable:

> *Había habido ya la guerra larga* (F. Díaz-Plaja, 1973: 518)
> There had already been the long war

## 1192 Splitting of *haber* and the Past Participle

As a rule, no other element is placed between the auxiliary and the past participle: contrast English *He has unfortunately left* with

Spanish *Desafortunadamente se ha marchado* (not *\*Se ha desafortunadamente marchado*).

**1193** In practice, the rule is sometimes broken, most commonly when the intervening element is a subject pronoun or a short adverb (although purists[65] insist that adverbs should not intervene):

> *Hubiera usted vivido mejor* (P. Baroja, 1946–51: VII, 889)
> You would have had a better life

> *Rosita había ya observado que ...* (J. M. Gironella, 1966c: 324)
> Rosita had already observed that ...

In the written language, other elements sometimes intervene, but the result is clumsy and not to be imitated.

> *Le habrá a usted contado la historia de la hermosa maestra* (J. A. de Zunzunegui, 1956b: 235)
> He must have told you the story of the beautiful schoolmistress

> *Había Fischer también pedido algún dinero prestado a Carvajal* (P. Baroja, 1946–51: VIII, 568)
> Fischer had also asked to borrow some money from Carvajal

> *No he – retiré las manos – hablado nada* (J. García Hortelano, 1979: 20)
> 'I haven't,' and I withdrew my hands, 'said anything'

## 1194 Repetition of *haber*

The auxiliary need not be repeated when two or more past participles immediately follow one another or when they are joined by a conjunction.

> *Nos hemos sonreído, abrazado, hablado* (T. Salvador, 1968a: 131)
> We have smiled, embraced and spoken

> *No era alta la ventana, pero pudo haberse matado o quebrado una pierna* (R. J. Sender, 1964: 320)
> The window was not high, but he could have killed himself or broken a leg

> *Casi todos sus hermanos se habían casado o partido* (I. Allende, 1984: 75)
> Almost all his brothers and sisters had married or left

Otherwise, the auxiliary should be repeated. Although this rule is not always observed in Spanish writing, a sentence like the following is inelegant and even unclear, and therefore is not to be imitated:

> *Había sido en España, en el segundo período constitucional, teniente de Caballería, y vivido siempre del juego y de otras trampas* (P. Baroja, 1946–51: VI, 146)
> During the second constitutional period he had been a cavalry lieutenant in Spain, and had always lived on gambling and other rackets

## 1195 Participle and Clitic (Unstressed) Pronoun

The clitic (unstressed) pronoun is never as a rule attached to the past participle in modern Peninsular Spanish.[66] However, in the following sentence, this rule is broken, presumably as a consequence of there being no auxiliary verb repeated with the second past participle, which is coordinate with the first:

> *En el tiempo que no le viera había crecido y héchose más hombre* (J. A. de Zunzunegui, 1956a: 68)
> During the time she had not seen him, he had grown and become more of a man
> (Note that *viera* functions as a pluperfect here (see **1015**).)

### Ser as an Auxiliary

**1196** *Ser* is not used to form the perfect and other compound tenses in modern Spanish, although occasionally relics of the older usage of *ser* as the perfect auxiliary of intransitive and reflexive verbs can be found:

> *Era llegado el momento* (M. Delibes, 1969b: 154)
> The moment had arrived

> *Son nacidos en Méjico* (R. Sánchez Ferlosio, 1971: 301)
> They were born in Mexico

Note that in such cases the past participle agrees with the subject in number and gender.

## (Semi-)Auxiliary[67] + Past Participle

**1197** The past participle may be used with *llevar, tener, estar, traer, quedar* and *dejar.* In contrast to the usage with *haber*, the past participle agrees in each case with the noun to which it relates: with *estar* and *quedar* it agrees with the subject of the verb, and with *dejar, llevar, tener* and *traer* with the direct object.

### 1198 *Tener*

*Tener* is increasingly commonly used in present-day Spanish with the past participles of transitive verbs.[68] It has a range of meanings.

### 1199 The Result of an Action

Whereas *haber* + past participle denotes an action in itself, *tener* + past participle stresses the completion of the action or the material or tangible result of an action. It is sometimes reinforced by the adverb *ya.*

> *Tu madre te tiene preparada una cena de todo tu gusto. Hay calamares rellenos* (W. Fernández Flórez, 1967: 114)
> Your mother has got you a supper ready with all the things you like. There's stuffed squid

> *Era una Orden de clausura para ingresar en la cual hacía muchos años que estaba reuniendo una dote y ya la tenía ahorrada* (C. Laforet, 1966: 101)
> It was a closed Order, and to enter it she had been getting a dowry together for many years; now she had it saved up

### 1200 Time

*Tener* + past participle may carry the implication 'for a long time now', and often must be translated by an adverb which indicates this. Sometimes it implies a notion of frequency.

> *Querido, ¿cuándo vas a comprarme la cajita de música que me tienes prometida?* (M. Delibes, 1969b: 155)
> Darling, when are you going to buy me that little musical box you've promised me for so long/you've always been promising me?

*El carbón era una cosa que teníamos olvidada* (F. Umbral, 1976a: 187)
Coal was a thing we had long forgotten

*Éramos ya una pareja veterana. Nos teníamos muy vistos* (M. Vázquez Montalbán, 1979b: 108)
We were a seasoned couple. We had seen a lot of one another (also: 'we'd had enough of each other')
(The author has commented to JdeB that the sentence carries the implications of *conocíamos todos los trucos* 'we knew all the tricks', *exceso de rutina* 'too much routine', *cansancio vital* 'being tired of such a life', but that it does not carry any aggressive overtone)

## 1201 Intensifying Meaning

This must usually be rendered in English by an adverb.

*¿No te tengo dicho que no quiero que afeites?* (S. Lorén, 1960: 32)
Haven't I expressly told you that I don't want you to shave?
(This also has the implication that the action is repeated: 'Haven't I told you repeatedly . . .')

*Se lo tienen merecido* (J. M. Gironella, 1966b: 121)
They've more than deserved it

*¡Qué callado se lo tenían ustedes!* (C. J. Cela, 1969: 335)
You've certainly kept that quiet!
(Note also the intensifying use of the reflexive *se*)

**1202** *Tener* + past participle may be passive in nature:

*Su compañera tenía prohibido pintarse* (J. M. Gironella, 1966a: 335)
His girlfriend wasn't allowed to use make-up

*Mi hija tiene terminantemente prohibido hacer amistades que no le corresponden* (S. Lorén, 1960: 259)
My daughter is strictly forbidden to have friends who are not of her class

Although it can also be used actively:

*Paulette tiene prohibido a Georges que lleve a Maurice a casa* (J. García Hortelano, 1982: 37)
Paulette has forbidden Georges to bring Maurice home

**1203** *Tener* as a (semi-)auxiliary may lose its literal meaning of 'have, possess' completely: cf. combinations like the following:

*La absolución de Hans Küng la tengo tan perdida como la de Wojtyla* (F. Umbral in *Heraldo de Aragón*, 30 December 1979: 32)
I have lost Hans Küng's absolution just as much as that of (Pope) Wojtyla

*Al parecer ese prelado era pariente lejano de ella y la tenía abandonada* (R. J. Sender, 1969c: 230)
It appeared that this prelate was a distant relation of hers and that he had abandoned her to her fate

## 1204 *Tener* and *haber*

The increasing frequency of *tener* + past participle raises the question of whether *tener* is in the process of replacing *haber* as the perfect auxiliary in modern Spanish. Certainly the process is very far advanced in the spoken language in Asturias and Galicia.[69] In the following examples, the distinctive meanings of *tener* + past participle described in **1198–1203** are only weakly present if at all, and *haber* could be used instead of *tener* without undue loss. This is especially clear in the second example, where the past participle is invariable, and in the third, where the construction is used with an intransitive verb.

*Su marido tengo entendido le dejó una tienda en San Francisco* (J. A. de Zunzunegui, 1952a: 25)
Her husband, so I understand, left her a shop in the Calle San Francisco

*Tengo visto en esta guerra muchos heridos* (R. del Valle-Inclán, 1963: 138)
I have seen many wounded in this war
(It should be remembered that the author was from Galicia)

*Yo tengo jugado muchas veces con una hermanica de ella* (R. J. Sender, 1965–6: II, 180)
I've played many times with a little sister of hers

*Manolo, ¿tienes esto cobrao?* (heard by JdeB in the Cafetería «Las Torres», Salamanca, in February, 1981)
Manolo, have they paid you?

## 1205 Separation of *tener* and the Past Participle

*Tener* is more regularly separable from the past participle than is *haber*:

> *Enviaron el telegrama a Trebujena (donde yo había dicho que teníamos hospedaje reservado)* (R. J. Sender, 1969d: 165)
> They sent the telegram to Trebujena (where I had said that we had accommodation reserved)

> *El comercio de segundo orden de la calle tenía en su casi totalidad apagadas las luces* (L. Martín-Santos, 1972: 61)
> Almost all the second-rate businesses in the street had their lights out

## 1206 Other (Semi-)Auxiliaries

Examples of other (semi-)auxiliaries used with past participles:

*llevar* + Past Participle

> *Él piensa que nos lleva engañados y va a salirle cara la equivocación* (R. J. Sender, 1964: 118)
> He thinks that he's got us fooled and his mistake is going to cost him dear
> (*Llevar* + past participle usually indicates that an action or state of affairs has already lasted for a time and cannot be considered as definitively ended:[70] i.e., that it can still have an effect in the future)

*Estar* + Past Participle

(See also **1240**.)

> *La madre la mira de arriba abajo.*
> *– ¿Dónde has estado metida?* (C. J. Cela, 1963a: 219)
> The mother looked at her from top to toe.
> 'Where did you get to?'

*Dejar* + Past Participle

> *Azaña había dejado dicho que no quería que lo moviesen de donde cayera* (F. Umbral, 1987: 88)
> Azaña had made it clear that he did not want to be moved from where he had fallen

*Traer* + Past Participle

> *Sacó del bolsillo de la famosa chaqueta unas fichas de cartulina blanca en que traía apuntadas las ideas maestras* (L. Carandell. 1970: 140)
> Out of the pocket of the famous jacket he pulled out some white record cards on which he had the key ideas jotted down

## 1207 The Place of the Past Participle

The past participle follows the auxiliary or semi-auxiliary, except when a special stylistic effect is required, as in the following example:

> *Pregonada fue a tambor y trompeta la guerra contra el rey de España* (R. J. Sender, 1964: 357)
> The war against the king of Spain was proclaimed with trumpet and drum

## 1208 *Estar* + *siendo* + Past Participle

This construction, which lays stress on the durative nature of the action, is frequent in modern Spanish, especially in Latin America, although it is criticized by purists.[71] *Estar* is sometimes substituted by a verb of motion such as *ir* or *venir* (see also **1255**).

(i) *El hecho está siendo comentadísimo* (E. Jardiel Poncela, 1969: IV, 417)
The fact is being greatly commented upon
(See **1230** on the use of affective suffixes)

(ii) *Aquella cruda alma de la ciudad iba siendo comprendida por Lorenzo* (R. Gómez de la Serna, 1959: 54)
That raw soul of the city was gradually being understood by Lorenzo

    (iii)   *Todos sus movimientos estarán siendo vigilados* (E. Parra, 1981: 140)
         A watch is being kept on all your movements

    (iv)   *El carácter arrebatado y fantástico del vasco depende, en parte, de pertenecer a un pueblo que va siendo absorbido* (P. Baroja, 1946–51: VI, 133)
         The impetuous and whimsical nature of the Basque depends in part on his belonging to a people who are steadily being absorbed

The (semi-)auxiliary may also be in a compound tense, although the result is stylistically even more cumbersome:

    (v)   *Los modelos que les habían venido siendo propuestos, no les ofrecían más alternativa que la de aburrirse o pecar* (C. Martín Gaite, 1972: 22)
         The models which had kept being proposed to them offered no other alternative than that of boredom or sin

See **1242** on *estar* + *siendo* + adjective.

## 1209 Past Participle + *que* + (Semi-)Auxiliary

This construction appears sporadically in the written language, and is equivalent to an adverbial clause of time introduced by *después que*, *en seguida que*, *en cuanto* or *luego que*.

*Leído que hubo la carta*
When he had read the letter

*Concluída que tuvo la obra*
When he had finished the work

*Encarcelados que estén los presos*
As soon as the convicts are in prison
(The subjunctive is used here as it would be in a temporal clause referring to the future)

*Apartados que fueron los combatientes*
When the combatants had been separated

*Herido que se vio*
When he saw that he was wounded

(All examples from *GRAE*, 427)

The past participle agrees in accordance with the rules for agreement in full clauses (cf. *los combatientes fueron apartados* as an equivalent to the fourth example above).

**1210** When this construction is used in modern Spanish, it has an archaic, ironical or pedantic overtone:

> *Y allí reside cierto vecino que, llegados que seamos, yo procuraré hacerle de menos* (R. J. Sender. 1964: 215)
> And there lives a rich man whom I will try and eliminate once we have arrived
> (Note also the archaic use of auxiliary *ser* with *llegado* in this example)

> *Contestado que hubo Pelegrín al oponente primero, se cerró el turno de discusión* (S. Lorén, 1955: 323)
> Once Pelegrín had answered the first opponent, the round of discussion ceased

> *Llegado que hubo a una pradera ... Vamos, queremos decir: en cuanto llegó a una pradera ...* (C. J. Cela, 1967b: 162)
> (When he got to a meadow ... (followed by equivalent clause using *en cuanto*))

## 1211 Repetition of the Verb: *lo lavó bien lavado*

This construction is mostly used with verbs which denote manual or mechanical actions carried out on objects (though see also third example below), e.g. *lavar* 'to wash', *fregar* 'to wash up', *teñir* 'to dye', *torcer* 'to wring', *picar*, 'to chop', etc., and it stresses the thoroughness or effectiveness of the action. In Spain it is typical of the spoken language; in Latin America it is found in higher registers.[72]

> *Tienes que torcer la ropa bien torcida* (Beinhauer, 1968: 295)
> You must really wring the clothes out

> *Metió en el hoyo el cántaro, lo tapó bien tapado* (Kany, 1951: 259)
> He put the pitcher in the hole and put the stopper in firmly

> *Me lavé todo bien lavado* (C. J. Cela, 1983: 20)
> I gave myself a really good wash

The Past Participle without an Auxiliary Verb

## 1212 General Rule

The past participle used without an auxiliary verb agrees in number and gender, like other adjectives, with the noun to which it relates.

> *Casi todos lo hacían con la boina puesta* (J. A. de Zunzunegui, 1952a: 37)
> Almost all of them did it with their bonnets on

> *Los cambios de ministros, las destituciones habidas, quedaban lejos* (J. M. Gironella, 1966b: 625)
> The changes of minister and the dismissals that there had been were far behind them

> *Para aquellos seres, dadas su edad o sus condiciones personales, no queda sitio en la ciudad* (M. Delibes, 1979a: 277)
> There is no room for those people in the town, given their age or their personal circumstances

The following sentence is an unusual example involving a passivized form of *dejar caer* 'to drop':

> *El hombre levantaba una piel y en seguida pasaba a otra, que a su vez era rasguñada, raspada, olfateada y dejada caer* (P. Neruda, 1976: 71)
> The man lifted one pelt and immediately passed on to another, which was scratched, scraped, smelled and dropped in its turn

## 1213 Special Cases: *excepto, incluso, salvo*

These irregular past participles are invariable in modern Spanish[73] and may be thought of as adverbs or even prepositions. *Excepto* and *incluso* are especially frequent. *Excepto* and *salvo* stand before the word or expression to which they relate; *incluso* more usually precedes, but may follow.[74]

> *Todos se habían acostado ya. Todos, excepto la rígida figura del timonel encerrado en su jaula de cristales* (M. Delibes, 1948: 195)
> Everyone had already gone to bed. All, that is, except the rigid figure of the steersman, shut in his glass cage

*Julio tocaba incluso las castañuelas* (J. M. Gironella, 1966a: 66)
Julio even played the castanets

*Será comerciante, o empleado del Ministerio de Agricultura, o quien sabe si dentista incluso* (C. J. Cela, 1963a: 239)
He must be a business man, or an employee of the Ministry of Agriculture, or, who knows, even a dentist

*En Londres conozco a poca gente, salvo a mis clientes* (I. Agustí, 1945: 99)
I know few people in London apart from my clients

## 1214 Remarks

*Incluido, incluyendo, inclusive* (and, of course, *aún* and *hasta* – see **598**) and, less commonly, *inclusivamente* and *incluyente* are used with approximately the same meaning as *incluso*: 'even; included'.

*A duras penas pudieron dominar a los polemizantes y ponerlos en la calle, incluyendo a Zacarías Smuts* (S. Lorén, 1971: 77)
They had a hard job controlling the troublemakers, including Zacarías Smuts, and putting them out into the street

*Había, inclusive, un antiguo funcionario conservador refugiado en la revuelta* (G. García Márquez, 1977: 155)
There was even a former conservative civil servant who had fled in the disturbance

*Incluido* normally agrees with the noun to which it relates:

*Todos los viajeros y los tripulantes, muertos, incluidas las lindas azafatas* (R. J. Sender, 1967: 170)
All the travellers and crew members dead, even the pretty stewardesses

But note also:

... *países del Caribe (incluido Cuba)* (J. Goytisolo, 1977: 232)
... Caribbean countries (including Cuba)

**1215** *Salvo*, as the irregular past participle of *salvar*, has an adjectival value in some cases, and then agrees with the noun to which it relates.

With the meaning 'safe': *Volvieron sanos y salvos* 'They returned safe and sound'

With the meaning 'excluded': *Salva sea la parte*, a euphemism for 'bottom, posterior (of a person)'

(Compare also *salvadas las distancias*, an expression used when setting aside a difference in age or position)

## 1216 *Debido a*

Note the difference between

> *Los desaciertos debidos a su mala gestión eran tales que ...*
> The blunders due to his bad government were such that ...

> *Los desaciertos, debido a su mala gestión, eran tales que ...*
> Due to his bad government, the blunders were such that ...

> (Both examples from Gili Gaya, 1964: 203)

In the first example above, *debidos* is an adjective which agrees with *desaciertos*; in the second, *debido a* is an invariable prepositional group, the equivalent of *a causa de* 'because of' or *en virtud de* 'by virtue of'. In the latter case, the phrase introduced by *debido a* is placed between commas. Some authorities consider the second construction unacceptable,[75] but it is now regularly found in literature and in the press, sometimes without the comma punctuation:

> *En algunos barrios vieron colas larguísimas debido a la progresiva escasez de muchos artículos* (J. M. Gironella, 1966c: 464)
> In some quarters they saw very long queues due to the increasing scarcity of many articles

> *Antonio Laínez hacía frecuentes viajes a París, Londres y Madrid debido a sus negocios* (M. Aub, 1963: 89)
> Antonio Laínez made frequent journeys to Paris, London and Madrid due to his business

## 1217 *Juntos (Juntas)*

The invariable prepositional expression *junto a* 'next to' should not be confused with *juntos (juntas)* 'together' (synonymous with *(con)juntamente*), the irregular past participle of *juntar* 'to join':

> *Dirijo algunas miradas a una señorita muy gorda que está junto a una señora muy flaca* (W. Fernández Flórez, 1967:17)

I direct the occasional glance towards a very fat young lady who is next to a very thin older lady

*Los gitanos del arroyo Abroñigal se acuestan junto a sus perros* (F. Umbral, 1966: 100)
The gipsies of the Arroyo Abroñigal sleep next to their dogs

*Todos los hombres juntos no valen una lágrima nuestra* (J. A. de Zunzunegui, 1952b: 49)
All men together are not worth a single tear of ours

*Pónganse más juntos. No tan juntos, por favor* (R. J. Sender, 1967: 154)
Get closer together. Not so close, please

*Convenció al notario Noguer y a su esposa para hacer el viaje conjuntamente* (J. M. Gironella, 1966a: 168)
He persuaded Noguer the lawyer and his wife to travel together

## 1218 *Hecho*

This very frequently used past participle may be the equivalent of *como*. It agrees in number and gender with the first term of the comparison (i.e. with the subject *estar*, etc., with which *hecho* is often used).

*Estás hecho un idiota* (I. Aldecoa, 1969: 176)
You're behaving like an idiot

*El niño, el perro y el zorro jugaban a la luz del carburo hechos un ovillo* (M. Delibes, 1968a: 55)
The child, the dog and the fox were playing in a tangled ball by the light of the carbide lamp

*Vivamos hechos unos bárbaros* (P. Baroja, 1960: 181)
Let's live like barbarians

**1219** Note especially the expression *hecho un basilisco*[76] 'terribly angry':

*La Paulina se va a poner hecha un basilisco en cuanto se entere* (C. J. Cela, 1963a: 286)
Paulina will be hopping mad when she finds out

**1220** For *(estar) hecho* and other expressions of 'becoming', see **1268**.

**1221** *Hecho* can also be used in the sense of 'agreed, OK':

– *¿Nos encontramos aquí, pasado mañana, a la misma hora?*
– *Hecho* (M. Aub, 1963: 88)
'Shall we meet here the day after tomorrow at the same time?'
'OK'

## 1222 *Lo* + Past Participle

The 'neuter' article *lo* (see **63**) can be used with a past participle as with an adjective, providing an economical construction which must often be rendered by a clause in English.

*Lo pasado*
The past

*Lo pasado, pasado, Paulino* (I. Aldecoa, 1969: 107)
Let bygones be bygones, Paulino

*Despechado por su fallo de memoria puesto a cuentas de lo bebido, agarró una gruesa piedra* (A. Carpentier, 1976: 62)
Filled with rage by his failure of memory on account of his having drunk so much, he seized a large stone

*A lo hecho, pecho* (A. M. de Lera, 1970: 164)
We must make the best of it

*Siento lo ocurrido ayer* (S. Lorén, 1971: 235)
I regret what has happened today

**1223** Note the very common expression *lo dicho* 'as I said':

*Bueno, pues lo dicho: hasta mañana*
Well, as I said: see you tomorrow

*Lo dicho: Antonio se ha vuelto loco*
As I said: Antonio has gone mad

(Both examples from Beinhauer, 1968: 111)

**1224** *Lo dicho* can of course have a more literal meaning:

*Briones dio cuenta al general de lo dicho por Martín* (P. Baroja, 1946–51: I, 249)
Briones gave the general an account of what Martín had said

– *¿Me perdonas lo hecho?*
– *Sí, te lo perdono. Pero vuelvo a lo dicho. Nunca más.* (I Agustí, 1957: 63)
'Do you forgive me for what I've done?'
'Yes, I forgive you. But I repeat what I said. Never again'

## 1225 Limpiado/limpio, llenado/lleno, hartado/harto

*Limpiado, llenado* and *hartado* are never used with *ser* to form the passive (cf. **1019**); thus:

| | | |
|---|---|---|
| Not *\*Fueron hartados de carne* | but *Se los hartó de carne* | 'They were stuffed full of meat' |
| Not *\*Fue limpiada la calle* | but *Se limpió la calle* | 'The street was cleaned' |
| Not *\*Fue llenado el local* | but *Se llenó el local* | 'The premises filled up' |

(Examples from *GRAE*, 419)

**1226** *Llenado* and *limpiado* are rarely used with adjectival value. Note how in the first example below *lleno* is used in parallel to the past participle *concluida* in an absolute construction.

> *Aquella tarde, concluida la tarea y lleno el carro de secos sarmientos, la cansada mula emprendió con lentitud la vuelta hacia el lugar* (P. Baroja, 1946–51: VI, 1006)
> That afternoon, when their work was done and the cart was filled with dry vine shoots, the tired mule slowly began the return journey to the farm

> *Sobre la mesa estaba el cenicero de metal, que ahora aparecía recién limpio* (C. J. Cela, 1967d: 139)
> On the table was the metal ashtray, which seemed to have been recently cleaned

The following example is therefore odd; *limpios* would be more usual than *limpiados*:

> *Eran unos metales verdosos que, limpiados, fulgían como si hubieran sido espolvoreados* (M. Mujica Laínez, 1983: 45)
> They were greenish metals which, when cleaned, shone as if they had been dusted[77]

**1227** *Hartado* is similarly only used in active compound forms: *se han hartado* 'they've had enough'.

*Harto* as an adjective implies '(more than) enough':

> *Estamos hartos*
> We've had more than enough/We're fed up

> *Estar harto de alguna cosa*
> To be fed up with something

> *Estar harto de dormir*
> To have overslept

> *Estar harto de vivir*
> To be tired of living

**1228** *Harto* also has an (invariable) adverbial use which must not be confused with its use in the examples considered so far.

> *El general tuvo plena conciencia de que su propia formación era harto deficiente* (J. M. Gironella, 1966b: 206)
> The general was fully aware that his own training was very inadequate

### 1229 *Pedir prestado*

There is no single-word translation of English 'borrow' in Spanish, and the past participle *prestado* is used with other verbs to render the notion. Note that in such expressions the past participle may be separated from the main verb and agrees with the direct object.

> *Pedí a Leticia su corazón prestado* (F. Umbral, 1979: 104)
> I asked to borrow Leticia's heart

> *Los toreros pidieron prestada la espada* (C. J. Cela, 1972: 59)
> The bullfighters asked to borrow the sword

> *Algo semejante le sucede si presta dinero o lo pide prestado, ya que en ambos casos Jacinto lleva las de perder* (M. Delibes, 1984: 81)
> Something similar happens if he lends or borrows money, since in either case Jacinto loses out

Note that *prestar* ('to lend' in Spain) is sometimes used in the sense of 'to borrow' in Latin America.[78]

## Suffixes with Past Participles

**1230**  Past participles may take affective suffixes (see **1319**ff.) just like the adjectives with which value they are so often used. The diminutive suffixes and -*ísimo* are those most frequently encountered.

> *Los niños están dormiditos* (C. J. Cela, 1963a: 213)
> The children are fast asleep

> *¡Quién estuviera como ella sentadita en el Cielo!* (R. del Valle-Inclán, 1963: 104)
> What I'd give to be sitting pretty in Heaven like her!

> *Tenía el ilustre periodista una sobrina ya entradita en años y sin carnes* (M. Aub, 1970: 14)
> The famous journalist had a niece who was no youngster and thin as a rail

> *La costumbre de pasear en coche descubierto estaba generalizadísima en la segunda mitad del siglo (XVIII)* (C. Martín Gaite, 1972: 31)
> The custom of riding in an open coach was very widespread in the second half of the (eighteenth) century

> *. . . por seguir la terminología de Mosén Escrivá en su leidísimo «Camino»* (J. A. Gómez Marín, 1972: 43)
> . . . following the terminology of Monsignor Escrivá in his widely read 'Camino'

When the past participle is used with *haber* and has no adjectival properties the addition of suffixes is very uncommon; however, odd examples are met:

> *. .. te he tomaíto* (= *tomado* + *ito*) *el cariño cuando menos lo pensé* (M. Machado, 1947: 19)
> . . . I took your affection when I least thought of it

# Special Problems with Spanish Verbs

## *Ser* and *estar*

**1231** The two Spanish verbs *ser* and *estar* in many cases correspond to the single English verb 'to be'; their use (they are never confused by Spanish speakers, incidentally) is therefore a special difficulty for English learners of Spanish.[1]

### 1232 Contexts in which the choice between *ser* and *estar* is clear[2]

*Ser*

(1) *Ser*, not *estar*, is used with a noun (see **1234**), a pronoun or an infinitive:

| | |
|---|---|
| *Soy abogado* | I am a lawyer |
| *Esta pluma es mía* | This pen is mine |
| *Vivir es sufrir* | Living is suffering |

(2) *Ser* is always used to introduce a 'cleft' sentence (see **1311**):

| | |
|---|---|
| *Fue entonces cuando le vi* | It was then I saw him |
| *Es Juan que/quien habla* | It's Juan speaking |

(3) *Ser* is used with constructions denoting possession or the material from which something is made:

| | |
|---|---|
| *El libro es de Pedro* | The book belongs to Pedro |
| *La caja es de madera* | The box is made of wood |

(4)  *Ser* indicates origin or provenance:

*Es de Madrid*　　　　　　　　　He is from Madrid

*Estar*

(5)  *Estar* is used with adverbs or adverbial phrases of place:

*Estoy aquí*　　　　　　　　　I am here
*Carlos estaba en Segovia*　　　Carlos was in Segovia

(6)  *Estar* is always used with the gerund:

*Pedro está trabajando*　　　　Pedro is working

## The Basic Meanings and Functions of *ser*

### 1233 *Ser* Expressing Existence

*Ser* has the basic meaning of 'to exist'; as a noun it means 'existence, being':

> *Margarita si no se ríe, sonríe, feliz de ser* (M. Aub, 1971: 126)
> If Margarita is not laughing, she is smiling, happy to be alive

> – *¿Por qué he de estarle agradecido a mi padre?*
> – *Por haberte dado el ser* (R. J. Sender, 1965–6: II, 81)
> 'Why should I be grateful to my father?'
> 'Because he gave you your existence'

In a more general sense :

> *Éramos doce o catorce* (E. Romero, 1963: 133)
> There were twelve to fourteen of us

Note also the expression *Era una vez . . .* (also *érase . . .* and *érase que (se) era . . .*) 'once upon a time':

> *Era una vez, hace muchos, muchísimos años . . .* (Fabiola, 1960: 1)
> Once upon a time, many, many years ago . . .

### 1234 *Ser* Expressing Equivalence or Identity

*Ser* expresses equivalence or identity between one thing and another:

*Pedro es alcalde* (Alcina Franch and Blecua, 1975: 900)
Pedro is a mayor

(Contrast the expression *estar de* + noun:

*Mi amigo Roberto está de embajador en Londres*
My friend Roberto is (posted as, acting as) the ambassador in London

*Ser* + noun indicates a profession, hence a regular attribute; *estar de* + noun denotes a particular appointment or function.)

*Hoy es jueves* (Alcina Franch and Blecua, 1975: 900)
Today is Thursday

*Ser inmortal es esperar la inmortalidad* (M. de Unamuno, 1967b: 23)
Being immortal consists of expecting immortality

In fact, it is a very general rule that a noun is never the complement of *estar*, only of *ser*. There are a number of idiomatic expressions in which this rule appears not to hold (*estar pez* 'to be totally ignorant', *estar fenómeno* 'to be fantastic', *estar cañón* 'to be fabulous, great'), but they are very limited and the noun may in any case be thought of as an adjective.[3]

### 1235 *Ser* as a Perfect Auxiliary

See **1196**.

### 1236 *Ser* as a Passive Auxiliary

See **970** and **1019**; also **1020-1021** on the contrast in this context with *estar*.

### 1237 *Ser de*

*ser de* = 'to become of':

*No sé lo que había sido de él* (E. Líster, 1977: 154)
I don't know what has become of him

**1238**  *Ser de* expresses possession, material or origin:

*La casa es de mi tío* (Alcina Franch and Blecua, 1975: 901)
The house belongs to my uncle

*La Constitución es de papel y la República de cartón* (M. de Unamuno, 1967b: 28)
The Constitution is made of paper and the Republic of cardboard

*El muchacho es de Madrid* (Alcina Franch and Blecua, 1975: 901)
The boy comes from Madrid

## The Basic Meanings and Functions of *estar*

### 1239 *Estar* Indicating Position

*Estar* is used to indicate position, even when this might be considered as inherent or permanent:

*No está en casa*
He is not at home

*Madrid está en el centro de España* (Gili Gaya, 1964: 64)
Madrid is in the centre of Spain

### 1240 *Estar* in Passive Sentences

The passive with *ser* has essentially the same meaning as the corresponding active verb, and the time at which the action takes place is the same as that denoted by the auxiliary verb. The passive with *estar*, on the other hand, denotes a resultant state.

The adjectival use of past participles with *estar* may be seen to be related to the *estar*-passive:

*Oye, Pat, creí que estabas enfadada conmigo* (J. M. Carrascal, 1973: 64)
Hey, Pat, I thought you were annoyed with me
(Something had made her annoyed)

*El árbol estaba ya muy carcomido* (M. Aub, 1971: 176)
The tree was already very rotten (i.e. in a rotten state)

### 1241 *Estar* + Gerund

*Estar* + gerund forms the progressive or continuous aspect in Spanish. See **1171**.

**1242** Mention has already been made of the construction *estar* + *siendo* + past participle (**1208**). *Estar* + *siendo* can also be used with a following adjective:

> *Pero no estoy siendo justo con la música* (G. Cabrera Infante, 1979: 47)
> But I am not being fair to music

> *Estoy siendo sincero* (T. Salvador, 1968: 126–7)
> I'm being honest

> *El partido está siendo vibrante* (heard by JdeB on Spanish Television, 23 June 1991)
> The match is really humming

### 1243 *Estar* + *que* + Verb

This construction appears in the spoken language, and intensifies the meaning of the verb:

> *Están que rabian, hombre* (A. M. de Lera, 1970: 92)
> They're really wild, man

> *Se ha enamorado de una de ellas y está que no vive* (Beinhauer, 1968: 276)
> He's fallen for one of them hook, line and sinker

### 1244 *Ser* and *estar* with Adjectives

Basically, *ser* may be viewed as expressing an 'essential' attribute and *estar* as an 'accidental' attribute. This general principle has been variously described as 'absolute' versus 'relative', 'objective' versus 'subjective', or 'inherent' versus 'non-inherent'.[4] The following series of examples illustrate the differences between *ser* and *estar* with adjectives.

### 1245 *Ser* + Adjective Denotes an Essential Characteristic; *estar* + Adjective Denotes Behaviour, an Accidental Circumstance

Some examples:

*Ser/estar alegre*

> *Bonifacio era muy alegre* (M. de Unamuno, 1967a: 49)
> Bonifacio was very happy

*Algunos días estaba alegre* (ibid.. 50)
Some days he was happy
(His happiness is not inherent, but occurs from time to time)

### Ser/estar feliz

*Ser feliz o desgraciado es una cuestión secundaria* (M. de
Unamuno, 1967b: 23)
To be happy or unhappy is a secondary question
(Happiness or unhappiness is here a general human
characteristic)

*Reconoció al León de Natuba por la mínima estatura. Lo besó
tiernamente, susurrándole: «Hijo mío, te creía perdido, tu madre
está feliz, feliz»* (M. Vargas Llosa, 1981: 288)
She recognized León de Natuba by his small build. She
kissed him tenderly, whispering, 'My child, I thought you
were lost; your mother is happy, so happy'
(The mother's happiness is here consequent upon seeing her
son again)

### Ser/estar orgulloso

*Soy muy orgulloso y siempre mantengo la palabra empeñada* (I.
Allende, 1987: 278)
I'm very proud (i.e. I have a proud nature) and I always keep
my pledged word

*Mary, Elisabeth y Kate estaban orgullosas de que su padre tuviera
importantes negocios en el Transvaal* (C. J. Cela, 1958: 101)
Mary, Elisabeth and Kate were proud that their father had
important business in the Transvaal
(Their pride is occasioned by a specific circumstance)

### Further Examples with *estar:*

*Estuve francamente simpática el resto de la tarde* (D. Fernández
Flórez, 1967: 27)
I behaved really nicely for the rest of the afternoon
(Implies that her normal behaviour is the opposite)

*Estate sonriente y amable* (J. A. de Zunzunegui, 1959a: 132)
Smile and be friendly
(Does not imply that the person addressed is inherently smil-
ing and friendly)

**1246** It may seem strange in the light of the foregoing that *estar* is regularly used with the adjectives *vivo* in its meaning of 'alive' and *muerto* in its meaning of 'dead'. But *vivo* and *muerto*, like *intacto* 'intact', *limpio* 'clean', *lleno* 'full'. *maduro* 'ripe', *roto* 'broken', *sucio* 'dirty', *vacío* 'empty'. etc. are seen in Spanish as states rather than properties, the possible or actual result of a process of 'becoming'.[5] Often the idea of 'still' or 'already' is implied.

> *Hay momentos en que comprendo que él está vivo y yo estoy muerto* (F. Umbral, 1979: 49)
> There are moments when I understand that he is alive and I am dead

> *Las personas que han visto San Sebastián dicen que está intacto* (J. A. de Zunzunegui, 1956b: 432)
> The people who have seen San Sebastián say that it is (still) unspoilt

> *A mí me va a dar vergüenza, porque estoy muy blanquita* (R. Sánchez Ferlosio, 1971: 42)
> I'll be ashamed, because my skin's (still) so white

**1247** Particularly difficult for English speakers to understand is the difference between *ser/estar casado, viudo, soltero,* etc.

> *El que mienta usted, ¿es casao?* (J. Goytisolo, 1981a: 29)
> Is he married, the one you mention?
> (A neutral enquiry: 'Is he a married man?' *Casao = casado*)

> *Hacía sólo un mes que estaban casaos* (ibid., 50)
> They've only been married a month
> (Focusing on their (new) married state)

> *Chufreteiro está viudo* (C. J. Cela, 1983: 19)
> Chufreteiro is a widower (has been left in a state of widowerhood)

Compare also:

> *Azucena Peaches me dijo de pronto: – Yo soy virgen, ¿sabes?* (F. Umbral, 1981: 65)
> Azucena Peaches suddenly said to me, 'I'm a virgin, you know'

> *¿Sabéis que Sofía está virgen?* (F. Umbral, 1966: 83)
> Did you know that Sofía is (still) a virgin?

**1248** Further adjectival contrasts with *ser* and *estar*:

| | |
|---|---|
| *ser borracho*<br>to be a drunk (an<br>inherent characteristic) | *estar borracho*<br>to be drunk (on a<br>particular occasion) |
| *ser bueno*<br>to have a good character | *estar bueno*<br>to be in good health; to<br>be delicious (of food) (cf.<br>*rico* below) |

*Ponme también salsa. Está muy buena* (S. Lorén, 1965: 53)
Give me some sauce too. It tastes delicious.

| | |
|---|---|
| *ser ciego* (see also **846**,<br>fourth example)<br>to be a blind person | *estar ciego*<br>to behave as if one is<br>blind |

*Soy ciego* (R. del Valle-Inclán, 1981: 44)
I am blind (said by Max Estrella, the blind protagonist).
But in the same work (p. 75), someone asks Estrella *¿Estás ciego?* 'Have you gone blind?' (as the result of a misfortune) and Estrella says (p. 77) *Hace un año que estoy ciego* 'I have been blind for a year' (thinking of it as a changed state)

*Debe de estar ciego de furor* (M. Mihura, 1981: 91)
He must be blind with fury

| | |
|---|---|
| *ser consciente*<br>to be aware<br>(This distinction is sometimes blurred in modern Spanish)[6] | *estar consciente*<br>to be conscious |

| | |
|---|---|
| *ser fresco*<br>to be cheeky, impudent | *estar fresco*<br>to be cool; also *¡estamos<br>frescos!* 'we're in a right<br>mess!' |

| | |
|---|---|
| *ser guapo*<br>to be handsome | *estar guapo*<br>to look elegant |

| | |
|---|---|
| *ser listo*<br>to be clever | *estar listo*<br>to be ready |

| | |
|---|---|
| *ser maduro*<br>to be mature (of a person) | *estar maduro*<br>to be ripe (of fruit, etc.) |

| | |
|---|---|
| *ser malo*<br>to be of a bad nature, to<br>have a bad character | *estar malo*<br>to be in a bad condition, to<br>be ill |

*Esta ostra está malísima* (A. de Laiglesia, 1972: 178)
This oyster is awful
(But: *Las ostras no son buenas para el hígado* 'Oysters are not good for one's liver' – presented as an inherent property of oysters)

| | |
|---|---|
| *ser pálido*<br>to have a pale complexion | *estar pálido*<br>to turn pale (with fright,<br>etc.) |
| *ser rico*<br>to be rich (wealthy) | *estar rico*<br>to be delicious (of food,<br>etc.) |

*La salsa está muy rica*
The sauce tastes very good

*Está (muy) rica el agua*
It's (really) lovely (of water in a swimming pool, for example)

and, with a sexual innuendo:

*Tu hermana, aunque no tenga tetas, está rica* (M. Delibes, 1987: 174)
Your sister may not have any tits, but she's a real dish

| | |
|---|---|
| *ser vivo*<br>to be intelligent, bright | *estar vivo*<br>to be alive |
| *ser sobrio*<br>to be of a sober<br>disposition | *estar sobrio*<br>to be sober (as opposed to<br>drunk)[7] |

## 1249 *Ser* + Adjective Represents an Objective Reality, *estar* + Adjective a Subjective Impression

With *VIEJO*

*Puedo establecer fácilmente mi diagnóstico. Soy viejo, ésa es mi principal enfermedad* (L. Buñuel, 1982: 247)
I can easily reach a diagnosis on myself. I am old, that is my main illness

*Él era ya mayor pero no estaba viejecito todavía* (F. Quiñones, 1979: 241)
He was no youngster, but he did not look a little old man yet

## With *JOVEN*

*Tú eres más joven, ¿verdad?* (J. García Hortelano, 1967: 23)
You are younger, aren't you? (comparing the age of two people)

*Y estás tan joven como cuando nació Susana* (J. M. Gironella, 1971: II, 42)
And you look just as young as when Susana was born (a husband paying his wife a compliment. Indeed, *eres tan joven* would be nonsense, since the woman is clearly older than she was)

Also:

*Las tortas fritas están sublimes* (J. Cortázar, 1974: 409)
Fried cakes taste sublime

## With *CALVO*

*Está calvo* is more likely to be used by someone who knew the person before he lost his hair[8] whereas *es calvo* is a straightforward objective statement. Alternatively, *es calvo* might be used of someone who is completely bald, while *está calvo* is used of someone who still has some hair left.

### 1250 *Ser* + Adjective Indicates an Absolute Value; *estar* + Adjective a Relative Value

Example:

– *Estás muy alto, ¿eh?*
– *Sí, señor, más que el año pasado* (C. J. Cela, 1963c: 170)
'You're a tall lad, aren't you?'
'Yes, sir, taller than last year'
(The use of *estar* implies that the boy has grown. In cases like this the use of *estar* often implies an idea of comparison.[9] For the straightforward description of an adult, *es muy alto* would be used)

## 1251 *Estar* + Adjective or Adjectival Phrase Indicates Location, Literal or Metaphorical

Examples:

> *Estaba arrodillado* (Gili Gaya, 1964: 64–5)
> He was kneeling down

> *Estaba fuera de sí* (J. A. de Zunzunegui, 1959b: 80)
> He was beside himself

## 1252 'Stylistic Exploitation' of *ser/estar*

Spanish authors are conscious of the contrast between *ser* and *estar*, and often exploit it to give a stylistic effect that is very difficult to render adequately in English.

> *Viejo no se es, se está* (J. A. de Zunzunegui, 1956b: 397)
> People are not old, they just feel old

> *Allí en frente, en el reflejo, estaba él y no era él* (I. Agustí, 1957: 437)
> There he was, reflected opposite, yet it was not him

> *Recuerdo entre los jóvenes compañeros de poesía y alegría a tantos que ya no están o que ya no son* (P. Neruda, 1976: 166)
> Among my young companions in poetry and happiness I remember so many who are no longer here or who no longer exist

> *Mi hermano continuaba estando, siendo tuberculoso y se pondría peor* (G. Cabrera Infante, 1979: 396)
> My brother continued to suffer from tuberculosis, he continued to be irrevocably tubercular, and he would get worse

> *¿Te gusta? Estoy muy fea . . . pero soy yo. Porque, ¿verdad que soy muy fea?* (J. M. Gironella, 1966b: 539)
> Do you like it? I look very ugly . . . but I'm me. Because I am very ugly, aren't I?

## 1253 The Impersonal Reflexive with *ser* and *estar*

Note that both *ser* and *estar* may be used in the impersonal reflexive:[10]

*Cuando se está alegre y se es feliz, con poco se vive* (J. A. de Zun-zunegui, 1952b: 221)
When you're happy and fortunate, you can live on very little

## 1254 *Ser* and *estar* + *por, para*

See **750–751, 774–775**.

## 1255 Replacement of *ser* and *estar* by 'Dynamic Verbs'

*Ser* and *estar* are often replaced by verbs of motion[11] which have lost a part of their original meaning and are clearly in a more or less advanced stage of grammaticalization (this is especially true of *andar*).[12]

*Cayóse de su caballo.*
*¡Parece que viene muerto!* (R. del Valle-Inclán, 1963: 57)
He fell off his horse
He seems to be dead!
(*Parece que está muerto* might be expected; *venir* and *muerto* are strictly speaking incompatible. On the other hand, the verb of motion is transferred, as it were, to the horse carrying the dead body)

*A su lado iba sentada una muchacha* (C. J. Cela, 1967c: 119)
A girl sat next to him
(A similar usage: the element of 'motion' is in this case a car)

*Yo iba ya en el vientre de Sa Malene cuando él la despidió* (A. M. Matute, 1977: 36)
I was in Sa Malene's tummy when he dismissed her
(The unborn child is not moving around in its mother's womb; the use of *ir* indicates rather that it necessarily accompanies its mother wherever she goes)

*Voy muerta – suspira* (J. L. Goytisolo, 1981a: 76)
'I'm dead,' she sighed
(*Voy* no doubt is equivalent to *estoy* here, but its use is connected with exertion (the speaker is a woman who has been working hard all afternoon))

*Luis andaba feliz porque había dejado el cigarrillo hacía un mes* (G. García Márquez, *Memorias de un fumador retirado*, in *El País*, 16 February 1983: 11)

Luis was happy because he had gone for a month without cigarettes

*La idea de que la Maga y Ossip andaban juntos se adelgazaba y perdía consistencia* (J. Cortázar, 1974: 98)
The idea that La Maga and Ossip were living together was wearing a bit thin and would no longer stand up

*Ketty andaba cambiándose de ropa* (F. Umbral, 1966: 31)
Ketty was changing her clothes

– *¡Hay que ir más despacio!*
– *¡Pero si voy parado!* (C. J. Cela, 1967b: 152)
'You should go slower!'
'But I'm standing still!'[13]
(This a slightly unusual example where the logical contradiction between *voy* and *parado* is exploited for stylistic effect)

*Estar* may also be replaced by a verb of motion when used with the gerund of *ser*:

*Creo que ya va siendo hora de dejar el tema del aborto* (Reader's letter in *El País*, 12 February 1983: 10)
I think it is now time to leave the topic of abortion
(See also **1208** (ii, iv, v).)

## Haber

**1256**  *Haber* is nowadays chiefly used as an auxiliary, while *tener* has the 'full' meaning of possession. This distinction is not absolute, however, and the two verbs have sometimes overlapping functions: we have already referred (**1198–1204**) to the important role of *tener* as a (semi-)auxiliary.

### 1257 *Haber* as a Verb of Possession (Archaic Value)

*Haber* may still occasionally be found with its older meaning of 'to have, to possess, to consider'.

In archaistic usage:

*¿Has galán?* (E. Quiroga, 1951: 101)
Have you an admirer?

In set phrases drawn from religious language.

> *Y eso no se lo perdono yo ni a mi padre, que gloria haya* (M. Delibes, 1967: 24)
> I can't even forgive my father for this, God rest his soul
> (*Que gloria haya* may be abbreviated as *q.g.h.*; variants are *que santa gloria haya* (*q.s.g.h.*) and *que Dios haya*)

In some still current expressions involving the past participle of *haber*, chiefly found in written language, such as *un hijo habido en su primera mujer* 'a son by his first wife', *habida cuenta de* 'taking account of' and *haber menester* 'to have need'.[14]

> *Dichas determinaciones tendían a dotar al Ejército del Pueblo de bases sólidas, habida cuenta de la prolongación de la guerra* (J. M. Gironella, 1966c: 412)
> These decisions tended to put the People's Army on a solid basis, taking into account the prolonging of the war

*Haber lugar* is used in legal language:

> *Se prohibe arrojar objetos a la vía bajo las responsabilidades a que hubiera lugar* (seen by JdeB in the Córdoba-Málaga TAF train, 24 February 1976)
> It is forbidden to throw things on to the track. Offenders will be held responsible for any consequences

Note also the use of *haber* as a noun:

> *Supone un sensible aumento de los haberes mensuales* (M. Delibes, 1968b: 190)
> It represents a noticeable increase in one's monthly income

## 1258 *Haber* as an Existential Verb (= 'there is, are')

*Haber* in the singular (present tense *hay*) forms the existential expression 'there is, are'. Note that in Spanish only the singular of *haber* is considered correct in this sense.[15] The past participle and infinitive are also used in this sense.

> *Lo ha habido, lo hay y lo habrá* (C. Sánchez-Albornoz, 1975: 194)
> (Of a link between Spain and Portugal) There has been one, there is one, and there will always be one
> *Julio hizo un resumen de las batallas habidas* (J. M. Gironella, 1966c: 656–7)
> Julio gave a summary of the battles there had been

*El muchacho creía en todos los Misterios habidos y por haber*
(J. M. Gironella, 1966a: 183)
The boy believed in all the Mysteries there had ever been and
ever would be
(*Habidos y por haber* may be regarded as a set expression: 'for
all time')

*En mi vida no había habido nunca una Ketty* (F. Umbral,
1966: 26)
In all my life there had never been a Ketty

– *¿No hay nadie fuera?*
– *Nadie, ¿quién va a haber?* (C. Martín Gaite, 1981: 199)
'Isn't there anyone outside?'
'No one, why, should there be?'

In many Latin-American countries the (old) form *habemos* is used
with the meaning of *hay*.[16]

## 1259  Idioms with *haber*: *habérselas*

The idiom *habérselas con* has the meaning 'to deal with, to be up
against, to have it out with'; the old form *habemos* can still be found
in this construction (see the third example below)

*Si tu madre supiera con quien se las ha Pilar, no le permitiría salir
con quien sale* (J. M. Gironella, 1966a: 519)
If your mother knew who Pilar knocks around with, she
wouldn't let her go out with who she does

*Comprendí que me las había con un indiferente* (R. Arlt,
1985: 166)
I saw that I was up against someone who didn't care

*Ya sabéis con quiénes nos las habemos* (*DD*, 214)
You know who we're dealing with

## 1260  *He aquí*, etc.

These expressions, sometimes involving a clitic (unstressed) pronoun, and behaving like a transitive verb (note the use of the personal *a* in the fourth example below, see **659**), are chiefly found in
the written language. *He* is invariable.

*Heme aquí* (*DD*, 219)
Here I am

*Y henos aquí, ya en Puerto Araguato* (A. Carpentier, 1976: 44)
And now here we are in Puerto Araguato

*He ahí el secreto de su seducción* (M. Delibes, in Coste and
Redondo, 1965: 234)
There's the secret of its appeal

*He aquí a tu madre* (*DD*, 219)
Here we have your mother

## 1261 *Ha* = *hace*

In archaistic literary use,[17] the form *ha* (also used in the imperfect
(*había*) and the future (*habrá*)) is synonymous with *hace* in 'ago'-
constructions (see **977**). It may precede or follow the time expression, though it almost always precedes in negative sentences.

*Saludamos a Paco Locedo, el hombre que, siglos ha, me descu-
brió el valium* (F. Umbral, 1985: 33)
We greeted Paco Locedo, the man who, centuries ago, discovered valium for me

*Ha pocos días ha muerto el cardenal Ottaviani* (*El Imparcial*, 15
July 1979: 3)
Cardinal Ottaviani died a few days ago

*Habrá ocho días que* ... (*Esbozo*, 292)
It must be two days ago that ...

*No ha mucho tiempo que* ... (*Esbozo*, 291)
It is not long since that ...

## 1262 *Hay que* + Infinitive

The impersonal *hay que* infinitive (also itself used in the infinitive)
expresses the idea of obligation.

*Hay que tener paciencia* (*Esbozo*, 447)
One must be patient

*Ya va a haber que darte la usía* (I. Aldecoa, 1970: 204)
People are going to have to be polite to you
(On the form of address *usía*, see **253**)

## The Expression of 'Becoming'

**1263** Unlike French (*devenir*) and German (*werden*), Spanish has no straightforward equivalent for English 'become', except for the very restricted *devenir* (discussed in **1269** below).[18] However, there are numerous words and expressions which permit the expression of this notion. They may conveniently be grouped into four categories.

### 1264 *Llegar* and *pasara* + *a ser*

*Llegar* and *pasar* + *a ser* are the most common of these verbs.

*Llegar a ser* expresses something (1) that can be considered as an end or a definite stage, or (2) that is presented as desirable and demands effort and/or time.

> *Quiero llegar a ser el mejor abogado de la ciudad* (J. M. Gironella, 1966b: 61)
> I want to become the best lawyer in the town

*Ser* may be omitted with an adjective or noun that is not further qualified:

> *Nadie está muy seguro de llegar a viejo* (W. Fernández Flórez, 1967: 101)
> No one is certain of reaching old age

*Pasar a ser* lays stress on the idea of change or transition:

> *Celeste está allí porque hace unos días ha pasado a ser sirvienta de los Ortueta* (S. Lorén, 1967a: 33)
> Celeste is there because she became a maid at the Ortuetas' a few days ago

### 1265 *Ir a dar (en)*

This implies that the result is not desired:

> *Calla y no hables más de esto, que vas a dar en loca.*
> *– En loca darás tú si sigues por ese camino* (J. A. de Zunzunegui, 1956b: 69)
> 'Shut up and say no more about it, or you'll go mad.'
> 'It's you that'll go mad if you take this any further'

*Ir (para)* can also be used in the sense of 'become':

*Los que vamos para viejos* (F. Umbral, 1979: 156)
Those of us who are getting on in years

*¿Y no pensaste nunca irte cura?* (C. J. Cela, 1983: 102)
Didn't you ever think of becoming a priest?

## 1266  A Single Verb

*Hacerse* denotes a slow development in which the subject of the verb cannot exert any influence on the action.

*¡No quiero hacerme viejo en este hoyo!* (J. Izcaray, 1961: 47)
I don't want to grow old in this dump!

However, it may also denote a more active role by the subject in the carrying out of the action:

*Uno de Gárgoles, que quería hacerse rico en dos años, se vino en bicicleta* (C. J. Cela, 1967d: 88)
Someone from Gárgoles who wanted to get rich in a couple of years, came up on a bicycle

*Meter(se)* is chiefly followed by a noun that denotes a profession or social status, and thus often implies something that is desired or sought. The use of the preposition *a* (less frequently *de*)[19] is optional.

*Mi tía Cecilia, a la muerte de la Joshepa, la criada vieja, decidió meterse monja* (P. Baroja, 1946–51: II, 986)
On the death of the old servant Joshepa, my aunt Cecilia decided to become a nun

*Al salir del cuartel, Gregorio Mayoral se metió a peón de albañil* (C. J. Cela, 1967b: 123)
When he came out of prison, Gregorio Mayoral became a builder's labourer

and the ironical

*Parecía que te ibas a meter de cura – dijo Pluto* (M. Vargas Llosa, 1973: 180)
'It looked as if you were going to become a priest,' said Pluto

*Ponerse* indicates a temporary state of affairs. It is never followed by a noun, only by adjectives, adverbs or manner expressions,[20] and may be thought of as similar in nature to *estar* (see **1244**ff.).

*Y volvió a ponerse roja* (R. del Valle-Inclán, 1963: 112)
And she blushed again

*Callaos y no os pongáis pesados* (J. A. de Zunzunegui,
1952a: 63)
Keep quiet and don't be so boring

*Quedarse* usually signals the definitive nature of a state of affairs.

*Quedarse viudo a los noventa años cae dentro de los usos del
Occidente* (C. J. Cela, 1963b: 269)
To be left a widower at ninety is part of the ways of the West

*Me quedaré ciega* (M. Vargas Llosa, 1973: 93)
I shall go blind

*La francesa resultó ser tan rosada, redonda y dulce, que quedó
encinta a los pocos meses* (I. Allende, 1984: 73)
The French girl turned out to be so pink, round and sweet-
natured, that she became pregnant within a few months

*Quedarse* is also used in a passive sense, as a replacement for
*ser* or *estar*:

*Lo habrá usted previsto todo para que los señores queden bien
atendidos* (I. Agustí, 1945: 96–7)
You must have thought of everything so that the gentlemen
are well looked after

*Por fin quedó aceptado el Proyecto que ofrecía la solución más
sencilla* (A. Carpentier, 1976: 154)
Finally the Plan which offered the simplest solution was
accepted

*Tornarse* and *volverse* (the latter is more frequent nowadays) are the
most neutral means of expressing a change in nature.
*Tornarse* is rarely followed by a noun.[21] It is chiefly used in connection with people, especially of a new physical or psychological state.

*Su respiración se había tornado ansiosa* (J. Goytisolo, 1960: 124)
His breathing had become anxious

*A tanto llegó el cansancio de Laureano, que perdió varios quilos
en pocas semanas y su carácter se tornó insoportable* (J. M.
Gironella, 1971: II, 329)

Laureano's fatigue reached such a pitch that he lost a lot of weight in a few weeks and his nature became unbearable
(See **2** for spelling of *quilos*)

*Volverse*, like *tornarse*, is generally used in connection with a people or personified things. Comparing the two, it becomes apparent that *volverse* (1) is used more often in connection with psychological than with physical characteristics, (2) that these characteristics are generally unfavourable, or presented as such, (3) that they have a more or less permanent nature, and (4) that the change denoted by *volverse* often has an unexpected or sudden nature:

> *¿Qué dices? ¿Te has vuelto loca?* (A. Casona, 1968: 91)
> What do you say? Have you gone mad?

> *Te has vuelto anarquista* (M. Aub, 1963: 15)
> You have turned into an anarchist

> *Arnaldo se volvió impotente por una mordedura de alacrán* (G. García Márquez, 1977: 368)
> Arnaldo became impotent as the result of being stung by a scorpion

> *Se había vuelto tacañísima con la luz* (C. Riera, 1991: 13)
> She had become very stingy with the light

> *Nos volveremos viejos esperando – dijo* (G. García Márquez, 1985: 115)
> 'We'll get old waiting,' he said

> *Las palabras se volverán verdad y vida* (J. Cortázar, 1984: 119)
> Words will become truth and life

*Convertirse* is used with a following noun where the stress is strongly laid on the 'full' meaning of *convertir* ('to change into'). Note, however, that the meaning is not as strong as that of English 'to convert'.

> *Como se trata de gentes que pueden convertirse en enemigos, lo más cómodo les parece eliminarles* (J. Goytisolo, 1960: 94)
> Since it is a question of people who could become enemies, the simplest thing is to eliminate them

> *La ropa interior femenina ha dejado de ser algo funcional y escondido para convertirse en un arma de seducción, sutil y sugerente* (*El Mundo*, 8 March 1990: 64)

Ladies' underwear has ceased to be something functional
and hidden, and has become a weapon of seduction, subtle
and suggestive

On the use of *ir* in the sense of 'become', see **1265** above.

## 1267 A Reflexive Verb

Such verbs may in themselves carry the notion of 'becoming', e.g.
*enfadarse* 'to get angry', *enloquecerse* 'to go mad', *enronquecerse* 'to go
hoarse', *cansarse* 'to get tired', *envejecerse* 'to grow old', *enriquecerse*
'to get rich', *ruborizarse* 'to go red, blush', *entristecerse* 'to become
sad', *enfurecerse* 'to become furious'. (*Enloquecer, enronquecer* and
*envejecer* also may have this meaning when used non-reflexively.)

> – *Mamá.*
> – *¿Qué?*
> – *Me canso* (C. J. Cela, 1967b: 39)
> 'Mum.'
> 'What?'
> 'I'm getting tired'

> *Y me pongo a pensar y me entristezco* (C. J. Cela, 1967c: 75)
> And I begin to think and I become sad

## 1268 *(Estar)* + *hecho*

It has already been pointed out (**1218-1219**) that *hecho* can be
used as an alternative to *como*. *(Estar) hecho* (followed by a noun)
may often be translated appropriately by 'to become'.

> *Estás hecho un hombre y muy guapo* – *le manifiesta* (J. A. de
> Zunzunegui, 1956a: 68)
> 'You've become a man, and a very handsome one,' she
> tells him

> *De recién casada estaba hermosa, gorda, reluciente, pero ahora, a
> pesar de no ser vieja aún, está ya hecha una ruina* (C. J. Cela,
> 1963a: 142–3)
> As a newly-wed she was beautiful, plump and resplendent,
> but now, in spite of not yet being old, she has become a
> wreck

> – *¿Y los nenes?*
> – *Hechos unos hombrecetes* (C. J. Cela, 1963a: 127)

'And the kids?'
'Quite grown up now'

## 1269 *Devenir*

*Devenir*, a borrowing from French, is increasingly found in the written language,[22] where it is used both as a verb and as a substantivized infinitive.

*Ocurrir es devenir. Una piedra no «deviene», sólo «es»* (S. Lorén, 1971: 148)
Happening is becoming. A stone does not 'become', it only 'is'

*Su responsabilidad devendrá histórica* (C. Rojas, 1970: 26)
His responsibility will become historic

*Las dos Españas ofrecen multitud de variantes, a las que el devenir histórico matiza cada día* (C. Alonso de los Ríos, 1971: 53)
The two Spains offer a multitude of variants, which historical development daily distinguishes further
(By 'the two Spains', Delibes means the conservative and progressive)

*El devenir* ('Becoming') is the title of a series of poems by E. de Nora (*Poesía*, 331ff.).

# *Deber*

## 1270 Expressing Obligation

English 'ought', 'should', 'have to' are translated by the tense of *deber* which would be the tense of the action of the verb itself:

*Los ciudadanos deben obedecer las leyes* (*DUE*, I, 862)
Citizens must obey the laws
(Compare: *Obedecen las leyes* 'They obey the laws')

*Debí figurármelo* (A. Gala, 1993: 50)
I should have realized
(Compare: *Me lo figuré* 'I realized')

The force of *deber* is strengthened by the use of the Conditional, the Imperfect or the *-ra* Imperfect Subjunctive:

*Deberías/debieras decírselo.*
You ought to tell him

*Debía volverme y mirarle a la cara, pero siento que no puedo, que me ruborizaría* (C. Martín Gaite, 1981: 123)
I should turn and look him in the face, but I feel that I can't, that I would blush

There are several possibilities for the rendering of English 'ought to have', 'should have', in Spanish. First, *deber* may be used in the tense corresponding to that of the action or state of affairs being envisaged:

*Debiste salir entonces*
You ought to have gone then
(The action *saliste* 'you left' is in the speaker's mind)

*Debías salir ayer*
You ought to have gone yesterday
(The speaker is describing the situation that applied yesterday: *tenías la obligación de salir* 'you were under an obligation to leave')

With the Conditional and the *-ra* form of the Imperfect Subjunctive, a Perfect Infinitive is used to make clear the reference to the past:

*Deberías/debieras haber contestado*
You ought to have answered
(Compare *deberías contestar* 'you ought to answer')

An alternative way of formulating the above construction is to use the Conditional Perfect or the *-ra* form of the Pluperfect Subjunctive with the Infinitive:

*Habrías/hubieras debido contestar*
You ought to have answered

## 1271 Expressing Supposition

Strictly, *deber* is followed by *de* when it denotes supposition. As in **1270**, the tense of the auxiliary is the same as the implied tense of the action or state envisaged:

*Debe de resultar muy caro*
It must be very expensive
(suggests *es muy caro*)

*Mucha hambre debió de tener para dedicarse a una alimentación tan indigesta* (**P**. Baroja, 1959: 219)
He must have been very hungry to adopt such an indigestible diet
(suggests *tuvo hambre*)

*Debía de ser muy difícil*
It must have been difficult
(suggests *era muy difícil*)

The Perfect Infinitive can be used with *deber* in the Present tense to indicate a supposition about the past:

*Debe de haber salido* (= *debió de salir*)
He must have left

**1272** Although purists insist on a distinction between *deber* and *deber de* being maintained, it is clear that there is considerable overlap in usage in modern Spanish:

*Deber* for *deber de*:

*No lo sentí llegar, debió subir de puntillas* (C. Martín Gaite, 1981: 157)
I didn't hear him come, he must have tiptoed upstairs

Compare in the same book:

*Lo del hotel de Burgos debió de ser el año 38* (ibid., 116)
The business of the hotel in Burgos must have been in '38

*Calculo que deben ser más de las tres* (J. Goytisolo, 1989: 27)
I calculate that it must be after three o' clock

*– Debes estar mal de la cabeza – se burló Mimí* (I. Allende, 1987: 248)
'You must be sick in the head', scoffed Mimí

*Deber* seems to be used quite regularly in the Perfect for *deber de*:

*Ha debido salir sin hacer ruido*
He must have left without making a noise

*Deber de* for *deber*:

*Marcos, como todo su pelotón, sabía lo que debía de hacer* (T. Salvador, 1968b: 309)
Marcos, like all his platoon, knew what he must do

# Poder

## 1273 Expressing Ability

*Poder* is used to express a physical or logical ability.

> *Se hace lo que se puede, jefe* (M. Vázquez Montalbán,
> 1979b: 90)
> You do what you can, boss

> *No puede ser el martes, sino el sábado* (I. Allende, 1987: 250)
> It can't be Tuesday, but Saturday

In the past, the choice between Imperfect and Preterite is governed
by whether a situation or an action is envisaged. The Preterite
often has the overtone of 'succeed in', 'manage to':

> *Aquella noche no podía dormir* (A. Gala, 1993: 113)
> That night I was unable to sleep
> (suggests a situation: *no dormía*)

> *Una decisión de tal magnitud no podía tomarse al azar* (I.
> Allende, 1987: 249)
> A decision of such magnitude could not be taken hap-
> hazardly
> (suggests a situation: *era imposible...*)

> *Nada pudo disuadirlo* (ibid., 249)
> Nothing could dissuade (succeeded in dissuading) him
> (suggests that he went ahead and acted in spite of
> dissuasion)

> *– Buenas tardes..., ¿tiene aspirinas? – fue lo único que pude decir*
> (ibid., 249)
> 'Good afternoon ... Do you have any aspirins?' was the only
> thing I was able [managed] to say
> (suggests *dije* or *logré decir*)

## 1274 Expressing Permission

In this use, *poder* is the equivalent of English 'may', 'might',
'can', 'could'.

> *– Podéis hablar – le dije* (A. Gala, 1993: 226)
> 'You may speak,' I said to him

- *¿Puedo quedarme en la tuya?* (M. Vázquez Montalbán, 1979b: 87)
'Can I stay in your house?'

The Conditional may be used instead of the Present to achieve a greater degree of politeness:

- *¿Podría hablar con usted?* (ibid., 92).
'Could I speak to you?'

Used in the Preterite, *poder* often has the implication of having gained permission:

*Al fin pude asistir a un colegio* (A. García Morales, 1992: 28)
In the end I was allowed to go to a school

## 1275 Expressing Possibility

Possibility in the future or present is expressed by the Present or Conditional tense of *poder*:

(i)   *Puede/podría venir mañana*
      She may/might come tomorrow

(ii)  *La visión de unos zapatos vacíos me hace imaginar sobre ellos a la persona que los ha llevado o podría llevarlos puestos* (J. Marías, 1989: 29)
      The sight of a pair of empty shoes makes me imagine in them the person who has worn them or who might wear/might be wearing them

Possibility in the past is expressed by a wide range of constructions similar to those used for *deber* when it expresses obligation (see **1270**):

(iii) *Antes de Franco, mis nociones de lo que pudiera estar pasando en el país eran confusas* (C. Martín Gaite, 1981: 130)
      Before Franco, my notions of what might have been happening in the country were confused
      (An alternative to *pudiera estar pasando* is *podría estar pasando*)

(iv)  *Podía haberse arreglado otra habitación cualquiera* (ibid., 163)
      Any other room could have been arranged

(Alternatives to *podía haberse arreglado* are *podría haberse arreglado, se habría podido arreglar, se hubiera podido arreglar*)

The use of the *poder* auxiliary in this sense often has an overtone of reproachfulness:

(v)   *Bien podías habérmelo dicho*
You might have told me

(vi)   *Podía haberse callado*
He/she could have kept quiet

(vii)   *Podría/habría podido ser más discreto*
He/she could have been more discreet

(viii)   *Hubiera podido invitarnos*
He/she might have invited us

(Examples (v–vii)  are from *DUE*, II, 788)

# Subject-Verb Concord

## General Rule

**1276** The general rule is that the verb agrees in number and person with its subject. When there is more than one subject, the verb is plural.

> *El niño jugó toda la tarde en el jardín* (*Esbozo*, 386)
> The child played all afternoon in the garden

> *Las niñas jugaron toda la tarde en el jardín* (*Esbozo*, 386)
> The children played all afternoon in the garden

> *Salieron en el examen problemas y preguntas muy dificultosos* (*Esbozo*, 387)
> Very difficult problems and questions came up in the exam

**1277** When there is more than one subject, and these belong to different persons, the first person takes precedence over the second, and the second over the third.

> *Usted y yo sabemos que hay sólo una solución* (J. C. Onetti, 1979: 30)
> You and I know that there is only one solution

> *Tú y él erais buenos amigos* (*DD*, 110)
> You and he were good friends

**1278** The subject is always implicit in the ending of a Spanish verb, and when nouns which are apparently third person are used with first or second person verbs, the first or second person meaning is retained:

*Entramos los cuatro en el comedor* (J. Ibargüengoitia, 1981: 7)
The four of us went into the dining room
(See also **732**, fourth example)

*Aludía con tanta frecuencia a su viaje que sus amigos llegamos a conocer de memoria los episodios más notables* (J. Ibargüengoitia, ibid.)
He alluded so frequently to his journey that we, his friends, got to know the chief incidents by heart

*Ahora os casáis muchos curas* (C. J. Cela, 1979b: 281)
Now a lot of you priests are getting married

Note that *nadie, ninguno,* etc., which are always used with a third person verb in English, may be used with different persons in Spanish:

*Ninguno estamos solos* (*DD*, 269)
None of us is alone
(Cf. *Ninguno está sólo* 'No one is alone')

*Acabamos de escuchar cosas que ya sabíamos y muchas que algunos ignorábamos* (M. de Riquer, 1967: 157)
We have just heard some things we already knew and many of which some of us were unaware
(The use of the first person plural verb allows the speaker to include himself amongst those who have learned something: to use the form *ignoraban* would be a rude implication that only some of the audience – and not himself – had heard things they did not know. For further similar examples see **401** and **409**)

## Special Cases

### 1279 Subjects Coordinated by *con, y* or *o*

When the two (singular) parts of the subject are joined by the preposition *con*, the verb may be in the singular or the plural, depending on whether the first noun is thought of as constituting the subject in its own right, or whether the two nouns are regarded equally.

*Pedro con su hijo fue a visitarnos* (*Esbozo*, 501)
Pedro came to see us with his son

(*Pedro con su hijo fueron a visitarnos* has the meaning 'Pedro and his son came to see us')

With two subjects joined by *y*, the verb can be in the singular only if the two are thought of as a unit:

*La compra y venta de estos objetos está prohibida* (*DD*, 112)
Buying and selling these things is forbidden

*En el mesón que en Toledo tenía el Sevillano y su mujer, había una linda moza* (Azorín, quoted in *Esbozo*, 502)
There was a pretty wench in the inn in Toledo which was kept by the Sevillian together with his wife
(*Tenían* is also grammatically correct; the plural form implies that the partnership is more equal: 'the Sevillian and his wife')

With *o*, the verb is in the singular if its action can be carried out by only one of the conjoined nouns:

*O Everton o Arsenal ganará la copa este año*
Either Everton or Arsenal will win the cup this year

In other cases, choice may depend on personal or stylistic factors: when only one of the conjoined nouns (the one nearest to the verb) is considered important, then the verb may be in the singular:

*Le atraía la hermosura de la moza o la amenidad del lugar* (*DD*, 113)
Either the beauty of the girl (or the pleasantness of the spot) attracted them
(Implying that it was really the girl's beauty; a plural verb (*atraían*) would give equal weight to the two nouns)

### 1280 Remarks

When the verb precedes a multiple subject, it often agrees only with the first noun (without there being any distinction in meaning of the type described above). However, this occurs mainly in the spoken language and is considered slipshod.[1]

*Lo que descubrió Hernán Cortés y sus compañeros* (*DUE*, II, 1503)
What Hernán Cortés and his companions discovered

**1281** Subjects conjoined by *como* 'like, as' and *junto con* 'together with' may take a singular or a plural verb, though the latter is preferred.[2]

> *La novela como el teatro, usan de estas malicias* (C. J. Cela, 1963c: 11)
> The novel, just like the theatre, uses these gimmicks

**1282** Common nowadays are agreements based on meaning rather than strict grammatical logic, where a singular noun is used in a generic sense:

> *Se pretende así librar al médico de la jornada continua que realizan actualmente* (*MEU*, 46, which comments that this construction is to be avoided at all costs)
> In this way it is claimed that doctors are freed from the continuous day that they work at present

### 1283 Collective Nouns and Related Instances

When the subject is a collective noun used in the singular, the verb is also in the singular, unless it is desired to call attention to the plurality of the group rather than to its totality.[3]

> *La escuadra atravesó el estrecho* (*DD*, 112)
> The squadron crossed the straits
> (The squadron is considered as an anonymous whole)

> *La mayoría daban pena* (F. Vizcaíno Casas, 1979a: 59)
> The majority took pity
> (The author is viewing the majority as a group of individuals)

> *Vuestra generación Camilo, fuisteis muy putañeros* (F. Umbral, 1985: 75)
> Your generation, Camilo, were a load of buggers
> (In this example the subject is thought of as *vosotros*)

> *También la ultraderecha tienen frases que son sincréticas* (words of the Spanish politician Alfonso Guerra, quoted in A. de Miguel, 1985: 26)
> The far right also have sentences which are syncretic

Following the general rule, the verb is generally in the plural when the collective noun is followed by a determining phrase which is itself in the plural,[4] although there are often exceptions to this principle.[5]

> *La mitad de los habitantes han emigrado* (*DD*, 112)
> Half the inhabitants have emigrated

But also:

> *Media docena de compatriotas me encarga que le escriba sobre algo muy concreto* (C. J. Cela, 1979b: 13)
> Half a dozen compatriots instruct me to write to you about something very concrete
> *Un centenar de soldados israelíes murió en esta ofensiva* (*El País*, 5 August 1982: 1)
> A hundred Israeli soldiers died in this offensive

**1284** When the subject is an acronym (even with plural meaning), the verb is usually in the singular.

> *CCOO intentará desdramatizar la negociación colectiva* (title of an article in *El País*, 5 January 1980: 1)
> *Comisiones Obreras* (a Spanish Communist Union) will try to pursue calm collective bargaining
> (Later in the same article a singular verb is even used with *Comisiones Obreras* written out in full)

> *EEUU insinúa que ha perdido el control de los acontecimientos de Líbano* (*El País*, 5 August 1982: 2)
> The US is insinuating that it has lost control over events in the Lebanon

The same is true of the name of an organization considered as a singular entity:

> *¿TIENES PROBLEMAS CON EL ALCOHOL?*
> *ALCOHÓLICOS ANÓNIMOS PUEDE AYUDARTE*
> (Advertisement read by JdeB in Granada, 17 February 1991)
> Problems with alcohol?
> Alcoholics Anonymous can help you

After *más de uno* the verb may be in the singular or plural:

> *Más de uno lo afirma/afirman*
> More than one says so

**1285** After a subject expressing a percentage, the verb may be in the singular or the plural:

> *58,7% de los informantes estudió en centros que enseñaban español* (M. Alvar, 1982: 17)
> 58.7% of informants studied in centres which taught Spanish
> (In the same article, Alvar uses *un 22,6% de los puertorriqueños* + plural verb, p. 19, *otro 15,3%* + singular verb, p. 23, and *un 28,6%* + plural verb, p. 26. etc.)

> *Un 7 por 100 de los hombres llevan barba* (O. Caballero, 1980: 21)
> 7% of men have a beard

(On the expression of percentages, see **220**.)

## 1286 Agreement with the Complement of *ser*

The verb *ser* sometimes agrees with its complement rather than with its subject. This is especially the case when the subject is a neuter pronoun or a collective noun.[6]

> *Eso son cosas que veías tú* (F. Umbral, 1985: 220)
> Those are things that you could see

> *Esta gente son profesores de idiomas* (*DD*, 112)
> These people are language teachers

## 1287 *Ninguno*

*Ninguno* on its own is followed by a singular verb. If it is qualified by a plural phrase (e.g. *ninguno de nosotros*) it may be followed by either a singular or a plural verb; additionally *ninguno de nosotros* may be followed by a first person plural verb (see **1277** above).

> *Ninguno de nosotros está solo* or *Ninguno de nosotros estamos solos*[7]
> None of us is alone

> *No cenaron ninguno de los dos* (C. Martín Gaite, 1980: 196)
> Neither of the two had any dinner

## 1288 *Soy yo el que/quien ...*

See **352**.

## 1289 Impersonal Verbs

Impersonal verbs like *llover* 'to rain', *relampaguear* 'to lighten', *tronar* 'to thunder', etc., may agree with a subject when used figuratively.

> *En 1900 se apagarían las luces y lloverían estrellas* (M. Vargas Llosa, 1981: 17)
> In 1900 the lights would go out and it would rain stars

> *El 15 de agosto, millares de paracaidistas americanos e ingleses llovieron en la región de Provenza* (J. M. Gironella, 1986: 313)
> On the 15th of August, thousands of American and British paratroopers rained down on the region of Provence

## 1290 The *Voseo*

See **255**.

# Syntax of
# Negative Elements

## General

**1291** Simple negation is expressed by placing the negative *no* before the finite verb or auxiliary to which it relates:

> *El sol no salió/No salió el sol* (Contreras, 1978: 75)
> The sun did not come out

> *No ha salido el sol*
> The sun has not come out

Note the difference in meaning between

> *No puede venir* (= *es imposible que venga*)
> He can't come

> *Puede no venir* (= *es posible que no venga*)
> He may not come

**1292** Other negative elements (see **1293**) may precede or follow the verb. When a negative follows the verb, the verb must be preceded by *no* or another negative element or context. When a negative precedes the verb, *no* is omitted. Thus:

> <u>No</u> vendrá <u>ninguno</u> de nuestros amigos
> or
> <u>Ninguno</u> de nuestros amigos vendrá
> None of our friends will come

> <u>Nunca</u> vendrá <u>ninguno</u> de nuestros amigos
> None of our friends will ever come

> <u>No</u> he leído <u>ningún</u> periódico (or, less frequently, *no he leído periódico <u>ninguno</u>*) (*Esbozo*, 412)
> I have never read any newspaper

## Other Negative Elements

**1293** The negative element preceding the verb may be a negative pronoun, adjective or adverb, or, as in the sixth example below, a negative prefix.

*Nadie podía recomendarme ningún libro interesante*
No one could recommend any interesting book to me

*Nunca había visto ningún espectáculo parecido*
I had never seen a spectacle like it

*No me gusta que nadie se humille así por mí* (M. Vargas Llosa1986: 73)
I do not want anyone to humiliate themselves like this for me

*Los indios casi nunca decían nada* (R. J. Sender, 1964: 264)
The Indians hardly ever said anything

*Los españoles apenas han hecho nada para aclarar su futuro* (J. Marías, 1976:101)
The Spaniards have hardly done anything to clarify their future
(*apenas* implies *casi nunca*)

*Parecen incapacitados para entender nada* (*Conversaciones con Monseñor Escrivá de Balaguer*, 100)
They seem incapable of understanding anything.
(*incapacitados* = *no capacitados*)

## Other Negative Contexts

**1294** A number of other elements in Spanish operate as negative contexts, and must be followed by negative forms. Verbs which are implicitly negative (see **1296**) do not require a preceding *no* when followed by a negative.

### 1295 *Sin (que)* as a Negative Context

*Me fui a España sin que ninguno de mis amigos lo supiera*
I went to Spain without any of my friends knowing

*Entramos y salimos sin que nadie tuviera sospechas* (J. C. Onetti, 1979: 139)
We went in and out without anyone suspecting

## 1296 Negative Implicit in a Verb

*A Cecilio Rubes le costaba eliminar ninguna frase* (M. Delibes, 1969b: 176)
It was difficult for Cecilio Rubes to take out any sentence
(*Costar* implies difficulty: compare *era difícil que eliminara ninguna frase*)

*Oficialmente don Felipe ignora que su hija tenga relaciones con nadie* (C. J. Cela, 1969: 323)
Officially Don Felipe does not know that his daughter is going out with anyone
(*ignorar* = *no saber*, and is hence thought of as negative)

*En una palabra me molesta atar mi vida a la de nadie* (M. Delibes, 1969b: 101)
In a word, I do not like linking my life to anyone else's
(Here the negative element is *molestar*: *atar mi vida. . .* is considered unacceptable or undesirable)

## 1297 Comparative as a Negative Context

A comparative also functions as a negative context.

*Usted ha viajado más que ninguno de nosotros*
You have travelled more than any of us (i.e. no one has travelled as much as you)

*La obra de Quevedo muestra mejor que ninguna otra la gravedad del conflicto* (J. Goytisolo, 1977: 122)
Quevedo's work shows better than any other the seriousness of the conflict (i.e. no other work shows it better)

– *¿Me quieres mucho?*
– *Mucho.*
– *¿Más que a nadie?*
– *Más que a nadie* (C. J. Cela, 1963a: 82)
'Do you love me a lot?'
'A lot.'
'More than anyone else?'
'More than anyone else'
(i.e., there is no one I love as much as you)

*Usted lo sabe mejor que nadie* (C. Fuentes, 1979: 14)
You know better than anybody

*Al pianista le gustaba más que nada la música religiosa* (P. Baroja, 1952: 63)
The pianist liked religious music more than anything (implying there was no other kind of music he liked as much)

Note also:

*Él sabe el idioma como nadie*
He knows the language better than anyone
(*como* = *mejor que*)

## 1298 Interrogative as Negative Element

Negative elements are used in rhetorical questions which suggest a negative answer. In such constructions no negative element before the verb is used. However, it is helpful to bear in mind that in statements corresponding to such questions, a second negative element would be present.

*¿Hice daño a ninguno de vosotros?* (*DD*, 268)
Did I hurt any of you?
(But *no hice daño a ninguno de vosotros* 'I didn't hurt any of you')

*¿Qué necesidad tenía de las bendiciones de nadie?* (R. J. Sender, 1967: 88)
What need had he of anyone's blessing?
(This implies *no necesitaba la bendición de nadie*)

*¿Qué daño hacíamos a nadie?* (A. M. de Lera, 1970: 138)
What harm were we doing to anyone?
(This implies *no hacíamos daño a nadie*)

*Pero a la edad de su hija, ¿quién le decía nada?* (J. Izcaray, 1961: 89)
But at his daughter's age, who could tell her anything?
(implying no one could tell her anything)

# Word Order

## Introduction

**1299** This Chapter deals only with the order of the major constituents of sentences. On adjective/noun order, see **166–177**; on the order of numerals with a noun, see **211**; on the order of enclitic pronouns with the verb, see **264–273**; on demonstratives, see **300**, and on *otro*, see **465–467**.

**1300** Spanish word order appears to be freer than English. However, it is important to realize that differences in word order in Spanish always correspond to sometimes quite subtle differences in meaning, differences which are often expressed in English by means of spoken stress (and hence not represented in the written form of the language).

## Declarative Sentences

**1301** We distinguish between 'unmarked' word order (in which no element in the sentence is given special emphasis) and 'marked' word order (in which stress is placed on a particular element in the sentence).

One very important factor to bear in mind in Spanish is that the last element of a declarative sentence tends inherently to carry stress, and that it is therefore in this position that distinctive information (e.g., the answer to a question) stands.[1]

## Unmarked Word Order

### 1302 Sentences Consisting of a Verb (with or without a Noun or Pronoun Subject) and Other Elements (Objects, Adverbs, etc.)

In unmarked order the subject precedes the verb, and objects and prepositional phrases follow:

*El cartero trajo una carta para mi mujer*
The postman brought a letter for my wife

The direct object normally precedes the indirect object, although the indirect object frequently precedes if the direct object is longer (and hence more 'distinctive'):

*Pago la botella a la mujer* (J. Goytisolo, 1989: 115)
I pay for the bottle for the woman

*Cinco siglos antes, la Cofradía de Ballesteros de Lovaina encargó a Roger van der Weyden, en 1435, una tabla para el altar central de la iglesia de Nuestra Señora Extramuros de Lovaina* (*El País Semanal*, 30 May 1993: 66)
Five centuries earlier, in 1435, the Crossbowmen's Guild of Leuven commissioned from Roger van der Weyden a panel for the central altar of the church of Our Lady Without the Walls in Leuven

Adverbs and adverbial phrases often follow the verb directly, in contrast with English:

*Conoce bien el inglés*
She knows English well

*Lola Flores rodó en Sevilla escenas de la película de su vida* (*ABC*, Seville edition, 10 June 93:107)
Lola Flores shot scenes from the film of her life story in Seville

But placing an adverb or adverbial phrase first or last in a sentence gives it rather more emphasis, and this is very likely to be done with longer adverbial phrases:

*La semana pasada telefoneé a su secretario* (J. Goytisolo, 1989: 96)
I phoned your secretary last week

*A partir de ese día Riad Halabí se consideró a sí mismo como un nativo de Agua Santa* (I. Allende, 1987: 133)
From that day on, Riad Halabí considered himself as a native of Agua Santa

*Muevo la cabeza negativamente* (C. Martín Gaite, 1981: 103)
I shake my head negatively

## 1303   Sentences Consisting of a Verb (with or without Enclitic Pronouns) and a Subject only

Both subject–verb and verb–subject orders are possible; the latter seems to be more frequent, to such an extent that it may probably be appropriately considered the unmarked order:

*Pasaron dos años y se consolidó la democracia* (I. Allende, 1987: 165)
Two years passed and democracy was consolidated

*A medida que avanzan las ciencias, la tecnología se hace más compleja* (*Gente*, weekly review in *Cambio-16*, 6 June 1993: 4)
As science advances, technology becomes more complex

*Gritaba el coronel cada vez que se desprendía de la cabeza de la columna* (C. Fuentes, cited in *Esbozo*, 396)
The colonel gave a shout each time he detached himself from the head of the column

Verb–subject order is especially favoured in the following cases:

(1)   Where the subject is a 'long' noun clause

*Aquel primer día me encantaron los círculos de colores que se veían a través del cristal y el extraño código mediante el cual avanzaban las fichas a tenor de los números que iba indicando el dado agitado dentro del cubilete* (C. Martín Gaite, 1981: 107)
That first day I was delighted by the coloured circles visible through the glass and the strange code by which the counters were advanced according to the numbers shown by the dice being shaken in the cup
(The subject of *encantaron* is *los círculos . . . cubilete*. Such sentences are often translated into English with passives, as above)

Verb–subject order is often used in Spanish passive sentences, especially where the subject is a long one:[2]

> *Ha sido votado por el Congreso un crédito para los damnificados* (*MEU*, 47)
> Money for the victims has been voted by Congress

(2) Where the subject is an infinitive or a clause.

> *Basta saber cuántos hay*
> It's enough to know how many there are

> *Me extraña que no se haya notado*
> I'm surprised it's not been noticed

(3) With verbs which do not take a direct object:

> *Me duelen los dientes*
> I have toothache

> *Me duele la cabeza*
> I have a headache

> *Me gusta este libro*
> I like this book

(4) In subordinate clauses where a non-finite form of the verb is used:

> *Habiendo llegado Juan/Al llegar Juan/Llegado Juan, comenzó la fiesta*
> When Juan (had) arrived, the party began[3]

(5) The adverb *ya* initially in a sentence normally requires inversion of subject and verb: *ya verá usted* 'you'll see'; generally in Latin America, however, and in parts of Spain, the order *ya usted verá* is found.[4]

The order subject-verb often places emphasis on the verb:

> *Ese órgano ya existe: no es necesario inventar otro* (*El País Semanal*, 7 August 1993:8)
> Such an organ already exists: it is not necessary to invent another

## Marked Word Order

**1304** There are more marked word order possibilities in Spanish than in English. The following are all the possible alternatives to the unmarked order sentence *El criado trajo una carta para mí* ('the servant brought a letter for me'):

*El criado trajo para mí una carta*
*Trajo el criado para mí una carta*
*Trajo el criado una carta para mí*
*Trajo una carta el criado para mí*
*Trajo una carta para mí el criado*
*Trajo para mí una carta el criado*
*Trajo para mí el criado una carta*
*Una carta trajo el criado para mí*
*Una carta trajo para mí el criado*
*Para mí trajo el criado una carta*
*Para mí trajo una carta el criado*[5]

In the above sentences, emphasis is generally given to the last element when the subject or verb stands first. When an object or prepositional phrase stands first, however, it is the first element that is given emphasis.

Some further examples of objects in initial position:

(i)   – *Dos padres tiene el pobrecito, eso es seguro* – *dijo Elvira* (I. Allende, 1987: 97)
'The poor little thing has got two fathers, that's for sure,' said Elvira

(ii)  *Bachillerato le tenía que haber hecho estudiar* (M. Vázquez Montalbán, 1990b: 18)
I ought to have had it (a dog) study for school exams

*Nada* is very frequently found before the verb as an object:

(iii) *El panorama de un Amurrio que nada tiene que ver con el pequeño pueblo idealizado por Jesús de Galíndez* (M. Vázquez Montalbán, 1990b: 10)
The view of Amurrio which has nothing to do with the little village idealized by Jesús de Galindez

## 1305 Remarks

Marked order does not normally produce ambiguity. In **1304** (i, ii and iii) the object cannot be construed as a subject in any meaningful way (in (i), additionally, the verb is in the singular while *dos padres* is plural).

When ambiguity might result from a change of word order, as in the following sentence

*El entusiasmo vence la dificultad* (Esbozo, 397)
Enthusiasm overcomes difficulty

Spanish sometimes (see **660**) uses the preposition *a* before the object if it is placed first:

*A la dificultad vence el entusiasmo*
Enthusiasm overcomes difficulty.

**1306** Except in sentences which consist only of a subject and a verb, the verb does not usually stand in final position. In sentences consisting of four or more elements, the verb is normally the first or second element.

It is possible, however, to find examples with the verb in final position in poetry and literary prose, but they are considered 'unusual' or 'affected':[6]

*La consigna de hoy se enuncia así: «Disciplina, nuestro orgullo es»* (J. L. Alcocer, 1978: 14)
The motto for today goes as follows: 'Discipline is our pride' (The stilted phraseology of the Francoist youth movement)

**1307** In the popular speech of some areas of Latin America, a (repeated) verb sometimes occurs in final position with emphatic meaning:[7]

– *¿Son muchas las yeguas?*
– *No, señora. Son ocho no más, son* (Kany, 1951: 267)
'Are there many mares?'
'No, ma'am. Only eight, no more than eight'

*Tengo sentimientos, tengo* (ibid.)
I sure got feelings

In Ecuador, Peru and Bolivia, the verb (not repeated) can be found in final position:

– *¿Y tú lo recomiendas a Luis?*
– *Sí señor, hombre bueno es* (Lapesa, 1980: 554)
'And you recommend Luis?'
'Yes, sir, he's a good guy'

**1308** Note the use of *él* and *ella* after adjectives or nouns in the popular speech of some areas of Latin America, with emphatic value:[8]

> – *Parece listo este Escopeta.*
> – *Sí, señora; pero . . . muy movido él* (Kany, 1951: 125)
> 'This Escopeta seems clever.'
> 'Yes, sir; but . . . very pretentious, he is

> *Por culpa de doña Melanía Querejazu, escritora ella y femi-nista* (ibid.)
> Through Doña Melanía Querejazu, who's a writer and a great feminist

## 1309 Stress

In Spanish, by contrast with English, spoken stress tends to fall only on the last element of the sentence:

> *A las siete vendrá JUAN*
> JOHN will come at seven

> *Vendrá Juan a las SIETE*
> John will come at SEVEN

Thus sentences with spoken stress elsewhere, such as

> *JUAN vendrá a las siete*

> *Juan VENDRÁ a las siete*

sound odd. (Compare the acceptability of English 'John will come at SEVEN/JOHN will come at seven/John will COME at seven', etc.)

## 1310 'Topicalization'

A common device for giving emphasis to a direct object or indirect object in Spanish is to place it as the first element in the sentence. Only one such element can be moved at a time, and an appropriate enclitic pronoun must also be used with the verb.

> Direct Object:

> *La última frase la he dicho tan bajo que no debe haberla oído* (C. Martín Gaite, 1981: 104)
> I uttered the last sentence so quietly that he couldn't have heard it

*Eso no lo entendíamos* (C. Fuentes, 1985: 15)
We didn't understand that

*A los hombres los guían intereses monótonos* (A. Gala, 1993: 17)
Men are guided by monotonous interests

Indirect Object:

*Al bandido le bastó una mirada para comprender que su enemigo se encontraba a salvo* (I. Allende, 1990: 146)
One glance was enough for the bandit to know that his enemy was safe

See also **281**.

## 1311 Cleft Sentences

Elements in a sentence can be given special emphasis by being introduced by a form of the verb *ser* (cf. English 'it was then that I saw him'). There are two points to note about the Spanish construction by contrast with the English:

(1)  The tense of *ser* is usually the same as that of the tense of the 'original' main verb: thus

**Fue** *Juan quien me lo* **dijo**
It was Juan who told me

(2)  Whereas in English a relative pronoun ('that', 'who' etc.) is used in such constructions, in standard Peninsular Spanish the appropriate relative adverb is the rule when an adverb is the·element being introduced:

*Fue* **en Madrid donde** *le conocí*
It was in Madrid that I met him

Further examples:

*Fue por entonces cuando don Miguel de Unamuno dio una conferencia en el Ateneo* (J. A. de Zunzunegui, 1956a: 188)
It was about that time that Don Miguel de Unamuno gave a lecture in the Ateneo
(The corresponding interrogative sentence would be *¿Cuándo dio una conferencia . . . ?*, and hence the appropriate relative adverb is *cuando*)

*Aquí es donde suelo yo comer* (P. Baroja, 1951: 86)
It's here that I usually eat
(*¿Dónde suelo comer?*)

*Y así es como he visto a Leticia* (F. Umbral, 1979: 112)
And so it was that I saw Leticia
(*¿Cómo he visto ... ?*)

*No me decía dónde era donde podía caer y si la caída sería mortal*
(M. Delibes, 1948: 134)
He did not tell me where I might fall and if falling would
be fatal

*Cómo más disfruta es ofreciendo recitales y explicando los
poemas al público* (*El País Internacional*, 23 February 1987)
What he enjoys most is giving (poetry) recitals and talking to
the audience about the poems

However, in Latin-American Spanish, *que* is often used in such
a context:[9]

*Tal vez fue entonces que cerró los ojos* (M. Puig, 1980: 95)
Perhaps it was then that he closed his eyes

*No recuerdo si fue en París o en Praga que me sobrevino una
pequeña duda* (P. Neruda, 1976: 237)
I cannot remember whether it was in Paris or in Prague that I
was assailed by a little doubt

## 1312 Inseparability of Nouns and their Qualifying Phrases

As in English, adjectives and qualifying phrases cannot be
separated from the noun or noun phrase to which they pertain.
Thus:

NOT *Vendo bicicleta para señora en buen estado*
BUT *Vendo bicicleta en buen estado para señora*
For sale: lady's bicycle in good condition

NOT *Sombreros para niños de paja*
BUT *Sombreros de paja para niños*
Children's straw hats[10]

Exceptions to this principle are found in poetry, or where there is a
deliberate intention to create ambiguity or humour.

Nevertheless, if a noun phrase is thought of as a single unit, then the adjective or qualifying phrase does not intervene in the noun phrase; contrast

> *Un libro de bolsillo extraordinario*
> NOT *Un libro extraordinario de bolsillo*
> An extraordinary pocket book
> (*Un libro de bolsillo* is thought of as a unit)

and

> *El libro extraordinario de mi amigo Pablo*
> NOT *El libro de mi amigo Pablo extraordinario*
> The extraordinary book of my friend Pablo
> (*El libro de mi amigo Pablo* is not thought of as a unit)

## Interrogative Sentences

**1313** In direct questions which require a yes/no answer, the verb may stand first:

> *¿Está mejor tu hermano?* (*Esbozo*, 396)
> Is your brother better?

> *¿No era ésa razón de sobra?* – dijo el coronel Frutos García (C. Fuentes, 1985: 13)
> 'Wasn't that more than enough reason?' said Colonel Frutos García

or the declarative sentence order may be preserved:

> *¿Tu hermano está mejor?*

In the latter case, the interrogative nature of the sentence is indicated in speech by the intonation and in writing by question marks *¿?*.[11]

**1314** Questions in Spanish may also be introduced by *¿es que ...?*

> *¿Es que no hay en este momento cosas interesantes que contar?*
> Aren't there any interesting things to relate at the moment?

> *¿Es que vas a venir o no?*
> Are you coming or not?

See also **581**, first example.

It should be noted that the use of *¿es que . . . ?* implies the idea of explanation or elucidation ('is it because . . . ?') as does the declarative *es que . . .* [12] In particular, it should be stressed that Spanish *¿es que . . . ?* is not equivalent to the more neutral French interrogative *est-ce que . . . ?*

> *Sí. Yo es que soy un frívolo* (F. Umbral, 1985: 163)
> Yes. It's because I'm a frivolous person

> *Es que es malo papá Telmo* (M. Delibes, 1987: 56)
> It's because Papá Telmo is bad

**1315** Another common way of forming questions in Spanish is to 'topicalize' (see **1310**) a noun phrase, especially a subject consisting of a number of words, by placing it first, and then to follow this with the normal declarative order. Note that the inverted question mark is only used before the question proper. Thus:

EITHER

> *¿No se opondrán a esas medidas los socios más prestigiosos de la asociación?*
> Will not the most prestigious members of the association be opposed to these measures?

OR

> *Los socios más prestigiosos de la asociación ¿no se opondrán a esas medidas?* (Van Dam, 1967: 382)

**1316** An interrogative pronoun or adverb always stands in initial position:

> *¿Cuándo quieres venir?*
> When do you want to come?

> *¿Quién te lo ha dicho?*
> Who has told you?

although the 'topicalization' construction exemplified in **1313** is also available here:

> *Este gobierno estúpido, ¿qué es lo que pretende?* (Contreras, 1978: 103)
> What is this stupid government trying to do?

An interrogative pronoun is normally followed immediately by the verb:

> *¿Qué quiere usted?* NOT *\*¿Qué usted quiere?*

However, in some areas of Latin America, subject pronouns are sometimes used before the verb in questions:

> *¿Qué tú quieres?* (Kany, 1951: 125)
> What do you want?

> *¿Por qué Ud. dice que yo soy el culpable?* (ibid.)
> Why do you say that I'm the guilty one?

> *¿Dónde yo estoy?* (Lapesa, 1980: 585)
> Where am I?

**1317** In indirect questions, the verb similarly immediately follows the interrogative pronoun:

> *Pedro pregunta qué quiere Juan* (NOT ... *qué Juan quiere*)
> Peter asks what Juan wants

However, in indirect questions introduced by interrogative adverbs (*¿cómo?* 'how', *¿dónde?* 'where'. etc.), it is possible for the subject to precede the verb, although the Spanish preference is still for the verb to precede the subject:[13]

> *Mi padre sabe dónde vive Juan/dónde Juan vive*
> My father knows where Juan lives

## Set Expressions

**1318** In a number of cases, the order of elements in set expressions differs from the corresponding English expression:

> *El altar y el trono*
> Throne and altar

> *Bajar y subir*
> To go up and down

> *La bandera de las barras y las estrellas*
> The stars and stripes

# Affective Suffixes[1]

## General

**1319** Not all the possible meanings and nuances of Spanish suffixes are examined in this chapter;[2] we limit ourselves to diminutive, augmentative and pejorative suffixes.

Affective suffixes have a high frequency in Spanish and have a wide range of expressive meanings, both literal and stylistic, which often pose considerable problems in translation. The range of nuances of some of these forms may give the impression of contradictoriness and of an unprincipled area of usage.

Many words formed with affective suffixes do not appear in the dictionaries. The numerous possibilities give Spanish vocabulary an 'open' nature: on the basis of existing 'traditional' words, new words can be created to denote, describe or qualify people, things or situations in an original way.

The translation of these suffixes into English is often difficult or impossible:

> *Platero! Platen! Platerillo! Platerete! Platerucho!* (J. R. Jiménez, *Platero y yo*, quoted in Berschin, 1986: 311)

## Forms

**1320** The addition of an affective suffix to a noun stem does not in the majority of cases change the gender of the original noun:

| (i) | *Un libro* 'a book' | → | *un librito* 'a little book' |
| (ii) | *Una mesa* 'a table' | → | *una mesita* 'a little table' |

However, the suffix *-n* always makes the noun masculine (although the feminine form *-ona* is also found in some instances (examples (vii) and (viii)):

| (iii) | *Una calentura* 'a fever' | → | *un calenturón* 'a high fever' |
| (iv) | *Una botella* 'a bottle' | → | *un botellón* 'a large bottle. magnum' |
| (v) | *Una jaqueca* 'a migraine' | → | *un jaquecón* 'a terrible headache' |
| (vi) | *Una memoria* 'a memory' | → | *un memorin* 'a prodigious memory' |
| (vii) | *Una mujer* 'a woman' | → | *una mujerona* 'a large woman' |
| (viii) | *Un(a) sinvergüenza* 'somebody shameless, a scoundrel' | → | *un sinvergonzón* 'a real rogue', *una sinvergonzona* 'a brazen hussy' |

The presence of a suffix sometimes necessitates a change of spelling:

| (ix) | *La vaca* 'the cow' | → | *la vaquita* 'the little cow' |
| (x) | *Una cerveza* 'a beer' | → | *una cervecita* 'a little beer' |

**1321** The most important affective suffixes in Spanish are[3]

| Augmentative suffixes | Diminutive suffixes | Suffixes with pejorative meaning |
| --- | --- | --- |
| *-azo* (f. *-aza*) | *-ito* (f. *-ita*) | *-aco* (f. *-aca*) |
| *-ón* (f. *-ona*) | *-illo* (f. *-illa*) | *-acho* (f. *-acha*) |
| *-oide* (f. *-oide*)[4] | *-ico* (f. *-ica*) | *-uco* (f. *-uca*) |
| *-ote* (f. *-ota*) | *-ín* (f. *-ina*) | *-ucho* (f. *-ucha*) |
| | *-ino* (f. *-ina*) | *-uelo* (f. *-uela*) |
| | *-iño* (f. *-iña*) | *-uzo* (f. *-uza*) |
| | *-ejo* (f. *-eja*) | |
| | *-ete* (f. *-eta*) | |

Examples:

| | | |
|---|---|---|
| *Un animal* 'an animal' | → | *un animalazo* 'a big animal' |
| *La casa* 'the house' | → | *la casita* 'the little house' |
| *La gente* 'people' | → | *la gentuza* 'the rabble' |

The above classification should not be taken too strictly: *-azo*, for example, can be used with pejorative as well as augmentative meaning and the pejorative *-uelo* may sometimes be used as a diminutive. (On the multiplicity of meanings of the suffixes, see the discussion of *-azo* in **1327**.) *Grandote* generally has a pejorative meaning: the suffix *-ote* gives the stem *grande* the additional meaning of 'too', 'excessively'.[5]

**1322** Sometimes suffixes are not simply added to the stem word: vowels are dropped or supporting vowels and consonants may be added. The following 'rules' apply to *-ito*, for instance:

| Ending of stem | + *-ito* suffix | Examples |
|---|---|---|
| *-a* or *-o* | The vowel falls and the suffix is added | *casa* → *cas-+ita* <br> *libro* → *libr+ito* |
| consonants except *-n* and *-r* | + suffix | *árbol* → *arbol+ito* |
| *-e*, *-n*, *-r* | + *c* + suffix | *hombre* → *hombre+c+ito* <br> *joven* → *joven+c+ito* <br> *mujer* → *mujer+c+ita* |
| monosyllabic words which end in a consonant or a diphthong | + *ecito* or + *c* + *ecito* | *flor* → *flor+ecita* <br> *pie* → *pie+c+ecito* |

But these 'rules' are not always strictly adhered to. *Jardinillo* and *mujerita* are found (especially in regional dialects) in addition to *jardincillo* and *mujercita*; an important exception to the 'rule' for words ending in *-r* is *señor* → *señorito*. Both *manita* and *manecita* are found as diminutives of *mano*.

**1323** Although primarily associated with nouns and adjectives, affective suffixes can be added to all grammatical categories apart from articles, prepositions and conjunctions.

(1) Suffixes with nouns. In addition to the usage with common nouns already exemplified, affective suffixes can be used with all kinds of proper nouns and with nouns denoting nationality, etc.:

*Cuatro madrileñitos iban hacia la costa caliente* (F. Umbral, 1972: 100)
Four little boys from Madrid were going to the warm coast

*Una españolaza* is, according to context, a 'heavy, very dark Spanish woman' or 'a magnificent example of a Spanish woman'[6]

*Usted comprende que lo importante de su viaje era ver a Chilito desde arriba* (P. Neruda, 1976: 349)
You understand that the important thing about his journey was to see our beloved Chile from above

*No es nada difícil, ¿verdad, Miguelón?* (S. Lorén, 1967a: 189)
It's not at all difficult, is it, Big Mike?

Diminutives of proper names sometimes differ markedly from the stem word: *José* → *Pepe, Francisco* → *Paco, María Teresa* → *Maite*, etc.

The diminutive forms themselves have a number of further diminutive variants: *Pepe* → *Pepito, Pepillo, Pepitín, Pepete, Pepón, Pepazo, Pepote, Pepino*; *Paco* → *Paquillo, Pacón, Pacolete, Pacorro*. Such forms (and there are many more possibilities) well illustrate the productivity of affective suffixes in Spanish.

(2) Suffixes with adjectives. The English translation must usually attach the affective idea to the noun.

*A este (niño) no lo quiso porque nació cieguecito* (C. J. Cela, 1963c: 136)
He did not want the little boy because he was born blind
(The use of the diminutive suffix also conveys a feeling of pity which is not easily rendered in English: cf. **1325**)

*Se pasó todita la tarde durmiendo* (*DUE*, II, 1331)
He spent the whole of the afternoon sleeping
(*DUE* comments that the diminutive has an emphatic value)

The affective suffix may also have an intensifying effect, which can be rendered in English by an adverb:

*Lo que va a pasar puede ser facilón* (E. Romero, 1963: 365)
What is going to happen may be extremely easy

(3)    Suffixes with cardinal and ordinal numbers.

*Querido Manu, cálmate . . . ¡si a ti cien mil beatas, ni te van ni te vienen! Es como si yo le doy cinquito al primer pobre que me encuentre en la calle* (J. A. de Zunzunegui, 1956b: 158–9)
Dear Manu, calm down . . . What are a hundred thousand pesetas to you? It's like me giving five miserable pesetas to the first poor man I met in the street
(The diminutive suffix reinforces the contrast between five and a hundred thousand)

*Y yo soy la primerita que se alegra* (Beinhauer, 1968: 239)
And I'm the very first to be pleased
(Here the diminutive suffix has an intensifying meaning: cf. *ahoritita* and *solitita* (**1324** (iii and iv))

(4)    Suffixes with adverbs and adverbial expressions. The following forms are fairly common: *ahorita* (<*ahora* 'now'), *a la mañanita* (<*a la mañana* 'in the morning'), *cerquita* (<*cerca* 'near'), *derechito* (<*derecho* 'right'), *en seguidita* (<*en seguida* 'immediately'), *hasta lueguito* (*hasta luego* 'so long'), *lejitos* (<*lejos* 'far'), *poquito a poco* (<*poco a poco* 'gradually'), *tempranito* (<*temprano* 'early'), etc. The *-ito* suffix is the one most generally used. The force of the diminutive suffix is usually to intensify the meaning of the adverb: hence *cerquita* has the meaning 'very close', *a la mañanita* 'first thing in the morning', etc.

*- Sí, señorito, ahora. – Afá hizo meliflua la voz. – Ahorita si te parece mejor – recuperó en tono duro* (I. Aldecoa, 1969: 67)
'Yes, young sir, now.' Afá's voice sweetened. 'Right now, if you think it best,' he continued, in a hard tone

(5)    Suffixes with verbs. For affective suffixes with gerunds and past participles, see **1164** and **1230**. We note here the use of the suffix *-ón* with verbal stems to form adjectives denoting the frequent or intensive nature of the action of the verb.

| | | |
|---|---|---|
| *comer* | → | *comilón* 'greedy, gluttonous' |
| *criticar* | → | *criticón* 'over-critical, niggly' |
| *dormir* | → | *dormilón* 'sleepyhead' |
| *faltar* | → | *faltón* 'untrustworthy, unreliable' |
| *jugar* | → | *juguetón* 'playful, frolicsome' |
| *mirar* | → | *mirón* 'nosey; voyeur (as noun)' |
| *preguntar* | → | *preguntón* 'inquisitive, nosey' |
| *replicar* | → | *replicón* 'argumentative' |
| *responder* | → | *respondón* 'cheeky, saucy' |
| *tragar* | → | *tragón* 'greedy, gluttonous' |

The suffixes are sometimes attached to verbal stems to form new verbs in -*ear* which express the ongoing nature of an action, or a repeated action:

| | | |
|---|---|---|
| *bailar* | → | *bailotear* 'to dance about' |
| *dormir* | → | *dormitar* 'to doze' |
| *besar* | → | *besuquear* 'to cover with kisses, to smooch, canoodle' |
| *lavar* | → | *lavotear* 'to wash quickly (and badly)' |
| *llorar* | → | *lloriquear* 'to snivel, whimper' |

Great care must be taken in using such words: *lloriquear* could not be applied to genuine grief; *corretear* 'to run about, chase around' could not be used of an Olympic athlete; *juguetear* 'to toy with' is inappropriate for a poker game with a million peseta stake!

(6) Suffixes with pronouns.

*Gracias, Josechu, no sabes cuantísimo te lo agradezco* (M. Delibes, 1969a: 293)
Thanks, Josechu, you have no idea how very grateful I am to you

*Me lo ha dicho todito* (*DUE*, II, 1331)
She has told me absolutely everything

(7) Suffixes with interjections. Most frequent are ¡*clarito!* (<¡*claro!* 'of course!'), ¡*cuidadito!* (<¡*cuidado!* 'careful!'), ¡*carambita!* (<¡*caramba!* 'goodness!, gosh!').

*Y cuidadito con mentar para nada la funeraria* (J. A. de Zunzunegui, 1958: 299)
And take good care not to mention the undertaker's/ funeral parlour

*¡Carambita con el hombre!* (Beinhauer, 1968: 77)
To hell with the man!

## 1324 Remark

A number of suffixes may be used in combination:

  (i)   *pícaro* + *ón* +*azo*   →   *picaronazo* 'real rogue'
  (ii)  *plaza* + *uela* + *eta*   →   *plazoletilla* 'little square'
  +*illa*
  (*ue* becomes *o* when unstressed: see also **916**).

Sometimes the same suffix may be repeated to reinforce the affective nuance; this is especially common in Latin-American Spanish:[7]

  (iii)  *Ahoritita nos bajamos, le dijo a Félix* (C. Fuentes, 1979: 18)
  We're going down right now, he said to Félix

  (iv)  *¿Yo solitita delante de todos los soldados?* (M. Vargas Llosa, 1983b: 12)
  Me on my very own in front of all the soldiers?

  (v)  *amigazazo* (<*amigo*) 'very good friend'
  *bocazaza* (<*boca*) 'very big mouth' (Monge, 1972: 241 n. 19)

## Meaning

**1325** The categories of diminutive, augmentative and pejorative used above represent the basic meanings of the affective suffixes:

*Diminutive:*

  *¡Que me mate usted! – le suplicó el hombrín* (J. A. de Zunzunegui,1959a: 34)
  'Kill me!' begged the little man

*Augmentative:*

  In M. Delibes, *Las ratas*, the parish priest is referred to as *el curón* ('the big priest'), and is described as follows:

*Don Zósimo, el párroco, levantaba dos metros y medio y pesaba 125 kilos* (p. 99)

Don Zósimo, the parish priest, stood eight foot high and weighed nineteen and a half stone (275 lb)

The use of the augmentative suffix here expresses admiration

*Pejorative:*

*Es gentuza y no veo por qué hemos de preocuparnos tanto por ellos* (J. M. Gironella, 1966b: 41)

They are common and I don't see why we have to worry ourselves so much about them

It is important to realize that these suffixes generally add an affective value to their stem word; diminutive and augmentative suffixes also have an emotional overtone which is often more important than any indication of size. The range of nuances is considerable: affection, friendliness, tenderness, love, admiration, politeness, pity, familiarity, joy, modesty (or false modesty), care with which something is done, safety and security, comfort, irony and mockery, mischief, euphemism and pejorative meaning, etc.

**1326** But in fact the meaning of the affective suffixes is not so easily described. Although *pelón* 'bald, having short hair' and *rabón* 'tailless, having a shorter tail than is normal'[8] have the augmentative suffix *-ón*, their meaning is clearly in contradiction to the augmentative idea. *Ratón* 'mouse' is also smaller than *rata* 'rat'. *Tristón* means 'somewhat sad'.[9]

Adjectives with affective suffixes can often be qualified by intensifying adverbs:

*Me siento muy tristona y alicaída* (D. Fernández Flórez, 1967: 371)

I feel very gloomy and downhearted

*Estaba muy malita, tú lo sabes. ¡Estaba tan malita!* (E. Quiroga, 1950: 85)

She was very poorly, you know, So poorly!

This adds to translation difficulties: *muy tristona* obviously cannot be rendered by '\*very somewhat sad', for example.

Apparently contradictory suffixes can be used in the same word:

*Nadie sabía si era una criatura magra y espigadita o gordezuela y culoncilla* (C. J. Cela, 1963b: 73)
No one knew whether she was a thin, slender baby or a plump, chubby-bottomed one
(The *-ón* suffix expresses the largeness of the baby's bottom (*culo*); the *-illa* suffix is used because it refers to a baby)

**1327** Another characteristic of Spanish suffixes is that the same form may have (very) different meanings. An example of this is *-azo*, which has at least the following meanings:

(1)    Augmentative:

*Se sentía tan lejos de aquellos tomazos que guardaba encima del armario* (J. M. Gironella, 1966b: 274)
He felt so far from those great tomes he kept on top of the wardrobe

This use of *-azo* is even more common in Latin-American Spanish, where it is used with adjectives as a kind of alternative to *-ísimo* (see **186**):[10]

– *¿Están feos?*
– *¡Feazos!* (Kany,1951: 51)
'Are they ugly?'
'Very ugly!'

*El patrón es influyentazo* (C. Fuentes, 1979: 257)
The boss is very influential

In the Peninsula, however, *-ísimo* is always used.

(2)    Favourable meaning:

*Y ese don Carlos no me negaréis que es un tipazo* (J. A. de Zunzunegui, 1958: 100)
And you won't deny that Don Carlos is a great guy

(3)    The addition of *-azo* to a word may indicate a blow given by the object expressed by the stem word:

*Volví a asestarle un nuevo derechazo en el estómago* (M. Delibes, 1948: 142)
I gave him another right-hander in the stomach
(In a footballing context, *derechazo* can also mean a kick with the right foot. Note also in this context *cabezazo* 'a header')

*¡Qué hachazo le dio!* (C. J. Cela, 1971: 75)
What a blow he gave him with the axe!

(4) A shot with a firearm: *fusilazo* 'rifle shot', *pistoletazo* 'pistol shot', *cañonazo* 'cannon shot', etc. *Balazo* may mean 'shot' or 'bullet wound'.

(5) *a* + noun + *-azo* + *limpio*. This common construction indicates an action repeated several or even many times. In spite of the plural meaning, the expression is always in the singular (never *\*a* + noun + *-azos limpios*). *Limpio* 'clean' adds a nuance of exclusiveness, 'just with'.

*Fue en la cárcel de Burgos donde uno de los condenados fue rematado a cristazo limpio sobre la cabeza* (F. Arrabal, 1972a: 159)
It was in Burgos prison that one of the condemned men was executed by having a crucifix hammered into his head

*Recorrieron el pueblo despertándolo a trompetazo limpio* (S. Lorén, 1967b: 290)
They went round the village blowing a trumpet to wake everyone up

(6) *-azo* with proper nouns. The suffix is used in this way to refer to political events associated with certain individuals. *El gironazo* (sub-heading in the *Heraldo de Aragón*, 2 January 1975: 30, referred to a spectacular and sensational appearance by José Antonio Girón de Velasco, the then Minister of Labour. The following have also been used recently: *pinochetazo* (the coup by General Pinochet in Chile in 1973), *espinolazo* (the coup by General Spinola in Portugal in 1974), *tejerazo* (the attempted coup by Lt.-Col. Tejero in Spain on 21 February 1981).[11]

**1328** In Latin-American Spanish, where undoubtedly these suffixes are more widely used than in the Peninsula, the affective meaning is often partly or wholly lost: many words with suffixes have become fully lexicalized, and one regularly encounters both in speech and writing forms like *ahorita, patroncito* and *con permisito* for *ahora* 'now', *patrón* 'boss' and *con permiso* 'excuse me'.

# Social Contexts in which Diminutive Suffixes are Used

## 1329 To or in Connection with Children

It has already been noted how the diminutive suffixes express affection, and it is therefore perhaps natural that they are often used in connection with someone who needs protection and tenderness; accordingly, these suffixes are used frequently in speaking to or about children.

## 1330 Children's Speech

Children themselves use many diminutive suffixes in their speech. Understandably, suffixes are therefore also used in texts which imitate children's language, indicate the childishness of a person or a situation, or to introduce a playful element.

## 1331 Women's Speech

Although statistical information is lacking, it appears that women tend to use diminutive suffixes more than men, and that men may avoid their use. The following examples illustrate some of the associations.

*Volvía con su mujer. «Mi mujerciña», pensaba, ruborizándose del diminutivo* (E. Quiroga, 1950: 169)
He returned with his wife. 'My little wife', he thought, blushing at the diminutive
The subject, Don Álvaro, is described as a real he-man. Does he blush at the diminutive because it reveals his feelings and because the use of such a suffix is considered rather effeminate?

*– ¿Tú qué dices, Lilito?*
*– ¡Oh, no me llames así, Paulina! Te lo suplico. Siempre te he dicho que no me gusta que emplees conmigo esos nombres horribles* (M. Delibes, 1969b: 39)
'What do you say, Lilito'
'Oh, don't call me that name, Paulina! Please. I've always told you that I don't like you using those horrid names with me'
(*Lilito* is the diminutive of *Cecilio*)

– *Esto es un disparate, Aurelito.*
– *No me vuelva a llamar Aurelito, que ya soy el coronel Aureliano Buendía* (G. García Márquez, 1977: 97)
'This is foolishness, Aurelito.'
'Don't call me Aurelito ever again, because now I am Colonel Aureliano Buendía'
(Buendía has just told his father-in-law that he is going to fight for the rebel forces in the civil war; he considers the use of the diminutive to be too closely associated with this earlier status of a son-in-law and inconsistent with his new status as a rebel soldier)

## 1332 The Regional Nature of some Suffixes

The *-iño* suffix is characteristic of Galicia (cf. **1331**, first example, which takes place in Galicia); *-ín* is typical of Asturias, *-uco* of Santander, *-ino* of Extremadura, *-illo* (or *-iyo*) of Andalusia, *-ico* of Murcia, La Mancha and especially Aragón and Central America.

# Notes

## Pronunciation

[1]There was, however, a marked tendency to anticipate the Academies' decision: DUE and the last edition of DD consider *ch* simply as *c* + *h* in alphabetical classification, for instance. Seco calls explicit attention to the matter in his *Advertencia preliminar*, *DD*, xx. DRAE, however, even in the 1992 edition, continues the traditional system.

[2]See *BRAE*, May–August 1991, 399–400.

[3]Following *Esbozo*, 133.

[4]*Esbozo* does not consider *rr* a letter in its own right.

[5]For further information, see Canfield (1981).

[6]Marsá (1986: 26); De Miguel (1985: 183–7 and passim); Alvar (1987).

[7]Marsá (1986: 33, 109); Malmberg (1947–8).

[8]See also *DD*, 119, which observes that the normal pronunciation of *coñac* is [koɲak] but that [koɲá] and [koɲás] are also common. *DRAE*, 398, accepts the spellings *coñac* or *coñá*.

[9]Lapesa (1980: 598).

[10]See also *MEU*, 152.

[11]See, for example, *DRAE*, 275.

[12]See De Bruyne (1986).

[13]*DD*, 326, points out that only in affected speech is *reloj* heard, but considers that the commonly used plural *relós* is vulgar.

[14]See, however, on the increased use of *k* in special cases, De Bruyne (1977, 1989).

[15]*Esbozo*, 124. Both spellings are equally valid, and the hesitation is clearly evident from the fact that a member of the Real Academia Española sometimes writes *quilómetros* and sometimes *kilómetros* (M. Alvar, 1982: 112 and 123). In contexts where *c* is possible, there is a clear tendency for *k* to be replaced by *c*. The spellings *folclor* or *folclore* are given in *DRAE*, 692 (though *DD*, 199, continues to mention *folklore*).

[16]See *Esbozo*, 37. At the IV Congreso de las Academias de Lengua Española (Buenos Aires, 1964), *yeísmo* was admitted, though it was advised that the difference between [ʎ] and [j] should be maintained in teaching.

[17]Lapesa (1980: 569–71).

[18]Confusingly enough, this term is occasionally also used for the acute accent (í).
[19]Salvador (1987).
[20]*DUE*, II, 1558. *DRAE*, 1464, however, gives the spelling *váter*.
[21]Lope Blanch (1968: 53–4). *Esbozo* does not otherwise make this distinction. It says correctly (133) that *x* is sometimes pronounced as [s] at the end of a word.
[22]Note that for *MEU* (22, 136) the only correct spelling for such words is with *x*. However, *DRAE*, 954 and 967, gives (without comment) the forms in both *j* and *x*. See also *DD*, 257–8.
[23]For further details, see Lapesa (1980: 570–1).
[24]*DRAE*, 19, 171, 336, 1510.
[25]In the majority of cases, *DRAE* indicates a preferred spelling.
[26]Marsá (1986: 30).
[27]The different possibilities are discussed in detail in *Esbozo*, 89–98.
[28]Cf. *Esbozo*, 67, n. 8.
[29]*MEU*, 25.
[30]At least for foreign learners: but see Gabriel García Márquez's recently expressed view (*La Vanguardia*, 5 October 1984, cited in *Boletín Cultural*, 37, November 1984, 10) that the written accents of Castilian should be suppressed.
[31]Marsá (1986: 69) gives a long list of similar cases.
[32]*Cartel* also has the meaning 'poster'. The variant *cártel* is only available with the meaning of 'cartel': *DRAE*, 301, gives both variants in this meaning, with the form *cartel* first.
[33]*DRAE*, 658, prefers the form *exegesis*.
[34]See *DD*, 329: the Academy prefers the form *reuma*, although *reúma* is more common.
[35]See *MEU*, 24, for a longer list.
[36]*DD*, 331.
[37]Lapesa (1980: 456): *MEU*, 119; *DD*, 166: Haensch (1984: 172).
[38]A more extensive list of rules for the use of capital letters in Spanish can be found in *Esbozo*, 144–5. See also *MEU*, 26.

## The Article

[1]*DD*, 24
[2]Fernández (1951: 170, n.1)
[3]The explanation in this connection is rather different: according to JdeB's informants BUS and ALV the function of the article is chiefly demonstrative and relates back emphatically once again to what has been already mentioned earlier in the sentence. LAP and MON consider the construction without the article as more typical of the written language.
[4]In his *Nicaragua tan violentamente dulce* (1984) J. Cortázar oscillates between *la Argentina* (pp. 21 and 111) and *Argentina* (p. 50 and passim).
[5]Kany (1951: 19) supplies interesting additional information about the use of the definite article with geographical names in Latin America.
[6]See Alcina Franch and Blecua (1975: 563); Fernández (1951: 295).
[7]Hernández (1979: 206).
[8]Fernández (1951: 296).
[9]Fernández (1951: 299).
[10]More information on the use of a definite article with proper nouns will be found

in Alcina Franch and Blecua (1975: 560–4), and in Marsá (1986: 127–9).
[11]Cf. Fernández (1951: 287).
[12]Fernández (1951: 103). J. Cortázar (1974: 195 and 197), seems to use *el absurdo* and *lo absurdo* more or less interchangeably. See also *Esbozo*, 409.
[13]Fernández (1951: 323) gives a few examples where the adjective or past participle remains unaltered.
[14]The examples and commentary in this section are based on Nieves (1984).
[15]For further commentary and examples, see *MEU* under *un* (154): also Lapesa (1987).
[16]*DUE*, I, 626. Fernández (1951: 405) and Alonso (1974: 152) are more permissive.
[17]Alonso (1974: 165).
[18]Fernández (1951: 278–9); Alonso (1974: 152–3).

## The Noun

[1]See also *Esbozo*, 174.
[2]But see the (partly) discrepant comments of Fernández (1951: 153).
[3]*DD*, 98.
[4]See *DD*, 173, who observes that many doctors use this word in the feminine.
[5] See Alvar and Pottier (1983: 48), and *DD*. 196 (*fantasma*) and 329 (*reuma*). *DD* does not mention the feminine use of *eccema*.
[6]See also *Esbozo*, 175, n. 14, with more examples.
[7]See R. Seco (1960: 19–20), and Fernández (1951: 163).
[8]In Bello (1972: xl and 222), the word is used in the feminine, though Cuervo, in one of his notes, uses it as a masculine.
[9]*DD*, 63
[10]See also *Esbozo*, 179.
[11]*DD*, 156.
[12]*Esbozo*, 81, 83 n. 46, 100 n. 38, 134 n. 34, 140 n. 43, etc.
[13]Haensch et al. (1982: 410).
[14]Kany (1951: 5–6) with examples.
[15]Haensch (1984: 172), who states that *la bikini* is typical of Argentine Spanish.
[16]*DD*, 156, mentions the masculine expression *(los) artes de pesca* 'fishing tackle'.
[17]*DD*, 253.
[18]Fernández (1951: 159), but for a counterexample, with commentary, see p. 160.
[19]Although there are exceptions on pp. 84 and 187.
[20]For example, C. J. Cela, M. Delibes, J. Izcaray, E. Quiroga, R. J. Sender, J. A. de Zunzunegui, etc.
[21]E. de Bustos Gisbert (1986: 130, n. 75) observes that *altamar*, *pleamar* and *bajamar* are changing to the masculine by analogy with *el mar*.
[22]*Huerta* is bigger than *huerto* according to *DRAE*, 797.
[23]*DRAE*, 330.
[24]Alvar and Pottier (1983: 391).
[25]*DD*, 292, observes: 'Hoy existe cierta prevención contra la forma *poetisa*, que con frecuencia se sustituye por *poeta*.' Indeed, J. Cortázar speaks of *la poeta salvadoreña Claribel Alegría* (1984: 70). However, in the latest edition of *DRAE* (p. 1156) *poeta* is given only as a masculine, *poetisa* still being cited as the feminine form.
[26]Alcina Franch and Blecua (1975: 520–1). *Esbozo*, 176, implicitly accepts *abogada*,

*ministra*, etc. by mentioning them along with other long-established terms like *licenciada*, *secretaria*, *tabernera*, etc. See also Hampares (1976) and Varela (1983).

[27]See also *DD*, 361, which gives as unacceptable the forms *mujer torero*, *(la) torero* and *la nueva torero*.

[28]Forms like *la ministro francesa* and *la ministro francés* make a somewhat strange impression as a result of the lack of agreement between noun and adjective and sound wrong to some people. Seco considers such constructions unacceptable and argues for the use of a feminine form of the noun, e.g. *la catedrática* (*DD*, 88 and 261-2). See also *MEU*, 33.

JdeB received a letter from the Fundación José Ortega y Gasset (Madrid) dated 27 July 1983 which referred to *nuestra Presidente Doña Soledad Ortega*.

[29]*MEU*, 154, nevertheless favours the form *travestido*.

[30]*(La) individua* and *(la) tipa* seem to be frequent today in Spain as well. See, for example, in two works in which popular speech is represented, *la individua* and *la tipa* in C. Pérez Merinero, 1982: 168, and *la tipa* in E. Parra, 1981: 111.

[31]See Kany (1951: 6) and Marcos Marín (1978: 263). Marsá (1986: 116) points out 'una tímida tendencia a la masculinización formal de algunos nombres', giving *modisto* 'couturier' as an example.

[32]Cf. *Esbozo*, 176.

[33]In the *Boletín de la Real Academia Española*, LXIII, Cuaderno CCXXVIII, January–April 1983, *jueza* is given as meaning both 'wife of a judge' and 'female judge'.

[34]According to *Esbozo*, 182, the plural is seldom used.

[35]*Esbozo*, 185, and Alcina Franch and Blecua (1975: 538).

[36]*DD*, 281, also mentions the plural *padres nuestros*, written as two separate words.

[37]Cf. *Esbozo*, 190, and De Miguel (1985: 186). Many grammars (e.g. Alcina Franch and Blecua (1975) and Fernández (1951)) do not deal with this problem.

[38]For further similar cases and commentary, see Lorenzo (1971: 35-6), E. de Bustos Gisbert (1986: 203, 205).

[39]*Esbozo*, 188-9. See, in more detail, *DD*, 43, and Fernández (1951: 179, n. 1).

[40]On foreign words in Spanish, see M. Seco (1977). See also *Esbozo*, 183-4, and Fernández (1951: 168).

[41]The extent of the confusion caused by such hispanized forms is evident from Madariaga (1966), who argues for a systematic way of hispanizing foreign words.

[42]Spanish version by P. Soriano (no date). Alcina Franch and Blecua (1975: 545), give *filmes* (whilst noting that the singular *filme* is less used than *film*), but J. Urrutia (professor in Seville) uses exclusively *filme* and *filmes* in *Imago litterae* (1984), passim. *DD*, 198, observes that both *film* and *filme* are used, and the last edition of *DRAE* (I, 643) gives only *filme*.

[43]See Marcos Marín (1972: 103). *Esbozo* considers *clubes* the correct form, but V. García de la Concha, professor in Salamanca, tells JdeB that *clubes* sounds pedantic to him. For further commentary on this problematic word, see M. Seco (1977) and *DD*, 100.

[44]F. Marcos Marín (1972: 103) records both *recordwoman* and *recordmana* (with plural *recordmanas*) as the feminine of *recordman* – anything can happen to a loanword!

[45]Seen by JdeB in February 1983.

[46]Note the orthographic variant *güisqui*, given in *DD*, 213 (and *huisqui* in the 5th edn, 347).

[47]*Esbozo*, 182–3.

[48]Both words are usually invariable according to *Esbozo*, 182–3. However, *médiums* and *memorandums* can be found (respectively in F. Umbral, 1976a: 123, and R. Ricardo Alonso, 1981: 50). See also Lapesa in Lorenzo (1981: 95). *MEU*, 34, recommends maintaining the Latin singular and using the hispanized form *memorandos* in the plural.

[49]*DUE*, I, 16, also gives *álbums* as a possible plural form. For a more detailed commentary, see Alvar and Pottier (1983: 37).

[50]Fernández (1951: 151) calls this phenomenon the *plural elíptico*.

[51]Examples from Kany (1951: 10–14).

[52]See Kany (1951: 12).

[53]See Fernández (1951: 176–8).

[54]Alvar and Pottier (1983: 58) speak of a 'plural interno'.

[55]Perhaps with a slight difference in meaning: see Fernández (1951: 176–8).

[56]See *Esbozo*, 187, DD, 206.

[57]See M. Seco (1977: 193ff), and for a convenient list of such forms, *MEU*, 87–93.

[58]See the humorous observations in De Miguel (1985: 120–1) and Marsá (1986: 105) (especially on Alianza Popular).

## The Adjective

[1]Beinhauer (1973: 153)

[2]Cf. Lapesa's *Contestación* in Lorenzo (1981: 96). He observes that it affects only singular nouns, and sees an explanation of the phenomenon in analogy with forms like *este alma*, *ese agua*, etc.

[3]For a more detailed account see *DD*, 103 and Coste and Redondo (1965: 120–1).

[4]Example from Fernández (1951: 121), who also gives further examples.

[5]For more examples and still further possibilities, see *DD*, 110–12.

[6]There are a number of interesting points and a detailed bibliography in Demonte (1982). See also Bosque (1982: 110–11 and 128–9).

[7]Pedro Salinas, the well-known essayist and poet (1891–1951), writes: 'The difference between the preposed and the postposed adjective is the following: the former enshrines an affective attribute; the latter a logical distinction . . . Therefore it is entirely permissible to say that the preposed adjective represents the intervention of the human element, of feeling, in the world of objective values represented by nouns . . . Preposed adjectives represent our way of feeling the realities of the world' (1967: 189–90). See also *Esbozo,*410.

[8]Alcina Franch and Blecua (1975: 509).

[9]See Fernández (1951: 148) for more commentary and examples.

[10]See *Esbozo*, 244, and Kany (1951: 29–31). Fernández (1951: 97) is of the opinion that the phenomenon is brought about by analogy with *cualquiera* apocopating to *cualquier* (see **430**).

[11]Esbozo, 194; Alvar and Pottier (1983: 38).

[12]Esbozo, 194, remarks that the non-apocopated form *grande* is found almost exclusively in literary language.

[13]*Esbozo*, 194–5.

[14]*DUE*, I, 423.

[15]*DUE*, I, 423.

[16]*DD*, 187 and 211.

[17]Fernández (1951: 123) gives more (learned) comparative forms.

[18]*DD*, 32 and 66.

[19]Fernández (1951: 135) mentions an example of *superior* followed by *de* (*una velocidad superior de los 126 kilómetros, ABC*, 6 September 1949: 19).

[20]See Lorenzo (1971: 177 and 195–200): arguments in favour of Lorenzo's hypothesis appear in Carabias (1978b). See also *MEU*, 56. It is certainly putting the matter too strongly to say today that the suffix 'sigue teniendo un marcado carácter culto' (Alvar and Pottier, 1983: 378).

[21]Kany (1951: 51).

[22]*Esbozo*, 196–7, from which all these examples are taken.

[23]Marsá (1986: 87).

[24]*DD*, 287.

[25]*MEU*, 39, mentions (and censures) the use of *más óptimo*, as, for example, in *\*obtener resultados más óptimos* 'to get more excellent results'.

[26]For more examples and some theoretical considerations, see De Bruyne (1974). More especially on the problems of translation, see De Bruyne (1980). The Spanish linguist E. Lorenzo (1971: 177, 195–200) gives an interesting explanation for the ever-increasing use of *-ísimo*: the phenomenon must be seen in the framework of a preference in Spanish for *esdrújulos* (i.e. words stressed on the antepenultimate syllable), an emphatic effect being sought by the use of such forms. F. Umbral comments on the emphatic use of *esdrújulos* in several of his works (1976b: 83: 1977: 133; 1979: 112). For more information and discussion, see De Bruyne (1984–5).

[27]Alvar and Pottier (1983: 356).

[28]Beinhauer (1968: 238). J. M. Gironella has more such forms in one of his last novels, (1971: II, 101 and 124).

[29]Beinhauer (1968: 256–7).

[30]On the adverbial use of the adjective, see also Lapesa (1977). *Esbozo*, 369, observes that in such constructions the adjective signifies a quality or characteristic of the subject but that at the same time it alters the meaning of the verb.

[31]Kany (1951: 32, 273).

## Numerals

[1]Cf. *Esbozo*, 242, and *DD*, 272.

[2]Cf. Fernández (1951: 458).

[3]Spellings like *treintaisiete* and *sesentaicinco*, which appear in a recent book by A. Berlanga (*La gaznápira*, 1984: 122 and 129) are considered unusual (at least in Spain). See *MEU*, 35, which further observes that no paragraph should begin with a numeral written in figures – but see also Marsá (1986: 90).

[4]For more examples of *mil y uno*, see DD, 369. *Esbozo*, 242, considers *ochocientos y un días* '801 days' exceptional.

[5]Fernández, 459.

[6]Cf. Alcina Franch and Blecua (1975: 666): *DD*, 96 (with further examples); Marsá (1986: 91): *DUE*, I, 625.

[7]*Esbozo*, 239–40 and Kany (1951: 31–2).

[8]*DUE*, I, 625.

[9]*Esbozo*, 241.

[10]*Esbozo*, 248.

[11]See also, with another example of this type (which is considered irregular), *DD*, 261.

[12]*Esbozo*, 238.

[13]Kany (1951: 11).

[14]*DD*, 197.

[15]Kany (1951: 11).

[16]*Esbozo*, 239.

[17]*MEU*, 37, *Esbozo*, 239

[18]Exceptionally in the written language and in set phrases *primo* is also sometimes found: see Fernández (1951: 460) and *Esbozo*, 244.

[19]*Esbozo*, 244.

[20]*DD*, 368 and 157, *MEU*, 36.

[21]Cf. Alcina Franch and Blecua, 667, *Esbozo*, 245, and, in more detail, *MEU*, 36–7.

[22]*Esbozo*, 245.

[23]Alcina Franch and Blecua (1975: 667) are of the opinion that this mistake is increasingly common in present-day Spanish.

[24]This example was contributed by Ricardo Senabre, professor at the Universidad de Extremadura in Cáceres.

[25]*DD*, 137.

[26]*Esbozo*, 246.

[27]Alonso and Henríquez Ureña (1955: 76).

[28]*Esbozo*, 246.

[29]*Esbozo*, 247, with commentary and examples.

[30]M. Seco (1977: 190) also mentions *septillizos* 'septuplets' and *octillizos* 'octuplets'.

## Personal Pronouns

[1]See Schmidely (1979: 233–42) and Fernández (1986a: 72–5).

[2]*Esbozo*, 422.

[3]Fernández (1951: 219–21).

[4]De Miguel (1985: 215–16); Cazorla (1987: 64).

[5]*Esbozo*, 145; *MEU*, 26.

[6]*Esbozo*, 342, n. 16; Fernández (1986a: 74–5).

[7]Kany (1951: 97–8).

[8]*Esbozo*, 343–4; Borrego Nieto (1978): Carabias (1 February 1978: 26).

[9]*Esbozo*, 344; Fernández (1986a: 73).

[10]Fernández (1986a: 73, 89–90).

[11]Kany (1951: 55); Lapesa (1980: 510–11, 580–1): Berschin (1987: 192).

[12]Kany (1951: 428).

[13]*DUE*, I, 1034.

[14]Kany (1951: 93–5).

[15]*Esbozo*, 342.

[16]Alcina Franch and Blecua (1975: 609).

[17]*DD*, 271.

[18]Kany (1951: 57–8).

[19]Lapesa (1980: 578).

[20]*DD*, 378.

[21]Malmberg (1974: 192).

[22]Alvar and Pottier (1983: 106); *DD*, 167: Hernández (1979: 297), Fernández (1951: 213); Fernández (1986a: 65–72).
[23]Lapesa (1970: 143).
[24]Schmidely (1979: 45).
[25]Lapesa (1980: 472); Kany (1951: 112–14).
[26]*Esbozo*, 425–7 and 466.
[27]*Esbozo*, 426: Kany (1951: 126–7).
[28]Martínez Amador (1961: 1229).
[29]*Esbozo*, 168.
[30]Martín Zorraquino (1979: 347ff).
[31]*Esbozo*, 423.
[32]Alcina Franch and Blecua (1975: 607); Bello (1972: 262): Fernández (1951: 202): Monge (1983: 447 and 1987); *Esbozo*, 204; Kany (1951: 102–7); Lapesa (1980: 577, 585–6); *DD*, 164.
[33]Penny (1986: 10); Mozos Mocha (1973: chs 1–2).
[34]*Esbozo*, 424.
[35]Alcina Franch and Blecua (1975: 607); *DD*, 164; Bello (1972: 262); Fernández (1951: 198–9); *MEU*, 54.
[36]Hernández (1979: 303): Fernández (1951: 199–200).
[37]*Esbozo*, 205; Llorente (1980: 25).
[38]Kany (1951: 107–9).
[39]*Esbozo*, 423; Fernández (1951: 203); *MEU*, 46: Kany (1951: 107–8); Lapesa (1980: 586).
[40]*Esbozo*, 206.
[41]Fernández (1951: 221–2).
[42]*Esbozo*, 381: Martín Zorraquino (1979: 280ff, 297ff, 320ff).

## Demonstrative Pronouns and Adjectives

[1]*MEU*, 24.
[2]Fernández (1951: 237); Lapesa (in Lorenzo 1981: 96); Martínez Marín (1982: 39–46).
[3]Fernández (1951: 253, 316); Alcina Franch and Blecua (1975: 626): *DD*, 183, 188.
[4]Fernández (1951: 262).
[5]Kany (1951: 136–8).
[6]Coste and Redondo (1965: 219–20).
[7]Keniston (1937: 103).
[8]*Esbozo*, 432.
[9]Fernández (1951: 254–5).
[10]Alcina Franch and Blecua (1975: 623).
[11]*DUE*, I, 227; *DD*, 47.
[12]Kany (1951: 269); Alcina Franch and Blecua (1975: 634).

## Possessive Pronouns and Adjectives

[1]*Esbozo*, 428–9, 211; Lapesa (1980: 581); Lorenzo (1981: 54).
[2]De Miguel (1985: 216).
[3]Kany (1951: 41–2).
[4]Fernández (1951: 228–9); Alcina Franch and Blecua (1975: 615).

[5]Fernández (1951: 232).
[6]Alcina Franch and Blecua (1975: 619–20): Kany (1951: 44–6): Alvar and Pottier (1983: 101).
[7]*Esbozo*, 430–1; Kany (1951: 44–5).
[8]Fernández (1951: 234).
[9]Kany (1951: 45).

## Relatives

[1]Fernández (1951: 347); Verdonk (1982: 257).
[2]*Esbozo*, 529.
[3]Umbral told JdeB that he chose this construction to avoid cacophony.
[4]*Esbozo*, 529–30; *DD*, 313.
[5]*Esbozo*, 225.
[6]*DD*, 316; *MEU*, 44. Ortega y Gasset uses *quien* with a non-personal antecedent, however (see 1985: 127).
[7]*Esbozo*, 220 and 531; *DD*, 316; Fernández (1951: 334).
[8]Alarcos Llorach (1982: 268).
[9]*DUE*, II, 1156.
[10]*DUE*, II, 985 (no. 8): *Esbozo*, 534–5.
[11]Alcina Franch and Blecua (1975: 1083–4).
[12]Fernández (1951: 338, 362, 364–8). According to BUS, CAR, HER, LLO, MON, SEN, VAQ, VAR and ZOR, *el que* and *quien* belong respectively to the spoken and written language; ALV comments that *el que* is more 'precise' than *quien*; LOP comments that *quien* and *el que* are used equally in many Latin-American countries; MOR that both forms can be used equally in written and spoken language, and RAB that *quien* is more formal.
[13]Fernández (1951: 452), who also gives *cual . . . cual* as a possibility.
[14]*Esbozo*, 530–1; Fernández (1951: 344).
[15]*DD*, 121.
[16]*Esbozo*, 222.
[17]Alcina Franch and Blecua (1975: 1034, 1086). But De Mello (1992: 67) is more permissive.
[18]*Esbozo*, 530; R. Seco (1960: 217): Marsá (1986: 147).
[19]*Esbozo*, 533; *MEU*, 44.
[20]Llorente (1980: 21); Marsá (1986: 147), sees the use as an affectation among uneducated speakers.
[21]Alcina Franch and Blecua (1975: 1088).
[22]*Esbozo*, 218, 533–4.
[23]*Esbozo*, 223; *DUE*, I, 818; Verdonk (1982: 260).
[24]Fernández (1951: 355).
[25]*Esbozo*, 534.

## Interrogative and Exclamatory Pronouns and Adjectives

[1]Bello (1972: 328).
[2]Fernández (1951: 321).
[3]*DD*, 316–17.

[4]Kany (1951: 48-9)

[5]Fernández (1951: 336); Hernández (1979: 313, 315); Alvar and Pottier (1983: 139).

[6]*Esbozo*, 116.

## Indefinite Pronouns and Adjectives

[1]*DD*, 369; Kany (1951: 142-3).

[2]*DD*, 369; Kany (1951: 143).

[3]De Bruyne (1972: 10- 13).

[4]Fernández (1951: 419).

[5]*DD*, 30.

[6]*DD*, 30; Fernández (1951: 402).

[7]Fernández (1951: 402).

[8]Fernández (1951: 417).

[9]R. Seco (1960: 194); *DD*, 30.

[10]*Esbozo*, 230.

[11]Martínez Amador (1961: 124); A. Bello (1972: 293); *DD*, 29; Fernández (1951: 420); Kany (1951: 143- 4).

[12]Fernández (1951: 104-5, 396); Martínez Amador (1961: 123); *Esbozo*, 415.

[13]Fernández (1951: 419); Kany (1951: 143- 4).

[14]Marsá (1986: 129); *DD*, 269.

[15]Fernández (1951: 418).

[16]Fernández (1951: 413).

[17]See also Smith (1991: 127).

[18]Fernández (1951: 420); Kany (1951: 143-4).

[19]De Miguel (1985: 140); Beinhauer (1968: 185).

[20]*Esbozo*, 356; Beinhauer (1968: 207).

[21]*Esbozo*, 213, Fernández (1951: 426).

[22]Kany (1951: 145-7); *Esbozo*, 231; *DD*, 125 (who sees the usage as one of hypercorrection); Alonso and Henríquez Ureña (1955: 100).

[23]*Esbozo*, 231; Fernández (1951: 425).

[24]*Esbozo*, 232.

[25]Beinhauer (1968: 150).

[26]*Esbozo*, 232.

[27]Kany (1951: 21).

[28]Perhaps a borrowing from French: cf. *le Tout-Paris*, etc.

[29]Fernández (1951: 436).

[30]Fernández (1951: 440- 1); *Esbozo*, 232.

[31]This interpretation was given by eight of the informants (BUS, HER, LOP, MON, MOR, SEN, VAQ). Five others (ALV, LAP, LLO, RAB, VAR) considered that the meaning was rather 'There are many good days ahead for Spain.' CAR, whilst admitting both interpretations, suggested that the sentence might have been modelled on *Aún hay mucho tajo por delante* 'There's still a long way to go'.

[32]Kany (1951: 312).

[33]*Esbozo*, 234; Fernández (1951: 448); *DD*, 291.

[34]*Esbozo*, 235; Fernández (1951: 409-10).

[35]*DD*, 34.

[36]*DD*, 34.

[37]Fernández (1951: 310, n. 1).

[38]Kany (1951: 138–9).
[39]*Esbozo*, 235.
[40]*Esbozo*, 235.
[41]Fernández (1951: 450).
[42]Fernández (1951: 451).
[43]Fernández (1951: 443n); *Esbozo*, 236.
[44]*DD*, 80.
[45]*Esbozo*, 236; Fernández (1951: 444).
[46]*DD*, 317.
[47]Kany (1951: 296); *DUE*, I, 885.
[48]Oliver (1985: 101); León (1981: 65); Umbral, (1983: 85, 243).
[49]Alcina Franch and Blecua (1975: 66).
[50]*DD*, 355.
[51]Many of the informants considered that *diversos* (and even more the singular *diverso*) following the noun to be pedantic or literary in tone. SEN thought the feature typical of political speeches. ZOR considered that *diverso* following the noun could also have the meaning 'complex'.
[52]Fernández (1951: 408).
[53]Fernández (1951: 226).
[54]Fernández (1951: 226).
[55]Fernández (1951: 226).
[56]*DD*, 262.
[57]All the informants accepted *mismo* in following position, though there were some different views on its connotations: BUS described it as 'muy vulgar' whereas MOR preferred it.
[58]Kany (1951: 311–12).
[59]Fernández (1951: 137); *DD*, 262.
[60]*Esbozo*, 212; Fernández (1951: 265); *DD*, 262, says that the usage is typical of official language; *MEU*, 45, deems it vulgar.
[61]Coste and Redondo (1965: 273).
[62]Fernández (1951: 266); *DUE*, II, 1252.
[63]Fernández (1951: 267–8).
[64]*DRAE*, 1371.
[65]*DUE*, II, 1253.
[66]Fernández (1951: 381).
[67]León (1981: 75).
[68]*DUE*, I, 1352; *DRAE*, 708.
[69]*Esbozo*, 248, which regards *sendos* as a 'learned' (*culto*) word; Fernández (1951: 461).
[70]*Esbozo*, 248; *DD*, 338.

## Impersonal Expressions

[1]De Kock and Gómez Molina (1982: 61).
[2]*Esbozo*, 382–3; Martín Zorraquino (1979: 150ff); Schroten (1972: 75–6); Cartagena (1972).
[3]Coste and Redondo (1965: 208).
[4]Berschin (1987: 200).
[5]León (1981); Lapesa (1987: 345).

## The Adverb

[1]*DRAE*, 916; *DUE*, II, 317.
[2]*DD*, 323.
[3]Kany (1951: 34); Vigara Tauste (1992: 233-4).
[4]*Esbozo*, 200; Stiehm (1975: 77-80).
[5]*DRAE*, 105; *DUE*, I, 190.
[6]Kany (1951: 412-13).
[7]Marsá (1986: 114); De Miguel (1985: 82).
[8]De Miguel (1985: 82).
[9]*DD*, 145.
[10]*Kany* (1951: 302-3).
[11]*DD*, 44.
[12]De Miguel (1985: 82).
[13]Kany (1951: 267). None of the informants had heard *casimente* used, except for VAR, to whom the observation on US Spanish is due.
[14]Kany (1951: 297).
[15]*DRAE*, 479.
[16]Kany (1951: 296).
[17]Kany (1951: 309-10); *DD*, 255.
[18]Kany (1951: 315-16).
[19]*Esbozo*, 140, n. 43.
[20]*Esbozo*, 72; *DD*, 58.
[21]Alcina Franch and Blecua (1975: 1111-12).
[22]Kany (1951: 415).
[23]Kany (1951: 276-8).
[24]*DD*, 344.
[25]Kany (1951: 327); Lapesa (1980: 591).
[26]*DD*, 255.
[27]Kany (1951: 331-2).
[28]*DD*, 51.
[29]Coste and Redondo (1965: 226); *DD*, 10.
[30]Kany (1951: 390); Llorente (1980: 452).
[31]*Esbozo*, 357.
[32]Kany (1951: 404).
[33]Kany (1951: 369-73).

## Comparative Constructions

[1]*DD*, 269. *DRAE* comments on the example cited that use of *no* is 'to intensify the affirmation of the sentence to which it belongs, fixing the attention on one idea as opposed to another'.
[2]See also *Esbozo*, 419.
[3]*DD*, 124.
[4]Fernández (1951: 452).

## Prepositions

[1]*MEU*, 64; Fernández (1986b: 148-90); Coste and Redondo (1965: 320-30).
[2]*Esbozo*, 373.

[3]*Esbozo,* 373c.

[4]Alcina Franch and Blecua (1975: 861); *DD,* 5; *MEU,* 67; Kany (1951: 1–2).

[5]*MEU,* 67.

[6]*Esbozo,* 374.

[7]JdeB consulted C. Hernández about this contrasting pair of sentences.

[8]Kany (1951: 334–5).

[9]Fernández (1951: 311).

[10]*Esbozo,* 439.

[11]Körner (1989).

[12]Kany (1951: 347–50).

[13]See also *DD,* 104, 169.

[14]Alarcos Llorach (1982: 257–9).

[15]*Esbozo,* 414–15; Alarcos Llorach (1982: 258).

[16]*Esbozo,* 402; Lapesa (1980: 469, n. 7); DD, 45, 82; Lázaro Mora (1982: 379–83).

[17]Kany (1951: 356).

[18]*Esbozo,* 522; Kany (1951: 353–4); *DD,* 134; Marsá (1986: 154–6); De Miguel (1985: 111).

[19]*DD,* 177.

[20]Kany (1951: 366–8).

[21]*MEU,* 119.

[22]*DD,* 219.

[23]*Esbozo,* 442; *DD,* 133.

[24]*Esbozo,* 442.

[25]F. Monge told JdeB that while *para* is not impossible in such cases, it sounds affected or foreign.

[26]RAE *Gramática,* 441; *Esbozo,* 70, 436; *DUE,* II, 805.

[27]E. Lorenzo (1971: 50–1) remarks that a sentence like *vine por ti* is ambiguous between *vine a causa de ti/vine a por ti.*

[28]*Esbozo,* 443; *DD,* 346.

[29]*DD,* 363.

[30]*DUE,* II, 1369.

## Constructions with Verbs and Nouns

[1]Kany (1951: 197–200).

## Conjunctions

[1]Although *Esbozo,* 506, recommends the use of a single *ni* before the last item in such lists, there is a clear tendency towards *ni* being used before all items: see *DUE,* II, 507.

[2]See also Beinhauer (1968: 333–6).

[3]Kany (1951: 393).

[4]De Bruyne (1982–3: 61–77).

[5]*Esbozo,* 517.

[6]See *DUE,* II, 1076.

[7]*Esbozo,* 517.

[8]*DD,* 314. The omission of *que* is also becoming more common in everyday language.

<sup>9</sup>See also Kany (1951: 395–400).
<sup>10</sup>Hernández (1979: 334) regards it as 'cacophonous'.
<sup>11</sup>*DD*, 342.
<sup>12</sup>See also Kany (1951: 400–2).

## The Verb: Conjugation

<sup>1</sup>*Esbozo*, 258. *-ear* is particularly frequent in the formation of neologisms.
<sup>2</sup>De Kock (1984–5: 33–7); *Esbozo*, 260.
<sup>3</sup>*Esbozo*, 252.
<sup>4</sup>*Esbozo*, 252.
<sup>5</sup>*DUE*, II, 1474.
<sup>6</sup>*Esbozo*, 291; *DD*, 216.
<sup>7</sup>*Esbozo*, 291.
<sup>8</sup>*DD*, 215; Marcos Marín (1978: 84); Llorente (1980: 30–1); De Miguel (1985: 192).
<sup>9</sup>*Esbozo*, 384–5; Kany (1951: 212–17); Hernández (1979: 141); Montes Giraldo (1982); Rabanales (1984: 56).
<sup>10</sup>*Esbozo*, 291.
<sup>11</sup>*Marsá* (1986: 83).
<sup>12</sup>*Esbozo*, 279–83.
<sup>13</sup>*Esbozo*, 279, n. 20.
<sup>14</sup>*Esbozo*, 280, n. 30.
<sup>15</sup>*DD*, 140.
<sup>16</sup>*Esbozo*, 284, n. 50; *DD*, 141.
<sup>17</sup>*Esbozo*, 280, n. 27.
<sup>18</sup>*Esbozo*, 281, n. 34.
<sup>19</sup>*Esbozo*, 284, n. 45; *DD*, 35.
<sup>20</sup>*Esbozo*, 273.
<sup>21</sup>Lapesa (1980: 470).
<sup>22</sup>*Esbozo*, 276–7.
<sup>23</sup>A fuller list is given in *Esbozo*, 287.
<sup>24</sup>*Esbozo*, 288, n. 68; *DD*, 292; *DUE*, II, 877–8; A. Bello (1972: 161); *Marsá* (1986: 245); Alonso and Henríquez Ureña (1955: 131).
<sup>25</sup>*Esbozo*, 287.
<sup>26</sup>*Esbozo*, 329–31.
<sup>27</sup>*Esbozo*, 335.
<sup>28</sup>*Esbozo*, 332–3.
<sup>29</sup>But see *DUE*, I, 708; *DD*, 110.
<sup>30</sup>*DUE*, I, 1243; *DD*, 191; there was similar disagreement among JdeB's informants. Fernández (1986b: 4) suggests a difference in meaning between *evacuo* and *evacúo* but does not elaborate further.
<sup>31</sup>*Esbozo*, 334.
<sup>32</sup>*Marsá* (1986: 115); *DD*, 305; De Miguel (1985: 81); *MEU*, 37.
<sup>33</sup>*Esbozo*, 301–2.
<sup>34</sup>*Esbozo*, 292; Alvar and Pottier (1983: 185).
<sup>35</sup>*Esbozo*, 294; *DD*, 383.
<sup>36</sup>Alcina Franch and Blecua (1975: 890).
<sup>37</sup>*Esbozo*, 308.

[38]Lapesa (1980: 470).
[39]In J. Goytisolo, (1981a: 52).
[40]Lapesa (1980: 470); *Esbozo*, 251–2.
[41]*Esbozo*, 299.
[42]Alvar and Pottier (1983: 230).
[43]*Esbozo*, 307; *DD*, 236.
[44]*Esbozo*, 297; *DD*, 372.
[45]*Esbozo*, 460, n. 2.
[46]*Esbozo*, 311.
[47]*Esbozo*, 311–13; *MEU*, 37.
[48]*DUE*, II, 1500; *DD*, 133.

## Use of the Tenses

[1]Fernández (1951: 212–39).
[2]*Esbozo*, 465.
[3]Fernández (1951: 239–84).
[4]*Esbozo*, 467.
[5]Fernández (1951: 270).
[6]Fernández (1951: 268).
[7]Beinhauer (1968: 348, n. 1). Note that the Academy (*DRAE*, 12) prescribes the spelling *acabose* without written accent.
[8]Barrera Vidal (1972) deals with this area in detail; see also Alarcos Llorach (1982: 46–9).
[9]Alarcos Llorach (1982: 24–5, 46–9).
[10]*Esbozo*, 466; Kany (1951: 161–4); MEU, 53; Lapesa (1980: 587–8).
[11]*Esbozo*, 469.
[12]*Esbozo*, 455, 470; *DUE*, II, 1473.
[13]Kany (1951: 152–5).
[14]Berschin (1986).
[15]*Esbozo*, 358, 471; Cartagena (1972).
[16]*Esbozo*, 473; Lapesa (1980: 480); Kany (1951: 159–60); *DUE*, II, 1498.
[17]MEU, 53, condemns this usage (but without suggesting alternatives).
[18]*Esbozo*, 359, 473; *DD*, 296–7; *DUE*, II, 1475, 1490; Lapesa (1980: 588–9); Kany (1951: 182–3); De Miguel (1985: 193). F. Umbral puts the phrase *se dijera que* 'it could be said that' in the mouth of E. Tierno Galván, who was known for his archaizing style of speech (1985: 146–7). Umbral himself uses the expression (1987: 72).
[19]All informants considered the use of *conociera* totally incorrect, though HER, SEN and VAR acknowledged that it might be a local archaism. LOP observes that the *-ra* form of the subjunctive is occasionally used as a conditional in Mexico. VAR reports its use in the Caribbean area, and RAB sees the usage as characteristic of the younger generation.
[20]*Esbozo*, 474–5; *DD*, 296.
[21]*DD*, 296.
[22]*Esbozo*, 468, 473.
[23]*Esbozo*, 477, 518–20.
[24]*Esbozo*, 519–20.
[25]*Esbozo*, 480; Alcina Franch and Blecua (1975: 807); Kany (1951: 170–4); MEU, 53.

[26]Thirteen of the informants considered *oyese* as the equivalent of *había oído* in this example; LLO equated it with *oyó*, and RAB and ZOR also saw this as a possibility.

[27]*Esbozo*, 480; Kany (1951: 170–4).

[28]*Esbozo*, 481, suggests that the *-ra* form is more typical of literary language and the *-se* form of uneducated speech; but this is highly contentious, and such authorities as Lorenzo, Cuervo and Lenz have different judgments. Alcina Franch and Blecua (1975: 808) find no difference between the two forms. In Latin America, the *-ra* form is more frequent, and the *-se* form is often felt to be higher in register: see Kany (1951: 171). See also De Kock and Gómez Molina (1982); Tavernier (1979).

[29]De Kock and Gómez Molina (1982: 65–6).

[30]Kany (1951: 185–6), and *DD*, 203 (Latin America); Lapesa (1980: 589) (Canaries).

## The Passive

[1]Much of the material in this section is drawn from Pountain (1993).

[2]See *MEU*, 48; Coste and Redondo (1965: 484).

[3]Fernández (1986b: 419ff).

[4]Examples (iv), (v) and (vii)–(x) are discussed in Pountain (1993).

[5]Gili Gaya (1964: 110); Alonso (1974: 242, n. 1).

[6]*MEU*, 48; Coste and Redondo (1965: 484).

## Use of the Moods

[1]*DUE*, II, 555.

[2]*DD*, 317.

[3]*Esbozo*, 456: Lorenzo (1971: 137).

[4]Kany (1951: 321–3).

[5]Coste and Redondo (1965: 438).

[6]*DD*, 258.

[7]*DD*, 11.

[8]See *DRAE*, 1317 (*seguramente*).

[9]Kany (1951: 321–3); *DUE*, II, 382.

[10]Lapesa (1980: 480) also mentions the use of the conditional in such cases.

[11]Beinhauer (1968: 311–12); Alvar and Pottier (1983: 134).

[12]*DD*, 283, considers it a Catalanism.

[13]*Esbozo*, 487: Coste and Redondo (1965: 442).

[14]Haverkate (1989: 119).

[15]Hernández (1979: 271).

[16]See also Fernández (1951: 326–7); Marsá (1986: 176): De Miguel (1985: 193).

[17]Fernández (1951: 344–5).

[18]*Esbozo*, 517; Hernández (1979: 79, 236).

[19]Fernández (1986b: 337–9).

[20]Fernández (1986b: 323–6).

[21]*DUE*, II, 1496–7; Fernández (1951: 328–9)

[22]This observation was made by ALV in connection with the examples discussed in **1044** and **1076**.

[23]The majority of the informants were agreed that such constructions are impossible in Spain and the standard language. HER reported their existence in Chile;

LOP described them as quite normal in uneducated Mexican speech, and VAQ thought them typical of some Puerto Rican dialects. BUS and MON perceived the possibility of a semantic difference between indicative and subjunctive. It is most likely that the *dudar que* and *dudar si* constructions have fused for such speakers (LAP's explanation).

[24]*Esbozo*, 456.

[25]*Esbozo*, 541.

[26]*DD*, 126.

[27]*Esbozo*, 548; *DD*, 146.

[28]*DUE*, II, 1226.

[29]*Esbozo*, 468, 554: *DD*, 300; *DUE*, II, 1471–2, 1490.

[30]*Esbozo*, 557; *DD*, 58: *DUE*, II, 1497.

[31]De Kock, Molina and Verdonk (1979: I, 115–18): Lázaro Mora (1982).

[32]*Esbozo*, 558; De Kock, Molina and Verdonk (1979: I, 115, n.2).

[33]*DUE*, II, 1497.

[34]MON considered that the subjunctive in such cases belonged to a higher register; LOP and MOR thought that the subjunctive was commoner in Latin America than in Spain.

[35]Lleó (1979: 5) comments: 'the speaker is convinced that the CIA played a role in the Chilean coup'.


## The Impersonal Forms of the Verb

[1]*Esbozo*, 483–99; Gili Gaya (1964: 185); De Bruyne (1976: 47–69).

[2]De Miguel (1985: 192–3).

[3]*GRAE*, 402.

[4]Gili Gaya (1964: 187); *Esbozo*, 483.

[5]*Esbozo*, 486, n. 2; *DD*, 231.

[6]*Esbozo*, 485–6.

[7]Kany (1951: 27–8).

[8]*Pace DD*, 4. Kany (1951: 25–7) notes this usage in many areas of Latin America.

[9]*DD*, 275.

[10]Kany (1951: 25–6); *DUE*, II, 1468: Coste and Redondo (1965: 476).

[11]*DD*, 4.

[12]*DUE*, II, 1468.

[13]*DD*, 269–70; Kany (1951: 316–17).

[14]CAR, LAP, RAB, VAR and ZOR were of the view that *sobre de* + infinitive is incorrect.

[15]Beinhauer (1968: 274, n. 174).

[16]Gili Gaya (1964: 191).

[17]Beinhauer (1968: 274, n. 174): *DUE*, I, 2; Lapesa (1980: 456), and especially MEU, 53. which recommends *procedimiento que ha de seguirse* or *que conviene seguir* in place of *procedimiento a seguir*.

[18]*DD*, 5–6; *Esbozo*, 438–9.

[19]Martínez Amador (1961: 763).

[20]At least since 1980 according to *DD*. 232 (with more examples). De Miguel (1985: 192) calls this usage the *infinitivo radiofónico*.

[21]*Esbozo*, 460, but also 143 n. 48, 362.

[22]Gili Gaya (1964: 143); *Esbozo*, 460.

[23]Gili Gaya (1964: 55, 142); *DUE*, II, 1476; Martínez Amador (1961: 765); Coste and Redondo (1965: 455–7).

[24]*DD*, 228; *DUE*, II, 1476; *Esbozo*, 143, n. 48.

[25] *DD*, 231; *Esbozo*, 143, n. 48.

[26]*Esbozo*, 143, n. 48.

[27]Lorenzo (1971: 98–9).

[28]Beinhauer (1968: 127); *DUE*, II, 1500; Hernández (1979: 387).

[29]Lorenzo (1971: 104).

[30]Alcina Franch and Blecua (1975: 747); *DUE*, I, 1393; Carnicer (1969: 120); Criado de Val (1972: 116); De Bruyne (1981).

[31]*Esbozo*, 488–9.

[32]*GRAE*. 410: *Esbozo*. 489.

[33]Gili Gaya (1964: 194).

[34] *Esbozo*, 490; *DD*, 207–8.

[35]*DD*, 208; R. Seco (1960: 225); Carnicer (1969: 122); *DUE*, I, 1394.

[36]MEU, 49.

[37]*Esbozo*, 491.

[38]*Esbozo*, 491–2.

[39]*GRAE*, 413 (n. 2a) and 414. See also *DD*, 208, and MEU, 50.

[40]Coste and Redondo (1965: 461).

[41]*Esbozo*, 488; Molho (1975: 702); Hernández (1979: 314); Luna Trail (1980: 101); *DUE*, I, 1394–5; MEU, 48.

[42]Lorenzo (1971: 99); *Esbozo*, 465.

[43]The responses of JdeB's informants were interesting on the usage of these words. ALV, CAR, LAP, RAB, SEN, VAQ, VAR and ZOR said that they would never use the term *bautizando*, and had never heard it. The other informants considered it a learned word; for BUS and MON the feminine form was completely unacceptable. But a canon of the Jaca cathedral told JdeB in August 1983 that he would quite naturally use *bautizando*, and the feminine form *bautizanda*. Nearly all the informants (all involved in education!) often use the forms *doctorando, examinando* and *graduando*, and *doctoranda, examinanda* and *graduanda* in the plural. LOP and LLO use *la doctorando* and *la examinando*. RAB says he uses the feminine forms *'aunque todavía predominan las masculinas'*.

[44]See Mozos Mocha (1973).

[45]*Esbozo*, 489.

[46]*DUE*, I, 1394.

[47]See *GRAE*, 416–17, *DD*, 209 and *DUE*, I, 1394.

[48]Cf. *DD*, 209.

[49]Following a suggestion by De Bruyne (1975: 31–4).

[50]This is suggested in the *GRAE*, 415, 458, note a.

[51]*GRAE*, 414.

[52]*DD*, 207; *Esbozo*, 490.

[53]*Esbozo*, 490.

[54]See Fernández (1986b: 531–9). Note this author's view that this construction appears to be very restricted with a negative adverb.

[55]Cf. Kany (1951: 238–9), who sees in this usage a possible influence from English. In Ecuador and southern Colombia *mandar* and *dar* are used in the same way. *Le damos vendiendo* and *te daré acompañando* simply mean *vendemos* and *te acompañaré* respectively.

[56]Gili Gaya (1964: 114–15).

[57]Luna Trail (1980: 209-10).
[58]Lorenzo (1971: 99-100).
[59]E.g. Criado de Val (1972: 116).
[60]See Kany (1951: 236-7), with examples from both colloquial and careful speech. The author also calls attention to the importance and frequency of this form in Old Spanish.
[61]Coste and Redondo (1965: 465).
[62]Marsá (1986: 201); *DUE*, II, 651.
[63]*DUE*, II, 1470 (*admitido esto, dicho esto*, etc.).
[64]*Esbozo*, 499.
[65]*MEU*, 56.
[66]*DUE*, II, 1469. *DD*, 284-5, observes that clitic pronouns with the past participle are sometimes encountered in Latin-American Spanish, especially in Mexico and Venezuela.
[67]*Esbozo*, 449.
[68]*Esbozo*, 449, considers the use of *tener* with intransitive verbs and with transitive verbs which have no direct object expressed to be incorrect: *\*Tengo estado en Montevideo, \*Juan tiene sido soldado, \*Tengo comido con gusto*. Alarcos (1982: 34) considers the use of *tener* + past participle to be mainly restricted to popular speech, and especially to the past participles of *decir, ver* and *entender*.
[69]*Esbozo*, 449-50. The past participle is invariable in such usage.
[70]Lorenzo (1971: 111-12).
[71]Criado de Val (1972: 116); Carnicer (1972: 43-5); Lorenzo (1971: 124, n. 26); *MEU*, 50; Kany (1951: 237-9).
[72]Beinhauer (1968: 295-6); Kany (1951: 259).
[73]*Incluso* is sometimes treated as a variable form: see *Esbozo*, 498.
[74]*DUE*, II, 109.
[75]Gili Gaya (1964: 203). *DD*, 136, however, despite censure in earlier editions, considers the construction now perfectly normal.
[76]Beinhauer (1968: 265, n. 156); Iribarren (1974: 626-7).
[77]ALV stated that *limpiados* was not impossible, and that it conveyed the idea of removing the oxide.
[78]*DD*, 299.

## Special Problems with Spanish Verbs

[1]See further Alcina Franch and Blecua (1975: 898-900) and Monge (1961).
[2]Based on Monge (1961: 213-14).
[3]*Esbozo*, 365.
[4]See for example Pottier (1970: 196).
[5]Gili Gaya (1964: 62).
[6]*MEU*, 110.
[7]De Miguel (1985: 205) denounces *estar sobrio* as an anglicism and recommends *estar sereno* instead.
[8]All informants except one (LAP) were in agreement with this judgement.
[9]*Esbozo*, 366; Alonso and Henríquez Ureña (1955: 123); Marsá (1986: 231).
[10]*Esbozo*, 368.
[11]Criado de Val (1972: 265-6).
[12]*Esbozo*, 369, and especially A. Alonso (1974: 190-236).

[13]Beinhauer (1968: 156ff.).
[14]*DD*, 258.
[15]*Esbozo*, 384–5.
[16]Kany (1951: 215–17).
[17]*DD*, 216.
[18]See Criado de Val (1972: 108).
[19]*DD*, 260.
[20]Coste and Redondo (1965: 506).
[21]Coste and Redondo (1965: 502).
[22]Criado de Val (1972: 108); *DUE*, I, 982; De Bruyne (1979).

## Subject–Verb Concord

[1]*DD*, 112.
[2]*DD*, 112.
[3]But see *MEU*, 46.
[4]*Esbozo*, 388; *DD*, 112; *MEU*, 46.
[5]Fernández (1986b: 456).
[6]*DD*, 112.
[7]See *DD*, 269.

## Word Order

[1]Though we believe this to be a useful pedagogical principle, it is far from adequate as an exhaustive rule. This question is investigated in detail by Contreras (1978).
[2]See also Fernández (1986b: 453–6).
[3]Examples from Schroten (1978: 17, 19–20).
[4]Kany (1951: 266).
[5]Gili Gaya (1964: 79).
[6]*Esbozo*, 398–9.
[7]Kany (1951: 266–7); Varela (1984).
[8]Kany (1951: 124–5).
[9]Lapesa (1980: 590–1); *DD*, 314; Hernández (1979: 121, 480) considers it a Gallicism.
[10]*Esbozo*, 406; *MEU*, 43–4.
[11]*Esbozo*, 396.
[12]Hernández (1979: 209).
[13]According to C. Gómez Molina of the University of Antwerp.

## Affective Suffixes

[1]See De Bruyne (1975).
[2]For a much more detailed account see Gooch (1967).
[3]See also *GRAE*, 22–4.
[4]De Bruyne (1989a).
[5]Interesting comments on the perjorative meaning of forms in *-ote* are to be found in Beinhauer (1973: 205).
[6]Translation from Gooch (1967: 215).
[7]Lapesa (1980: 583–4).
[8]*DRAE*, 1217.
[9]*DRAE*, 1439.
[10]Lapesa (1980: 584).
[11]See also De Bruyne (1978).

# Bibliography

*(A) Dictionaries*

Casares, J. 1942: *Diccionario ideológico de la lengua española*. Barcelona: Gili.

*DD* = Seco, M. 1970: *Diccionario de dudas y dificultades de la lengua española*. Madrid: Aguilar, 5th edn.

*DRAE* = Real Academia Española 1992: *Diccionario de la lengua española*. Madrid: Espasa Calpe, 21st edn.

*DUE* = Moliner, M. 1966–7: *Diccionario de uso del español*. Madrid: Gredos, 2 parts (reprinted 1982).

León, V. 1981: *Diccionario de argot español*. Madrid: Alianza Editorial.

Martínez Amador, E. 1961: *Diccionario gramatical*. Barcelona: R. Sopena.

Oliver, J. M. 1985: *Diccionario de argot*. Madrid: Sena.

Reyes, A. 1947: *Diccionario (francés-español y español-francés)*. Madrid: Reyes.

Sainz de Robles, F. C. 1953: *Diccionario de la literatura, II*. Madrid: Aguilar.

Umbral, F. 1983: *Diccionario cheli*. Barcelona: Grijalbo, 9th edn.

Van Dam, C. F. A. 1969: *Spaans Handwoordenboek, I, Spaans-Nederlands*. The Hague: Van Goor, 4th edn.

*(B) Newspapers and Magazines*

*ABC*, Madrid
*Aragón Expres*, Zaragoza
*Boletín Cultural*, Madrid
*BRAE* = *Boletín de la Real Academia Española*, Real Academia Española, Madrid
*Cambio 16*, Madrid–Barcelona
*Cinco Días*, Madrid

*Diario 16*, Madrid
*El Alcázar*, Madrid
*El Imparcial*, Madrid
*El Independiente*, Madrid
*El Mundo*, Madrid
*El Norte de Castilla*, Valladolid
*El País*, Madrid
*El Periódico*, Barcelona
*Heraldo de Aragón*, Zaragoza
*Informaciones*, Madrid
*Ínsula*, Madrid
*Interviú*, Madrid–Barcelona
*La Estafeta Literaria, revista quincenal de libros, artes y espectáculos*, Madrid
*La Vanguardia Española*, Barcelona
*Muy Señor Mío*, Madrid
*Tiempo*, Madrid
*Ya*, Madrid–Barcelona

## (C) Works on Spanish

Alarcos Llorach, E. 1982: *Estudios de gramática funcional del español*. Madrid: Gredos, 3rd edn.

Alcina Franch, J. and Blecua, J. M. 1975: *Gramática española*. Barcelona: Ariel.

Alonso, A. 1974: *Estudios lingüísticos (temas españoles)*. Madrid: Gredos.

Alonso, A. and Henríquez Ureña, P. 1955: *Gramática castellana, segundo curso*. Buenos Aires: Losada, 13th edn.

Alonso, D. 1981: El español, lengua de centenares de millones de hablantes, sus problemas a fines del siglo XX. Proceedings of I Simposio Internacional de Lengua Española (1978). Excelentísimo Cabildo Insular de Gran Canaria, pp. 419–26.

Alvar, M. 1982: Espanol e inglés. Actitudes lingüisticas en Puerto Rico. *Revista de Filología Española*, 62: 1–38.

Alvar, M. 1987: *El lenguaje político*, Fundación Friedrich Ebert, Instituto de Cooperación Iberoamericana.

Alvar, M. and Pottier, B. 1983: *Morfología histórica del español*. Madrid: Gredos.

Alvar Ezquerra, M. 1982: Diccionario y gramática. *Lingüística española actual*, 4.2: 151–207.

Barrera-Vidal, A. 1972: *Parfait simple et parfait composé en castillan moderne*. Munich: Hueber.

Beinhauer, W. 1968: *El español coloquial*. Madrid: Gredos, 2nd edn.

Beinhauer, W. 1973: *El humorismo en el español hablado*. Madrid: Gredos.

Bello, A. 1972: *Gramática.* Caracas: Ediciones del Ministerio de Educación.

Berschin, H. 1986: Futuro analítico y futuro sintético en el español peninsular y americano. *Revista de Filología Románica,* 4: 301–8.

Berschin, H., Fernández-Sevilla, J. and Felixberger, J. 1987: *Die spanische Sprache : Verbreitung, Geschichte, Struktur.* Munich: Hueber.

Borrego Nieto, J. et al. 1978: Sobre el tú y el usted. *Studia Philologica Salmanticensia,* 2: 53–69.

Bosque, I. 1982: Más allá de la lexicalización. *Boletín de la Real Academia Española,* 52: 103–58.

Bustos Gisbert, E. 1986: *La composición nominal en español.* Salamanca: Universidad de Salamanca.

Canfield, D. Lincoln 1981: *Spanish pronunciation in the Americas.* Chicago and London: Chicago University Press.

Carabias, J. 1978a: Vestimenta y tuteo. *Heraldo de Aragón,* 1 February: 26.

Carabias, J. 1978b: Esdrújulo. *Heraldo de Aragón,* 1 September: 22.

Carnicer, R. 1969: *Sobre el lenguaje de hoy.* Madrid: Prensa Española.

Carnicer, R. 1972: *Nuevas reflexiones sobre el lenguaje.* Madrid: Prensa Española.

Cartagena, N. 1972: *Sentido y estructura de las construcciones pronominales en español.* Concepción: Instituto Central de Lengua de la Universidad de Concepción.

Cartagena, N. and Gauger, H. M. 1989: *Vergleichende Grammatik Spanisch-Deutsch,* 2 vols. Mannheim–Vienna–Zürich: Dudenverlag.

Cazorla Prieto, L. M. 1987: Consideraciones sobre la oratoria parlamentaria actual. In M. Alvar, 1987 pp. 59–70.

Contreras, H. 1978: *El orden de palabras en español.* Madrid: Cátedra.

Coste, J. and Redondo, A. 1965: *Syntaxe de l'espagnol moderne (enseignement supérieur).* Paris: Sedes.

Criado de Val, M. 1972: *Fisonomía del español y de las lenguas modernas.* Madrid: SAETA.

De Bruyne, J. 1970: Vertalingen van 'worden' in het Spaans. *Le Linguiste-De Taalkundige,* 5–6: 1–6.

De Bruyne, J. 1971: Das Partizip I und fast gleichwertige Formen im Spanischen. *Linguistica Antverpiensia,* 5: 7–14.

De Bruyne, J. 1972: De betekenis en de grammaticale waarde van 'uno' in het hedendaagse Spaans. *Le Linguiste-De Taalkundige,* 6: 10–13.

De Bruyne, J. 1973: Les néologismes espagnols formés au moyen du suffixe '-oide'. *Linguistica Antverpiensia,* 7: 27–35.

De Bruyne, J. 1974: Over het gebruik van het Spaanse suffix '-ísimo'. *Linguistica Antverpiensia,* 8: 7–16.

De Bruyne, J. 1975: Over samenstelling door suffixen in het Spaans. *Linguistica Antverpiensia,* 9: 7–169.

De Bruyne, J. 1976: Enkele toelichtingen en bedenkingen bij de definitie van de infinitief door de 'Real Academia Española'. *Linguistica Antwerpiensia,* 10: 47–69.

De Bruyne, J. 1977: Analecta en commentaar in verband met de letter 'K' in het Spaans. *Linguistica Antverpiensia*, 11: 17–26.

De Bruyne, J. 1978: Acerca del sufijo '-azo' en el español contemporáneo. *Iberoromania*, 8: 54–81.

De Bruyne, J. 1979: Complementos de 'Esbozo de una nueva gramática de la lengua española' – II (Notas sobre 'devenir'). *Romanistisches Jahrbuch*, 41: 249–61.

De Bruyne, J. 1980: Acerca de la traducción de '-ísimo'. *Lingüística Española Actual*, 2.1 (January): 27–37.

De Bruyne, J. 1981: Het 'gerundio' in het moderne Spaans. *Linguistica Antverpiensia*, 15: 7–73.

De Bruyne, J. 1982–3: Algunos aspectos de la polivalencia de la conjunción 'que'. *Linguistica Antverpiensia*, 16–17: 61–77.

De Bruyne, J. 1984–5: Antología esdrújula. *Linguistica Antverpiensia*, 18–19: 15–28.

De Bruyne, J. 1986: ¿Una desheredada del alfabeto español? (Acerca de la letra 'h' en el español moderno). Proceedings of VIII Congreso de la Asociación Internacional de Hispanistas, Providence, Brown University, 22–7 August 1983. Madrid: Istmo.

De Bruyne, J. 1989a: Antolojoide. *Boletín de la Real Academia Española*, 69: 91–130.

De Bruyne, J. 1989b: Nota sobre 'sendos'. *Romanische Forschungen*, 101, 2/3: 273–80.

De Bruyne, J. 1989c: La 'k', ¿Hija natural o 'enfant terrible' del alfabeto español?. *Revista de Filología Española*, 69: 97–117.

De Kock, J. 1948–5: Des noms donnés au passé composé en espagnol ou de l'importance relative de la terminologie grammaticale. *Linguistica Antverpiensia*, 18–19: 33–7.

De Kock, J. and Gómez Molina, C. 1982: Concordancias e índices automáticos a disposición de la enseñanza del español, lengua extranjera. *Lingüística Española Actual*, 4.1: 47–82.

De Kock, J., Gómez Molina, C. and Verdonk, R. 1979: *Gramática española*. Leuven: Acco, 3 parts (with additional material by W. Brems in part 3).

De Mello, G. 1992: 'Cuyo' y reemplazos por 'cuyo'. *Anuario de Lingüística Hispánica*, 8: 53–69.

De Miguel, A. 1985: *La perversión del lenguaje*. Madrid: Espasa-Calpe.

Demonte, V. 1982: El falso problema de la posición del adjetivo: dos análisis semánticos. *Boletín de la Real Academia Española*, 52: 453–85.

Duviols, M. and Villégier, J. 1960: *Grammaire espagnole*. Paris: Librairie Hatier.

*Esbozo* = Real Academia Española 1973: *Esbozo de una nueva gramática de la lengua española*. Madrid: Espasa Calpe.

Fernández Ramírez, S. 1951: *Gramática española. Los sonidos y el pronombre*. Madrid: Manuales de la Revista de Occidente.

Fernández Ramírez, S., ed. J. Polo 1986a: *Gramática española: 3.1: El nombre*. Madrid: Arco.

Fernández Ramírez, S., ed. I. Bosque 1986b: *Gramática española: 4 El verbo y la oración*. Madrid: Arco.

García Berrio, A. 1976: *La lingüística moderna*. Barcelona: Planeta.

Gili Gaya, S. 1964: *Curso superior de sintaxis española*. Barcelona: Vox, 9th edn.

Gómez Torrego, L. 1988: *Perífrasis verbales*. Madrid: Arco.

Gooch, A. 1967: *Diminutive, augmentative and pejorative suffixes in modern Spanish*. London: Pergamon Press.

*GRAE* = Real Academia Española 1931: *Gramática de la lengua española*. Madrid: Espasa-Calpe.

Haensch, G. 1984: *Neues Wörterbuch des Amerikanischen Spanisch und neues Wörterbuch des Kolumbianischen Spanisch. Hispanorama (Mitteilungen des Deutschen Spanischlehrerverbands)*, 36: 167–76.

Haensch, G., Wolf, L., Ettinger, S. and Werner, R. 1982: *La lexicografía*. Madrid: Gredos.

Hampares, K. J. 1976: Sexism in Spanish lexicography?. *Hispania* 49: 100–109.

Haverkate, H. 1989: *Modale vormen van het Spaanse werkwoord*. Dordrecht: Foris Publications.

Hernández, C. 1979: *Sintaxis española*. Valladolid: published by the author, 4th edn.

Iribarren, J. M. 1974: *El porqué de los dichos*. Madrid: Aguilar, 4th edn.

Kany, C. 1951: *American-Spanish Syntax*. Chicago: University of Chicago Press, 2nd edn.

Keniston, H. 1937: *Spanish syntax list*. New York: Henry Holl.

Körner, K.-H. 1989: Der Agensausdruck beim Reflexpassiv im Spanischen aus syntaxtypologischer Perspektiv. In *Variatio Linguarum: Beitrage zu Sprachvergleich und Sprachentwicklung: Festschrift zum 60. Geburtstag von Gustav Ineichen*. Wiesbaden: Steiner.

Lapesa, R. 1968: Sobre los orígenes y evolución del leísmo, laísmo y loísmo. In *Festschrift W. von Wartburg*. Tübingen: Niemeyer.

Lapesa, R. 1970: Personas gramaticales y tratamientos en español. In *Homenaje a Menéndez Pidal*, 4, *Revista de la Universidad de Madrid*, 19, no. 74.

Lapesa, R. (ed.) 1977a: *Comunicación y lenguaje*. Madrid: Karpos.

Lapesa, R. 1977b: Tendencias y problemas actuales de la lengua española. In R. Lapesa (ed.), pp. 203–29.

Lapesa, R. 1980: *Historia de la lengua española*. Madrid: Gredos, 8th edn.

Lapesa, R. 1987: El sustantivo sin actualizador en español. *Estudios lingüísticos, literarios y estilísticos*, Universitat de Valencia, 2: 57–68. (See also E. Lorenzo.)

Launay, M. 1980: Acerca de los auxiliares y frases verbales. *Lingüística Española Actual*, 2.1: 123–30.

Lázaro Carreter, F. 1980: *Estudios de lingüistica*. Barcelona: Crítica.

Lázaro Mora, F. A. 1982: Sobre 'aunque' adversativo. *Lingüistica Española Actual*, 4.1 :123–30.

Lleó, C. 1979: *Some Rules in Spanish Complementation: Towards a Study of the Speaker's Intent*. Tübingen: Niemeyer.

Llorente Maldonado de Guevara. A. 1980: *Consideraciones sobre el español actual*. Supplement to *Anuario de Letras*, 18.

Lope Blanch, J. M. 1971: *El español de América*. Madrid: Alcalá.

Lorenzo, E. 1971: *El español de hoy, lengua en ebullición*. Madrid: Gredos, 2nd edn.

Lorenzo, E. 1980: *El español y otras lenguas*. Madrid: Sociedad General Española de Librería.

Lorenzo, E. 1981: Utrum lingua an loquentes? (Speech delivered on 22 November 1981, with a reply by Rafael Lapesa). Madrid: Real Academia Española.

Luna Trail, E. 1980: *Sintaxis de los verboides en el habla culta de la ciudad de México*. Mexico: Universidad Nacional Autónoma de México.

Madariaga, S. de 1966: ¿Vamos a Kahlahtahyood? *Revista de Occidente*: 365–73.

Malmberg, B. 1947–8: L'espagnol dans le nouveau monde. *Studia Linguistica*, 1: 79–116; 2: 1–36.

Malmberg, B. 1974: *La América hispanohablante*. Madrid: Istmo, 3rd edn.

Marcos Marín, F. 1972: *Aproximación a la gramática española*. Madrid: Cincel.

Marcos Marín, F. 1978: *Lengua española, Curso de orientación universitaria*. Madrid: Noguer.

Marsá. F. 1986: *Diccionario normativo y guía práctica de la lengua española*. Madrid: Ariel.

Martín Zorraquino, M. A. 1979: *Las construcciones pronominales en español*. Madrid: Gredos.

Martínez Marín, J. 1982: 'Este agua' y construcciones afines en español actual. *Lingüistica Española Actual*. 4.1: 39–46.

*MEU* = Agencia Efe 1985: *Manual de español urgente*. Madrid: Cátedra.

Molho, M. 1975: *Sistemática del verbo español*. Madrid: Gredos, 2 parts.

Monge, F. 1961: Ser y estar con participios y adjetivos. *Actes du IXe Congrès International de Linguistique Romane*. Lisbon: Centro de Estudos Filológicos.

Monge, F. 1972: Sufijos españoles para la designación de golpe. In *Homenaje a Francisco Ynduraín*. Zaragoza: Librería General, pp. 229–47.

Monge, F. 1983: Notas a una hipótesis sobre el leísmo. In *Serta Philologica F. Lázaro Carreter*. Madrid: Cátedra, pp. 441–53.

Montes Giraldo, J. J. 1982: Sobre el sintagma 'haber' + sustantivo. *Thesaurus*, 37.2: 383–5.

Mozos Mocha, S. de los 1973: *El gerundio preposicional*. Universidad de Salamanca.

Nieves de Paula Pombar, M. 1984: *Contribución al estudio de la aposición en español actual*. Anexo 20 a *Verba, Anuario galego de filoloxia*, Universidade de Santiago de Compostela.

Penny, R. 1986: Patterns of language change in Spain. Inaugural lecture, Westfield College, London, 26 November.

Porroche Ballesteros, M. 1988: *Ser, estar y verbos de cambio*. Madrid: Arco.

Pottier, B. 1970: *Lingüística moderna y filología hispánica*. Madrid: Gredos.

Pountain, Christopher J. 1993: Aspect and Voice: questions about passivization in Spanish. *Journal of Hispanic Research*, 1: 167–81.

Rabanales, A. 1984: ¿Qué es hablar correctamente? *Revista de Educación*, Santiago de Chile, August: 49–58.

Real Academia Española 1961: Gramática de la lengua española, nueva edición. reformada, de 1931. Madrid: Espasa-Calpe (=*GRAE*).

Real Academia Española 1978: *Estatutos y reglamento de la Real Academia Española*. Madrid.

Rósenblat, A. 1965: *El castellano de España y el castellano de América*. Caracas: Cuadernos del Instituto de Filología Andrés Bello, 2nd edn.

Salvador. G. 1987: *Lengua española y lenguas de España*. Barcelona: Ariel.

Schmidely. J. 1979: *La personne grammaticale et son expression en langue espagnole*. Paris: Champion.

Schroten, J. 1972: *Concerning the Deep Structures of Spanish Reflexive Sentences*. The Hague–Paris: Mouton.

Schroten, J. 1978: Marking rules and the underlying order of constituents in Spanish. *Utrecht Working Papers in Linguistics*, 6: 1–28.

Seco, M. 1977: El léxico de hoy. In R. Lapesa (ed.), pp. 181–201.

Seco, R. 1960: *Manual de gramática española*. Madrid: Aguilar, nueva edición revisada.

Smith, C. C. 1991: The anglicism: no longer a problem for Spanish? In *Actas del XIII Congreso Nacional de AEDEAN (Tarragona, December 1989)*, University of Tarragona, pp. 119–36.

Stiehm, B. G. 1975: Spanish word order in non-sentence constructions. *Language*, 51: 49–88.

Tavernier, M. 1979: La frecuencia relativa de las formas verbales en *-ra* y *-se*. *Español Actual*, 35/6: 1–12.

Van Dam, C. F. A. 1967: *Spaanse spraakkunst*. Zutphen: Thiene, 3rd edn.

Varela, B. 1983: *Cuerpo de tentación, pero cara de arrepentimiento. Diálogos*. Mexico. Colegio de México, 109: 23–8.

Varela, B. 1984: Argentinismos y cubanismos. *Romance Notes*. 24. 2: 123–31.

Verdonk, R. 1982: Relatieve frequentie en grammaticaonderwijs: de Spaanse 'pronombres relativos'. *Handelingen van het 2e Fakulteitscolloquium (over Linguïstische en socio-culturele aspecten van het taalonderwijs), Ghent, 24–26 November, 1982*, University of Ghent, pp. 256–63.

Vigara Tauste, A. M. 1992: *Morfosintaxis del español coloquial*. Madrid: Gredos.

## (D) Primary Sources

Acevedo, E. 1969: *Cartas a los celtíberos esposados*. Madrid: Magisterio Español.

Acevedo, E. 1972: *El caso del analfabeto sexual*. Barcelona: Planeta.

Aguirre, F. 1972: *Itaca*. Madrid: Ediciones de cultura hispánia.

Agustí, I. 1944: *Mariona Rebull*. Barcelona: Argos.

Agustí, I. 1945: *El viudo Rius*. Barcelona: Argos.

Agustí, I. 1957: *Desiderio*. Barcelona: Planeta.

Aínsa, F. 1984: *Con acento extranjero*. Buenos Aires: Nordan.

Alberti, R. 1981: *Marinero en tierra*. Madrid: Losada.

Alcocer, J. L. 1978: *Radiografía de un fraude*. Barcelona: Planeta.

Aldecoa, I. 1969: *Gran sol*. Barcelona: Noguer, 3rd edn.

Aldecoa, I. 1970: *El fulgor y la sangre*. Barcelona: Planeta, 3rd edn.

Allende, I. 1984: *La casa de los espíritus*. Barcelona: Plaza y Janés, 3rd edn.

Allende, I. 1987: *Eva Luna*. Barcelona: Plaza y Janés.

Allende, I. 1990: *Cuentos de Eva Luna*. Barcelona: Plaza y Janés.

Alonso, D. 1974: *Prólogo* to *Poema de mio Cid*. Barcelona: Juventud, 2nd edn.

Alonso de los Ríos, C. 1971: *Conversaciones con Miguel Delibes*. Madrid: Magisterio Español.

Alonso de Santos, J. L. 1987: *La estanquera de Vallecas*. Madrid: Ed. Antonio Machado.

Alvar, M. 1975: *Islas afortunadas*. Madrid: La Muralla.

Alvar, M. 1984: *El envés de la hoja*. Zaragoza: Diputación Provincial, Institución Fernando el Católico.

Arlt, R. 1985: *El juguete rabioso*. Madrid: Cátedra.

Arrabal, F. 1972a: *Lettre au général Franco* (bilingual edition). Paris: Union générale d'éditions.

Arrabal, F. 1972b: *El triciclo*. Madrid: Escelicer, Colección Teatro.

Arreola, J. J. 1986: *Confabulario definitivo*. Madrid: Cátedra.

Asenjo Sedano, J. 1978: *Conversación sobre la guerra*. Barcelona: Destino.

Aub, M. 1963: *Campo del moro*. Mexico: Joaquín Mortiz.

Aub, M. 1970: *La calle de Valverde*. Barcelona: Seix Barral.

Aub, M. 1971: *Las buenas intenciones*. Madrid: Alianza Editorial.

Azorín 1964: *Capricho*. Madrid: Colección Austral, 4th edn.

Balmes, J. 1959: *Cartas a un escéptico en materia de religion*. Madrid: Colección Austral, 4th edn.

Baroja, P. 1946–51: *Obras completas*. Madrid: Biblioteca Nueva 8 parts.

Baroja, P. 1951: *Los últimos románticos*. Madrid: Colección Austral, 3rd edn.

Baroja, P. 1952: *Las noches del Buen Retiro*. Madrid: Colección Austral, 2nd edn.

Baroja, P. 1955: *La estrella del capitán Chimista*. Madrid: Colección Austral, 2nd edn.

Baroja, P. 1956: *El laberinto de las sirenas*. Madrid: Colección Austral, 2nd edn.

Baroja, P. 1958: *Las inquietudes de Shanti Andía*. Madrid: Colección Austral, 5th edn.

Baroja. P. 1959: *Los pilotos de altura*. Madrid: Colección Austral, 3rd edn.

Baroja, P. 1960: *Paradox Rey*. Madrid: Colección Austral, 3rd edn.

Baroja, P. 1961: *La casa de Aizgorri*. Madrid: Colección Austral, 5th edn.

Baroja, P. 1964a: *El mayorazgo de Labraz*. Madrid: Colección Austral, 3rd edn.

Baroja. P. 1964b: *Las veleidades de la Fortuna*. Madrid: Colección Austral, 3rd edn.

Berlanga, A. 1984: *La gaznápira*. Barcelona: Noguer.

Blanco Aguinaga, C., Rodríguez Puértolas J. and Zavala, I. 1979–81: *Historia social de la literatura española*. Madrid: Castalia, 3 parts.

Blasco-Ibáñez, V. 1963: *Cuentos valencianos*. Madrid: Colección Austral, 4th edn.

Botrel, J. F. and Salaün, S. 1974: *Creación y público en la literatura española*. Madrid: Castalia.

Bryce Echenique, A. 1981: *Tantas veces Pedro*. Barcelona: Cátedra.

Buero Vallejo, A. 1966: *Historia de una escalera*. Madrid: Escelicer.

Buñuel, L. 1982: *Mi último suspiro*. Barcelona: Plaza y Janés.

Caballero, O. 1980: *Titulares de España*. Barcelona: Planeta.

Cabrera Infante, G. 1968: *Tres tristes tigres*. Barcelona: Seix Barral, 2nd edn.

Cabrera Infante, G. 1978: *O,* Barcelona–Caracas–México: Seix Barral.

Cabrera Infante. G. 1979: *La Habana para un infante difunto* Barcelona–Caracas–México: Seix Barral.

Cabrera Infante, G. 1982: *Exorcismos de esti(l)o*. Barcelona: Seix Barral, 2nd edn.

Camba, J. 1964: *Aventuras de una peseta*. Madrid: Colección Austral, 7th edn.

*Canciones populares españolas* n.d.: Universidad de Zaragoza. Cursos de verano en Jaca.

Carandell, L. 1970: *Celtiberia Show*. Madrid: Guadiana de Publicaciones.

Caro Baroja, J. 1969: *Ensayo sobre la literatura de cordel*. Madrid: Publicaciones de la Revista de Occidente.

Carpentier, A. 1971: *Los pasos perdidos*. Barcelona: Seix Barral.

Carpentier, A. 1976: *El recurso del método*. México–Espana–Argentina: Siglo Veintiuno Editores, 14th edn.

Carrascal, J. M. 1973: *Groovy*, Barcelona: Destino.

Carrera, M. A. 1986: *Costumbres de Guatemala*. Guatemala: Librerías Artemis y Edinta.

Casares, J. 1961: *Cosas del lenguaje*. Madrid: Colección Austral.

Casona, A. (edition and study by J. Rodríguez Richart) 1968: *La dama del alba*. Madrid: Alcalá.

Castillo Puche, J.-L. 1951: *Con la muerte al hombro*. Madrid: Biblioteca Nueva.

Castillo Puche, J.-L. 1970: *El vengador*. Barcelona: Destino.

Castro, A. 1970: *Aspectos del vivir hispánico*. Madrid: Alianza Ed.

Castro, A. 1973: *La realidad histórica de España*. México: Porrúa, edición renovada.

Cela, C. J. 1957: *La obra literaria del pintor Solana*. Madrid: Papeles de Son Armadans.

Cela, C. J. 1958: *Mrs. Caldwell habla con su hijo*. Barcelona: Destino, 2nd edn.

Cela, C. J. 1963a: *La colmena*. Barcelona–Madrid: Noguer, 5th edn.

Cela, C. J. 1963b: *Garito de hospicianos*. Barcelona: Noguer.

Cela, C. J. 1963c: *Nuevas andanzas y desventuras de Lazarillo de Tormes*. Barcelona: Noguer, 8th edn.

Cela, C. J. 1967a: *La familia de Pascual Duarte*. Barcelona: Destino, 16th edn.

Cela, C. J. 1967b: *El gallego y su cuadrilla*. Barcelona, Destino, 3rd edn.

Cela, C. J. 1967c: *Pabellón de reposo*. Barcelona: Destino, 4th edn.

Cela, C. J. 1967d: *Viaje a la Alcarria*. Madrid: Colección Austral, 4th edn.

Cela, C. J. 1969: *San Camilo 1936*. Madrid–Barcelona: Alfaguara.

Cela, C. J. 1971: *El molino de viento (y otras novelas cortas)*. Barcelona: Noguer, 2nd edn.

Cela, C. J. 1972: *Toreo de salón*. Barcelona: Lumen.

Cela, C. J. 1973: *El tacatá oxidado*. Barcelona: Noguer.

Cela, C. J. 1979a: *Gavilla de fábulas sin amor*. Madrid: Bruguera.

Cela, C. J. 1979b: *Los sueños vanos, los ángeles curiosos*. Barcelona: Argos Vergara.

Cela, C. J. 1983: *Mazurca para dos muertos*. Barcelona: Seix Barral.

Cela, C. J. 1988: *Cristo versus Arizona*. Barcelona: Seix Barral.

Cela, C. J. 1989: *Nuevo viaje a La Alcarria*. Barcelona: Plaza y Janés.

Cela, C. J. 1991a: *Cachondeos, escarceos y otros meneos*. Barcelona: Plaza y Janés.

Cela, C. J. 1991b: *Desde el palomar de Hita*. Barcelona: Plaza y Janés.

Cervantes, M. 1960: *El ingenioso hidalgo Don Quijote de la Mancha*. Madrid: Colección Austral, 21st edn.

Chacel, R. 1981: *Barrio de maravillas*. Barcelona–Caracas–México: Seix Barral, 4th edn.

Cierva, R. de la 1975: *Historia del franquismo, Orígenes y Transfiguración*. Barcelona: Planeta.

Comellas, J. L. 1967: *Historia de España moderna y contemporánea*. Madrid: Rialp, 2nd edn.

Conde, C. 1979: *Poesía ante el tiempo y la inmortalidad (Discurso pronunciado el 28 de febrero de 1979 en su recepción pública)*. Madrid: Real Academia Española.

*Conversaciones con Monseñor Escrivá de Balaguer* 1968: Madrid: Rialp.

Cortázar, J. 1973: *Libro de Manuel*. Buenos Aires: Sudamericana, 2nd edn.

Cortázar, J. 1974: *Rayuela*. Buenos Aires: Sudamericana, 17th edn.

Cortázar, J. 1981: *Los Premios*. Barcelona: Bruguera, 2nd edn.

Cortázar, J. 1984: *Nicaragua tan violentamente dulce*. Barcelona: Muchnik.

Dalí, S. 1983: *Diario de un genio*. Barcelona: Tusquets.

Daudet, A. 1968: *Fulanito* (translated from the French *Le Petit Chose* by J. Gallego de Dantin). Madrid: Colección Austral.

del Moral, C. 1974: *La sociedad madrileña fin de siglo y Baroja*. Madrid: Turner.

Delibes, M. 1948: *La sombra del ciprés es alargada*. Barcelona: Destino.

Delibes, M. 1967: *Siestas con viento Sur*. Barcelona: Destino, 2nd edn.

Delibes, M. 1968a: *Las ratas*. Barcelona: Destino, 5th edn.

Delibes, M. 1968b: *Vivir al dia*. Barcelona: Destino.

Delibes, M. 1969a: *Cinco horas con Mario*. Barcelona: Destino, 4th edn.

Delibes, M. 1969b: *Mi idolatrado hijo Sisí*. Barcelona: Destino, 3rd edn.

Delibes, M. 1972: *Un año de mi vida*. Barcelona: Destino.

Delibes, M. 1974: *El príncipe destronado*. Barcelona: Destino, 2nd edn.

Delibes, M. 1975: *Las guerras de nuestros antepasados*. Barcelona: Destino.

Delibes, M. 1976: *S.O S.* Barcelona: Destino.

Delibes, M. 1977: *Aventuras, venturas y desventuras de un cazador a rabo*. Barcelona: Destino.

Delibes, M. 1978a: *El disputado voto del señor Cayo*. Barcelona: Destino.

Delibes, M. 1978b: *El tesoro* Barcelona: Destino.

Delibes, M. 1979a: *Castilla, lo castellano y los castellanos*. Barcelona: Planeta.

Delibes, M. 1979b: *Un mundo que agoniza*. Barcelona: Plaza y Janés Ed.

Delibes, M. 1980: *Viejas historias de Castilla la Vieja*. Madrid: Alianza Ed.

Delibes, M. 1981: *Los santos inocentes*. Barcelona: Planeta.

Delibes, M. 1983: *Cartas de amor a un sexagenario voluptuoso*. Barcelona: Destino.

Delibes, M. 1984: *Parábola del náufrago*. Barcelona: Destino.

Delibes, M. 1987: *377A, Madera de héroe*. Barcelona: Destino.

Díaz-Plaja, F. 1966: *El español y los siete pecados capitales*. Madrid: Alianza Editorial.

Díaz-Plaja, F. 1973: *Otra historia de España*. Barcelona: Plaza y Janés, S.A.

Díaz-Plaja, G. 1967: *La dimensión culturalista en la poesía castellana del siglo XX* (Discurso de recepción en la Real Academia Española – y contestación del Excmo. Sr D. Martín de Riquer). Madrid: Real Academia Española.

Díaz-Plaja, G. 1981: *Figuras (con un paisaje al fondo)*. Madrid: Espasa-Calpe, S.A.

Donoso, J. 1980: *La misteriosa desaparición de la marquesita de Loria*. Barcelona–Caracas–México: Seix Barral.

Edwards, J. 1971: *El peso de la noche*. Barcelona: Seix Barral.

Edwards, J. 1985: *La mujer imaginaria*. Barcelona: Plaza y Janés.

*El Año Literario 1974–1979*. Madrid: Castalia.

Escrivá de Balaguer, J. M. 1965: *Camino*. Madrid: Rialp, 23rd Spanish edn.

Fabiola 1960: *Los 12 cuentos maravillosos*. Madrid: Sinople.

Fernández Flórez, D. 1967: *Lola espejo oscuro*. Madrid: Plenitud, 7th edn.

Fernández Flórez, D. 1973: *Nuevos lances y picardías de Lola espejo oscuro*. Barcelona: Plaza y Janés, 7th edn.

Fernández Flórez, W. 1967: *Las gafas del diablo*. Madrid: Colección Austral, 8th edn.

Fernández Santos, J. 1977: *Los bravos*. Barcelona: Destino.

Fernández Santos, J. 1982: *Jaque a la dama*. Barcelona: Planeta

Franco Salgado-Araujo, F. 1977: *Mi vida junto a Franco*. Barcelona: Planeta.

Fuentes, C. 1979: *La cabeza de la hidra*. Barcelona: Argos Vergara S.A.

Fuentes, C. 1985: *Gringo viejo*, México–Madrid: Fondo de Cultura Económica.

Gala, A. 1993: *El manuscrito carmesí*. Barcelona: Planeta, 19th edn.

Gan Bustos, F. 1978: *La libertad en el W. C. (Para una sociología del graffiti)*. Barcelona: Dopesa.

García Hortelano, J. 1967: *Nuevas amistades*. Barcelona: Seix Barral, 5th edn.

García Hortelano, J. 1979: *Cuentos completos*. Madrid: Alianza Edilorial.

García Hortelano, J. 1982: *Gramática parda*, Barcelona: Argos Vergara.

García Lorca, F. 1955: *La zapatera prodigiosa*, in *Obras completas*. Madrid: Aguilar, 2nd edn aumentada.

García Márquez, G. 1985: *Cien años de soledad*. Barcelona: Plaza y Janés, 6th edn.

García Márquez, G. 1985: *El amor en los tiempos de cólera*. Barcelona: Bruguera.

García Morales, A. 1992: *El sur*. Barcelona: Anagrama, 16th edn.

García Pavón, F. 1971: *Las hermanas coloradas*. Barcelona: Destino.

García Pavón, F. 1972: *Vendimiario de Plinio*. Barcelona: Destino.

García Pavón, F. 1977: *Los nacionales*. Barcelona: Destino.

García Pavón, F. 1980a: *El último sábado*. Barcelona: Destino.

García Pavón, F. 1980b: *Una semana de lluvia*. Barcelona: Plaza y Janés.

García-Badell, G. 1971: *De las Armas a Montemolín*. Barcelona: Destino.

Garriga, R. 1979: *La Señora de El Pardo*. Barcelona: Planeta.

Garriga, R. 1980: *Nicolás Franco*. Barcelona: Planeta.

Gironella, J. M. 1966a: *Los cipreses creen en Dios*. Barcelona: Planeta, 40th edn.

Gironella, J. M. 1966b: *Ha estallado la paz*. Barcelona: Planeta.

Gironella, J. M. 1966c: *Un millón de muertos*. Barcelona: Planeta.

Gironella, J. M. 1971: *Condenados a vivir*. Barcelona: Planeta, 2 parts.

Gironella, J. M. 1986: *Los hombres lloran solos*. Barcelona: Planeta.

Gómez de la Serna, R. 1959: *La mujer de ámbar*. Madrid: Colección Austral, 6th edn.

Gómez de la Serna, R. 1979: *Greguerías*. Madrid: Cátedra.

Gómez Marín, J. A. 1972: *Bandolerismo. santidad y otros temas españoles*. Madrid: Miguel Castellote.

Goytisolo, J. 1960: *Duelo en el paraíso*. Barcelona: Destino, 2nd edn.

Goytisolo, J. 1977: *Disidencias*. Barcelona–Caracas–México: Seix Barral.

Goytisolo, J. 1978: *Libertad, libertad, libertad*. Barcelona: Anagrama.

Goytisolo, J. 1981a: *La chanca*. Barcelona–Caracas–México: Seix Barral.

Goytisolo, J. 1981b: *Fiestas*. Barcelona: Destino.

Goytisolo, J. 1985: *Coto vedado*. Barcelona: Seix Barral.

Goytisolo, J. 1986: *En los reinos de Taifa*. Barcelona: Seix Barral.

Goytisolo, J. 1988: *Señas de identidad*. Barcelona: Seix Barral, 7th edn.

Goytisolo, J. 1989: *Campos de Níjar*. Barcelona: Seix Barral, 5th edn.

Grande, F. 1985: *Agenda flamenca*. Seville: Editoriales andaluzas unidas.

Grandes, A. 1990: *Las edades de Lulú*. Barcelona: Tusquets.

Grosso, A. 1978: *Los invitados*. Barcelona: Planeta.

Gutiérrez-Solana, J. 1972: *La España negra*. Barcelona: Seix Barral.

Hargreaves, R. 1986: *Don Tacañete* (translated from the English *Mr Mean*). Madrid: Alhambra.

Ibargüengoitia, J. 1981: *Los conspiradores*. Barcelona: Argos Vergara.

Icaza, J. 1980: *Huasipungo*. Barcelona: Plaza y Janés, 2nd edn.

Izcaray, J. 1961: *La hondonada*. México: Palomar.

Jardiel Poncela, E. 1969: *Obras completas*. Barcelona: Ahr, 5th edn.

Jardiel Poncela, E., *Amor se escribe sin hache*, in *Obras Completas*, IV.

Jardiel Poncela, E. 1973: *Un marido de ida y vuelta*. Madrid: Colección Austral.

Jardiel Poncela, E. 1977: *La mujer como elemento indispensable para la respiración*. Barcelona: Ahr.

*La Codorniz: Antología 1941–4* 1987: Madrid: Aznao.

Laforet, C. 1966: *Nada*. Barcelona: Destino, 17th edn.

Laiglesia, A. de 1972: *Te quiero, bestia*. Barcelona: Planeta, 7th edn.

Larra, M. J. de 1966: *Artículos de costumbres*. Madrid: Colección Austral, 9th edn.

Lázaro Carreter, F. 1972: *Crónica del diccionario de autoridades (Discurso leído el día 11 de junio de 1972 en el acto de su recepción en la Real Academia Española)*. Madrid: Real Academia Española.

Lázaro Carreter, F. 1985: *Las ideas lingüísticas en España durante el Siglo XVIII*. Barcelona: Crítica.

Lera, A. M. de 1970: *Las últimas banderas*. Barcelona: Planeta, 18th edn.

Líster, E. 1977: *Memorias de un luchador*. Madrid: I: G. del Toro.

Lorén, S. 1955: *Cuerpos, almas y todo eso*. Barcelona: Corinto, 2nd edn.

Lorén, S. 1960: *El baile de Pan*. Barcelona: Planeta.

Lorén, S. 1962: *Las cuatro vidas del doctor Cucalón*. Barcelona: Planeta, 2nd edn.

Lorén, S. 1965: *Siete alcobas*. Barcelona: Planeta, 2nd edn.

Lorén, S. 1967a: *El pantano*. Barcelona: Plaza y Janés.

Lorén, S. 1967b: *Una casa con goteras*. Barcelona: Planeta, 7th edn.

Lorén, S. 1971: *V.I.P.* Barcelona: Destino.

Lorén, S. 1975: *Clase única*. Barcelona: Planeta.

Lorén, S. n.d.: *La rebotica*. Zaragoza: Ediciones del Pórtico.

Machado, M. 1947: *Soleares*, in *Obras Completas*. Madrid: Plenitud.

Malinow, I. 1983: *La fascinación*, Buenos Aires: Emecé.

Marañón, G. 1952: *Raíz y decoro de España*. Madrid: Colección Austral.

Marías, J. 1976: *La España real*. Madrid: Espasa Calpe, 4th edn.

Marías. J. 1989: *Todas las almas*. Barcelona: Anagrama.

Marsé, J., 1982: *Útimas tardes con Teresa*. Barcelona: Seix Barral.

Martín Gaite, C. 1968: *El balneario*. Madrid: Alianza.

Martín Gaite, C. 1972: *Usos amorosos del dieciocho en España*. Madrid: Siglo Veintiuno de España.

Martín Gaite, C. 1978: *Las ataduras*, in *Cuentos completos*. Madrid: Alianza.

Martín Gaite, C. 1980: *Fragmentos de interior*. Barcelona: Destino, 2nd edn.

Martín Gaite, C. 1981: *El cuarto de atrás*. Barcelona: Destino.

Martín-Santos, L. 1972: *Tiempo de silencio*. Barcelona: Seix Barral, 9th edn.

Matute, A. M. 1977: *Los soldados lloran de noche*. Barcelona: Destino.

Maurois. A. (tr. R. de Hernández) 1968: *Disraeli*. Madrid: Austral, 18th edn.

Medio. D. 1958: *Nosotros, los Rivero*. Barcelona: Ed. Destino, 7th edn.

Mendoza, E., 1985: *La verdad sobre el caso Savolta*. Barcelona: Seix Barral.

Mihura, M. 1981: *Tres sombreros de copa*. Madrid: Cátedra, 5th edn.

Mingote, A. 1988: *Dos momentos del humor español*, Discurso de ingreso en la RAE, 28 February, Madrid: Gráficos Vidos.

Montero, R. 1979: *Crónica del desamor*. Madrid: Debate, 6th edn.

Moreno-Durán, R.-H. 1981: *El toque de Diana*. Barcelona: Montesinos Ed.

Mujica Lainez, M. 1983: *Bomarzo*. Barcelona: Seix Barral, 2nd edn.

Muñoz Molina, A. 1990: *El invierno en Lisboa*. Barcelona: Seix Barral.

Neruda, P. 1976: *Confieso que he vivido –Memorias*. Barcelona: Seix Barral.

Onetti, J. C. 1979: *Dejemos hablar al viento*. Barcelona: Bruguera Alfaguara, 2nd edn.

Ortega y Gasset, J. 1959: *Estudios sobre el amor*. Madrid: Revista de Occidente, 12th edn.

Ortega y Gasset, J. (ed. R. Senabre), *Espíritu de la letra*. Madrid: Cátedra.

Parra. E. 1981: *Soy un extraño para ti*. Barcelona: Cátedra.

Paz, O. 1971: *Corriente alterna*. México–Buenos Aires: Siglo Veintiuno Editores, 5th edn.

Pemán, J. M. 1972: *Ensayos andaluces*. Barcelona: Planeta.

Peñuelas, M. 1969: *Conversaciones con R. J. Sender*. Madrid: Magisterio Español.

Pérez Merinero, C. 1982: *Las reglas del juego*. Madrid: Cátedra.

Posse, A. 1990: *La reina del Plata*. Barcelona: Plaza y Janés.

Pozuelo Escudero, V. 1980: *Los últimos 476 días de Franco*. Barcelona: Planeta.

Puig, M., 1980: *Maldición eterna a quien lea estas páginas*. Barcelona–Caracas–México: Seix Barral.

Puig, M. 1989: *Boquitas pintadas*. Barcelona: Seix Barral, 3rd edn.

Quiñones, F. 1979: *Las mil noches de Hortensia Romero*. Barcelona: Planeta.

Quiroga, E. 1950: *Viento del Norte*. Barcelona: Destino.

Ramón y Cajal, R. 1966: *Charlas de café*. Madrid: Colección Austral, 9th edn.

Ricardo Alonso, L. 1981: *El Supremísimo*. Barcelona: Destino.

Ridruejo, D. 1976: *Casi unas memorias*. Barcelona: Planeta.

Riera, C. 1987: *Cuestión de amor propio*. Barcelona: Tusquets Editores.

Riera, C. 1991: *Contra el amor en compañía*. Barcelona: Destino.

Riquer, M. de 1967: *Contestación . . .* , see G. Díaz-Plaja (*La dimensión culturalista . . .*).

Roa Bastos, A. 1977: *El trueno entre las hojas*. Barcelona: Bruguera.

Rojas, C. *Por qué perdimos la guerra*. Barcelona: Nauta.

Rojas, C. 1982: *El sueño de Sarajevo*. Barcelona: Destino.

Romero, E. 1963: *La paz empieza nunca*. Barcelona: Planeta, 13th edn.

Rulfo, J. 1981: *Pedro Páramo*. Barcelona: Bruguera.

Sábato, E. 1981: *El escritor y sus fantasmas*. Barcelona–Caracas–México: Seix Barral, 8th edn.

Sábato, E. 1983: *El túnel*. Madrid: Cátedra, 9th edn.

Salinas, P. 1967: *Ensayos de literatura hispánica*. Madrid: Aguilar, 3rd edn.

Salinas, P. 1972: *Literatura española siglo XX*. Madrid: Alianza, 2nd edn.

Salvador, T. 1966: *Los atracadores*. Barcelona: GP.

Salvador, T. 1968a: *Diálogos en la oscuridad*. Barcelona: Bruguera.

Salvador, T. 1968b: *División 250*. Barcelona: GP, 4th edn.

Sánchez Ferlosio, R. 1971: *El Jarama,* Barcelona, Destino, Colección Ancora y Delfín, 11th edn.

Sánchez-Albornoz, C. 1975: *Mi testamento histórico-politico.* Barcelona: Planeta.

Sánchez-Albornoz, C. 1977: *Siete ensayos.* Barcelona: Planeta.

Sender, R. J. 1964: *La aventura equinoccial de Lope de Aguirre.* Madrid: Magisterio Español.

Sender, R. J. 1965–6: *Crónica del alba.* Madrid: Alianza Editorial.

Sender, R. J. 1967: *La llave (y otras narraciones).* Madrid: Magisterio Español.

Sender, R. J. 1969a: *Epitalamio del prieto Trinidad.* Barcelona: Destino, 3rd edn.

Sender, R. J. 1969b: *La luna de los perros.* Barcelona, Destino.

Sender, R. J. 1969c: *Mr. Witt en el cantón.* Madrid: Alianza editorial.

Sender, R. J. 1969d: *La tesis de Nancy.* Madrid: Magisterio Español, 3rd edn.

Sender, R. J. 1970: *Siete domingos rojos.* Buenos Aires: Proyección.

Sender, R. J. 1972: *Relatos fronterizos.* Barcelona: Destino, 2nd edn.

Sender, R. J. 1979: *La mirada inmóvil.* Barcelona: Argos Vergara.

Skármeta, A. 1986: *Ardiente paciencia.* Barcelona: Plaza y Janés.

Tellado, C. 1984: *Necesito aprovechar la vida.* Barcelona: Bruguera.

Tierno Galván, E. 1984: *Bandos del alcalde.* Madrid: Egraf.

Torrente Ballester, G. 1975: *El Quijote como juego.* Madrid: Guadarrama.

Tudela, M. 1970: *Cela.* Madrid: Epesa.

Umbral, F. 1966: *Travesía de Madrid.* Barcelona: Destino.

Umbral, F. 1969: *Si hubiéramos sabido que el amor era eso.* Barcelona: Destino, 2nd edn.

Umbral, F. 1972: *Amar en Madrid.* Barcelona: Planeta.

Umbral, F. 1973a: *Carta abierta a una chica progre.* Madrid: Ediciones 99.

Umbral, F. 1973b: *Retrato de un joven malvado.* Barcelona. Destino.

Umbral, F. 1975: *Diario de un español cansado.* Barcelona: Destino.

Umbral, F. 1976a: *La guapa gente de derechas.* Barcelona, Luis de Caralt Editor, 2nd edn.

Umbral, F. 1976b: *Las ninfas.* Barcelona: Destino.

Umbral, F. 1977: *La noche que llegué al café Gijón.* Barcelona: Destino.

Umbral, F. 1979: *Los amores diurnos.* Barcelona: Kairos.

Umbral, F. 1980: *Los helechos arborescentes.* Barcelona: Argos Vergara.

Umbral, F. 1981: *A la sombra de las muchachas rojas.* Madrid: Cátedra.

Umbral, F. 1985: *Mis queridos monstruos.* Madrid: El País.

Umbral, F. 1987: *Memorias de un hijo del siglo.* Madrid: El País.

Umbral, F. 1989: *El fulgor de África.* Barcelona: Seix Barral.

Unamuno, M. de 1967a: *El espejo de la muerte.* Madrid: Colección Austral, 6th edn.

Unamuno, M. de 1967b: *Visiones y comentarios.* Madrid: Colección Austral, 3rd edn.

Urrutia, J. 1984: *Imago litterae*. Seville: Alfar.

Uslar Pietri, A. 1983: *La isla de Róbinson*. Barcelona: Seix Barral.

Valle-Inclán, R. del 1963: *Sonata de otoño y sonata de invierno*. Madrid: Colección Austral, 4th edn.

Valle-Inclán, R. del 1981: *Luces de bohemia*. Madrid: Colección Austral, 13th edn.

Vallejo-Nagera, J. A. 1980: *Concierto para instrumentos desafinados*. Barcelona: Argos Vergara.

Vargas Llosa, M. 1973: *La ciudad y los perros,* in *Obras escogidas*. Madrid: Aguilar.

Vargas Llosa, M. 1981: *La guerra del fin del mundo*. Barcelona: Plaza y Janés.

Vargas Llosa, M. 1983a: *Contra viento y marea (1962–1982)*. Barcelona: Seix Barral.

Vargas Llosa, M. 1983b: *Pantaleón y las visitadoras*. Barcelona: Seix Barral.

Vargas Llosa, M. 1986: *La chunga*. Barcelona: Seix Barral.

Vázquez Montalbán, M. 1979a: *La cocina calalana*. Barcelona: Península.

Vázquez Montalbán, M. 1979b; *Los mares del sur*. Barcelona: Planeta.

Vázquez Montalbán, M. 1983: *Los pájaros de Bangkok*. Barcelona, Planeta.

Vázquez Montalbán, M. 1990: *Galíndez*. Barcelona: Seix Barral.

Vilallonga, J. L. de 1980: *La nostalgia es un error* Barcelona: Planeta.

Vizcaíno Casas, F. 1976a: *Café y copa con los famosos*. Madrid: Sedmay Ed.

Vizcaíno Casas, F. 1976b: *La España de la posguerra 1939–1953*. Barcelona: Planeta, 4th edn.

Vizcaíno Casas, F. 1978: . . . *y al tercer año resucitó*. Barcelona: Planeta, 7th edn.

Vizcaíno Casas, F. 1979a: *La boda de señor cura*. Madrid: Albia, 12th edn.

Vizcaíno Casas, F. 1979b: *Hijos de Papá*. Barcelona: Planeta.

Zunzunegui, J. A. de 1952a: *Beatriz o la vida apasionada*. Madrid: Colección Austral.

Zunzunegui, J. A. de 1952b: *Ramón o la vida baldía*. Madrid: Colección Austral.

Zunzunegui, J. A. de 1954: *La vida como es*. Barcelona: Noguer

Zunzunegui, J. A. de 1956a: *El camión justiciero*. Barcelona: Noguer.

Zunzunegui, J. A. de 1956b: *El hijo hecho a contrata*. Barcelona: Noguer.

Zunzunegui, J. A. de 1958: *El barco de la muerte* Madrid: Colección Austral, 2nd edn.

Zunzunegui, J. A. de 1959a: *Los caminos de El Señor*. Barcelona: Noguer.

Zunzunegui, J. A. de 1959b: *La úlcera*. Madrid: Colección Austral, 2nd edn.

Zunzunegui, J. A. de 1971: *Una ricahembra*. Madrid: Prensa Española, 4th edn.

# Word Index

References are to sections, not to pages.

siéntesen 267
signo
  signos de admiración 18
  signos de exclamación 18
-sigo 284
simple 173
simular 795
sin 80, 774, 780
  sin + *infinitive* 780,
    1104, 1110, 1111, 1112,
    1114
  sin embargo de 1096
  sin otra preocupación 462
  sin problema 781
  sin que 1070
  sin (que) 1295
  sin querer 1113
  sin yo saber 1085
sino 823, 834
  no ... sino 838
sino que 837
sinvergüenza 105
-sión 107
siquiera 1066
sistema 102
situar 932
so 782, 889, 911
  so capa de 782
  so pena de 782
  so pretexto de 782
sobrar 801, 813
sobre 784
  estar sobre sí 787
  sobre + *infinitive* 1108
  sobre de + *infinitive* 1108
sobrio 1248
solamente 596, 642
solazarse 809
soldar 918
soler 637, 795, 918
solicitar 795
solitita 1324
sólo 570, 586, 596, 642,
  1097
  con sólo 1097
  sólo + *infinitive* 1102
  sólo con 1097
soltar 918
soltero 1247
sonar 675, 918
sonreír 924
sonreírse 821
soñar 810, 918
sor 32

su 320, 322
subir 802
sucio 1246
suelto 1176
suerte
  de suerte que 1058
suficiente 742
sufrido 1178
sugerir 927
sumo
  a lo sumo 65
super 194
superar 660
superávit 139
superior 155, 184, 591
superiora 155
suplicar 1038
suponer
  es de suponer que 1031
supuesto 170
suspirar 814
sustituir 660
suyo 320, 329, 341

t 2
tabú 127
-tad 107
tal 74, 514
  como si tal cosa 528
  con tal (de) que 823, 1070
  cual ... tal 518
  el tal 517, 522
  la tal 522
  ¿qué tal? 525
  tal como 527
  tal cual 519
  tal de + *adjective* 526
  tal vez 631, 1027
  tal y como 527
  tal ... cual 523
  un(a) tal 516, 522
  y tal 524
talmente 529
tamaño 74, 170
también 570, 621
tampoco 621, 628
tan 369, 370, 570, 575,
  1058, 1139
  tan + *adjective* 650
  tan + *adjective* +
    como 650
  tan + *adjective* + *noun* 76
tantísimo 491

tanto 170, 486, 570, 574,
  647, 1139
  cuanto más/menos ...
    (tanto) más/menos 647
  otro tanto 465
  tanto + *noun* + como 650
  tanto más ... cuanto
    que 647
  tanto que 1058
  tantos otros 465
  tanto ... como 657
  tanto ... cuanto 651
  tanto ... que 652, 657
  un tanto 397, 492
  y tantos 490
tardar 809
  a más tardar 1100
tarde 143, 597
tatuar 932
te 238
tejerazo 1327
telegrafiar 931
tema 102
temblar 198
temer 795, 848, 1033, 1037
templar 920
tempranito 1323
temprano 597
tenazas 141
tender 802, 918
tener 79, 664, 901, 936,
  940, 945, 948
  tené 949
  tener + *past
    participle* 1198
  tener + X años 36
  tener por 771
  tenerlas 282
tentar 803, 918
teñir 924, 1211
tercero 178
terminar 805, 814
ternísimo 187
ti 238, 239
tía 33
ticket 138
tiempo
  a tiempo 632
tientas
  a tientas 678
tiernísimo 187
-tigo 284
tijeras 141
tilde 17, 109